Beiträge zur Praxeologie / Contributions to Praxeology

Series Editors

Bruno Karsenti, Paris, France
Erhard Schüttpelz, Siegen, Germany
Tristan Thielmann, Siegen, Germany

Die „Beiträge zur Praxeologie / Contributions to Praxeology" setzen sich zum Ziel, die Praxis allen anderen Erklärungsgrößen vorzuordnen, und die theoretischen Grundbegriffe aus dieser Vorordnung zu gewinnen, zu klären oder zu korrigieren. Sowohl die Arbeiten von Wittgenstein als auch die von Schütz und Garfinkel verweisen auf eine gemeinsame mitteleuropäische Genealogie der „Praxeologie", die bis heute allerdings weitgehend unbekannt geblieben ist. Die Reihe will sich daher in drei Stoßrichtungen entfalten: durch philosophische Theoriearbeit, durch empirische Beiträge zur Theoriebildung und durch Beiträge zur Revision der Wissenschaftsgeschichte.

Die Bände der Reihe erscheinen in deutscher oder englischer Sprache.

Niklas Woermann

Seeing Style

How Style Orients Phenopractices across Action, Media, Space, and Time

Niklas Woermann
Department of Business and Management
University of Southern Denmark
Odense M, Denmark

ISSN 2946-0158 ISSN 2946-0166 (electronic)
Beiträge zur Praxeologie / Contributions to Praxeology
ISBN 978-3-662-69184-7 ISBN 978-3-662-69182-3 (eBook)
https://doi.org/10.1007/978-3-662-69182-3

Funded by the Deutsche Forschungsgemeinschaft (DFG, German Research Foundation) –
Project-ID 262513311 – SFB 1187.

© The Editor(s) (if applicable) and The Author(s), under exclusive license to Springer-Verlag GmbH, DE, part of Springer Nature 2024

This work is subject to copyright. All rights are solely and exclusively licensed by the Publisher, whether the whole or part of the material is concerned, specifically the rights of translation, reprinting, reuse of illustrations, recitation, broadcasting, reproduction on microfilms or in any other physical way, and transmission or information storage and retrieval, electronic adaptation, computer software, or by similar or dissimilar methodology now known or hereafter developed.
The use of general descriptive names, registered names, trademarks, service marks, etc. in this publication does not imply, even in the absence of a specific statement, that such names are exempt from the relevant protective laws and regulations and therefore free for general use.
The publisher, the authors and the editors are safe to assume that the advice and information in this book are believed to be true and accurate at the date of publication. Neither the publisher nor the authors or the editors give a warranty, expressed or implied, with respect to the material contained herein or for any errors or omissions that may have been made. The publisher remains neutral with regard to jurisdictional claims in published maps and institutional affiliations.

Cover illustration: © Paul Masukowitz

This J.B. Metzler imprint is published by the registered company Springer-Verlag GmbH, DE, part of Springer Nature.
The registered company address is: Heidelberger Platz 3, 14197 Berlin, Germany

If disposing of this product, please recycle the paper.

One can learn to ski only on the slopes and for the slopes.

Martin Heidegger (cit. in Gadamer 1994: 115)

We want to walk: so we need friction. Back to the rough ground!

Ludwig Wittgenstein (2009: § 107)

To my parents

Acknowledgements

This work would have been impossible without the help, openness, camaraderie, and dedication of my informants on and off the mountain. I owe them deep gratitude. Some sections of chapter seven have been published in Woermann (2017): "It's really strange when nobody is watching. Enactive intercorporeality and the Spielraum of practices in freeskiing." in Christian Meyer / Ulrich v. Wedelstaedt (Eds.): Moving Bodies in Interaction–Interacting Bodies in Motion: Intercorporeality, interkinesthesia, and enaction in sports. Amsterdam: John Benjamins, pp. 215–242. Most of the empirical material discussed in this work was collected for my dissertation at the University of St. Gallen under the supervision of Thomas Eberle, on which the present book is based. Over the past decade, my ideas have been developed, tested, amended, and updated in exchanges with countless colleagues to whom I am deeply indebted. First and foremost, I want to thank Karin Knorr Cetina, Ted Schatzki, Elizabeth Shove, and Hubert Knoblauch. All remaining errors and shortcomings are my own. The work presented here was in part supported by grants from the Swiss National Fund SNF, the German Research Foundation DFG, as well as the University of Southern Denmark research fund.

Contents

1	**Introduction: Why Phenopractices?**	1
	1 Purpose, Topic, and Form of the Present Work	1
	2 The Field of Freeskiing	6
	3 Theoretical Approach and Stance	8
	4 The Focus: Intelligibility and Vision	11
	5 The Foundation: Ontology and Epistemology	13
	6 Outline of the Present Work	16
2	**Vision—Seeing Lines**	19
	1 Introduction: The Line	19
	2 The Threefold Line	23
	Excursus: The Diverging Focus of Theories of Social Practices	26
	3 Reading (Mountain) Faces	27
	4 From Seeing Terrain to Gazing at Landscapes	30
	Excursus: Situation Theory and Situated Awareness in Psychology	35
	5 Seeing as Interaction: Formulating and Showing a Line	36
	Excursus: Knowledge and (Pheno-)practices	48
	6 Professional Vision	53
	Excursus: Affordances	57
	7 The Technical Dimension of Seeing	58
	Excursus: Distributed Cognition	60
	8 Situated Seeing	62
3	**Perception—Figuring Out the Visual Field**	65
	1 Introduction: On the Ridge	65
	2 Seeing as Opening	68
	3 Seeing-of and Seeing-in	70
	4 Towards an Ethnography of Visual Fields	73
	Excursus: Extending Ethnomethodological Studies of Vision	74
	5 The Janus Face of Vision	80

6	The Restless Eye	82
7	Visual Routines	84
8	The Gestalt and the Roots of Practice Thought	87
9	Gestalt-Seeing as Visual Cognition	90
10	The Temporal Structure of the Gestalt	92
11	Blending In and Standing Out	96

Excursus I: Husserlian Phenomenology, Gestalts, and the Practice Turn 99
Excursus II: Husserl on Eyeball Movement and Seeing Figures 102

4 Movement—The Phenomenal Field 117

1	Riding Down	117
2	The Paradox of Ethnographies of the Body	122
3	Achieving Amalgamation	123
4	Sensing the Dys-Appearing Body	128
5	The Phenomenal Field of Practices	131
6	The Moving Body in the Phenomenal Field	135

Excursus: Merleau-Ponty from a Phenopractice Perspective 137

7	Subjectivity and Intersubjectivity	140
8	Seeing, Apprehension, and 'The Brain's Way of Touching'	143
9	The Normativity of Perception	147
10	Two Ways of Seeing: Pragmatic Versus Epistemic Seeing	149

Excursus: Does Vision Science Necessarily Lead to Cognitivism or Mentalism? 154

5 Things—The Amalgam 157

1	Introduction: The Love for Equipment	157
2	The Amalgam of Practice and Its Material Aspects	160

Schatzki on Materiality: Elements Versus Arrangements 162

3	Zeug and Ding	164
4	The Ski-In-The-Amalgam: What is a Ski?	166
5	Flex Curves—Good Data as Bad Science	170
6	On Understandings, Aspects, and Elements	175

Excursus: Post-Structuralism, Postmodernity, and Performativity 178

7	Enduring Elements	184

Excursus: The Epistemology of Phenopractice Thought 186

8	Bodies and Artefacts	190
9	Foregrounding and Sublating	193
10	Knowing Your Style	194
11	The Visibility of Things: What is a Good Ski?	196

6 Community—Style 205

1	Introduction: The Silence of Style	206
2	The Centrality of Style	208
3	What is Style?	209
4	"You can't Wear Your Skis to School"—Symbols of a Lifestyle	213

Contents xiii

	5	Style of Life or Style of Conduct?	217
	6	Towards Defining Style: Seeing versus Talking	221
	7	Style in the Media	226
	8	Cultures of Style? Contra the Praxeological Perspective on Style	229
	9	Is Style Embodied?	236
		Excursus: (Mis)readings of Practice Theory and their Roots in Wittgenstein on Techniques and Rules	239
	10	The Learning Body and Neural Pluralism	243
		Excursus: Bourdieu's Individualistic Reading of Language Games	247
	11	Storing and Transporting Style	253
7	**Emotion and Space—The Arena**	257
	1	Introduction: "It's Really Strange When Nobody is Looking"	257
	2	The Need for Teleoaffectivity	260
	3	Emotional Energy	262
		Excursus: Interaction Ritual Chains	265
	4	Visual and Verbal Pushing	268
	5	Drive, Attunement, and Mood	272
	6	Enter the Arena—Seeing Seeing	274
	7	Visual Space: The Arena as a Stylescape	277
	8	The Kicker as a Visual Arena	279
		Excursus: Foucault, Power, and Phenopractices	283
	9	Position and Posture	286
		Excursus: Why the Arena is not a Ritual	289
	10	Space and Spacing	295
	11	Landscape and Taskscape	298
	12	Commonality and Orchestration	301
8	**Time and Action—Flow**	305
	1	Introduction: On Riding	305
	2	Flow: The Temporal Order of Riding	307
	3	The Action-Present	309
	4	Action from a Phenopractice Perspective	310
	5	Flow in Minds and Markets	312
		Excursus: The Sociology of Flow	313
	6	Taking a Turn in the Krimml	316
	7	Seeing as Steering: Crucial Points	317
	8	The Organization of Practical Intelligibility	322
	9	Stream and Flow	325
	10	Look Where You're Going: The Collective Management of Action	329
	11	A Schutzian Account of Flow	334
	12	Projecting and Grasping Actions	335
	13	Sedimentation and the Body	341
		Excursus: Action and the Body in Husserl	342

	14	The Problems of Projecting	347
	15	Reprise: Projecting, Deciding, and the Flow of Conduct	353
	16	Schutz and Schatzki: The Givenness of Order and the Temporal Rift	355
	Excursus: Schutz and Heidegger		357
	17	Consequences: From Flow to Style	360
9	**Understanding and Media—Seeing Style**		**363**
	1	Introduction: Of Beauty and Repulsion	363
	2	Face Recognition and Style Recognition	365
	3	The Mirror System	369
	Excursus: Do Mirror Neurons Verify Praxeology?		372
	4	Basal Understandings versus Action Understandings	378
	5	Sketchiness	381
	6	Understanding Style and its Roots in Epistemic and Pragmatic Seeing	384
	7	Regularity versus Similarity	386
	8	Judging: Contests and the Anti-Competitive Ethos	388
	9	The Instructed Flow of Judging	392
	10	Juxtaposing Media	401
	11	Seeing a Trick as Gestalt-Seeing	404
	12	Talk and Action	407
	13	Intelligibility and Understanding	412
	Excursus: The (Too) Many Faces of Intentionality		415
	14	Attunement and Expression of Style	420
	15	Seeing Style in Media: Lebenswelt Pairs	425
	16	Beautiful Errors	429
	Excursus I: A Tyranny of Style? Wittgenstein on Images		431
	Excursus II: Luhmann and the Self-programming of the Artwork		437
10	**Invention—Emergence and Stabilization**		**445**
	1	Introduction: Alaska, the Motherland	445
	2	Emergence and Evolution	446
	3	Circulation and Invention	448
	Excursus: The Organization of Normality		451
	4	Mobility, Access, and Natural Laboratories	453
	5	Orientation and Prefiguration	457
	6	New Ways of Seeing	458
	Excursus: Lifestyle Sports, Job Markets, and the Habitus		461
	7	From Orientation to Innovation	465
	8	Inventing Problems, Finding Solutions: How Skiing was Born	467
	9	Teleoaffectivity and Self-Explanation	471
	10	Style and Paradigm Shifts	475
	11	What is Skiing? The Paradigmatic Understanding of Going Down	477
	12	Defining Moments: Demonstration and Competition	480

	13	Media of Dissemination: A Short Visual History of Skiing.	483
	14	Media of Deliberation: Talking Skiing	487
	Excursus: Communication from a Practice Perspective		490
11	**Innovation—Coordination and Evolution**		**493**
	1	Introduction: Unfree Skiing?	493
	2	Organizations: Ski Instruction	496
	3	Symbiotic Fields: Ski Racing.	502
	4	Media Systems: The First Freestyle Revolution	508
	5	Fit to Media Forms.	517
	6	The Birth of Modern Freeride	521
	7	The Sponsor System	525
	8	Authenticity: Skiing and Being	527
12	**Summary, Conclusion, and Outlook**		**531**
	1	Style and Lifestyle: From Symbol to Tool.	532
	2	New Theoretical Perspectives	534
	3	Phenopractice Theory: Key Axioms	540
	4	Avenues for Developing Phenopractice Theory.	546

Appendix: Phenopractice Methodology 549
  1 Theory, Methodology, and Methods in the Practice Turn. 549
  2 Participation and Observation. 552
  3 Observability: Understandings, Intelligibility, and Publicness. 554
  4 Delineating Empirical Phenomena 557
  5 Intelligibility: Can there be an Adequacy Criterion? 559
  6 Validation: Ensuring Adequacy. 561
  7 Generalizability: Average, Typical, or Normal? 564
  8 Conceptualizing Normality. 566
  9 Data, Elements, and Media. 568
  10 Research Procedure of this Work 572

References 585

Index 621

Chapter 1
Introduction: Why Phenopractices?

1 Purpose, Topic, and Form of the Present Work

The fundamental topic of a theory of the social is the nature of intelligible social order. How does observable orderly social conduct come about? Or, more simply put: How do we do what we apparently do? In recent decades, practice theory has emerged as a prominent school of thought offering a convincing and coherent answer. Its conceptual framework integrates key insights from a century of social thought on the basis of philosophical thought by Wittgenstein and Heidegger. This work seeks to extend and inspire the growing family of practice theories by focusing on practices whose performance is oriented by style. Understood in Wittgensteinian terms, style offers a concept to grasp the linking of practices in a number of important ways that feature prominently in different fields of social theory and everyday life: lifestyles, thought styles, and cultural, artistic, or semantic styles for example. This work suggests that apprehending and expressing style qua the conduct of phenopractices is a theoretically under-appreciated way of linking doings and sayings into practice bundles. Focusing on the visual dimension of practices, I will show empirically that both the local order of practice performances and the long-term evolution of practices can be enabled and organized through style. Beyond its empirical relevance for large parts of contemporary culture and consumption, discussing style is theoretically insightful for practice theory at large because style differs from other forms of linking in that it is immaterial (unlike artefacts or tools) but cannot properly be verbally explicated (unlike discourses, norms, or rules). As such, style offers a fresh perspective from which to think through some fundamental practice-theoretical questions, for example those about the nature of practice elements, of social order in the context of rules and regularity, or of action and practical intelligibility. Each chapter in this work is therefore dedicated to a different fundamental theoretical concept such as

© The Author(s), under exclusive license to Springer-Verlag GmbH, DE, part of Springer Nature 2024
N. Woermann, *Seeing Style*, Beiträge zur Praxeologie / Contributions to Praxeology,
https://doi.org/10.1007/978-3-662-69182-3_1

action, emotion, or media. Crucially, understanding how styles help reproduce and link practices requires paying systematic attention to the experiential dimension, because style needs to be felt, sensed, or seen. For this reason, this work integrates insights from phenomenology as well as recent research at the intersection of phenomenology and neurosciences which offer rich inspiration but also considerable provocation for practice thought. On the one hand, phenomenological aspects and insights tend to feature at the margin of practice theory because most accounts aim to grasp the larger nexus of practices and their long-term emergence, evolution, and disappearance. On the other hand, those practice theorists who do pay close attention to action, interaction, and experience often do so by building on subjectivist assumptions and formulating implications in terms of subjectivities and subjectivation. This work seeks to find middle ground between both positions by conceptualizing style as a social rather than a subjective phenomenon linking practice performances across large communities as well as space and time. Therefore, the focus is on the social prefiguration and situated ordering of experiences in practice performance, instead of accounting for the (possibility of social order despite the) idiosyncrasies of individual conscious experiencing.

In sum, this work presents a suggestion to further develop contemporary practice theory by offering *a theory of phenopractices,* understood as the (large) subset of *social practices whose conduct can express style and can therefore be oriented by style.* I will call the result of my considerations "phenopractice theory" mainly for practical reasons, as a shorthand to pinpoint a particular (pro-)position within the family of practice theories. The term "phenopractice theory" on the one hand denotes the importance given to phenomenological problems in designing the theoretical arguments. Although practice theory is successful and convincing because it allows to abstract from the intricacies of individual situated performances to the general features of practices, the intelligibility of performances as the performance of one particular practice is key to their reproduction or existence and therefore requires theoretical attention—as much as necessary, but as little as possible. On the other hand, the prefix "pheno-" invokes the Ancient Greek phaínō, meaning "to bring to light, to make appear." It is thus a reference to this work's particular focus on the visual dimension of social practices and performances to explain the intelligibility of situated social order.

Because it seeks to address the problem of social order by starting with the problem of intelligibility, my discussion of phenopractices is based on a social ontology rooted in the phenomenology of Heidegger and Wittgenstein and building (primarily) on the thought of Harold Garfinkel and Ted Schatzki. The present work compares phenopractice theory with, and defends it against, alternative sociological accounts of social practices and closely related phenomena such as action or knowledge. It does so by examining a fascinating empirical case: the visual practices of the German-speaking freeskiing subculture, a dynamic and rapidly growing lifestyle sport similar to snowboarding. This case is used to demonstrate the plausibility and adequacy of the theoretical concepts and serves as a basis to test, criticize, and develop said concepts. This strategy implies that very general notions such as meaning, temporality, or space are discussed with regard to very specific practices such as watching a freeski-video, skiing down a dangerous mountain face at high speed, or trying to learn difficult acrobatic ski tricks. Such practices are without a doubt particular and sometimes extreme. But although freeskiing and lifestyle sports more generally are important and interesting phenomena in their own right, it is not my aim to develop something like a theory of freeskiing, but rather to advance theory vis-à-vis freeskiing. I believe that not despite, but because of being somewhat exotic, freeskiing practices offer an excellent opportunity to challenge and refine existing accounts of social order. Let me briefly explain why.

Practice theorists claim that even the most mundane social practices necessitate a broad range of skilful accomplishments and finely ordered details which we routinely take for granted and which are thus difficult to observe and reflect upon. Although a number of research methods and strategies have been devised to overcome this obstacle (some of which I will employ), appreciating and systematically documenting the quotidian characteristics and taken-for-granted prerequisites of everyday practices remains a difficult challenge. In some way or another, the researcher will either need to manipulate, interrupt, or alter the conduct in order to gain a distanced perspective; or she needs to record or measure the conduct in order to subsequently re-interpret these pre-produced data. From a practice perspective, there is a danger that by doing so, the researcher will effectively study the details of manipulated, interrupted, altered, or staged-and-recorded conduct rather than normal conduct per se. In contrast, studying a set of special, even extreme practices avoids these pitfalls to a certain extent. Freeskiing practices in particular, I will show, are highly fragile as they demand the fine-tuned alignment of many different aspects such as material tools, interaction patterns, embodied routines, emotions, moods, spatial arrangements, and so on. Consequentially, freeskiing is rich in moments of failure, surprise, doubt, difficulty, learning, trying, and near-disaster which to some degree prevent these aspects from melting into a transparent, uneventful, and indiscernible stream of routine conduct.[1] Under the premise that the very basic nature of social order and conduct is not essentially unique and incomparably different in freeskiing as opposed to social life per se, it should consequentially allow rich insights into the ways in which such aspects can relate and intertwine to form the fabric of ongoing social life.[2] More to the point,

---

[1] It is important to note that my own situation as an 'apprentice' of freeskiing was arguably especially helpful towards this. Since being a relatively experienced skier and former ski instructor, I was able to accomplish and experience freeskiing first hand; but because I was not familiar with its specifics before beginning my research, I needed to learn and come to understand step by step what accomplished freeskiers simply take for granted and thus hardly notice any longer. See the appendix for a more detailed discussion of methodological questions.

[2] Referring to Garfinkel's "unique adequacy principle" (Garfinkel/Wieder 1992), some ethnomethodologists have argued that one cannot make such a provision, in that the phenomenon of social order in one particular field is incomparably different from all others. As I will show in the appendix, this interpretation goes too far. After all, it does itself build on the provision that ethnomethods and social order per se share basic characteristics across all fields of inquiry.

social theorists usually claim to make general arguments and provide accounts of universal social phenomena such as time and space. Consequentially, said arguments and accounts can legitimately be expected to work just as well if applied to a possibly exotic, but nevertheless global, popular, and persistent set of subcultural practices.

By analysing and discussing the details of the artful accomplishment of freeskiing practices, I will necessarily and purposefully simultaneously provide a rich account of the freeskiing experience and culture. Accordingly, this work can alternatively just as well be read as an ethnography of the freeskiing subculture, especially since each chapter attends to a different typical practice taking place in a different corner of the freeskiing universe, such as planning a route in the backcountry, checking out a new ski model on a trade-fair, or judging freestyle contests. There is, however, one caveat such a reading requires: It is not my foremost goal to provide a complete description of all aspects of freeskiing; and the selection, order, and depth of presentation of my topics follows the needs of the theoretical discussion, not the other way around. Sadly, this means that I will not be able to present all the empirical insights I arguably gathered during more than four years of fieldwork comprising participant observation, video and audio recording, interviews, and document analysis. Some of the aspects I had to leave out here are chronicled and analysed elsewhere (Woermann 2010, 2012a, 2012b, 2013). Nevertheless, I believe that I am able to cover most of the things that freeskiers deeply care about. I do spend considerably more effort and words in order to provide a thick description of my empirical topics than a purely theoretical discussion that is only seeking to provide some examples or a nice framework would. There are three reasons for this: First, I believe that providing a lively image of this fascinating subculture that reflects a number of interesting developments in our contemporary consumer society is a worthy end in itself. Accordingly, I have tried to separate the main text that gives an account of freeskiing practices and then interprets and explains it in terms of practice theory from purely theoretical excurses (in grey boxes), which ponder theoretical alternatives and discuss abstract theoretical issues. Although the line is often difficult to draw, my idea is that a reader skipping all these 'grey boxes' will gain a complete picture of my theoretical positions and the empirical insights it is build on, but will miss most of the reasons why I have chosen certain explanations or theoretical notions over others, and which problems I see in rival explanations. Second, many of my theoretical arguments built on specific particularities of the situations and momentary contexts in which freeskiing happens, and are only plausible and coherent if understood against this rich empirical background. Further, I believe that attention to and insight into details necessitates a good sense of the different dimensions of the overarching context; for example freeskiing's intensive visceral experiences of danger, euphoria, and exposure, or a basic grasp of the technological or historical horizons within which freeskiing happens. In sum, I believe that my detailed theoretical account does not simply frame or illustrate my theoretical line of argumentation, but makes it possible in the first place. Third, to some extend my empirical accounts function as a piece of 'theoretical ethnography' in that they directly drive my theoretical findings, including my terminology. A number of authors I build on have followed a related principle when conducting "empirical philosophy" (Mol 2002) or "applied philosophy" (H. L. Dreyfus 1979; see Kelly 2000); and in twisting the idea around, Wittgenstein's work can be read as an "imaginary ethnography" (Gebauer 2009: 236): in these cases, empirical phenomena themselves are taken to provide theoretical arguments.[3] In comparison to these, theoretical ethnography as I understand it shares the conviction that lived life provides rich theoretical insight, but differs in that it uses laymen's folk theories and folk terminology as itself offering (possibly) adequate theoretical concepts or arguments. For example, at several points my writing ethnography and writing theory coalesce in that freeskiers' folk theory and folk terminology provide me with concepts and terms (such as "style" and "flow") which I adapt and integrate into my overall theoretical construct—in both cases because they arguably allow me to grasp a certain sentiment until now amiss in the literature.

To summarize: Although this work is about freeskiing, it is primarily a work of theory. Its main goal is to lay down a coherent account of a theory of phenopractices. By moving systematically from one empirical site to the next, it takes a series of key theoretical topics (such as meaning, action, or space) into focus in order to assemble a string of arguments that link together within a general theoretical perspective on social practices. Any author drawing on practice theory needs to content with the fact that it represent a family of theories rather than a unified position, and that the focus and purpose of the 'family members' is stratified along different dimensions. Because of my focus on intelligibility, seeing, and style, the discussion will take as its starting and reference points two accounts of practice theory that offer situated concepts of intelligibility and social order: the works of Ted Schatzki and Harold Garfinkel. This combination might seem unusual or surprising, because both ethnomethodologists (Lynch 2001) and Schatzki (1996: 178) have rejected each other's position. However, I believe that these rejections are each born out of a superficial reading of one another and that in contrast, both share a number of fundamental convictions, especially because they both build on Heidegger and define all meaning as manifesting in local contexts only. Still, both differ greatly in their style of arguing, the topics they cover, and the data they draw on: Schatzki provides an abstract theoretical vocabulary which has often loosely referred to in empirical research but seldomly been applied strictly, while ethnomethodology understands itself as a 'radically empirical' enterprise and distances itself from abstract theory per se (although addressing fundamental theoretical questions, see Lynch 1999). Precisely because of these differences, however, I argue that both positions are complementary to a considerable extent; especially in that ethnomethodologists have developed a number of empirical methods and

---

[3] Harold Garfinkel (2002) goes a step further by insisting that the phenomena ethnomethodology seeks to 'describe' must be discovered first hand, and thus his writings are not meant to actually contain theoretical arguments in written form, but rather "tutorials" on how to personally reproduce their real-life experience (see Rawls 2002).

a detailed methodology but decline to take a more long-term view on the social, while Schatzki's work remains mostly silent on questions of methodology (and epistemology) but develops a more systematic account of pan-situational relations and developments. I do not claim, however, that my account will or can do full justice to both positions at the same time—quite to the contrary, I will interpret both in my own ways and deviate on a number of issues.

The following chapters will each cover a different theoretical issues intricately linked to the core theme of intelligibility of and through style. Intelligibility of any kind, I will argue, can only and exclusively transpire in concrete situations; and situations, in turn, are established or opened up through the situated unfolding of social practices. On this basis, I hope, theoretical coherence will be achieved in this work in that the different topics of inquiry will turn out to be different aspects or dimensions of situated conduct, or rather of the situated accomplishment of stylized social order that enables intelligibility. But does this perspective not contradict the idea that freeskiing is a subculture, or maybe a lifestyle sport community? After all, these notions seem to imply a social whole that needs to be studied: the group, tribe, symbolic universe, or cultural field as one given unit. Does the practice approach, in other words, necessitate breaking freeskiing down into a series of dispersed and possibly disparate practices taking place in different sites? As one will see, my perspective indeed differs in important ways from the bulk of established studies of lifestyle sports; and this yields a number of important implications. But before attending to them, one needs to ask in which way one can think about a subculture as being composed of different practices in the first place. Towards an answer, let me first sketch out what freeskiing is.

2 The Field of Freeskiing

Freeskiing is a lifestyle sport subculture comprised of two interconnected yet different subgenres: Freestyle[4]—performing aerial tricks over ramps, in half-pipes, or on other obstacles such as handrails—and freeriding—powder skiing in steep and unprepared terrain, often including aerials or cliff-drops. Freeskiing forms an aesthetic universe of its own, structured by a "style" that permeates bodily movements, clothing, video, music, product design, language, and lifestyle. It is organized not via a centralized body such as the international ski federation FIS, but consists of globally dispersed communities of freeskiers, each of which form a small minority in the ski resorts dominated by classic alpine skiing. On the other hand, it is a globally movement tightly connected via the internet and regular scene-specific events or contests. Freeskiers, I argue, can be understood as an avant-garde, crossing boundaries and transforming established practices of

---

[4] What I refer to here exactly is the emerging lifestyle sport called Newschool Freestyle which is different from the "Oldschool" Olympic sport of Freestyle or Trick skiing.

skiing; driven by a curious passion or devotion. In order to be properly understood, I suggest that freeskiing needs to be seen as more than just symbolic action, as a quest not just for economic success, group status or gold medals, but something more abstract, yet at the same time more real: as a bodily, material, social and aesthetic phenopractice. More to the point: as a field of different context-dependent phenopractices which together form the sphere of freeskiing. Since this work aims to develop a coherent understanding of the interrelations and dynamics of pheno practices, its scope is not only confined to training and performing the sport itself, since this would render invisible the wide range of specific practices which stand as inevitable prerequisites to the athletic accomplishments. Instead, practices of preparing for and discussing training runs, shooting and watching ski films and photos, or testing skis will be studied symmetrically. The basic assumption is that they can only be adequately grasped in context of each other, each being oriented to the others in a certain way. However, these phenopractices on the other hand do constitute particular situations of conduct; each necessitating specific skills, being subject to certain environmental contingencies and producing particular dynamics. Therefore, this work attempts to capture these practices as local, situated and contingent accomplishments on a micro level primarily from a perspective derived from ethnomethodology—but it does so with a distinctive focus on how each of such situated accomplishments momentarily and locally (re-) produces certain 'objects' it orients to, which constitute the central 'elements' of freeskiing. For example, it will examine how skiers or videographers (re-) construct a certain run or trick that was just performed as being meaningful, cool, instructional, and so on. To take another example, it will look at how marketers on a trade fair, together with visitors cooperatively construct material objects as being desirable products with certain attributes. As in both cases certain versions of what has happened (this movement on skis was a rad Japan Double-Mute Switch Rodeo) or will happen (this ski will easily float in deep powder) are made present, the relevancy of and interrelation to (past or present) practices of freeskiing is locally reproduced in each such situation anew. The coherence of the field of freeskiing will thus not be understood as a fixed social structure (be it explicit or implicit, subconscious or intentional), but as an ongoing processual achievement within each local situation that is coordinated through a common reliance on a certain set of understandings and by virtue of a shared orientation towards a certain style of conduct. This conception has to two mayor consequences for the scope and organization of this work: On the one hand, it looks at quite distinct fields of phenopractices (such as sport, media, marketing or product design) which all share a very important denominator: they form an integral part of the freeskiing subculture and committed freeskiers typically engage in all of them. Because the phenomena which this work examines are constituted through finely coordinated details, it must rely on data able to exhibit such minutiae, such as recordings of naturally occurring situations or videos of gestural coordination. On the other hand, such an undertaking can easily result in an unmanageable avalanche of data when applied to a field of practices that is too wide, making a coherent interpretation impossible. Therefore, the study focuses on certain practices deemed central to the respective field of phenopractices, by zooming in on typical situations the observation of which will be embedded into a more general ethnographic account of its contexts.

Crucially, even though I speak of a subculture, freeskiing will not be framed as a community of people in the classic sense, that is, as a group of like-minded individuals. The way I presented the project thus far, this conviction appeared to be a direct and inevitable effect of taking a practice perspective on such a subculture. This perspective contrasts with a prominent and rich school of thought that employs practice theory to study lifestyle sport cultures, subcultures, or culture more generally with a focus on subjectivation and subjects as 'carriers of practice' sharing certain (embodied) knowledge or dispositions (Brümmer/Alkemeyer 2017). A core proposition of this book is that style needs to be conceptualized as a social rather than a subjective phenomenon if it is to be theorized as linking practice performances across large communities as well as long stretches of space and time. Therefore, the focus is on the social prefiguration and situated ordering of experiences instead of (idiosyncrasies of) individual conscious experiencing. Because prior work on (life-)style is dominated by (more or less) subjectivist accounts, I will continuously draw out the contrasts and disagreements-in-detail despite the shared interest and motivation of these practice-based accounts and mine. Rather than proving the ultimate superiority of one theoretical account over the other, this procedure is simply a productive tool for theory development and refinement. Clearly stating identities and differences within practice theory approaches can only help furthering its appeal.

Any authors seeking to theorize phenopractices will encounter a practice theory literature rich in empirical nuance and insightful arguments, but also marred by incoherent uses of terminology and incompatible methodologies or underlying assumptions. During the last two decades, theories of social practices have received considerable attention in sociology, cultural theory, and philosophy, as well as in many more specific fields such as human geography, management studies, or artificial intelligence. However, some of the broad reception might be due to the fact that social practices is a concept at the core of a Venn diagram of an unduly large array of theoretical positions. Despite powerful attempts to order and consolidate the field, key points of contention remain. By calling my proposal phenopractice theory rather than practice theory proper, I hope to avoid adding to the confusion by marking clearly that I am offering a specific version of the theory, an alternative rather than a revision. In other words, my suggestion should be easy to distinguish and dismiss (if necessary).

3 Theoretical Approach and Stance

The first task in proposing a phenopractice theory is to clear the ground on which to erect the theoretical edifice by clarifying what common ground exists with established works on practice theory, and where lines of thought branch off. For this reason, I will consistently try to make clear why certain concepts or terms are

3 Theoretical Approach and Stance

being chosen over which preeminent alternatives; and I will attempt to trace back the roots of the arguments that are being exchanged over the issue. Frequently, these roots are to be found in philosophy rather than sociology itself. Once that happens, I will not go much further once a philosophical a-priori has been unearthed since discerning its general validity or logical coherence is a matter best left to philosophers themselves. I will not, for example, make an extensive case for why I follow just this one particular of the (at least) two competing readings of Wittgenstein's notion of rule-following, since detailed discussions of the arguments and counterarguments are already plentiful. Neither will I attempt to decide whether Heidegger got it right when he transformed Husserl's thought. However, I deem it fundamentally important to acknowledge that, for example, Schutz relies on Husserl when he conceptualizes action, while Schatzki follows Heidegger; and that certain postulates of Husserl are thus in turn shared by those sociologists building on either Schutz or Husserl. Only after these presuppositions have been clarified I will proceed to try and establish the logical coherence of my preferred theoretical notion as well as its plausibility vis-à-vis the empirical data at hand. In doing so, I will at times argue for the implausibility (but usually not the incoherence) of rival understandings delineated from alternative philosophical postulates, but I should caution that I cannot and do not claim to be able to 'disproof' said fundamental postulate in this way. Despite the space devoted to theoretical alternatives, in other words, my aim is to argue for a specific understanding rather than against another. I selected the optional positions I discuss on the basis that I consider them to be adequate alternatives, i.e. they can be applied well to the empirical case at hand and in some of their arguments, they are relatively close to practice theory; but they nevertheless differ in important ways in other aspects—not the least important of which is frequently their philosophical a-priori basis. In contrast I do not, for example, discuss rational choice theories at any length because they seem neither adequate to explain freeskiing, nor do I see the danger that one might mistake practice theory for a rational choice theory. In effect, my account will on the one hand concern several prominent positions such as Schutz, Goffman, and Bourdieu; but on the other hand, it will also attend to more specific arguments, especially those which seem relevant for topics such as style or vision. Finally, because I strive to discuss different topics and different theoretical alternates chapter by chapter, I will sometimes use the same or very similar arguments repeatedly and in quite different contexts. For example, I will use the argument that social order is grounded on similarity rather than regularity—which is drawn from Wittgenstein's discussion of rule-following and family-resemblance—both to reject notions of social space deducted from ritual theory and to counter praxeological readings of the impact of mirror neurons on taste and distinctions. I do not consider this a sign of redundancy in a strict sense, but rather of logical coherence of my line of argumentation. Precisely because a definitive and relatively small set of philosophical a-priories underpins the practice perspective on all sorts of different phenomena or questions, I suggest considering it as a theoretical position in its own right rather than a mere mishmash of disparate insights or a superficial revamping of well-known classics.

A key effect of theorizing phenopractices in particular, instead of practices per se, is the pivotal importance of Heidegger for developing the argument. Heideggerian thought is at the root of many, but crucially not all theories of social practices. At first sight, this might be surprising, since it is after all Wittgenstein's philosophy which is commonly regarded as the root of practice theory (being the origin of the very term 'social practices'). However, I argue that the realm of practice thought is partitioned into two mayor factions that differ in their reading and use of Wittgensteinian philosophy, and that the origin of their disparity lies in the fact that one of them additionally builds on Heidegger, while the other does not. Theorizing phenopractices therefore offers an opportunity to deepen and develop Heideggerian thought on social practices. The key effect of invoking Heidegger, I will show, is a strictly situated view of practical conduct according to which all social order must be tied to local sites or clearings. While Wittgensteinian thinking can be aligned well with this situated perspective, Wittgenstein can alternatively be read as implying that social practices or forms of life are characteristics of groups of people, e.g. by virtue of embodied knowledge. This division between a situated and a 'forms of life' notion of social practices is arguably at the root of both many (though not all) disagreements within the practice 'camp' and of misconceptions held about practice theory by 'outsiders.' Put in broad terms, I hold that especially those authors building on Bourdieu's praxeology adhere to a reading of Wittgenstein that effectively frames it as an anthropology (see Gebauer 2009), while Schatzki as well as many ethnomethodologists (see Garfinkel/ E. Livingston 2003; Lynch 2009) understand it more 'radically' as providing an ontology of factual 'social things' (see below for my use of the term ontology). Interestingly, those forming the latter of the two 'factions' have been quite clear and explicit about the nature of the disagreement, but as far as I can see, their arguments have unfortunately neither been acknowledged nor refuted by the other group.[5]

Consequently, sorting out the differences between versions of practice thought rooted in anthropological ontology on the one side, and a theory of social practices building on a site ontology in the wake of Heidegger on the other is a key step towards formulating a phenopractice theory, that is, a practice-based alternative to traditional subject-centred phenomenology. The best way to systematically do so, I suggest, is to return to the phenomenological questions deliberated by Wittgenstein and Heidegger that are at the root of contemporary practice thought. Although most sociological contributions to practice theory do not discuss phenomenology explicitly, at the heart of each version of practice theory lays a certain understanding of the nature and constitution of meaningful social order and meaningful experiences of lived life. More to the point, both Wittgenstein and Heidegger considered themselves phenomenologists; but both also sought to

---

[5] For example, Schatzki explains the considerable distance between his position and that of Bourdieu and Giddens as a direct consequence of his reliance on Wittgenstein and Heidegger (e.g. 1996: 153); ethnomethodologists have uttered similar sentiments (Lynch 1997, 2001).

argue (in different ways) against the phenomenology of consciousness as funded by Husserl (as did other key forefathers of contemporary practice thought such as Merleau-Ponty and Gurwitsch). At the core of the phenopractice-project, one could very well say, lies the attempt to separate or expel meaning or intentionality from consciousness—and from the subject. Such a move evidently implies far-reaching consequences for both theory and methodology. In order to be able to trace them throughout my discussion, I will focus on a specific aspect of social practices, the importance of which is a direct consequence of my interest in phenomenology: intelligibility.

4 The Focus: Intelligibility and Vision

Towards making the case for a coherent theory of phenopractical perspective based not only on Wittgenstein, but also on Heidegger, the present work focuses on a specific dimension of social life, both in terms of empirical findings (and the methodology I therefore applied), and in terms of the theoretical standpoints I discuss. The central topic of this work will be observability or intelligibility. How is it possible, it will be asked, that participants of the social world come to identify things, understand how things are, determine what to do, show successfully what they can do, and so on. Focusing on intelligibility will allow me to approach certain issues central to sociology from a distinct angle and formulate new answers: Most importantly, these are issues which are frequently discussed under the terms identity, knowledge, and action. In short, I aim to formulate an account of how it becomes intelligible or observable what someone or something is, knows, or does. The crucial point is that I aim to provide an account which explains these phenomena without accounting for them by virtue of identity, knowledge, or action itself. Instead, I will offer a different explanations which systematically undercuts these categories by treating them as effects of underlying entities: social practices. I focus on intelligibility, in other words, because it provides a platform to tackle a number of fundamental questions in order to show, in each case, what kinds of answers and open questions a practice theory perspective produces. On the other hand, this focus on intelligibility still leaves open a potentially overwhelming range of things to study vis-à-vis the manifold practices even within a specific subculture such as freeskiing. In face of the breadth and diversity of the issues and theoretical viewpoints I seek to address, some further focus and selectivity is necessary for the project not to explode. For this reason, I will focus on the visual dimension of social practices.

Throughout the book I will apply a consistent focus on the visual dimension of the different practices that together make up what is called the freeskiing subculture. To this end, I will examine visual displays and practices of showing on trade fairs, cameramen's views of freeskiing action, collective watching of freeski movies, the scrutinizing gaze of judges during freestyle competition, and more. While all of these practices need to be taken as instantiations of some common, general nature of looking-at-something-in-order-to-see-something that relies on the use of vision, they are at same time very different; being situated in very different circumstances and making use of different technological tools, social interactions and spatial arrangements in systematic ways. Therefore, they point to the ubiquity of seeing and the inherent embeddedness of most social conduct into visual order as a fundamental dimension of social orderliness per se. Much of the work in visual sociology is concerned with some form of visual art or craft such as painting, film, or advertising and thus might tempt one to see visual culture as a specific field rather than a dimension of culture in general. In contrast, the approach guided by practice theory I will follow highlights the general relevance of the visual in almost all moments of lived social life—even for those athletic practiced which appear to be 'only' motor exercises at first glance. I stress that I focus on the visual *dimension* of the topics I will explore, for example the visual dimension of the social production of space or bodily routines in the realm of human vision. Accordingly, I do not generally neglect all non-visual phenomena, but I centre my discussion on their relation to or intertwining with vision and the visual. On important case that comes to mind is language and language use: I do not devote a specific chapter entirely to language, but I analyse ways of speaking and functions of words several times, taking particular interest in how speaking accompanies, influences, or fails to express seeing and visual order.

My focus on vision has two main reasons. First, there is the empirical importance of all things visual in freeskiing. Although the visceral experience of skiing is of course of outmost importance, freeskiing is also a thoroughly visual culture. After all, in freeskiing, the performance or aptitude of an athlete cannot be measured metrically but must be judged by eyesight in terms of aesthetic qualities such as the calmness, elegance, or perfection of movements. What is more, freeskiers show an almost never-waning interest in freeski pictures and films, and the next best thing to being on the snow for them is to indulge in a visual feast of perfectly composed skiing images. Freeski magazines show jaw-dropping stunts performed against the stunning backdrop of a magnificent sundown over pristine mountain ranges, and freeski-DVDs feature heli-skiing in the most exotic locations produced by international, highly professionally companies with multi-million dollar budgets (Kay/Laberge 2003). Besides consuming photos and videos, producing them is an important aspect of the subculture. Photo- and video-equipment is a ubiquitous sight in snowparks where freeskiers hang out, and often includes sophisticated helmet cameras, fisheye lenses, and camera booms. Between two attempts of a trick, during lunch breaks, or at the end of the day in the campervan, freeskiers frequently huddle together around a screen and assess what they have recorded, commenting on everything from a rider's stability in the air to the snow-quality of the landing, the stylishness of a new pair of baggy pants, or the planar composition of a picture. My discussion of style in this work is in part an effect of this empirical predominance. However, I also stress that this glossy and polished side of the freeskiing subculture is only its most refined and most aesthetic form of manifestation; and that visual style also plays a much more mundane and even functional role for the everyday achievement of freeskiing practices. Only on the basis of the everyday practices of seeing, I will argue, one can—and should—attempt to understand the impact and role of the professionalized global freeski mediascape. The second reason for my focusing on vision is theoretical in nature. As I will show, many key ideas that led to contemporary practice theory have their roots in thinking about and experiments with vision, and particularly in gestalt theory. This influence is for example reflected in Wittgenstein's notion of family resemblance and his philosophy of the image (D. Mersch 2006; Richtmeyer 2009); in Heidegger's visual metaphors such as 'clearing' or 'unconcealment' and his focus on sight (W. McNeill 1999; Protevi 1998); or in the importance of the term 'horizon' for phenomenology in Husserl (who also drew on vision science and gestalt thinking, see Rang 1990) and later in Merleau-Ponty and Gurwitsch, who likewise derived the notion 'phenomenal field' from the visual field. Therefore, if one attempts to disentangle and delineate the different versions and aspects of practice theory, the visual seems to be a good place to start from.

5 The Foundation: Ontology and Epistemology

The last thing I need to clarify before I can get this account underway, finally, is to sketch out my own theoretical a-prioris. It should be clear that I will presuppose the notion that social practices are responsible for the phenomenon of social order. But what exactly does that mean? Are they simply a theoretical fiction, maybe or a phenomenal effect of some basic human capacity? What is left to be defined, in other words, is my stance on the social world per se. My basic suggestion is simple: Take practice theory to be an ontology. Then ask about intelligibility. Assume that social practices are the ontological condition of possibility of phenomenological experience. The project of this work and the specific perspective on social thought it operates from are therefore grounded in a basal distinction: ontology and epistemology. It holds as an a-priori postulate that every epistemology (or phenomenology) must be based on or carry an ontology. Its proposition is: While most sociological[6] theories provide epistemologies of the social or phenomenologies of the social based on a (implicit) individualist ontology, practice theory develops a *social ontology* whose phenomenology and epistemology of the social has not yet been sufficiently addressed. The term epistemology can denote a range of different things within social thought, particularly because the realms of phenomenology and epistemology seem to intertwine and overlap as soon as the social is concerned. Let me therefore clarify my use of the terms for the sake of this distinction. In my use of the term, ontology is the study of what is. In a strict sense, ontologies are not explanations, but philosophical a-priori postulates, descriptions of given basic qualities, structures, and laws governing a certain

---

[6] Henceforth, I will exclusively refer to sociological theories, explanations, or methods concerned with meaning (in a broad sense) when talking about sociology.

realm: things as they really are. Therefore, ontologies are not concerned with an explanans, but provide the bedrock of one's explanandum. An ontology *of* the social in my terms is thus a theory about the nature of the social. Further, a *social* ontology is a view on the world that understands social life as (part of) the primordial soup from which facts, things, and subjects spring from (see also Schatzki 2002: 124). In contrast, I understand phenomenology in the broadest sense as the study of meaningful phenomena, as an enquiry of how meaningful worldly things and events present themselves. In this sense, meaning and existence are not to be equated, and the unfolding of meaning must not necessarily take place in consciousness. Contrary to those sociological theories which equate sociality and meaningfulness (most precisely stated by Luhmann 1995a), social ontologies grant social elements existence independent of—though possibly related to—the occurrence of meaning. In the same vein, what I call ontology should also be contrasted with epistemology or the study of knowledge and knowing. In a way, this already follows from the fact that many sociological authors develop epistemologies based on phenomenological concepts, and that philosophers of social epistemology usually include perception and experience into its realm (e.g. Goldman 2010). For reasons of clarity I should nevertheless state that epistemologies of the social in my terms are theories of the social treating it as having the form of knowledge, being brought about by (action directed by) knowledge, or acting socially as a form of knowing (for an overview, see Knoblauch 2005a). As I stated, epistemologies and phenomenologies always carry an ontology, that is, they imply something about the ways things are beyond the realm of meaning or knowledge. As Schatzki (2002: 124–132)—to whom this discussion is obviously indebted—shows, this ontology is frequently individualistic or, as others have argued, anthropologic (Luckner 2008; Luhmann 1995b), sometimes despite certain authors' assurance to the contrary.

From this position, I believe, the project of theories of social practices can be stated most clearly: to provide a social ontology of the social rather than an individualistic ontology of the social. Many of the misunderstandings and unfruitful quarrels surrounding the current debate on practice thought can, I hope, be avoided if one accepts that what is put forward are non-individualistic, but nevertheless ontological propositions. Unfortunately, sociologists are often not very keen on discussing ontologies at extensive length—and understandably so, since after all, it is the social that they are interested in and experts of. Ontology, in contrast, seems to smack of metaphysics or—as Luckmann (1973) implies—deliberating ontology means to spin cosmology, to reach for the stars and loose footing in the social every day. By turning to ontology, many thus seem to fear, they will find themselves in a realm of speculation, haruspication, and proclamation cut off from solid empirical reasoning. In my view, this mistrust is unwarranted. For one, ontologies are of course still theories, not revelations; thus they are both contingent and can (and should) be informed by empirical insight and logical coherency. Far from delivering themselves to postmodern arbitrarity, they principally demand to be measured against an eminent standard of both plausibility and flexibility in application. Crucially, I further hold that despite their prejudices, sociologists are necessarily and ubiquitously in the business of invoking ontologies anyways. Yet while frequently priding themselves of their reflexivity (and often justifiably so), many seem to be somewhat uneasy and quiet about this fact and therefore try to hide ontology in the closet for things not to be discussed in public. By developing epistemologies or phenomenologies of the social, they might hope to avoid the deep waters of philosophical ontology through building on postulates about the individual, the contingency of which they often leave to philosophers or anthropologists. Alas, their hope is in vain.

To be sure, by no means do I intend to claim that sociological individualists or individualists-in-disguise have not been able to produce important, valid, or coherent insights. Precisely because philosophical a-prioris lie outside of the reach of sociological reasoning per se, their sociological arguments can be, and often are, entirely coherent. Even though delivering depth and precision, however, they are still entangled in problems of their own; problems that one might try to avoid by discussing ontology more explicitly, thus dragging it into the limelight of sociology and its methods. Where do I locate these alleged problems of the ontology of what I called phenomenologies and epistemologies of the social? Arguably unlike Schatzki, I suggest that their ontological postulates are not strictly confined to individualism (or anthropology) alone, because the ontology of any epistemology or phenomenology necessarily includes assumptions about the nature of knowledge or meaning, respectively. When undertaking the study of social phenomena as a study of meaning or knowledge, the social is thus implicitly granted ontological status to the extent that it is composed of meaning or knowledge. In effect, such works apply a mix of a largely implicit 'semi-social' ontology of the (epistemology of the) social, and an individualistic ontology of the (epistemology of the) social; oscillating back and forth as need arises. Trying to avoid this impasse by re-tying social epistemology to the individual or by reducing practice thought to notions like embodied knowledge or the habitus does not solve but only deepen the problem. In my view, this has been seen maybe most clearly by Niklas Luhmann and led him to try to develop an epistemology of the social purified from all underlying 'anthropo-logic' ontology. If one insists that epistemologies unavoidably carry an ontology (as I do), however, Luhmann's brilliant social epistemology of the social suffers from requiring an extremely reduced ontology entirely modelled after and confined to the ontological qualities of meaning, e.g. in that events cease to exist in the same instance in which they begin (Luhmann 1995a, 1996a). Therefore, Luhmann's ontology has drawn widespread criticism and continues to pose problems in terms of methodology.

Practice theory as I understand it, one could say, starts from the same diagnosis but proceeds in the other direction by holding that, rather than trying to abolish ontology altogether, it should be untied from any inherent individualism still governing it. Therefore, what I suggest is attending to ontology sociologically. Arguing with a social ontology, I hold, benefits sociology because it allows it to re-explicate, re-consider, and re-arrange the a-priori postulates it operates from—without, of course, being able to remove them. Instead of schematically applying traditional individualist ontologies to practice thought, one might as well take a closer look at the shifting of relations between ontology, phenomenology, and epistemology implied by an explicitly social ontology (for example by Schatzki). This is precisely the aim of this book. And the issue within which these shifting relations are reflected is the question of the epistemology and phenomenology of elements of practices. In this work, I suggest that theorizing phenopractices requires a particular understanding of the relation between the practice as an arrangement and its elements. I embrace the difficult, yet central assertion of practice thought that practices can only said to exist or happen in the form of an ordered whole (a site) and that the meaning or order of a practice cannot be reduced to, encapsulated in, or fully represented by single entities other than the practice itself, such as accounts, rules, or objects. In my view, accepting this premise is fundamental to envisioning practice theory as a non-individualist *ontology* of the social, which I deem as the core of the practice project. Consequentially, I accept that intelligibility cannot occur outside of the situated unfolding of phenopractices. However, I suggest that neither premise does automatically imply a radically situationalist and effectively fragmentarist ontology that holds that no enduring qualities whatsoever exist outside of social occurrences. That every concrete social occurrence of order is unique in its detail (and the details of its context) does not render the existence of regularity or self-identity impossible. It only implies that they cannot directly transpire in moments of social life. A social ontology, finally, makes assumptions about the nature and prerequisites of such regularities or enduring entities underlying social order—only that the regular entity it takes for granted does not happen to be an individual 'Anthropos.'

> "To include epistemological questions concerning the validity of sociological knowledge in the sociology of knowledge is somewhat like trying to push a bus in which one is riding." (Berger/T. Luckmann 1966: 13)

To speak in the words of Berger and Luckmann: This work hops on to a different bus than many other theories of the social. Let's see where the ride will take us.

6 Outline of the Present Work

The purpose of this work is to develop and defend phenopractice theory by examining the visual dimension of freeskiing in order to understand how intelligibility is produced within them. The outline of the different chapters is as follows:

The second chapter will discuss *observing* and identifying as interactive, situated, and multi-modal accomplishments, thus sketching out the basic premises of the phenopractice perspective. The case that will be discussed is a practice freeskiers call 'reading faces,' that is, figuring out attractive lines of descent through dangerous mountain terrain by inspecting and discussing it from afar.

The third chapter focuses on *sensory experience* and the bodily foundations of perceiving and spells out theoretical consequences for intelligibility and meaning.

6 Outline of the Present Work

In this chapter, I will look in some more detail at the optical and neural underpinnings of human vision and how they are reflected in phenomenology and especially gestalt thinking—both in the history of ideas and in contemporary theory.

On this basis, the fourth chapter then examines the sensory experience of skiing itself in order to sketch out how *bodily movement* enables and influences observing, and how—turning the question around—the body and movement themselves become intelligible for us.

The fifth chapter analyses a classic question of epistemology: how do we gain insights into and understandings of particular things or material *objects*. The case at hand will be—not surprisingly—the ski; or, more precisely: the different ways and techniques to learn about, (visually) represent, and test the specific qualities of a ski.

In the sixth chapter, I turn to the role of *style and symbols* in order to explain how performances come to mean or express something. Here, I will chronicle the role and function of that peculiar quality that freeskiers consider to be outmost important: style.

Subsequently, chapter number seven describes freeskiers' interactions, performances, and spectatorship in the funpark and discusses the dual role of first, *emotions*, and second, *space* for accomplishing intelligibility and as enforcing mutual observation.

The following eight chapter seeks to explain the intelligibility of *action*, that is, how actions make sense to the actor; particularly with regard to their temporal structure. Returning to the dangerous mountain backcountry, I will assess the freeriders' ways of learning and controlling their high-speed skiing.

Chapter nine discusses the function of *media* and mediatized observation or understanding by asking what precisely it means when freeskiers say that a performance, image, or video has style; and by virtue of which local practices they manage to discern and agree on visible style.

The tenth chapter, uses this discussion as a foundation to examine how understandings evolve and spread, thereby enabling the *dissemination* of phenopractices by tracing the history of freeskiing, but also modern skiing per se, which turns out to be partly driven by the specific performativity of skiing as well as the necessities and dynamics of visual media that helped popularize, transport, and teach skiing around the world.

The eleventh chapter, finally, applies the findings collected about the nature, function, and dissemination of style to describe the *evolution* of the global skiing world and especially the several style 'revolutions' (freeskiing being only the latest) that have rocked it in the last century. Here, I will attempt to explain on the basis of their dependence on visible style and visual media why certain mutations of skiing have matured into popular subcultures of their own, while others have been marginalized.

In addition to the theoretical and empirical discussion, the *methodological appendix i*n chapter twelve will consider how the ethnographic researcher him- or herself observes, gains insights, and comes to understand pheno practices; not to a small extend by relying on eyesight or cameras.

Presented like this, it seems that I plan to discuss a collection of relatively disparate topics or issues. Yet in my view, they are not only all tightly interwoven and co-dependent, but—according to the practice perspective—they are also merely different aspects of a social life organized by one universal set of underlying principles or relationships. Therefore, because practice theory treats these different phenomena as effects or dimensions of the same basal processes, it will be possible to assemble, step by step, one coherent phenopractical theory account.

Chapter 2
Vision—Seeing Lines

Wilde Krimml, Zillertal, Austria

1 Introduction: The Line

Early in the morning, when the coming day resonates only in a weak inkling of its later glistening brightness behind the distant peaks to the east and the empty, rock-riddled vastness of the Wilde Krimml just subtly looms among the edgeless blue-grey of the first dawn, nothing but the piercingly cold wind is sweeping along the deserted alpine mountains' sharp ridges. The wind runs over the gently curved snow of cornices, it soughs through the narrow ravines between small hilltops and towering cliffs that string along the ridge all the way up to the summit of the Rifflerkogel, and then it pushes down through the couloirs and gorges that stretch from the ridge down into the vast bowl's width. As it forms small swirls along the

© The Author(s), under exclusive license to Springer-Verlag GmbH, DE, part of Springer Nature 2024
N. Woermann, *Seeing Style*, Beiträge zur Praxeologie / Contributions to Praxeology, https://doi.org/10.1007/978-3-662-69182-3_2

brinks, it carries along some snow crystals sparkling in the first light of the day. It is the only motion detectable up here, high above the tree line on a clear January morning in the Kitzbühler Alps. Apart from the soft, howling sound of the wind it is completely quiet. Soon, when the sun will emerge from behind the surrounding peaks and turn the clam blue-grey of the snow-covered mountainsides into a glistening, seemingly endless white against which only some black rocks will stand out in stark contrast, a "smooth space" (Deleuze/Guattari 1987) par excellence will stretch out. Under a clear blue, cloudless sky lies a contour-less, homogenous, almost form-less white. One might see it as an empty canvas onto which the art of the social can freely paint its sign and symbols as it sees fit. A vacant space of nothingness that can be filled with our ideas and creativity and will hitherto stand testament to precisely what these ideas have been. Or so one might think.

In my view, this idea—however dear to theorists eager to demonstrate the omnipotence of the social—is misleading. After all, it already requires one to see the perfectly contingent, form-less white *as* something (in this case, white, form-less, spacious, fill-able, and so forth). It must, in other words, bear intelligibility; just like any other space or structure or situation or activity or culture or society in which the signs and symbols and actions and intentions and decisions that allegedly make up the social are theorized to happen. It might seem to be the most banal assertion in the world that something (some realm or locale or site) must be seen or understood as being something before one can analyse how and why it is whatever it is. In fact, some theorists tell us that anything can be seen in everything; that any form can be understood to depend entirely on the subjective knowledge, culture, or social disposition framing the viewpoint one might take. But I do not happen to think that this is true. Towards showing why, I will not make an abstract argument on why anything can be seen in everything, but instead suggest taking a closer look at what happens when we see something in something. And while just about anything could be chosen to serve as an empirical example of such a something to be examined, I will use the case of the homogenous white surface of the Wilde Krimml on a clear winter morning after fresh snowfall—simply because I hope it will be as interesting and instructive a case as I can find, precisely because it is so far detached from most common topics of theorizing about intelligibility and social order. In doing so, I will examine visibility in order to understand intelligibility—a procedure that might not yield a complete picture, but which, as it will become clear, allows me to stand on the shoulders of several giant thinkers that have primarily focused on vision like I do. In this first empirical chapter, I will thus detail the ways in which a small group of remarkably skilled practitioners work out what there is to see in the face of the Krimml, this majestic but also perilous powder-filled mountain-flank, in order to sketch out some of the key challenges one arguably needs to tackle to adequately conceptualize the phenopractical production of intelligibility. Because it is intelligibility which, I maintain, must take place in order for any kind of unfolding of something social to happen.

But if, one might ask, intelligibility allegedly has such specific prerequisites, how can I be sure that there actually is something to be seen in the formless white surface of the Krimml? Because, I answer, the fact that the Krimml has indeed been the site of understanding, that one could indeed see that this surface exhibits certain intelligible forms, has left a trace. Since later, when the day draws to an end in late afternoon, there will still be a calm, white emptiness be visible in its last light, beginning to dive back in to the grey of dusk. But for one difference: between the cliffs, in the middle of a couloir's white, there will be a track. A deep, even scar in the soft powder that starts up on the ridge, at the edge of the cornice, leads straight down into the steep channel, then sways right in a big turn, raising slightly up the counter-slope before it takes a little narrower a turn to the left, returning to the vertical of the slope line only to lead dead straight towards a small cliff at the sharp edge of which the track ends. Three meters below, under the craning rock spur, a small crater has been smashed into the otherwise untouched surface, the snow sprayed from it in a perfect circle. Out of the crater, again, runs the track, first following gravity straight down towards the valley, then in a long curve to the left and then back again to the right, scattering the light powder to both sides over the slope in perfect symmetry, finally between two sharp-edge rocks and on into the wide ramp of the slope, at the bottom of which the track takes a last, sweeping move to the right. Silently, the wind blows over the long, elaborate carving in the spotless surface. Slowly, it begins to fill it up with loose snow. The day dawns, the surface is untouched; the day goes down, a trace remains. Sociology has a big word for the cause of this small difference: society. The track in the snow, I will show in this chapter, bears witness to conduct both artful and extreme which took place on this slope during the course of the day. It remains there as the physical desiderate of a multi-dimensional amalgam, a concurrence of space, body movement, technology, interaction, emotion, and visuality. But almost everything that unfolded during the day, interfolded back again until the end of it. Before, there was a mountain with some snow on it, and afterwards, there is a mountain with some snow on it. In between, it is a world.

A track is an irregularity in an otherwise smooth, even slope. The powder has been impressed and was sprayed over the surrounding surface. Almost any observer could be convinced that this trace is a cast from something, a track by something that moved through the snow. Adults familiar with Western culture will probably agree that it must have been humans using suitable gliding tools, a skier or snowboarder, an athlete. Most of them will also notice the steepness of the slope, the numerous sharp cliffs, or the raw harshness of the terrain. Many will subsequently comment on the presumed rider, his courage, his madness, the danger of his conduct, and that they themselves would never do something like this. Those, finally, who can exhibit more experience in observing alpine sports might possibly compare this particular track to those of other athletes and might see how it stems from a skier and not a snowboarder. They would determine that this track consists of far longer turns than the short wavelike patterns that classic off-piste skiers produce, that they are much less symmetric and exhibit a different rhythm. They would understand that going over the cliff and impacting into the powder below was not a fateful accident, but rather a planned feat. Maybe they would even, by looking at the shape of the impact and the continuing track, be able to tell that the rider did not crash, but kept on riding. And probably they would then call what they see extreme, and quite often plain stupid.

If one would ask those who call themselves freeskiers about this track of compressed and shuffled snow, they would talk quite differently than anybody else. They would call this track a {line},[1] and they would talk about radicalness, about symmetry and {speed}, about beauty and {spray} and, time and again, about {style}. In their words, the mundane trace in the snow turns into a freeride line, into an object of importance and beauty that one enjoys watching and discussing. In conversations—and in movies, magazines, and internet forums—the complex dimensions of such a line will gradually unfold: technical difficulty, safety, access routes, drop-ins and escape lines, snow conditions, speed, exposure, visibility, light conditions, aesthetic quality of the line and the mountain, avalanche risk, possible variations, dependency on favourable weather, and many other factors can subsequently become of importance. Within different conversational situations, the self-same line can refer to a seemingly endless range of topics—but never to all of them simultaneously. The artistry of communication thus lies in making something distinct, graspable, and connectable present *within* the line that would not be there otherwise. Apart from certain specialized professional or scientific perspectives, most observers focus their attention on the action performed earlier. The line testifies that at this particular spot, somebody did something: he or she went down the mountain. The line is the track of an individual, an athlete—a single, rapid, dangerous, skilful, brave, heroic act, a dauntless testament to will. A trace—a man[2]—a feat. This logic is dutifully carried forth by today's freeskiers following a

---

[1] Expressions in definite brackets indicate words that are used to signify German-speaking freeskiers' folk terms which are derived from or equal to English words. The German freeskiers' frequent use of such terms is testament both to the American origin of the sport, the international character of the scene (e.g. in that most freeski movies which German freeskiers watch are in English), and the general sound of coolness and expertise these expression carry in the German-speaking (youth) context. Through my writing in English, much this omnipresent mimicking of American youth slang thus regrettably disappears from the data.

[2] Neither here nor on any other occasion do I intend to create the impression that women are not able or not meant to ski down a mountain or to do any of the other various things this book will be about. But I also do not take the view that it is in any way helping the situation of women 'per se' in society if I will continue to repeat this trivial fact permanently from here on. Quite the opposite, this would mean playing down a problematic fact: Many of the narratives and ideals of freeskiing have their roots in a modern Alpinism and thus a world-view that a) demands virtues such as braveness, self-reliance, unconventionality, and dominance and b) at the same time identifies them as typically male (for an extensive discussion of gender in lifestyle sports in general and snowsports in particular, see Atencio/Beal/Wilson 2009; Beal/Wilson 2004; Frohlick 2005; Stoddart 2011; Thorpe 2008, 2010; Wheaton 2000a). The role of female freeskier within the scene and its media is thus characterized by the fact that they seem to fit into this scheme although they are 'actually' women. I deem it wrong to adhere to this binary logic by pointing out that women can also be freeskier or freeskier also be women. In sum, my ethnographic descriptions of freeskiers are gendered and usually imply that riders are male in order to stay true to the freeskiers' own language and perspective: Almost all statements I make about riders refer directly to concrete situations or formulations I have personally witnessed (i.e. I try to

path blazed by 19th-century British alpinists, modern ski athletes, and professional ski instructors.[3] It is misleading.

2 The Threefold Line

Of course, a line is the product of skiing down a slope. However, the constitution of such a track is the result of much more than just said skiing per se. The actual practice of sliding-down-this-slope can only be an element in a chain of specialized practices which only together enable and form freeriding. Two levels of such an embedding need to be differentiated. One the one hand, the practice of skiing down must be surrounded by an adequate habitat of practices which provide the basic prerequisites it relies on. Ski equipment and clothing has to be bought, the gear has to be serviced and tuned, a suitable group of companions has to be assembled, travel, accommodation and food has to be organized, the techniques of the body have to be trained, and so on. In other words: An important part of freeriding actually takes part off the snow. The 'molecule' that is freeriding, so to speak, is composed of different atoms which are—within their specific tension towards each other—connected into a whole of specific character. Nevertheless, these complementary practices do happen in a considerable temporal and spatial distance from the concrete conduct of skiing down, and if they would be recombined in a different ways, they might form a different complex of practices—that of surfing, for example. Some of these indispensable neighbouring 'atoms' of preparation and reflection will be subject to a closer examination in the following chapters, and I will make some specific suggestions how their relations and cross-dependencies can be conceptualized, because they turn freeskiing into what it is. But even if one takes into account that the lone rider needs to be well equipped, trained, and nourished, it would still be misleading to assume that once this has been accomplished, he can just start on top of the mountain and begin going down. Apart from those practices that happen off the snow, the conduct[4] on the snow is also made

---

give examples or quotes for every general statement) even if I do not always quote skiers word-by-word. Consequentially, they overwhelmingly concern male participants since a majority my informants was male, reflecting the nature of the scene. In contrast, when I make general or theoretical statements, I freely mix the male and female form. (i.e. I avoid writing 'he or she' and instead randomly use either of them.)

[3] See chapter ten on the historical advent of freeskiing and its ideals from early alpinism, professional competitive sports and finally (post-)modern lifestyle-sports.

[4] I will frequently use the term "conduct" throughout this text, because I regard it as more neutral and more general or encompassing than, for example, the term "action", which needs to be treated with caution from a practice perspective (see Chap. 7). I find this term particularly apt because of the semantic origins and connotations it resonates: The latin *conductus* or "what has been lead together" functions as a reminder that accomplishing practical conduct implies the

up of numerous highly skilful practices that enable and frame the actual riding down. Together they comprise that complex of practices which the riders call a {run}—a cyclic sequence from starting the ascent to the return to (usually) the starting point, for example a lift station. Using the terms suggested by Schatzki (1996), one might thus say that doing a run is an integrative practice, a bundle of more basic (so-called dispersed) practices that practitioners weave together, being coordinated by, inter alia, certain overall ends such as producing a great line or 'tasks' such as not dying in an avalanche. Like an atom core, the ride down is encircled by complementary practices without which it could not be: planning the route, coordinating the group, preparing the last bits just before skiing down, or assessing and reflecting on the line directly afterwards. An observer foreign to the scene will—informed by the freeskiers' self-portrayal or media image—most likely mistake the core activity, the extreme act skiing down itself, as equivalent to a freeride run as a whole. Within the freeriders' everyday conduct however, said act can naturally only be a part of the whole—although it is the most important part. By virtue of complementary practices, the core practice of riding a line is ultimately embedded into the rich tissue of social practices which comprise what I will loosely call the subculture of freeskiing or simply the freeskiing universe. In doing so, I seek to avoid the pitfalls of a long-standing and twisted debate within sociology regarding a number of alternative categories that have been suggested for phenomena similar to freeskiing: scenes (Hitzler/T. Bucher/Niederbacher 2005; Hitzler/Honer/Pfadenhauer 2008), communities or communities of practice (Bauman 2001; Lash 1994; Wenger 1999, 2007), tribes (Cova/Kozinets/Shankar 2007; Maffesoli 1996a, 1996b), fields (Kay/Laberge 2002; Thornton 1996; Wacquant 2004), and small life-worlds (Honer 1995, 2007; B. Luckmann 1978), to name the most pervasive concepts. At the most basic level, I do not apply these concepts (although I will discuss an number of them) because they are based on an individualistic ontology, that is, they would force me to conceptualize freeskiing as a group of people, while I plan to look at it as a nexus of practices. To be sure, the term subculture is commonly used in the same sense, as denoting a community of members who share certain aspects of identity (see Crosset/Beal 1997; Gelder/Thornton 1997; Hebdige 1979; Huq 2006); but in my view, the term culture per se does not actually necessitate and maybe not even warrant equating it to a group of individuals. Thus, I employ the term subculture simply to denote that there is a field or sphere of freeskiing practices which belong to, but are also different from, skiing practices more generally. It will not be until relatively late in this work that I will be able to define what precisely ties these practices together (in a nutshell, a shared orientation to freeskiing style), but for now it suffices to say that they are interrelated and co-dependent in several ways. One dimension in which the

---

successful combination of different resources (see the notion of amalgamation I introduce in Chap. 2); the *conductor* is someone in charge but not directly in control; and even the Spanish *conducer*—to ride—names a particular mode of action that seems not only important when studying skiing, but also useful for a practice perspective per se (as I will detail in Chap. 3).

integral interdependences of these various practices manifest is the language of freeskiing. Freeriders call what they undertake by a word that can denote three quite different things: lines.

The line forms the core of freeriding, its central object, and the focal point of all activities—freeriding means {ripping lines}. A line is—abstractly defined—a route through a mountain face or down a slope, a geometrical curve that describes a passage over ground. It is always influenced by the present terrain, and sometimes even predefined by it (for example when riding down a narrow chute), but it also—and this is crucial—unfolds freely within these given boundaries. Depending on how it is engraved into the landscape, a line can be fast or dangerous, stylish or photogenic, but also slow or boring according to the preference system of the freeriders. From this abstract definition, it is not yet evident how the word "line" refers to not one but three different things. If, however, one observes the practices of freeskiers more closely, it becomes apparent that the word "line" denotes the differing products of different practices. First, the expression 'line' describes a possible route through a face—a route that can be seen and discussed from afar. Typically, this happens at the beginning of each run, but some lines are being watched by a rider for years, patiently waiting for the right snow and weather conditions and eagerly anticipating the perfect moment to finally rip it. "Down there to the left is another phat line!"[5] [M][6] an informant exclaims while we talk about a specific slope. Second, a line is ridden in a concrete moment, it is an action: "Peter has just ripped a sick line, really phat!" [R][7] or "Right in the middle of my line, a massive avalanche went off." [M][8] The word "line" thus describes a concrete conduct just like a lap raced by a race driver. Third, a line is also a visible track in the snow like that which I described at the beginning of this chapter.

---

[5] „Da links ist noch so eine geile Line drin." Although I conducted fieldwork in different countries and although freeskiing is an international scene in which English is mostly spoken whenever riders from different countries meet, the majority of my field data is in German (including various local accents and Swiss German). I will provide the original quote in a footnote whenever it has been translated, but I am aware that important shades of meaning are inevitably lost.

[6] I use abbreviations to signify the format of field data from which a specific quote is drawn in order to make transparent the contextual origin of each quote (see the methodological appendix for my reasons why).

I will use the following abbreviations: Any statement I make without stating sources is a finding gained from my general ethnographic work and thus stems from my fieldnotes and ethnographic memos. Scientific sources are quoted in brackets as it is common practice. If I quote from publicly available material that I consider a field-specific document such as an article in a freeski magazine, I will quote it "(author, year, [D])." Quotes from documents without a named author (such as leaflets or ads) carry just a [D]. The other types of data are signified as follows. [I] = formal Interview with open recording; [M] = quote from memory from an informal interview or conversation. I recorded these quotes usually a few minutes after the conversation, trying to memorize the exact quote. [R] = audio record from a naturally occurring conversation.

[7] „Peter ist grad so ne geile Line gefahren, superkrass!"

[8] „Mitten in der Line ist mir auf einmal ein Monsterschneebrett abgegangen."

Once the line has been completed and is carved into the snow, it can now be the topic of discussion and considerations of certain qualities—and most importantly, it serves as testament to the rider's achievement, resplendently on the mountainside for everybody to see (see Geisler 2003: 63–66). In the following, these three forms of the line will be discussed sequentially, as three steps in constituting the track left over by the end of the day. However, as the freeriders' language shows, these three cannot be kept sharply separate in reality. A potential line is itself always a reference to the concrete riding, every run that is just being done immediately produces a (more or less aesthetic) track, and each visible trace always points back to a concrete run done by somebody, making use of the possible lines given by the terrain.

Excursus: The Diverging Focus of Theories of Social Practices

> One reason why it might be useful to consider phenopractices as a particular case of social practices in general are the theoretical challenges created by the need to differentiate between the concrete and local (re-)production of social order and interrelated webs of complementary practices, and the notable rift which separates the treatment the problem receives in different strands of practice-minded theories of the social. In Latour's Actor-Network-Theory, for example, the technical components of social practices come to be seen primarily as representatives or outcome of spatially and temporally distant practices. As an 'immutable mobile', e.g. the Berlin Key (Latour 2000) refers back to those intertwined practices of normalization and technology development which have been cast into iron to become the guiding conditions for each concrete act of unlocking the door in the moment of turning the key. The dynamics of the network which this theory emphasizes results from the interactions of spatially and temporally dispersed practices, such as—to name a well-know example—the nesting habits of crabs on the ocean floor, the discursive craftfulness of the lobbying of fishing industry representatives and the laboratory experiments of marine biologists (Callon 1986). Accordingly, the central position of technological artefacts within the theory stems from their ability to allow such dispersed practices to influence each other (see especially Latour 1996a). In a different fashion, but from a similarly overarching perspective, Bourdieu (1979, 1987) understands fields as transgressing time and space, and answers the consequential question of their interrelation by attributing to the habitus the function of 'transporting' acquired capital. Both schools of thought thus observe social practices with regard to their role in the development and sustainment of societal structures. Therefore, they are interested in the elements which make up the 'thing' called society and focus primarily on the characteristics of its atoms, so to say. On the contrary, ethnomethodology (Garfinkel 1967, 2002) concerns itself nearly exclusively with these 'atoms' themselves—or

even their core. The 'resolution' of empirical ethnomethodological studies with regard to the finest details of these basal elements (such as adjacency pairs, for example) is correspondingly high, but at the same time it becomes apparent that certain interdependencies simply cannot adequately be taken into account from this perspective. An instructive example of this lack is provided by the study by Baccus (1986), which is on the one hand able to demonstrate the skilfulness of the life-threatening repair work on rims of truck wheels with great precision, but on the other cannot, with the theoretical vocabulary at hand, really grasp the dynamics of the legislative regulation of safety norms for the self-same rims over time. Accordingly, although the ethnomethodological *Studies of Work* were of great value for my analysis of many aspects of freeskiing, it can already be stated that this problem of conceptualizing overarching order will need further elaboration throughout this work. Schatzki's account of social practices, finally, in my view seeks to embrace most of the ethnomethodologists' arguments about situated order while focusing more on the transitive relations and patterns throughout lived social life (see especially Schatzki 2002) without relying on assumptions about social wholes such as Bourdieu's fields. Towards this end, he conceives practices as related not alone through (material) actors or shared bodily dispositions (to some extent similar to the habitus), but as also united by rules, understandings, and teleoaffective structures (see especially Schatzki 1996: 184–192). In my view, this has the effect that, while his account seems sometimes somewhat lacking in focus in that he provides rather long lists of cross-influences and forms of relation, it opens up much more theoretical flexibility in accounting for social order per se. More specifically, I suggest that the ethnomethodological inquiries into the details of situated conduct show that practitioners use a range of resources to reproduce and account for (seemingly) stable phenomena of social order, for example talk *and* gestures *and* objects *and* gazes *and* explicable rules *and* emotions. Zooming in on just one of them just in order to suit the demands of a certain theoretical lens would just seem inadequate (cf. Nicolini 2012). On the other hand, I also believe that the relatively broad range of aspects and topics that Schatzki includes necessitates that special attention is given to the specific ways in which practitioners come to deal with and 'pick out' the various procedural tools available to them. Consequentially, this is precisely what I try to do in the present work.

3 Reading (Mountain) Faces

"For me special about freeriding [sic] is having the possibility to search for any mountain, hike up there and ski right this one special line you have been looking at." Tine Huber, professional freerider (Huber 2009; [D])

We reach the Krimml in the late morning. A sharp wind has been blowing through the Zillertaler Alps since nightfall, sending clouds torn into streaks of bleak grey through the gaps between the sharp peaks. It is bitterly cold as we sit in the small chairlift that takes us up onto the ridge between the two small hilltops and into the heart of the Wilde Krimml. Tom and I cannot wait. That one crucial chairlift opened only after some considerable delay, because the wind was too strong. But now, at last, we are standing on the top, with the rugged width of the Krimml bowl stretching out below us. In order to access the unmarked terrain beyond the boundary of the ski area, we would need to turn left now and then trudge uphill through the deep powder fenced off by the side of the slope. But we turn right instead, skiing down the groomed slope, taking big turns, being slightly bored. While it would be routine for a classic alpine skier to take the slope, it is remarkable for a freerider—this is a lost chance to rip the precious powder that waits off-piste. Still completely untouched, the virgin powder glares under the sun. Now we need to be quick, before the clouds will block the sun again, or worse, it gets tracked by somebody else. Still, Tom skis down the boring slope without hesitation, in order to "watch from below" [M] as he explains to me while already beginning to move downwards. As the slope reaches the centre of the high valley, he stops by the side of the slope and immediately begins to inspect the couloirs that now lay in front of him on the opposite side of the bowl of the Krimml (Fig. 2.1). I stop next to him. Motionless, we stand for a couple of minutes, our heads steadfastly turned towards the rock-cluttered mountainside.[9]

After about twenty seconds, Tom begins to comment on the current situation of the {face}, which I confirm or comment on sparingly. He seems content: there was more snow blown into it than we thought, and nobody else seems to have tracked it yet. He begins to explain the face. The wind is coming in from the left side today ("That's the only direction that's actually bad for the Krimml." [M][10]); the sun will shine on that part longer and on those only briefly; and there the snow conditions will accordingly be fluffier and deeper as opposed to there. These are the drop-ins we could use, and this is how we can hike there. These wind lips up on the crest can be pretty dangerous, so make sure to stay nice and clear towards the other side. In this way, step by step, the concrete freeride-face that we are about to rip unfolds from the scenic mountain panorama in front of us. In the course of our conversation, the nondescript white surfaces and the distant

---

[9] All pictures in this chapter (apart from fig. 2.3) have been taken on the specific day I describe and show the east face of the Krimml that the text is concerned with. Therefore, they are more than a pure illustration, allowing apprehension of the situation and my analysis in an additional, a visual dimension. Just like each text, they also have a distinct logic, and their own particular meaning. Despite a forceful tradition in Western modernity they should therefore not be taken as an equivalent copy of the lived, concrete reality present that day. Rather, they provide the reader-viewer the opportunity to open up an additional dimension of understanding and hopefully add a further layer of insight.

[10] „Das ist die einzige Windrichtung, die schlecht für die Krimml ist."

3 Reading (Mountain) Faces   29

Fig. 2.1 Two riders gaze into the east face of the Krimml that is discussed in this chapter. The picture illustrates the initially confusing perspective they take, but it lacks spatial depth: The cliffs in the centre are about 700 meters away and between 4 and 12 meters high. The Rifflerkopf that can be seen in the background is considerably further away and much higher than the cliffs in the foreground

contours of the cliffs and spines merge into an ensemble, into features of a face that opens up options for riding (Fig. 2.2).

Freeriders establish a specific relation towards a mountain face that sets them apart from other visitors to the high alpine regions. While tourists see an impressive, yet inhospitable panorama, ski tourers focus on ascent routes, mountaineers on suitable spots for bivouacking, and ice climbers on climbing routes (e.g. T. Bucher 2000). Freeskiers, however, see lines. They inspect singular elements of a face with great precision, but they see them as attributes of a possible descent, as references to the challenges and opportunities of a specific freeride line. Seeing and then riding lines is what constitutes their sport at its core, a feature it shares with a number of 'freeride' sports, skating, and parkour (Buckingham 2009; Braune 2021).[11] The seemingly simple constitutional principle of finding and following lines has been generative for a whole range of rich cultures of movement, testament to the often-overlooked complexity and richness of the universal human practice of moving across spaces in reflection of abstract cultural principles (that can be rational, spiritual, technical, intellectual or technical in nature). Importantly, the generative force of an abstract form such as a straight line when bodily enacted interactively in a lived environment is irredeemably intertwined

---

[11] Parkour can be defined as the never-ending "to find the most direct path between two points [in an urban or buit landscape] and to overcome any obstacle within that path, using only one's own physical and mental capacities" (Braune 2021). It offers therefore a great example of how a simple, geometric rule produces and requires and enormous creativity and variety in terms of embodied, emplaced rule-following.

Fig. 2.2 The same freeride face seen from the chairlift, from about 1 km away. From this perspective, a large part of the 'seeing' of the line is taking place—subject to an eventual shift through the moving of the lift

with visual practices that lend it form, function and feasibility. In freeskiing, watching faces is, on the one hand, an indispensable preparation procedure for every run and a possible life-saver. When skiing down through the face from the top at high speed, one needs to be able to orient very quickly using certain landmarks memorized earlier, or otherwise one might take a wrong turn and fall into an abyss at any moment. On the other hand, this practice of watching is a central and enjoyable practice within freeriding. It is not by accident that the freeskiers talk about "reading faces" as if they were trying to uncover the character of a man by studying the wrinkles and lines on his face. As if looking into an old man's weather-beaten visage, feelings of respect, unease, or distrust arise. Much more often than immediately necessary, freeskiers continue to stare at mountainsides with fascination. Examples are plentiful: When driving down a mountain pass, the peaks and couloirs around them inevitably catch their eyes. A large poster print of a wild mountain range adorns the bedroom. Movie sequences and high-res pictorials show nothing but mountain sides deeply covered in snow. But why?

4 From Seeing Terrain to Gazing at Landscapes

That gazing at a landscape is not an anthropological universal, but a specifically cultural and therefore contingent practice can, on the one hand, be demonstrated by the fact that different communities or experts will focus on different aspects within the same view. On the other, it can also be made apparent by pointing to the historical evolution of the concept of the landscape per se (see Edensor 2012). Bucher (2003) traces its emergence back to an exact date. On April, the 26th 1336, the poet Petraca climbed the peak of Mount Ventoux and subsequently reported on the vista he gained. Through the following centuries, an extensive genre of landscape painting developed, fostering an—historically volatile—cultural perception of landscapes. Idealized visions of Arcadia or stereotypical representations of national identities dominated the common view of the landscape through various epochs. The classical sociological understanding of landscapes begins with Simmel's essays "On landscape" (1913) in general and on "The Alps" (1911) specifically. Already here, he presents landscapes as the product of a "peculiar mental process" which is based on a "forming gaze of men." Like an artist, he argued, an onlooker only ever picks out a part and treats it as the whole (Simmel 1913). Therefore, he cannot grasp the sublime of the totality of the Alps within one secluded form, but has to rely on excerpts (Simmel 1911). Generally, the Alps are probably the single landscape whose perception has undergone the most profound historical alternations. It was not until the 18th century that scholars and artists discovered the sublime and the romantic Alps (A. Bucher 2003). They thus developed the well-known stereotypical view on the formerly bleak and dangerous landscape that monopolize Simmel's essay as much as the postcard vistas of the modern 'tourist gaze' (Urry 1990). The breakthrough of the sublime and aesthetic Alps into the canon of mainstream culture was arguably brought about by the emergence of the mountain film in the 1920, which institutionalized views of the Alpine landscape that still dominate its media representations today (Bogner 1999; Rentschler 1990). Arguably not by accident, these mountain films where also ski films. And even despite their up-to-date subcultural street-style appeal, the countless photos and videos in freeskiing media carry forth this visual and epistemological tradition almost unaltered. All they add to the quintessential images of the Alpenglow over pristine, untouched valleys is the silhouette of a freerider performing a scenic spray turn.

Both in pictures and when watching them 'live,' however, it is indeed not the mountains themselves that receive such heightened attention, but rather the almost sacral element of snow which provides a magic touch and transforms the visible alpine world into the specific environment[12] that attracts and preoccupies the rider almost inescapably. It turns barren mountain slopes into what Edensor (2012) calls a "vital landscape"—textured, temporal, and tactile. Freeskiers relate to snow with an almost philosophical attitude. "No Snowflake ever falls in the wrong place." [D] declares an ad from a freeski company, quoting an old Zen dictum[13]—wherever snow can be found, it calls upon the rider as there is no place in the world one should not ski. The freeskier finds complex beauty in snow-covered terrain, an outworld secluded from the everyday lifeworld, an enchanted dimension, "Powderheaven." To him, fallen snow possesses deep fairness, a suggestive

---

[12] I here allude to the notion of environment which Luhmann (1984) developed—but which is also already evident in Simmel's Essay on the Alps (1911).

[13] At least this saying is quoted as stemming from Zen in several sources, for example by Krieger (2002: 31).

pulchritude of almost physical attraction[14] because, despite outwardly calmness and immobility, it is always a reference to movement. The smallest impulse, the most subtle prod is enough, and powder-snow will ripple, slide, sag, spray. A steep mountain covered in deep powder thus represents the edge between just fine and already too much, the thin line between terra firma and the bottomless abyss. When a rider looks calmly down into a couloir disappearing into the cliff below, it almost screams back at him in challenging silence. Because as he eyes the flank of a mountain, he sees a movement, a recumbent ensemble promising fast-paced dynamics. Skiing down a steep slope is a kind of controlled dropping, it is a forward-downward movement never of oneself alone, but always of a larger whole—much like a wave—, a movement of the body, the head, of gear and, above all, a movement of snow that becomes part of the flow, sloshes to the side, slides down from behind, cushioning and enwrapping the rider, popping him out and shoving him downwards. Seeing snow, inspecting a face thus always means seeing a potential movement, an order that is only preliminary frozen and static, only in need of a small impulse to head towards the valley floor, the skier in its white midst—or rather with his head high above it.

A rider reading a face does thus not just apprehend it in its totality, but subdivides it into legs of a run, into phases of the continuous movement of a skier. He sees {turns} and {drops}, assumes sharp rock edges hidden under the smooth with surface, guesses where dangerous avalanches might go off, and tries to anticipate the route of {slough}[15] funnelling down the slope. Does the rider thus enter into a silent dialogue with the face as he watches it? A forceful cultural tradition easily leads us to interpret his relationship with the mountain in this way (cf. Simmel 1911, 1913): as an idea unfolding inside the head, as a play of thoughts, or a silent yearning, or a mental self-complacency, or as cognitive application of knowledge. At this point, I neither intend to differentiate and dissect these understandings, nor to repudiate them completely. Even if one understands sociology to be able to mobilize the strange forces that enable some to read others' minds, I believe that there is not much to gain from such an exercise for my task at hand. Since this work focuses on the topic of intelligibility, I will have ample possibility to return

---

[14] It is not by accident that fresh powder invites allegories of physical attraction and erotic conquest such as the quintessential talk of 'virgin powder'. The cultural framing of sex and powder skiing show several parallels such as practices of yearning, consumption of suggestive images, rhythmic entrainment of the body, accompanying cries of joy and subsequent bragging rights.

[15] Slough develops from the thin layer of very light snow that is often the topmost stratum of fresh powder. When a rider cuts through the snow with high speed, small 'avalanches' of this very light snow are ticked off. In itself, this rippling of light crystals is harmless, but fast runs on steeper slopes can cause large clouds of slough that would block the rider's vision. Thus, the need for so-called slough-management arises, that is, choosing a route that avoids the downward-sliding slough. As a freeski wiki article explains: "Slough management starts before you even on top of the line. It starts when you're in the heli (or hiking/skinning up) and you start to visualize where the slough is going to funnel into (…). Once you can visualize that, you can plan your line." (EpicSki Community 2009; [D]).

to this important point. For now, it suffices to note two things: First, such considerations deem it both necessary and adequately possible to distinguish between observer and observed within the process of observation. An epistemological process or ontological accomplishment is typically understood as a confrontation of two clearly demarcated and stable entities, and influence of one onto the other is frequently assigned to one of each parties to a certain degree—typically followed by the inescapable haggle between determinism of given structure or objective quality versus relative freedom of subjective mindsets. However, I understand a theory of social practices to take on a different phenomenon: neither the subject, nor the object, but the *unfolding* of practices *within* which both subjects and objects might or might not become visible. In other words, one could attempt to use the notion of social practices as an epistemological tool to step beyond the dichotomy of observer and observed—something that I will not try to push through in a swift theoretical proclamation but venture to substantiate empirically throughout this book. To be sure, trying to find a 'third way' between subjectivism and objectivism has in a way been the core mission of sociology ever since the earliest classic authors' transgression of this dualism through their addressing that crucial realm lying between those two extremes: the social. At the same time, it is fascinating to see how many schools of social thought are able to define themselves through the claim that they are the ones who are now able to finally correctly sort out the exact workings of this dialectic of subjectivism and objectivism. Although this strategy thus has a very noble tradition full of achievements, one may still wonder if sociological work does indeed need the phantasmagoria of those two never-lands in order to know its own doings—especially since at least since Freud on the one and Heisenberg on the other side, neither subjectivism nor objectivism are what some sociologists liken them to be.

Second, for now I therefore simply want to proceed with a careful empirical observation: When freeriders read faces, this does not only occur—if ever—silently and invisibly within the consciousness of a single individual, but it can be observed quite well and quite frequently. If one looks close enough, reading faces is almost never mute, but quite articulate as freeriders who look at mountain sides very frequently begin to talk to one another. They coordinate their line of sight, reciprocally exchange comments or at least minimal utterances, and through this elaborate the elements of a face and the lines in it step-by-step. A line thus typically originates in a lively interaction between members of a shared situation, and it is not brought into being through the spoken word alone, but especially by way of pointing at the mountain side. Inter alia for this empirical reason, my analysis thus commits itself to what Edwards (2006) has called the "rich surface of the social." It undertakes the attempt to take the visible and hear-able seriously and to examine its 'superficial' structures as precisely as possible instead of rashly proceeding towards the hidden, deep structures allegedly able to explain the phenomena relevant to this study. The level of detail within the following account will therefore exceed that usually expected from a common ethnographic description. But it is—I believe—only under the 'sociological microscope' (Büscher 2005a) that one can fully grasp how, for example, a line cannot just 'be there,' but must instead be the product of a situated, contingent and—more often than not—interactive process. In the same manner, the nature of a given slope as the basis from which a line is planned cannot simply be a linear consequence of a pre-given physical shape of the mountain. (Given for whom? Through what?) Instead, it is a processual or methodologically elaborated form—and this form of the mountain face thus depends on the characteristics of this process as well as on the characteristics of the rocks themselves.

If one observes the conduct of reading a face in detail—for example by recording it on video and then analysing it frame-by-frame as I will do soon—, it becomes clear that the freeriders work out lines in sequences. Through gestures and words they elaborate specific points in the face which they then use as positions from which they describe the course of a line (Fig. 2.3). It seems important to point out the complex nature of the task at hand: Recognizing or drawing a line on paper is easy, but if we try to describe a line verbally, we need to resort to defining points in space which can then function as anchors to the line connecting them. It is thus not necessarily surprising that the freeriders spend most of their effort to establish a common understanding of certain points or spots in the face—and then only add: "Go from here to there." The following excerpt from such an interaction demonstrates the refinement and extraordinary level of detail of this process. My analysis draws on the rich tradition of Conversation Analysis and especially the techniques developed by Charles Goodwin (1994, 1995, 2000a,

Fig. 2.3 Two freeriders looking at a face while standing on a groomed slope, discussing lines

2000b). These methods are, however employed in the context of a research project that has aims and ontological premises that are quite different from those of a 'classic' CA study (see Heath/Hindmarsh 2002; Hindmarsh/Heath/Luff 2010; Knoblauch/Schnettler/Raab/Soeffner 2006; Schnettler/Raab 2008). I want to point out that the *selection* of the exact sequence chosen for detailed analysis is in this case explicitly guided by ethnographic research logic. As a participant, I observed many such conversations of which I was able to videotape some, and I see this one as sufficiently typical to be deemed absolutely 'normal' by the standards of my informants (who have explicitly confirmed this assumption in a feedback-interview). In contrast to this 'classic' ethnographic procedure, CA studies seldom comment on how the reduction from hundreds of hours of taped material to an analysed sequence of a mere ten seconds was achieved. While they deem *any* naturally occurring situation as suitable object of analysis per definitionem, it is—at least in contemporary studies—not just any situation they choose to analyse. Their reliance on member's expertise consequently remains implicit, yet indispensable (ten Have 2002).

Excursus: Situation Theory and Situated Awareness in Psychology

The situated perspective in theories social practices finds its equivalent in psychology in situation theory (Barwise 1989; Greeno 1994) and the notion of distributed situated awareness (Salmon et al. 2007), which understand cognitive accomplishments not as purely mentally, but situatedly elaborated achievements. Since they share both topics and some central arguments with practice theory, let me briefly sketch out why I nevertheless refrain from building on these psychological works more extensively. Situation theory builds inter alia on works from conversation analysis, especially those by Schegloff (1972), and from workplace studies by authors such as Suchman (1987) or Hutchins (1995). On the one hand, psychological situation theory thus comes quite close to many aspects of a sociological theory of social practices. On the other, it needs to be noted that the model of an interactive, locally coordinated analysis of situations as an alternative to notions of solemnly individual, mental interpretation of information does (at least partly) embrace a view in which the respective situationally produced findings come to be seen as only a-posteriori symbolically mediated version of information still objectively given ex-ante in the environment. In other words, to a certain degree these psychological theories still reproduce ontological reifications of facts given objectively outside of situations (of fact-finding). In a literature heavily focused on empirical cases, it does not always become clear whether the proponents of situation theory understand practices as interpreting or information-constructing. Accordingly, the question remains unanswered whether a local and interactive epistemic conduct constructs or simply unveils its respective environment. Seen in this light, it might not be incidental that situation theory builds almost exclusively on examples in which people analyse a (social) environment which has been pre-interpreted in that it was purposely designed to be rich in symbols and prescriptive patterns. Mathematical procedures, flight-control rooms, supermarkets, airplane cockpits, or copy machines have all been carefully designed in order to evoke a certain 'informational state' on the part of their users as reliably as possible. In this regard, the mountain slope discussed here might serve as an instructive example since the orientation of the freerider is not already framed by a designer who has at least tried to make certain options more visible or inviting than others. Even so, riders reliably manage to elaborate a common orientation. Notably, they achieve this by making use of anything pre-interpreted in the widest sense, such as visible tracks of others or opinions uttered by companions, before orienting towards 'nature' per se.

5   Seeing as Interaction: Formulating and Showing a Line

Tom and Steffi are sitting in the Krimml Xpress chairlift that takes them up towards the next run. While sitting, the north face of the Krimml extends right in front of them. They have already completed a run, and now they are planning the next through the powder that is still untouched. Steffi declares that Tom knows this area much better; therefore she will be choosing a route close to his. Subsequently, Tom begins an extended explanation of the options for skiing the Krimml's face offers, detailing the one he seems intent to take. Both riders are sitting in the lift chair looking at the mountain keeping their torsos still, while Tom is stretching out his right arm (towards the face and into the field of vision of the two) and accompanying his words with lively gestures (Fig. 2.4).[16] Although this situation is immediately understandable for those present, one might still ask what exactly the apparent clarity of the topic of the conversation results from. Both riders are surrounded by mountains—how do they know which segment of the slope is meant? A closer examination reveals that an answer is not provided verbally, but through the positioning of bodies within the situation. The orientation of the body towards a specific mountain slope picks out this slope as the topic of the conversation (cf. Kendon 1990 on the role of body positioning for the definition of interaction contexts), and the line of sight the specific part of the slope which is of

---

[16] In many ways, this formation is quite similar to the spatial order of Powerpoint-presentations (Knoblauch 2008; Schnettler/Knoblauch 2007)—and is hardly by coincidence that the face-to-face orientation characterizing such presentations is made up for by intensive use of gestures in this case.

Fig. 2.4 Steffi and Tom (behind her) sitting in a chairlift facing the slope of the Krimml. Steffi listens intently as he explains a line of descent, using his arm to point out terrain features

interest (C. Goodwin 1995, 2007; C. Goodwin & M. H. Goodwin 1996; Mondada 2012). In contrast to everyday conversations, however, this alignment of bodies is prefigured through the technical apparatus of the chairlift. A massive safety bar prevents the skiers from choosing any other sitting position, thus one is downright forced to look straight onto the mountain. Therefore, it seems not implausible to mirror Schivelbusch's (1986: Chap. 4) argument that the introduction of the railroad in the 19th century led passengers to engage in a new, "panoramic" way of seeing and ascribe the prominent role of visuality in skiing in part to the fact that a skier necessarily spends a large part of his time on the mountain sitting or standing in lifts. After all, this material set-up makes it almost impossible *not* to direct one's gaze at the mountains and the other skiers—in a way, both are thus mechanically predestined to be frequent topics.

As Tom begins to formulate the line through the Krimml-face, he proceeds sequentially, much like someone marking two points and then drawing a line to connect them. First, he defines a precise position, a waypoint within the face, and then he describes a second position that serves as a destination to be reached from the first. Subsequently, this position is then turned into another starting point for the next segment of the route. Periodically, Steffi acknowledges that she was able to follow the description, asks additional questions, or utters some comment. Described in such a general way, the task at hand seems rather unremarkable. But when one takes a closer look, it becomes apparent that sitting out here in the cold wind, preparing oneself to risking one's life in the dangerous, manifold vastness of the Krimml and faced with myriad details of a route to be worked out by merely looking from far away, a fine-tuned assortment of conversational details is necessary to establish the situated accountability of a particular line.

The following analysis of video clip will focus on two short consecutive segments of Tom's explanation which together take no longer than ten seconds to show in exemplary detail just how the riders manage to collaboratively figure out precisely what it is that is to been seen as being a suitable line of descent within the vista of the slope. Illustrating my analysis on the basis of several video stills, this particular case of socially seeing a line will help me to sketch out some general considerations about the nature of socially situated seeing. The conversation between the riders was recorded while sitting next to the two in the lift, so that in the still images, Steffi can be seen in the front, whereas Tom is hardly visible apart from his arm stretched-out towards the mountain side in front of both. I subdivided the video into logically coherent parts. A still from the beginning and the end of each part is shown, plus an overlay of the frames in between to illustrate the exact movement of the hand and arm.

Frame/Sec.		Movement of hand and arm	Spoken words
1–11/ 0.00–0.44		Hand centred in front of the face, opened to the left. Then moved to the upper right by moving the whole arm.	Tom: "Now to the right…" („Jetzt rechts…")

1) At first, Tom begins his description of the preceding segment of the line by demonstrating the movement of an imaginary rider to the right. By describing this part, Tom moves seamlessly from one segment of the line to the next—this particular move of the rider is the endpoint of the prior segment as well as the starting point of the next. When reading a face, the riders construct each line as a continuous object, so that each step of the explanation depends on contextualization with reference to the prior elements of the line. (The formulating of a line starts with constructing a special element, the drop-in.) In order to comprehend the explanation, the listener always needs to know where 'one' is right now, that is, he needs to see the current position of the imaginary rider of the line in the face. The description of a line depends to a large extent on indexical expressions such as 'here', 'there' or 'to the right'. The indexicality of such space-defining expressions (Schegloff 1972 calls them "locational pro-terms") is not only an unavoidable feature of such description, but it appears on two levels simultaneously, underlining the complexity of the task. Each formulation of a line not only references a certain spot ("over there") indexically, that is, as bound to a certain viewpoint and situation; but it also needs to describe the destination one should steer towards from this point on. Therefore, it needs to identify a spot or movement in relation to the current indexical position in the face. For example, relative to the rock that lies relative to the current standpoint of the descriptor to the right there is a wind lip to the left that needs to be approached but must stay on your right. In order to be able to grasp the complexity of this indexical positioning in a more reliable way, the freeriders' language is enhanced by an additional directional spatial dimension apart from those present in everyday language. Apart from left, right, above and below, they distinguish between {rider's left} and {rider's right}. These terms denote those directions that the rider will experience as his 'natural' left and right once he is at a certain position in the mountain face, moving downwards and in the direction implied in the description of the line. The freeskiers thus construct an in-situ geography based on a directional grid that stretches out not from the current point of the speaker, but is based on the expected experience occurring within the planned practice of riding down the face (or what human geographers and neuroscientists call its allocentric geometry). The spatial order of the line is not just established with reference to the physical shape of the mountain, but bound to the experiential dimension of the practice of riding the line itself. Freeriders thus develop a strictly relational instead of an absolute spatial order (see Löw 2001)—similar to sailors who orient by distinguishing windward and leeward rather than left or right during sailing.

2) When seen from afar, the surface of a snow-covered slope forms an amorphous, homogenous plane. In order to still be able to describe a specific route, the freerider depends on using particular elements of the slope as landmarks since each position in the face is elaborated in relation to certain cliffs, trees, and so on. The identification of these landmarks—and not the actual route—makes up the mayor part of the work[17] of formulating a line. Said identification is indeed the most central challenge: while the slope is quite far away, elements like rocks are looking quite similar and are hard to distinguish. To complicate things further, the rider needs to be able to identify the same objects again once he will be skiing down the face at a rapid speed, thus he needs to choose elements that will be clearly identifiable from different angles. This work of spotting a viable route through the face and identifying reliable landmarks in order to follow it correctly is one of the core competencies of freeriding. As an internationally successful freerider explains in an interview:

> "At the beginning you think if you can ride with nice, big turns, you're a good freerider. (…) But when I started attending contests, I quickly realized that you need more than just technique. Firstly, you need a lot of experience and a trained eye, to see the right lines and be able to react quickly during a run (…)."[18] (Polzer 2009, [D])

---

[17] I use the term "work" in the universal sense of the ethnomethodological Studies of Work by Garfinkel (1986), which in turn build—albeit in a distinctive way—on Schutz' (1945: 537) definition that "Working is action in the outer world, based upon a project and characterized by the intention to bring about the projected state of affairs by bodily movements."

[18] „Am Anfang denkt man, wenn man gut Kurven fahren kann, ist man ein guter Freerider. (...) Als ich dann aber zu den ersten größeren Contests gefahren bin, habe ich schnell gemerkt, dass es mehr braucht als nur Technik. Zum einen braucht man viel Erfahrung und ein geschultes Auge, um die richtigen Lines zu sehen und während eines Runs schnell reagieren zu können (...)."

5 Seeing as Interaction: Formulating and Showing a Line

Next, Tom starts to describe riding over a small rise, a wind lip in the face. To identify it exactly, he tries to find a precise expression from the vocabulary of freeriding. Thus, a short pause appears in his talk. If a rider misunderstands such an instruction, grave accidents can easily happen, for example when one attempts to jump down a cliff that has no proper landing below it. But at this crucial point, Tom does not need to resort to language alone. While talking, he points towards the lip with his hand and arm, and at the same time also uses the iconic abilities of his hand by forming the lip with his palm and fingers.

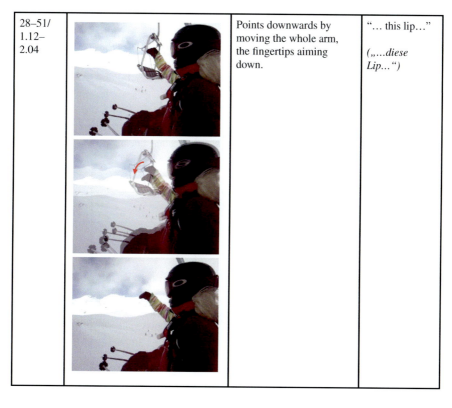

| 28–51/ 1.12– 2.04 | | Points downwards by moving the whole arm, the fingertips aiming down. | "… this lip…" („…*diese Lip…*") |

3) Having decided to use the term "lip" instead of "crest" or "hump", Tom continues his explanation. The lip formed by his hand now becomes dynamic. It moves downwards in order to demonstrate the direction of the ride while the fingertips are now stretched out, pointing downwards as well. With a single gesture, Tom thus points toward the element in the face, mimetically forms it with his hand, demonstrates the direction in which to ride by moving his hand, and additionally signals this direction with his fingers. This detailed, dynamic, and complex instruction takes no longer than a single second—but it forcefully shows the precision and diligence the riders apply when orienting within a face. At the same time, it makes apparent that a line can only result from the relation of the static elements of the face and the dynamic movement of

the rider: within Tom's formulating, the lip and the riding over the lip become the same thing. The ingenuity of this highly (sub-) culturally specific gestures demonstrates that pointing should not be misunderstood as a monothetic universal repertoire of humans 'per se' (Wilkins 2003). Just like language, it is instead not only specific to different cultures, but also to concrete situations. In addition, the descriptive gestures encountered here undermine the strict dichotomy between deictic and iconographic gestures predominant in linguistics (cf. D. McNeill 1992). Goodwin's (2003) alternative suggestion to differentiate between the indexical and iconic component of a gesture seems to be more apt in that it undercuts this strict duality. However, Goodwin's expression "indexical component" seems somewhat problematic as well, because even a purely iconic gesture must necessarily be indexical in an ethnomethodological sense in that its specific meaning can only emerge from a concrete situation. Therefore, it seems more sensible to distinguish the deictic and the iconic component of every necessarily indexical gesture.

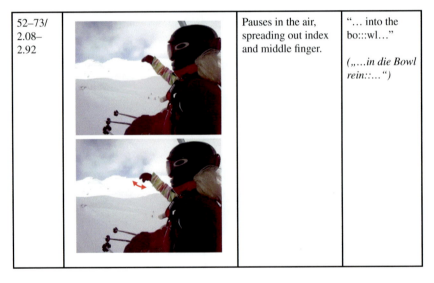

| 52–73/ 2.08–2.92 | | Pauses in the air, spreading out index and middle finger. | "… into the bo:::wl…" („…*in die Bowl rein::…*") |

4) In contrast, the following segment of the line is formulated with a little less finesse, because for a freerider, it follows logically from the preceding step. The route over the lip leads down into a {bowl}, a small, round depression in the slope. Again, it becomes apparent how the line is being formulated from the perspective of an imaginary rider in the face. When one rides over the lip, the bowl 'opens up' in front of oneself—while Tom's hand is still forming the hump of the bowl, his index and middle finger open up below it in a movement Goodwin (2003) aptly calls "pointing as demonstration."

5 Seeing as Interaction: Formulating and Showing a Line 43

74–77/ 2.96–3.08		Pauses shortly.	Prolonging the last syllable while pondering "in::::" ("rein:::")
78–95/ 3.12–3.8		The fingers 'step back into line'; raises the arm sharply and the hand closes slightly to form a 'claw'.	"Hhh." (draws breath)

| 96–184/3.84–7.36 |  | On the outstretched arm, the hand moves sharply down and back up again, the middle finger stretched out pointing. | "… and then the lip quasi points to the crest."

(„…und dann zeigt die Lippe ja quasi so auf die Kuppe.") |

5 Seeing as Interaction: Formulating and Showing a Line 45

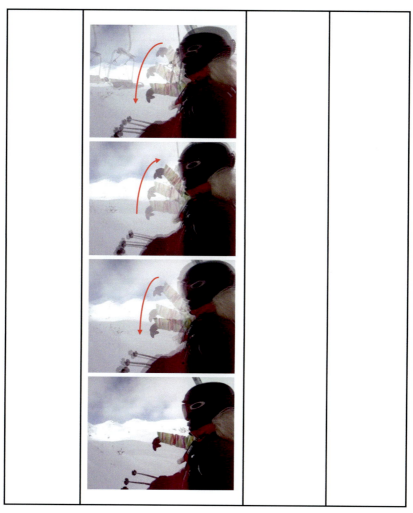

5) At this point, Tom is confronted with another difficulty. After the bowl, open terrain spreads out, offering different options for continuation. Thus, the description must be especially precise, but at the same time the terrain does not offer many clear reference points. For this reason, Tom now continues with a very lively gesture that he repeats four times. With a movement of his whole arm, Tom formulates the direction within the face. To define said direction, he cannot rely on absolute orientations such as north or south, nor can he for example name the exact degree of inclination of the part of the slope one should ride on. Without instruments, such instructions are impossible to follow. Instead, he again makes use of a clearly identifiable aspect—in this case a feature of an element he has already successfully defined, an element that already 'exists' within his formulation, so to speak: the wind lip. He now describes the

direction to take as an imaginary extension of the lip. In his own words, the lip itself becomes an active agent. The lip is pointing towards the next important waypoint, in this case a crest. This pointing of the lip is again additionally underscored through gesturing. Tom continues to form a hump with his hand, but this hump now moves up and down, so that the imaginary open space that needs to be crossed opens up below it. The hand no longer points directly towards the relevant object, but it becomes a dynamic element on a virtual map unfolding in front of Tom and Steffi. The movement of the arm demonstrates the direction which the lip points, and again this gesture is underlined by an outstretched finger. This pointing technique is thus similar to the "creative pointing" which Knoblauch (2008) discovered in his study of PowerPoint-presentations. By moving his (laser) pointer in a certain way, a presenter is able to add additional layers of meaning not present in the visual display on its own, for example because this type of pointing illustrates a dynamic movement across the fixed plane of the image—much like the direction into which the windlip is visibly pointing within Tom's formulating the line.

| 185–221/7.4–8.84 | | Waits. | Steffi: "Mh:m." |

6) Because the definition of this position in the face could not be tied to any fixed anchors, it was relatively complex to formulate and prone to misunderstandings. Tom now pauses relatively long compared to the preceding segments, implicitly asking Steffi for a sign of acknowledgement or a question. She complies by uttering a short affirmation. Seeing the line in the face is not an isolated, purely individual act in this situation, but an interactive conduct between several collaborators. In freeskiing, such an episode of seeing happens typically in one of two ways: First, in the course of a hierarchically organized instruction in which one of the speakers is ascribed significantly greater experience and thus authority with regard to this particular face so that he primarily formulates the face while the others present only signal their apprehension. Second, in a more egalitarian format where several speakers discuss different options interchangeably. In both cases, the successful construction of the line over the course of the conversation requires the continued attentiveness and engagement of the participants, which is continuously made visible within the conversation itself (e.g. through respective utterances, eye contact, or nodding). The freeskiers' expert knowledge expressed in seeing (as opposed to riding) a 'good,' save, aesthetic line is therefore at least partly understood as a *local* knowledge (see below). Even the world elite of pro-riders routinely relies on local guides to

5 Seeing as Interaction: Formulating and Showing a Line   47

instruct them about the specific local terrain. Similarly, in the example examined here, Steffi actually has more experience in freeriding and formal training as a mountain guide that Tom lacks—but he is much more familiar with the Krimml as its his 'home spot.' This local expertise additionally plays an important part for the construction of subcultural identities through making someone what freeskiers call a {local} of a certain area, and thus literally places people on the map of freeskiing.

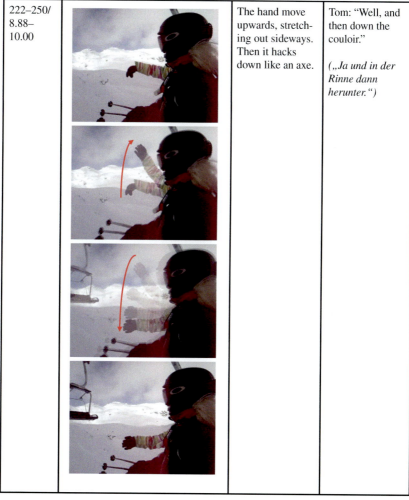

| 222–250/
8.88–
10.00 | | The hand move upwards, stretching out sideways. Then it hacks down like an axe. | Tom: "Well, and then down the couloir."

(*„Ja und in der Rinne dann herunter."*) |

7) Now that this intensive preparation of the next step is complete, the further continuation of the line is quite obvious to see, because a small chute extends right below the crest that was just reached. To a freerider, such a couloir expresses an 'invitation' to ride it straight and with high {speed}. Thus, Tom

lifts his hand as he did in the preceding sequence, but this time his hand no longer resembles the lip. Instead, he stretches his hand straight out and lets it fall down like an axe cutting through the air. This expressive, swift gesture is full of dynamic and stands in sharp contrast to the earlier one that was describing a movement of a rider and not a feature of the terrain. The mellow ride down into the bowl in step IV. was signalled by a subtle spreading of two fingers, but now the ride continues with high speed vertically down. The structure of the slope and the dynamics of the ride become one: a steep couloir implies a swift ride with a clearly defined finish (the end of the couloir), a gentle bowl in contrast requires calm cruising that allows preparation of the next segment as the rider will need to choose a new direction very soon. In this way, the form of a line is not only based on the shape of the terrain and the bodily ability of the rider, but also pays testament to the orientation work necessary throughout the run. And accordingly, the formulation of each line involves much more than merely mentioning the existing rocks or snowfields, it refers to a dynamic practice *in* the face: the riding of a line.

This detailed account examined only a small excerpt of ten seconds from a conversation of maybe ten minutes that is repeated in a similar form again and again throughout a typical day of freeriding. Yet these few seconds already display the central characteristics of such instructions: to see a line means to formulate a line (in the sense of "formulating place," see Schegloff 1972). Seeing a line is a situated, sequential, interactive, bodily, and epistemic (or creative) practice—a continuous social production of an abstract object that is woven in view of the mountain side. Seeing a line is thus not just an expression of purely conceptual or mental knowledge, neither is it a direct output of something that was previously given in memorized form, nor is it a disembodied process happening invisibly in the head of the rider.

Excursus: Knowledge and (Pheno-)practices

The use and exact meaning of the term knowledge within the practice perspective is both ambiguous and contested. Reckwitz (2002a, 2002b), for example, treats knowledge as a crucial element of all practices and see the contribution of practice thought to sociology in its specific conceptualization of embodied knowledge. Accordingly, he defines practices as "bodily anchored behavioural routines that are carried by collective implicit knowledge" (2016: 163; my translation). Some practice theorists have argued that this has led to a problematic "neglect" of "theoretical forms of knowledge" that needs to be reversed without reverting to mentalism (Schmidt 2017: 141). Schatzki, in contrast, seems to have stopped using the term knowledge in his later writings and instead speaks about understandings which incorporate capabilities of the type "knowing how to do X"—and notably, knowing

5 Seeing as Interaction: Formulating and Showing a Line

is always used in its progressive form by him (see e.g. Schatzki 2002: 77–78). What is more, Schatzki has rejected Turner's (1994, 2001) weighty critique of practice theories precisely on the ground that Turner treats practices as 'chunks' of tacit knowledge (Schatzki 2002: 69–74). Nevertheless, because the precise meaning of the term knowledge is contested, it would be perfectly possible to argue that the ability to see a freeride line in the manner just described represents a certain type of knowledge. The different strands of practice theory that have emerged in Germany over the past two decades share such a focus on knowledge and demonstrate the fruitfulness and flexibility of a knowledge-centred reading of practice thought. Working in the long shadow of Schutzian Wissenssoziologie—whose affinities with (pheno-)practice theory I discuss in chapter seven—and using the highly influential early paper by Reckwitz (2002a) as a reference point, the shared rejection of mentalist concepts of knowledge and individualist conceptions of experience and action unites a broad range of works whose underlying ontologies differ. Alternatively, implicit knowledge is theorized with reference to Bourdieu's habitus (Gebauer/Alkemeyer/Flick 2004, Brümmer/Alkemeyer 2017; Schmidt 2012), Foucauldian discourses and dispositifs (Reckwitz 2004, 2006b; Prinz 2014; H. Schäfer 2016), or Garfinkel's radical reformulation as ethnomethods (Meyer/v. Wedelstaedt 2017). Each approach, applied to befitting empirical cases, brings out different facets that I will discuss in the respective chapter focused on that topic. Of particular relevance to this work are naturally practice theoretical accounts of sports and (life-)style that argue on the basis of non-mentalist or ethnomethodological conceptualization of knowledge (e.g. Alkemeyer/Buschmann 2017; Schmidt 2012, 2017). I will dissect many of their arguments in detail throughout this work, with a focus on clarifying the subtle difference in the approach or reading of certain concepts or sources (in particular readings of Wittgenstein). As it is often the case with positions that are broadly similar but distinct in detail, these critical discussions might give a false impression. Many of my findings could adequately be rephrased in terms of a study of something like "the practical knowledge of seeing"—but this would stand in the way of my larger project of developing a phenopractice perspective on style that attends to experiences as invoked and ordered by practices and not subjects. Therefore, I will follow Schatzki and largely refrain from using the word "knowledge" because it is prone to imply misleading 'mentalist' misconceptions despite all best intentions to the contrary. Phenopractice theory postulates a locus and modus operandi of the 'social construction of reality' which differs in several important ways from a classical view focusing on meaning-making in subjective consciousness. Generally, I argue that from a practice-based view, knowledge can be applied as a very general term in that *every* practical accomplishment (and thus any ordered situation) is treated as the result of (practical) knowledge, and thus every situation becomes an exemplar of knowledge-in-use or 'doing knowing' (an argument primarily made with regard to ethnomethodology, e.g. ten Have 2002; Lynch 2002). But if one chooses to do so, the question remains precisely which difference one is trying to make if every doing expresses some form of knowing in the first place. Consequentially, I hold that the use of the notion 'knowledge' within the practice turn is always slightly problematic. On the one hand, theories of social practices share important theoretical roots with the sociology of knowledge (or Wissenssoziologie) since they base the orderliness of the social world at least in part in the existence of a canon of competencies that could well be labelled knowledge. In this vein, Reckwitz underlines the "implicitness of knowledge" (2006a: 707; my translation) as a "foundational intuition" of all theories of social practices since he sees the dissociation from primarily cognitive concepts of knowledge as a central common ground of the various theories within the 'family' of theories of social practices. However, the question is what exactly a fruitful 'non-cognitive' notion of knowledge should entail and how the relation between knowledge and practice (i.e. practices of knowing) should be understood. Frequently, the notion of "Know-How" in contrast to "Know-What" is posed as an alternative that aptly expresses the embodied character of pragmatic competencies. The notion of implicit or tacit knowledge, however, has been criticized by many to escape precise definition (H. M. Collins 2001; Gourlay 2006; S. P. Turner 1994). As the discussion about the relationship between conversation and cognition shows (see Molder/Potter 2005), referring to implicit knowledge leaves unanswered the question of whether knowledge is generally inexplicable, or whether implicit and explicit knowledge always appear side-by-side, or whether explicit knowledge has mental correlates, or—finally—whether every seemingly explicit piece of knowledge is only the result of a situated production or practice of demonstrating or formulating knowledge which is in itself an irredeemably embodied competence (Matthews 2009; Rammert 2007a, Schmidt 2017). To pick an exact position within this field of possibilities seems to be neither possible nor necessary in the face of the empirical case discussed here. Instead, I will build on Schatzki's notion of understanding which arguably bypasses much of the vexed debate by seeking a more general answer to the question by virtue of what some doing constitutes the doing of a certain practice—the provisions of which can arguably not be reduced to individual or subjective features anyways. Further, whenever (at a few occasions) I employ the vocabulary of knowledge, I will do so in just this sense: I will speak of the *expression* of knowledge (usually because the freeskiers themselves would put it this way), a formulation that leaves completely open by virtue of which such situated expression has been brought about.

By virtue of being the performance of a practice, seeing a line is tightly anchored in the concrete situation. As a bodily act in the here and now, it is interwoven with the specific possibilities of the concrete situation, but also subject to its contingency. This becomes particularly evident when one considers an especially prominent feature present in virtually every conversation freerider hold about lines: pointing. It seems almost impossible for riders to talk solemnly with words vis-à-vis a mountain; almost always, they make use of arms, hands, or ski poles as well. It is within these gestures that the line can really spring to life, it is here where it is made bodily and interactively present to the here and now. And it is also the frequency and extensiveness of pointing that provides an important step towards understanding seeing as an act of embodied apprehension (see Chap. 4).

From a theoretical perspective, pointing as an element of conducting a social practice can help to sketch out a more specific position within the broad family of practice theories (cf. the contributions in Meyer/v. Wedelstaedt 2017). First, the present analysis of reading a face makes it clear that pointing does not only represent a reference to something already given. Instead, pointing constructs its object carefully and in various ways, and this construction work in turn depends on the competence of the observing freerider. Therefore, a constructivist view in the widest sense ensues. Second, pointing is nevertheless a bodily act that is necessarily locally situated; it is as such beyond the reach of those theories which place knowledge or culture on a purely semantic or mental level (cf. Reckwitz 2002a). Third, reducing the nature of practices to purely pre-semantic, bodily routinized conduct (as Bongaerts 2008 suggests in order to equate practices with behaviour or Verhalten in a Schutzian sense) is unjustified and reductions. In contrast, Goodwin (2003) powerfully demonstrates empirically a point made by Wittgenstein (1995a: 56), who saw pointing as "one of the most fundamental language-games:" Gestural pointing can only be used successfully as a form of communication if it happens within the frame of a situation in which the type of conduct, object shown, and showing actant have been already narrowed down sufficiently—an accomplishment which is most frequently (and often with superior efficiency, precision, and finesse) achieved through the use of language (cf. Mondada 2012). Consequentially, a practice-based perspective applied beyond the most basic forms of human conduct cannot do without taking into account the enormous potency to differentiate that semantics make available in social conduct. After all, it is this power to differentiate finely which renders possible so many of the seemingly mute, reflex-like practices—be it because language use remains a constant backup option for remedying failing gestural communication, or be it because language is frequently irreplaceable as a tool to instruct or teach such 'mute' body techniques. The voicelessness of many practices, in other words, should not be mistaken for a silence of the social world which facilitates their very existence.[19] To conclude, formulating a line should be understood as an pheno-practice, as a selecting of features of the environment accomplished in-situ which is reconstructed within the framework of a conversational practice—and thus as a practice which is always partly bodily, but is nevertheless grounded in the capacities of language use.

Pointing is an act of selection par excellence. A particular detail is made to stand out from the rest of the slope and identified as something that is a natural part of a line for a freerider (such as a wind lip or a cliff). In this way, Tom selects every segment as one particular option from within an extended space of potentialities. The mountain slope is cluttered with many smaller and larger terrain features, and accordingly almost endless possibilities for riding a line exist—at least theoretically. The work of formulating a line thus consists of selecting and presenting a single optional route in order to make it addressable—and thus also rejectable. Not until both riders see the same line, they are able to discuss whether it is too difficult, too dangerous, too boring, etc. Only after Tom has finished his explanation, Steffi can formulate her own plan by simply saying: "Ok, then I will keep to the right of you and just leave the cliff alone" [M].[20] The line has now become a thing with attributes, a thing relative to which one can position oneself or other things. This is a dual accomplishment: On the hand, I have shown that the concrete line has been chosen among a broad range of similar options. On the other, a line must not be defined to narrowly; it needs to be described in a way that allows a subsequent run to be identified as riding *this* line regardless of minor discrepancies, because the track described at the beginning of this chapter cannot ever be produced a second time. Every rider follows a line in unique ways, every run ends up somewhat different than planned—a turn ends up being bigger, you drop down slightly further to the right, a couloir turns out to be a little steeper and faster than you thought. The description that Tom delivers is in a way already prepared for this fact, since regardless of all detail, it is still quite imprecise. How exactly one should ride through the bowl, when exactly one should drop into the chute, where exactly a turn to the left should start is not defined. Thus, it 'fits' a large number of concrete runs that could be described and understood as this particular line.

In view of this double fuzziness, one could think that a line is something not really binding, a vague interpretation, or a playful suggestion. But in the freeskiers' language, a line is treated quite differently. Here, a line is an object that is just there just waiting to be discovered. For example, an instruction on how to ride big mountain lines begins with the simple statement: "You can find lines

---

[19] A similar argument could be made with regard to technical instruments. For example, when Latour (1996a) argues that it is artefacts and not "symbols" that allow humans (but not animals) to erect complex societies, he remains silent on the fact that probably all advanced tools or material structures in turn require language use to be designed or implemented into routine practice. He himself needs about ten pages of text to *explain* the use of the Berlin Key (Latour 2000) that is supposedly able to "do things without words."

[20] „Ok, und ich halt mich dann immer etwas rechts davon und lass halt das Cliff aus."

everywhere."[21] ([D] Häusl 2008: 22) In everyday conversations, one finds typical phrases like: "To the left there lies another phat line."[22] [M] or "The couloir straight across that face, that's also a really sick line."[23] [M]. I did not observe a single instance where the basic existence of a line was questioned or denied—a critical comment would instead typically point out that this line is too dangerous, difficult to enter, or nearly impossible to ride. The current (snow-) conditions, however, are not decisive for the existence of a line. Freeriders talk about lines that finally became doable after they have been observing them for months or even years because the snow and weather were eventually ok (e.g. Häusl 2008 [D]). In the freeskiers' language, in their texts, movies, and videos, lines are objects fixed in space, causing the attractiveness of certain resorts or mountains. In this spirit, the leading German special-interest magazine writes about the Dachstein resort: "But most {jibbers} don't know that down towards the valley some very fine lines are waiting for those peeking across the border of the funpark."[24] ([D] Mandl 2009: 66) In the folk language of freeskiing, lines are even objects one can own, that somebody is entitled to: "No, no. You saw it, so it's yours!" [M] Tom shouted when his mate Peder asked him if he would not prefer to do this beautiful drop they are just inspecting. In this terminology, all traces of hesitation, sequentiality and relativity that characterize a line in the stage of concrete description are gone.

6 Professional Vision

Accordingly, the line as a social object exists in two ways. In the language, in texts, narrations, or videos it is a static thing in the environment; it lies in a slope of a specific mountain. In lived interaction, on the other hand, it is elaborated step-by-step; it grows through the sophisticated gestures of Tom and under (or, rather, in) the critical eyes of those present. The 'reading' of the face of the Krimml can thus be understood as constitutive work which makes the line present as a line in the social world of freeskiing, so that now Steffi can talk about 'this line'—as a plan, a challenge, or even a dream. This making-accessible of an object to a specific expert discourse or practice has been termed professional vision by Charles Goodwin (1994). It is the ability of an expert to make a certain relevant object visible for his community of practice (in the sense of Wenger 1999). Goodwin differentiates three steps of this process. First, coding, which involves the attribution of a visual phenomenon to a certain differentiation scheme which is part of the specific expertise of the respective expert culture. Second, highlighting, which

---

[21] „Lines könnt ihr überall finden."

[22] „Da links ist noch so eine geile Line drin."

[23] „Die Rinne da quer durchs Face, das ist auch so eine krasse Line."

[24] „Die meisten Jibber wissen aber nicht, dass ins Tal hinunter einige sehr feine Lines auf diejenigen warten, die über den Park-Rand hinausschauen."

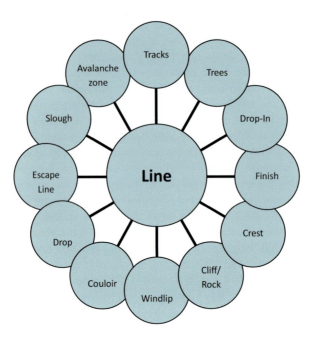

Fig. 2.5 Taxonomy of the components of a line

consists of pointing out certain elements thus framed as being especially important or decisive for the given problem. And third: the production and interpretation of graphical representations of such relevant elements (C. Goodwin 1994). Although Goodwin refers specifically to professionals such as lawyers or archaeologists, the process of describing the line by Tom that was analysed above matches this scheme quite well. In the course of his description through words and gestures, Tom performs coding, that is, he assigns certain visible attributes of the slope to certain semantic categories with which freerider usually describe a slope. This established vocabulary can be subsumed into the folk taxonomy shown above (see on folk taxonomies Maeder/Brosziewski 1997) (Fig. 2.5).[25]

While Tom needs to elaborate the exact position of these elements carefully, their general attributes are already clear to Steffi and him because a freerider knows the relevant difference between, e.g., a couloir and a bowl, just like he knows how to handle slough and whether a cliff is dangerous. The different elements of the line, in other words, point to "category bound activities" in the

---

[25] In contrast to the formalized and standardized schemata used by the archaeologists in Goodwin's example, such a taxonomy is to be regarded as an informal differentiation scheme that is not fixed in a materialized form, but should be rather understood in terms of an ethnographic semantic (Maeder/Brosziewski 1997).

sense of Harvey Sacks (1994) (although this notion originally refers to persons or members): Certain elements are coupled with respective actions or ways of skiing. Parallel to such 'coding,' Tom also performs 'highlighting' in each segment in that in a second step, certain elements are assigned a heightened relevance as they become especially important e.g. as landmarks for orientation. Another good example are {drops}—cliffs that are suitable to jump down from—, which are a frequent topic although they were absent from the sequence analysed above. Drops are the highlight of every line they're built into, and advanced freeriders observe faces primarily with regard to interesting and suitable drops. The third element of Goodwin's model of professional vision, graphical representations, are typically absent from a freeride-situation on the mountain—but nevertheless, visual representations do play a very important role in the freeski scene (see Chap. 5). Although freeriding is without a doubt a sport that is very demanding athletically, the freeriders regard this professional vision and not body control as the key competence necessary for big mountain skiing. From an analytical point of view, physical training and athletic skills are no doubt indispensable to be successful freerider. However, these bodily competences are not very often an evident concern during everyday routine, partly because much of the actual technique of skiing needs to be a routinized skill happening partly unconsciously in order for the rider to be able to focus on picking the right line instead of thinking about how to steer his skis into the next turn (see Chap. 4 for details). Accordingly, the introduction to freeriding quoted above explains:

> "The art of big mountain lines is not so much about riding skill—that's a prerequisite anyways—but about visualizing the route (…)."[26] ([D] Häusl 2008: 22)

In the same way, pro riders explain their competence primarily as a *competence of seeing* that is the result of living in close and frequent contact with the mountains. For example, the legendary extreme skier Stefano de Benedetti narrated his metamorphosis from a normal skier to a member of the "mountain people" in the following way:

> "When you live in touch with the mountains (...) your vision changes completely. And after three or four years, I could see the possibility to ski where nobody saw it." (Obernhaus 2008: 26:30; [D])

At first sight, this is a surprising statement: A legendary skier should distinguish himself through his skiing abilities—and not through the mere seeing of possibilities! But, as the fifth chapter will demonstrate, seeing and moving coalesces in the practice of riding down a line—and visual orientation is the decisive component of the two. However, this quote does not only point to the fact that seeing a good line is an important prerequisite for a successful run, it also reveals a deeper connection. Tom's description does refer to the slope he points out, but he does

---

[26] „Die Kunst der Big Mountain Lines liegt nicht so sehr im Fahrkönnen – das ist sowieso Voraussetzung –, sondern in der Visualisierung der Route (…)."

not describe the slope itself, for example its beauty. Instead, he formulates the options for riding that this slope affords. To be precise: he articulates the options to ride this particular part of the slope under these particular circumstances in a way typical for freeriders. The actual topic of his talk is thus the *affordance* of the face, those options for action that the face opens up, those possibilities it invites to explore like the urban landscape invites the traceurs of parkour (Braune 2021). In Goodwin's (2000a) terms, the affordances of the slope are thus part of the "activity system" of the situation of pointing and can therefore gain different shapes according to the respective framing of the situation. For example, the framing would be different for a ski tourer than for a freerider, and the affordances expressed in ironic exaggeration differ from those in serious planning.[27] The crucial point is that these possibilities only exist relative to a particular rider and a particular style of riding. Schatzki (2002: 229) formulates accordingly: "An individual does not, so to speak, stand self-contained over against a landscape of qualified paths. Rather, she or he is present, or implicated, in the contours and textures of the landscape." In the same sense, but more specifically referring to the phenomenology of gazing, Wylie (2006: 519) notes: "[L]andscape is not a way of seeing the world. Nor is it 'something seen', an external, inert surface. Rather, the term 'landscape' names the materialities and sensibilities with which we see." While medium sized cliffs provide Tom affordances for drops between six and eight meters, larger cliffs of 15 or 20 meters do not pose affordances, but threats to him. For a professional rider, on the other hand, things would be different: since a professional can typically drop cliffs that high, they posses an affordance. Seeing a line almost always means seeing a line *for oneself*—a line one could at least imagine being able to ride. A line therefore relates the rider and the mountain in a specific way; it is equally influenced by both and functions as a liminal object between them. There are, nevertheless, specifically framed situations in which one would talk of doing this one really sick line one fine day, or in which one would comment on a certain line (for example in a picture) in a more general way. However, such situations occur quite seldom, and as soon as the formulating of a line refers to a concrete line vis-à-vis oneself, riders are reluctant to suggest specific routes to one another. In the high mountains, everybody has to choose his own risk level and his own path. It is important to note that Tom does not actually instruct Steffi where to ride; indeed, he does not even suggest a route for her. Instead, she had stated earlier that she will ride where he rides, and it is in response to this that he describes what he intends to do.

---

[27] Apparently, Goodwin builds directly on Goffman's (1974) frame analysis.

Excursus: Affordances

The concept of affordances is used in different ways in the literature, and thus some clarification seems necessary. Within the framework of Ecological Psychology, Gibson (1986) introduced the concept and used it to describe the attributes of an environment as a correlate of those possibilities for action that it opens up for a specific actor/observer. Although he develops his concept specifically with regard to the visual perception of possibilities for movement through the material environment (and thus with regard to the exact same problem that freeriders need to solve when they read a mountain face), he defined the affordance of an environment as an ontologically given attribute that is dependent upon the physiognomic aptitude of the specific observer, but not upon his goals, attitudes or any cultural framework. The affordance itself only changes to the extent to which the relation of observer and environment changes (for example if he gains or loses certain skills, or the environmental factors change), but it is *not* dependent on the perception of the actor—an objective possibility does still exist, even if one does not subjectively 'believe' in it. For Gibson, an affordance is always ontologically given and not the result of a mental or cognitive interpretation—and for this reason his approach has been called "the direct theory of visual perception" (Jacob/Jeannerod 2003: 157). It is under this premise that Gibson discusses the fact that one can sometimes fail to spot an opportunity (which nevertheless exists): in his terms, seeing an affordance requires successful and 'correct' information processing. Therefore, the original concept of affordance postulates not an observational relativity, but an observer relativity that is based on objectively given facts—only that objectively given attributes of the environment need to be put into relation with objectively given possibilities for actions. While the original theory is decidedly anti-constructivist in nature (Greeno 1994), the notion of affordance gained considerable influence in the literature on product design—but notably only after it was rephrased quasi-phenomenologically by Norman (1988; see McGrenere/Ho 2000). In contrast to Gibson, Norman applies the concept with regard to *perceptible* affordances and focuses on the discrepancy of "perceived" and "real affordances" as a key problem in design. At the core, his argument is that products like software should be designed in a way that makes it possible for users to understand which functions they offer. While in this version the perception of an affordance is dependent on the cultural background of the user (or his knowledge), the affordances themselves are now seen to be universally given rather than observer-specific (McGrenere/Ho 2000)—which stands in sharp contrast to Gibson's original model. In Norman's notion, the reason for the fact that an affordance always exists relative to an actor is shifted from the bodily abilities to the interpretative acts of consciousness.

Sociology (and especially STS) took up the concept of affordances with regard to technical products. However, the concept remains subject to controversial discussion in sociology as much as in the design literature, especially because several different authors take it to offer a middle course between the (alleged) determinism of classical positivist positions and the (alleged) total relativism of radical constructivism. Unfortunately, these authors define the concept in differing ways, depending on the schools of theory to which they subscribe (e.g. compare the variation across Akrich/Latour 1992; Bloomfield/Latham/Vurdubakis 2009; W. Gibson 2006; Hutchby 2001, 2003; Rappert 2001; and Streeck 1996). Since an affordance is a liminal entity between subject and object, this continuing discussion mirrors the differing positions of the two basic readings of affordances (ontological-individualistic versus phenomenological-subjective) within the respective theories. At this point, it should suffice to state that I am using the notion of affordances in accordance with the original concept with regard to the visual perception of a natural environment, but that I treat it as a product of a local performance of a phenopractice and thus not as universally given: A perceptual or phenomenological affordance is a possibility (one might say 'invitation') to perceive that opens up towards a practitioner within conduct of a phenopractice. This definition is sufficient at this point since the contingency which emerges during the formulating of an affordance can be addressed as a feature of the observation itself without creating a necessity to define its general attributes further. It is, in short, enough to say that a rider sees and says that a line is possible and that he could always do this seeing and saying in a different way.

7 The Technical Dimension of Seeing

As I have shown, the perception of the freerider is not actually directed towards with the face per se, but rather to the practical affordance for riding within it—that is, with lines. These lines, however, are not only dependent on the features of the terrain (to be precise: the features of the terrain which are relevant to the line as they emerge within the inspecting of the slope), but also from the technical equipment such as the ski that makes the riding of the line possible. A good example is what freeskiers call a {switchline}. Over the last three or four years, very wide powder skis have been developed that enable the skier to ride backwards through deep powder. With the addition of such a ski to the freerider's gear, a powder slope that was hitherto rather gentle and wide and thus boring because slow gains the affordance of a switchline, therefore becoming quite interesting to many accomplished riders. Because of the given inclination, spatial order, and available equipment, the skier could ride this slope backwards, thus copying a practice that has lately appeared increasingly often in freeski movies and is regarded technically challenging as well as playful and progressive. Accordingly, in this season Tom has begun to keep his eyes open not only for nice cliff-drops, but also for suitable switchlines. An interesting question, one might add, is how switchlines have been 'invented' together with the development of new types of skis and how the new trick has been disseminated through freeski media so that it has become a 'must-have' for Tom's own freeski videos. In other words, switchlines offer a very instructive example of how technological developments can (without planning) carry the affordances of certain practices within them, which will then begin to spread as the new equipment does (for reasons other than this new affordance). As chapter ten will sketch out, a practice might then be picked up by the (subcultural) media and thus become part of the aesthetic canon of the subculture so that it gains status-inducing distinction value and with through this will be finally emotionally charged.

The observation of the slope, however, is not only structured by certain socially disseminated subcultural schemes such as those just mentioned, but it is also directly coupled to a riders' concrete situational setting, for example because his material equipment influences the affordances he is able to see in a face. Such a change in the *visual* perception caused by changes to the technical gear available which unfolds new affordances within a given material environment is reflected in a quote by Shane McConkey, a pioneer of Ski-BASEjumping. This especially extreme version of freeriding consists of the rider jumping over a very high cliff (such as the Eiger north face) at the end of his line in order to open a parachute after a short free fall and finally land safely. Although this free fall itself does obviously provide an enormous 'kick' for the rider, McConkey describes something totally different as the primary effect of this new technique. For him, the new lines that become possible now that he does not have to take into account a safely skiable end point of his lines:

> "With the addition of a parachute to my skiing gear, I'm looking at these mountains through totally different goggles than all the other skiers." (Obernhaus 2008: 1:07:50; [D])

The technical equipment of the rider therefore has a direct influence on the actual practice of skiing, and also an *indirect* influence on the complementary practices in which the skiing is embedded. Of the numerous factors that influence if and how a rider skis a face—if, for example, he attempts a certain cliff-drop or a particular couloir—many do not actually influence the run directly, but rather indirectly, by taking effect through the complementary practices that form the habitat of the core practice of descending. Most important of these complementary practices is the seeing of the line I discuss here, but the ascent to the drop-in of the line would be another example: if the ascent is too difficult or dangerous, an otherwise attractive line will not be ripped.

Excursus: Distributed Cognition

The relevance of technical equipment for situationally achieved orientation surfacing here bears some resemblance to the theory of distributed cognition developed primarily by Hutchins (1995). He proposed a notion of *situated cognition* as coordination work which must not be reduced to mental processes alone. His notion does not only share important characteristics with the empirical case at hand here, but, as Pylyshyn (1999, 2000) argues, is a phenomenon primarily rooted in the specific (and often neglected) ways in which human vision and 'visual cognition' works (see next chapter). Hutchins observed that tasks usually considered cognitive work that supposedly happens 'in the brain,' are actually interactional work that makes use of a range of different cultural and especially material resources, and which should therefore be seen as a distributed process. This view was developed primarily in the course of detailed ethnographic studies of navigation procedures aboard ships (Hutchins 1995) or airplanes (Hutchins/Klausen 1998) in which special instruments arguably play as much a central role as thinking humans do. Hutchins' research methodology bears many similarities with ethnomethodological works; not only in terms of the density and form of the data used, but also in the basic theoretical orientation towards the processual order of the concrete situation instead of a focus of singular actors—but the author remains silent about this. (There is no need here to speculate about reasons; however it seems evident that Hutchins (1996) regards cognitive psychologists and not sociologists as the primarily relevant audience.) Although the orientation "in the wild" that Hutchins (1995) discusses is equally evident in the case examined here, and although in both cases material equipment has a large influence on the way the orientation is conducted, an important difference in the role of the material remains. In contrast to naval navigation with the help of sextants or airplane piloting through the use of instruments for measuring and data storage, the skiing equipment does not assume a role in the reading of face that can be sensibly understood as fundamental for processes of cognition in the way Hutchins suggests. The only instruments which are of direct functional use in the observation of the slope are the ski goggles the rider wear (which allow a contrast-rich sight despite the blinding white of the snow) and the ski poles and gloves that acquire an additional role as primitive pointing devices. The theory of distributed cognition, however, refers to "rationalized and historically stabilized settings where problems and their solutions have been crystallized in physical artifacts" (Hutchins 1996: 67). The given case does not precisely fit this definition and is thus instructive in multiple ways. First, it points to the fact that it is only a certain type of 'problem' that seems to cause such technical crystallizations of solution procedures while others do not. For only a few of the many reoccurring problems in mountaineering, solutions through instruments of the type that Hutchins discusses have been successfully developed. For example, calculation tables aid decision-making about the danger of avalanches (Engler/J. Mersch 2006; Munter 1997), but they are not used widely by freeskiers. Although the danger of avalanches has always been faced by ski mountaineers, it is only lately that technical crystallizations of safety procedures have emerged—without much success. Second, material equipment can be relevant for order-producing social conduct in two different ways. One the one hand, a direct participation of some kind, for example when a computation table 'calculates' figures or a display 'memorizes' values (Hutchins/Klausen 1998); and on the other, an indirect influence, for example when the material gear transforms the object of the observation (by changing its affordances). Accordingly, the equipment of ski-BASEers emulates the affordances that are the object of the orientation process, while the modus of the conduct itself—the inspecting, pointing, commenting, asking—remains the same (cf. Preda 2000 on the role of artefacts in rule-following). Third, this case can help to make apparent how the different theories that have been developed with regard to similar empirical phenomena of technically supported decision processes apply different delimitations between the elements involved. For example, in his discussion of Hutchins' work, Bruno Latour (1996b) repeats his pledge for a complete levelling of any subject-object-distinction and presses for acknowledgement of the equal partaking of technical and human actors in the accomplishment of navigation. In the network that ANT postulates, the ski goggle that facilitates the observation, the human eye, the rider's body and the parachute of the ski-BASEr all gain so-called "symmetric" roles since they are all co-constitutive—resulting in a loss of differentiation between the indispensable (the eye) and the adequate (goggle) or between the object-transforming (parachute) and process-facilitating (goggle). Hutchins' persistent orientation—on the other hand—towards phenomena that fall into the realm of cognitive psychology narrows down the focus of the discussion in a way that excludes certain decisive dimensions apparent in the example of reading a face. The relevance of the additional affordances opened up through the addition of the parachute for the orientation of the rider in the face would escape the view of the scientific observer since they do not directly belong to the actual instance of what Hutchins calls 'cognition,' but are instead relevant for its object. (Compare the marginalized role of the specific qualities of the Palau, the ship on which Hutchins (1995) conducted his observations.) Additionally, Hutchins concerns himself with a *situated* and not only a *distributed* notion of cognition, and defines the second simply as a special case of the first that lends itself more easily to examination (see Hutchins 1996). However, in the face of the possibility of a limitation of cultural preference or predisposition towards technical solutions to only certain types of problems and situations that I proposed above, one needs to ask whether these two types of cognition do not indeed do represent fundamentally distinctive types. In other words, Hutchins seems to build his research upon a rationalistic notion of problems which hides the fact that it is by no means unquestionably given what will be considered a problem when, and how exactly a 'good' solution looks. One could therefore question whether diagnosing a constitutive role of material instruments is not necessarily depended upon an unquestioned givenness of the principal aim of the observed conduct (the ship must enter the harbour securely, the airplane has to climb to a new route). If so, one could further imply that the openness that is characteristic of instrument-free reading of faces by the freeriders is not only prevalent on practical grounds, but much more for cultural reasons that have their basis in the subcultural-specific understanding of a successful run as an expression of individuality through variation.

8 Situated Seeing

In conclusion, it has become apparent that the seeing of the line is situated in two ways: One the one hand, it is subject to the contingency of the situation in that the concrete state of things given here and now shapes aspects of the line. Throughout formulating the line, riders often judge the momentarily state of the snow, the current development of the weather, the present danger of avalanches, their personal physical and motivational condition, and so on. Moreover, reading a face is neither a standardized analysis nor a formalized process; but instead, the dynamics of the conversation itself can influence the seeing of a line. For example, one might come up with an idea, but then the conversation turns to another feature of the face and the original idea is subsequently dropped. On the other hand, as the influence of technical equipment exemplifies, the practice of seeing is also situated in a second sense. It is situated not only in the local social order, but also in a superordinate social order which for example consists in the evolutionary development of the gear the skiers use. Therefore, the seeing of a switchline or a skiBASE-line is not only the result of a local conduct that led to the 'just-here-and-just-now-and-just-like-this' of the seeing, but it is as well an element of the translocal, long-term process of the development and dissemination of skiing switchlines or skiBASEing. The last chapter of this work will shed more light on such processes of evolution and dissemination—partly because they are not as abstract and distant from the "real thing" of "just" skiing down a slope as one might conceive them. To the contrary, they are so tightly interwoven with the situated, local practices of freeriding that they deeply influence them even before the rider has only made his first turn.

But what does this initial empirical observation of the freeriders' ways of seeing imply for the theoretical project of this work? More generally speaking, both seeing-in-interaction and the influence of technology on seeing are examples for how the relevancy and influence of allegedly 'external' factors manifest in the situation itself; and both therefore point to the fundamental situatedness of all intra-situational order. In other words, I suggest that both the rich detail captured in the video analysis of freeskiers' situated and interactive seeing and the inherent influence of the skier's equipment on their ways of seeing demonstrate a co-dependence and functional coherence of different 'layers' or aspects of social practices that is manifest already in the visual dimension alone. Consequently, I argue that in order to adequately grasp freeskiing's organized artfulness, one needs to attend to seemingly disparate topics of inquiry within a unified theoretical and methodological framework—a framework that theories of social practices provide. To this end, phenopractice theory is proposed in order to complement the existing literature on visual practices. Developing this alternative framework seems necessary because said literature either a) remains relatively limited in scope in that they restrict themselves to specific aspects such as the role of images (e.g. Burri 2008) or talk-in-interaction (e.g. C. Goodwin 2000b); or b) attends to interrelations and dynamics on a rather abstract macro level (e.g. Bourdieu's [1977, 1984] studies of 'whole' societies or Foucault's [1976, 1977] discussions of gaze and power); or c) unpacks the complex nature of the situated production of relevancies and intelligibility in practices of seeing in sufficient detail but remains tied to an individualist ontology when doing so (by theorizing seeing as performed by active subjects possessing implicit knowledge [see especially Prinz 2014, 2016]).

I propose that a viable theoretical alternative can be formulated by drawing on the work of Ted Schatzki, who discusses modes of relatedness or 'hanging-together' of social practices extensively and coherently (see especially Schatzki 2002). In line with the insights just gained, he does not suggest that all practices are related or co-relevant, for example in that they are all permeated by power or all reproduce social capital; but instead argues that only practices of a certain type (he calls them 'integrative practices') are coordinated by means of social order which are—and this is crucial—bound to and transpire in social *sites* rather than individuals or social wholes. Throughout the following chapters, I will draw on his arguments and concepts to a varying extend; and I should note that also I deviate from his account in important matters such as the role of technology. For now, it suffices to conclude that his philosophical account shares a fundamental premise with my theoretical standpoint which became empirically evident in the freeskiers' ways of seeing a line: The notion that whatever aspect is considered to influence or frame a concrete moment of situated conduct must bear on the intelligibility of said situation.

Nevertheless, I also feel that Schatzki's remarks on epistemology remain relatively brief; particularly because situational order per se is not a topic he dwells on for any length. The freeskiers' practices of seeing just presented, however, have arguably shown that to understand just how interactively seeing a line prior to riding *frames* (rather than informs, predetermines, or limits) the actual riding, a theoretical framework seems necessary that acknowledges the 'epistemological primacy' of the situation, i.e. the fact that all relevant factors or forces must 'show up' in the concrete situation rather than on abstract levels of (theoretical or statistical) aggregation alone. In the ethnomethodological tradition, but also in phenomenological works by authors such as Merleau-Ponty, deep theoretical and empirical insights into these issues have been gained; and therefore I will attempt to combine some of these with Schatzki's overarching theoretical framework. It seems to me that specifically within the practice literature focused on situational order, authors have to an unduly large extent relied on phenomena of sequentiality to underscore concepts designed to grasp the interrelation and co-dependency of separate situated (and not just visual) practices. To be sure, my examination of situatedly seeing a line did emphasize the importance of the sequentiality of lived conduct as well, and argued that many phenomena of social coordination can be explained by the fact that different practices happen consecutively, in series, or in repetitive patterns (see on the topic of routines and repetitive orders of consumption practices Shove/Trentmann/Wilk 2009). But as the subsequent discussion of the notion of affordances evidenced, practical conduct can only be influenced by or oriented towards certain limited and selected aspects of instances of prior conduct, and thus sequentiality per se is not sufficient a concept to account for more complex or long-lasting forms of relatedness of situated practices. Accordingly, I suggest that sequentiality is not sufficient a concept to account for a range of related phenomena captured in everyday terms such as attention, interest, sense-making, focus, care, absorption, and so forth. In other words, I argue that in order to get a coherent grasp on the forms or processes through which 'macro' dynamics, complementary practices, or extra-situational prerequisites relate to and bear on situated conduct, it is necessary to inquire in more detail into the ways in which they (or their 'products') might take presence, stick out, or become relevant in concrete, local situations of conduct. Therefore, I am convinced that any inquiry into broader meshworks and dynamics of social practices must be rooted in a thorough and coherent discussion of precisely *how* observability and intelligibility are achieved and organized in concrete, situated unfoldings of social practices; and in line with the overall focus on this work, I will concentrate my arguments on the visual dimension of observability and intelligibility. The following chapter seeks to lay a solid foundation for this project by taking a closer look at the details of visual perception and the theoretical and phenomenological arguments or lines of thought the study of human vision has inspired. To this end, I will follow Tom and Steffi as they make their way up towards the ridge of the Krimml and to the drop-in of the line they have just seen.

Chapter 3
Perception—Figuring Out the Visual Field

1 Introduction: On the Ridge

The sign speaks loud and clear: "ATTENTION! You are in high-alpine terrain! You are leaving the controlled and secured ski resort. Risk of avalanches! Crash hazard!" Below the sign, a rope swings lazily in the chilling wind. Coloured bright yellow, it fences off the piste—marked, secured, and controlled—from the surrounding mountain terrain. For most ski tourists and those commentators in the mainstream media that seem prone to moralizing every time the news report another victim of avalanches, it separates the realm of the sane and normal from that of the irresponsible daredevils. For the freeskiers, it separates the uniform, nondescript, and boring tourist repository from the real mountains. For a ski tourist, the open mountain terrain behind the rope is a no-go area, beautiful to look at but otherwise almost non-existent: Empty, unknowable, indifferent. For the freeriders, it is everything they care about. The {backcountry}, a land of promises and freedom. Challenging, but quiet; bleak, but beautiful; familiar, but alien. In comparison, the piste is to them what Marc Augé (1995) called a non-place: Mundane, undistinguishable, and tiring; a functional, crowded, over-controlled space not too different from an airport corridor.[1] Passing through it is primarily a necessary evil rather than the objective of an expensive holiday. (And indeed, freeskiers often seem intent to make sure that all these tourists take notice of just how mundane and boring pistes are to 'real mountain people.')

---

[1] As the example of a ski piste demonstrates, Augé's critique is better understood as a critique of practices of "doing place" rather than places per se (and, for example, their architecture). Spinney (2007) elaborates this point with regard to the visual and bodily aspects of cycling practices in the city.

Without hesitation, Tom heads straight towards the barrier rope as we leave the lift, still assorting his gloves and poles while he already slides across the piste. Nonchalantly, he lifts the rope with his pole and slips under it, showing complete disregard for its symbolic function. Ignoring the curious looks of the tourists standing by, we follow him and begin to climb the short, steep wall of hard snow behind the barrier. Within two minutes we have cut a corner—and suddenly the resort, the tourists and lifts and pistes all seem miles away. Just like every other time I step out into open mountain terrain, I am immediately captured by the same powerful impression: Silence. The sublime tranquillity of the open range enwraps me; the visible features of the environment seem strangely detached or secluded, and I feel thrown back onto myself, forced to focus on my solitary being within this wide vastness. The only sounds I hear emanate from my immediate surroundings: The snow crunching under my skis; my breath steaming out of my mouth into the crisp, thin air; the blood throbbing in my ears because of the steep climb.

Quickly my senses adapt, and these details converge and retreat into the background as the visual takes centre stage again. What a view! After a short but laborious climb, we stop where the range of the Krimml unfolds again in front of our eyes, but now from a very different angle, looking from the side (Fig. 3.1). Nobody says a word as we all stand and intently study the face one more time. In silence, I try to relocate the important points of orientation I intend to follow in the face: The drop in, the first bowl, the small couloir. I reassess the route, trying to estimate the quality and layering of the snow on the basis of what I have learned by trudging through the powder up to this point. On the exposed ridge we are currently standing on, the wind has formed a hardened top layer called windpress that carries a curved pattern much like the sand on a beach. But below, the snow seems soft and nice; and more importantly, the wind will have carried the loose powder into the chutes between the ridges, piling it into knee-deep patches of powder-heaven. Tom points at some key segments in his line again, remarking how the snow looks fine but we should stay away from the wind lips on our way up. Steffi agrees. We start hiking again, traversing a gentle slope, then scrambling around some sharp rocks, manoeuvring careful as we are now on a ridge dropping steeply to the left and right. Far down in the valley, we can see the black roofs of Zell am Ziller. We continue in silence for some fifteen minutes, at times warily circumventing blocks of sheer black rock with our skis still strapped on, but quickly and with ease traversing the small patches of powder in between. At first, we follow a narrow path in the snow left by others, but soon their tracks end—thank god, further up there will be fresh powder lines left for us! Tom starts to trudge a new track into the untouched powder. I follow with growing anticipation, from time to time catching a view of the ragged, beautiful wilderness around us, but mostly concentrating on neither losing sight of those in front of me nor my precious balance on the narrow ridge. Finally, he pauses. We have reached the drop in.

"And if thou gaze long into an abyss, the abyss will also gaze into thee," Nietzsche (1967: 54) wrote metaphorically. While the Krimml is not an abyss—at least not for a competent freerider—there is something engulfing about standing

1 Introduction: On the Ridge

Fig. 3.1 Tom and a colleague on a ridge in the Krimml, peeking down into a line. (c) Martin Schalk for sofa movielab

close to an edge and staring down. For most people looking down from a tower or lookout, the gaping emptiness right in front of them gains and immediate, almost overwhelming presence, and almost immediately they start figuring out the vague contours of things down below. Those that seem to be completely unaffected by heights, that are able to carry on with the things right in front of them without attending to the seemingly dramatic background, in contrast impress and bewilder most of us. To be sure, right now we are not standing in front of a drastic vertical drop, but nevertheless, the vista down into the line absorbs us. We are standing in silence for several minutes, everyone intently mustering the perspective unfolding in front of us.

2 Seeing as Opening

Freeskiers have, I hope to have demonstrated, a different view on mountain-slopes than 'tourists', especially those slopes they are about to ski. Thus peeking down into the chute from the narrow ridge does not capture us because it stimulates a vague foreshadowing of the horror of falling down into an abyss, but still it grabs our attention and holds on to it. It does so by virtue of our knowing that we will drop down into it very soon, and thus it is both enticing and challenging, demanding preparation, care, and joyful optimism. Even as I sit and write, I can vividly remember a number of such moments of looking into a line I was about to ride. As every freerider will assert, reaching a drop-in and looking down into the line is always a special moment, not only because it demands focus and care, but also because it invokes a transgression of a certain kind, a shift in perspective that goes hand-in-hand with a shift in the current modus of being per se: Just now, from this particular point, the line *opens up* in front of you. Even more than the reading of the face I already discussed, this crucial moment is a key element of freeriding that remains largely invisible and neglected by an outside view. In what follows, I will try to unpack what precisely is going on when a freerider is 'just' looking down, taking into account a range of intersecting processes and sentiments colluding in this special moment. At the core, what I argue is that when I describe the experience of staring down as the *opening up* of the line, it is precisely this that Schatzki (1996: 115) terms the "opening of a site,"[2] the beginning unfolding of a different practice. And quite some time before I will actually 'drop' into the line with my whole body, it is my vision which carries this fundamental process of opening up.

The perspective onto the line Tom, Steffi, and I are gaining now is very different from the one established down below, as shown in Fig. 3.2: Not only are we now looking from a very different angle and distance so that it takes some skill to be able to see the same line established earlier, recognizing the landmarks figured out and following the possible paths leading towards them; and not only do we do so mostly in silence and without much pointing, everybody now focusing on his or her line in solitude-in-co-presence. But crucially, it seems to me that the prospect of actually skiing the line is now much more concrete and immediate, and this has profoundly changed our way of looking *at* it; it is now more a way of looking *into* it, as well as more immediately looking *forward to* it. This gradual transition points towards the range of different aspects or functions that make the skill of seeing lines so important for both freeriders themselves and for my goal of understanding the freeskiing practices and the subculture around it. Looking into the line from up here means critically assessing what is possible, feasible,

---

[2] Schatzki actually writes about "the opening of a space of places" in this first book on social practices (Schatzki 1996: 115) and introduces the more general concept of the site only later (see specifically Schatzki 2002: 141–147). It will become clear later that I embrace the notion of the site in the sense of Heidegger's term *Lichtung* (or clearing) from which Schatzki partly derives it.

2 Seeing as Opening 69

Fig. 3.2 Tom's view down into his line shortly before dropping in. The image is taken from a helmet camera he carries to document his pursuits; the angle is slightly broader than that of the human eye. Unfortunately, contrast is poor in this picture, hiding most of the crucial details of the slope

or promising and how dangerous and demanding it might be; and looking from a different angle and at closer distance now provides many new and possibly contradicting clues for answering such questions. One might call this practice decision making or risk assessment, but it would be very misleading to understand it as a systematic, neutral assessment of all options which are first spotted and then judged: As I discussed in the second chapter, the sheer number of possible combinations of 'single' options and their details is far too high for such a procedure to be considered thorough or systematic,[3] and instead, the assessment is inherently framed or situated by the options and ideas already developed earlier while looking from below. But even more importantly, the necessary balancing of opportunities and dangers is experienced as an emotional and intuitive *bodily* process of

---

[3] The factors important to the question of how and where to ski theoretically include the snow's depth, density, and layering; the danger of avalanches, slough, ice, hidden rocks, or falling and the existence of according "escape lines" or emergency reactions; the steepness, openness and exposition to sun and wind—and all this for any reachable point in the slope that can each be approached with different speed, care, or force and from different directions; factors which in turn depend on the 'options chosen' to be taken prior and consecutive to skiing that spot, and much more. One would be led to ask an endless succession of questions such as: "If coming with speed out of that couloir and taking a sharp right turn towards this windlip at that spot might cause a small avalanche to go off, will I be able to escape to the left by going straight into the bowl and still avoid crashing into that rock given that there seems to be very harsh snow in front of it?"—*and* then judge the 'fun factor' or 'risk value' of different combinations of possible answers.

Fig. 3.3 Another drop-in in the Krimml that has already been used by several riders. While this perspective provides not much vision onto the actual slope down to the right, the structural details of the snow can be seen well in the foreground, providing clues on how deep and hard the snow will be below

'feeling right or wrong' about things which might then successively be questioned and considered in acts of more schematic or 'technical' reason. For example, one might be convincing oneself to either listen to or ignore the uneasiness felt in the stomach by calling oneself to consider 'facts' like today's official avalanche danger report or a certain danger evaluation schemata. And it is from this stage of getting a feeling for the slope below that a crucial transition needs to be achieved (see Fig. 3.3): Moving away from the initial critical stance that is so vital for keeping freeriders from making one of the fatal mistakes that tragically happen all too often in this sport, and building up the emotional momentum that allows for the confidence, focus, and easy playfulness that are necessary to ride a difficult line not only successfully but also safely. Looking forward to go is, in other words, a crucial and integral part of knowing where to go.

3 Seeing-of and Seeing-in

Before I can proceed to discussing the details of seeing-while-riding, however, some more general considerations regarding human vision are due in order to be able to untwist the overlapping modes and functions of seeing that make freeriding possible. Towards this end, I begin by highlighting a series of rifts that exist between different ways of seeing: A rift between standing down there in the valley, talking, looking for a suitable line, planning and being excited; and standing here, exposed, looking down to where I will drop into, knowing that I will drop very soon. My current practice of seeing seems more fundamentally about, or oriented by, riding the line—foreshadowing, questioning, and then embracing it; so that in a way, riding down this line has already begun to unfold within my vision while I am still standing at the edge. This sentiment is matched by experimental findings from neuroscience arguing that vision indeed functions as a simulation of action, a foreshadowing of the near future that is not just a mental "fantasy," but a process carried by nerve endings and muscles of the full body (Berthoz 2000). However, another rift separates my current situation fundamentally from what will happen soon. Once I physically drop into the action, things will be fundamentally different since vision is itself a crucial dimension of the actual bodily accomplishment of skiing. This second rift is arguably even more severe: The difference between the seeing *of* the line and seeing while being *in* the line—seeing while being in the action of riding and, simultaneously, as part of that self-same action. These two practices of *seeing of* and *seeing in* are perfectly natural twins for every freerider, yet they seem to casually cross boundaries of social thought that are carefully respected by most authors of theory. From the jovial, dynamic, sometimes superficial realm of conversation and social cooperation, I am suddenly thrown into the almost existential confrontation of myself and the mountain, a single mind or body out in the wilderness. To simply call both instances of seeing "situations" and examine them side-by-side means to roam borders between abstract, pondering philosophy and solidly grounded empirical studies of social interaction; between answers to the most general questions about man or life, and fine-grained portraits of fleeting local meaning. The rift between these ways of seeing is therefore not only important for me right now, standing here alone on the ridge in the cold wind and the bright sun, collecting myself to drop into the line. This difference is, I will argue, also of crucial importance for a sociological understanding of seeing per se, because it is directly connected to the question which theory to employ when discussing vision as a social phenomenon. At the core, the importance of this difference between separate ways of seeing and the reason for my extended discussion of it comes down to this: I argue that there is more to vision than perception (in an epistemic or conceptual sense) and especially with regard to movement, the visual system carries further functions than only the recognition or production of perceived meaning. What I will suggest to do is to treat these additional functions as *social* phenomena in their own right, so that the social framing of perception is not seen as the sole basis of the sociality of human conduct. Therefore, social theories that take perception as their sole point of reference potentially do not suffice to describe this rift adequately, but neither do they, of course, lose their relevance entirely.[4] Accordingly, addressing these different modi of vision will require an elaboration of a range of fundamental questions about both theories of social practices and the methodology they imply and rest on—questions that will require drawing on an range of different theoretical resources from philosophy, sociology, and neuroscience.[5] If one accepts that the phenomenon I try to discuss—the role of the visual orientation in riding a line—happens at least partly subconsciously, data stemming from public social interaction alone can no longer suffice to develop deeper explanatory momentum; yet personal ethnographic observations are evenly insufficient to the task as they can only reflect my conscious experience. Thus, while the opening empirical chapter of this work argued primarily on the basis of what I called the rich surface of social interaction—the openly observable locus of the production of social order—, the next two chapters in contrast attempt to shed some light on the bodily and only partly conscious processes of movement and perception that make up a core part of the resources that allow for a practical constitution of social order on the slopes. Building from such diverse sources and then working my way back towards theoretical coherence shares some qualities with learning freeriding: Looking from afar, it seems quite clear where one needs to go and which turns to take—but eventually going down bit by bit necessitates much more sorting out of delicate matters than one would have expected. I will, in other words, need to ask the reader for some patience when I now turn towards more general questions of theory and method, as I am getting the gear ready before we can actually drop into the action of freeriding and on towards the colourful life of the freeskiing scene.

---

[4] If one considers a theory as being exclusively grounded in philosophical (or other) postulates concerning processes of perception (i.e. an epistemology), then I would suggest adding to those foundations and thus going beyond those theories.

[5] While grounding sociological concepts in philosophical thought is widely practiced, attempts of relating sociology to findings from neuroscience are few in comparison (cf. the works collected in Zaboura/Reichertz 2006; see Behrend 2007 for a critique)—if considered apart from a) those works that seem to rather boldly equate neuroscientific thought with sociology, often using Mead as their sole sociological point of reference (e.g. Franks 2010); and b) a number of works who pick out singular neuroscientific findings (especially regarding the so-called mirror system) to connect them to a praxeological perspective (Kastl 2004; Lizardo 2007, 2009; Lizardo/Strand 2010; Schmidt 2008, 2017)—I will discuss these works in Chaps. 7 and 9. This general reluctance is probably not only due to the relative newness of some (but not all) of these findings, but rather because both their claims to factual truth and their methods are not unproblematic when seen from the perspective of a sociology of culture or knowledge. Nevertheless, I believe if handled from a critical stance and integrated in a fitful manner, some findings nevertheless can provide valuable resources for theorizing phenopractices. I will repeatedly return to my reservations against and respecification of several general assumptions of neuroscience throughout this chapter.

4 Towards an Ethnography of Visual Fields

The peculiar situation of the opening up of a line—of standing on an edge and looking down—can be instructive towards a more general understanding of the practices that produce our vision, one that can serve as a theoretically guided foundation to studying the visual aspects of the structure and dynamic of freeskiing as a whole. As I have mentioned in the introduction, throughout the book I will apply a consistent focus on the visual dimension of the different practices that together make up what is called the freeskiing subculture, in the hope of being able to track the cultural 'logic' that might manifest in formative principles or aesthetic rules and ties them together: their style. Because every practice has a visual dimension,[6] I do not aim to develop a theory of visual practices on that basis—that would just mean to re-write a general practice theory. Instead, I take practices of seeing (a particular form of visual practices) as a key form of what I call phenopractices, that is, practices whose performance is organized by style. To this end, I will examine visual displays and practices of showing on trade fairs, collective watching of freeski movies, the judging gaze of athlete collectives in funparks, and more. While all of these practices need to be taken as instantiations of some common, general nature of looking-at-something-in-order-to-see-something that relies on the use of vision, they are at same time very different, being situated in very different circumstances and making use of different technological tools, social interactions and spatial arrangements in systematic ways. As I have demonstrated in the second chapter, it would be futile and misleading to try to isolate the 'seeing itself' from these supposedly 'external factors,' as this would effectively destroy the respective phenomenon at hand: a situated, multidimensional social order oriented towards the perceptibility of a certain visual phenomenon. The *empirical* object of enquiry of this chapter thus cannot be vision per se, but this specific practice of seeing normally occurring within the world of freeskiing. Yet in aiming towards developing some general considerations about phenopractices, the way of seeing I discuss here seems at least to be more basic or 'pure' than others, because it does not happen within direct interaction such as talking and pointing. Since the situational arrangement of standing on and staring down the mountain (me, my equipment, and the mountain) is less complex than that of, say, a group interaction

---

[6] Maybe this is an exaggeration and one can think of an example of an entirely 'blind' practice. But if so, then the absence of visual dimension would still be highly formative for its performance, and thus the visual would still matter. In most cases I can think of, however, performances are framed by darkness rather than blindness, and as Cook and Edensor (2017) show, darkness means that visuality (and the lack thereof) becomes more, not less, important during performance. I should add that my argument that a theory of the visual dimension of practices ends up being a theory of practices in general is not only an empirical one. Rather, as I will seek to show throughout this book, the philosophical arguments and concepts underpinning practice theory have their origins in discussions of visual phenomena (such as Aspect-seeing in Wittgenstein, Gestalt thinking, or Heidegger's clearing).

in a funpark (various people, purposefully built obstacles, visual equipment such as cameras, etc.) it makes it easier to discuss certain aspects of seeing practices that will also be part of most other typical situations—specifically the role of the body and movement. Discussing these aspects now should help to be able to better appreciate and compare the differences and similarities to more complex situations where video recordings, interaction rituals, or social relations gain much higher relevance. It should be noted that while I present phenopractices as static and local at this point, I have not lost sight of my goal to consider circulation and change of phenopractices. My motivation to proceed from a static towards a dynamic perspective is somewhat didactic in nature, because accounting for change from a practice perspective amounts to the vexed problem of explaining dynamics with routines. In this part, I thus want to demonstrate that the stability or persistence of practices (see Schatzki 2010a) that e.g. makes it so difficult for policy makers to keep people from eating unhealthy or wasting energy (Shove 2010) is ultimately rooted in the fluidity and indeterminacy of concrete situations and the fundamental necessity to manage and overcome them each another next first time. By 'zooming in' on (and almost exaggerating) the complexity of achieving order despite being carried forth in an almost overpowering perpetual stream of situational particulars, I aim to highlight the fact that practices are first and foremost ways of staying afloat in that stream; so that only changes that do not seem to entail the danger of rocking the boat a tad too much—changes that can be interwoven smoothly into the flow rather than bringing it to a crunching halt—stand a chance of blending into the durable pattern of normality.

Excursus: Extending Ethnomethodological Studies of Vision

> It is important to note that in analysing seeing during skiing, to a certain degree I aim to extend (but not reject) the established canon of the by now 'classic' studies of practices of seeing grounded in ethnomethodology (e.g. Büscher 2006; C. Goodwin 1995, 2000b; C. Goodwin/M. H. Goodwin 1996; Heath/vom Lehn 2004; Hindmarsh/Heath/Luff 2000). As I argued in the second chapter, what Goodwin called "professional vision" captured the practices of seeing a line in a mountain face very well, and it seemed hardly necessarily to move beyond their focus on situated talk and interaction. I should explain why I nevertheless deem it both feasible and necessary to extend these studies both in terms of theory and methodology at this point. As I argued in the introduction, authors developing theories of social practices are quick to acknowledge the importance of embodied seeing and situated vision as a *dimension* of social practices—but few dwell on the specific nature of this dimension, while most others treat it as a homogenous 'building block' of practices essentially alike others. Furthermore, the extended body of empirical works on practices of seeing which have demonstrated that seeing is not a purely subjective or mental act but a shared

practice building on resources such as interaction and material technology (cf. the overview provided by C. Goodwin 2000b) tend to focus on either a) the role of bodily gaze or gestures for the interaction orders ("activity systems" in Goodwin's (2000a) terms) that seeing is embedded in; or b) visual media such as images, videos, or spatial settings and the practices of seeing organized around them (e.g. Mondada 2012). These are, without a doubt, very important aspects of visual practices, and their study has been key to demonstrating the social character of vision in the first place. However, I also hold that there is no need of treating these phenomena as *all there is* to seeing as a practical accomplishment. In my view, some authors are too swift in declaring studies of specific types of visual practices to provide us with a sociology of 'the visual' in toto (e.g., Burri [2008] claims to provide a "Sociology of the Visual" by way of equating image practices with the visual). Vision is, however, a dimension of almost all social practices and a crucial element of many mundane routines and even basic emotional states (think of fear in the dark)—something quite different from the specifics of 'doing images' or pointing during conversations. To be fair: Most authors—especially those arguing with ethnomethodology or conversation analysis—are more careful to point out that they confine themselves to interaction as the essential 'the site of the social' they are concerned with (C. Goodwin 2000b). Seen from their perspective, one might argue that in what follows I move beyond the boundaries of interaction as I follow Schatzki (2002) in treating practices per se as 'the site of the social' to be studied. My work would then be seen as profoundly detached from those studies of vision undertaken in ethnomethodology and conversation analysis, since I study a different phenomenon, build on different theory, and apply a different methodology. While obviously my methods do differ at least to a certain extent, I do not share this view with regard to the phenomenon and theory. I call my aim extending rather than replacing or rejecting ethnomethodological studies of seeing because I hold that neither the phenomenon I study nor the theoretical foundations applied can (or need to) be distinguished as differing sharply from them.

Let me first discuss the question of the commonality or difference of the phenomenon studied. For studies building on ethnomethodology or conversation analysis, it is crucial that all action observed is conducted by members of a situation, because any social order perceived to be reaching beyond a concrete situation will not be treated as 'actual' social order in its own right, but rather as an effect of (e.g. a gloss produced by) a different situation. Therefore, the phenomena of visual order these studies of seeing are concerned with must be shown to be orders of that very situation. For example, in his much-cited handbook article summarizing the analysis of practices of seeing, Charles Goodwin (2000b: 157) details that what is studied within this canon are the social production of either "visible bodies" or "seeable structure in the environment." One powerful example he discusses repeatedly is a situation in which a student of archaeology is instructed by a instructor to see certain relevant traces in a patch of dirt, which happens partly through talk and pointing gestures, but crucially also through gaze orientation: The instructor looks intently at the phenomena to be seen so that the student can register the instructor's direction of gaze (by looking at her face) and mimic it; and in turn, the instructor will at times check whether the student does look at the right spot (by looking at the student's face). The visible orientation of one's gaze, in other words, is used systematically as a resource to establish (relative) coherence of vision of "seeable structure in the environment." Are the visual orders of freeriding that emerge during my day out in the Krimml with Tom and Steffi oriented towards the same kind of phenomena? I would argue they do: For freeriders, the meaning of freeride lines emanates from their style, that is, the rider skiing smoothly and making creative use of the mountain face. What freeriders seek to produce through riding can thus precisely be summarized as a certain type of "visible bodies" moving through "seeable structure in the environment," and therefore, an ethnography of the visual orders of freeskiing is indeed concerned with those phenomena Goodwin suggest. However, how does my study of the social production of vistas of bodies and environments differ from the established canon, and why? Specifically, I would argue, because I deem it difficult to *isolate situations of interaction* as an exclusive field of inquiry in the way EM- or CA-based studies of vision claim to be able to (cf. Nicolini 2012: 150–152, Schmidt 2016). Take, for example, the delineation of interaction as the exclusive field of inquiry that Goodwin (2000b) provides at the very beginning of his handbook article:

"A primordial site for the analysis of human (...) action consists of a situation in which multiple participants are attempting to carry out courses of action together while attending to each other, the larger activities that their current actions are embedded within, and relevant phenomena in their surround." (C. Goodwin 2000b: 157).

Can riding down a line in the Krimml be regarded such a situation and thus a "primordial site"? As I will demonstrate, what a rider attends to during riding does indeed include, first, "relevant phenomena in their surround" such as rocks or windlips, second, "the larger activities that their current actions are embedded within," such as the prior mutual agreement not to ride to aggressively and keep sufficient distance because of the danger of avalanches (and also, more generally: to do 'proper' freeriding and not boring ski mountaineering), and third, "each other," for example when riding towards your friend currently filming you in a way that will look good on the video later. Crucially, when I say "attend," I do not simply refer to the fact that the rider will *look out* for these things, but also to the fact that he will simultaneously need to make sure that he *looks like* he is attending to these things as he will be judged upon it. Freeriding is after all a dangerous activity that you do not just perform together with anybody, but rather only with those who you know you can trust to take care and do the right thing. The nexus of complementary practices called freeriding, in other words, is in part held together by certain moral obligations, for example to help one another if necessary, but also those to "be a cool guy"[7]—and therefore, *all* practices conducted in situations of freeriding together need to exhibit a certain level of constant attention and adherence to such mutual obligations.

In conclusion, I argue that the visual dimension of practice of riding a big mountain line consists in the production of visible bodies and seeable features of the environment by way of orienting vision towards the others, the relevant action framework, and the surrounding in the mutual production of both individual gaze and visible attention. In freeriding, vision and social visibility coalesce as mutually elaborating aspects of a situated and social visual order; just like gaze in conversations is both visible and directs vision. But is this enough to argue that the phenomenon under study does match the definition provided by Goodwin? As it becomes apparent now, this depends on the understanding implicit in his use of three expressions: "situation," "together," and "while attending to". For the freeskiers on the mountain, it is pretty clear that they go skiing together, share the same situations and are attending to each other. However, with regard to 'classic' ethnomethodological studies of practices of seeing (e.g. those within the workplace studies), interaction defined as "acting together in the same situation while attending to each other" always describes a much more narrow spatial setting: face-to-face interaction in a setting of immediate co-presence. In other words, those who are taken to be members of the same situation are usually not more than an arm's length away from each other since they for example man the same control room (Heath/Luff 2000) or play hopscotch together (C. Goodwin/M. H. Goodwin 2001). A freerider skiing down a line does clearly not fit into this narrow spatial format. But can it be justified to limit the studies to such a narrow framework given the qualities ascribed to interaction between members of the same situation? I do not think so.

In ethnomethodological studies, the "public visibility" of visual orientation is treated as the key quality of interaction situations in which visual practices can be mutually elaborated (cf. C. Goodwin 2000a). But public visibility is by no means an exclusive character of action in close spatial proximity, for example acting while being in the same room. As I have argued, a freerider in the midst of a mountain face is very much publicly visible, and the performative aspect of his sport is of great relevance to him.

---

[7]What I refer to here are the mechanisms of inclusion and exclusion at work in the often loose group formations within a lifestyle sport scene. In short, two overlapping factors are at work with varying relevance: friendship and skill—and at least the latter must be visibly performed.

Going further, one might also well argue that much about our everyday conduct in public places happens in a way *as if* we would be watched doing it. In fact, the very example of learning to see like an archaeologist discussed by Goodwin (2000b) builds on the premise that the student will *continue* to orient her gaze in a certain way as if the teacher would be looking. The performative character of practices, in other words, does not cease just because the immediate attention of an audience is possible, but not guaranteed. But is the sequential production of visible, mutual, and continuous attention not exactly what these studies seek to demonstrate? This question leads to the second aspect besides spatial order that the sharp distinction between actions (or practical conduct) carried out in interaction versus actions carried out alone (which do not feature in EM studies of vision) seems to rest on: temporal order. Interaction as "acting together in the same situation while attending to each other" implies, after all, that things are done at the same time—coevally, in Garfinkel's (2002) words. But exactly which kind of temporal order of events is treated as an instance of "at the same time" in ethnomethodology, for example in the case of the instruction of archaeologists? As I will detail below, the immediate focus of human vision can only capture a rather small field. Therefore, the members of the situation who Goodwin describes cannot look at each other *and* the phenomena to be elaborated at the same instance, but they do so *sequentially*. In other words, EM-based studies of vision treat the orientation of somebody's vision as a mutually elaborated feature of the interaction (rather than a situated practice carried by the individual) because it is frequently instructed, checked, and sometimes corrected by gazing back and forth between face and object—and this sequence is emphasized as a core feature of this situation. The existence of a sequential order of the situation is therefore necessarily based on the fact that intervals can be observed during which the members of the situation *continue* to look on their own, before checking back if the other is visibly looking the right way. Both the scientific analyst and the members engaged in the situation can therefore witness any type of visual social order of the situation only because they are able to infer that practices of seeing are continuing in the same way *independently* during moments in which they are not being observed. That these durations of unobserved continuity are rather short in the cases discussed in the literature, is, in my view, not a theoretical need but rather the result of a specific preference on behalf of the researchers: a preference for situations of conflict (C. Goodwin/M. H. Goodwin 2001), instruction (C. Goodwin 1994), risk (C. Goodwin/M. H. Goodwin 1996), or other types of 'trouble' (C. Goodwin 1995). Therefore, I argue that in Goodwin's definition quoted above, the meaning of the expressions "situation," "together," and "while attending to" all emanate from an implicit assumption of a relatively close temporal succession of acts of gaze orientation towards the other—but a precise theoretical understanding of how long practices of focusing something can be carried out independently before another instance of direct orientation towards the other must reoccur in order to be regarded as interaction is not provided. Both the spatial and the temporal border of what should be considered one interaction situation as opposed to another remain, in other words, blurry (cf. Mol 2002, Schmidt 2016).

Therefore, can one really say that professional vision (understood as a socially organized visual practice) as the phenomenon studied is a phenomenon that is precisely and exclusively carried by situations of immediate co-presence—in which case such situations should indeed remain the exclusive domain of studies trying to grasp such phenomena? This would arguably trap us in what Levinson (2005) called interactional reductionism. Or could one say that the same phenomena can *also* be carried by situations in which, for example, onlookers are more spatially dispersed or even only an unknown, but possible feature? As it should have become obvious, I argue for the latter view, because simply speaking, I do not believe that the phenomenon of socially oriented seeing simply vanishes with spatial proximity of others. Thus, I deem situations of 'direct interaction' to be a very valuable, but not the exclusive domain in which to study practices of seeing. The social order that is taken as the exclusive phenomenon of ethnomethodological studies of seeing cannot claim to be grounded in precise temporal or spatial identity, but is a social order only by way of implying or 'having trust' in the fact that interaction partners will continue to see what they are seeing just when they are looked at, and that they enjoy essentially the same perspective as the other members (Nicolini 2012: 150–152). This is, crucially, also the premise that the observed participants of the situation must build on themselves. The phenopractical perspective I propose, just like other theories of social practices, operates on the assumption of greater stability or persistence of practices than the 'strict' studies in ethnomethodology and especially conversation analysis—but at the core, they make an identical assumption about the existence of a *duration* or continuity in practices. As I will detail, in my view such an assumption of meta-temporal and meta-spatial stability lies at the core of any theory of social practices.

Ethnomethodological studies of practices of seeing which treat vision as a feature of 'public' situations rather than subjective acts of consciousness or purely individual perception necessarily imply continuing duration of practices oriented or acquired in interaction beyond their immediate inclusion into interaction. Professional vision as understood by Goodwin is, in other words, an inherently social phenomenon not exclusively carried in conversation or communication; it is a social practice carried by situated bodies. For this reason, I understand the phenopractical analysis of 'vision in action' as an extension of these studies rather than a rejection. I build on the same premises and observe essentially the same phenomenon; but I carry the analysis further, towards practices of seeing more 'extreme' (in terms of speed and danger, for example) and happening within an interaction framework that is spatially and temporally stretched out further. Both of these features—speed and expansion—will also make it necessary to undertake an extension not only in terms of theme and methodology, but also in terms of the theoretical foundations of studies of practices of seeing. In conclusion, phenopractice theory does not claim a completely different position, and it does not seek to propose ideas or notions which are incommensurable to, or fully rejecting an ethnomethodological conception of vision. Instead, I deem it necessary and promising to spell out in some more detail certain notions of what I consider to be the mostly implicit philosophical a-priori assumptions that ethnomethodological studies of vision rest on.[8] In short, argue that these studies, although sometimes claiming to be a purely empirical enterprise solemnly documenting things as they are, at least to some extent build on certain understandings of human life, perception, and the social laid down by Wittgenstein and Merleau-Ponty, and my aim is to return to these writings to re-examine them, especially with regard to vision. Because coincidentally or not, although both philosophers have informed ethnomethodology as well as social theories of practice primarily through their general considerations concerning language and the body, both originally developed their ideas to a substantial extent with regard to a more specific topic: seeing (see Stengel 2003 for an extensive recapitulation). When using practice theory to discuss practices of seeing, most authors build indirectly (via the detour of Schatzki or Garfinkel, for example) on the general ideas of Wittgenstein and Merleau-Ponty, so it seems sensible to instead return directly to the more specific thoughts on seeing they laid down.

5 The Janus Face of Vision

Staring down into the drop in of the line in this face of the Krimml and trying to literally figure out what I will be doing very soon, I try to visually work out two basic aspects of the ride I will soon drop into: where and how to ride, and which obstacles and dangers to avoid. In the analysis of reading a mountain face in interaction, it already became clear that pointing out or highlighting plays a crucial

---

[8] It should be noted that Rawls (2008), in contrast, argues Garfinkel developed his theoretical notions coevally and completely independently of Wittgenstein. Nevertheless, ethnomethodology is frequently considered as expression several notions central to Wittgensteinian thought (Heritage 1984; Lynch 1992a, 2001; Sharrock/Button 1991); while Merleau-Ponty is one of the few authors Garfinkel (2002) cites (and recommends for "misreading").

role in establishing visual order vis-à-vis a mountain face, and that what is to be seen is elaborated sequentially by first highlighting and then relating certain crucial points that carry or anchor associated meaning in the framework of the current practice. In the course of talk and interaction, one might therefore say, a web of visible nodes is spun and superimposed onto the vista of the mountain face, bringing certain forms to the fore and thus simultaneously framing everything else as part of essentially homogenous patches of background. I have argued that the practices of 'distributed vision' examined in the prior chapter shape the way freeriders see mountain slopes. But what does that tell us about the *practice* of looking intently at something per se? Is the spinning of a web of meaning I described something that can only happen in the course of talk and interaction? And if not, how does something similar happen in the course of staring in silence? In developing an answer, one will realize that vision is a Janus-faced process: One the one hand, it entails bodily functions like eye movements and is thus subject to the laws of optics and biology, but on the other, it is a process of perception, a manifestation of meaning we can be consciously aware of. The question of how both aspects should be related within theory has of course divided philosophers and scientists since thousands of years, and thus any answer I can propose will be in good company of an almost endless list of alternatives. I will discuss some notions of what it means to see—or more precise: to stand and look at an object in front of oneself—in order to develop a phenopractice perspective on these understandings. To this end, two major streams of thought and scientific practice can be compared, juxtaposed, and combined: The *phenomenology of vision* which more or less directly inform (cultural) sociological understandings of seeing, and the experimental psychophysics and *neuroscience of vision*, which has very often been the starting point of philosophical accounts. I will, in other words, look Janus into the eyes from two different directions—yet this does not mean that what I look at are two different creatures.

What does it mean to see something? In other words: Which processes need to be accounted for when examining the practice of staring down into a drop-in? For an answer, consider images 2.2 and 2.3 once again. On a basic level, what the rider needs to figure out is the spatial setting in front of him: Is that rock small and close by, or large and far away; how steep is the chute over there; and is this couloir really wide enough to make some proper turns? Furthermore, he or she must successfully recognize the landmarks pointed out earlier, that is, he or she must distinguish singular objects as standing out from the surrounding and identify their shape on the basis of how they looked from down below, from a different angle. Finally, as I will detail below, freeriders need to 'read' the surface of the snow in order to learn about the conditions awaiting them during the ride: If the snow is hard or soft, deep or shallow, if there are rocks or edges hidden right under the surface, if they might release avalanches, and so on. Considering seeing at this abstract level, one might easily adapt a technical terminology and say the rider needs to gather information by identifying distinct objects, recognizing their identity by linking their shape to what he saw before, evaluating certain qualities judging from their surface, and calculating their position in three-dimensional space.

Yet as I have argued, by doing so one would essentially *miss* what it means to see a line, both because terms like information-gathering, recognizing, evaluating, and calculating do not adequately capture the experience I have standing on that ridge (the phenomenological argument), and because we cannot be sure that other instances of practices we call information-gathering, recognizing, evaluating, and calculating, for example those in an office, have anything in common with what is happening in the Krimml (the situated-practice argument). But on the other hand, striving to avoid this technological or rationalist fallacy by instead offering a colourful description of my experience and the uniqueness of being-there-just-now would not help much towards grasping the bodily aspect of vision. In other words, although it is inherently problematic, it is equally unavoidable to build on certain general assumption and findings at this point—and maybe paradoxically I suggest that in order to avoid a rationalist fallacy, it seems sensible to build on even more general and thus somewhat de-humanized understandings from experimental psychology and neuroscience instead.

At the core, what the freerider's 'visual system' needs to perform are two basic functions: First, in order to see e.g. a 'bump' or depression in the otherwise even slope or order to estimate the snow quality at a certain spot, he needs be able to contrast different shades of white, and moreover, he thus needs to recognize certain shapes in order to identify something as a rock, a bowl, and so on. On a conceptual level, he needs to conduct what is called *contrastive identification* (see below). As I will show, the vista of a snow-covered mountainside is generally an environment that makes these basic 'tasks' rather difficult to accomplish, because the setting and the task of skiing require working out spatially complex relations (for example, there is not one flat plane but parts with various inclinations) and grasping subtle differences in shades of grey under changing lighting conditions. The importance of seeing and the visual within freeskiing, I believe, stems to some degree from these demanding circumstances of the core practice of skiing. One will be hard-pressed to find a practice where 'getting' a slight change in the shading of a white surface that is partly in the shadow and partly sparkles in the bright sun while moving through it very quickly can make such a big difference. If one portrays freeriding as an extreme sport because of the extreme level of skills it requires, contrastive identification could be considered among those skills. But what is it that the eye does to accomplish this feat?

6 The Restless Eye

In the second chapter, I used stills from a video of seeing-in-interaction to document how seeing is achieved through bodily motions. Given the right equipment like an eye-tracking device, I could repeat this analysis of the publicly visible bodily work of seeing with regard to the process my own body undertakes more or less privately as I am standing on the edge, figuring out the visual field (see for example Duchowski 2007). A remarkably similar process would become visible:

6 The Restless Eye 83

If I would attach a small camera recording the restless and immensely rapid movement of my eyeballs and their perpetual repetitions of establishing and abandoning focal points,[9] I would document how the meaningful impression that I gain through staring down emerges while 'my' eyes perform rapid sequences of movements called saccades.[10] The eyeball meanders, its focus rushes up and down, criss-crossing the visual field, *working out* what is there to see. Of course, eyeball movement and having a specific phenomenal impression is by no means the same thing, and it was after all Wittgenstein who outspokenly warned against thoughtlessly equating a bodily state or process with the specific thing we express in sentences such as "I see X." But on the other hand, if I am to include bodily movements as a crucial aspect of social practice into my inquiry, then these kinds of movements seem definitely important to consider.[11] Not only are seeing and eyeball movement intimately connected in our everyday experience of vision when we look at others or into a mirror, but philosophers and (neuro-) scientists also commonly embrace their mutual dependence in some way—yet not without disagreeing on many of the details of the interrelation between eye fixation, visual attention, and the visual perception of something. The idea to record eyeball movement and the fixation of specific points within the visual field in experiments in the hope to gain a window to what goes on inside the head has been followed at least since the 16th century (Wade 2007). In my view, it is crucial to note that, despite certain assurances to the contrary, the fundamental assumption of visual attention (that focusing something relates to being visually aware of it) and thus the direct relation of body movement and perceptual awareness continues to be the basis for almost all philosophical and sociological understandings of vision. In other words, as a sociologist one does not even need to take all scientific 'facts' at face value to acknowledge their importance; it would instead suffice to accept the role they played in informing those philosophical or anthropological views one in turn builds upon. But before discussing how the eye's saccades and

---

[9] Regrettably, it was not possible to actually install and use the necessary equipment in the rough environment of the Krimml, but I can see no reason why the result one would have obtained would differ from the general results that have been identified without exception whenever such studies of eyeball movement have been undertaken (Duchowski 2007). In other words, this description builds on scientific accounts of the *normal* workings of the visual apparatus. I will detail below in why ways I regard normality as the adequate foundation (and aim) of studies of phenopractices.

[10] I do not intend to say that saccades should be considered the universal bedrock of all human vision or that the brief account I present here is the only way vision can work. There are, for example, persons who cannot move their eyeballs and instead revert to moving their whole head in a similar fashion, which allows them to engage in practices involving vision in a basically normal way (Martinez-Conde/Macknik/Hubel 2004). Instead, what I suggest is, first, that certain routinized patterns of bodily movement necessarily serve as the basis to conducting more complex practices involving perception, and second, that these routines must be normal *at least for the respective practitioner*.

[11] For an overview of arguments made within psychology about the key role of the body for perception see Gibbs (2006).

the phenomenology of vision might relate, I need to sketch out in more detail what happens as a vista is worked out. In doing so, there is a certain danger of involuntarily portraying the process as something that somebody 'does,' simply because I am bound by the mechanisms of language. I will therefore copy the fashion of neuroscientists and speak of the visual system as the 'actor' in this little tale, but I need to emphasize that I do so for lack of better options: Neither do I want to embrace the implications of a lingo in which for example 'the mind' does the thinking, and even less do I want to imply that what is happening on this basic level of human vision should be termed action at all. This, of course, poses two further important questions: How can such basic bodily processes be understood from a practice perspective; and under which circumstances should one then speak of action—if at all? An answer to both questions will be developed, respectively, in the fourth chapter focusing on the body and in the eighth considering action. But for now, let's take a closer look at the eye.

7 Visual Routines

When the rider is trying to spot sharp rocks lurking dangerously just under the surface of the powder, or certain landmarks he saw earlier when reading the face, his visual apparatus engages in what neuroscientists call contrastive identification. As the name suggests, this process has two aspects that intertwine: contrasting and identifying. Contrasting, to begin with, is the most basic function any type of biological eye can perform on the basis of two photoreceptor cells being exposed to light of different intensity or colour, or the same cell being exposed to different levels over time. The complex human eye contains a great number of such cells, which are arranged in different areas of the retina each reacting to different aspects of exposure such as colour or basic shapes. Crudely said, eye movement has a key function for this reason: In order to 'get' a particular quality of something (such as the more fine-grained details), light stemming from a specific point is directed to the area on the retina where suitable receptor cells are positioned. From a biological viewpoint, all complex forms of vision are thus derived from the most basic 'mechanism' of 'getting contrasts' by what one might call second-order contrast: Contrasting different contrasts, for example comparing a dark spot that was present a moment ago and that has now vanished with the dark spot now lying right next to the original position; which would imply that the dark patch has moved (or the eye has moved in relation to it). Here lies the reason why (eye) movement is so essential for seeing: it allows the visual system to 'produce' certain contrasts on purpose. This also crudely describes what happens in the process of focusing something: To get richer contrast from a certain spot in the visual field, this spot needs to be moved to the centre of the field so that the light coming from it will fall on the fovea, the area at the centre of the retina where a high density of specific photoreceptors is found. Because of the retina being divided into different 'zones', in other words, human vision is inherently dualistic even on a biological level, comprising both foveal (or in-focus) and para-foveal (or out-of-focus) vision: Everything the visual system takes into sharp focus carries a corona of slightly blurred co-presentations. What I called working out a visual field therefore happens on the basis of focusing different elements one after another—and for our impression of a given view to emerge, some kind of synthesizing these 'snapshots' into one view has to take place (Duchowski 2007: 11). Therefore, the biology and the phenomenology of vision differ dramatically: While images are seemingly given to us at once in their totality, the eye proceeds sequentially. Up to this point, my description of the process of vision contained no news to well-established cultural theories of the visual: Said antagonism between totality and sequentiality has been widely noted and discussed by phenomenologists, cultural anthropologists and sociologists concerned with vision at least since Mannheim (1972) and arguably lies at the root of most processual concepts of meaning, particularly in the wake of Husserl (see below). Therefore, from a sociological viewpoint it is less of a question whether the meandering saccades of the eyeball are important at all, but rather what precisely to make of them in detail. And it is in these details, I propose, where one encounters differences that will prove crucial to opposing philosophical and sociological accounts of vision.

As I will discuss, focusing is central to a number of bodily functions (such as grabbing a ball flying towards one), but for now it suffices to say that focusing is probably the most basic bodily routine with regard to vision one can find. In my view, this insight is quite remarkable, because it directly implies two fundamental characteristics that will be essential to the account of visual practices I propose: The biological layout of our eyes already implies that first, our 'raw' visual field (or what Husserl calls 'hyletic data') is always *inherently ordered around something* because necessarily, something particular is in focus, at the centre, and in the foreground; and second, that seeing anything always happens on the basis of *bodily movements*—movements which, in turn, also need to be *directed at something* in some way. Remarkably, this basic physiological account of vision already contains two central sentiments of practice theory in a nutshell: The inherent orderliness of any given meaningful setting (such as the visual field), and the fundamental directedness of the routines carrying such a setting. But this supposed directedness of the eyeball movement immediately poses a question that will be of key importance to different versions of phenomenology: How does the visual system 'know' where to move the eye? Resting on one focal point for a split-second, where to 'hop' next? After all, saccades do not occur randomly, flip-flopping back and forth through the visual field, but they follow what is called *scanpaths*, for example by tracing the edges of a geometrical figure that dominates the visual field (Noton/Stark 1971). Crucially, throughout more than fifty years of research, not just one, but two types of answers to these questions have been developed, so that today it seems uncontested that two processes work in conjunction to produce human vision. Vision is therefore understood as a process with two converging aspects: a "bottom-up" part in which basic clues within the environment of the current focus are recognized and followed up, and a "top-down" part in which visual routines are invoked, that is, certain basic patterns of eye movements are followed, directing focus (or visual attention) to certain areas where something important is to be 'expected' (Ullman 1984). In my view, this duality is so important because it seems to hint at two basic sentiments of meaning and culture sometimes treated as mutually exclusive (although a saccade does not simply equal the constitution of meaning, of course): In the bottom-up part of vision, one might say that the image guides the eyeball, thus focusing is a reaction to what is already given in the environment. In the top-down part, however, search patterns can be culturally invoked, for example when Westerners not only read text from left to right 'automatically', but also scan images in the same basic way. Let me consider both processes in a little more detail: The bottom-up process of saccade succession happens based on the (low resolution) peripheral vision which accompanies every given focal point. Therefore, this "preattentive stage" of vision happens *without* moving the eye and without us being aware of what we see (Doll 1993; Treisman 1985). In the course of it, certain elements of the visual field 'stick out' in that colour, size, orientation, and motion are captured in the periphery of the current focus so that consequently, these areas are focused by moving the eye accordingly. Each focus then results in a new periphery and thus new 'points of attraction'; so that as a result the eye is 'hopping' from one element to the next while working out the whole of the visual field. However, such serial scanpaths alone cannot account for the ability to acquire holistic visual scenes (Duchowski 2007: 224): Empirically it is not the case that serial paths follow a strict order directly invoked by, for example, the geometrical figure that is being looked at; but to the contrary, the order in which an 'identical' figure is scanned might differ from one instance to the next and across cultures (Noton/Stark 1971). Saccade sequences, in other words, are as well in part established by what is called *visual routines* (Ullman 1984), by patterns of saccades that work 'top-down' and not as simple reactions to momentarily given stimuli. These routines, however, do also not happen randomly (they eyeball does not, for example, always repeat a certain pattern), but they are fundamentally *dependent on the situation* (Pylyshyn 2001). They are invoked according to a) the current situation given (e.g. entering a full bar as opposed to dwelling on a piece of art) and b) the task or project currently carried out (e.g. looking for a familiar face and not the restroom entrance). Consequently, cognitive scientists refer to the phenomenon as "situated vision" (Pylyshyn 2001)—and in my view, the parallels to sociological concepts of situated action (Garfinkel 1967; Mills 1940) and vision as a situated activity (C. Goodwin 2000b) are neither superfluous nor coincidental.

Visual routines, I suggest, can be characterized as basal social practices in the sense of practice theory: They are routinized ways of moving the body which are both fundamentally situated and characterized by their being directed at something. Therefore, by pointing to the fundamental role of routinized bodily movements for visual perception, can I consider the issue settled and from now on simply refer to the bodily routines as the new 'ghost in the machine' that governs whatever happens when we see something? Or, since those routines are said to be depending on the current situation and project, am I not simultaneously and paradoxically subscribing to both behaviouralism claiming the environment causes perception as a reaction, and cognitivism postulating what we perceive is effectively what we *want* to perceive? In other words, what precisely is it that these routines do, and what kind of a middle ground do I suggest them do cover? These questions have of course been asked in various versions, and in the particular case of visual recognition, the problem can be restated as follows: The existence of visual routines alone cannot be the full answer to what cognitive psychologists call the scene integration problem, that is, the question of how the visual system can grasp the overall basic structure of the visual field—for example in order to employ further adequate visual routines (Duchowski 2007: 7; Pylyshyn 2001). Therefore, I still need to qualify the nature of the directedness of saccades more precisely. Towards this, I need to introduce a concept which was developed within experimental psychology of vision but has had a lasting impact on philosophy and sociology as well, a concept that in my view is at the root of the contemporary practice turn: The notion of the gestalt.

8 The Gestalt and the Roots of Practice Thought

"There you can see his line." Tom looks to our right. I can see a chute cut through the sharp rocks; long, narrow, slightly bent, and very steep. "Yeah. That's crazy." "He somehow slid in from the side, and then just [went] straight down."[M][12] Of course I can see the line—it is right there.

As I demonstrated in the prior chapter, seeing freeride lines is a crucial accomplishment in freeriding and amounts to a complex, inherently situated interactive process; and as I just argued, at the core of this interactive process one encounters another complex, inherently embodied process. But discussing the interrelated details of vision yields the danger of one fundamental, astonishing fact being buried under all the particulars: When we see a line—just a normal line on a white sheet of paper, a line of trees flanking the road—*it is just there*. Right in front of us. We get it immediately and we can judge very confidently that this is indeed a line. Draw a line onto a piece of paper. The most simple thing in the world. And as the short fieldnote excerpt above shows, this basic ability does not vanish just because we are standing on a mountain: Over there, I see a line of snow running between the rocks. What I am trying to point at is that human vision has a fascinating duality which gestalt-psychology tried to capture (Koffka 1999; Köhler 1969) and that can fruitfully integrated into practice theory (v. Wedelstaedt/Meyer 2017): Vision is not just a process happening in sequential details, but it also characterized by forms of meaningful order that are given as a whole, in toto, and at once. And these wholes, gestalt theory argued, are *not* just mental constructs, but inherent to seeing itself. In other words, at least to some extent, seeing means seeing gestalts. What exactly is a gestalt? Consider the line as one of the most basic

---

[12] „Er ist so seitlich reingerutscht und dann einfach straight runter."

examples: Like a rectangle, a line is a shape we can clearly identify regardless of its size, colour, orientation in space, or the environment it is embedded into. Not only can we draw a line long before we can walk or speak, but our visual system can also pick lines out from crowded backgrounds extremely fast—in fact we even tend to see continuous lines even when they are comprised of distinct points with gaps laying between them (as in seeing a line of trees). In other words, pragmatically a line is a very simple thing. Yet trying to give a concise definition of the logical or geometrical concept of the line requires surprisingly complex descriptions. Examples include: A straight or curved continuous extent of length without breadth. An infinitely large number of indefinitely small points that are directly adjacent to each other and lie in the space between two separate points. A common mathematical definition even applies a clever trick: a line is the trace of a point moving into a certain direction. Interestingly, this 'definition' is essentially an instruction of how to visualize a line mentally, much in the way of Wittgenstein (2009, § 66) demanding: "Don't think but look!" So what do we see when we see a gestalt? In my view, the core concept has been summarized well by phenomenologist Aaron Gurwitsch:

> "By 'Gestalt' is meant a unitary whole of varying degrees of richness in detail, which, by virtue of its intrinsic articulation and structure, possesses coherence and consolidation and, thus, detaches itself as an organized and closed unit from the surrounding field." (Gurwitsch 1964: 115)

A gestalt is a coherent whole that seems to impose itself, that we can hardly avoid seeing because it is in some way prior to other things within the visual field: We can 'see' three distinct lines rather than a triangle, but initially, we will see the triangle. Although the term gestalt is usually associated with the top-down theory of vision, this should *not* be taken to mean that what this theory suggests is that a gestalt is simply imposed by 'the mind.' Instead, the argument is that the process of grasping the visual field has a top-down structure in that each detail focused is contrasted against the general pattern of the visual field rather than the adjacent details captured in peripheral vision (as in bottom-up vision). A gestalt arises from a background that 'fits' or carries the current gestalt in that one can say that the current visual field that has a "gestalt-contexture" providing a specific context (the thematic field) (cf. Arvidson 1992). To clarify the idea, let me contrast this proposition to a 'classic' account of seeing a line using the notions of expectation and judgement such as this one: The freerider sees the line because he expects to see it on the basis of prior experience; in other words he 'looks for' typical telltale signs of lines the visual field; and once he has spotted a possible candidate, he evaluates whether the details of what he sees matches his conceptual knowledge about how lines look. Note, however, how talking about knowledge leads seamlessly to verbally turning the whole process into something the freerider wilfully does. As I will make clear in detail below, I believe this effect is a persistent danger when employing the notion of knowledge: Considering that what I tried to describe above is a sequence of minimal saccades lasting only fractions of a second, one can indeed say that applying a visual routine can be considered a skill or competence and thus know-how, a kind of knowledge. But terming the saccade a skill or know-how does not really express much about the *order* of the scene integration that seems to guide scanpaths across the visual field. Here, gestalt thinking suggests a different approach: To consider the whole not as given by its parts, but the parts as given consecutively to the whole.

But as it stands, is this approach really convincing? Do we not nevertheless have to ask: Where does the whole come from? What precisely is happening when Gurwitsch (1964: 115) postulates that a gestalt "detaches itself"? At the core, the definition of the gestalt I quoted has not provided an answer to the question of whether the synthesis of different sensory minutiae into a coherent whole is the result of an interpretation in the sense of an intervention of the mind, the brain, or cognition. Historically, the core impetus of the gestalt-movement was the rejection of the "constancy hypothesis" of visual perception which states that separate sensory stimuli reach us 'directly' or in 'raw form' and thus as separate impulses or events which are only consecutively synthesized into larger wholes (Rang 1990). But here we have to ask: What does it mean to say that stimuli reach us—who is "us?".

Trying to discern the roles of entities like the brain, the mind, the body, cognition, consciousness, and so on leads to debates that are notoriously difficult, bitter, and long—and the notion of the gestalt is inherently tied up in these debates, partially because vision is among the key subjects of them. The importance of the gestalt notion stems from the fact that it served as a bridge between disciplines: Developed within experimental psychology, the gestalt-argument was first adapted for the philosophy of perception and subsequently for sociological theory. The extended history and the various interpretations of the term 'gestalt' would easily fill an extended volume of its own, but in brief, I suggest that the notion of the gestalt is at the historical and intellectual root of contemporary practice theory—or what Schatzki (2002) calls site ontologies—because it functioned as a prototype of the idea that meaning should be conceptualized as an order inherent to a given setting. Practice thinking sprung forth from the gestalt idea along two lines: On the one hand, Gestalt psychology had a major impact on the 'turn' that Wittgenstein (arguably) took in his later life and which culminated in the writing that was published as the *Philosophical Investigations* (see Gebauer 2009; Stengel 2003). On the other hand, the philosopher Aaron Gurwitsch made converging Husserl's phenomenology and gestalt-thinking his lifetime project. Gurwitsch not only influenced Husserl's thinking to some extent (see below), but more importantly, he was a mayor inspiration to two of his students who are key intellectual forefathers of the contemporary practice theories: Merleau-Ponty (Carman 2008: 20) and Garfinkel (Fele 2008). But while the adaption of the gestalt notion proved very fruitful, I would argue that it also implied a significant switch that needs to be considered when discussing gestalt-thinking: What was a hypothesis to be tested (and eventually refuted to some extent) in a scientific debate became a philosophical concept employed towards formulating an answer to a fundamental enigma: the relation between 'us' and 'the world'. Thus, while the philosophers used the data of the scientists and discussed their experiments, they were engaged in a fundamentally different enterprise. In fact, the theory whose name they employed did not actual support the point they were trying to make: The original gestalt-psychology contains a naturalistic view on perception, directly equating a perception to a local stimulus in our sensory system—a fact well noted by its philosophical readers like Wittgenstein or Merleau-Ponty (Stengel 2003: 56 fn147). Therefore, when discussing the notion gestalt, it is imperative to discern between the scientific findings that led to the gestalt-hypothesis and the philosophical *idea* of the gestalt. To a large extent, this amounts to discerning the two Janus-faces of vision I mentioned earlier—the phenomenology and the neurobiology of vision—, but as I also pointed out, I do not believe one can or should separate them into entirely exclusive spheres. In other words, when phenomenological philosophers discussed findings from gestalt-experiments, they did not do so from an entirely neutral stance, but (to some degree) they relied on them as providing grounding to their thought. Therefore, I will first roughly assess to which extent this ground has moved since the 1920s by sketching the contemporary landscape of experimental findings about gestalt 'detachment', before I synthesize what I consider the key features of a philosophical take on gestalts.

9 Gestalt-Seeing as Visual Cognition

From the perspective of contemporary vision science, the question of how we come to see a gestalt 'automatically' is but one version of a phenomenon that can be found in several different variations. I introduced the gestalt-notion with regard to the question of how a series of temporally separate saccades can be prefigured by seeing a unified figure in a field, which is one of the four classic topics of gestalt-debates. The second classic phenomenon—arguably the one discussed even more extensively by the philosophers who embrace gestalt-questions—is the question of colour-synthesis[13]: One the one hand, we synthesize our perception of the colour of a surface and the shape of an object into seeing a coloured object, yet on the other, we are also able to distinguish between, e.g., red light shining on a white surface and white light shining on a red surface. Thus we are synthesizing colour and object in some cases, but not in all. The third problem at least to some degree discussed by gestalt-thinkers is that of multisensory convergence, or the question why stimuli of different senses (like hearing tones and seeing colours) affect one another, and whether this effect emerges only in the brain. To the fourth topic, finally, I will return in the coming chapter: To this day, psychopathological phenomena play a key role in vision research in that certain patients exhibit grave inhibitions regarding some practices involving vision (e.g. pointing to an object)

---

[13] See for a critique of Husserl's discussion of the problem Rang (1990); and for a concise summary of Wittgenstein and Merleau-Ponty on the same question Stengel (2003).

but nearly none in others (e.g. grabbing an object). As I will argue, these cases are on the one hand especially important from a (pheno-)practice perspective in that they provide 'naturally occurring' data, but on the other, they also pose specific problems to philosophers.

Over the last 80 years of research, the number of phenomena considered as belonging into the same basic category of effects relevant to gestalt philosophy has risen considerably, so that they are today considered as a whole class of their own: In between what is termed "low-level vision"—or the reflex-like reaction of the eye to basic stimuli in para-foveal vision—and "high-level vision"—or the conceptual interpretation of visual content on the basis of memorized knowledge—, a third type called "mid-level vision" is being discerned (Cavanagh 2011). Vision scientists have framed this field under the label *visual cognition*[14] in order to summarize a range of visual routines which attend to different tasks through what is defined as "unconscious inference" about how different elements within the visual field relate (Cavanagh 2011; Ullman 2000; Wagemans 2001). Such routines include, for example, grasping basic relations such as "inside," "behind," or "tangent"; linking shadows to the objects casting them; comparing proportions; discerning movements; and so on. Looking at all these problems in detail will be neither necessary nor possible for me, but what is crucial is that they are all understood to happen prior to processes leading to awareness of the conceptual content of the visual field. Notions like "awareness" or "conceptual content" are, of course, highly contested, and therefore these findings alone cannot be conclusive towards reframing a phenomenological term like consciousness. Moreover, from a strict constructivist viewpoint (e.g. Luhmann 1995a) such processes could well be understood as instances of observation of rather than entanglement into the environment. Therefore, all I want to suggest right now is that from a practice perspective which is trying to reframe the 'site' of the production of social meaning, the findings about visual cognition all point to the situatedness of perception and the role of bodily routines for it. From this perspective, it is indeed questionable whether instances of, e.g., high- and mid-level vision can really be 'purified' in the laboratory; and that certain 'tasks' can really be said to be 'solved' by singular routines, since the proper demonstration of having solved the tasks on behalf of the participants requires an extended number of complementary social accomplishments and practices. Precisely how such scientific 'facts' regarding our body can be relevant towards a sociological practice perspective is an important question that will have to wait to be answered until I have provided a more concise account of the body. For now it suffices to say that I am not concerned with the problem 'where' in 'the body' certain details of perception happen, i.e. if the nerve

---

[14] The logic behind applying the term 'cognition' in this case is basically the same as in the case of distributed cognition discussed earlier; or in phrases like "cognition on the ground" (Maynard 2006) or "cognition in the wild" (Hutchins 1995): A view on certain aspects of practices as tasks to be done or projects to be solved that, albeit being functionalistic, seeks to overcome the classic account of 'thinking' and purely mental ratio.

endings that supposedly 'do' these things sit on the retina or in the frontal lobe. What seems important, however, are the differences in *quality* such 'localizations' by scientists can imply—for example, whether or not the content of certain visual routines lends itself to reflection; or how and how fast the socialization into a (sub) culture might impact on said routines, e.g. considering deeply emotional reactions to seeing a beautiful line as opposed to their mere 'technical' recognition.

But before returning to those findings from the field of visual cognition that seem especially interesting in light of this work, let me try to delineate a more general understanding of mid-level vision that can be used to contextualize the philosophical adoptions of gestalt-thinking that I will turn to next. What is key about the findings of visual cognition is that our vision happens through making use of routinely developed distinctions on a level that is adequate to the task: While every visual field we look at could be broken down into ever-smaller units, or seen as parts of a huge whole, this would be unhelpful in most cases, and therefore our pre-reflexive processing of visual input already imposes a 'suitable' level of aggregation (Jacob/Jeannerod 2005: 140). Visual routines, in other words, are instances of *figuring out* in the true sense of the word in that they are oriented by figures (figural forms) to be seen in the visual field. And maybe this helps to clarify why I see an essential connection between the scientific findings about vision and theories of social practices (in terms of topics, notions, and their genealogy): If visual routines are practices of figuring out, then they might help us to get to the core of the phenomenon of *prefiguration*—in my view a key idea of practice theory which after all tries to describe, in Schatzki's (2002: 44) words, "how at any moment the site of the social prefigures the flow of activity by qualifying the possible paths it can take."

10 The Temporal Structure of the Gestalt

In order to clarify why and how I deem gestalt-thinking to be at the core of practice theory per se and an understanding of phenopractices such as practices of seeing in particular, I will now try to trace out some further key characteristic of the philosophical implications of the notion of the gestalt. For sociology, what proved crucial about the gestalt-thesis is that it turns the traditional concept of constructionism around: It no longer asks how we are able to routinely assemble the (essentially) same meaningful entities from the stream of unconnected details fired at our senses, but instead holds that visual perception happens to a large extent on the basis of a gestalt-order that is already given—without necessarily detailing 'by whom' it is given. The meaning of the details within the visual field, in other words, are said to be constituted on the basis of this overall order rather than the other way around. For example, it has been shown that visual attention (on the basis of gaze fixation) of an object cannot be equated to selecting the *whole* object (or what the scientists unreflexively treat as 'actually' being an object), that is, co-selecting all relevant and non-relevant features of the object at once

(Wegener/Ehn/Aurich/Galashan/et al. 2008). Instead, the suppression of non-relevant features is an intrinsic part of establishing visual attention even on a neural level (which is in turn a prerequisite to any kind of awareness or action regarding the object). In other words, we do not first see things and then process their specific features, but by suppressing certain features we work out that certain objects are there to be seen. Conclusively, the coherence of a gestalt results from the functional meanings of its parts—that is, the relevancy they gain within the overall gestalt. For this reason, each perceptual detail can only carry meaning which is *functional,* meaning that stems from its 'fitting in' or 'being helpful towards' achieving the perception of the total gestalt—its meaning emerges, so to speak, by deduction from the final figure. It is on the basis of this point that gestalt-philosophers make their arguably decisive point: They deduct an understanding of the *temporality of perception* which is crucially different from proponents of what one might term 'individual interpretation theory.'

Importantly, according to Gurwitsch (1964, 1970) the notion of the gestalt implies, that our perception of a field has a temporal order that is invoked or carried by the current gestalt schema: When we establish meaning sequentially, we do so by following a specify order intrinsic to the field itself. For example, in the case of saccades, our focus of perception moves not arbitrarily from one moment to the next, but according to a pre-given sequence. But this sequence is *not* a projection independently imposed by our mind on our eye on the basis of retrospection (or retention), thus it is not just an expectation given by memorized knowledge. Instead, Gurwitsch holds that the direction our stream of consciousness takes depends on the theme implied by the current field through three conjunctions: The coherence of the resulting impression with a gestalt, the relevancy of the different details to the gestalt, and the marginal co-presence of certain aspects (Arvidson 1992). In other words, what Gurwitsch emphasized is that the 'path' our visual attention takes is original to the given details *of the field itself.* Let me clarify the origin of this idea: The sequential organization of our visual perception is often illustrated by using ambiguous figures such as the Necker cube, a 2D drawing of a cube that we can be seen as a 3D object either protruding from the page or as being carved into it—but never both at the same time. Switching between these two impressions is possible, but it takes some effort, since our perceptual system seems to 'insist' on keeping the currently achieved gestalt coherence. While these simple illusions so popular among authors seem to do the job of demonstrating the sequentially of grasping gestalts well, I think they can be somewhat misleading because they do not bring to light the nature of this sequentiality. Because, when e.g. taking the example of the Necker cube, it is easy to argue that our visual perception is quite *independent* of its given object and rather depends primarily on our internalized expectation or mental attitude in that we can mentally teach or 'tell' ourselves to switch from seeing one of the two possible figures to seeing the other. But such an understanding runs contrary to what I regard as the core argument of gestalt theorists, namely that the sequential organization of a perception follows *not* from cognitive typifications alone, but from the overlapping of bodily routines and the features of the concrete situational environment. Therefore, what such illusions demonstrate most vividly in my view is the fact that it is only in very specific situations containing very particular, abstract, and artificial graphical displays devised with great care, that for brief moments, more 'pure' cognitive patterns can take the lead and induce certain perceptual content on us. In the vast majority of normal situations, however, such a definite reign of the mind over what we see does not occur.

At the core of the philosophical gestalt-perspective, I suggest, one finds the idea of meaningful order that is prior to, or already given with, our engagement with a situation so that it needs at least in part to be understood as a condition rather than a result of this engagement. However, this basic concept does not really specify what it is that 'gives' the gestalt order whenever practices happen. Here, several different accounts seem possible, and while it can hardly be said that any single author discussing gestalt ideas with regard to vision focused on just one of them exclusively, the approaches do differ with regard to the aspect they emphasize:

a) One might state that the order perceived is 'in' the visual field in ontological terms—the physical order of the things thus 'guides' our vision in that it is 'directly' picked up. For example, one can experimentally produce the effect that objects lying close to each other are seen as being even closer as they actually are—in other words, the 'objective' order of the field is amplified by the visual system so that the gestalt already physically given prefigures our vision. The clearest proponent of such a view is probably the ecological theory of vision (J. J. Gibson 1986), which has also been called "the direct of visual perception" (Jacob/Jeannerod 2003: 157).

b) As a variant of a), the inherent order of the visual field can be understood as already 'physically' given in that this order is seen as a practical accomplishment in concrete, often intersubjective situations. This view has most explicitly been expressed by Ethnomethodology through emphasizing that every social situation must already have what is called an "authochtonus order" in the form of gestalt-coherence without which we would not be able to perceive it meaningfully (Garfinkel 2002; Fele 2008).

c) Gestalts can be regarded as the result of subconscious and/or non-mental bodily routines. In this view, what is emphasized is that those instances often termed interpretation, knowledge, or culture are in fact processes, skills or entities operative only at a 'second level' in that the more fundamental bodily routines work prior to them. Additionally, one might emphasize that such routines work beyond our awareness or conscious attention, so that once reflexive interpretation 'kicks in,' part of the 'epistemic' work has already been done. On the basis of this version, authors might variably hold that concepts like interpretation, knowledge, culture, consciousness, or awareness should either be abandoned or extended to include these basal routines.

d) Gestalts can be seen as mental patterns or implicit knowledge that can be explicated, and that therefore vision is semantic[15] in character. Empirically, various studies have shown that vision has semantic aspects—for example, one usually needs to be verbally told that e.g. the famous duck/rabbit drawing in Wittgenstein's *Philosophical Investigations* can be seen in two versions to be able to indeed see both versions. The semantic nature of vision is, however, also heavily contested by proponents of the versions a)—c) (see Ingold 2000; Noë 2004).

Given these different options, where should one position the practice perspective? In my view, practice theory not only seeks to embrace and combine all four versions, but also argues that discerning them is difficult, if not impossible and carries the risk of a one-sided view. The crucial advantage of the notion of social practices, in other words, is that it does not force one to deny or ignore the role of the unconscious or the material, but instead insists of their mutual dependence. Committing to 'the site of the social' as a multidimensional realm, in other words, is employed as a remedy against the monism sometimes caused by one-sidedly only a slim selection of scientific findings in order to localize where meaning dwells. But at least in the case of vision, despite (or because of) all their sophisticated equipment and complex formulas, one cannot say that vision scientists themselves are able to give a very concise and sophisticated account of the locus and nature of the coordination of visual routines and the synthesis of their products. Consider, for example, this account (from a top-level research paper authored by a Harvard professor):

> "This idea of a common space and a common format for exchange between brain centers has been proposed (…) as a central bulletin board or chat room where the different centers post current descriptions and receive requests from each other like perhaps 'Vision: Are there any red things just above the upcoming road intersection?'" (Cavanagh 2011: 4)

Instead of battling about where precisely the emergence of meaningful order manifest in seeing is to be located, I suggest that practice thought provides a framework within which scientific insights aiming at different levels or loci of (visual) perception can be coherently integrated—if one can develop a suitable understanding of the way in which phenopractices and their elements (such as bodily routines or material orders) relate. This is precisely what I aim to do in this chapter. A key point in this discussion of how the intelligibility of meaningful visual order is accomplished via the integration of the different levels of human vision is the notion of *intentionality* one implies from the gestalt-thesis, because intentionality (be it as a form of volition or as a field-like quality) has been traditionally considered as the force driving such accomplishment of intelligible order. Therefore, the

---

[15] Note that frequently, authors from cognitive psychology or neuroscience suggest that gestalt-vision is conceptual in character. In doing so, they often—but not always—imply that such concepts can necessarily be expressed semantically without explicitly saying so, and without acknowledging how problematic this assumption is (Clark 1997).

key contribution of gestalt thinking to social theory arguably lies in the relation of intentionality and volition it implies, for example in regard to our perception of action (see Chap. 8). And this is precisely the point where the visual illusions which philosophers arguing with gestalt-notions such as Wittgenstein (i.e. his drawing of the duck/rabbit) become important: Crucial to the notion of the gestalt is the possibility of the *gestalt-switch*, the fact that the same image can be seen as two mutually exclusive, yet equally 'real' versions. But as we all can experience vis-à-vis these images, we cannot just *choose* to switch our view at will and in the middle of seeing, but we must somehow manage ourselves to achieve the effect. Seeing the duck or the rabbit is, in other words, not just an interpretation that can be superimposed at will over given visual data, but instead a processual manifestation we can hardly 'escape' from. Of course, the existence of this effect cannot be taken as an empirical finding like those I collected by hiking up the ridge of the Wilde Krimml. Instead, in this work I treat the visual effects of seeing gestalts as paradigmatic for phenomenal fields per se (a move I share with many authors, as I will show). It seems to me that it is no coincidence that many of those theories accused of intellectualism or an exaggerated distance from everyday life discuss only those specific visual fields one will encounter when sitting at a desk and fixating a simple object or a carefully crafted drawing of an optical illusion. The visual fields I encountered by following the freeskiers into the backcountry of the Krimml are of course quite different in nature—but my examination of them shares the core sentiment with the experiments with and discussion of optical illusions: namely, that it is 'at the edge' of our capabilities where many insights occur. Just like in skiing, it is when things go partly wrong, that we learn the most.

11 Blending In and Standing Out

Having emphasized the multiplicity of empirical phenomena studied in contemporary visual cognition research, and pointing to the variety of interpretations prevalent in philosophical readings of the gestalt, how can I claim that all these diverse experimental findings about various processes share a common gestalt-perspective, and why do I think they can be instructive for phenopractice theory? Because in my view, at the core of the gestalt as a philosophical notion lies an inherently *reflexive* approach to knowing about the world—an approach that some scientists and philosophers implicitly share: The different routines and patterns that cognitive psychologists and neuroscientists 'discovered' are necessarily traced out under the assumption of seeing as an inherently ordered or purposeful whole that 'works'—in other words, proponents of visual cognition or situated vision treat *seeing itself* as a gestalt. And not by coincidence, the same approach is also shared by the phenomenology of Merleau-Ponty[16] (2002: 112 ff.), who not only extensively discusses the findings of the gestalt-psychology of vision, but emphasizes that we "have" our body because we always perceive it as a whole, not as a sum of organs.[17] Practice theory itself, I believe, follows the same fundamental ratio: Just like scientists devising particular experiments under the assumption that vision (whatever it might be) already works and therefore ask how this detail contributes to the whole; just like we ourselves can only focus our attention on a single bodily sense or body part within a given, working whole body, practice theory holds that each element or aspect or basal routine only has meaning or order by virtue of it being situated within a 'working' whole (Schatzki 2002). To emphasize this fundamental point: The gestalt-argument foundational for practice thought is that only by starting from a greater whole that is already given, already 'up and running,' *any* kind of detail, element, or routine can be understood—and since the basic quality of the social world is its intelligibility, one can even say: only then can it be. If the core 'move' of practice theory lies in differentiating single practices (as entities) from overall human praxis (Reckwitz 2002a: 249), then this is an outcome of just this fundamental understanding: One can take a certain single practice to be contributing to human praxis (and gain some insight into how this happens) only on the basis of the assumption that this praxis already 'makes sense' in some way. What I try to suggest is that certain recurring discussions or discrepancies with practice thought have their common root in this basic 'move.' For example, I described freeskiing as a molecule and practices as its atoms always in need of complementary atoms and noted how different strands of practice theory look at empirical 'fields of order' of very different magnitude (e.g. Garfinkel and Bourdieu). Within the contemporary practice discourse, moreover, there are ongoing debates about if and how different levels of practices can be discerned, if one should distinguish dispersed and integrated practices, how elements of practices can be said to be basal elements and not itself composed of elements (or even practices), and so on (e.g. Schatzki 2002; Shove/Pantzar 2007; Warde 2010). By no means do I intend to say that these discussions are not important, but what I believe is this: they cannot reach a rock bottom, as one will always find electrons within atoms and quarks within electrons and strings within quarks. At least not via empirical observation or logical arguments, but only by adhering to some common definition would one be able to open the second-last matryoshka and find her daughter who is finally solid and un-openable. And more importantly, whenever one sets out to examine any matryoshka, one has already taken her out of a larger mother-figure one thus implies to have a gestalt of her own.

---

[16] For a practice perspective on vision partly grounded on Merleau-Ponty see Ingold (2000: 262–266).

[17] And as Stengel (2003: 57) argues, it is also shared by Wittgenstein when he holds that every sentence can only be understood as a part of language game—that is, as a part of an already meaningfully ordered whole.

Transposing these general considerations back to the realm of vision and visual practices, I suggest that the core understanding of the gestalt-perspective leads to a specific notion of visible order as carried in the modus of *blending in and standing out*. A respective foundational understanding of visibility has been elaborated by a number of authors studying vision from a range of disciplines: Building on the works of Gestalt psychology (Köhler 1969), Wittgenstein (1995b, 2009) developed the philosophical notion of Seeing-As or the seeing of interchangeable, yet mutually exclusive *aspects* in a given vista; while Merleau-Ponty (2002) uses the same sources to develop a phenomenology of (visual) perception grounded in the differentiation of *foreground and background* (see Stengel 2003 for the commonalities in Wittgenstein and Merleau-Ponty); Luhmann (1995a) roots his sociological theory by following the imperative of mathematician Spencer Brown (1971) to "Draw a distinction!" as the basal operation to establish meaning, and connects this notion with the differentiation of *form and medium* introduced by gestalt-psychologist Fritz Heider (1926); and Heidegger (1962) engaged in "seeing phenomenologically" in order to unfold his analysis of *Dasein* as a pragmatic being-in-the-world attending only to certain selected things as *present-at-hand* and others remaining in the background of being *ready-to-hand* (see for the parallels between Heidegger and Wittgenstein Taylor 1995). Within the contemporary discussion, Schatzki (2002) grounds his theoretical conception of the social in an understanding of *sites* as constellations of relatedness that provide intelligibility and illustrates this understanding with the example of looking at a landscape (2010b) (as does Ingold 2000). Each of these accounts, of course, differs in perspective and methodology so that it would necessitate a detailed treatment of its own which I cannot provide in this work. And while I will return to specific points of these different works, it should for now suffice to say that I hold that they all share a basic common sentiment stemming from common roots in Gestalt psychology which I deem fundamental for any treatment of vision from a practice perspective. I should stress that this common sentiment lays *not* just in the fairly basic understanding that seeing a pattern entails superimposing a somewhat abstract meaning structure over a given visual datum; but rather that a) one cannot first analyse the given background and then deduct the existence of a pattern e.g. by mentally testing the 'fit' of possible candidates for things to see, but that to the contrary, the foreground is always *given with* a certain background; and that b) it is (at least to some degree) the order embedded in the *pattern* itself that structures the sequential process of figuring out the visual field; yet c) while this does not imply a predetermination of the resulting impression by the abstract pattern since visual routines nevertheless at least in part depend on the details of the object in question. When I hold that the selection of sources I build on is—surprising as they may seem—neither eclectic nor incommensurable, this is because I consider this basic concept to be common to all of them. More specifically, I hold that the three strings I aim to weave together into a phenopractice theory—Schatzki's conception[18] of practice theory, Merleau-Ponty's studies of the phenomenology of perception, and neuroscientific findings about vision—can indeed be fruitfully understood as *aspects* of the same phenomenon of vision coming to light vis-à-vis this phenomenon in alternating stances.

One last point: it seems to me that in my discussion so far (and sometimes in discussions within the practice turn in general), there is an elephant in the room: Husserl. Practice thought is at the core a deliberation of the nature of meaning and the conditions of intelligibility and therefore, it is essentially (though not exclusively) a phenomenological enterprise. Yet while a certain indebtedness to Husserl is quickly acknowledged by many, he is often equally quickly dismissed as still captured in Cartesian thought, as ignoring the role of movement, or as overlooking the notion of the gestalt. At least with regard to Husserl's writing on vision, however, none of these three accusations is true. For the remainder of the chapter, I will therefore look at Husserl's account of vision in more detail. I will argue that, while Husserl's adaption of the gestalt poses less of an antipode to practice-thinking than it is often claimed, it does pose important question with regard to the phenomenology of movement and action. In summary, I will try to show that Husserl is right to emphasize the role of intentionality for visual perception and that his should not be equated to an intellectualist nor a strictly subjectivist[19] conception—but it will have to be discussed whether it is necessarily an individualist notion or else can be integrated into what Schatzki (2002) terms collectivist ontologies. The problem with Husserl's account of vision, however, is that he insists on consciousness as the sole locus of any synthesis of meaning. In consequence, his account could be called 'particularistic' in that it treats the sensation of meaningful forms as always given in almost infinitesimally small and isolated particulars, as well as 'pseudo-voluntaristic' in that he treats all bodily movements as manifesting in consciousness exclusively in the modus of volitional action. In order to develop an alternative, I will conclude, one might look to Merleau-Ponty and need to examine the role of the body and movement in some more detail.

Excursus I: Husserlian Phenomenology, Gestalts, and the Practice Turn

> Without a doubt, the works of Edmund Husserl are to be found among the philosophical conceptualizations that have had the greatest impact on sociological thought. This importance, however, is equally documented by those sociological thinkers seeking to adhere to the core principles of his

---

[18] Schatzki does not embrace the notion of the gestalt explicitly, but I would hold that the gestalt is a more specific version of his general concept of prefiguration being a relation among components of arrangements contained in a site. Specifically, because he characterizes them not as general (macro-social) structures directly invoking specific actions, but rather as contained in the local order of the site (Schatzki 2002: 44 f.).

[19] Subjectivist in the sense of an individualist solipsism, that is, since Husserl points to the transcendental character of the noema.

phenomenology and their methodological implications, most notably Alfred Schutz and his successors like Berger and Luckmann, and those for whom Husserl serves as a reference point from which to distance their position, among them those subsumed in the practice turn. For Reckwitz (2002a: 247), for example, Schutz' theory is the prototype of all forms of what he calls "mentalist 'subjectivism'" because its theoretical roots lie in Husserl's concept of the mind as "the sequence of intentional acts in consciousness." However, it is not quite as clear as it seems how wide the gap between Husserlian phenomenology and practice theory really is. Without pretending to deliver a complete discussion of this vexed question at this point, several reasons can be stated against painting practice thought as a wholehearted dismissal of Husserlian thought. First, the basic understanding of meaning as an ongoing stream, and its inherent directedness towards concrete objects is without question fundamental for the basic move of theories of practices to explain intelligibility through routinized conduct. Consequently, the major forefathers of contemporary practice thought all explicitly build more or less directly on Husserl, although by altering or extending his concepts: Heidegger, Merleau-Ponty, Bourdieu, and Garfinkel are all a case in point.[20] In turn, it remains an open question whether these thinkers should be read as overcoming or continuing Husserl's phenomenology (e.g. for the case of Heidegger see Smith 2007: 407; and for Merleau-Ponty see Toadvine/ Embree 2002). Second, it would be misleading to think that within theories of practice, there is no place left to account for intentional thoughts, beliefs, will, purposes, and similar 'mental' or conscious phenomena. The crucial difference, rather, is that their functional or causal role in explaining situated conduct is being questioned by considering them not as presiding over but an epiphenomenon of lived human life.[21] Third, Husserl developed and changed his position over time (see e.g. Smith 2007), so that embracing or denouncing his work in toto is always likely to miss out on certain aspects. Fourth and more specifically with regard to the topics of core relevance to phenopractice theory, Husserl's work is sometimes portrayed as outright neglecting a) the role of the body, b) the existence of pre-conceptual sentiments, and/or c) the role of gestalts or the horizon for the process of perception. In so far as these points are routinely raised by referring to

---

[20] The relation between Wittgenstein and Husserl is more complex as it is unclear whether they read each other. In any event it seems clear that they dwelled on similar problems and Wittgenstein explicitly discusses phenomenology as a "grammar" (Smith 2007: 411–414).

[21] Schatzki, for example, writes: "The only form of coexistence that can occur outside the mesh of *all* practices and orders is intentional relatedness, especially thoughts about others." (2002: 150; original emphasis) The practices and orders he refers to, to be sure, being the site of the social itself.

Merleau-Ponty or Heidegger as their proponents, there is grave danger of oversimplifying their arguments since—as both authors of course acknowledged—Husserl does indeed discuss all of these issues at some point, seeking to integrate them into his phenomenology. Husserl emphasizes the role of the body specifically with regard to the visual perception of material objects and space (see below); pre-conceptual sentiments or perceptions of various sorts do feature in his thought (but are considered as only pre-phenomenal, "hyletic" data that still need to undergo active apperception to gain their phenomenal relevancy; see Eberle 1984: 22); and finally, in the course of attending to gestalt-ideas, the notion of the horizon is discussed several times (however his discussion of the horizon arguably remains somewhat inconclusive and of lesser importance to the overall theory; see Smith 2007: 290–294). In other words, while there are without question important discrepancies between Husserl's approach and a practice-based view, they are not rooted in the fact that he simply ignores a whole class of phenomena, but instead in that he conceptualizes them differently. If one is to acknowledge that there is a phenomenological aspect to the question of how social practices work, then a closer look at Husserl's thoughts on bodily routines is due—especially with regard to vision.

In my view, this remains also true in the face of the argument that, if building on Husserl's phenomenology, body functions per se should not be considered by the sociologist since sociology's exclusive concern should be the realm of meaning, thus only if the body emerges as a meaningful entity (for example within talk), it should be studied as such. Studying freeskiers' bodies, for example, would thus amount to studying if and how bodies are subjectively perceived and/or intersubjectively addressed within the subculture. However, while Husserl does indeed hold that bodies can only become relevant *for the subjective actors* insofar as they are 'featured' in consciousness, one cannot infer that he did not acknowledge the bodies' relevance *for perception* per se—thus implying their relevance for the social scientist concerned with the question of how intelligibility is possible. Quite to the contrary, one crucial reference point for Husserl's phenomenology was the scientific view of human vision based on experiments which was state of the art at his time: von Helmholtz work on visual perception (Rang 1990). It is for this reason that for example the term "adumbration" (*Abschattung*) plays a central role in Husserl's general conceptualization of perception as a process of identifying the same 'thing' within a series of inherently different perceptual impressions. Notably, the critique that the gestalt psychologists brought forward against Husserl's thought—which I characterized as a crucial basis for the move to de-centre the subject when considering visual perception—originates from challenging exactly those assumptions which Husserl adopted uncritically from von Helmholtz (Rang 1990: 299–309).

In a way, one could thus say that the question of what happens when our eyes scan a visual field lies at the historical root of the gap that exists today within sociology between approaches based on subject-centred versus practice-centred theories of the social.

But if there is a common historical root and if the 'ancestral' authors of today's 'antagonist' sociological camps built on the same authors and the same empirical cases with regard to vision, how did the impression emerge that both are so squarely separated (cf. Burri 2008)? In my view, the main reason is partly to be found in the *topics* rather than theories alone that scholars within a certain tradition attended to. What I discuss here are, one might say, the 'basics' of vision; the ubiquitous processes that take place when we engage in such mundane, even boring practices like grabbing a tube of toothpaste or walking down the street. Yet this mundane version of human vision has a much more elegant, prestigious twin: vision in visual arts. And while Husserl concerned himself with both art and pale mundanity, most authors in philosophy and sociology building on him did not, confining themselves mostly to the visual glamour and complexity of the art world—Heidegger and Schutz[22] are a case in point. Especially for sociologists of culture working in this tradition, understanding visual art has been the prime path to understanding visual culture and eventually vision per se—after all, this approach was already embraced by Mannheim. But while it has proven very fruitful, I think this approach also yields the danger of becoming so fascinated with the many levels and complexities of the visual arts that the many levels and complexities of 'basic' vision are being overlooked, leading authors to deduct findings about one of our most fundamental and routine ways from being, knowing, and feeling from a sphere of carefully staged visual effects, performances, and concepts. Here, I believe, lies the deeper reason for my deviation from certain understandings of vision deemed 'classic' in cultural sociology.

Excursus II: Husserl on Eyeball Movement and Seeing Figures

I argued that the gap that exists today between a (hermeneutic) sociology focusing on the subject and a practice-oriented sociology focusing on situational order can be traced back to a long-standing philosophical argument regarding the proper conceptualization of human vision. Of course, the relation of sociological theories in the wake of Husserlian phenomenology

---

[22] Note that I am not referring to Schutz' work per se, which is of course concerned with everyday life, but rather the context in which the details of vision are discussed by him.

and practice theory is both complex and contested. But if one accepts my proposition, then the decisive point is the notion of the gestalt, in that it was central for the critique of Husserl's understanding of consciousness voiced (inter alia) by Merleau-Ponty and Gurwitsch. However, as I mentioned it would be simplistic to differentiate between phenomenological concepts of vision pre and post gestalt-theory, because in fact, Husserl did already integrate it into his thinking (Drummond 1979; Rang 1990). And since the basic postulates of gestalt-theory have arguably been confirmed and refined in psychology and neuroscience, there is much debate on whether Husserl's concept of vision on these grounds needs to be abandoned (e.g. Schlicht 2008), has been confirmed as basically correct (e.g. Gallagher 2005), is in need of important adjustments (Drummond 2009; Pacherie 1999), or is simply not concerned with issues these theories or experiments touch upon. While I will obviously not be able to retrace this discussion as a whole, I believe it is important to clarify Husserl's position with regard to gestalts because they are of continuing importance to contemporary sociology of action and knowledge. To this end, I will focus on those parts of Husserl's voluminous oeuvre that explicitly cover embodied vision and the role of the gestalt without being able to track how these parts relate to the overall work in all cases. In detailing Husserl's 'version' of gestalt-thinking, I will also briefly refer to the phenomenological critique it received, especially from Merleau-Ponty—without intending to comment on the question whether the differences found contradict certain arguments made about the congruence of both authors' general phenomenological positions or not (see Zahavi 2002). In order to understand why Husserl interpreted gestalt-ideas so differently from those who followed him, it seems useful to start by considering the chronology of his writing and the position from which he approached them. When Husserl considered the notion of the visual field and role of bodily movement, gestalts, and the horizon for its constitution after writing the *Ideen* I, he had already laid down the basic foundations of his grand theory and formulated key postulates (Rapic 1991). Always striving to achieve overall logical coherence in his work, when he integrated central concepts from gestalt theory, he adapted them so that they would fit into his strict system of thought that separates the realms of Nature, Consciousness, and Culture (Smith 2007). Therefore, the key question Husserl tried to answer with regard to human vision is the same he asks in terms of perception per se: How can we determine the identity of an object over the course of separate, necessarily non-identical impressions (or "adumbrations") of it? For an answer, he points to our ability to move our body and its parts in order to gain different perspectives that are non-identical but intersecting, thus unravelling what becomes the 'essence' of our understanding of the object

(Drummond 1979). But in doing so, he imposes from the start that the seen object needs to be 'assembled' from separate 'bits' rather than accepting what is arguably the core of the gestalt-idea: that any single object is instead 'singled out' from an already given whole that is at least to some degree coherent in itself.

Husserl attends to the role of gestalts[23] in visual perception primarily in the lectures posthumously published as *Ding und Raum* or "Thing and Space" (1997). The view he develops in this relatively early work is not identical with his mature work and especially the *Ideen II* where he briefly mentions the gestalt as well (see Carman 1999 for a critique of the account of vision in the *Ideen II*), because he is still concerned with the empirical manifestations of the subject before fully embracing its transcendental character later on (Rapic 1991). Since the notion of the transcendental subject is inherently problematic from a sociological viewpoint (as, for example, Schutz has argued [Eberle 1984, 2010]) and since it is precisely Husserl's interpretation of empirical results that is of interest here, I will restrict my discussion to this work.[24] In *Thing and Space*, Husserl specifically emphasizes the role of the moving, "lived body" or *Leib* for the constitution of the visual field, which he characterizes as a perceived three-dimensional "space field" that has to be constituted on the basis of the two-dimensional "oculo-motor field" our senses provide (Husserl 1997, § 58). The general idea that our ways of moving and our ways of seeing are tightly intertwined is therefore already clearly present in his work—after all, the pragmatist thought of William James was an important inspiration and reference point for him (Smith 2007: 20), although he also sharply distanced himself from pragmatism by introducing the notion of conscious intentionality to conceptualize perception.

---

[23] Note that I am referring to the principle idea of the gestalt as sketched out above. Husserl does explicitly use the term *Gestalt*, but (with some exceptions where he seems to equate it to the terms *Figur* and *Form*) he uses it only to refer to the three-dimensional shape of an object as opposed to a two-dimensional shape which he calls *Figur*. Therefore, I regard both *Gestalt* and *Figur* to be instances of gestalt perception in my definition; and I primarily discuss Husserl's treatment of the 2D *Figur* because this is the case with regard to which Husserl discusses the role of eyeball movements in detail.

[24] In other words, although being problematic, the notion of the transcendental subject is not what is a issue with regard to vision and the body. One could also say: Should one bear the hope that if only we could somehow 'remedy' Husserl's arguments from his reliance on the transcendental subject, we would gain a perspective that can be aligned with the empirical findings of psychology and neuroscience or practice theory, then this hope would seem futile—at least if assessed on the basis of Husserl's own thought as presented here.

Husserl's (1997: 152) rectangle: "a rectangle resting in an arbitrary, resting environment".

Within the frame of this work, Husserl (1997: 149–153, § 51) explicitly discusses a problem central to the gestalt-movement: What happens when we look at a drawing of a simple figure, for example a rectangle?[25] Can one say that the whole of the gestalt 'imposes itself on us,' so that in the words of Merleau-Ponty (2002: 9) "this elementary perception is already charged with a meaning?" To answer the question, Husserl asks us to consider what happens when we see the rectangle. He holds that, as our focus wanders from one corner of the rectangle to the next in a sequence from a to d, we successively see four different preliminary figures or images he calls "pre-'empirical'": First, we see a line connecting two points, then two lines standing at an angle of 90°, and so forth. Husserl now asks how these different figures are connected, that is, why we focus them in this particular order.

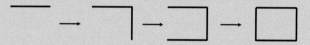

The sequential constitution of image appearance of the rectangle as accompanied by the kinaesthesia of our eyeball-movement according to Husserl (1997: 151).

In his answer, Husserl (1997: 152) to some extent follows gestalt-theory and argues that each of these figures "points to its neighbour" in that they are "directed at each other and through each other" so that they are "carrier of intentions which run through them." Here, his formulations come remarkably close to not only gestalt-theory, but even the language of contemporary practice theory: The figures Husserl characterizes in this way are, after all, *Bildeindrücke* or image appearances, and therefore they are neither physical nor logical forms, but *acts* of consciousness—it is the act of seeing the

---

[25] Husserl also extensively discusses the question of colour perception which was central to early gestalt-theory—and in doing so draws several problematic conclusions (see particularly Rang 1990: 318 ff.). I restrict my discussion largely to the question of eyeball movement because of the significance of bodily movement to practice theory and freeskiing, but similar arguments could be made in the case of colour synthesis.

figure that *carries* an intention, the act *directs* towards synthesizing the whole of the gestalt. In seeing the rectangle, Husserl postulates, each image appearance corresponds to a kinaesthetic appearance, that is, a perception of a corresponding bodily movement 'opening up' a specific sensual content. Reading only this passage, one might think that Husserl does indeed embrace an embodied notion of perception, an understanding of visual perception as a stream of acts which by virtue of their being the invocation of a coherent figure directly imply the consecutive movement of the eyes—figure, eye movement, and intention would intertwine.

But for Husserl, the connection between eyeball movement and coherent impression of the figure does not stem from any deep-rooted body schema as Merleau-Ponty would have it, but is instead a just *type*, "a formal unity of the sequences" (Husserl 1997: 154) which we employ to 'decipher' a given mass of sense data by apperception. In other words, for Husserl the rectangle must be composed from sides and corners rather than the other way around. Why? Husserl argues that the "kinaesthetic eye appearance" K (*Kinästhetische Augenempfindung;* 1973: 177) and the "image appearance" b (*Bildeindruck*) do not "fall together," that is, they cannot be meaningfully connected: What I see cannot induce how I move my body, for example how I move my eyeballs, because depending on the current situation, the same movement of the eyes can lead to very different visual data—e.g. looking to the left before and after I turn around. Therefore, it follows that for Husserl, K is to be understood as something *independent* from the environment: Moving my eyeballs from left to right yields always the same K, but it yields different image impressions depending on my position in space (Husserl 1997: 151). "To every position in the visual field" he writes "there corresponds a sensation of the position of the eye (…) and every visual line that the gaze runs over has a correspondence in a continuous kinaesthetic sequence." (1997: 144) For this reason, the relation of K and b is not one of "empirical relation of motivation" (1997: 149), but they are merely "phenomenologically related in a certain sense." (1997: 151) At the core, what Husserl implies is that the relation between K and b is one of expectation and confirmation: Because of our experience, we know that if we are to move in a certain way in relation to the object we are looking at (which will in turn result in the sentiment of a K), we will gain a different perspective on the object and thus a different b. For this reason, Husserl imposes an important differentiation in his discussion of the rectangle: He postulates that the kinaesthetic appearances themselves *do not* point to each other and do not carry intentions. Moving our gaze along a line, he would for example contend, does not in itself prompt us to continue the imaginary line any further. The reason for this lies in the specific definition of the kinaesthetic appearance Husserl builds on: For him, kinaesthesia has a twofold character in that it is not only a specific sensory impression of movement occurring in the respective "kinaesthetic system" (in this case the eyes), but it necessarily also contains a "moment of spontaneity," i.e. it is *always* simultaneously perceived by us as the result of an act of will—movement can only be experienced in the modus of "I move my body" (Mattens 2010). According to Husserl (1973: 282), our movement of the eyeballs in seeing the shape of a rectangle is, in other words, perceived by us as something we did, and for this reason he holds that kinaesthetic appearance and visual appearance do not have an "essential," but only a "functional" connection (1997: 144; see also Drummond 1979: 24).[26]

In my view, the postulate that eyeball-movement is always perceived as caused by the subject is a critical point in Husserl's account, and it leads towards a highly important question with regard to sociological theories of action which will be discussed in Chap. 8. At the core, what I want to suggest is that on the one hand, Husserl is right to note that what he calls kinaesthetic appearances K are of functional importance for visual perception; but on the other hand, that the terms he uses to define K are at least ambiguous, even misleading—his application of the notion confuses what I hold to be different things. To support this claim, let me first detail the correctness of the functional reason Husserl gives. His basic argument is that the visual system needs kinaesthetic appearances to discern whether it was us or the environment that has moved. In other words, this association between K and b is necessary, because if we move our eyeballs, our visual field moves as well, yet we do not attribute this change of the visual data to be caused by a movement of the objects themselves, but rather by our own movement (Husserl 1973: 176; Rang 1990: 77 fn64). Therefore, if our consciousness is to be the locus of such attributions as Husserl holds, even the most minimal eye movements must somehow feature in consciousness, and they must do so in a way that makes it possible to link them to the change in the visual field. In this regard, Husserl's theory is logically coherent, since this is precisely the role of the K defined as sensory data which are attributed be caused not by some external factor, but by what is the conscious

---

[26] It is important to note that Husserl does postulate a *functional* moment to be active in visual perception. At the core, I would argue that what phenomenology and practice theory share is a functionalistic view of visual perception in that both see the question of how intelligibility is possible as fundamental. And this is also the deeper reason why I suggest the philosophy of Schatzki and certain insights from evolutionary neurobiology go together quite well. In other words, the key difference between a gestalt-approach to vision and one grounded in Husserl is not the functional perspective per se, but rather the question how or where the functional element is located in the respective views. It would therefore be misleading to use functionalism as a label to denounce the practice-oriented perspective on perception and separate it, for example, from phenomenology based on Husserl.

'representation' of the body, the *Leib* or lived body.[27] But the problem is: Does this justify equating the K to appearances in the modus of "I can"?

The question Husserl answers with the notion of K—how we are able to discern seeing movement from our movement during seeing—still today ranks among the core questions in experimental neurosciences (Berthoz 2000). But the answers that we have today do not necessitate us to understand this problem as one solved by consciousness in Husserl's sense: While he holds that the movement sensations (the K) motivate the image appearances, today it can be said that bodily movements themselves fulfil this function (cf. Drummond 2009). Moreover, from the perspective I take here, it is highly problematic to treat the kinaesthetic sensations which eyeball movements supposedly cause as identical to the kinaesthesia of movements in general. Yet this is precisely the view not only manifest in certain misleading formulations of Husserl (see Mattens 2010), but more crucially also follows logically from the fact that he treats walking around a large object and moving one's eyeballs as essentially identical in terms of the relation of K and b that it yields (Husserl 1997: § 53). As part of this problematic generalization, he grounds his discussion of the role of eyeball movement for visual perception on the differences that results from holding the eyeballs (or the body) still as opposed to moving them. For example, Husserl (1997: 149) writes: "If now, with the K-location of the eye, have a certain partitioning of the image in the visual field, and I desire to have another one, (…) I know at immediately what movement of the eye I have to carry out."[28] By formulating in such ways, what Husserl originally portrayed as a sedimented, almost automatic process becomes easily equated with a motivation to act; and consequentially, what I identified as visual routines earlier can all too easily become characterized in ways such as this: "the percipient can activate the K-system." (Drummond 1979: 25).

But why does Husserl choose a terminology so close to action and volition when it would be sufficient to define that the K appear as non-random and attributable to the body? For an answer, one needs to consider the role of the eidetic reduction which Husserl took to be his primary method, and its relation to the notion of the horizon—another notion which Husserl shares with gestalt-theory buts uses in a very different manner. Husserl emphasized the role of the horizon in his later works (Rang 1990; Smith 2007: 290 f.), noting the importance of the potentiality that every meaningful

---

[27] Which is why Luhmann (1996b: 34) holds that Husserl's differentiation between noema and noesis is essentially a distinction between self-reference and other-reference.

[28] „Habe ich jetzt bei der K-Lage des Auges eine gewisse Bilderverteilung im visuellen Feld und will ich eine andere haben, (…) so weiß ich sofort, welche Augenbewegung ich auszuführen habe."

event implicitly contains—a potential, however, that can never be fully realized. Crucially, Husserl takes the horizon to be (nothing but) a manifold (*Mannigfaltigkeit*). In his view, a perception[29] opens up a horizon of possibilities of meaning, and this field of possible meanings corresponds to a set of perceptions that would fit into this field, in Husserl's (1991, § 135) words a "manifold of possible noetic events" which, despite being slightly different, would lead one to perceive the essentially same thing (the same "eidos"). A manifold, in other words, is mass of 'raw' (or hyletic) data which can *possibly* be interpreted as confirming the current conceptual view an observer holds. Therefore, the horizon does not order or direct the sequentiality of visual perception per se; but rather, it will be in need of being interpreted or ordered itself before it can contribute to the perceived validity of our experience. Such horizons of expectation, Husserl postulates in line with his general strive to build a general and systematic theory, are nothing endemic to embodied vision, but rather a subtype of what happens during perception in general: Especially in his later works, he equates the conscious acts of appresentation and apperception with the inner and outer horizon of an object (Eberle 1984: 23), so that whatever we do while using our vision becomes but one version of the prototypical process of epistemic recognition in general. Therefore, not only is Husserl's horizon not directional in itself, but moreover, it is also not a feature of the current situation and its gestalt, but instead something that the individual observer 'carries' by his virtue of being conscious, an expectation based on sedimented experience.

We can see now that from a practice perspective, the problem with Husserl's account of vision is that he insist on consciousness as the sole locus of any kind of synthesis of meaning, and in consequence his account is what one could call particularistic in that it treats the sensation of meaningful forms as always given in almost infinitesimally small and isolated particulars as well as pseudo-voluntaristic in that it treats all bodily movements as manifesting in consciousness exclusively in the modus of volitional action. One can thus conclude: Integrating the gestalt-notion into his model is not per se a problem for Husserl, it even supports his argument because it demonstrates the social predetermination of basic perception (and for this reason, Gurwitsch [1964] understands his work as a continuation rather than critique of Husserlian ideas). But when it comes to the question of *how* such patterns are carried and in which process the synthesis of the gestalt takes place, Husserl needs to insist on the uniqueness of consciousness as

---

[29] Precisely: the noematic sense in it.

the sole locus of intentionality and thus meaning-emergence.[30] For this reason, the movements of the eyeball need to be transposed or translated into representations in consciousness—and at this point arguably a 'translation error' occurs: The eidetic reduction of our conscious awareness of movements to one general type of kinaesthesia forces one to either systematically exclude the constitutive role of the saccades as "pre-empirical" and essentially meaningless, or to exaggerate them into wilful action.

Arguably, the consequences of Husserl's particularism of hyletic data and the separation of sensation and meaning synthesis have been most clearly spelled out by Niklas Luhmann (Luhmann 1995a, 1996b; Nassehi 2009). Put in his terms, the horizon refers to a range of possible meaningful ways of continuing the process of meaning-making. Luhmann (1996b) argues that if taken seriously, Husserl's duality of noesis and noema implies a strict separation of consciousness and world, and that these terms correspond to the concepts of self-reference and external reference as equally reflexive operations of closed meaning systems, including, but not limited to, consciousness. Therefore, Luhmann (1996) holds that his theory of systems of meaning strictly separate from each other is the logical consequence of Husserl's view that the same event has diverse properties in that it happens simultaneously within the separate "regions" of Nature, Consciousness, and Culture (see also Smith 2007: 161–168). But Luhmann is also very explicit about the role of the body with regard to meaning-making that results from such a conceptualization: Meaning remains restricted to the realm of consciousness and the social systems, but the body itself is a biological system not directly involved in the production of meaning (Fuchs 2005; Luhmann 1995a).

Essentially equating the kinaesthesia of eyeball and full body movement as a result of the urge to separate 'pure' consciousness from the

---

[30] More specifically, what is problematic about this insistence is that the inherent dualism it invokes leads to a persistence of a bipolar subject-object opposition that seems overly difficult to overcome. For example, Smith (2007: 306 f.) accuses Gurwitsch of postulating a "neo-phenomenalist model of noema" in which the different appearances of an object are considered as qualities of the object itself—the noema is thus a structural part of the intended object rather than the content of the act of intending. In my view, this critique is exemplary in that it contains a frequent misconception that arises from treating the *impression* that 'the' single observer confronts 'a' single object in general as proof of an unquestioned and implicitly presupposed duality of the two (cf. Carman 1999): For Smith, meaning can only be "in" acts of consciousness of the observer or "in" the observed, so that should someone deny the constituting role of the consciousness, we are left with the object as the sole carrier of intelligible meaning. But the option he does not take into account is to conceptualize what he calls acts not as purified acts of consciousness, but rather as *bodily* acts of which 'the' object (which is really an aspect of an object-world) is but one constituting part, like a high-heel is part of a contemporary Western 'elegantly feminine' way of walking.

'natural' body is, however, not the only part of Husserl's concept that has been exposed to criticism. Two further points need to be carved out. To this end, I will first compare Husserl's account to more contemporary findings about the physiology of eye movements during seeing geometrical figures; and second, I will refer to a critique stemming from within phenomenology, namely the points raised by Merleau-Ponty. Let me begin with the understanding of eyeball movement Husserl implies. In summary, one can conclude that although Husserl embraces some aspects of gestalt-thinking, his account differs in several important points from the notion that the synthesis of a visual field happens through visual routines which are applied according to their functional relevance in relation to the inherent organization of the field. Specifically, he transposes the empirical movements of the eyeball into instances of kinaesthesia (K) in consciousness, but these K differ in four important regards from the original conceptualization of concrete movements in gestalt-theory: First, K are independent of the environment (they are not situated nor part of a field) in that they are appearances I experience in the form of 'my body gives me this feeling.' Second, the K are occurring sequentially, but they are not in themselves inherently linked to one another (one K does not lead to the next). Third: Therefore, the actual eye movements are preconceived acts not invoked by the inherent order of the gestalt but motivated by consciousness. And fourth, it follows that the image-impression of seeing the full gestalt figure at once is seen as the result of a *recursive* synthesis of the independently given 'data points' performed by consciousness. In other words, Husserl does not embrace the understanding of the specific temporality of meaning arguably key to gestalt-thinking (namely, that the gestalt is prior and not successive to the unfolding perception).

As I have noted, it can be shown in experiments that the eyeballs can hardly be said to actually ever "rest" on an object and that quite to the contrary, our impression of a static stare is an effect of bodily motion itself rather than the sort of zero-condition Husserl takes it to be. What appears to us as a still image in fact results from a *process* of stabilizing an image on the retina during which the eyeballs do not remain absolutely immobile, but are constantly in slight motion, 'drifting off' and then 'jumping back' into a position that enables effective stimuli (Martinez-Conde/Macknik/Hubel 2004; Pritchard 1961). Moreover, restricting the discussion to eyeball movement seems somewhat arbitrary from a contemporary perspective, since the eye continuously performs a number of other movements as well, particularly those related to focusing the lens. In other words, Husserl develops his account of the stream of consciousness in precisely the opposite direction in which our visual system is found to work in more contemporary experiments: He begins with a still image and then discusses how it carries a horizon of possible perspectives on the same object which would confirm its identity. In the course of this, he holds that these appresentations are based on the subjective experience of seeing essentially identical objects which provided such perspectives after moving accordingly. His argument is that our conscious awareness of an object is thus composed in the modus of "I can" (I can move around and would see this kind of perspective) and the differences in perceptual data we associate with a specific movement in relation to an object are the crucial source of our knowledge about it. Yet, if one does not study the conscious impression, but instead observable visual routines, it becomes difficult to argue that the identity of an object is essentially a protention of movement and the according perceptual changes regarding the object. Whatever the phenomenological experience, the very stillness of the image itself is already based on 'purposeful' (non-random) bodily movement, and so is the identifying protention of movement, since it is defined as the difference between the current state of stillness and the anticipated new state of stillness after the movement. In other words, since the eyeballs are not still anyways, intending a specific K (the perception of a movement) alone is not sufficient to lead to a predefined shift in our field of vision and thus a specific or precise datum to be given to our senses.

One might object that Husserl (e.g. 1997: § 45) does leave room for minimal subconscious movement to exists without calling into question his concept, because he emphasizes that movement is only relevant if it is perceived and thus results in kinaesthesia—small distortions of our perception of something caused by minimal subconscious eye movement could potentially just be 'remedied' by consciousness as being insignificant adumbrations of the same thing, as Rapic (1991: XI) suggests. But on the other hand, as I have shown, eye movements are presented by Husserl as being crucial towards gaining a coherent understanding of something as being a thing in the first place—and these constitutional eyeball movements can be minimal in amplitude as well (for example if we figure out the small printed rectangle Husserl himself uses as an example). Indeed, there is a whole range of visual effects that are in constant need of remedy, and eye movements play a crucial role in doing so, including the blind spot in the centre of our visual field, the reflection of our own eyes on our retina, as well as several types of fading effects (Martinez-Conde/Macknik/Hubel 2004). Thus, if one suggests to stick to Husserl's account by acknowledging there might be certain non-random eye movements which help our vision but qualifies them as irrelevant to conscious perception because they are not accompanied by conscious kinaesthesia, then he would a) have already embraced at least a basic notion of bodily routines as constitutive for perception and b) would face the problem of discerning minimal movements accompanied by kinaesthesia from those featuring in consciousness only as meaningless distortions. On which grounds could one justify such a sharp distinction? After all, Husserl himself held that already minimal eye movements lead to a series of conscious acts according to his model: "the slightest oscillation of the eye already brings into play intention and fulfilment." (Husserl 1997: 87 fn3)[31] Thus at the very least, one might say that from the perspective of cognitive psychology and neuroscience, Husserl's account of eye movement as being essentially identical to moving the whole body becomes less plausible if applied to these myriad basal movements within the eye. As I will argue, this equation is even more problematic because eye movement and fixation are crucial prerequisites to our ability to move the whole body—shifting our gaze from left to right is not a homunculus of walking around an object, but instead a key part of it.

Let me now attend to the crucial 'other side' of vision: its phenomenology, and specifically the phenomenology of moving our body and the conscious availability of the kinaesthetic appearances K. Does it make sense to say that, for example, the impression of moving the eyeballs precisely horizontally by 30° is essentially always the same, but only yields different external images? Merleau-Ponty was arguably the phenomenologist to most outspokenly criticize this assumption (Carman 1999): He holds that a phenomenological study that is trying to unearth how we perceive our own gaze as a thing for itself is doomed to fail. Not only, he argues, are most scientific findings about vision gained in artificial contexts; but more importantly, trying to exercise an "attention to the pure visual" will lead the phenomenologist astray. Instead, his topic should be the "natural attitude of vision in which I make common cause with my gaze and, through it, surrender myself to the spectacle" (Merleau-Ponty 2002: 263). Not only is it the natural attitude that dominates our live, but moreover, the specific awareness of certain details of visual effects—such as the gestalt-switch vis-à-vis visual illusions—is only possible because and insofar as these situations *differ* from normal visual life. In the context of this general rejection of Husserl's attempt to isolate the essential moments of conscious acts (in the eidetic reduction), Merleau-Ponty (2002: 322–327) also discusses the constitution of visible space through eye movement. Although he does not explicitly refer to Husserl in this passage (but see Merleau-Ponty 2002: 53–57), it seems quite clear that he responds directly to his conceptualization. Quoting findings from gestalt-psychology but emphasizing that they are in need of a phenomenological framing, he outright rejects Husserl's assertion that we

---

[31] Notably, Husserl adds: "But the lightning flash in the middle of a stormy night?" and thus arguably points to a weak point of his assumption that the eye movements underlying visual recognition can be entirely traced back to intentionality: The flash might well illustrate his point that our vision is usually driven by certain expectations and we almost need to 'recover' if we are surprised by visual events and quickly need to make sense of them ex-post. But if so, where does the intentionality emerge from which 'motivate' the eye-movements that enable us to see the flash in the first place? The flash itself?

can be aware of our eyeball movement. Consequently, he denies that it is on the basis of kinaesthesia that, whenever a shift occurred in the visual field, we conclude whether we have moved in relation to the object or the object has moved in relation to us.

> *"In fact, this analysis is entirely artificial, and such as to conceal from us the real relationship between our body and the spectacle. When I let my gaze wander from one object to another, I am by no means aware of my eye as an object, as a globe set in an orbit (...). The figures of the alleged calculation are not given to me." (Merleau-Ponty 2002: 325).*[32]

Instead, Merleau-Ponty points out that our visual perception of movement is based on grasping the movement of different objects within our visual field *relative to each other* rather than relative to ourselves, something we do by focusing one aspect of the field (not necessarily a single object) and then discern movements in peripheral vision (Merleau-Ponty 2002: 325 f.). Crucially, he adds, it follows that visual fixation *precedes* any perception of movement and thus objects and space. But in natural settings, we cannot choose these "points of anchorage" at will, because "they do not present themselves directly to perception, they circumvent it and encompass it by a preconscious process, the results of which strike us as already made" (Merleau-Ponty 2002: 326). At the core, Merleau-Ponty argues that what gestalt-appearances demonstrate is that the content we perceive is not the result of an intentionality that is exclusively carried by a substance-less or even transcendental consciousness, but that instead:

> *"Beneath the intentionality of the act or thetic intentionality, and as its condition of possibility, we found an operative intentionality already at work prior to any thesis or any judgment, a 'logos of the aesthetic world.'" (Merleau-Ponty 2002: 490).*

What is manifest in this excerpt is how in Merleau-Ponty's philosophy, the routines of what is today called mid-level vision or visual cognition are embraced as a "sort of operant reason" of perception (Merleau-Ponty 2002: 57). And while these routines seem to stand as rather isolated mechanisms in cognitive neuroscience, Merleau-Ponty deducted deep-reaching consequences from their empirical existence, concluding that movement can only be perceived as happening between two objects and thus within a *field* given in the relation of a foreground and a background—and that our own lived body might be one of those objects given as an effect of the field. Bodily movement, in other words, becomes both a fundamental and preconscious prerequisite to perception and an important aspect of our phenomenology

---

[32] I made some slight adjustments to the English translation based on the German text (Merleau-Ponty 1974) in order to maintain what I consider the superior precision but also sharpness of critique of this version.

of being in the world. What saccadic eyeball movement effectively means, Merleau-Ponty concludes, is "that as long as we live we remain committed [literally: "engaged", N.W.], if not in a human setting, at least in a physical one" (2002: 326). Doing justice to Merleau-Ponty's multi-faceted phenomenological argument regarding movement will require a more detailed discussion, but even more importantly, it needs to be put into the particular context of movement called freeskiing. For now, one can conclude that in response to Husserl's engagement with gestalt-ideas, three notions become of key importance for developing a theory of phenopractices: First, the decisive shift that field-theories arguing with gestalts try to undertake can be understood as a redefinition of Husserl's notion of *intentionality*—an argument most explicitly made by Aaron Gurwitsch (1964). A second crucial area of interest emerged from gestalt-debates in questions about the form and quality of bodily *movement*, both in regard to their position within an ontology and their phenomenological character. And third, this question further points to the condition of *normality*—for example as a bodily state—which seems an essential grounding necessary to discern the two other notions. But in order to discuss possible answers to the complex question of how we experience movement, I suggest we should finally return back to the snow-covered cliffs of the Krimml, and get ready to move.

Chapter 4
Movement—The Phenomenal Field

1 Riding Down

"The thing is to move, to have your body moving through the elements" (Jean, pro freerider; [I])

My turn. Tom disappeared a few minutes ago, trailing a small cloud of fine snow crystals gleaming in the sun as he went. I waited for him to reappear into sight far down below, near the bottom of the wide bowl of the Krimml. It looked effortless yet energetic how he was speeding through the untouched white of the outrun, taking a very long turn to slowly lose the enormous momentum he had gathered in the steeper part of the slope. Smoothly, he came to a stop on the small dome where we had decided to meet up. Immediately, he turned around to eye the track he just left, and then watch us follow him down the face. I was second to drop, then Steffi would ride a line in the chute further to the left. I had completed most of my preparation routine earlier on; retightening the top buckles of my ski boots, checking the straps of the helmet and backpack, making sure the emergency release handle of my inflatable avalanche-airbag-system was not entangled and sat within easy reach on my left chest, selecting the right song on my MP3-player and starting it at the right moment so that my favourite part should kick in just as I would be gathering speed, zooming down into the steeper parts of the slope.

I look down at me once more—everything is in place (Fig. 4.1). I pull the upper end of my left glove with my right, making sure it is tight, then the right glove with my left. I look up and firmly grab the poles that were dangling from my wrists. I fixate a small rock further down that marks the entry into the chute I plan to speed through. When shooting video, freeskiers would now start counting down dramatically: "{Three… Two… One… Dropping!}" No need for that now, no one is around to hear me. I briefly stretch out my fingers once more, then clutch the grips of my poles again, a bit tighter this time. I click my poles together twice,

---

© The Author(s), under exclusive license to Springer-Verlag GmbH, DE, part of Springer Nature 2024
N. Woermann, *Seeing Style*, Beiträge zur Praxeologie / Contributions to Praxeology, https://doi.org/10.1007/978-3-662-69182-3_4

Fig. 4.1 Gathering focus just before dropping in. (This and the following are still images from a helmet cam worn by Tom [not me] during a run in the Krimml. They give an idea of the first-person view of freeriding in the Krimml to illustrate my description.)

Fig. 4.2 Dropping in. The steeper parts of the slope lie behind the rocks in the centre, the bottom of the bowl is barely visible in the background (in the shadow)

gathering focus. Tick. Tick. Here I come. I lean forward and push myself over the edge with both poles, making a slight skating step to gather momentum (Fig. 4.2). Off I go.

A slight, cold wind hits my face as I gather speed. My skis sink deep into the soft powder, disappearing below the perfect surface. Then they start to float; the ski tips reappear from under the snow, and I get this feeling of lightness. Traversing straight through the gentle slope, I wait until I gain additional speed, then I lean into a big turn to the right (Fig. 4.3). Oops, that was a bit too early. The turn ends up being much shorter than what I had wished for, since the edges cut deeper into the snow than I thought. I lost more speed than I intended to. I had told myself earlier that I should really aim for more speed this time, avoiding those slower, semi-short turns I still habitually tend to resort back to. (After all, it did take me enough time to learn them in the first place.) This is supposed to be freeriding. Let it run. "Speed is your friend," they say.

1 Riding Down

Fig. 4.3 The first turn

I briefly think how I must look a bit flimsy from down below, already putting the brakes on after barely having started. Yet while having this brief thought, I am already in the next turn that followed almost automatically after the first. For an advanced skier, taking a turn to stop is quite a different move from taking a normal turn which sends the body swinging over to the other side, thus leaning into the consecutive turn. It would be easy to fall into a rhythm of short turns now—but what I need are bigger turns, more speed. The slower my speed is in relation to the radius of my turns, the lesser the degree to which I can 'rely' on the soft snow to carry me safely and lean into it with the full weight of the body (see Loland 2007). Carving through wider turns at lesser speed feels a bit like balancing along on the edge of the turn.[1] It is hard to describe what I feel and do during the next turns, how I eventually manage to ski wider, longer, and faster turns. Maybe I can say: there is something like a voice-over to my ongoing skiing, one telling myself to produce bigger turns. While I keep myself in the routinized flow of riding down, there is something I try to achieve on top of it. The ongoing riding streams along as it should be, and I try to give it a certain twist as I work on to keep it going. Keeping balance and rhythm; making the movement flow from one turn into the next; sensing the right kind of resistance under my skis as I sink in not to deep to

---

[1] I cannot, of course, provide an extensive treatment of the physics of powder skiing (see Lind/ Sanders 2010). Briefly and technically speaking, I need to incline my skis as I take a turn and lean against the centrifugal force as in taking a turn on a bike. Leaning in too far in relation to the speed, I would fall inwards; standing too upright, I would fall outwards. But unlike on a bike, my speed and weight also push the skis into the powder snow, and while this is necessary to create a resistance to 'lean against', the skis also need to stay afloat or would otherwise stop me abruptly. Moreover, I am conducting an athletic practice, so keeping the balance is not just a question of finding the right angle of ski and body in relation to speed and radius, but much more importantly a question of how to bend my torso and how to hold my arms and knees, especially given that I do not just seek to keep the balance but ride my skis in a way that will allow me to deal with unpleasant surprises, e.g. unexpectedly hitting a stone hidden under the snow (see Loland 1992, 2007).

stay afloat, but deep enough to keep the 'grip'; my arms moving back and forth, poking one pole forward into the snow to initiate the next turn, then 'circumventing' it (as it feels) and then thrusting the other shoulder forward to lean firmly into the turn—these things are only at the periphery of what I am knowing and doing, if at all. I keep an eye on them, I might say, but I do not focus on any of them in particular, rather trying to keep them in proper place. They seem to be sensory conditions under which I am skiing; not events, but states. Themselves aggregated effects of an exorbitant number of details of movement and inclinations and pressure on limbs I could potentially sense individually, they flow together to form feelings of aspects going well or not so well. Some of these 'background-conditions' seem more general, such as keeping balance or rhythm, but they go hand-in-hand with those specific to powder skiing, such as 'pushing' through the apex of each turn with grip and control. What carries me down is an overall impression that I am doing fine; an impression that is composed, I would say, of several aspects that are *just about fine*, things I keep at bay and have an eye on, such as my balance. Together with the wind in my face, the sense of acceleration and my seeing that I approach the rock, these aspects form what my skiing is for me, a somewhat odd or indirect feeling of keeping myself in a state of riding, of having myself sent on the journey well.

For now, it works quite well. The turns become wider; I gather speed (Fig. 4.4). Yeah! I smile to myself; both because I am happy and because I know I can push myself to 'getting into it' by smiling and challenging myself, which in turn will make me perform better. Wohoo! I have almost reached the rock that serves as my landmark to the entrance of the chute I want to speed down. The chute opens up before my eyes as I draw nearer; steep and not too wide, yet filled with deep, soft powder. Gathering speed in a difficult and potentially dangerous terrain, I am now feeling a bit wary. A lot of things can go wrong. I am riding more or less at the edge of my abilities—of course, since this is why I can be proud afterwards. I know I am potentially getting myself into something here. This uneasiness (not outright fear, I would say) works against my ambitions to do it right this time, to get more speed, wider turns. Have confidence! It will be fine! I do not suggest I

Fig. 4.4 Balancing on the edge of a turn

1 Riding Down

Fig. 4.5 Shortly before entering the couloir that starts to the right of the windlip in the centre

am having some sort of complex inner dialogue at this point, but for all of what I remember, there are two sides to the experience: On the one, the uneasiness in the stomach and the routines of taking slower, safer turns being always on the verge of kicking in; and on the other, me 'reminding' myself to go for it, to trust today's good conditions, to follow the others in what they did only moments ago. And indeed, convincing myself that I am doing great, the music now pumping in my earplugs, I go for it.

I will, I think to myself, take two turns through the whole of the chute—not more. Coming in with a left turn, then one right there halfway down, then another slight left as I come out of it, and then I can speed just straight on and into the wide, gentle outrun of the slope (Fig. 4.5). In making this 'plan,' I am thus tricking myself into riding fast: taking just two turns in the narrow, steep chute means I will be going almost straight down. Once I am underway, I cannot just stop this process; if I begin with this speed and angle, there is no way I can just 'decide' to take it slower once I am halfway down. And this exactly why I do it, this is how I push myself to my personal edge—by withholding myself the opportunity of being 'flimsy' and taking it slow in the last second, because once I entered the chute in this way, the only safe way to get out of it is going fast and smooth. Speed is your friend.

I feel the acceleration as I dive down into the narrow tube, now focusing fully on the spot of my next turn (Fig. 4.6). I cut through it smoothly, going fast and faster, leaning directly into the next turn. Watch out for the slight compression at the lower end. Another wide turn to the right. The wind hisses through the straps of my helmet next to my ear. Stay nice and low now, push down firmly on both skis. Suddenly, a rock appears on my left, quite close to where I want to pass. I have hardly realized that I must not hit it and then—it is already behind me. I am in the outrun, zipping through the deep fluffy stuff. Just keep it running, you are already losing speed. A flash of euphoria as I realize that I did it. Nice {big turns} just like I should. I am smiling broadly as I cruise over to where Tom is standing. Yes! This is freeriding.

Fig. 4.6 Speeding down into the bowl; another skier's track joins from the right

2 The Paradox of Ethnographies of the Body

This account is, of course, a complete misrepresentation of what it means to ride a line in the Krimml. To be sure, I do not want to claim the experience is so grandiose that I do not find words for it, joining the chorus of heroic ballads praising the magic of being 'in the zone' that is being sung by big mountain skiers since the days of their 19th century Alpinist forefathers. But still, when I re-read my description, almost everything that was important about the moments of riding seems to be absent: The thin, crystal-clear air I breathe, the bright sunlight flooding the immense scenery, the whole strange banality and joyful stress of skiing, and, most important: The sight, the feeling of being-here and looking-at and about-to-ski-this-thing-just-now. The vividness and importance of my vision can hardly be understated. Consider this quote from Glen Plake, an icon of the ski movies from the 'early days' in the nineties that pioneered contemporary Newschool freeskiing:

> "I am not an adrenaline junkie. I have a respect for visions. I have a desire to visualize something and put it into my body and make it work." (cit. in: Kerig 2008a: 181)

Indeed, this is the key aspect of my own experience that I struggle to convey: How it feels to look at something and then 'put it into my body and make it work.' The images I inserted into the text above cannot quite represent these impressions, as they merely share some of the content I saw when getting into taking the turns. That images as much as texts are insufficient to convey the totality of a subjective experience is of course common-sense within the ethnographic research tradition today. But besides this incompleteness of representation, I want to point out that there is something else that is also lost in an ethnographic text: the structure of the experience, the hierarchy of its layers. Particularly, what is missing from my description is the dominance the visual gains during the skiing—and the extent to which remembering the skiing equates to visualizing what I think I saw as I went down. Pushing aside vision, the brief moments I described as 'telling myself something' move to the foreground without necessarily belonging there, because they are so much easier to convert into written words. In my recollections of riding, the images I saw dominate, punctuated by things I 'told' myself. Conversely, the most crucial aspect of achieving skiing is mostly reduced to a slight background hum to the experience: the body. Therefore, an ethnography of skiing is confronted with a paradox: Technically or physically, it is clear that bodily movements are essential to freeskiing; yet my bodily experiences seem somewhat blurred and indirect to me. In this chapter, I will try to frame this paradoxical rift and develop a clearer perspective on the intelligibility of the body within a practice view, both in terms of the theory per se and in terms of the methodological implications that follow from it. In theoretical terms, the issue at stake is to explain how practical understanding is possible with regard to the body: How do we know that we do what we do, and how do we know what we can do? Answering this question will also prepare a discussion of understanding in general from a practice perspective which can be found in the following chapter. I should note that, in the phenopractical perspective I suggest, the issue of practical understanding is considered separately from what is termed practical intelligibility, i.e., what makes sense for a practitioner to do—or put in more familiar terms: choosing paths of action. Since both practical understanding and practical intelligibility coalesce in the unfolding of a practice into praxis, however, some issues of practical intelligibility will be foreshadowed in this part of the work as well.

3 Achieving Amalgamation

In my discussion of the minute details of human vision in the third chapter, I described vision as a Janus-faced process that entails both bodily workings—especially movements—and phenomenological occurrences or perceptions. I noted how both movement and perception are intertwined and co-constitutive, but by no means synchronic or strictly coupled, because many (minimal) movements go unnoticed. For example, visual attention (the current eye fixation) and conscious attention can diverge to an important degree. While I hope I was able to convey some important insights on the organization of the visual field and eye-movements that underlie conscious visual perception, my account did not provide the full picture of the complex relation of vision and movement because both micro-movements like saccades and the routines of so-called visual cognition happen almost entirely below the radar of conscious attention. Riding down a line in the Krimml, however, yields a different picture: by no means is this form of bodily movement confined to 'subconscious' or rather preconscious,[2] 'pre-cognitive' routines.

---

[2] I adapt the term 'preconscious' from Merleau-Ponty (2002). While I will use it somewhat interchangeably to the term subconscious, I prefer the former term because a) it avoids associations with the Freudian unconscious and especially what I consider rather speculative theorizing about

Instead, body movement itself not only can be a conscious experience—sometimes exhilarating, sometimes mundane—, but rather, it must be consciously perceived so that it can be 'steered' by the practitioner. One can, in other words, discern three levels or modi of relevance of bodily movement for conscious (visual) perception: a) as a background routine carrying perception; b) as a 'topic' of consciousness; and c) as a perception that functions as a pragmatic resource in the course of conducting a practice.

However, in my discussion of visual routines, I also cautioned against what I called the monism of theories of visual perception that try to reduce vision to a single or singularly dominant process or domain such as consciousness or situational order. I then commended the practice perspective as an alternative able to integrate different findings about vision, for example from experimental vision science and phenomenology. The empirical underpinning of this effort to broaden the scope beyond the borders of subjective consciousness and draw on somewhat diverse theoretical sources is to be found in the nature of the experience I just described. The experience of riding is, I argue, not simply manifold—composed of various different elements—but *polyvalent*—serving several causes simultaneously. For example, the proprioception of riding through deep powder is both a source of great joy and provides the crucial clues towards simply staying alive and well during this dangerous endeavour. The polyvalence of experience thus points to the fact that the sensory 'scape' enwrapping me is not just a complex cacophony of details, but necessarily already in order, oriented towards certain practical demands. For this reason, I suggest that any sensible account of vision-in-movement (and the visual dimension of practices more generally) needs to be grounded in an adequate understanding of the phenomenology of bodily movement in which vision is embedded. Therefore, before vision itself will move back into the limelight, this chapter undertakes to develop a theoretical account that can capture the specific nature of the experience of bodily movement. On the one hand, skiing down a steep slope is a fragile and complex arrangement of bodily movements and reactions, sensory processes and adaptations, technological workings and physical events; and on the other, it represents itself to me somewhat fuzzily and indirect, but all in all as a working *whole*, as one 'thing': skiing. The specific form of movement on skis requires a continuous adaption to ever-changing circumstances, and much of the micro-adaption happens subconsciously and in ongoing cooperation with a multi-sensuous observation of and focus on the current environment. Therefore, even scientists trying to model and measure so-called biomechanics of

---

the 'social unconscious'; and b) since talking about something unconscious always yields the question by virtue of what someone has at some point become aware of, and thus conscious about, it while at the same time being entitled to considered it inherently fenced off from all consciousness. More to the point, we do at some point consciously realize more or less all the bodily movements that express the preconscious processes I am interested in—which is why I can discuss them in an ethnographic study.

skiing to define 'optimal' techniques have been forced to conclude that achieving the 'correct' interplay of the different kinetic aspects crucially depends on bodily rhythm and, in the end, the phenomenology of the skiing body (see for the phenomenology of skiing Loland 1992, 2009). Reacting smoothly to losing critical grip under one ski can become routinized as a normal ability that all but disappears among the manifold impressions that the complex coordinated movements of the body during freeriding create. The established practices of skiing (as well as practices of learning skiing) are thus not only ways of handling the body and the ski equipment, but also ways of purposefully managing or directing sensual perception, focusing on key components and avoiding inhibiting distractions. For this reason, I argue, the notion of the gestalt is crucial to the perspective I suggest, because it not only expresses the inherent directedness of the organisation of experience, but also offers a concept to grasp the form of this organization as a background-foreground relation. Being able to do something as complex as powder skiing, in other words, seems only possible because I only need to be dimly aware of much of what is happening during skiing but without it being entirely impenetrable either. Should I fall, for example, I would 'lose my balance' and usually recall it as such, thus referring to a certain state that vanished in an unfortunate accumulation of non-descript details, and would usually not actually know that I was leaning a little too far to the left and not raising the right arms sufficiently to counterbalance—but as I will show, I can work out what needs to be done better on the basis of knowing that what I lost was my balance. Thus, instead of understanding myself to be undertaking an enormous number of parallel processes and functions, I am doing a single thing: a practice. It is in this sense that I frequently apply the term 'in conduct of a practice,' since *conductus* means "what has been brought together" in Latin.[3]

Grasping the fragile act of freeriding from the viewpoint of the practitioners therefore demonstrates that theories of social practices should not be misunderstood as disregarding the subjective viewpoint of the social actor (I will return to this important point). Instead, the notion of social practices describes a fundamental necessity for anyone willing to do something (including things not as daredevil as extreme skiing): That he or she can count on the fact that first, all in all 'things will work'—a huge number of things, to be precise—and second, that they will do so without the need to take care of or even notice them in detail. Accomplishing a practice means to throw oneself into a highly complex process, an interplay of many interrelated particularities and dynamics that cannot and must not be present to one in detail all at the same time—but still must somehow be available as a whole that one can know and steer. What I will call the amalgamation of numerous

---

[3] With a precision lacking the English language one could define in Latin what I will call amalgamation as *conducens cuducturus* or "being in the process of bringing together what is going to having been intended to be brought together."

aspects[4] into one single practice, in other words, is not some unfortunate mishap hindering the diligent work of the student of a practice (be it for the sake of learning or science), but instead a fundamental prerequisite to accomplishing anything. For it is only in the format of the 'block' of a practice that the almost countless particulars of every doing can be treated as intelligible, i.e. as perceivable and manageable. Amalgamation, I should emphasize, does not describe a phenomenological process or effect but an *ontological* quality of phenopractices themselves. The argument which I will develop is not about, for example, multisensory convergence as an accomplishment of consciousness, kneading together various sensory ingredients poured in from above into the bowl that is the subject. As I noted, I will attempt to discern the relation of bodily movement and perception, and the starting point for this attempt is the diagnosis that movement is part of the amalgam of practice, essentially indivisibly interwoven with and knitted together by micro-routines, physical effects, spatial orderings, and more. The specific experience a practitioner has—or rather, the practitioner which the experience produced by a practice has—is therefore by me considered to be multifaceted; because it is an effect of amalgamation rather than being a domain of synthesis of isolated details delivered by different senses. To reiterate this point: I want to argue that the amalgamation of what are commonly regarded different entities such as the body, material tools, or emotions into mere aspects of a practice is a general and pervasive condition of social order carried by situated practices. As I will detail below, the amalgam describes an ontological feature of practices, an ordered hanging-together of elements some of which are necessarily physical, material, or biological. It does not describe the emergence of meaning in an abstract domain.

This understanding yields important consequences for any sociological attempt to analyse social order as an unfolding of polyvalent and partly 'material' phenopractices. Particularly, it implies that bodily routines or sensory organs cannot be seen as particulars working in isolation which is in turn the reason why consciousness is no longer considered the sole locus of synthesis of sensory data and, effectively, meaning. For example, when studying bodily conduct such as skiing from such a phenopractice-perspective, it seems almost impossible to differentiate between the parts of the body engaged in sensing at any certain time. If, during a turn the edge of left ski is almost losing its grip on the slope, forcing the skier to

---

[4] My use of the term 'aspect' is loosely rooted in Wittgenstein's discussion of aspect perception or Seeing-As. Like in the cases of 'background/foreground' and 'figure,' however, I use it to refer to general phenomena that occur beyond the realm of vision, while Wittgenstein discussed aspects only as a visual phenomenon. Note that for Wittgenstein, not all seeing is a case of Seeing As in that perceiving aspects is a specific, non-ubiquitous form or modus of seeing (Gebauer 2009: 208–215; Glock 2010a). Likewise, I do not suggest that aspects of an amalgam appear in the phenomenal field all the time or necessarily, or that all aspects of an amalgam must appear at all. As I will discuss in Chap. 3, the appearance of aspects is a phenomenon of finite duration (like Wittgenstein's aspect seeing) and is best described as an act of sublation in Hegel's sense.

react quickly in order not to fall: Does the left foot recognize that? Or is it rather the skin on the sole of the foot? The left leg? The hip? The vestibulum in our inner ear where our apparatus of balance 'resides'? The nerves that make all these attributions possible? The frontal cortex where the 'information' is processed so that a perception of slipping can arise? The same is true for a study of embodied vision, because it is necessarily a study of eyes-in-use within a body. As much as all body 'parts' (which can only really be parts during an autopsy) are naturally understood as interconnected and working together within one body in our everyday understanding and conduct,[5] as much seems the eye to be one—if especially capable—instance *within* a working whole.[6] Even the most minute steps of visual perception (the saccades) happen in concert with the other senses such as the tactile abilities of the body or hearing (Walker/Doyle 2003). If, for example, neuroscientists emphasize that "multisensory convergence is the rule" (Berthoz 2000: 59), they refer to visceral processes happening within the sensory organs themselves rather than a mental, ex-post "fusion of content." This is especially true in situations of swift movement, when visual and vestibular information are used concurrently to determine the speed, direction, position, and posture of the body (Berthoz 2000: 66)—for example in freeriding. Contrary to the neuroscientists' somewhat idealistic portrait of the body as highly functional problem-solving apparatus, however, the cooperation of senses is not exclusively of beneficial character. For example, for many novice skiers, ski edges screeching over ice patches in a slope are one of the most feared impressions because they impose the fear of falling—to the point that the unnerving screeching sound seems to become an obstacle in itself when they try to master icy slopes. In other words, it is not only difficult to ascribe certain successful practical accomplishments to singular bodily functions, but it is also difficult to single out failure or problems of single functions—let alone discern if there might be a 'suboptimal' performance on behalf of one body part cancelled out by the 'superoptimal' of another. Given this predicament, on which grounds can a detailed study of vision as a phenopractice, and therefore as a bodily practice, be undertaken? How to get hold of bodily states and processes? And, most importantly: If one is to undertake an ethnography of vision as a situated, bodily practice, precisely what is the object of enquiry? How can I conceptualize

---

[5] Annemarie Mol (2002) demonstrates forcefully how the seemingly singular body is in fact situationally enacted in multiple ways, and thus could be termed a "body multiple". Consequently, in her view, the body-whole as the corpus and locus of a singular person on the one, and a specific body part as the focal point of a medical examination on the other hand, are principally only "enacted side-by-side" (2002: 149)—and only on this basis further forms of inclusion and interference of parts and the whole can be enacted or negotiated. The notion of enactment Mol develops comes very close to the phenopractice perspective taken up in this work (see also Chap. 5 for a discussion of her work).

[6] The 'holistic' understanding of perception as something achieved by all sense simultaneously (merged in the perceiving body) was an important foundation for Gibson's 'ecological theory of perception' that was discussed in Chap. 2 (see Carman 1999: 221).

practices in such a way that the result is neither an ethnography of the body nor of situations (or situational order), but phenopractices per se? In the remainder of this chapter, I will try to sketch out my understanding of the relation of perception and the body in order to develop such a concept of social practises.

4 Sensing the Dys-Appearing Body

The suggestion that my body is—like everything else—tightly baked into an amalgam I call practice seems somewhat counter-intuitive in light of our everyday experience of the body as an independent entity roaming about the world. Therefore, I will begin my re-assessment of the body-in-practice with a closer look at the phenomenology of the moving body as a physiognomic thing and use it as a basis to develop my understanding of the relation of movement and perception. Reflecting on my experience of the body during riding the Krimml, the first and most basic feature is the *absence* of most of its details and the myriad functions it fulfils during the ride. I do not feel the pressure on my knees, I do not realize how I spread out my arms and turn my torso to keep my balance, and I am not aware how I press my toes into the soft foam of the ski boots in order to control the direction of the tips of my skis—or rather, I am not *specifically* aware of all those things. What I *do* know is how 'it' feels to ski, how it feels to get a turn just right, or how it feels if my skis almost lose the grip and I nearly crash. Although my body is doing the actual work, I perceive its functions more like the familiar background noise in my office: If I pay too much attention, then this will keep me from doing my intended work, but fortunately I also do not need to, because if something uncommon should happen, I will usually realize it just from casually overhearing it. If the pressure on my knee gets almost overwhelming, if the flailing of my arms threatens to harm the smoothness of my ride, or if my toes start to hurt from clinging desperately into the inner boot, I will realize this consciously and react. In his phenomenological discussion of "the absent body," Drew Leder (1990) notes how the body "disappears" within successful routines, but can reappear as the dysfunctional and thus "dys-appearing" body in problematic situations. Applying Heidegger's (1962: 98 f.) differentiation between tools that are usually *zuhanden* (ready-to-hand) and thus there to use, and broken tools which are only *vorhanden* (present-at-hand) or merely present, Leder argues that our actions are usually embedded into an experience of a body that does not need much attention because it is always ready-to-hand.[7] This, however, changes as soon as the body

---

[7] It seems important to note that Leder makes an argument concerning the similarity of the phenomenology of tool and body which I share. Despite Leder's (1990: 33) assurance to the contrary, I would, however, argue that the ontological argument which Heidegger makes about tools frames them as fundamentally distinct from the body. Heidegger (1962: 97) applies the distinction of *vorhanden* and *zuhanden* in his discussion of the pragmatic character of *Zeug* (loosely

4 Sensing the Dys-Appearing Body

does not fulfil our high expectations: "At moments of breakdown I experience *to* my body, not simply *from* it." (Leder 1990: 83 f.) The hurt or hindered body now moves back into the foreground, demanding attention and blocking out other things. The muted perception of my body is thus a necessary if not essential part of the routine of riding, because it allows me to take on other complex tasks such as seeing my route. However, whenever some aspects of my body experience do take centre stage, this routine is broken.

If I do experience problems within my riding, I often react by silently telling myself do this or that as a response, and sometimes this practice of telling myself actually results in me physically whispering short commands to myself, for example to ride more upright and lean properly into the initial phase of the next turn. Yet, as much as the normal routine of riding, such 'states of emergency' remain fundamentally inaccessible to me. Simply being willing not to lose grip or balance does not help much, but rather this would only lead me to being tense and stressed which does not contribute towards riding better at all. Within actual riding, my 'control' of my body and my equipment necessarily consists of various 'ways-of-making-myself-doing-it-right' combined with various 'ways-of-letting-myself-know-that-I-am-doing-it-right' that I need to achieve as situational accomplishments each time anew.[8] For example, I have learned that by riding more upright and bending my knees further, I will gain a better balance and develop more appropriate pressure on the balls of my foot—to be precise, this is the technical explanation I have come to know during my formalized training as a ski instructor. In other words, I try to affect the inner workings of my riding body indirectly through what one could call 'access points' of bodily practice—Arnold Gehlen (1988: 176) develops a similar notion of *Knotenpunkte* or crucial points (see Chap. 7).

This way of dealing with the constant imperfection of my movements hints towards another form in which aspects of my body can 're-appear' apart from their 'dys-appearing' when something goes wrong: exercises. Learning skiing consists primarily of two types of practices: 'Just' riding and thus learning-by-doing on the one hand, and specific training exercises on the other. Many, if not all of these exercises, I would argue, have the purpose of making a specific bodily mechanism

---

translatable as equipment or tools) and the specific form of *Dasein* or being-in-the-world it evokes (see H. L. Dreyfus 1991; Luckner 2008), but for him the body is in contrast necessarily a given part of our *Dasein*—it is always already there. He specifically writes: "So one cannot think of [Being-in] as the Being-present-at-hand of some corporeal Thing (such as the human body) 'in' an entity which is present-at-hand." (Heidegger 1962: 79) Not the least, the very notion of being ready-to-hand uses the hand itself as the reference point for this state of being, so that a hand cannot really itself be ready-to-hand.

[8] The experiences I describe are, of course, heavily influenced by the fragile nature of the practice of freeriding, or rather by the nature of me riding as fast and as steeply as I can just about handle. As a theoretical argument I would uphold this understanding for the practice of everyday walking-down-the-street as well, but its phenomenological gestalt is obviously very different.

become present to the skier and thus manageable for him in some way—with the former being a crucial prerequisite to the latter. One particularly apt example[9] is an exercise that I often used to great success when teaching skiing as a professional instructor. The purpose of this exercise is to improve the bodily position of the skier through making him or her rotate his torso towards the valley (or the outward ski) during turning. This is practiced by tying two ski poles to the hips of the ski student so that they run parallel to the shoulders. Notably, these poles by no means provide a mechanical help to perform the rotation; they only signal the respective angle of the hip. With their help, the ski students can *see* how they rotate their torso during skiing by observing the pole ends extending from their body to the left and right. Once they can continuously see the angle of the torso, the ski students usually improve their movements rapidly. The exercise therefore works because it is able to produce what Larissa Schindler (2009, 2010, 2011) calls *vis-ability*: The students develop a visual way of knowing whether they are doing skiing the way they should be doing it *while* they do it, and only now they can learn to know what it feels like doing it right.[10] Teaching and learning skiing, the example illustrates, happens through carefully arranged phenopractices, that is, exercises designed to make accessible a particular embodied experience aligned with motor routines.

To be sure: This exercise of making visible hip rotation is alien to the freeskiing culture, since it lacks the elegance, playfulness, and individual freedom the freeskiers search for. Therefore, they *purposefully* rob themselves of the useful effects of certain exercises—they even do not simply ignore them, but their ignorance towards organized training settings is actually part of their cherished cultural ethos. It will be necessary to postpone an answer to the question of why this happens. For now, one will have to do with the observation that learning about your body and thus learning skiing is not the exclusive domain of formalized exercises. Instead, in the case of freeriding it almost exclusively happens via "just riding." Yet what I want to argue is that the principle through which said learning happens is in essence the same as in the exercise I described. On the one hand, because—as I will show—the playful "cruising around" of the freeriders does nevertheless contain a number of aspects of more formal training. And on the other, because

---

[9] Formal exercises are just one possible way of spreading knowledge nested within specific ways of bodily routines. Larissa Schindler (2009, 2010) has conducted an extensive study exclusively concerned with this question.

[10] Note how the verbal rule ("Keep the poles attached to your torso at a 90° angle to your skis throughout the turn.") does not actually provide a precise program to memorize and follow. Instead, the students need to first start skiing and only then can check the conformity of the outcome with the rule; and thus they begin to correct their way of moving so that what they see will start to fit the rule. This specific practice of seeing thus provides a very apt example of Wittgenstein's understanding of rule-following (see Chap. 7) or Garfinkel's (2002) notion of instructed action as a situated, reflexive observation-and-correction of oneself towards the aim of being able to present one's own doing as a doing that fits the description the rule has given—a reflexive production of the validity of rules.

more fundamentally, all forms of formal or informal, more or less scripted forms of skiing enforce continuous observation, variation, and adaption of movements and thus shape or train one's ways of skiing in some aspects regardless of the type of situation. Therefore, considering the exemplary exercise I described provides a useful empirical step-stone to the argument that the state and doings of our body are neither just accessible to us, nor are they inaccessible per se. Instead, the type and range of our body perceptions are a quality of our bodily practices: What and how much we can sense depends on the phenopractice in question in that certain aspects of our body usually 'stick out' within a certain practice—pending, of course, certain particularities of the concrete situation. In order to become better 'riders' or rather 'helmsmen-passengers' of our bodies, we systematically make use of these variations in the phenomenological landscape of bodily practices, working[11] on certain highlighted bodily aspects at a time, while others remain in their muted routine. In the example of the exercise I described, bending the knees and positioning the skis still needs to be done properly and simultaneously to keep skiing, yet the student cannot pay much attention to it. In other words, learning how to move in a particular way and environment happens through a succession of 'spotting' a 'cause' of a 'problem,' paying attention to that particular area and managing the 'source' of the 'problem' appropriately—only that all of these need to be aspects of multi-modal practices happening in real time. The example of the ski-school exercise is therefore instructive because it shows how this form of training relies on a didactic setting that combines material (ski-poles), spatial (groomed, empty, not too steep piste), social (instructor-student relation), visual ('sticking out' of ski poles), linguistic (useful instructions), and various other resources in order to relatively reliably reproduce the intended 'feel'—a specific formation of experiences typical for this practices for which I will propose to use the term phenomenal field.

5 The Phenomenal Field of Practices

The notion *phenomenal field* was introduced by Merleau-Ponty (2002) in the context of his criticism of what he termed empiricists and intellectualist concepts of perception; with both the critique and the term being adoptions from Gurwitsch's (1964) earlier work "The field of consciousness." Pointing to the fundamental role of bodily movement for perception, the phenomenal field denotes a key "dimension of our bodily embeddedness in a perceptually coherent environment" (Carman 2005: 51). As I discussed in the last chapter, the term 'phenomenal field' is therefore applied as a generalization of certain properties of human

---

[11] When I use the terms *work* or *working* I refer to the ethnomethodological understanding of work as a situated accomplishment rather than a mechanistic procedure (Garfinkel 1986, 2002).

visual fields that were encountered by experimental Gestalt psychology and then adapted philosophically. Consequently, what Merleau-Ponty seeks to express is not only that all perception is embedded into a context, but moreover that this context is organized as a field of coherence, that it can serve as a background which foregrounds a specific form or gestalt to be seen. It is in this sense that I will make use of the term phenomenal field in phenopractice theory. On a basic level, I simply seek to express the idea that every practice turns a 'phenomenal face' towards the practitioner engaged in the practice and that this 'face' (which is also an interface) is a central quality of this practice. Of course, such a definition immediately calls forth a series of pressing questions about the specific nature of such a phenomenal field, the process of its constitution, and specifically the role of the body and consciousness in it. These complex issues will need to be dealt with step by step and in the context of my empirical material. I need to point out that in doing so, I will in important ways deviate from the phenomenological thought of Merleau-Ponty (2002), so that my use of the term 'phenomenal field' cannot necessarily be equated to his. For now, it should suffice to say that I apply it in a somewhat narrow sense, as simply denoting a totality of perceptions given to a practitioner in the course of unfolding a particular practice. For the cause of terminological precision, I should add that by defining the phenomenal field to be a feature of a practice, I do not imply that all of the 'meaningful content' of an instance of concrete praxis should be considered as either carried by or definitive for the phenomenal field of a practice currently unfolding. Furthermore, it should be noted that in my terms, the phenomenal field is neither the temporal or spatial place where a (pheno-)practice unfolds, nor is it what Schatzki (2002) calls the site of the social, but instead an *effect* of the unfolding of a practice in concrete praxis, and therefore it is what I will call the "normal" experiential scape a practitioner encounters vis-à-vis the practice.[12] Recalling my account of the visual field should help to sketch out some basic features of phenomenal fields: Although the visual field is given to us as a totality, as containing 'all there is to see' at this moment from this perspective, it is the result of bodily processes (which do not necessarily, however, start from 'nothing' or chaos and only eventually assemble 'something'). As such, every element of the field gains meaning in relation to the other particulars—a quality which extends to its very virtue of being a particular entity in that it depends on the overall field whether a detail will stand out or is conflated with other details. Therefore, the phenomenal field is both ordered, contingent, and multi-modal. Moreover, everything we find in a visual field can be subjected to closer inspection; we can (usually) step closer and see its details. As I noted in the last chapter, both Husserl and Merleau-Ponty use the term horizon to capture this 'unfold-ability' of things perceived; but while Husserl describes the horizon as a manifold of possible meaning invoked by the intentionality of consciousness (as a protention), Merleau-Ponty portrayed the horizon as part of

---

[12] See Schatzki's (2002: 143–147) corresponding remarks on sites versus fields.

5 The Phenomenal Field of Practices

the physical world to be explored via bodily movement and thus carried at least in part by unconscious motor intentionality (Protevi 1998). I believe that two different issues are at stake here: Endorsing Luhmann (1995a: 74–77), I think that by abstract definition meaning can be described to carry a "horizon of potentialities" within its actuality, a corona of things co-noted and paths not (yet) taken. The fact that phenomenal fields contain things that can be 'followed up,' however, is a more specific case. Building on the notion of affordances introduced in chapter one, I will speak of *phenomenological affordances* to describe possibilities or 'invitations' to perceive that exist (not just hypothetically) for the practitioner within a phenopractice and which can therefore orient his further conduct.[13] As a set of phenomenological affordances, the content of a phenomenal field is always given as a mutually constituent foreground-background relation, as instances of blending in and standing out. To be clear: In this use of the term phenomenal field, entities that would be 'generally' or 'physically' regarded as perceivable are *not* necessarily considered a part of the field, since I hold that one core reason for the ubiquity and totality of social practices is the need for reduction of complexity (in a Luhmannian sense) of the enormous avalanche of particulars towards a range of perceivables that can be normally handled within that practice. As I will detail below, the workings of human vision are a case in point, as the visual system can only focus a small section of the visual field at a time (an even smaller fraction of what a person could see when moving his head and looking into every direction), just like a sentence can only include so many meaningful points at a time. The phenomenal field of a practice thus contains considerably less than the totality of the perceivables of that situation (howsoever that totality could be ascertained), but possibly more than what a single individual perceives in a concrete unfolding.

Until now, not much has been said about the *relation* of phenomenal field and practice. Therefore, a fundamental question is left unanswered: What and how can we (as practitioners) know about practices in the first place? What can a phenomenal field tell us about the practice it is an effect of? I have thus far argued that the overlapping, intertwining, and polyvalence of different aspects of my experience

---

[13] Note that I am following Gibson's (1986) original conception of an affordance as a potential for action which is both perceivable and feasible for the particular actor in question. This original conception differs from its later 'phenomenological' reinterpretation which contrasts "perceived" and "real affordances." A phenomenological affordance in my sense it therefore necessarily never 'hidden' and always 'actionable'; it is a potential to further unfold the current and concrete bodily experience that is carried by the particulars of the practice itself (rather than subjective consciousness). This notion is thus directly related to my notion that particulars have duration, which I will detail below. Phrased in Schatzki's (2002: 44) terms, phenomenological affordances are part of the prefigurations which practices invoke rather than being part of (practical) understandings held by practitioners. Therefore, this concept is effectively the application of his claim that practical understandings alone do not determine action to the case of practices of perception (see Schatzki 1996: 169–167, 1997).

are not the result of an (ex-post) synthesis undertaken by consciousness, but instead evidence of a prior and unavoidable amalgamation of different aspects within each practice; and furthermore, that practitioners' experiences are an effect of the phenomenal field of practices. My account so far might seem somewhat misleading in this regard: Am I, the reader might ask, not simply inserting the phenomenal field in between practitioner and practice, thus creating a pseudo-phenomenological no man's land neither conscious nor material? I do not. Which is why I speak of the phenomenal rather than phenomenological field, I might add. The phenomenal field is a feature of a practice in that the unfolding of said practice creates a figure-background coherence invoking certain experiences (n.b.: synthesized experiences rather than punctuations of sense-data) for the conducting practitioner. In a very specific way, phenopractice theory is therefore indeed a 'direct' theory of perception in the sense of Gibson (1986), as no self-referential process happens 'in-between' the perceived entity such as a red ball, and the sense impression of the red ball—*but* only in the sense that a) perceiving as a concept, and b) the ball as a physical object, and c) red as an understanding, and d) various bodily routines, and e) 'ecological' factors such as light conditions are considered as *organized features* of a 'constellation'[14] or what Schatzki (2002) calls a site. Instead of presuming the ontological existence of two super-temporal entities (the ball and the 'perceiver') and then conceptualizing perception as a temporal process happening 'between' them, I treat all of the above as features of one enduring coherence. Again, this definition is linked to the distinction between practices as entities and praxis as their temporal unfolding. For now, the key conclusion is that questions about properties of the phenomenal field—for example, what the field 'tells' us about the practice—are in fact questions regarding the form of relatedness of the aspects and dimensions of a practice, the 'elements' of a 'hanging-together' (Schatzki) that has what Garfinkel called "said-and-shown Things in synaesthesia of witnessed particulars." (Garfinkel/E. Livingston 2003: 22) Answering questions regarding the phenomenal field, in other words, must happen by providing more details on what I called the amalgam of practice. In Chap. 4, I will sketch out my understanding of the amalgam in more detail, especially with a view on material aspects of practices. One important issue will be the question whether elements of practices can be said to have what Shove et al. (2012) call "a life of their own", that is, if they have qualities existing independently of practices—and if so, how these qualities influence phenopractices and feature in phenomenal fields.

---

[14] I use the term 'constellation' because this astronomical metaphor nicely illustrate the idea how stable congregations of independent, enduring particulars produce patterns of 'bits' which stand out of a background carry figural entities, even if (or because) they move across said background coherently. Thus, my use of the term differs from that of Frers (2007a) who employs it to give different answers to similar questions.

6 The Moving Body in the Phenomenal Field

To fill this abstract postulate with life and concreteness, let me return to the phenomenology of the body and bodily movement—which was, after all, Merleau-Ponty's central topic (Carman 1999, 2005). From a phenopractice perspective, we can say that if we sense the body, it always stands out of a phenomenal field, or more precisely, the phenomenal field of a practice. As each practice provides us with a typical "directorial orientation in an environment, in a materially inhabited space" (Carman 2008: 64), it provides us with a certain sense of our body. The phenomenal field of a practice—or, in Garfinkel's (2002: 98) terms: the phenomenal field properties of a concrete situation[15]—and thus certain features of our practical environment, form the indispensable background against which we gain the possibility of experiencing our body and the world per se. The phenomenal landscape of a practice is never painted by one sense in isolation: We can see how our hip turns, hear how the neck crackles if we make a wrong move, or sense pressures on parts of our skin. Seeing, hearing or feeling the body necessarily happen within practices, and it is thus always embedded into a range of sensual perceptions—muted or amplified according to the phenomenological set-up of the respective practice. Merleau-Ponty emphasized that the body plays a very distinct role in this interplay of field and perception, because it is in turn itself a necessary prerequisite of the existence of any perception and thus any phenomenal field. The body, he concluded, is never just given to consciousness on its own, but the givenness of the world is instead a crucial prerequisite to sensing the body: "I am conscious of my body via the world" (Merleau-Ponty 2002: 82), yet, in an almost dialectical inversion, "consciousness is being-towards-the-thing through the intermediary of the body." (2002: 159 f.) To make this point—and the departure from earlier phenomenological thought it represents—very clear: Merleau-Ponty did not just mean to say that the distinct role of the body springs from the fact that we perceive with sensory organs so that the perceptions stream 'through' our body before they reach our consciousness, but that the phenomenal field of a practice is constructed through the body itself—specifically because it is constructed through bodily *movement*. However, the importance of movement for perception per se was already acknowledged by Husserl, not to mention even Descartes (Carman 2005: 68). As I detailed, Husserl acknowledged at least with regard to vision that perception happens on the basis of movements, but effectively insisted that perceptions of earlier movements suffice to explain the occurrence of further movements

---

[15] In his later works, Garfinkel builds on Merleau-Ponty as well as his teacher Gurwitsch when he continuously emphasizes that it is the nature of each "thing" to occur necessarily within a phenomenological field. For him, it is thus a core policy that ethnomethodology "elucidates each thing in and as of an ongoing course of instructably produced and instructably witnessed endogenously coherent phenomenal field properties." (Garfinkel 2002: 98; see also A. Rawls 2002: 8 fn13).

so that conscious perception can be explained on the basis of conscious perception. Therefore, Merleau-Ponty argued against Husserl that a 'pure phenomenology' which considers only the subjective conscious experience does not suffice to explain simultaneously what is perceived and on the basis of which it is perceived and argued that the primacy of the sensual body invalidates hopes to purify universal essences of perception, for example via eidetic reduction. Instead, he emphasized, phenomenology needs to acknowledge the intrinsic immersion of the body into the surround:

> "Our body is not in space like things; it inhabits or haunts space. It applies itself to space like a hand to an instrument." (Merleau-Ponty 1964: 5)

Merleau-Ponty's notion of an intertwining of movement and sight is thus based on the basic observation that practices of seeing heavily depend on the body to open up the necessary lines of sight, for example through achieving a suitable posture or keeping the right distance to the object of inquiry. Practices such as scrutinizing or taking a closer look are intertwined with specific bodily movements and postures: Leaning forward, protruding the head, squinting one's eyes, and so on. In this way, our body is essential to provide us with what Merleau-Ponty calls our 'grip' on the world—moving in ways that are organized towards certain perceptions (Carman 2005: 69). A key implication of this insight that Merleau-Ponty emphasized in his earlier work (especially 2002) is the alternative understanding of intentionality he drew from it: While for Husserl intentionality is a process of immaterial consciousness, Merleau-Ponty describes motor intentionality as carried by the body as a whole. Consequently, since it is the task of phenomenology to study intentional acts, bodily movements need to be included into a phenomenological investigation not just as a type of content (i.e. kinaesthesia), but as a form of intentionality enmeshed with perception in its own right. In his later work, Merleau-Ponty drew the more far-reaching conclusion that body and world intertwine in what he called the chiasm, especially in that "the visible world and the world of my motor projects are each total parts of the same Being." (1969: 255) As much as the body for him is a lived body, the world is a lived world as well—a world we see, touch, and move through.

> "Immersed in the visible by his body, (…) the see-er does not appropriate what he sees; he merely approaches it by looking, he opens himself to the world." (Merleau-Ponty 1969: 256)

As I have shown, this description matches my own experience of seeing-while-riding-a-line quite well: What I see, what I focus and inspect along the route is not something I do in the sense that I chose or decide to undertake it; but it is instead as much a consequence of my route and the environment through which I travel as my own wilful pursuit. I do not stare down that couloir because of some aesthetic interest in its rock formation, but as I speed towards it my eyes are guided towards it as much as they guide my path into it. In Merleau-Ponty's (1968: 131) words the world "… is much more than the correlative of my vision, such that it imposes my vision upon me as a continuation of its own sovereign existence."

From a phenopractice perspective, this idea yields three important consequences: First, it requires developing a more suitable understanding of Merleau-Ponty calls "the world," which I suggest is provided by the notion of practice (see the excursus below). Second, it implies that vision and its content cannot be thought of as subjective (in that it is carried by individual consciousness) but as inherently tied to the course of our current activity; an understanding that needs to be adequately expressed in theoretical terms. And third, this visual experience and the phenomenology of vision and movement it implies provides me with the task of accounting for it in light of the state of the art of the neurological underpinnings of human vision. Before proceeding with this latter task at the end of this chapter, I will tackle the second point by discussing the normativity of bodily perception after the following excursus.

Excursus: Merleau-Ponty from a Phenopractice Perspective

> Merleau-Ponty's bodily phenomenology remains somewhat marginal to contemporary practice thought (outside of Germany). With the notable exception of Tim Ingold's work (2000: 262–266), Prinz' (2014) Foucauldian practice account of seeing, and a number of authors focusing on sports from a practice perspective (e.g. Alkemeyer/Buschmann 2017), the key works by Schatzki or Reckwitz, for example, note the theoretical affinities with regard to the conceptualization of knowledge or the body, but refrain from integrating detailed arguments into the practice vernacular. Those authors who argue more strictly along the line of Bourdieu's praxeology refer to it in passing (e.g. Lizardo 2007), as evidence for the general importance of embodied perception but without discussing his more specific arguments (which arguably differ quite a lot from a Bourdieuian viewpoint). Many discussants of practice theory thus seem to look at Merleau-Ponty predominantly as a phenomenologist in the classic sense, i.e. as thoroughly adhering to subjectivism (e.g. see Bongaerts 2007). This is somewhat surprising, since first, he directly extended on the work of Heidegger,[16] who considered himself a phenomenologist as well and plays an increasingly important role in contemporary practice thought (see especially Schatzki 2010b); and second, Harold Garfinkel and other ethnomethodologists have since long made use of Merleau-Ponty in a thoroughly non-subjectivist manner (see Fele 2008; Garfinkel 2002; Garfinkel/E. Livingston 2003). Consequentially, contemporary practice theorists drawing on Garfinkel have pointed out the affinities and made important steps towards integrating key concepts such as intercorporeality (Meyer/v. Wedelstaedt 2017). In order to extend this

---

[16] For Merleau-Ponty's use of and divergence from Heidegger see Protevi (1998) and Carman (2008: 42–43, 112–113).

fruitful line of thought but pay dues to the entrenched scepticism towards Merleau-Ponty's phenomenology, I briefly need to sketch out how I intend to align it with a practice—rather than conscious-centred theoretical framework. To begin with, several authors have noted that the broad strokes Merleau-Ponty's view on the body converge with that of Wittgenstein's (e.g. Stengel 2003). Yet while some seem to take that as a warrant to rephrase Wittgenstein's concept of language games to a system of embodied and perceptual routines, Schatzki (1996: 51) is among those who object against such a reduction of social life to bodily expressions and instead point to the multiple dimensions of social practices, for example artefacts and explicit rules. In doing so, however, Schatzki in turn neglects the details of Merleau-Ponty's work, which he dismisses as "aiming to reduce (…) linguistic meaning to behaviour" (Schatzki 1996: 49). I will not discuss this claim in detail; in part since Schatzki does not substantiates this critique further, but more generally because his position on linguistic meaning notwithstanding, the value of Merleau-Ponty's work seems obvious for developing precisely what Schatzki stays largely quite about: a phenomenology based on a social ontology rooted in Wittgenstein and Heidegger. Therefore, while I embrace Merleau-Ponty's core argument concerning the body, I also seek to expand this line of reasoning beyond phenomenology and towards a practice perspective. Specifically, while such a perspective arguably agrees with Merleau-Ponty's findings regarding the ways we experience with and through our body, it also takes into consideration several other aspects or dimensions of practices apart from the body. But while my position does hold these aspects to be co-carrying what one might call final meaning, it does not contend that they carry intentionality (according to my limited use of the term, see Chap. 8) and therefore, the perspective I unfold should not be mistaken for a phenomenological approach thusly defined. More sharply put: In my view, in the Phenomenology of Perception, Merleau-Ponty somewhat freehandedly extends phenomenology's domain of relevance to include various physiognomic phenomena (e.g. when discussing psychological experiments at length) because he labels them as instances of bodily movement carrying intentionality. This however, makes it difficult to discern the borders of relevance, i.e. what kind of phenomena should no longer be considered by his phenomenology—after all, the relevance of conscious awareness can no longer serve as a useful distinction in this regard.[17] A practice approach does not share this predicament since it does not define intentionality as a virtue of all aspects of practices but as tied to human conduct or

---

[17] In his later work, Merleau-Ponty himself came to the conclusion that "the problems in Phenomenology of Perception are insoluble because I start there from the 'consciousness'—'object' distinction" (1968: 200; see also Carman 2008: 120–124).

activity (e.g. Schatzki 2002: 44). For this reason, I will undertake a kind of 'reorganization' of Merleau-Ponty's vocabulary in an attempt to develop a more precise notion of bodily movement. Specifically, I deem it important to distinguish the perpetual stream of micro-movements such as saccades from whole practices of moving ourselves—such as skiing through powder—which relate to specific *experiences* of acting and moving. In other words, in contrast to Prinz (2014, 2016), I will reframe his conceptual terms to distinguish the perception of movement as a feature of the phenomenal field of a practice from bodily movement constituting said field—not because I wish to argue that both are not intimately related, but in the sake of conceptual clarity. A crucial first step is replacing his notion of 'the world' with that of 'practice': Merleau-Ponty (2002), as well as Wittgenstein, unfolds his argument primarily with regard to the relation of 'the body' and 'the world' as two universal entities or abstract domains (see Stengel 2003). As I have argued, such a conceptual duopoly (in its particularism still reflecting Husserl's idea of separate realms) is difficult to sustain, not only with regard to the ontology (which does not need to be a concern for the phenomenological philosopher), but also the phenomenology of bodily praxis: Just like I can have a headache but otherwise feel fit and well, I can simultaneously steer a car with one hand and gesticulate with the other while I talk on the phone, and the driving can be dull while the conversation yields trouble. Therefore, the permeable situatedness in the world which the body unfolds and which unfolds the body could be as well understood as an immersion into concrete practices, a concrete 'slice' of the lived world happening in socially preconfigured situational instances—in Merleau-Ponty's own words: "the situation of the body in face of its tasks" (2002: 115). Particularly, I would suggest (along the lines of thought of Gurwitsch 1964) that the notion of a generality of 'the world' cannot be sustained in light of the *temporal* structuredness of social situations, situations that have been prepared and are preconfigured by elements such as materials, semantics, or spatial arrangements. Using a distinction employed by Schatzki (2002: 65), I could thus say this field-concept of perception is contextualist rather than nominalist: Rather than treating perceptual impressions as events occurring within a universal domain of essentially homogenous particulars (such as meaning), I treat them as existing only in specific, delimited contexts—practices.[18]

---

[18] This does neither imply that practices in themselves are not meaningful entities, nor that they are entities that are nothing but meaningful.

7 Subjectivity and Intersubjectivity

Before turning towards these important forms of organization of the phenomenal field, however, another feature of my proposition to consider phenomenal fields as effects of practices needs to be spelled out. Particularly, I need to clarify further how this phenopractical proposition relates to a key term in 'classic' phenomenology and sociological theory grounded in phenomenology: the subject. As I have noted, the practice turn can be read as an undertaking to de-centre subjective consciousness as the sole domain of meaningful order considered relevant for sociological enquiry. But notably, I do not suggest that this move should be equated to a disregard of the importance of the subjective point of view. The way I presented it, the phenomenal field needs to be understood as intimately tied to what Merleau-Ponty calls the phenomenological body, the body-in-action as perceived by the practitioner. It follows that from a phenopractice perspective, it is mandatory to observe social order in the form in which it presents itself to the practitioner—a position e.g. reflected in Schatzki's postulate that practices are regimes of practical intelligibility and activity, both of which must be understood as phenomena pertaining to practitioners engaged in a practice. Not by coincidence, "understandings" are a key 'ingredient' of every social practice according to Schatzki's account of them. This emphasis on understanding is indeed shared by the *Lebenswelt*-school of thought in sociology, which has since long held that the subjective perspective on meaning as it presents itself to an actor should a) be taken as the object of sociological enquiry and b) provides the relevant methodological lens through which to collect data and 'understand' social life. But while I agree with the latter conclusion and thus rely on ethnographic data, I do not think that an 'egocentric' understanding of social order vindicates restricting sociological enquiry to the subject as the sole locus or generator of said order. In other words, I share the view arguably popularized in sociology by Harold Garfinkel that "the actor's point of view (…) no longer [has] to be thought of as belonging to individual actors." (A. Rawls 2002: 60) In the words of ethnomethodologists Sharrock and Button (1991: 156 f.): "The 'primacy' which the 'actor's point of view' has so far been given is not the result of a reductionist commitment, an insistence that 'social reality' can be decomposed into an ensemble of individual points of view." My definition of phenomenal fields shares this understanding in that it regards phenomenal fields as a quality of a practice rather than subjective consciousness. In other words, the field contains phenomenal affordances which are necessarily affordances *for* a practitioner in the practice, and it contains phenomenal details which are perceptible in this way exclusively *by* practitioners in the practice.[19]

---

[19] My conception is thus somewhat similar to the term envelopment (or Einhüllung) used by Frers (Frers 2007a, 2007b) to describe a phenomenological 'enwrappment' induced by situations such as being in train terminals, but also things like sunglasses, headphones, etc. Envelopments, he writes, "dampen or filter perception" and "direct attention and activities to certain areas" (Frers 2007b: 34).

The notion of consciousness raises multiple issues that are notoriously difficult to discern, in particular issues pertaining to its form, structure, or means of accessing and representing its content. I hope it has become clear that a phenopractice perspective does not, or at least not primarily, try to develop answers to such questions. In a strict sense, one could say that while theories of social practices do require that people can have understandings and become consciously aware of certain things, they do not per se seek to make far-reaching arguments about, and deep inquiries into, the nature and content of consciousness (and especially not as taken in isolation)—simply because they do not consider consciousness as the crucial phenomenon at which to look in order to explain action, intelligibility, meaning, and social order. This situation has led many proponents of practice thought to state that such explanations are instead to be found in the realm of the subconscious, especially in the form of a Bourdieuian habitus. From my perspective, however, this conclusion is unjustified: Saying that the structures or processes which govern or constitute action, order, and meaning are not identical with consciousness and saying that said structures or processes do not feature in consciousness at all are two pairs of shoes—the latter claim being far more ambitious, harder to uphold and substantiate methodologically, and arguably doomed to fail. In this work, in contrast, I subscribe to the former claim, which explains why I rely on my personal experiences and participant observations of skiing in terms of methodology, but also raises some important questions to be answered with regard to it. I will refrain from doing so right now and instead refer the reader to the methodological appendix specifically addressing the implications of my concept of the phenomenal field, among related issues. Moreover, the considerations regarding practical intelligibility and understanding flow and emotions that I develop will help towards fleshing out my approach more fully. For now, it should suffice to state that phenopractice theory avoids the predicaments of studying consciousness by way of a definition: Phenopractice theory is not concerned with the content of subjective processes; but it is inter alia concerned with phenomenal fields of normal practices.

In addition to the issue of subjectivity, let me also provide a brief comment on the related issue of intersubjectivity (cf. Meyer/v. Wedelstaedt 2017). In the 'classic' view of the individualist sociology of action, the fact that perception itself can be perceived led to a series of complex and escalating implications. Because the actor perceives that his perceiving is being perceived by others, and thus tries to be perceivable as perceiving in a certain way, and thus needs to perceive if and how his perceiving is perceived by the others without being perceivably doing so, which necessitates him to speculate about the perceive-ability of his perception of the other's perceiving of his perceiving their perception of his perception, which in turn... Since theories of social practices do not subscribe to theoretical individualism and do not consider meaning as being produced by individuals in any strict sense, or intelligible order as exclusively tied to individual subjects, intersubjectivity does not figure as an extraordinary case or problem in these theories but is universally presupposed in the very existence of practices (see Schatzki 1997). This is not to deny that practical conduct or human activity is a phenomenon that is specific to human involvement (contrary to Latour's claims) and that the unfolding of any practice into lived praxis is not tied to the involvement of skilled practitioners (Preda 2000; Schatzki 2010b). Yet while different accounts of practice thought seem divided over the question whether more than one practitioner can be 'in' an ongoing practice, my position is this: Just like practice theories' conceptualization of material objects implies no principal difference between one or more objects being entangled in one practice; and just as it makes no general difference how many body parts are active in conduct of a practice, there can be more than one body or consciousness involved. In short, I suggest making a distinction between the social and the bodily dimension of practices: The co-presence of others does for itself neither imply that they are part of the same conduct, nor that they are necessarily engaged in the same practice. While one could say that they are part of the same situational praxis (however some ambiguities remain about where one situation ends and the next begins), their relation to the practice necessarily depends on the particular structure of said practice. In the case of freestyle skiing in a funpark that will be discussed in Chap. 6, for example, something like an audience and a performer can be distinguished. While it is clear that performing a trick and watching a trick are two different practices, I will also argue that both usually require the co-conduct of more than one person, so that those present are engaged in more than just one practice (which seems a common feature of everyday life). Because phenopractice theory distinguishes between the practice per se and the phenomenal field it effects, moreover, the classic question about the role of the social other—*Alter*—can be respecified as the simpler question if and how others feature in the phenomenal field. And thus the answer simply is: it depends on the practice in question. In the case of conducting a performance, for example, the presence of bystanders might be initially noticed, but consecutively pushed to the margins of attention, whereas when in watching someone else intently, one's own doings can almost disappear. In other words, because intelligible meaning is conceptualized as something occurring *for* a practitioner in a situated unfolding rather than in an individual consciousness, having more than one consciousness-carrying body on location does not change the fact that it depends on the order of the situation if and how their relation is organized in any manner. That said, I stress that I consider the social dimension of situated interaction as outstandingly important, especially for human vision. My point is rather that I do not believe that being confronted with Alter's co-presence is an extraordinary challenge threatening to throw our human life off the rails in that it requires all sorts of complex and reflexive cognitive moves to manoeuvre through 'double contingency,' or as Luhmann (1995a: 109) put it, the predicaments arising if "two black boxes, by whatever accident, come to have dealings with one another"—since that unfortunate accident is just everyday lived social life. To stay with the metaphor: From a (Heidegger-inspired) practice perspective, two black boxes in a pitch-black room will not notice each other in the first place; and hence I am more inclined to ask: How and why do they switch on the light? Cranky metaphors aside, accounts of practice theory that can be described as site ontologies in Schatzki's (2002) sense locate social order and meaning at precisely the locus which traditional microsociology termed the interaction order, and while they acknowledge that it often makes a difference in praxis whether said order is manned by one or several practitioners, it does not make a fundamental difference in theory. One important consequence of this view is that I will argue (in concordance with Schatzki and others), that the teleo-affectivity of conduct is tied to the current situation rather than the subject in question, for example in that the emotional drive that 'motivates' freeskiers to engage in ever-new dangerous stunts is frequently and critically something that is shared by a group of skiers practicing together (in that euphoria as well as fear seem to be highly contagious) rather than something experienced in isolation. At the core of this phenomenon, I believe, lies the fact that perception in and for movement is very often normatively 'keyed' in such a way that seeing and feeling intertwines.

8 Seeing, Apprehension, and 'The Brain's Way of Touching'

The cold wind sweeping over the rugged face of the Krimml has begun to push the dark clouds away, so that patches of blue can be seen in between the pale grey of the sky. All morning, Tom has been concerned about the weather. A few clouds blocking off the sunlight are enough to make freeriding difficult, if not impossible; and being caught in fog up on an alpine peak is outright dangerous. Visibility remained a frequent concern not just on this particular day: Lighting conditions that are any less than perfect receive constant attention from freeskiers, in open terrain as much as in snow parks (Fig. 4.7). As I have shown, the line as a seen object to a large degree prefigures where and how a freerider will ski. What needs to be added to this assessment is that the process of seeing itself, or to be precise, the modality of seeing also configures where and how one will ride: Testament to the sociologically under-appreciated importance of light and its immediate links to shared emotions (Edensor 2012), perfect sunshine stimulates riders, while poor visibility slows them down and can even make them timid. Emotionally and pragmatically, riding within certain landscapes is directly tied to the visual affordances present according to current weather conditions. The best example for this are so-called {tree-runs}, lines in sparse wood ridden almost exclusively on days of bad weather: While the trees hinder high speeds and big turns, they provide much-needed guidance in terms of orientation and inclination of the slope (and reduce the risk of avalanches). For freeskiers, a terrain is thus not only characterized by its affordances for movement, but also its *visual affordances*, both in terms of orientation and visibility.[20] This is not just because poor visibility can completely

---

[20] The same is true for cycling in the dark. For an insightful discussion of affordances and apprehension in cycling at night, see Cook and Edensor (2017).

Fig. 4.7 Tom figuring out a line during a tree-run in bad weather conditions. He is about to drop in between the two small bushes in the centre and then head straight down. Without the clear contours of the trees below, the inclination and shape of the slope would get lost in shades of grey

inhibit any sophisticated skiing, but rather because visibility regulates the capacity to ride in that the speed, style, and layout of a line need to be adapted. In cloudy conditions, the contours of cliffs or windlips begin to blur into a landscape composed of various shades of white and grey. It becomes ever more difficult to distinguish the different types of snow from afar, to differentiate between hardened firn or ice and fluffy powder, or to spot small rocks covered only by a thin layer of snow. Furthermore, with fading light it also becomes increasingly difficult to estimate the inclination of the slope (and thus the speed of the ride) as well as the distance of objects. All this forces the rider to refrain from pushing his limits and keeping a 'reaction reserve' in his bodily movements that allows him to react swiftly to sudden changes in snow quality or to absorb unforeseen drops in the slope. Riding posture, body tension, and skiing technique are adapted accordingly and (given ample experience) almost automatically: the knees are bend further, the force exercised during a turn is reduced, and one's centre of gravity is lowered. If a good skier is forced to ride in dense fog, she will try to cling to the slope and "see with the knees" as ski instructors call it aptly: Instead of spotting the surface conditions with the eyes and adapting proactively with the whole body, the rider needs to adapt reactively to what he feels while skiing by 'keeping slack' in the knees [M]. This coupling between vision and the sensual capacities of our muscles such as the arms and legs not only demonstrates that our senses always work in conjunction, but also the fact that one sense can overtake the role of another to a certain degree. If vision is bad, the extremities as well as our proprioception—our sense of balance and acceleration—can take over some of the coordination work usually done via visual orientation—but only if one benefits from sufficient experience. Throughout the process of becoming a more able skier and during my work as a ski teacher, I have observed the opposite process as well: While beginners can hardly assess the features of the snow surface right in front of them and need to react with hectic movements every time they encounter an icy patch on a slope or some really heavy slough, more accomplished skiers routinely spot such irregularities and adapt anxiously at first, automatically later. In other words: because they can *see* that this is going to be a slippery spot, they do not need to *feel* it to react—or, as Merleau-Ponty put it: "Vision is the brain's way of touching" (cit. in Berthoz 2000: 11). Just as in the seeing of the features of terrain, the rider is able to increase his competence in riding because he is enabled to accomplish sensory and visual perception in a meaningful succession and can thus learn to replace sensing slippery, icy patches of snow with seeing them early on, and—vice versa—to replace seeing an apt rotation of his hips with more directly sensing it. This very basic, yet very powerful division of labour between the senses was also described by Arnold Gehlen (1988, p. 174): "Visual perception assumes control of experiences formerly obtained through tactile perception."

It seems clear that this basic flexibility of our senses to fulfil multiple roles is a key resource for our achieving fragile conduct such as freeriding. But while this basic ability might seem relatively uninteresting and ordinary if taken for itself, it leads to some deep and important theoretical consequences if one considers how these different abilities or dimensions of bodily perception and activity are coordinated and correlated. For our body-in-conduct does not simply alternate between these modes of figuring out and reacting, picking them like tools from a box one after another. Instead, as riding through foggy weather makes clear, they are co-present to different degrees and on different levels, organized into variable and overlapping constellations: Even while 'the eye' is still trying to make out whether the slightly darker spot in the snow is a dangerous rock hidden under the surface or just a shadow (thus 'running' certain visual routines of contrastive identification), 'the torso' will already build up additional tension that would be needed for manoeuvring around it at the last moment, while 'the knees' relax further in anticipation of a pending impact. The crucial point here is that this multimodality is a) organized at least in part in a pre-reflexive and pre-conscious manner and b) amounts to a capacity of embodied apprehension (Cook/Edensor 2017). To an often astounding extend, the body seems able to sort out itself with a foresight our conscious self seems to be unable to muster, regaining our balance before we even realized we were slipping, time and again getting us out of situations in one piece we did not actually see coming—that is, as I will show, if this 'we' is our own body, we did indeed see it coming quite literally, we just did not consciously know that.

In the history of practice thought, our capacity for embodied apprehension is arguably a cornerstone much like (and linked to) the idea of the gestalt (von Wedelstaedt/Meyer 2017). It features prominently in the later works of Wittgenstein (see Gebauer 2009: 86–101); and it is arguably at the root of Heidegger's treatment of coping (H. L. Dreyfus 1991, 2008; Ennen 2003) as well as his notion of spatiality as bound up with paths of action and bodily orientation (see Schatzki 2010b). It is central for Bourdieu's theorizing about the habitus (e.g. Bourdieu 2000: 128) and his contemporary defendants (e.g. Lizardo/Strand 2010); and it has inspired arguments as diverse as Nigel Thrift's discussion of "pre-cognition" (see Laurier 2011; Thrift 2004a, 2004b) and (arguably) central aspects of Garfinkel's notion of situated perception and order (see especially the discussion of embodied sight in Garfinkel 2002: 207–216). I will refrain from exploring the details of these arguments as well as the complexities of the neural processes probably underlying them for now; and I will only foreshadow the argument I will later pursue by pointing out: When certain effects (i.e. prefigurations and orientations of bodily conduct) of such pre-conscious sensori-motor routines surface in the social world (in the form of bodily doings), they would frequently be considered as *mental* conditions from a Wittgensteinian perspective:

> "In Wittgenstein (…) mind is a collection of ways things stand and are going (for someone) that are *expressed* by bodily doings and sayings." (Schatzki 1996: 23; original emphasis)

Without sorting out the argument and its implications in detail, I only note that this definition is so broad that many cases of what I called embodied apprehension on the basis of vision falls into this domain. The core reason is that from a phenomenological[21] perspective, the assortment of phenomena I described is united by the fact that they are linked to an underlying normativity (in that things are going good or bad; or in that we are reluctant and insecure rather than determined and careless) and are closely linked to emotional states. As I will seek to show, while we are frequently not fully aware of the content our body's apprehension, we nevertheless take care. This caring about the way our body is exposed to the world is for example evidenced by the fact that the influence of visibility is not limited to the physical style of freeriding, but matters even more for aspects of attitude, motivation, and confidence. As I had to experience many times, poor visibility can block a rider mentally as it inflates fears of failure and distorts the fragile balance between the challenge chosen and one's confidence in one's own aptitude. Reduced visibility often sets into motion a downward spiral of excessive caution, inhibiting tension, improper riding, and consequential frustration resulting in an even more negative attitude. In effect, abilities that one seemingly just 'has' can dwindle rapidly. At times, I had to witness myself sliding miserably through the fog like an absolute beginner, continuously cursing my less-than-meagre

---

[21] Phenomenology understood in a broad sense, i.e. including the thought of Wittgenstein, Heidegger, and Merleau-Ponty.

performance. In this way, seeing the terrain is not just a matter of noticing an environment within which the 'actual' skiing happens, but it is an integral part of the act and art of riding itself. For this reason, I argue that practices of seeing occurring during riding are very different in nature from the preparatory practice of reading a face that were discussed in the first chapter. While these practices of seeing *a* line were best characterized as complementary to the practice of riding—they are instrumental but separate—the practice of seeing *in* the line are integral to riding: they are a core aspect of the bodily accomplishment of riding. I suggest that this sentiment translates into the proposition that phenomenal fields are bound to specific (pheno-)practices rather than the world per se, and that it lends itself particularly well to a key aspect of Merleau-Ponty's thought: the normativity of our bodily orientation.

9 The Normativity of Perception

"Bodily capacities and dispositions," Carman (2005: 70) summarizes Merleau-Ponty's position, "establish a *normative* domain without which perception could not be intentional." As the experience of powder skiing demonstrates, feelings of uneasiness or 'just-rightness' play an important role in the organization of bodily perception, especially for focusing or diverting attention. I suggest that, in light of conceptualizing perception as a background-foreground relation, this normativity of bodily orientation should be understood as a modus of taking care of the background of the current attention focus, and as a result of our ability to process several clues parallel and 'stay in touch' with the current situation on multiple levels. One example I have discussed are deep-rooted visual routines which can for example alert us to sudden movement in parafoveal vision so that we can see something coming in the corner of our eyes very shortly before it hits us—like the rock I nearly hit when speeding out of the chute, already intuitively bodily avoiding it while 'mentally' still only thinking "Oh, there is a rock I did not expect." One might object that such rapid 'shock-reactions' of foregrounding background features that demand immediate attention cannot be equated to a phenomenon Merleau-Ponty (2002: 20) describes as a "vague feeling of uneasiness." However, I suggest that this example demonstrates in its more dramatic form what is a ubiquitous process, namely the 'maturation' of something foreshadowed by what one might call pre-conscious rather than subconscious perceptual synthesis of background features of the current field. In doing so, it underlines the importance of bodily routines or reflexes—squinting, flinching, ducking—and embodied emotions for this 'keeping in touch with' the background of the phenomenal field. In its more subtle and less adrenaline-drenched versions, such normative para-attention continuously accompanies situated perception focused on key objects and objectives: If, for example, we spot a pile of things that seems out of balance, we do not experience this as a rational assessment in lieu of our knowledge of Newton's laws. Rather, it is that from glance over, we get a vague sense that there is something fishy about this pile, so we stop short and—to speak with Heidegger (1962; see H. L. Dreyfus 1991: 240)—we start to *care*; we now realize that it looks unstable, about to tip over, so we keep an eye on it like a mother keeps an eye on the child playing on the floor while she keeps chatting. We grasp the imbalance 'intuitively,' we first have an unspecific idea and then see this imbalance as a feature of the pile, like the freerider sees that this windlip is about to cause an avalanche, or like "one sees the weight of a block of cast iron which sinks into the sand" (Merleau-Ponty 2002: 267). The normative framework of perception, one can conclude, is an effect of a synthesizing process of various subtle routines of perceptual organization of background features that are held available for heightened attention in the form of an unspecific 'look and feel' that the phenomenal field offers, a perceptual synthesis which—Merleau-Ponty emphasizes— is fundamentally bodily. This normative and largely emotional dimension of the phenomenal field, it follows, is not an unfortunate by-product, but a highly functional feature that allows for an effective organization of perceptual attention both laterally and temporally. The organized background of the field is thus essential, because it is here where all focused objects of thought and action must originate and rise from, "as a storm imminent in storm clouds." (Merleau-Ponty 2002: 20) It should be clear that matters of background-organization and ongoing para-attention are central to the core questions of this work, namely, how visual practices (or the visual dimension of phenopractices) are organized, in which ways freeskiing is a visual culture, and which views on theories of social practice can be derived from these findings. As Merleau-Ponty (2002: 7) argues: "We must recognize the indeterminate as a positive phenomenon. It is in this atmosphere that quality arises."

At the beginning of the last chapter, I described that a freerider looks down into a couloir he is about to drop into in a quite different manner than a tourist marvelling at the landscape. Given the discussion just provided, I suggest that this effect can be traced back to the normative orientation of the phenomenal field in light of the bodily movement currently impending for the former, but not the latter. In the words of Ingold (2000: 198–199), the explanation would thus be that while the latter is indeed seeing a landscape, the former sees a task space, a realm of paths of actions to take and challenges to overcome. From a 'theory of action'-perspective, one might argue that this observation simply proves that our perception depends on what Alfred Schutz called our attitude: Knowing that we are about to ski, we interpret the given sense data differently, that is, in light of the task at hand. On this basis, it seems quite plausible to assume that not just this 'knowing' what one is about to do and the framework of interpretation of visual cues it implies, but also the various ways of getting to know what to do (such as someone telling me, and my understanding and memorizing his words) happen within the same realm: consciousness. In comparison to this clear and unified explanation, the account I just gave seems rather unsophisticated in its alluding to a "vague feeling" reflecting "embodied apprehension" and a "normative orientation" of the phenomenal field rather than the actor himself. More to the point, it seems that practice theory is trying to have the cake and also eat it when suggesting that ends or tasks (such as intending to move towards a certain rock) co-define almost all moments of conduct but refuses to accept that human action is the dominion of volition and consciousness. However masterful it might be, in the end of day Merleau-Ponty's philosophical account of the phenomenology of vision and movement stands pitted head-to-head against Husserl's philosophical account on the same matter. Beyond the empirical argument just presented, can one further underpin the concept of a phenomenal field that is oriented, but not necessarily consciously so? How can one, in other words account for the preparation of bodily movement through seeing without building on conscious intentionality? One way, I suggest, is to develop phenopractice theory by returning to the kind of sources that Husserl and Merleau-Ponty had turned to as well: The contemporary state of the art of vision science.

10 Two Ways of Seeing: Pragmatic Versus Epistemic Seeing

The optical, anatomical, and neural underpinnings of human vision, I have shown earlier, have been and still are a source of inspiration, irritation, and (more or less) plausible arguments for or against phenomenology, epistemology, and social thought—especially through the gestalt movement. In continuing this tradition, I have surveyed some basic contemporary scientific findings and theories regarding visual routines and (mid-level) visual cognition in order to assess competing accounts of human practices of seeing and their social nature. I will now follow this path further by discussing the visual processes behind bodily movement and activity. Out of the four 'classic' problems that informed gestalt thinking (see Chap. 2), three are problems of synthesis: assembling a single figure over the course of temporally separate saccades; synthesizing impressions of colour and an object's shape into seeing a coloured object; and multisensory convergence or the cross-influence of, e.g., hearing and sight. While I believe that I have discussed the neural roots and philosophical implications of these phenomena at sufficient length, the fourth problem requires additional treatment; in part because it is especially relevant to practice thought as well as the topic of freeskiing, and in part because very significant additional insights have been gained since the likes of Goldstein and Merleau-Ponty discussed these cases. The basic phenomenon in question was that certain patients were able to grab and use a tool or object, but unable to point at it or name it (or the other way around). In the "Phenomenology of Perception," Merleau-Ponty (2002) provided an extensive discussion of the infamous "Patient Schneider," and used his case to support his argument that there must be a kind of "intentionality already at work prior to any thesis or any judgment" (2002: 490)—a *motor intentionality* (see on Merleau-Ponty on "Patient

Schneider" Carman 2008: 111–123; Jensen 2009). Expressed in contemporary terms, some patients suffer from a brain lesion inhibiting certain visual systems causing either so-called associative agnosia—i.e. the inability to identify or draw the shapes of objects—or apperceptive agnosia—being unable to grab or use things they can readily identify (see Jacob/Jeannerod 2003: 73–104 for an overview). To be sure, such pathological cases alone cannot adequately inform a phenomenological analysis of unimpaired human life. However, we can also observe very similar phenomena in everyday conduct: For example, we can see a ball flying towards us out of the corner of our eye and catch it, but then we need to look again at the object now in our hand to determine its colour (Jacob/Jeannerod 2003: xii). In the decades since Merleau-Ponty's writing, increasingly more refined laboratory experiments have been developed to study the effect; e.g. asking subjects to grab or recognize objects while making use of elaborate optical illusions. In addition, neuroscientists are relying on experiments with mammals and—increasingly—on fMRI-data in trying to discern the different brain areas activated during solving different visual tasks. While especially the latter two approaches are inherently problematic (and will be scrutinized sceptically below), the fundamental conclusion supported by decades of research in several related disciplines is quite clear: 'Seeing for perception' and 'seeing for action' are two fundamentally different processes (Berthoz/Petit 2008; Clark 1999; Goodale/Milner 1992; Goodale/Milner/Jakobson/Carey 1991; Jacob/Jeannerod 2003). Crucial to this so-called dualistic approach to human vision is that this distinction does neither just refer to a functional nor to a purely philosophical difference—though both types of implications are of cause under discussion—but describes an *anatomical* structure: Different nerve systems and areas of the brain (within the cortex) are carrying the two different visual systems. In effect, "the same objective stimulus can undergo two basic kinds of visual processing according to the task." (Jacob/Jeannerod 2003: xii) On the one hand, there is what comprises consciously seeing and recognizing an entity in our everyday understanding, the form of vision I will call *epistemic vision* (following Jacob/Jeannerod 2003) and others term "visual awareness" (Clark 1999). On the other hand, one can distinguish a preconscious (or subconscious) "visuomotor perception" or "vision for bodily movement" that can be called *pragmatic vision*, which enables bodily actions such as moving or grasping.

At first sight, it seems tempting to suggest that the neuroscientists' distinction between epistemic and pragmatic vision can be more or less directly matched with Merleau-Ponty's distinction between conscious intentionality and subconscious motor intentionality, or even Heidegger's distinction between singular things that stand out ready-at-hand (Ding), and things merely ready-to-hand (Zeug) in the immediate surround. However, as my discussion will show, this would be as much a misleading simplification as it is a confusion of categories. It is important to note that from the viewpoint of cognitive psychology and neurosciences, a whole umbrella of neural systems, cognitive routines, and/or brain areas is responsible for the various ways in which our body keeps what Merleau-Ponty[22] called its "grip on the world." They have been embraced or loosely referred to by philosophers and social scientists to various degrees and in various depths. Nevertheless, it seems to me that an overwhelming majority of those treatments that lie in proximity of the practice turn draws explicitly or implicitly on those modes of pre-conscious embodied apprehension that depend directly on the visual system, although of course not all forms of bodily skills, intuitive reactions, tacit knowledge, etc. do. For these two reasons, the literature on social practices, situated (interaction) order, and embodied action form a densely interwoven rhizome of arguments within which identical or related phenomena acquire half a dozen different names—e.g. what neuroscientists call mindreading is social cognition for psychologists, a performance for cultural theorists, interaction order for micro-sociologists and collective intentionality for philosophers. Depending on their scientific position and interest, the intimate and non-conscious coupling of vision and body movement has prompted authors to re-asses notions such as action (Alvarez 2010; Berthoz/Petit 2008; Chapman 1991; C. Goodwin 2000a; Pacherie 2008; Schatzki 2010b), cognition (Ballard/Hayhoe/Pook/Rao 1997; Coulter 1991; Gallagher 2005; Hutchins 1995; Jacob/Jeannerod 2003; Lynch 2006), intentionality (Becchio/Bertone 2004; Carman 2005; Gurwitsch 1970; Jensen 2009; Merleau-Ponty 2002; Searle 1983), or emotion (R. Collins 2004; Hochschild 1979; Riis/Woodhead 2010; Giacomo Rizzolatti/Sinigaglia/F. Anderson 2008; Schatzki 2002; Schlicht 2010). While my discussion touches upon these (and other) points in one way or another, by necessity it cannot hope to cover the full range of the ways in which authors within the practice turn have made use of the finding that epistemic and pragmatic vision are inherently distinct, let alone sort out all their arguments against rival, but related uses of such findings. Yet while both my discussion of scientific findings as well as of their philosophical or sociological interpretations need to be selective, I also believe that a number of contradictions or pseudo-antagonisms can be clarified by relating them to one overarching framework. Both in defending a phenopractice-theoretical account as well as in assessing alternative viewpoints, I will thus strive to return to the fundamental distinction between epistemic and pragmatic vision and the two distinct neural systems carrying them.

---

[22] In his *Phenomenology of Perception*, Merleau-Ponty (2002: 116–158) undertakes a similar appropriation when he extensively discusses the case of "Patient Schmidt" which he takes from early psychological studies of related disorders. However, his distinction of proprioception (perceptual self-awareness) and conscious observation of other objects should not be conflated with the distinction between pragmatic and epistemic seeing I use here, although they are frequently quoted in support of the former (see also Jensen 2009 for a critical discussion). First, proprioception refers to the much wider realm of all perceptions of the body, such as sensing temperature. Second and much more fundamentally, Merleau-Ponty makes a phenomenological observation and thus a philosophical point with regard to conscious experience—an experience that does not include neural networks which might be engaged in its production (Carman 2008: 116–119). Moreover, as I have discussed above, I regard proprioception in Merleau-Ponty's sense not as a universal sense given to man per se, but as a component and result of specific practices that provoke and make use of proprioception.

In order to avoid misunderstandings, I want to stress that both of these types of vision need to be understood from within a practice perspective—as inherently depended on and the co-product of situational order, bodily routines, material constellations, and so on. Most importantly, I do not suggest that epistemic and pragmatic seeing are (pheno-)practices in their own right, for example in that a practitioner might at some point conduct epistemic seeing and then switches over to epistemic seeing. Instead, I argue that they are *aspects* of human vision; and as such they are thoroughly baked into the amalgam of lived conduct, contributing in distinct ways and in varying extent to our situated accomplishments. At any moment of lived live, both forms of vision are involved—but not necessarily in all doings we engage in, as the example of grabbing a ball without having seen its colour demonstrates: Surely, there was something that we were consciously looking at (something we know and could identify) when suddenly the ball came flying—it is just that recognizing the ball was not an aspect of catching it. In this sense, epistemic and pragmatic vision can be incremental to phenopractices to varying degrees and with varying importance. By calling them aspects of practices, it is implied that I do not consider pragmatic and epistemic vision as purely cognitive phenomena in the sense cognitive psychologists and most neuroscientists do. From a sociological point of view, one cannot fail to notice how the apodictic tone of their findings necessarily obscures its origin in the highly specialized (and opportunistic as well as political) epistemic practices in the context of the laboratory (see especially Knorr Cetina, 1981, 1999); and not surprisingly, they have been criticized in this vein (e.g. Briscoe 2009). What is more, much of the work of cognitive psychologists and neuroscientists consists in seeking to purify (or rather mutilate) "the" act of seeing objects in general. In most cases this is done by reducing the scope to observing reactions to artificial tasks of grasping an object by hand in experiments—and quite often, even this practice is only undertaken in an environment of 'virtual reality.' The laboratory purification of the practice thus consists in systematically robbing the actor of the richness of multimodal resources that are essential to achieving conduct deemed successful within naturally occurring situations, as ethnomethodological studies of practices of seeing have demonstrated time and again. In this vein, what I have called practices of seeing are thus instances of epistemic seeing only in so far in that they are organized in a way to allow the specific visual perception of respective epistemic objects—however, as most other practices, such practices almost always simultaneously depend on instances of non-epistemic seeing in order to be accomplished. More specifically, I reject arguments suggesting that "visual phenomenology (…) can arise only from [epistemic] processing (…) that we have linked with recognition and perception" (Milner/Goodale 1995: 200). In contrast, I hold that visual meaning can never effect from epistemic vision alone. To this end, I have argued that visual perceptions are inherently bodily in that they arise from a phenomenal field of social practices which are necessarily carried by and dependent on the position, orientation, and posture of the body. In doing so, I have also argued for a 'situated' phenomenology (as well as an underlying social ontology) that treats the meaningfulness of lived live as dependent on and carried by a broader range of bodily processes than the 'cognitive' phenomenology Milner and Goodale seem to suggest—or than Husserlian phenomenology would suggest. Notably, my account does *not* suppose that epistemic and pragmatic vision are in perpetual felicitous co-existence: Although vision scientists overwhelmingly embrace a kind of optimistic functionalism that implies that our visual systems do nothing but dutifully solving pre-given and fully transparent tasks of some sort, I am deeply sceptical about such technomorphism, and instead hold that said systems neither just 'know' what to do, nor necessarily refrain from getting in each other's way when doing whatever they do. In other words, since I treat both intelligibility and activity as arising situatedly and in the dimension of meaning, I believe that, insofar as the visual is involved, either of the two can only be successfully accomplished if the epistemic and pragmatic aspects of vision can be suitably aligned. I argue that this situation is exemplified by the freeskiers' different practices of seeing: In the understanding of neuroscience, reading a mountain face from a distance is a very different practice from inspecting its surface while riding through it; and the somehow fuzzy or movement-drenched memories the freeriders carry forth from the slopes are of this very nature because they do stem from an altogether different practice than calm inspection. In this view, the key challenge of seeing during freeriding lies in managing both the demanding non-epistemic, visuomotor seeing necessary for the immediate movement, and the epistemic recognizing or spotting of the landmarks that serve as 'entry points' for riding into the next segment. Consequentially, the difficulty and fragility of freeriding would to emanate to a considerable extent from the fact that this management or alignment has to happen smoothly in the midst of the continuous temporal advancing of the unfolding of praxis. This argument leads to a last, pivotal point: If it is true that epistemic and pragmatic visual routines can entangle in unproductive ways, and if both are at least in part pre- or subconscious in nature, then a theoretical treatment of the visual dimension of intelligibility and activity needs to account for the disentangling or aligning or management of these two by some pervasive feature of human live other than consciousness or cognition. As the reader might have guessed, the present work is designed to show that situated order is responsible for this organization of vision, and that said order can be suitably accounted for by the unfolding of phenopractices. In the next chapter, I therefore provide a discussion of understanding and intelligibility as accomplished across phenopractices conducted on the basis of epistemic *and* pragmatic seeing, and I will later complement it with an account of human activity as conducted on the basis of an artful combination of these two forms of seeing. Both discussions, I might add, will flesh out my notion of the phenomenal field of practices in more detail.

Excursus: Does Vision Science Necessarily Lead to Cognitivism or Mentalism?

It might seem problematic, if not outright wrong to adopt arguments from what I subsumed under the umbrella of vision science, i.e. especially cognitive psychology and neuroscience, into a practice-based perspective—after all, mentalism and cognitivism are precisely the two theoretical traditions practice thought tries to overcome (e.g. Reckwitz 2002a). Nevertheless, I argue that integrating findings from cognitive sciences to overcome cognitivism does not mean trusting the cat to keep the cream, but rather strengthening the argument and widening its scope—as long as sufficient attention to the details of argument and methodology is being paid.[23] For one, I have noted that both Wittgensteinian philosophers of mind and practice-minded sociologists have already embraced many of the scientific findings and theories I make use of in some way or another, and I have also sketched out which kinds of uses I deem adequate and why. With regard to the dual approach to vision, however, a more specific problem arises and needs to be discussed: the problem of representationalism. Overwhelmingly, vision scientists are representationalists, that is, they describe vision as a procedure in which mental representations undergo a certain processing, e.g. of identifying or acting towards something. The question thus is: How can one draw on such (alleged) representationalism without falling prey to mentalism and/or subjectivism? For one, I have in Chap. 2 rejected the notion that the (hypothetical) occurrence of mental representations alone warrants considering meaning as happening within human consciousness as a closed realm or self-referential system. Expressed in the terms of the philosophy of mind, one might thus agree with Clark (1998) that anti-isolationism—the notion that the mind or cognition is not what he calls an "inner symbol flight" during which the mind first elaborates complete mental representations of the outer world (e.g. calculating 3D mental maps from 2D visual input) before reacting on them—does not automatically imply the conviction that there can must be no mental representations whatsoever. Following this path of thought, I suggest that on closer inspection, certain varieties of representationalism are indeed compatible with site ontologies or the notion that meaning arises for practitioners in situations. As Ennen (2003) works out nicely, although phenomenologists, neuroscientists, and cognitive scientists all discuss mental representations as a concept, they use the term quite differently. What is crucial for my question at hand is the difference between

---

[23] For this reason, I deem it at least as important to point out the limitations and problems of existing practice-theoretical arguments that embrace (neuro-) scientific findings as forwarding arguments of my own—which is why I discuss Lizardo at some length, for example.

what Clark (1997, 1998) calls weak versus strong representations: Weak representations are conceptualized as mental correlates of situational features; mental states that vanish if the object of reference disappears. Strong representations, in contrast, are understood to be "de-coupleable surrogates for specifiable (usually extra-neural) states of affairs" (Clark/Grush 1999: 8). In other words, assumptions and findings about weak representations, and the theoretical models building on them, might be cognitivist or mentalist as well as individualist in nature (and they usually are)—but from my perspective, they are nevertheless fully compatible with theoretical arguments about situated order, intelligibility, cognition, or action. Ethnomethodologists, for example, might "deliberately abstain from the use of mental mechanisms" (Garfinkel 1996: 13) since they hold that "there is no reason to look under the skull since nothing of interest is to be found there but brains" (Garfinkel 1963: 190). While this implies that neuroscientists—who study almost exclusively weak representations (Ennen 2003: 301)—try to answer questions ethnomethodologists do not bother to ask; it also means that their answer can be seen as supporting and enhancing theoretical accounts of situated cognition and order (cf. Coulter 1991). I argue that many of the details of neuroscientific explanations in vision science are simply irrelevant from this perspective—but this does not mean that the overall findings as well as *some* details of explanations can deepen, but also challenge a practice-based view. Jacob and Jeannerod (2003), for example, make a long and detailed argument that visuomotor perceptions are conceptual rather than non-conceptual content (or "direct" in the sense of J. J. Gibson 1986)—but as long as it is assumed that these conceptual representations "fall silent"—as Ennen (2003: 301) puts it—as soon as their referent vanishes, I can see no reason to demand that all traces of representationalism must be eliminated from cognitive sciences, as Sharrock and Coulter do (1998a, 1998b). In contrast, I suggest that Schatzki's (2002: 79) postulate that what he calls practical intelligibility (rather than skills alone) largely determines what people undertake to do links up well with findings presupposing weak representations—and thus it is somewhat unwarranted to reject them wholeheartedly, as Schatzki (1997: 303) does, just because from a Wittgensteinian standpoint, they are strictly speaking mentalist. No one, after all, would earnestly deny that our brain is deeply involved in our seeing and doing things; or that when we grasp a moving object we have somehow 'foreseen' its speed and direction in some way or another. That said, I caution that whether or not conceptual (motor-) representations can be adequately translated into language or abstract logical relations is quite a different question—and indeed the point that needs to be critically raised against many, if not most neuroscientific accounts of vision and conduct (see Schatzki 1996). In sum, I embrace

Ennen's suggestion (2003) that neuroscientific models inferring weak representations can be matched to Heidegger's and Merleau-Ponty's notions of actors' engagement in the world, but add that their content cannot be adequately expressed in language or logic and only manifests indirectly (e.g. in outward behaviour and/or measurable electric 'activity' in brain areas).

Chapter 5
Things—The Amalgam

1 Introduction: The Love for Equipment

"This morning, I didn't know if I should take [this ski] for today. But when I wake up and my new skis are standing next to my bed… That's my groom—I have to ride him today!" [M][1] Tina is exaggerating—but just a bit. Her eyes are sparkling as she looks down onto the brand-new pair of Dynastar Legend Pro Rider on her feet. And yes, she probably should not have taken the new skis today: The layer of fresh powder is still pretty thin, so there is a good chance that she will hit a rock hidden under the snow and add a nasty scratch to the skis' base. But when you wake up and the first thing you see are your new skis smiling at you—who could resist the temptation? Not Tina. "Ohh, he looks sooo god!" [M][2] Her groom-metaphor is of course a welcome opportunity to crack a round of sex-related jokes during our long lift-ride up onto the Schaufeljoch towering above the Stubai glacier. But then there is a grain of truth in it: After all, it is a men's ski model—heavier, longer, stiffer—and that matters to her, since it means they are made for more speed, more power, and more radical lines. "These girlie skis are not for me." [M][3]

Pete: "So, did you get yourself the new Wall?" [M][4] The last time I saw Pete I was still renting out some battered-down freestyle ski, and I had told him I would buy my own pair soon. As we meet again about two months later on the parking lot in Zell, the first thing he asks me is if I got the skis.

Me: "No, I got last year's model. I didn't really feel like paying a hundred Euro extra just to get the new [graphic] design." Of course, Pete will know that Völkl did not actually redesign their flagship freestyle ski this year, but only changed the graphics on the

---

[1] „Ich wusst ja nich heut morgen ob ich den nehmen soll für heut. Aber wenn ich aufwach und mein neuer Ski steht neben meinem Bett. das ist mein Bräutigam, den musst ich fahrn heute."
[2] „Ohh, der sieht so gut aus!"
[3] „Mit diesen Girlie-Ski kann ich nichts anfangen."
[4] „Hast dir den neuen Wall [ein Skimodell] geholt?"

© The Author(s), under exclusive license to Springer-Verlag GmbH, DE, part of Springer Nature 2024
N. Woermann, *Seeing Style*, Beiträge zur Praxeologie / Contributions to Praxeology, https://doi.org/10.1007/978-3-662-69182-3_5

157

Fig. 5.1 Skis left lying around carelessly on a freeski contest

topsheet. I turn half-way to Tom, who is standing next to us: "Since they changed practically nothing else, did they." [M][5] It is half a question, half a statement. It is what I read on the internet, browsing through the endless discussions about this season's new skis. Tom should know, since he is sponsored by Völkl and has skied both models.

Tom: "They feel the same when you ride them. The lamination, between the core and the base-layer has gotten a bit better." [M][6] (Fig. 5.1)

From my fieldnotes from a trip to Laterns, 15.2.09.

"Fred is really into bindings. Today, he is riding his JPvsJulian-clone from Pale [a cheap copy of a well-known backcountry-ski model he got from eBay] that have centrally mounted Naxo [bindings]. 'No idea how you can come up with the idea of mounting this binding centrally.'[7] But they're not soft or wobbly—unlike the recent test in the Skiing [magazine] said. For his Big Daddy (his deep-powder ski which is even more wide and hard) he treated himself with the Duke [a much more expensive binding]—although the sole argument justifying the higher price should be the greater stability compared to the Naxo. But he just loves bindings. 'I also have a Rossignol XYS200. It goes from 12 to 19, that's so crazy.[8] They just go CLACK and you're glued onto your skis.'[9] I agree, that is pretty crazy. I ask him which he needs such high DIN settings. 'Well, I actually use 14.' So he could have just gotten a standard freeride binding instead of fiddling with a used professional race binding."

---

[5] „Nee, den vom letzten Jahr. Ich hatte keinen Bock, für das aktuelle Design hundert Euro mehr auszugeben." (halb fragend an Tom): „Denn sonst hat sich ja praktisch nix geändert."

[6] „Das Fahrgefühl ist das Gleiche. Die Verbindung zwischen Belag und Kern ist etwas besser geworden."

[7] „Wie jemand auf die Idee kommt, die zentral zu montieren, ist mir auch schleierhaft."

[8] He is talking about the DIN setting scale that allows for adjusting the release force of the safety mechanism. Most bindings go up to 10, which is sufficient for expert on-slope skiing. Downhill racers use settings of 20 and higher.

[9] „Ich hab noch ne Rossignol XYS200. Die geht von 12 bis 19, dass ist so krass. Das macht so KLACK und dann bist du darauf festgebombt."

1 Introduction: The Love for Equipment

Tom his really happy with his new Völkl Chopsticks. "What really surprised me was how hard they are on your knees. Every single bump hits you straight away, no absorption at all. (...) I mean I knew that you can't really carve them and that they are really hard on your thighs, but I didn't expect this. But then they're also really cool when you land in powder. You're not, like, slamming in, but you sink in slowly just a bit at first. And it doesn't pop you out straight away, but you sink in and then smoothly ride straight out." [M][10]

From my fieldnotes, Zell am Ziller, 30.1.09

"Tom broke his skis during training some weeks ago, that is, completely, topsheet and core. At first he didn't even realize it, probably it happened as he crashed on the rails. He just kept skiing normally for the rest of the day. It probably felt a bit spongy, he says, but the skis were old anyways, and because the edges had cracked it felt spongy anyways. Not before he was down in the valley he saw that the ski was really broken all the way through."

From an interview, 4.10.08

Me: "So you're waxing [your skis] yourself?"

Tom: "Yeah, I always do that myself. I do the edges myself as well. That is really important that they are not sharp, otherwise you'll break your neck [when grinding] on a box. (...) So [preparing my edges] is really important for me, it puts me at ease. (...) And if the hole for the bindings are drilled [into a new pair of skis]. That is also something I really care about. I have to be there. I mean, I know Stefan will do it right. But I have to see that." [I][11]

Freeskiers really care about their gear. On and off the mountain, they spend endless hours discussing the pros and cons of certain models or technical details of shape and material, exchanging tips about this one guy at the Arlberg who sells gear out of his ramshackle cellar for fabulous prices, and stories about a friend who bought Russian counterfeit powder skis that aren't actually that bad. They debate the pricing strategies of a Scandinavian beanie brand and the quality of zippers on some ski wear brand and the advantages of bamboo ski cores. They know their stuff. For one, the type, quality, and state of someone's gear serve as markers of his skill and style preferences. The pros, for example, will have next season's model already from about mid-February onwards (after the large trade

---

[10] „Was mich total überrascht hat war wie die in die Knie gehen. Da hauts dir jeden Buckel direkt ungefedert rein. (...) Das man die kaum Carven kann und dass die mega in die Oberschenkel gehen, war mit klar, aber damit hab ich nicht so gerechnet. Aber dafür ist es halt auch supergeil beim Landen im Powder. Da schlägst du nicht so ein, sondern sinkst erst so ein bisschen gebremst ein. Und es federt dich dann nicht so raus, sondern du sackst ein und fährst dann locker nach vorne raus."

[11] „Ja, das mach ich immer selber. Die Kanten schleif ich auch immer selber. Das ist wichtig, dass die abgeschliffen sind, sonst packt man sich ordentlich auf die Fresse auf ner Box. (...) Das ist mir wichtig und das gibt mir auch Ruhe. (...) Und wenn die neuen Löcher gebohrt werden, das ist auch sowas. Das ist mir echt wichtig, da muss ich dabei sein. I mein, I weiß ja der Stefan macht das richtig. Aber ich muss das sehen."

fairs took place), and after a few weeks their gear will already look used and battered, thus signalling how much they ski. But then equipment is so much more than just a symbolic marker. It can protect or endanger the rider, give confidence, or disappoint, it must be groomed and looked after, and it can challenge or hinder or help. Gear is not just in between you and the mountain; you are *in* the mountains *in* your gear. Therefore, it is hardly surprising that freeskiers care about their gear in that they regularly attend to it and talk about it (see for a similar case Dant/Wheaton 2007; and Wheaton 2000b on the role of material in windsurfing). Indeed, it would be fair to say that riders love their gear; just like Parisian engineers loved the ARAMIS automated metro systems (Latour 1996c) and development workers love the Zimbabwe Bush Pump (de Laet/Mol 2000). But how do they *know* about their gear in the first place? After all, I have argued that material elements are tightly baked into the amalgam of practices. How are skiers sometimes absolutely sure about how well a ski works and how hard it is on their knees in specific snow conditions, when on other occasions they do not even notice that their skis have broken? What, in other words, does it mean to know about material things-in-practice?

2 The Amalgam of Practice and Its Material Aspects

Assuming that we routinely and interchangingly rely on two separate and distinct modi of visual perception which I suggested to call epistemic and pragmatic vision does not only require me to adapt the theoretical notion of intentionality and action accordingly; it also raises the question how one can conceptualize intelligibility, understanding, and—ultimately—meaning in light of this fundamental insight. How to best think about the social infrastructure at work in our gaining insights, that is, when we see something as something? In the first two chapters, I argued that seeing and recognizing something is a practical accomplishment that is inherently social, situated, and enmeshed into bodily work; and that the 'logic' of the body and the situation prefigure our visual insights to a considerable extent. Concluding that consciousness and conceptual knowledge determine our ways of knowing in isolation would be misleading. In search of an alternative, I adapted Merleau-Ponty's notion of the phenomenal field and incorporated it into phenopractice theory. My main objective was to get a coherent grasp on the complex problem of how we perceive from and to, with and within our body; being 'viatores mundi' perpetually en route, steering, passengering, riding body-vehicles of the strangest kind and feeling fully in charge nevertheless. Let me now turn to the *inanimate* things that are alive in the actors' world. Epistemic and pragmatic vision are both frequently concerned with material objects of some sort. Consequently, the meaning an object gains in the social world cannot be reduced to those aspects epistemic vision alone can pick up. The freeskiers' never-waning interest in, and heartfelt enthusiasm about, skiing gear, for example, is by no means solemnly motivated by allegedly 'superficial' qualities like shape, colour, or branding, and thus the purely symbolic meaning they might have. Skiers, I believe, truly care about equipment; and like a sailor encapsulated in his boat in the middle of the ocean, they have good reason to do so. As the case of Ski-BASEing in the first chapter demonstrated, once put into use, material objects can have a profound impact even on supposedly 'intellectual' and non-technological practices such as looking at a mountain. One advantage of the concept of the phenomenal field that I advertised is that it enables a symmetric perspective on the different aspects simultaneously and co-dependently shaping and challenging our perception-in-conduct, e.g. the material and the embodied or the interactive and the spatial.

Yet this notion also raises an important question: If all seeing and knowing happens in practical conduct, and if everything that is put into conduct is baked tightly into an amalgam, can we still understand anything about things themselves rather than momentary amalgams? To be sure, my characterization of amalgamation should not lead to the impression that I am arguing that within a phenopractice, a few stable or basic or ontological features (like those of the body or the material) become mixed up with 'messy' social things. What I call the amalgam of a practice is not a cocktail of solid building blocks with an added twist of 'cultural' chaos or 'social' self-reference. Instead, I argue that holding that congregations of distinct elements evoke meaning-in-relation does not imply that said elements must have fixed and independent meaning in themselves, that is, if taken out of any context. In other words, I simply refer to aspects of an amalgam to denote that there is no way of getting any of them 'out' of a specific practice or praxis per se, neither empirically nor analytically. It is in this sense that philosopher Volker Caysa (2008) understands all worldly entities to be depended on the level of the "empractical," that is, being firmly enwrapped in basal (bodily) practice. Any instance of knowing, analysing, or seeing any part or building block of a practice can only be achieved in the course of a practice—often a practice of observing which is *different* from the practice the supposed 'object' of observation is an amalgamated aspect of. Therefore, one could say that any epistemological operation should be considered as an act of sublation or *Aufheben* in the sense of Hegel in that something is elevated from the background to the fore, but simultaneously taken out of the context that provided its original meaning. This notion of phenopractice as sublation is a direct consequence of the concept I discussed in Chap. 2: that a fundamental duality of blending in and standing out forms the basis of a processual constitution of meaning. Generalizing from the finding that seeing a figure is a twofold process of relating background and foreground, it is argued that all attempts of singling out any aspect equates to foregrounding rather than separating it from the background practice. In my view, what is significant about this idea is its dual nature. On the one hand, it is a constructivist concept that acknowledges the reflexive and inherently social origin of meaning: Just like seeing a figure means detaching it from its background in a top-down process driven by 'cognition' or 'memory' (e.g. being told to look for a duck rather than a rabbit enables us to 'find' the duck 'in' an ambiguous duck/rabbit figure), observing or knowing something about something is primarily an effect on the *process* of observing or knowing rather than the observed or known thing itself. On the other hand, however, the idea is not a version of 'radical' constructivism or radical reflexivity, because it describes a routinized organization of affordances rather than an autarchic invocation of meaning as an alien essence existing in another realm or on a different plane (such as secluded consciousness or social superstructures). Seeing can teach us, I believe, how 'top-down' and 'bottom-up' processes can intertwine to from a situated epistemological act, so that a), insisting on either of the two as the only 'true' source of meaning or identity seems unjustified, and b), although acknowledging the unshakeable situatedness or 'haecceity' of all knowledge or observations, one might still expect quite rigid mechanisms at work behind the seemingly arbitrary surface of postmodern rhizomes. Of course, generalizing the case of vision into such an 'epistemology of social practices' amounts to mere theoretical speculation, because thus far, nothing but perception with and of the body has been discussed. Indeed, I hold that many of the misunderstandings within the practice turn stem from some authors' unfortunate self-restriction to discussing the body and embodied sociality, thus mistreating the practice turn as largely tantamount to the so-called body turn (Gugutzer 2006; Shilling 2003), the performative turn (Fischer-Lichte 2004; V. W. Turner/Schechner 1988), or theories of embodied knowledge and skills, particularly by reading (and reducing) Bourdieu to this aspect (such as Wacquant's [2004, 2005a] "carnal sociology"). Consequently, sorting out the differences between what one could summarize as pragmatist, praxeological, and performative versions of practice thought rooted in individualist ontology on the one side, and a theory of social practices building on a social ontology (especially in the wake of Heidegger) on the other is a key aim of the following chapters of this work.

Schatzki on Materiality: Elements Versus Arrangements

Notably, in describing material objects as elements of practices, I deviate from Schatzki's account of practice theory. In Schatzki, practices are anchored in what he calls material arrangements, but material elements themselves are not part of practices. He distinguishes objects or arrangements of substantial entities ("people, artifacts, living organisms, and things" [Schatzki 2002: 22]) from activities or practices (which are composed of activities); and criticizes ANT and authors like Pickering for ascribing intentional action to objects (Schatzki 2002: 189–210). He holds this distinction to be important because:

> *"The enabling and constraining effects of objects and arrangements on activities are relative to actor's ends, projects, hopes, fear, and so on. Objects, if you will, make a contribution, but the nature of that contribution depends on us." (Schatzki 2002: 117).*

However, Schatzki's rejection of Actor-Network-Theory in particular and what he calls posthumanist theory in general is not as decisive or complete as it may sound—in fact, I believe that, according to his own terminology, the distinction he seeks to draw between practices and material arrangements is not as clear-cut as he sometimes suggests. First, one needs to note that he explicitly marks this distinction between objects and practices as not referring to an ontological difference:

> "*Practices are intrinsically connected to and interwoven with objects (i.e., substances). The differentiation of practices from orders is not, therefore, a division into distinct ontological regions. Rather, it is an analytic distinction between components of a single mesh." (Schatzki 2002: 117).*

Further, he drops the idea upheld in his first book that doings as well as activities are necessarily human doings, stating clearly: "I no longer (…) restrict the expression 'doing' to bodily human doings"; and provides as examples of agents: "a practice, a person, a text" (Schatzki 2002: 191). To be sure, he then goes on to emphasize the "unique richness" of human agency and ultimately advises to take up a "cautious humanism" (2002: 210) which acknowledges the limited, but notable importance of nonhuman agents, yet nevertheless insists on the centrality and, if you wish, superiority of human action for social life. In writing this, however, I should be quick to remind the reader that Schatzki employs a quite specific notion of action and activity; and that for this reason he is not the hidden individualist he appears to be here in this brief explanation. Nevertheless, I also suggest that Schatzki's allegedly strict distinction between material arrangement and practice is at least blurred: By postulating that material artefacts can be understood as agents undertaking doings (2002: 191), it is implicated that said entities themselves carry forth practices, since practices are bundles of doings. More specifically, he writes: "If Y is an articulation of intelligibility, the agent is whatever articulated it (a practice, a person, a text)" (2002: 191)—and at least in my use of the term intelligibility this implies that tools or texts can be, and frequently are, constitutive parts of social practices in that they underwrite both understanding and intelligibility. Thus, while I share his general sentiment regarding both the centrality and uniqueness of the contribution of human activity to the unfolding of social order and the important but less capable influx of material tools (or texts), I do not think that the exclusion of material objects from social practices is a) formulated theoretically in an entirely satisfying way in his writings, and can b) be stringently upheld in empirical arguments. For both reasons, I argue contra Schatzki that material arrangements do not just 'anchor' phenopractices but should be considered elements of them. Regarding the empirical point b), my line of reasoning is that practices are required to gain insight into features of the material world, and even to gain an understanding of materiality as singular entities at all. Thus, one cannot empirically know, first, how and what materialities themselves are, and second, in which way materialities

> could be 'outside of' and anchoring practices. In other words: Since my account ties intelligibility or observation to practical and situated conduct, there can be no empirical basis for or realization of the theoretical argument that material arrangements are anchoring practices from below rather than featuring in their midst. To be sure, this alone does not devalue the argument's logic per se—but then I hope to demonstrate that there is also no theoretical need to uphold this specific reservation against the enmeshment of material elements into practices.

3 Zeug and Ding

Several authors have suggested that the core innovation of contemporary practice theory lies in integrating theories of performativity or embodiment more fully with the STS-tradition of conceptualizing the social nature of the material (Reckwitz 2002a, 2002b; Schatzki 2001)—although the intertwining of things and embodied *Dasein* was, of course, already a key topic of Heidegger (H. L. Dreyfus 1991; Luckner 2008). Following this tradition, I will over the following pages examine empirical cases which are at the core versions of a problem that is central to Heideggerian philosophy of technology: How can a thing, a *Ding-an-sich,* stand out of the ubiquity of material tools, settings, or surrounds—in Heidegger's words, "the totality of equipment" or *Zeug* (1962: 97). How this problem is related to my earlier discussion of the phenomenology of vision should be clear: This question is somewhat absent from Husserlian phenomenology,[12] because a perceived thing equates to a single noema—although it is of course part of the stream of consciousness and usually enmeshed into various apperceptions, it is in principle already singled out as a given unit (or even just one act in consciousness). Heidegger, in contrast, starts from the opposite direction, so to speak, and inquires into the prerequisites of the possibility of perceiving something as a single object with qualities distinct from its immediate use-in-context (Luckner 2008: 46–52). As with all other key theoretical arguments I try to embrace, I hold that this line of reasoning is not only theoretically convincing, but also simultaneously grasps an important facet of the empirical case at hand—it directly resonates with the freeskiers' everyday concerns. In particular, Heidegger's perspective highlights the enormous difficulty posed by freeskiing practices such as testing equipment, making a buying decision, or optimizing one's gear. As I will detail, the challenge

---

[12] As we have already seen several times, Husserl's writing is open to contradicting readings depending on which parts of his multifaceted oeuvre are read in which way. Authors disagree whether Heidegger should be considered as arguing in line with Husserl on this issue, or not (Dostal 1993).

3 Zeug and Ding

arising within such practices is twofold: In order to learn about or acquire the routinized use of a tool, it needs to be made standing out as an observable entity—but the condition towards which the adequacy of the object and its use needs to be assessed is its future quality as a Zeug, as a smoothly integrated and almost invisible detail of practical conduct.

Let me illustrate this point by looking at a ubiquitous and fairly nondescript piece of skiing equipment which nevertheless plays an important role and has evolved over the course of a complex history: ski poles. At first sight, poles seem so simple an object and marginal to the whole enterprise of skiing. In fact, one of the first things beginners have to learn is that they must *not* 'really' use the poles during riding, in the sense that they lean on them or try to brake or steer with them. "Just hold them in your hands and forget about them," they are told, "and make sure they do not even touch the snow." Indeed, one key innovation in the advent of alpine ski technology and technique has been to stop using ski poles for steering or breaking during riding, and thus switch from using one long, sturdy pole to two much lighter ones (Allen 2008). A further important step into the same direction of reducing the in-use remark-ability of the ski pole was the introduction of alloy poles in the 1960 which were much lighter and easier to hold in hand (Fry 2006a: 80). But then why do you need poles in the first place? Sure, the poles come handy when traversing a plane, but skiers hardly ever do that. Ski poles are not cheap, they have to be carried around all day, and in crashes they pose an additional risk of injury often underestimated.[13] Throughout the history of skiing, innovators and tinkerers have suggested to delete poles from the practice of skiing: ski racers in the 1920s (Allen 2008: 13), 'Oldschool' freestyle skiers of the 1970s (Fry 2006a: 223), so-called "extreme-carves" of the 1990s, and last but not least 'Newschool' freestylers from 2000 onwards. But none of these repeated 'revolutions' succeeded to any greater extent. In the case of freeskiing, for example, some known and respected superstars performed without poles in a very well-received ski movie, but their innovation in style was—unlike most other stylish little details seen in movies—not widely adapted—and more lately, the protagonists of the trend-not-to-happen apparently went back to using poles as well. Poles, it turns out, are important for almost all types of skiing because they a) help to provide much-needed balance and b) are used to organize the bodily rhythm of skiing by initiating a turn by 'pointing into it' with the pole and then planting the pole softly into the snow to turn 'around' this imaginary pivot—a swift and subtle move executed without any force; not more than a short flick of the wrist in skilled skiing. In other words, they are an interesting showcase of how seemingly trivial pieces of technical equipment can fulfil a pivotal role in phenopractices not because they transfer physical forces or have mechanical effects, but because they help to align epistemic and pragmatic vision, as well as body posture and movement: They

---

[13] Both freestylers and freeriders have special techniques of holding their poles: A ski pole getting caught in a beginning avalanche can easy drag you into it (because of its strap), and thumbs jolted or wrenched because of crashing with poles are all too common among freestyle skiers.

support the smooth transition from making out a crucial point, heading towards it, and realizing the turn in that the eye's 'pointing-by-fixation' becomes an embodied pointing with the pole, which fluidly transmutes into physically organizing the body posture adequate for leaning into the beginning of the turn. Yet bodily routines like keeping balance and coordinating movements already underway happen almost entirely outside of our immediate awareness—despite or because of their fundamental importance. Ski poles have to amalgamate smoothly with these most 'natural' and fragile bodily routines, and indeed they are largely intuitive to use. But, paradoxically, their very importance and high demands in usability make both designing and marketing ski poles especially difficult: Blending into the flow of epistemic-to-pragmatic vision during skiing is obviously very different from standing out epistemically on the crowded shelves of a ski-shop. For customers, it is very difficult to see in a pole-on-the-shelf that it will make a good pole-in-use that is easy to forget about since it works just fine. Accordingly, among all segments of ski equipment, both innovation and competition are probably on the lowest level in the ski pole market. Expressed in the terms of Heidegger (see H. L. Dreyfus 1991: 240): as Zeug-in-use, ski poles do not concern *(besorgen)* remarkable things, and thus they feature only marginally in skiers' care *(Sorge)*. Who cares about ski poles?

To be sure: Ski-poles, I argue, are but one very clear example for a general problem one always faces when trying to understand what and how a material piece of equipment is. For this reason, I will now look at ways of looking at material tools in more detail with regard to a more complicated, but also more insightful case: the one piece of equipment that freeskiers probably do care about the most, and which they thus try to grasp in its specific qualities as a *Ding* most attentively and diligently: the ski. When it comes to knowing about a particular ski, freeskiers, unlike most 'casual' skiers, are not only at the receiving end of marketing brochures, brand image claims, pricing structures, or advice offered in ski shops. Instead, many of them engage in practices of testing a ski from time to time, taking up and focusing on the material object, actively trying to tease out the particular nature of this particular piece. They engage, one might say, with passion and expertise into "a determination of the structure of the Being which entities possess." (Heidegger 1962: 96).

4 The Ski-In-The-Amalgam: What is a Ski?

For obvious reasons, the specific qualities of a ski are of great interest to advanced skiers: Does it float easily in deep powder? Is it easily manoeuvrable at lower speed, or instead stable and reliable at high speed? For a freerider, it is clear that choosing the right ski matching current snow conditions, the terrain one plans to ride in, and the manoeuvres one intends to make (such as 'hucking' cliffs to try tricks versus going for speed in Big Mountain lines) has a large effect on how well one will do on the mountain. Testing and debating a ski's qualities is an important genre of both freeskiers' everyday talk and various subcultural media such as websites or special-interest-magazines. Consequently, ski manufacturers both big and small invest much effort into determining the qualities of new ski models they ponder to build. The market segment for freeski is both fragmented and developing rapidly, so that new and improved models are expected by customers form every brand every season anew. For these reasons, ski prototypes are crucial for manufactures to succeed, ski tests appear regularly in freeski media, and shop owners conduct test of their own in order to decide which ski to put on display this season. In all these cases, more experienced freeskiers are often asked to help out, be it because they are sponsored by manufactures or shop-owners and thus can be 'put to work,' or be it because they will receive some media exposure in return. And since both media exposure and having sponsors are key indicators of status within the freeski community, ski testing is often part of what it means to be an accomplished and well-connected freeskier. Testing skis, in other words, is important for freeskiing in various ways. There is only one problem: in a strict sense, a practice for testing a ski does not exist. That is, there is no dedicated practice of testing, no commonly accepted method using specific tools and workshops and exact measures and clear categories of description. As a website for ski builders explains: "There's only one real way to test your skis: ride them, and ride them hard." (skibuilders.com 2004, [D]) (Fig. 5.2).

This is, of course, a bit of an exaggeration: For more than a century, the ski industry has continuously evolved, refined, and repeatedly revolutionized the technology behind skiing; introducing bamboo cores and leather lashings, fibreglass coatings and plastic boots, graphite poles and piezoelectric vibration absorbers, GPS-guided piste grooming machines and laser-sensors in fully automatic ski edge-grooming robots (see Fig. 4.2 and Fry 2006a: 71–123 for an overview of the technological history of skiing). At the centre of this astounding technological

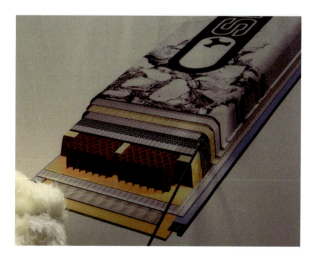

Fig. 5.2 Showcasing a ski's hidden qualities. (At a trade fair.)

evolution often stood, of course, the ski itself (e.g. Masia 2005). Transformed by wave after wave of innovation and market re-segmentation, generations of engineers have modelled, sketched, calculated, simulated, measured, and tried skis in various ways; and ski building has grown into a complex engineering discipline of its own (Lind/Sanders 2010). But despite the impressive range of scientific and 'exact' methods employed by engineers and developers, none of them can really determine the qualities of a prototype when it comes to actual skiing. From an exact engineer's point of view, skiing is a nightmare. For them, skiing is the interplay of a tool and a substance in the course of a movement, just like plane flying through air or a knife cutting wood. But the ski-tool oscillates between being used for carving, floating, grinding, and gliding; and snow as a substance is variably solid and stable like ice or drifts and flows like a fluid, changing density, weight and temperature in the process (Armstrong/Brun 2008; Grey/Male 1981). Additionally, a ski is built as a fibre-reinforced polymer composite so that its assembly is done by 'baking' together several layers of wood, plastic, fibre-glass, and steel with the help of gel coat, high pressure, and heat. The exact interplay of these heterogeneous layers and the precise impact of fiddling with various conditions of the moulding process remain largely a matter of trial-and-error, gut feeling, and experience. The crown of all this unreliable over-complexity, of course, is the human skier with his unrealistic expectations, imperfect postures, unreliably biomechanics, anti-rational addiction to fads and fashions, and—probably worst of all—his surprisingly profound aptitude of compensating for shortcomings of his equipment without even realising it. "A ski is equal to a black box," [I][14] a ski development engineer and experienced ski test supervisor told me.

To be sure: The engineers I spoke to portray the ski as some kind of unfortunate exception in terms of complexity and resistance to proper planning and measurement (not without occasionally priding themselves to be among the few able to cope with the challenge nevertheless). From a practice perspective, however, it is expected that at close observation, all forms of testing and measuring run into comparable problems and respective ways of remedying the inherent complexity of objects-in-use for purposes of engineering's exactness and scientific truth. Whether or not one shares this perspective on professional engineering is, in any event, of secondary importance to the following account, because said account is concerned with the freeskiers' own ways of knowing about skis. To some extent, freeskiers take principles of engineering science and especially engineering methods for granted, partly because some of them are, and others closely collaborate with, ski construction engineers. But as I will show, their methods, descriptions, and understandings also differ in important ways—which is why many approach the engineers' confident displays of technical perfection with some ironic distance (see picture). I want to underline that I do not consider this as an obstruction to getting a clear view on ways of knowing or realms of knowledge, for example in order to contrast professionals and laymen, scientists and everyday actors, or even

---

[14] „*Ski gleich Black Box.*"

4 The Ski-In-The-Amalgam: What is a Ski?

theorists and practitioners. Freeriders taking a friend's new ski for a test rider are, of course, as much practitioners as are engineers programming finite-element simulation models of vibration absorption in fibreglass layers. Therefore, I hold that accomplished freeskiers testing skis provides what Garfinkel (2002: 108) calls a "perspicuous setting" precisely because they roam the borders of codified professional practice and the informal pragmatism of enthusiastic hobbyists (being sometimes paid, partly professionally educated, and to varying degrees embedded into professional business operations). However, while I think one can well say that they are sometimes engaged in bricolage—in tinkering and puttering—I, crucially, do not suggest that they are *bricoleurs* as Levi-Strauss (1966) would have them, unsystematic laymen excluded from the strict world of engineers' rigor. Indeed, although sociology provisions several competing versions of interpreting the following case of 'looking at something (such as a ski) in different ways' as demonstrating the existence of separated abstract realms or structures of meanings, I will not embrace them here. A first alternative would be to see them as an effect of the existence of multiple social realities, systems, or discourses, for example scientific versus mundane. Another would treat them as competing perspectives in the sense of a subjective, volitionally chosen stance or viewpoint.[15] A third version, finally, would see them as proof of divergent sets of background knowledge being applied, possibly in the context of cultures of expertise (Honer/Maeder 1994) or as proof of (nothing but) embodied skills or a habitus (Schmidt 2006). None of these readings of the case, however, matches practice theory's central paradigm that *understandings*[16] are carried in social practices rather than subjects or superstructures. Therefore, if I am to survey freeskiers' ways of understanding skis towards discerning the nature of the amalgam of practice, I approach them from a different perspective: I treat them as different phenopractices employed towards the end of 'getting to know' a ski—specifically, and arguably not by accident, these practices are at least in part ways of seeing skis and

---

[15] The notion of perspective seems especially important with regard to the topic of seeing. Especially the historical development of the central perspective in visual arts has been discussed widely, predominantly by authors arguing for a view on vision grounded in the sociology of knowledge or action (see Raab 2008: 35–45). While I agree that forms of organisation of an image (such as the central perspective) can indeed imply a certain way of observing—e.g. from a specific distance and position and focusing on a particular detail (usually in the centre). I do not, however, believe that just because art from this period implies or seeks to demonstrate the subjectivity of vision, one can infer that it must be anthropological subjects who 'pick them up.' In fact, one might as well interpret this case as showing that the very priority of the seeing subject itself is nothing but an effect of a certain style of image composition.

[16] I borrow the term understandings from Schatzki. Note that therefore the term "understandings" should not be taken to mean mental states or events in consciousness. As Schatzki (1997: 303) makes clear: "Understanding et al. are not states of an abstract mental or real underlying apparatus that are causally related to actions. They are, instead, conditions of human existence" in Wittgenstein's sense. I will also embrace Schatzki's distinction between practical understandings and general understandings later on.

ways of looking at skis. Consequently, the fact that different conclusions about or different 'versions' of the ski are being produced will be attributed to the differences between phenopractices, while the humans, skis, and/or symbolic universes (etc.) engaged in said practices are considered as remaining essentially the same (or their variety as not being of necessary relevance to the phenomenon of difference). One important difference that I will focus on is that between two different kinds of backgrounds effective in those practices of understanding skis: In the first case, the foregrounding of the character of the ski will occur in the course of juxtaposing the ski and mechanical tools or material against material, while in the second case, the material ski as a *Ding* will be made to stand out against the body as a *Zeug* made of flesh.

5 Flex Curves—Good Data as Bad Science

Of course, certain qualities of a ski can be measured metrically: its length and weight, the stiffness of torsion, the radius cut into its shape, and so on (see Lind/Sanders 2010). One interesting tool in this regard are so-called flex-curves, graphs produced to enable engineers to see (rather than calculate) the 'hidden' qualities of a ski (see Fig. 5.3). In these graphs, a line is used to describe the flex of the ski, that is, the stiffness defined as the force in Newton that is necessary to bend the ski vertically at this point by one millimetre. For freeskiers (as well as ski manufacturers, vendors, or journalists), the flex or stiffness of a ski is an important aspect of a ski's "character" that frequently features in descriptions of a ski, be it in marketing brochures or ski tests, and various terminologies or numerical systems for rating ski flex are used. One typical way of practically assessing a ski's flex can be frequently observed when experienced skiers 'check out' ski models at a shop or trade fair (see the picture on the following page): They grab the ski by its tip with one hand (its bottom end standing on the ground) and then push forcefully onto the ski with the other hand so that it bends and they thus feel the flex. In contrast, proponents of flex curves or a standardised flex index suggest that, rather than using such 'ways of the hand,' skiers should rely on systematic measures instead. In the freeski community, one particular method and according sets of data annually produced by a Norwegian freeride enthusiast (see Hals 2007, 2011) has received considerable attention on the discussion forums and bulletin boards of the dominant freeski-websites (e.g. epicski.com 2007; skibuilders.com 2006; tetongravity.com 2006; [D]). I will examine these discussions as fascinating documents of online sense-making in the course of a—somewhat failed—attempt to establish acceptance of a specific practice of observing and describing how a

Flex curves and SFI 2008

Each ski is placed in a hidden layer. To visualize them, click the "eye buttons" in the layers menu on the left. Some PDF readers don't allow layers. If you are a MAC user, all the curves will probably appear at once. In that case, save the pdf and open it in a layer compatible PDF reader (like Adobe Reader).

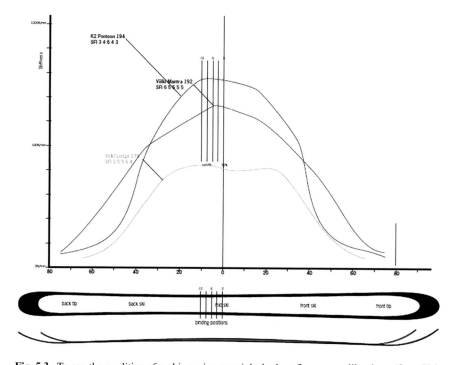

Fig. 5.3 To see the qualities of a ski, engineers might look at flex curves like these (from Hals 2007; [D])

ski's flex 'is' among a community of ski experts.[17] In doing so, I take up the inventor's own explanation of what flex curves are needed for: "We cannot discuss ski flex when we don't know what ski flex is." (Hals 2011; [D]) Flex curves, in other words, are a way of knowing a ski—a way of knowing conducted by looking at the graph and relying entirely on epistemic vision in doing so.

---

[17] Since I am making an argument with regard to the lived praxis of freeskiing, internet postings discussing practical action (rather than first-hand observations) might be seen as inadequate sources of data. I should therefore clarify that the fact that the flex of a ski is an important aspect of its character and that various phenopractices are employed to find out about it is a general finding of my ethnographic work, that is, I have participated in and observed these practices first hand (for example when buying my own skis) and discussed the issue with several freeskiers and professional ski developers. I concluded that a) several different practices of testing or 'knowing' flex co-exist, and b) online discussions are one important form of debating or learning about ski

As such, flex curves are instructive in two regards: First, they come with extensive fine prints explaining various measures of standardization, compensation, and recalculation that had to be conducted to produce 'accuracy.' (see Hals 2007, 2011; [D]) Therefore, they are the product of practices of purification, inscription, translation, and representation of data that have been intensively studied in the context of science (e.g. Callon 1986; Knorr Cetina 1981, 1999; Latour/Woolgar 1986; Lynch/Woolgar 1990). But second, unlike in the case of professional science, the freeskiers seem much less willing to accept the authority of accuracy. In particular, the freeskiers I observed knew such graphs but considered them not much use because they only give hints, allowing for no more than a broad qualification of a ski such as: A long, stiff ski with a large radius is great for taking big turns at high speed. Moreover, online discussions are dominated by critical enquiries into the methods applied, the units chosen, the appropriate forms of presenting or reading the data, and so on (e.g. epicski.com 2007; skibuilders.com 2006; tetongravity.com 2006; [D]). At the core, I want to argue, the discussants defend different understandings of *what* a ski is and, consequently, what qualities need to be measured or which methods yield authority in terms of the relevance and correctness of said qualities. For example, while for some it is clear that the ski binding is not part of the ski itself and must thus be ignored, others object that nobody rides a ski without a binding, plus a ski-with-binding would yield quite different flex data. More specifically, many riders object to the data recorded for some specific model and claim that they personally *know* this very ski to be different. Predictably, those defending the method do so by building on what one might call a scientific regime of justification (in the sense of Boltanski/Thévenot 2006), for example by juxtaposing thought and fact, myth and reality:

> "The ski is thought to be a soft ski, but test show that the ski is very stiff underfoot and has a soft front tip. (this is also correct according to K2's website) People seem to get very engaged, and sometimes a bit angry, when the reality does not match the myth." (Forum post signed by the 'inventor' of the flex-index [skibuilders.com 2006]; [D])

Notably, the many critics of the method do not dispute the ideas of precise data and measuring per se. Instead, they question the very legitimacy of measuring in a workshop and using machines as a path to accurate, *scientific* data and thus as a source of authority:

---

flex, a way of 'doing flex' if you wish. (As far as I have observed, online forums are generally important within freeskiing in that they are frequently used by many and considered an inherent part of the global freeski community [be it in a positive or negative way] by all participants I encountered or spoke to. Geisler's [2004: 47, 94] ethnography of the German freeski-scene reports the same finding.) Therefore, I treat online discussions about Hals' FSI-method as one particularly instructive and well-documented example of a general phenomenon regarding practices of testing skis, and I consider these texts as 'naturally occurring data' providing insight into one way of 'doing being a freeskier.' I do not suggest they faithfully document workshop practices of testing ski flex, but that they are a key elements of freeskiers' phenopractices regarding skis.

5 Flex Curves—Good Data as Bad Science

"The data seems inaccurate for skis I am very familiar with. (…) You can grab a ski and flex it and get better data, or ski it. This is likely bad science." (Forum post (epicski.com 2007); [D])

What is drawn into question, in other words, is not the idea that a ski should be observed as a technical object, or that this problem falls into the realm of science, but instead the very practice which enables the skiers to observe the relevant particulars of a ski. Rather than looking at a flex curve, the quote suggests, one should either flex the ski 'by hand' as shown in Fig. 5.4, or better even, bring the flex to life by skiing it. A ski's character, it is argued, depends on the interplay of many minute details, and instead of capturing and then adding them up to a sum of 'data points,' the interplay of several elements of the practice of skiing has to be made happening for the ski's gestalt to appear. For example, it is clear for a ski-builder that a softer 'flex' of the shovel of the ski effects the skiing in wind-pressed, hard snow. But will it also work in conjunction with the stiff centre of the ski? Does the softer tip not matter because there is sufficient grip at the centre, or would the ski binding need to be mounted a tad further back to make it work? But if the binding, and thus the centre of gravity, is moved further backwards, does the softer tip still retain its favourable impact on softer, deeper snow? Or will it make the skier lean further forward to cut into a turn, thus nullifying all positive qualities? Answers

Fig. 5.4 Flexing a ski. (At a trade fair.)

to such questions, skiers argued both in interviews I conducted and in online discussions, cannot be gained in the workshop or with the help of measuring instruments, because they relate to effects that do not appear unless the skis are used for skiing. Therefore, while the skiers agree that a ski is a physical object that can and should be aptly described as a sum of discernible and relevant characteristics, they express contesting understandings of the circumstances, practical methods, and relevancies that enable the 'discovery' of the true features of the ski as a material object.

Moreover, what is in question with regard to the skis is not so much the concept or nature of the ski as a whole, but more frequently and importantly what measurable units should be considered as being one single quality of a ski and what are two separate units in need of differentiation, possibly adding that one of them needs to be ignored as it distorts the data. For example, on the one hand the very usefulness of the flex-curves-method is supposed to stem from the fact that it enables the observation of the combined and overlapping effects of, e.g., the ski's wooden core, its fibre glass layers, and the thickness of the steel edges. The length of the ski, on the other hand, is considered as disturbing the data and, as the self-proclaimed 'inventor-owner' of the method explains, needs to be compensated for (Hals 2007; [D]). Not all discussants accept this particular point; and even more objections are raised in similar matters, e.g. if and how the chamber (the horizontal 'bend') of the ski should be accounted for. Instead of measuring the flex-relative-to-length, it is argued, one should measure the flex-relative-to-length-and-chamber. But the 'inventor-owner' rejects the idea:

> "When measuring skis I am absolutely confident that we can not mix different characteristics into one unit. Even if it is absolutely true that all the different characteristics infect on how the ski performs. A term of 'stiffness combined with camber' would be absolutely useless, because you would not be able to separate the two values afterwards." (Forum post signed by the 'inventor' of the flex-index [skibuilders.com 2006]; [D])

This quote expresses, I suggest, a central proposition of practice theory: What a physical object is and which characteristics it (or anything else) has, depends on the practice within which it appears.[18] "When measuring skis," for example, certain terms and characteristics might become observable, but they still remain "absolutely useless" given the practice at hand. Moreover, the core process towards achieving intelligibility is just not one of imposing differences, i.e. depending on whether one is able to keep apart A and B, but rather a process of assembling and discerning: What to conflate? What should stand out? When—inter alia—relying on epistemic and pragmatic processing in variable ratios, which combination of background details add up to exhibit an intelligible and relevant gestalt? As information theorists have argued since long, gaining information depends on making selections and thus on ignoring as much as attending (Ashby

---

[18] Notably, this proposition is by no means shared by all authors within the practice turn, for example not by Schatzki (2002) or Giddens (1984), but by Reckwitz (2002a) or Shove (2007).

1958; Shannon 1948)—however, contrary to some authors (such as Luhmann 1995a), I do not believe that this implies that *every* whole we perceive, or reference only results from an assembling of effectively infinitesimally small singularities (see below).

6 On Understandings, Aspects, and Elements

I want to suggest that disagreements of the kind the freeskiers have about the proper methods of getting to 'know' a ski are instructive not because they demonstrate that categories of observation are contingent and that measuring 'facts' is a rhetorical or political process (e.g. Suchman 1994). Rather than suggesting that categories such as the flex contain a logic of their own essentially different from the 'actual' ski, I hold that from a phenopractice perspective, the case of the flex curves is to be understood as an instance of *Seeing-as* in the sense of Wittgenstein (2009; see Gebauer 2009): as practices of observing a certain kind of physical objects as having a) a set of characteristics-in-context that can b) be practically validated within some (not all) of these specific contexts. Using the terminology coined by Annemarie Mol (2002), the ski is thus considered a multiple; that is, although every phenopractice provides a different 'version' of the ski, these are understood as different perspectives on aspects of the same entity.[19] Before I continue my discussion of the amalgam of practice and the take on materiality it implies, I should explain this particular Wittgenstein-inspired perspective on the social nature of understandings a bit further (building on, but also diverging from Schatzki 1996, 2002). Let me use the ski flex as a perspicuous case by giving an account of the ski flex as a 'social thing' in the sense of Garfinkel (2002), as something that (at least for freeskiers) exists and influences skiing and other activities.[20]

---

[19] Mol (2002) undertakes a "praxiography" of a range of different practices of diagnosing, observing, and treating the same 'thing' (an illness) quite similar to my discussion in this chapter. Although these practices, produce incongruent versions of the illness and the ill body, she argues "that there is manyfoldedness, but not pluralism" (Mol 2002: 84) in the sense that the body itself is neither fragmented nor plural, but only the practices of knowing it are.

[20] Garfinkel uses the term 'social thing' to describe social phenomena which are situatedly and accountably achieved in concrete situations in such a way that they are evidently not unique, but general and expectable 'facts' of life: "Each *thing* (…) consist of accountable phenomenal-field-properties-in-and-as-of-the-generality of that *thing* (…)." (2002: 99; original emphasis) Garfinkel suggested that such in-situ 'social things' are to be understood as the empirically in-detail manifestations of Durkheim's (arguably merely aphoristic) 'social facts' (see Greiffenhagen/Sharrock 2009; Lynch 2009; A. W. Rawls 2009). Schatzki's definition of practical understandings as *bundles* of abilities of "knowing how to X, knowing how to identify X-ings, and knowing how to prompt as well as respond to X-ings" (2002: 77) in my view comes very close to Garfinkel's account of ethnomethods. The key point in both cases is that they consist (at least) in 'pairs' of understandably acting and actively understanding which together constitute or carry phenomena. The meaning of a word, for example, is carried at the very minimum in saying the word and understanding it—both of which can only amount to what they are in a certain context.

In other words, I will define that within freeskiing,[21] understandings of what a ski flex is exist; and I will use this fact in order to illuminate the meaning of the following central postulate of practice theory (at least according to Schatzki):

> "What something is is, fundamentally, what it is understood to be. Understandings (...) are carried in social practices and expressed in the doings and sayings that compose practices." (Schatzki 2002: 58) *and*

> "People share an understanding of a word or action when they use that word or carry out the action intelligibly to one another." (Schatzki 1996: 110)

To illustrate what is meant by saying that understandings, e.g. the understanding of a ski flex, are *carried* by social practices and *expressed* in doings and sayings, let me consider again the case of testing the flex by hand. In a ski shop or in a ski manufacturer's booth at a trade fair, one will usually find the different ski models lined up on the wall, accompanied by lively descriptions like this one:

> "Our custom weave fibreglass creates tremendous torsional stability while allowing easy longitudinal flex to initiate turns and absorb terrain." (Liberty Skis 2010; [D])

Colourful marketing prose like this, everyday wisdom suggests, needs to be greeted with scepticism because it tries to put the product into a favourable light irrespective of the products actual features. A common sociological version of this notion is the assertion that the text uses symbolic or semantic means to imbue the ski with a certain meaning, a meaning the customer will hopefully internalize. This internalization of symbolically mediated meaning, in turn, is in this view held to happen by way of perceiving, recognizing, and interpreting signs that are taken by the customer to be referring to the ski (and possibly also mistrusted by reason of his background knowledge regarding the tricks of marketing). A practice perspective, however, would suggest a different account, one that can be clarified by paying close attention to what almost all visitors on a trade fair booth (and most experienced ski buyers in shops) routinely do after or even before reading the text: They grab the ski and test the flex in the way I described above, by pushing down onto it to 'get a feel' of flex. From a constructivist viewpoint, the text and the pushing-down, the doing and the saying, could be considered two separate communicative events, or expressions of different forms of knowledge held by different persons. From a practice perspective, however, the flex is carried by the *interplay* of doings and sayings (in turn carried by a combination of epistemic and pragmatic engagement). Expressed in ethnomethodological terms, the flex is not just a way of describing a ski, but a phenomenon that is "instructably observable and instructably reproducible in and as the phenomenal field's (…) ordered details of structure" of the practice of 'feeling' the flex (Garfinkel 2002: 149). The facticity and relevance of the flex, in other words, is rooted in "praxeological validity" because, firstly, it is provided by way of its practical, 'hands-on' availability; secondly, it can be expressed and mediated in verbal or written form; and thirdly

---

[21] More precisely: freeskiing as a community forged by a field of freeskiing practices.

and crucially, in that both 'doing' and 'saying' are related in such a way that the one reliably demonstrates the relevance and correctness of the other (Bjelić 1992, 1995; Garfinkel 2002, 2007; Garfinkel/Lynch/E. Livingston 1981; Lynch 1993, 2009). Notably, it is neither implied that talking about the flex produces some alternative reality in which the flex is made to exists, nor that talking works as a self-fulfilling property conjuring up the flex's facticity, and also not that talking about the flex expresses a condition of the world existing independently of the talking. Instead, the phenomenon of the flex is established on the basis of coherences: Given (inter alia) necessary skill, the printed text-on-display can be read as coherently making a statement about the flex of the ski; and grabbing and pushing the ski in a certain way produces a phenomenal field in which the customer can feel the flex. Moreover, while some authors suggest a "praxeological approach to subjectivation" (Warnier 2001) and understand the grabbing-and-flexing as a manual way of internalizing the ski's flex (thus adhering to an individualist standpoint), ethnomethodologists emphasize that the latter coherence is established situatedly and "instructedly," i.e. on the basis of, but not fully determined by the instruction (see A. W. Rawls 2011). The validity of the flex, in other words, is the result of the situated interplay of the skill of flexing, the ski's qualities of producing-the-feeling-of-the-announced-flex-if-flexed-in-the-right-manner, the text announcing 'what to look for' in flexing the ski, and possibly several further conditions, such as the visibility of the customer's expertise, or his moral entitlement to forcefully bending a ski that is not his own. (Indeed, testing skis in this way surely has a performative quality, especially because less experienced bystanders are often afraid the brand-new ski will break.) Therefore, the argument goes, the flex cannot be said to reside in any of those conditions alone; in particular not in the 'instruction' or 'rule' provided by the text, or for that matter in the embodied skill or the material object if taken in isolation (Schmidt 2022).

This latter point is particularly important with regard to the various versions of practice theory that diverge from my viewpoint (see Schatzki 1997, 2002: 194–203 with regard to the following examples; and Schatzki/Knorr Cetina/von Savigny 2001 for the wider discussion): For example, one might hold with Bourdieu that the individual having the embodied skill of (visibly) 'getting' or perceiving the flex—the Habitus carrying practical understanding—is the sole or predominant carrier of the flex's social existence. Alternatively, one might read Latour's claim that objects possess actorship as implying that things carry and independently enforce social orders. Both positions would be rejected from the 'Wittgensteinian' or 'Heideggerian' reading of practice theory popularized by Schatzki (as they would by ethnomethodology)—notwithstanding, of course, discord on whether or not Bourdieu or Latour 'really' made these arguments. Notably, this rejection should not be mistaken for a disagreement over the importance of one element of practices versus another; nor as blatantly overlooking the container-in-context argument Bourdieu and Latour are accused of making, i.e. that the Habitus is embedded in a Habitat or that ANT's actors are parts of networks. Instead, it is rooted in the fact that Schatzki's version of practice thought conceives every social practice as a *nexus* in itself, as "a spatial–temporal manifold

(…) whose constituents form a nexus—as opposed to an aggregation—in existing only in conjunction with other members of the manifold." (Schatzki 1997: 285)[22] Strictly speaking, Schatzki's thought implies a shift in the unit of sociological inquiry and a different concept of the 'format' of sociality in that 'the social' is *not* just said to happen or take place in occasional congregations of the 'pieces' that eventually (in the true sense of the word) add up to sociality, but instead that—turning the concept around—these situated occasions "express" the social, that is, social practices as the common determining force of all instances that can be identified as unfoldings of said practice (cf. Reckwitz 2000b for a critique of Schatzki's use of the term "express"). Social practices lie, so to speak, above and beyond both concrete occasions of sociality and single elements of practices. This statement, however, is not just a preference on behalf of the practice theorist, but a consequence of the following insight: What something intelligibly is (in which way it can be said to have socially relevant existence, rather than physical being), can never be defined or instantiated by singular events, but needs to be understood as the effect of an enduring coherence. The flex of a ski as a social phenomenon, for example, cannot be equated to the sum of several distinct social events in which the flex's existence is 'made to happen' by way of performance, because each of them exhibits certain situational contingencies that have nothing to with the flex—and, as ethnomethodologists would add, this mundane indexicality is itself a resource that is strategically used to uphold the situations' coherence. Consequentially, one might imply (in a possibly postmodernist manner) the irredeemable indeterminism of all things and/or the effectively arbitrary nature of all apparent commonalities of said events. This position has been taken up by some proponents of a strand of practice thought which I subsume under the (somewhat imprecise) label performative practice theory. They amount to a radical challenge of not only the classic concepts of knowledge and action, but a (more or less complete) rejection of the idea that the (social) world is inherently determined or ordered in some way (transparent to us or not).

Excursus: Post-Structuralism, Postmodernity, and Performativity

> My discussion of practices of knowing and observing in this chapter bears many resemblances to a stream of literature focusing on so-called knowledge practices, practical ontology, and the sited or spatial nature of knowledge. More precisely, while the STS-literature on these topics is rich and

---

[22] I edited this quote for reasons of clarity. In full it reads: "a spatial—temporal manifold *of actions* whose …" (my emphasis). Since I will discuss the notion of action in detail later (in Chap. 7), I excluded it here because Schatzki's notion of action differs in important ways from that held by the sociology of action (and our everyday notion). As he notes immediately after the above quote, he seeks to oppose "individualist theories (…) tying the identity of particular actions to properties of individuals who perform them." (Schatzki 1997: 285–286).

varied, I suggest that the arguments and studies put forward by Annemarie Mol and John Law (Law 1994, 2004; Law/Mol 2002; Mol 2002) come close to the line of argumentation I have pursued here, and can be treated as exemplary for the literature on social practices that locates itself within the realm of post-structuralism and/or post modern sociology. Building on the tradition of Actor Network Theory (since Latour/Woolgar 1986) and the study of socio-technical systems it inspired (Bijker/Law 1992), Law and Mol have developed the study of the 'social enactment' and circulation of technological and material objects into a study of objects of knowledge (not unsimilar to the way Knorr Cetina [1997] conceptualizes 'epistemic objects' in the wake of Rheinberger [1997]). Consequently, just like the observation of the local enactment of things such as the Zimbabwe Bush Pump (2000) led to diagnosing the "fluidity" of technology, they now draw the same conclusions about what they consider the "enactment of realities." Their argument comes in two versions which arguably mirror the two central pillars of most postmodern or post-structuralist accounts of social practices: Mol (2002) explicitly seeks to develop a *philosophical* account of ontology, albeit one she describes as "empirical philosophy" which is based on and elaborated alongside an ethnography (Marres 2004). Law (2003, 2004), in contrast, makes primarily a *methodological* argument based on this philosophy; both in that he criticizes social science methods and by effectively suggesting that the scope of our methodological means impose tight limits on what can and should be said in theory. Both components are, I suggest, not just tightly intertwined (since both authors have collaborated for many years); but the way in which they relate exemplifies the problematic tendency I sense in what I call the performative perspective within practice thought: Rich empirical findings are used as a basis not only for weighty attacks on methodology, but as prescribing a kind of theoretical chastity which I find troublesome. Since empirical findings show that reality itself is not coherent, the argument goes, the known attempts to develop coherent theoretical accounts of the social world are infested with "perspectivalism," or the urge to provide a single perspective on the world, and presuppose "a classic Euro-American version of out-thereness" (Law 2004: 52), thus being a deeply flawed project better abandoned. The clearest example is Annemarie Mol's (2002) discussion of "The Body Multiple" which considers practices of observing or knowing about a disease as performances[23] which are bound to specific sites and situations (in the hospital or laboratory). Crudely said, Mol does for atherosclerosis what I have just tried to do for the ski flex. But in contrast to my attempting to draw conclusions about *intelligibility*,

---

[23] Mol (2002: 41) mentions that she considers enactments as equivalent to performances and uses the term only to avoid the entrenched theoretical battles about the proper use of the term.

Mol considers the performance of practices as enactments of *ontology*. Her conclusions are far-reaching: "Ontology," she writes, "is not given in the order of things," but instead, "ontologies are brought into being in (…) sociomaterial practices" (2002: 6). Thus, "the relation of objects is not hidden in the order of things, but enacted in complex practices" (2002: 150). She concludes:

> "If practice becomes our entrance to the world, ontology is no longer a monist whole. Ontology-in-practice is multiple." (Mol 2002: 157)

The predicament with this use of the term 'ontology' is that a theoretical statement about ontology-in-practice is not a statement about the ontology *of* practices. If assessed on the basis of the way I defined these terms in the introduction, Mol conflates ontology and epistemology: The social ways of knowing about (an aspect of) reality become a description of how reality itself is—multiple. Expressed more generally, what I call the performative view holds that since performances in praxis are indexical and contingent, so must be that what they are performances *of*: reality, sociality, practices (cf. Eberle 2000a). Now, the conflation of epistemology and ontology is itself an exercise in ontology; a philosophical postulate of how the world is that—arguably— needs to be both logically consistent and plausible in light of empirical (and everyday) findings. It requires us to take certain things for granted and draw certain implications. Thus one might ask: How do authors like Mol or Law conceptualize a world in which mundane ways of knowing are not just events in reality, but in which reality is *nothing but* what is "made" in mundane ways of knowing?[24] In other words: If lived life is a social performance, what does the stage look like? Unfortunately, while both Mol and Law are concise in their rejection of philosophical realism (as well as subjectivism), the reader is largely left in limbo about how to think about the world instead. They confine to making rather vague and tentative suggestions such as "we live in an underdetermined world" (Mol 2002: 165) or "the world is largely messy" (Law 2003: 3)—suggestions that stop short of taking, for example, a clear constructivist standpoint and describing the world as *un*determined or completely unordered. In effect, the theoretical account of ontology offered by Mol and Law remains ambiguous. To be sure, this effect is not accidental, since many 'postmodern' theorists seem simply content with drawing (alleged) certitudes into question rather than daring answers of their own. Mol and Law sometimes appear to operate in this modus; for example when, just after presenting their case for 'things' as being manifold and tied to sites, they conclude:

---

[24] "This, then, is the crucial question in a world where ontology is accepted to be multiple: what is being done and what, in doing so, is reality in practice made to be?" (Mol 2002: 159 f.).

> *"Things add up and they don't. They flow in linear time and they don't. And they exist in a single space and escape from it." (Mol/Law 2002: 21; original emphasis)*

The point is not only that it would be helpful to know just *how* things are inherently tied to sites but then manage to escape from them anyways; but rather, that the things' alleged capacity for adding up and not adding up and flowing and standing still and existing spatially and escaping sounds like an announcement of a detailed elaboration of a theory of things, an ontology of time and space and movement and addition and thing-hood—but this elaboration does not take place. Instead, we are left with statements such as: "Perhaps the in-here is being *made* by its visible out-there realities, or *caused* by them" (2004: 55). Perhaps? To be fair, this situation is not due to error or neglect, but instead stands at the core of the carefully crafted argument: That reality is inherently multiple, incoherent, and/or fluid. But the problem with this postmodern or post-structuralist ontology is: that is all. Nothing more is being said, no further qualifications are made. To be sure, I agree that identities, truth, or knowledge only occur in practices that are bound to situations, and that the incongruencies or contingencies that result need to be and are routinely remedied or glossed or managed through practices of coordination or what Law (1994) called modes of ordering; and that both Law and Mol provide many captivating and valuably insight into their functioning. But this alone does not imply that an empirical or theoretical analysis of the (social) world must therefore restrict itself to attending to *nothing but* these modes of ordering. Instead, I can think of two other reasons that could be given for exercising this kind of ontological frugality: a) One could hold that the finding that reality is multiple or fluid implies that no (theoretical) inferences about this reality should be made. Or b), one might argue that the description of the reality and its objects presented by Mol and Law is complete and makes further qualifications or explanations unnecessary. I will first assess point a) and argue that this position is difficult to agree with. Then, I will attend to point b) and show that the account of ontology given from their performative perspective is incomplete and should be complemented with an account similar to that which I develop in this work.

From my perspective, refraining from drawing specific conclusions about the character of the (social) world could be motivated by at least three quite different convictions; and I am not quite sure which of the three holds in the case of Mol or Law. They might subscribe to it either because there is no order or stability inherent in the world at large; or because one cannot hope to unveil said order; or because doing so is simply not of interest for sociology or "empirical philosophy." Let me briefly assess these three options. The last point, I hold, is plain wrong: There can be no question that the nature of order, however contrived, is of key interest to social thought. The first possible argument, in turn, has been elaborated, disputed, and defended by proponents and antagonists of various versions of constructivism in great detail.

Frankly said, I consider not linking up to these important discussions by leaving one's explicit stance in limbo—as Mol and Law do—simply a missed opportunity. This leaves the second argument, which is the one that particularly John Law seems most drawn to. For example, he states that "events and processes (…) necessarily exceed our capacity to know them" (2004: 6; emphasis removed). Drawing directly on Mol's work, Law (2003, 2004) thus attacks the methodology of the social sciences for trying to represent or circumscribe the social world in an orderly way despite the fact that it is actually "messy." Reality, he holds, is "unknowable in a regular and routinised way" and suggests "disciplined lack of clarity" as a methodological remedy (2003: 3). In a similar vein, Mol and Law (in writing together; 2002: 1) argue against the excessive reduction of complexities which amounts to simplification and "impediment to understanding." Their point is surely valid to some extent, but it is also one that has troubled sociologists ever since the very emergence of the discipline. Indeed, in a different text, Mol and Law (2002) themselves go on to accept the point made by social constructivism: That some reduction of complexity is an unavoidable precondition for understanding or knowing per se. However, they seem to consider this an issue of methodology alone; as one that can be solved by developing adequate methods of collecting data and representing the social world and by otherwise abstaining from trying to describe phenomena that cannot be adequately grasped. The problem, of course, is that any kind of methodology for studying and writing about the social must itself be rooted in theoretical a-prioris; they necessarily adhere to—dare I say?—a theoretical perspective of which we do not know whether it "knows" the world in an adequately coherent way. But then I doubt that rejecting logical coherence for not being a sure sign of an inadequate theory or account of the social is a highly difficult position—in fact, it defeats itself in that it would require that one does *not* coherently adhere to the requirement not to write coherent arguments… In contrast, social theorists today have a number of concepts at their disposal which can serve as a foundation for assessing accounts of social order other than the troublesome 'classic candidates' truth or facticity: adequacy, methodological fruitfulness, or empirical plausibility, to name just a few. The underlying question, it seems, is whether or not a theory is something else than an (empirical) description. In my view, the answer is clearly: yes. Just how social theory is different from, but accountable to, empirical descriptions of the social can be framed in a number of powerful ways—Schatzki, for example, provides a specific and arguably useful definition (2010b: xv–xvii).

Let me now turn to point b) and ask whether Mol and Law's performative ontology is complete and coherent, so that one might as well accept it and hitherto exclusively study the modes of ordering they urge us to attend to. To this end, it must first be emphasized that, despite their rejection of the idea that a theory can capture the reality that is 'out there,' both authors of course do make very specific theoretical claims about the objects of knowledge they write about. Law, for example, negates that "we live in a single natural or material reality" (2003: 6) with the argument that objects can often "overlap, but they are not the same" (2004: 55). Accordingly, he paraphrases Mol as not having shown "that reality is fragmented" but rather, that "different realities overlap and interfere with one another." (2004: 61) Law, in other words, makes an ontological statement in that he discusses reality's being such-and-such. But what does it mean to say that an object, indeed anything, overlaps? Here, the effect of conflating ontology and epistemology becomes clear: Rather than saying that *practices* overlap and interfere with one another, it is concluded that the 'objects' they produce overlap and interfere. Therefore, it becomes visible what separates the performative or postmodern practice thought from the one phenopractice theory is based on: For Mol and Law, it is the *object* of inquiry—reality itself—, which is a manifold (e.g. Mol 2002: 157); while phenopractice theory follows Schatzki when he suggests that, instead, the nexus of practices is a manifold. In effect, one can argue that while the body, for example, indeed appears as polyvalent or manifold in praxis, it does so *within* a manifold of practices. But if so, then the multiplicity of the body-in-praxis which Mol accurately describes does not necessarily document the nature of the body itself, but rather the nature of the way in which the various practices relate. Notably, this does not at all imply that the body could not *also* have the character of a manifold in some respect; it only means that not all objects of knowledge, all aspects of reality are ontologically manifold or multiple or fluid in their entirety. Quite to the contrary, it seems very plausible to assume that some objects in or of reality (however conceived) have some enduring features (other than multiplicity)—and if so, they can and should be described by social theory. One way to account for manifoldedness-in-praxis as well as an ontology of enduring qualities of objects is the notion that practices which are manifold share elements which endure but are enmeshed or amalgamated into unfolding practices at any moment of lived social life. Such an account, I hold, can adequately explain the pervasive phenomena Mol and Law chronicle. Nothing in such an account, however, suggests that "events and processes (…) *necessarily* exceed our capacity to know them" (Law 2004: 6; emphasis altered) or that reality is "unknowable in a regular and routinized way" (Law 2003: 3). In fact, I believe the phenomena Mol and Law capture demonstrate just the opposite: That it is *only* in regular and routinized ways that we can know, and that we live through events and processes in awareness to just that extend to which they *do not* exceed our capacity to know them.[25]

---

[25] These remarks, of course, depend on what one suggests what it means to know. Indeed, what I intended to show was just that: The account of knowing given in postmodern social theory is inadequate.

7 Enduring Elements

Instead of taking something like the flex to be nothing but a nexus of ways of flexing, i.e. contingent performances-in-practice, an important strand of practice thought holds that such events should instead understood as effects or—as Schatzki puts it more conservatively, using the words of Wittgenstein—*expressions* of underlying stable structures—arrangements called social practices. I should stress once again that this structure—which I located interchangeably under, above, and beyond the events—must *not* be equated with structures the events or situated unfoldings themselves share, such as the word "flex" or the physical structure of skis. Rather, the social existence of the flex as something that can be understood (or simply: can be), is something that 'stands out against' the ordered background of occasions of doing the flex as a gestalt; and the order of said background is the "hanging-together of things, the existence of nexuses" Schatzki (2002: 18) calls social practices. It follows that this order is to be understood, as I have noted, as enduring (but of course not as endless), and not as a perpetual stream of evanescent occurrences. The core assumption of phenopractice thought, to sum up, is quite straightforward: There is something about a ski's flex that makes a flex just what it understandably is, and it continues to be so while day after day, different people read the marketing text, grab the ski, and flex it, or employ sophisticated machines and procedures to measure and chart it. While there is no doubt that the strength and pattern of the ski's fibreglass layers are but one important factor for the enduring of this coherence, I hope to have demonstrated that ways of flexing by hand, or understandings of what a flex is and how it can be made instructably observable, play an equally important role. Furthermore, because the flex can only become intelligible in the ordered details of a phenomenal field, it prerequisites the situated accomplishment of the amalgamation of the phenopractices' polyvalent elements, for example so that the practitioner can attend to the resistance offered by the ski as exhibiting the flex rather than the posture of his body. And while pushing down on the ski in this way happens concurrently with the unfolding of almost countless other details (such as keeping balance) and is thus temporally current or progressional, neither the flexing as a way to check out a ski's flex nor the ski are sequential in nature (see Chap. 8). For this reason, I suggest to speak of entities such as the ski or the body as *aspects of the amalgam* of skiing, or more precisely as a dimension of a practically accomplished amalgamation that can become observable in a certain way if the details of the ongoing practice are organized in such a way that it 'sticks out' as a figuration in the way foreground and background relate. I have claimed earlier that I do not believe this conceptualization necessarily implies a 'radical' notion of meaning as effectively occurring in a separate, non-material realm or system. Instead, by observing the unfolding of social praxis, I witness *inter alia* the unfolding of physical processes. When practitioners engage in practices, physical qualities reappear in the form of different aspects: the body, material objects, spatiality, and so on.[26] Expressed in the terminology proposed by Sørensen (2009), I could also say that I distinguish between material and materiality: I consider material *entities* as phenomenal effects of practices, while it is the amalgamated *dimension* of materiality which can be said to be affecting phenopractice. To sprinkle physical qualities across a range of different aspects in this way might not seem helpful from a physicist's point of view—but just the human body alone is simultaneously a physical, chemical, biological, physiological, kinetic, neurological, cybernetic, social, and cultural phenomenon. Notably, I do not argue that skis 'have' certain flex qualities only as long as they are in the workshop or on the mountain, as if the physical object itself would be different. Instead, I propose that it is only testing-through-measuring, testing-through-flexing, or testing-through-skiing which provides 'access' to said qualities otherwise inaccessibly baked into the amalgam of practices. I consider the ski as an amalgamated aspect of such practices—that is, I purpose to consider the ski as an existing material thing with physically *stable* properties and not just as an illusion created by skilful manipulation of instruments and senses. In doing so, I imply that material arrangements can shape or prefigure phenopractices in important ways, only some of which have the effect that material objects 'stick out' phenomenologically and thus appear to practitioners engaged in conduct. Note that in social theory, a number of different notions of, and approaches to, the trope of a social form of memory and/or memories of the social have been developed. From the perspective taken here, it follows that two different phenomena should be differentiated in this regard: One the one hand those focusing on what I would consider stable features of enduring elements, for example material (or materialized) memory (W. Gibson 2006; Hargadon/Sutton 1997; Latour 1991; see also Reckwitz 2002b) as well as bodily or embodied forms of memory[27] (Hahn 2009; Mauss 1973; Wacquant 2005a). While such arguments and findings could be cited as supporting my view that elements abidingly invoke prefigurations, my view would also suggest that, if taken in isolation, said findings are in danger of overemphasizing a single aspect while possibly neglecting others. On the other hand, authors have discussed the memory or memory-like processes of overarching entities such as organizations (Spender 1996; Walsh/Ungson 1997), systems (Luhmann 1996a, 2000a: 230–233, 2000b: 576), and—last but not least—practices (Schatzki 2010b: 216–221). This second form of memory, I emphasize, cannot be adequately explained by pointing to elements alone, but rather point to a separate kind of phenomenon: the 'storage' and transport of *ways of amalgamation* of elements as opposed to the storage and transport of elements themselves. In different but related ways, this phenomenon will be at the heart of the discussion

---

[26] I am aware that I also frequently label them dimensions of practices. I do this to emphasize their coexistence and mutual relevance for the way things are; my use of the term 'dimension' should be read in the sense it is used in ('postmodern') sociological writing, not as referring to dimensions in the strict sense of theoretical physics.

[27] Note that this literature is also entangled with that on tacit or embodied knowledge in very unfortunate ways (H. M. Collins 2001; Gourlay 2006).

throughout the second half of this work, and the notions of style and media of dissemination will be pivotal parts of my argument.

However, just saying that the ski's characteristics such as the flex only become observable vis-à-vis the ski-in-movement or ski-in-a-practice does not sufficiently describe the position of phenopractice thought—in fact, this proposition still lends itself well to individualist accounts of observation as a form of 'grabbing and holding fast' fleeting details of the stream of perception. In contrast, I need to add that in order to be intelligible, continuing movement or unfolding needs to exhibit enduring conditions rather than only dynamic interplay. As I defined with regard to the phenomenal field, features observable-in-practice are effects of enduring constellations, which is why movement must be transposed into a *condition*—and this is precisely what the very definition of the ski flex expresses as "force in Newton," in other words, the currently effective potential for acceleration of the ski's mass. However, it would be misleading to say that the difference between dynamic unfolding and static states (or qualities) occurs only when the ski is 'put into use'—for example by skiing it—, because the ski always needs to be—literally—put into practice (e.g. of measuring) to become observably intelligible in the first place. The conversion of a dynamic unfolding into enduring conditions has been traditionally treated as occurring only in the process of observation or interpretation, and thus as being the unique capacity of subjects or conscious observers made possible by their ability for retention. This view has received increased criticism (especially from STS) over the last decades, and while I agree with Preda (2000) that humans must nevertheless be involved in order to be able to speak of activity (cf. Schatzki 2002: 194–203), I argue that the invocation of (transiently) enduring and (sufficiently) stable conditions is neither exclusive to conscious sense-making nor solemnly possible retrospectively. Therefore, I suggest that the freeskiers' disagreements about how the ski flex should be measured and expressed is not just an ex-post deliberation of adequate descriptions and their justifications, but similar to a clash of what Knorr-Cetina (1999) calls divergent epistemic cultures: The engineer mounting the ski onto a machine in the workshop and the skier undertaking a test ride do not just apply different frames of reference, but are engaged in different bodily, material, and spatial practices carrying fundamentally different understandings of what observation is, who should observe, what data is, and so on.

Excursus: The Epistemology of Phenopractice Thought

Generalizing the notion of the gestalt from an empirical phenomenon in human vision to a philosophical take on the nature of all social meaning as a foreground-background relation, I hold, implies a specific epistemology as a central part of phenopractice thought. I will avoid slipping into a lengthy discussion of facets of epistemological theory at this point, in part because I believe this whole work can be read as a comment on questions of epistemology and phenomenology. But broadly speaking, I suggest that while such a practice-based epistemology builds on the general foundations of any constructivist or constructionist thought which points to the inherently social nature of meaning, it does so with a slight twist to the argument. An epistemology of sublation does indeed acknowledge the reflexivity of meaning (or knowledge) in that it holds that any aspect of social practices can only be known or accounted for within and through further social practices. However, in my view, this point does only imply a 'strong' program of "radical reflexivity" as championed by some ethnomethodologists (Pollner 1991) if considered in isolation, as if it was the only defining feature of such a theory. In a similar vein, I would also be reluctant to paint such an epistemology as a version of "radical constructivism" (e.g. in the fashion of von Glasersfeld 1996). In a way, there is something banal about the self-proclaimed radicalism of the insight that all *social* meaning is the result of *social* processes, at least from a sociological point of view. How far-reaching the implications of the reflexivity of social practices effectively are (for example with regard to methodology) depends, I think, to a great extend on the assumptions about stability or identity of patterns or meaningful formations one holds, and less on the very revelation of fundamental reflexivity per se (see below). As I have noted, practice theories treat the perceived stability of the world (such as the stability and reliability of my own body) as an effect of contingent social processes, but nevertheless, they emphasize the stability or reliability of these processes themselves—and as I have argued, it moreover seems plausible to expect a high degree of stability in the parts or elements of said processes, particularly if they are material or physical in nature. But how, one might ask, can one conceptualize this antagonism of the free-flowing contingency of abstract meaning and the supposed stability of physical 'elements'? If social meaning is not to be understood as the immaterial ether of Husserlian consciousness, nor as exclusively bound to ephemeral speech acts in discourse, how can one still uphold its reflexivity without falling back to postulating behaviourist automatisms?

Towards an answer, I think, the notion of meaning as a foreground-background relation is essential, because it allows conceptualizing self-reference without having to postulate a strict separation of realms or levels such as consciousness/world or system/environment. (Nota bene: it does not necessarily force one to negate them, either.) Since meaning is conceptualized as a structure (or, as Schatzki [2002: 18–25] would have it: as an arrangement[28]), it is reflexive in the sense that the meaning of any part of the structure is reflexively co-constituted by its virtue of being part of the self-same structure—meaning is a relation, not an essence. But unlike dualist conceptions of the type of 'form and medium,' where order is constituted only on one side, namely the form (Heider 1926; see especially Luhmann 1990), it is assumed here that foreground and background are *mutually* constitutive rather than unidirectionally dependent. Therefore, one must not suppose that everything which lies 'beneath' the currently processed 'bit' of meaning—the current event—, must be completely meaningless, arbitrary, or over-complex because the only way for it to be meaningful would be to stand in the limelight of the meaningful present. The idea that foregrounding parts of the background requires 'backgrounding' the foreground does not imply that this background is either essential (a positivistic view) or meaningless (a 'radical' constructionist view). This latter point is crucial: At the core, most constructivist theories of meaning (and Husserlian phenomenology) invoke an extreme form of the classic Aristotelian distinction between *morphe* and *hyle*, form and matter (see Ingold 2010, 2011 for a critique of this duality). Therefore, they argue (in a de Saussurian spirit) that one or more strictly separate realms or spheres of meaning must exist, because meaningful forms can only emerge on the basis of distinctions or patterns logically independent of the objects or media they are applied to, and henceforth these distinctions or patterns must be exclusive to said spheres. The objects of observation, it follows, are in turn inherently *not* meaningful (at least with regard to the domain in question), and can, as Luhmann (1990, 1995a) argues with great precision, effectively be thought of as nondescript and fully homogenous. In contrast to this view, I suggest that meaningful forms or gestalts can be explained as aggregations of details or particulars *without* having to imply that these details need to be entirely homogenous or nondescript in order for the resulting gestalt to be 'more than the sum of its parts.' If the ski, for example, is understood as a congregation of physical

---

[28] Schatzki's version of practice theory does not introduce the notion of a background-foreground relation, gestalts, or a similar concept. In my view, however, he implies a similar concept in that he holds that meaning derives from activity—and activity, in turn, is governed by what he calls practical intelligibility, that is, "what is signified to someone" as making sense to do in the course of an action (Schatzki 2002: 56, 76). In any event, he shares the particular point made here: He identifies meanings as something that entities possess within arrangements (or orders) and states that "meanings of social entities derive *in part* from a context" (Schatzki 2002: 20; my emphasis). More explicitly, he describes arrangements as being composed of "substances" or "abiding objects that bear properties" (2002: 23) and holds that meanings of entities can occur which are not part of current practices (not "intentionally set up in practices") but only happen in their context (2002: 101).

elements, there is no need to hold that (logically or physically) its basal elements form just an amorphous mass of atoms or quarks. Instead of "pulverizing" the ski in this way, it seems more sensible to consider constellations of such hypothetical basal elements as having discrete and relevant qualities—such as crystalline structures providing a certain level of rigidity.

A related issue is the question whether *all* meaningful wholes perceived or referenced should be considered as the product of an 'assembling' process just because *many* indeed are. Affirming the question leads to a concept of meaning or elemental wholes as derived from effectively infinitesimally small singularities (a thought most clearly expressed in Luhmann 1990). But consider, for example, the case of vision: visual meaning as featured in the visual field is derived from contrasts photoreceptor cells can pick up. The basal elements of visual meaning, therefore, are not evanescent singularities in a strict sense because they necessarily have a minimum extension in both space (in the visual field) and time because there is a certain, relatively stable threshold of stimulus intensity that either activates the *whole* cell to 'fire' a neurotransmitter for a minimum *amount* of time—or not (S. E. Palmer 1999). Of course, (conscious) visual perception of something requires the activation of several more (but not too many) cells in conjunction and thus happens on the basis of aggregation—but what is aggregated are nevertheless 'chunks' of a set size or extension: we do not not see single atoms because of aggregation, but because they are considerably smaller than photoreceptor cells. Even if one is referring only to meaning as processed in consciousness (as e.g. Luhmann does), there is no real reason why, and explanation of how, the "chunks" of stimuli emerging from cells would be pulverised into singularities without extension and duration. The implications of this argument are important: Conceptualizing meaning as an undivided *stream* (as it is common in phenomenology since Husserl) is in a strict sense a misrepresentation of something that is 'just' a *succession* of what Schatzki (2010b) aptly calls episodes.[29] At the core, my argument is that one can uphold claims about the continuing existence of certain ontological properties of objects (inter alia) despite their apparent dis- and re-appearance in the course of varying phenopractices without having to conceptualize them as instances of interpretation on behalf of an independent observer. The reason is that differing practical circumstances can sufficiently explain this phenomenon, particularly because these invoke differing *levels of aggregation* of details into units of enquiry or observation (see Schatzki 1996: 201). Let me also point out that this perspective additionally contains a specific approach to the duality—or even inherent contradictions

---

[29] The alternative I suggest is to conceptualize flow as a not-ubiquitous state of a succession of meaning rather than treating meaning as perpetually streaming in a strict sense (see Chap. 7).

of—practice-theory conceptions of materiality that Shove, Pantzar and Watson discuss (2012). Theories of social practices emphasize, on the one hand, how material objects can only become intelligible or socially effective in the course of local practices, or what I call amalgamation; but on the other, they foster interest in the forms and regimes of dissemination, circulation, and recombination of material 'elements' of practices, which might be conceptualized as systems or mobilities (de Laet/Mol 2000; Shove/Pantzar 2005b, 2007; Shove/Pantzar/Watson 2012; Urry 2000). A phenopractice-theoretical notion of social order as a constellation of amalgamated details within a figure-background relation provides a conceptual framework compatible with such a dual view on 'elements' of practices in general and materiality in particular, because the gestalt-order of the practice is not implied to be the exclusive realm of duration of qualities inherent to 'things' in the most general sense.

8 Bodies and Artefacts

Having conceptualized material artefacts as aspects of the amalgam of practice, let me now consider the second key form of background a ski is judged against by freeskiers: the body-in-movement. As I noted, many freeskiers question the validity or applicability of how a ski comes to be seen in the course of workbench practices like measuring the flex—but everybody, ski developers and engineers included, seems to agree that test riding a ski is a valid and crucially important way of finding out about a ski. On closer inspection, however, test riding becomes somewhat problematic in itself. In fact, the very concept "test riding" seems a combination of slightly antithetical components: Riding is a fragile, somewhat fuzzy exposure to the ongoing stream of life characterized by a highly complex time structure, while testing implies repeatability, accuracy, and generalizability. Most importantly, however, understanding test riding requires figuring out the reflexive relationship between bodies and artefacts. What does it mean to observe a ski as a thing-currently-used-in-skiing while skiing it? After all, the phenomenology of skiing is not really amiable to this task: As I ride down the Krimml, I experience my skis as the outer borders of the moving self, so that although it is actually my skis which are physically losing grip on a patch of ice or plunging deep into the snow, I would naturally think and talk about myself 'doing' this. When a skier experiences skiing, the physical object 'ski' will under normal conditions be present only para-attentionally, in convergence with many other details. Like the different body parts which are not usually experienced as singular entities during riding, the material tools of riding such as the boots, the skis, the gloves, and the poles are routinely taken for granted by the practitioner. Arguably, there would be no way one could learn to ski smoothly if one would not 'think with his skis,' if one would not intend to move the skis in a certain manner rather than just moving legs and feet so that they might move the ski in that way. Physical tools are, in other words, not only an inherent part of a phenopractice if observed from the outside, but within the experience of the practitioner engaged in the respective practice, they also appear as naturally embedded aspects rather than artificial add-ons. How does the ski tester cope with this predicament?

When testing a ski, a rider will take a prototype into different types of mountain terrain and try to 'get a feeling' how the ski 'is,' what kind of 'character' it has. Rather than producing a set of numbers, or what engineers would consider an 'exact' definition of the qualities of the ski, such test rides result in verbal assessments such as the following[30]:

> "Very agile and good fun in the woods. The ski floats almost right from the start and it is almost impossible to make the shovel cut under. In open terrain, it conveys an extremely stable and safe feeling, accelerates enormously and does not even slow down through turns." (Posting in a forum on freeskiers.net; [D])[31]

Such descriptions mix anthropomorphic characteristics and technical 'facts' quite freely and often alternate between broad generalizations (*"Did everything well all week long"* [D]) and detailed accounts of specific events. Notably, the skis are described as actors in such texts, so that skiing a particular way is something that *they* do—in contrast to, e.g., a description of a run in freeride competition where it would surely be the skier who *"accelerates enormously and does not even slow down through turns."* In everyday language, the amalgamation of practitioner and tools within a practice is thus routinely reflected: It seems perfectly clear that a man-sliding-on-ski is an entity that deserves a category of its own—the skier. Unlike a man-in-shoes or a man-holding-skis, object and body merged within the practice seem to be so essentially different that they make a general distinction from ubiquitous forms of just 'using' or 'wearing' objects necessary.

---

[30] This is an account by an 'amateur' ski-builder (a creative consumer or prosumer) about his newest model posted in an online freeski-forum. Very similar reports are to be found in special interest magazines or can be heard on trade-fairs when the season's new ski models are being discussed. Regarding the empirical data this section is based on: Initially, I planned to observe a prototype testing routine first hand, but I did not succeed in gaining access, because companies are understandably secretive about their product development. However, I did conduct a number of interviews with ski developers and manufacturers, ski shop owners, authors of ski tests in different ski magazines, as well as freeskiers who had been asked to help in testing prototypes for their sponsors. From these sources, I concluded that neither test procedures nor the categories applied to test and describe skis differ much between laymen building and trying out skis, professional ski manufacturers, and test reports in ski magazines. To be sure, certain discrepancies would arise upon closer inspection of the detailed test procedures, but for the limited sake of the more general argument I am making regarding 'feeling' a ski, they seem neglectable.

[31] „Im Wald sehr agil und spaßig. Der Ski schwimmt beinahe aus dem Stand heraus auf und es ist quasi unmöglich, die Schaufel zum Abtauchen zu bringen. Im offenen Gelände vermittelt er ein extrem stabiles und sicheres Gefühl, beschleunigt enorm und wird auch durch Turns nicht langsamer."

Despite their mundanity, fusions of human bodies and material objects have been (re-)discovered and debated several times in social theory, often as part of a quest to question certain notions of the body, the material, or both. Two important conceptualizations of body-object fusions (similar to the skier skiing skis) available in the literature are the cyborg (Featherstone/Burrows 1995; Haraway 1991) and the hybrid (Callon 1991; Latour 1991). But since skis do not replace body parts as in cyborgs and are not as permanently coupled with humans as hybrids, both notions seem unfitting in this case (see Dant 2004). More generally spoken, the plethora of possible forms of recombination and cross-influence of bodies and objects draws into question the usefulness of the distinction in the first place: Material objects and structures can be in bodies, attached to bodies or body parts, present-in-hand or present-at-hand (in the sense of Heidegger), enwrap the body or its parts, or be under, over, next to, and around it—and all this in various obvious or not-so-obvious, helpful or restraining, permanent or periodical ways. When to speak of one entity, when of two? Which to ascribe actorship to, and how much? Assuming that practices necessarily have a material dimension amalgamated with the bodily dimension relieves not only the practitioner, but also the scientific observer from the imperative to reify distinctive entities in the first place, especially if this happens in order to question the very distinction between man and material he or she just established. Instead, the focus is shifted to the question of when and how objects, just like bodies, 'show up' as an entity in the course of the conduct of phenopractices themselves. When and how do they 'stick out' of the phenomenal field? In other words, because the theoretical approach I try to follow is somewhat more radical, the empirical instead of the theoretical role of materialities and body-object assemblages shifts back into focus.[32] Therefore, when the ski test report breaks out of the mundane pattern and describes the ski as an actor, I will neither interpret this as providing proof for an ANT-perspective, nor will I argue that this role-switching only happens in the texts or verbal comments of the skiers, as a way of reinterpreting the exact same doing. Instead, I hold, it reflects a modus of the organisation of attention during riding and thus a different approach to, or style of, the practice of skiing. A freerider taking part in a competition, after all, will 'go at' riding down a particular line quite differently from the same rider asked to test a prototype—something Heidegger (1962: 96) calls "putting ourselves into a position" (*Sichversetzten*). Note, however, that from this perspective, attention does not automatically imply a mental activity or mindset, since for example visual attention (focus) cannot be equated to conscious attention but is driven by embodied micro-routines. From a phenopractice perspective, the difference between a freeride run as part of competing in a freeride event versus testing a ski is not aptly described as just a different way of 'thinking about' that run, since it entails a different focus, different emotions, a different body tension, and—quite literally, as I try to argue in the following parts—a different way of looking at this very run.

---

[32] Consequently, the amount of scientific attention sometimes devoted to cyborgs and their look-alikes seems rather surprising from my perspective.

9 Foregrounding and Sublating

Expressed in the terms I suggested, one could say: Foregrounding that a ski is, e.g., "aggressive" or "playful" can only happen against the background of skiing because these aspects only show up during skiing. Moreover, upon close inspection it becomes clear how background and foreground are mutually intertwined or co-constitutive. Compare, for example, test-riding with the training exercise I discussed earlier: In this case, ski students were made aware of their hip rotation through attaching ski poles, thus allowing them to observe their body via the equipment. In contrast, the test rider must observe the ski equipment via his body, so that the body functions as the 'access point' to the qualities in question. Body and equipment, in other words, not only co-construct the practice of skiing as a prerequisite of observing the skiing body or the skiing ski; but towards observing either of the two, the other needs to be employed in the course of organizing the experience of the practitioner in such a way that he or she can 'single out' and observe an aspect of the unfolding phenopractice as a documentation of the qualities of 'the' ski or 'the' body.

Notably, what is of interest here is not only that the ongoing skiing is a condition of the character of the ski becoming observable so that the ski is what one might call a "performative artefact" (Suchman/Trigg/Blomberg 2002: 175). More importantly, what the test rider is trying to evaluate is how the ski conditions the riding, e.g. making it easier or more difficult to control. Knowing about this ski, in other words, results from assessing how background and foreground relate, so that in the above test report, the ski is "agile and good fun" if one is "in the woods," while "in open terrain", it is instead "stable and safe." Crucially, this notions of figuring out as practically establishing a certain relation of foreground and background of a practice should not be simplified into a truism such as 'certain qualities appear only in certain environments.' Neither do I want to argue that the impression or judgement of the test rider is—strictly speaking—contingent or arbitrary just because both categories "agile" and "in the woods" are open to interpretation. In fact, as several of my interview partners assured, different experienced ski testers will come up with remarkably similar characterizations of the same ski model after testing it separately.[33] Thus, I argue that describing the character of a ski is an act of sublation, a lifting out of context and thus overriding certain aspects of skiing-this-ski, because 'getting to' the ski requires (em-)practically foregrounding certain aspects of the amalgam of skiing while backgrounding others. Such foregrounding, then, cannot mean that the ski is dissolved away or unhinged from the amalgam of skiing, because for the ski to appear in focus, the

---

[33] Particularly, this was emphasized by the editor of the leading German freeski magazine with vast experience in ski testing: He had overseen systematic tests of thirty or forty new ski models each season over the course of eight years, where each ski was tested by four or more riders [I].

amalgamation of skiing must have already been accomplished: First and foremost, the ski tester needs to take a practical interest to 'get the skiing going', and only in the course of this he can hope to learn something about the ski he is skiing.

10 Knowing Your Style

Now the challenge or even paradox that sublation is can be seen more clearly: As I have described, accomplishing skiing depends on 'assembling' the flow of skiing as a *whole*, as a unity both a) in terms of ontological or physical factors—so that the density of snow the angle of the ski, and the pressure applied by the skier link up favourably—; and b) in terms of the phenomenology of skiing, in that the skier must be able to orchestrate his various bodily doings to the rhythm of the ongoing concerto of multiple experiential details. The task of singling out a particular quality such as the agility of the ski against this dual background requires the skier to work into the opposite direction, so to speak: It is not just that focusing on a single aspect too much can cause a failure to conduct the phenopractice in toto— e.g., losing balance while concentrating too much on the ski's feel—but moreover, conducting a practice always means remedying indexicality (in Garfinkel's terms), evening out particulars, or achieving coherence despite and 'over the ground' of myriad imperfections by relating or assembling such minutiae into a sufficiently coherent structure. Thus, if a certain quality is supposed to stick out or show up in the course of doing the practice, this is always somewhat antithetical to the ubiquitous coherence as a fundamental quality of any intelligible practical conduct. Conducting a practice, in other words, always carries an inherent tendency to compensate for a range of distinctive factors, so that grasping the distinctiveness of just this ski is inherently difficult. Again, I must emphasize that this inherent compensation is a bodily and physical process rather than a 'mental' interpretation. In my view, this is exactly what Heidegger[34] seeks to express when he cautions:

> "The achieving of phenomenological access to the entities we encounter, consists rather in thrusting aside our interpretative tendencies, which keep thrusting themselves upon us and running along with us, and which conceal not only the phenomenon of such 'concern', but even more those entities themselves as encountered of their own accord in our concern with them." (Heidegger 1962: 96; original emphasis)

Indeed, the skier cannot hope to find out about the 'real' ski by trying some sort of ex-post 'reverse engineering' or 'de-interpretation' of his experiences of the test skiing's details in order to reduce or translate it into the 'normal' details of

---

[34] Authors are divided on the question of whether or not Heidegger considers things to have properties independent of our practices of making sense of them (regardless of their being either available or occurent), but as this chapter should have made clear, I read him in the sense that they do, thus siding with Dreyfus (2001).

unconcernedly skiing the ski. It is not by coincidence that organizers of a ski test ask the rider to "ski hard" and then immediately afterwards write down "just how it was:" 'getting to the ski' must happen within skiing itself, in a modus of being concerned with the ski (to use Heideggerian terms) rather than some mental remedying of the skiing's concreteness, which would amount to being concerned with the testing rather than the ski per se.

What makes observation or epistemic acts contingent, therefore, is not that elements or (material) factors themselves need to be particularly malleable or unpredictable, but instead, that a practice is necessarily a highly adaptable or flexile process in that various combinations of different micro-routines can yield the same overall pattern. Again, this is reflected in the practice of testing skis. As an experienced ski developer explains:

> "The important thing in testing is that you can differentiate why a ski is good: Because you are used to it or because it really matches your style of riding?" [D]

Skiing successfully requires continuously adapting to various conditions such as the quality of the snow or the steepness of the slope. Of course, this adaptation also includes the specificities of the material used, for example in that a stiff, long ski requires more force to be skied effectively. When the test skier finds a ski to be agile, for example, is that because he is skilled and agile himself, or because the conditions are favourable, or because the ski could be called agile? Can he control the ski well at high speeds because the ski affords such control, or just because the terrain affords it? To make matters worse, the longer one will use a piece of equipment, the better one will be able to adapt to its particularities—as, e.g., every car driver realizes when he switches 'his' old car for a new one. As the above quote documents, the ski testers try to solve this problem by relying on an implicit assumption about the speed of accustomization: The very first turns with an unknown ski are not considered 'realistic' in that adaption is deemed unnecessarily insufficient; and after a certain time span has passed, 'figuring out' the ski is considered no longer possible as well, because now, the adaption has come too far, the skier is 'getting used' to the ski and thus routinely adjusting for, and thus backgrounding, most of its particularities. In summary, testing skis can be understood as foregrounding a piece of equipment, an aspect of the practice of skiing, in a gestalt switch: During a competition or a normal training day, the skier seeks to accomplish a certain personal style of riding as emanating from, becoming observable in, the course of the particulars of his ongoing riding; but now he needs to treat this style as a given background against which the character of the ski comes to be seen. Note that in doing so, according to the above quote the skier uses "your *style* of riding" as a background against which the 'fit' of the ski under the circumstances of 'normal' adaptation to its particularities is to be measured. In other words, the skier assumes that he 'has' one given way of riding which the ski should support rather than distort. This view seems to suggest that one's style of riding is simply an effect of sedimentation over time, a certain way of skiing one acquires by riding over and over again. But while there is surely some truth to this image of style, I will also argue that it is misleading and oversimplified. Just like a ski, one's personal style of riding is of course also something that becomes visible only against a certain background, for example when performing a certain trick in a certain way under 'normal conditions' and with 'normal equipment.' In other words, why should the argument I made about understanding material elements as a situated accomplishment in this chapter not also hold in a similar way for the observation of what Garfinkel (2002: 216) called "transparent embodied achievements"? Just like the ski flex as a social thing is *also* a physically existing quality which's remark-ability is carried by the interplay of doings and sayings, a stylish line or trick can as well be seen as an entity in the form of an embodied skill or tacit knowledge—but just like pointing to the ski's materiality does not suffice to adequately grasp the social conditions of its availability, treating a skill as a stable feature inherent in a body alone does not explain its intelligibility at all. In my view, some of the perspectives routinely described as practice theories treat embodied skills or dispositions as factual entities in just this sense without considering the very *practices* carrying their availability. Therefore, I argue that in order to grasp what style is and how it works from a phenopractice perspective, one first needs to develop an adequate account of the relation of bodily technique, material technology, and language use within practice thought. As a step-stone towards developing such an account of such an abstract and immaterial social thing such as style, let me first look at some implications of the account of getting to know something as stable as a ski in this chapter. "Fair enough," one might ask, "so there are many ways of observing or understanding a ski in practice, and understandings about skis are carried across the various moments of situated praxis. But what does this mean for the skis themselves? If this is the case, what is a good ski?"

11 The Visibility of Things: What is a Good Ski?

At the core, skiers in a shop or on a trade fair are concerned with a straightforward question: Which ski is good? Based on the above examinations of the freeskiers' ways of finding out one can, I believe, also gain some interesting insights on a related question of key interests to both sociologists of consumption and technology, as well as marketers: What is a good ski? More precisely, from a perspective that is fundamentally concerned with meaning and intelligibility, the above question translates to: What kind of ski will be come to known as a good ski? As I argued in extenso, I do not suggest that the social meaning of a ski among freeskiers is essentially independent of the material features of the artefact 'ski,' and neither that it is just a representation. However, my account has also not been positivistic in that said meaning can only be carried by and unfolded in phenopractices of testing and judging skis. A ski that will be come to known as a good ski must therefore first and foremost be a ski that will fare well in such practices—which are, I argued, related but different from practices of 'just skiing.' With regard to the classic controversy of whether it is only product quality that counts for a

11 The Visibility of Things: What is a Good Ski?

product's success in the long run, or whether it is in fact artful marketing (advertising, pricing, promotion, branding, and so on), I therefore arrive at a mixed conclusion: As far as freeskiers choosing skis are concerned, testing and test results in a wide sense play an important role—especially test reports in magazines or in web forums, opinions and hearsay from other riders, and personal testing routines from flexing a ski in-store to systematically testing several models. Advertisements, promotional texts and the like do not seem to have much of a direct impact on these ways of finding out about a ski, because freeskiers do not expect them to have the necessary validity of truth. However, such messages can nevertheless be an important indirect structuring factor, because they can function as *instructions* that "configure reception" (see Garfinkel/Liberman 2007; Heath/vom Lehn 2004) by explaining what there is to look for in assessing a particular product, for example directing attention towards the fact that the ski is particularly lightweight or has a particular flex. From a phenopractice perspective, though, the instruction alone can never provide praxeological validity as it has to be put into practice; and if it is, the outcome of the instructed practice can never be ensured by the content of the instruction (Garfinkel 2002; A. W. Rawls 2011). Promotion and advertising, in other words, can indeed frame the judging of the product, but only by potentially prefiguring phenopractice rather than by invoking symbolic meaning. In doing so, moreover, it is flanked by various other sets of instructions, for example flex curves or other's test reports and opinions.

But then what about the ski? As Lucy Suchman (2007; Suchman/Blomberg/Orr/Trigg 1999) has argued forcefully, artefacts can be self-instructive in that they prefigure their user's practices in way that is helpful towards successful accomplishments. At first sight, because she developed her argument primarily on the basis of more complex machines that have user interfaces, the case of the ski as a material mono-block and 'black box' seems to belong to a different category. Nevertheless, I suggest that I have demonstrated the opposite to be true: In test-riding the ski, for example, what counts is what one might call the sense-ability of the ski's specific features, that is, whether or not the attentive test-rider can, in the riders' own words, grasp "what the ski wants." [M] What makes imbuing a ski with such a quality so challenging is that, in order for such characteristics to unfold and thus potentially be attended to, the ski must also possess what one might call *amalgamate-ability*. It must, in other words, first facilitate its own being-woven into the unfolding of the test practice, fitting smoothly into its particular arrangement, before second it can thus stick out in a positive manner—a manner, moreover, that needs to be complementary to the instructions in light of which the testing happens, be it bold announcements made by the manufacturer or unfavourable prejudices held towards the products' brand. Note that this situation is more complex than the description of the success factors for the circulation of technological goods that de Laet and Mol (2000) have put forward: In assessing why a certain type of water pump is extraordinarily successful, they emphasize how the pump is "fluid" in that it is flexible enough to appear favourably to those assessing it from quite different angles: engineers, development workers, village communities, and so on. Their account seems to suggest that what they call the fluidity or elasticity of technology is an unequivocally positive characteristic as well as one depending primarily on technological finesse (of building redundancy into mechanical parts, for example). However, they also mention that in order to work in a certain context, adequate instructions are a key prerequisite (2000: 231)—those manning the sites across which the pump circulates need to understand it in the first place. And as the case of the ski shows, the flexibility or elasticity of a technological good is actually a potential *obstacle* to understanding, because the good does not stand out of the site of its use, and/or because it is unable to instruct the practitioner about its qualities. What needs to be added to the account of de Laet and Mol, I suggest, is the fact that what they call fluidity is an *accomplishment elaborated across sites* rather than a feature of the good, and while elasticity is surely an important prerequisite in many cases, it can be contra-productive as well. What is more, making sure that a good fits into many different sites successfully is not necessarily only a matter of shaping the product, but it is just as much a matter of moulding the sites accordingly—which is maybe why most companies spend more money on marketing communication than product development.

To conclude, a ski's character as grasped by the freeskiers results from the coherence of the figures it gains within various phenopractices of testing, judgment, and debate which in turn are prefigured by marketing communications (as instructions) as well as physical qualities of the ski, but also a wide range of other factors that can prefigure practices in various ways. Despite the potential complexity of this poly-determinism, however, one key point of the notion I propose is straightforward: The ski as well as the marketing communication matter *only* insofar as they prefigure the practices of testing or judging, *not* in terms of whatever qualities they might have as well. Particularly, it is suggested that, first and foremost, a ski is 'good' if it lends itself well to testing it positively—which is not the same as, e.g., lending itself well to 'just riding' it for years on end. Let me illustrate this point with regard to the never-ending parade of innovations and revolutions the ski industry churns out year after year: While every major ski manufacturer announces a mayor innovation almost every season, very few of them ever really take hold. One important reason why some innovations 'stick' and other do not could be their vis-ability, and particularly, their in-store vis-ability (Fig. 5.5): In the more mainstream ski market, most customers have much less expertise about ski technology and test methods, so that they on the one hand rely on test results they found in the media or online, and on the other have to figure out which ski to take while standing in a ski shop, confronted with some twenty or thirty different models lined up in front of them. A fair share of these models allegedly contains some brand-new technology allowing, better, faster, easier skiing. Now, which one to pick? Most innovations concern structural details of the skis which remain hidden. For example, various vibration absorption mechanisms have been invented, but all lie invisibly under the ski's polished surface. The manufacturers try to compensate for this lack of visibility by printing ever-new colourful logos, names, and visualizations onto the skis—some even include miniature versions of graphs similar to the flex curves I have shown above. Such printed messages,

11 The Visibility of Things: What is a Good Ski?

Fig. 5.5 Establishing the praxeological validity of a ski's carved shape (on a trade fair)

however, are hardly *instructive* in the way described above, as they merely depict characteristics, but do not allow the customer to 'see for themselves,' or—even better—grab and feel for themselves and thus establish praxeological validity.

Consider in contrast to this onslaught of soon-forgotten novelties what proved to become the two key innovations in ski design during the last twenty years: the carving ski and the rocker ski. In both cases, the innovation is clearly present in the form of the ski itself: while classic ski where longer and had straight edges, carving skis are very obviously waisted, being much thinner in the centre and broader at the shovel and the end. Both in the shop and on the slopes, skiers could immediately *see* that these skis were different. What is even more important, when they got curious and tried to grasp what was different about these new skis, they could be instructed about how the radius literally cut into the ski translates directly into skiing turns of that radius on the slopes. To be sure, waist-shaped skis have a long and complex history and only enjoyed eventual breakthrough decades after the first prototypes where developed (on the evolution of modern ski shape see Masia 2005)—an interesting case of how material artefacts, commercial organizations, and shifting rules and norms intertwine as consumer markets and consumption practices shift (see Cochoy 2009; Pletz 2010 for insightful studies of similar historical cases). In very broad terms, it can be said that carving skis struggled because they required a different skiing technique, so that their dissemination got entangled into the notorious conservatism of ski instruction, racing, and standardizing bodies (freedom from which is also meant by the 'free' in freeskiing). But regardless of whether they were seen as positive or negative, carving skis were rapidly accepted and talked about as being obviously different and new, a crucial threshold that most innovations in ski design never pass.

During my fieldwork on the world's largest winter sport industry trade fair, the ISPO held annually in Munich, I could observe a similarly important innovation emerge: the so-called rocker ski (see e.g. Spiegel Online 2010; [D]). Unfortunately, I do not have the space to spell out how various institutions such as special-interest and mainstream media, independent shop owners, large buying syndicates, and many others work together—as well as against each other—in their hope to have found "the next carving ski" [D], the next mayor innovation that makes every customer buy a new pair of skis. Instead, I will only focus on key point: the practical visibility of the innovation, and the collective efforts of manufacturers, marketers, and the media to produce it. Again, the rocker is an innovation in the shape of the ski. Classic skis have a so-called chamber, so that when they are laid flat on the ground, they only touch the ground at the shovel and the end but bend upwards in between. Rocker skis, in contrast, have an inverse chamber at the front and a normal chamber at the centre and back—for now, I will omit what this means in terms of actually skiing the ski. What is important, however, is this: An average skier will not be able to spot the difference between a ski with and without a rocker if both are just standing or lying in front of him or her—until he or she is instructed to produce the visibility of the rocker. When rocker skis were first introduced on a larger scale at the ISPO in 2010, several methods of instruction towards practically seeing the rocker technology could be observed on the booths of those manufacturers trying to popularize rocker ski as an instructably observable normal innovation. One important means were illustrations and displays with schematic sketches of the rocker technology.

As Fig. 5.6 shows, such displays are not photos or 'realistic,' detailed drawings of skis-that-have-a-rocker, but deliberately and carefully designed abstract depictions that use scale and colour to produce the visibility of the *figural principle* that is supposed to result from the rocker technology itself. Therefore, they not only carry an air of technical precision and engineering authority, but crucially, are meant to convey the *gestalt* of a rocker, the conceptual figure that is visible when one is seeing a rocker. Taken in isolation, these displays cannot enable the on-looker to see a rocker ski (since the ski is absent), just as a rocker ski alone will not visibly have a rocker unless seen by a suitably instructed onlooker under the right conditions. If combined in a suitable manner however, the facticity of the rocker technology arises from the visible coherence of drawing and ski. Of key importance towards establishing this coherence by instructing trade-fair visitors to establish the rocker's praxeological validity were interactive practices of instructed

11 The Visibility of Things: What is a Good Ski?

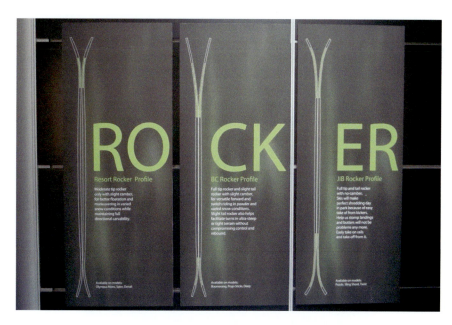

Fig. 5.6 Schematic display of different forms of rockers that are depicting the figural order rather than actual look of skis. (Originally almost 2 meters high, on a trade fair)

seeing. The manufacturers' marketing personnel was practically demonstrating the rocker's newness or remark-ability to their customers—the shop-owners—so that they, in turn, could later practically demonstrate it to the end-customers visiting their shops. The practice works something like this: Both skis of a pair are lifted up and held side by side with their bottom surfaces (that are usually sliding on the slow) leaned against each other. With the upper part of the ski being at head-height, the 'instructor' will move his head so that he can look at the skis exactly from the sides. In other words, he produces a vista of the skis that is structurally coherent with the technical drawing shown above: From this perspective, the skis are almost reduced to two lines (compare the image to the right and on the previous page). And while it is very difficult to spot a slight bend within in a three-dimensional plane that is looked at from an angle (and often impossible to see if looked at directly from above), the eye's visual routines can follow the contours of geometrical figures (such as lines) against a relatively homogenous background very well—the unusual curvature of the ski stands out quite clearly. In other words, once the 'student' emulates his instructor's posture and line of sight—*et voilà*: he can see how the skis, instead of running almost parallel like usually, fan out at the top. Now that the rocker being a feature of the ski has been established in the visible gestalt of the skis as exhibiting the figural coherence that belongs to rocker ski, the marketing professional can continue to explain how the rocker technology—as an abstract principle—"works" and, consequentially, which beneficial characteristics are justifiably to be expected from this particular ski. As the images document, the situated work of seeing the rocker must not necessarily happen in the course of an interaction between marketer and customer (Fig. 5.7).

Instead, skilfully composed spatial and material arrangements of drawings, texts, and objects can equally enable conducting the practice of seeing the rocker—given of course, a suitable level of attention, interest, and cooperation on behalf of the practitioner. If so, the on-looker can gradually establish and 'appropriate' the understanding that these skis are innovative by looking back and forth between the instructional text, the accompanying sketch illustrating the theoretical concept, and the aptly positioned ski (Fig. 5.8).

In my view, the fact that seeing the rocker can happen variably as a case of instruction-in-interaction or instruction-by-display nicely illustrates an important postulate of (pheno-)practice theory, namely that different arrangements of activities (in Schatzki's sense), materialities and ends or projects can form versions of

Fig. 5.7 Instructedly seeing the rocker as a feature of the ski

11 The Visibility of Things: What is a Good Ski?

Fig. 5.8 Instructedly seeing the rocker as a feature of the ski

the same practice carrying the same understandings, in this case the rocker. Of course, practices of seeing a rocker like those I just detailed are not the only format in which the rocker ski must succeed in being sense-able as a useful innovation in order for the technology to become widely disseminated. Of particular importance, for example, are the practices of test-riding I described earlier, that is, whether this ski shape does indeed perceivably prefigure them in the ways the manufacturers announce they do figure skiing, namely making turning on hard slopes easier and floating in soft powder happen faster. Again, I emphasize that for the technology to be a success, these positive effects must not necessarily also occur when an average skier uses the ski. However, a first crucial prerequisite for the dissemination of an innovation in ski equipment clearly is being fulfilled by the rocker: Its novelty and functional principle is instructably observable despite the complete absence of snow that characterizes the environments within which it has to excel, namely trade fairs and ski shops. More fundamentally, the rocker-ski's long-term success depended on whether or not it matched the style of riding a sufficient number of skiers strove to accomplish at the time—a style which will in turn be influenced by the use of the rocker ski itself, for example in that it makes skiing off-piste easier and thus possibly more popular. As Stephen Fry's (2006a) rich account of the history of skiing details, the style of skiing predominant or deemed 'correct' at certain points in time has always depended on the interplay of several factors, such as the technology available, the terrain skied, or the forms of instruction and learning applied. The introduction of motorized grooming of slopes, for example, required pistes wide enough to operate these machines efficiently, and the wide, well-groomed slopes in turn influenced the way skier's skied (Fry 2006a: 53). The wider, faster turns that became more common were best matched by using longer, more stable skis—skis which required a refined technique when used on steep, hard slopes. The history of skiing, in other words, bears rich testament to the fact that the evolution of the style of a phenopractice is dependent on a nexus of various interrelated elements that cannot be untangled by applying coarse schemata. Grasping the evolution and dissemination of a phenopractice, as well as the success and failure of product innovations, therefore crucially depend on deeper insight into the nature and function of the style of a practice. Before moving to discussing the evolution of skiing throughout the last century, I will therefore first take a closer look at the pivotal theoretical notion of style itself.

Chapter 6
Community—Style

Tom riding a line near Zell am Ziller [D]. © Paul Masukowitz

1 Introduction: The Silence of Style

"What *can* be shown *cannot* be said," Wittgenstein stated (1990: 79; original emphasis)—and many think that he also managed to show it. In this chapter, I will discuss style in freeskiing, its practical accomplishment, its intelligibility, and what I consider its function. But in doing so, I will not be able to convey just what exactly it is that a freeskiers sees when he sees style. I cannot quite muster the words to describe the beauty of a perfect powder turn. Not for a lack of romantic prose or cheesy metaphors, but because you cannot say what you need see. For this reason, I hope that I will manage to "mean the unspeakable by clearly displaying the speakable," as Wittgenstein (1990: 77) put it. But before I do that, in seeking to provide at least an idea what freeskiing's style is all about, I will put pictures rather than words. They are, I should add, not simply any freeskiing pictures, but some of the best which Tom and his friends have produced during four seasons of shooting skiing. Therefore, they are not documenting what a dedicated freeskier like Tom is doing in the sense that they merely record it. Rather, they are what freeskiing is all about for him: producing beautiful, stylish images and videos is his first and foremost goal in freeskiing (right after experiencing a great time on the mountain, that is). For example, he no longer takes part in contests, but his sponsors still support him because images such as these appear on freeski-websites or can be used as promotion material. These images, in other words, are documents of athletic achievements as much as they are creative works of art, shot and edited by him and his colleagues from a small group of semi-professional enthusiasts who produce freeski- and surf-DVDs and pictures in their free time to sell them online. These images, in other words, are the result of a considerable

Fig. 6.1 [D]. © Klaus Kock

1 Introduction: The Silence of Style

Fig. 6.2 [D]. © Paul Masukowitz

investment in time and resources; of endless hours of searching for new spots, breathtaking sceneries, and perfect lighting conditions; and of laboriously hiking through the deep powder, then crouching in the snow, camera in hand, and waiting until the riders have climbed up the opposite slope in order to speed down in a flash, producing mere seconds of material for the next movie clip. They are the product of huddling around the screen in a wrecked campervan back down on the parking lot of the lift station at the end of the day, eagerly looking for great catches and sorting out the countless misses, debating quality and style, pointing out flaws and trying to find ways to get it right next time. They are the outcome of even more hours of sifting through hundreds of shots; editing, cutting, and optimizing them; uploading them on YouTube and posting them on Facebook walls, then discussing once more about their beauty and style and that unfortunate small shadow falling onto the line in the upper right corner. These images are objects of envy, pride, and never-waning fascination. For freeskiers, they surely *have* style. Thus, they are pictures that might perhaps *show* you style as well (Figs. 6.1 and 6.2). I hope they speak to you.

2 The Centrality of Style

In addition to being of key interest to members of the subculture, I argue that Style is a central bearing point of the social nature of freeskiing practices, and therefore a key topos for a study of the freeskiing subculture. In this chapter, I will thus look in detail at how style manifests in the freeskiing world, how freeskiers come to understand and (re-)produce style, and how my findings align, but also contrast, with the descriptions and theorizations of style and its social role (e.g. in symbolizing identity or distinction) that have been developed in sociology. In the notion of style, in other words, sociological theory and the emic self-description of freeskiers meet; and therefore I will distinguish between Style (writ large) as a topic, product, or dimension of freeskiing; and style (in small letters) as a general theoretical notion of core importance for a proposed phenopractice theory. As explained in the introduction, the core project of phenopractice theory is to integrate phenomenological considerations (rooted in Heidegger and Wittgenstein but updated to the current state of the art by taking into account certain neuroscientific findings) into a practice theory framework. To this end, the theory requires a conceptual micro–macro link that can explain how practices (and their elements) as enduring macro-entities bear on the experientially organized minutia of situated performance. To be clear, all versions of practice theory need to formulate an answer to how this linking function is being fulfilled, and in doing so point to more than one linking process while putting special emphasis on one: skilled coping, the structured structuring of the habitus, rule-following, or material affordance and agencement, for example. Seeing and expressing style falls into this category of theory concepts, which means that I do not wish or need to claim that is the only linking process, or that it replaces all of the prior concerns. Instead, as my detailed discussions of functional equivalents should show, style is just a necessary addition to the notional arsenal because it can explain a form of relational ordering that is different in structure and effect and insufficiently understood in its workings. Through prefiguration and orientation via the phenomenal field, style organizes practice performances in a different (for example visual) mode, a mode that is implicit and non-regular, but can nevertheless utilize various media, thus aiding and enabling practice reproduction, dispersion, and evolution.

Freesking style makes these qualities particularly obvious and empirically evident. In freeskiing, style is polyvalent in that on the one hand it links macro-social, cultural, or community-wide structures or topics of interest; but on the other it is also of great relevance to the concrete, micro-level, and situated conduct of a practice. Style is meaningful on the macro level, because the "family" of freeskiers can be defined as composed of those who know Style, and also because Style 'circulates' globally and thus fosters global coordination and cohesion across the different local 'pockets' where freeskiing happens. It is also super-individual and not subjective: The biography or social background is not important if somebody is observed with regard to Style, and neither is the current situation per se. The only question freeskiers really care about when looking at a performance or a visual representation of freeskiing action is: Does it have Style, or not? Further, when I say that freeskiers care about Style, I mean this quite literally, as well as in the sense of Heidegger, in whose work care is a central term (see Chap. 6). Consequentially, Style is important for and reproduced in all key practices which together compose the freeskiing subculture, such as getting sponsors, gaining respect, or winning a contest. Another aspect which makes Style central for freeskiing is the fact that being able to see Style works as a proof of membership, of belonging to the community. Notably, this is not just a social procedure of distinction and symbolic demonstration of membership; but arguably, it also constitutes a momentary, situatedly produced kinship based on a shared fascination and attunement, as the next chapter will detail. For these reasons, I will develop the argument that freeskiing exists as a subculture on the basis of Style: doing freeskiing means doing Style, or more precisely: by virtue of being oriented to freeskiing Style, a doing (such as skiing) becomes practicing freeskiing. Importantly, my argument will entail that 'doing Style' should not be equated to performing certain symbolically relevant bodily movement patterns—or mastering a technique—per se, but that only within the framework of a certain type of collaborative social conduct, such movements can a) be practically achieved, and b) become observable as stylish in freeskiing's particular way.

3 What is Style?

"Phh, (.) that's hard to say. (2s) You just see it." [I][1]

"But that is really a matter of gut feeling. Well it's, (.)—there is no model how it should be optimally, unless you watch the videos of the pros, [and] then you say: 'Oh look, how he's doing it.'" [I][2]

For a freeskier, there is no question that Style is *the* decisive category in their sport: Well-known riders are praised and envied for their Style; freeski movies and pictorials are judged with regard to the question whether or not they show {stylish} tricks or lines; sponsors' team-managers pick athletes according to their Style [I]; and spectators of, rulebooks for, and judges at freeski competitions all emphasize that showing Style is key to winning [I, R, D]. But despite this fundamental importance, freeskiers are hard-pressed to say what Style actually *is*. In formal interviews just like in everyday talk, they would usually hesitate, search for words, and point to a concrete example instead, for example by showing a picture, video, or naming a known freeskier.

---

[1] „Puhh, (.) das ist schwer zu sagen. (2s) Das sieht man halt."

[2] „Des ist aber ne reine Gefühlssache. Also es wird, (.) es gibt ja kein Leitbild wies optimal sein sollte, es sei denn man schaut sich die Videos von den Pros an, sagt dann: 'Ach guck mal, wie er's macht."

"Bene, for example, his 9er, they clearly have Style." [M][3]

Not surprisingly, such answers did not quite satisfy me. But if I pressed further and asked which specific visible features of a performance or movie need to be there to conclude that a trick or line has Style, my informants did really only mention one point in different versions: The movements have to be "clean" or "smooth," and there should be no hint that an attempt was {sketchy}, that is, there was no fidgeting or floundering. This basic condition for having Style is a foremost goal of every freeski athlete, second only to the basal aspiration of not crashing:

> "Because for me, aesthetics are really my focus, are really important. For me at that moment, when I go onto such a box, [it's important] that I am as smooth as possible, that I look as good as possible and stuff like that. [I]"[4]

But this definition ex negativo does not quite work either: A performance or picture of a trick that is clean and not sketchy is by no means necessarily stylish. For example, even some of the world's best freeskiing pros are sometimes attacked bitterly in online discussions or blog posts for having a Style that is "too clean," which comes close to having no Style at all. Many freeskiers are worried that, as competitions get more professional and more formal, those riders who show what freeskiers call technical tricks—i.e. very difficult tricks that are performed without much spirit or Style—will win out over those how perform stylish tricks—technically less difficult tricks that have that special something. Style, one can conclude, is a highly important and multi-layered category in freeskiing, but it can hardly be put into words: While a host of folk terms for different combinations and versions of tricks and grabs exists, the taxonomy for Style and the 'tonality' of a performance's Style is strikingly limited. Despite the frequent and compassionate discussions about a rider's Style, it is mostly only qualified as "sick," "smooth," "incredible," "great," and so on—in other words: in a generally positive manner. The only added precision found in ways of talking Style is that this generic praise can often be referring to a particular trick in someone's repertoire (e.g. "a perfect and stylish Switch Double Corked 1080° Japan") or a part of the sequence of a trick (e.g. someone is considered "the king of the after-bang" [a small trick or gesture performed after landing the main trick]). But crucially, freeskiing's folk taxonomy is not quite able to pinpoint just *what* it is that makes sick Style sick, or which types or genres of 'sickness' one can find.

Generally said, the freeskiers' folk-term "Style" refers to an aesthetic category; the visual impression of a trick or a line: on the one hand, the trick or line should look controlled and determined, but at the same time fluent, playful, and creative. Notably, despite their difficulties in formulating definite criteria, freeskiers can

---

[3] „Der Bene jetzt zum Beispiel, seine 9er, die ham' auf jeden Fall Style."
[4] „Weil für mich Ästhetik total im Vordergrund steht, total wichtig is. Für mich is dann, wenn ich so auf'ne Box drauf geh, [wichtig] dass ich möglichst weich bin, möglichst schön aussehe und sowas."

3 What is Style?

find a broad consensus on whether or not a trick had Style with relative ease—although they can surely spin endless arguments when comparing individual pro athletes, or about controversial decisions made at contests. But by and large, these are disagreements in detail are made under the shared assumption that, by looking at two stylish tricks, 'everyone who knows' can agree that both have Style, but that there might be disagreement about which one had a bit more Style than the other. In addition to the 'tidiness' of the conduct of a trick, Style has an individual, creative aspect in that the rider makes his own interpretation of a known trick visible.

> "I find it important that you have your own style of riding, that not everyone tries to copy the others. (…) You know, a 360 can look different 3000 times if 3000 different people do it. But really completely different." [I][5]

For a trick to have Style, in other words, it must on the one hand visibly conform to the pre-given schema, so that a performance can be taken to be a successful attempt of the trick; but on the other hand it must also exhibit a certain deviance from the norm that must, however, by no means resemble an accident, mistake, or loss of control.

> Pete: "Just the other day, we saw this video where someone is only doing a switch zero [a straight jump without any rotation] over 25 meters."
>
> Jo: "He doesn't move a millimetre while he is in the air. He's just looking the whole time [mimics someone looking calmly ahead while holding a grab]. Wuuuh. Wup! And he lands."
>
> Pete: "That looks phat."
>
> Me: "Yeah."
>
> Jo: "Looks so phat. Because, in the air, he is just like—totally cool." [I][6]

In effect, Style oscillates between conformity and deviance while expressing intentionality: It must be discernible from what freeskiers call a {clean} trick, but it must also express a certain internal logic, a kind of stylistic program. As the quote demonstrates, Style is understood as a quality that is separate from technical difficulty. In fact, it often expresses a playful and somewhat ironic stance towards the athletic challenges of doing freeskiing. One telling example is a short scene in a freeski movie, in which a rider approaches a box (a box-shaped obstacle that is about half a meter high, 40 cm wide, several meters long and has a slippery surface across which riders usually 'grind' sideways) but then, instead of grinding over its surface, simply jumps neatly over the whole length of the box, almost, but *just not* touching it with his skis. This little move was neither very easy nor

---

[5] „Ich finds au wichtig, dass man so sein eigenen Style beim Fahren hat, dass net jeder probiert da einen zu kopieren. (…) Also, nen threesixtie kann 3000 mal anders aussehen, wenn das 3000 unterschiedliche Leute springen. Aber wirklich komplett anders."

[6] A: „Letzens ham wir wieder nen Video gesehen, wo einer nur n Switch Zero gemacht über 25 Meter." – B: 2Der bewegt sich halt keinen Milimeter in der Luft Der guckt die ganze Zeit so (macht eine Pose nach) Wuuuh. Wup! Und landet." – A: „Das sieht geil aus:" Ich: „Ja." – A: „Sieht geil aus. Weil der halt einfach in der Luft – total cool… "

too difficult and surely does not constitute a 'real' trick in the freeskiers' eyes, but it functions as an expression of both athletic control and creative playfulness, like an improvisation over the topic of grinding on a box, so to speak. To be sure: Such extravagant performances are only one form of the more general dimension "Style" that should be part of every jump or line a freeskier undertakes; little gestures or typical postures that are supposed to make every rider's performance stand apart from the others. If a certain form of deviance from the average has been repeatedly observable vis-à-vis a rider's performances, freeskiers are able to recognize one another on the basis of their Style of movement alone—a genuine visible identity as a freeskier has emerged.

> "If you see Patrick Hollhaus [a well-known local rider] doing [that trick], you can spot him among thousands. If he does this jump and you can't see the face of this guy, you can precisely tell that this is him, because he... Just how he does this grab, nobody else does it like that." [I][7]

Importantly, freeskiing's Style is not only something that nobody but freeskiers performs (by virtue of it being freeskiers), it is also something that only freeskiers can reliably see. In contrast, laymen unacquainted to freeskiing frequently do not 'get' a sense of Style at all: Watching a freeski movie for the first time, inexperienced spectators are struck by the repetitiveness of the images: A skier in colourful baggy clothes speeds towards a ramp, flies briefly through the air while performing wild rotations, lands—cut. The next sequence starts, another freestyler in colourful baggy clothes, another ramp made of snow, another three or four seconds of swirling through the air, another hard landing—cut. The initial fascination with the athletic skill can quickly give way to the realization that these images do not cause the same fascination for the layperson. More precisely said, laymen look for different things in watching freeskiing: They are drawn to the spectacular, such as very high jumps or multiple somersaults that accordingly dominate depictions in mainstream media and are emphasized in events tailored towards a more mainstream audience, e.g. those held in large cities like London or Zurich. In contrast, freeskiers not necessarily take much interest in just those tricks which are mainstream media's favourites, because they focus their attention on those details of Style to be found in much less dramatic moves such as sliding over handrails. The difference is even observable in the way the on-lookers react to a certain jump: While the uninitiated—those who freeskiers call "tourists"—will exclaim "Ohh!" and "Ahh!" as if they are watching fireworks, freeskiers will calmly and respectfully nod at a good performance, briefly 'applaud' a more impressive feat using their poles, and only rarely actually cheer at spectacular accomplishments. Back- and front-flips, for example, appear especially spectacular and awe-inspiring to less experienced audiences; but they are not seen too often in 'insider'

---

[7] „Wenn du da den Patrick Hollhaus [ein bekannter Fahrer] siehst, wie der den [Trick] macht, kannst, siehst du den unter 1000. Wenn der den springt und du siehst das Gesicht net von dem Typ, kannst du genau sagen, dass er das ist, weil er... So wie der das einfach macht mit dem Grab, das macht keiner sonst."

competitions or training. While these tricks are no doubt difficult and dangerous to perform, they are neither considered by freeskiers as the most difficult ones, nor as those that are the most interesting (these are off-axis rotations and complex jibbing tricks)—since they often do not show a lot of Style. In conclusion, seeing Style requires expertise, it is an embodied and emotion-laden skill. In order to be able to see Style, everyone agrees, you need to have been part of the scene for some time.

"I think you have to be in the scene for a bit in order to be able to see that." [I][8]

In terms of the time freeskiers spend conducting a number of different practices in the funpark, *watching* others training is the most prevalent of all, especially since training itself means to a large extend waiting in a queue or sitting in a lift, time that is almost invariably spend watching the performances of other riders. The process of socialization into the subculture is inherently tied to acquiring the capability to see Style: Regularly and attentively watching enables participants to grasp freeskiing's specific level of aesthetics, especially if it is done together with other freeskiers. At some point, one will be able to share the involuntary, 'heartfelt' euphoria and excitement that freeskiers feel and express when witnessing a really stylish trick or line. Such emotional practices of taking care are fundamental to their cohesion as a group as well as, as I will try to show, for the emotional drive or motivation that enables freeskiers to continue attempting dangerous and often painful tricks or lines in the first place. For these reasons, I argue that Style is of central importance to freeskiing, and that freeskiing could aptly be described as a community of style in the sense of a community of practice of seeing Style. This finding seems to bear some resemblance to the common characterization of freeskiing as a lifestyle sport, a typification that has inspired a strong and broad tradition in the sociological literature on sport and subcultures. The phenomenon of Style, however, differs from the common understanding of lifestyle in important ways.

4 "You can't Wear Your Skis to School"—Symbols of a Lifestyle

As the categorization 'lifestyle sport' already expresses, the decisive feature of what has alternately been called "action sports," "new sports," "Californian sports," or "extreme sports" is widely seen in their connection to, and blending into, a whole lifestyle—epitomized by the surfing lifestyle (for an overview, see e.g. Bette 2004; Rinehart/Sydnor 2003; Wheaton 2004a). Two aspects are frequently deemed crucial. First, the fact that participants of these sports follow the conventions of the sport subculture not only during the athletic practice itself, but also in their general life: Clothing, music, ways of talking and moving,

---

[8] „Ich glaube man muss schon n bisschen in der Szene sein, um das sehen zu können."

friendships, sometimes political views, and frequently ones' more general view on life match those of fellow participants. Expressed in the terms of practice theory, elements of the sport practice such as skating shoes or surfing brands are spilling over into everyday life. A large majority of authors thus highlights the symbolic aspect of lifestyle sports, and many explain participation in such sports as a form of identity work, as either a construction of, expression of, or play with one's personal identity and/or gender (e.g. Beal/Wilson 2004; Le Breton 2000; P. Donnelly/Young 1988; Frohlick 2005; Robinson 2004; Thorpe 2008; Wheaton 2000a, 2019; T. Williams/P. Donnelly 1985). In discussing the symbolic production or expression of identity by way of style, however, it seems that one can never be quite sure to which extend such symbolic expressions are 'true' or 'fake'—including the theoretical question of whether the symbolic layer of social life is thought to have some underlying 'true' level (candidates being true experience, honest expression, authentic being, socio-economic realities, real power structures, etc.), or not. Accordingly, for participants, companies, the media, and theorists, authenticity is often an issue spawning endless debates about if and why and how someone or something is really, really real (Atencio/Beal/Wilson 2009; Beal/Weidman 2003; Beal/Wilson 2004; Force 2009; Stranger 2010; Wheaton 2004b; Wheaton/Beal 2003; Wheaton/Thrope 2021). The second important reason to talk about lifestyle sports is the fact that—beyond symbolism, brands, and the media—avid participants often organize their whole life around the sport: jobs, careers, place of residence, friends, partners, and families are 'arranged' so as to fit the demands of maximized and optimized sport participation (T. Bucher 2000; Geisler 2003; Rinehart/Sydnor 2003; Wheaton 2000b, 2003, 2019), as well as risking their life and health in conducting the sport (Atencio/Beal/Wilson 2009; Celsi/Rose/Leigh 1993; Hunt 1995; Robinson 2004; Stranger 1999). In practice parlance, one could thus say that the sporting practices metastasize and start to push many other practices of lived life to the side.

As far as freeskiing is concerned, all these aspects of lifestyle seem relevant and valid to some extent. From the ski-manufacturer selling surprisingly many t-shirts "because you can't wear your skis to school" [I], to the Facebook-profiles of my informants adorned with a picture of skiing action rather than their face; from those for whom studying at a university in the Alps seemed much more important than the precise degree chosen, to the fact that many, if not most seemed to know someone who had 'stayed on the mountain:' Defined like this, freeskiing surely is a lifestyle sport. However, I will not focus on the trope of lifestyle in detail in this work. For one, the literature on lifestyle and lifestyle sports is already rich and plentiful. More importantly, the concept of style I develop here answers to particular theoretical questions at the heart of phenopractice theory which are only of indirect interest to the lifestyle literature. In a nutshell, research on lifestyle focuses on the distribution and development of said lifestyles on a macro level and relies on theoretical models of lifestyle reproduction borrowed from other (practice) theories. Summarizing a complex field of research, I suggest that predominant concepts of lifestyle take two major forms which are distinct from the theorization of style developed in this work. First, many authors treat following or performing a certain lifestyle as equivalent to making use of certain symbols such as clothing or brands in a (sub-) culturally specific manner. For example, Schäfer (2022) structures his practice-theoretical ethnography of the skateboarding subculture along what he considers the three dimensions bodies, spaces, and signs. However, I will argue equating the notion of style to a repository of distinctive symbols is theoretically problematic, particularly from a practice perspective. Arguably, it is also a distortion of the original notion of 'style of life' that was introduced to sociology by Simmel (1976), for Simmel rooted his understanding in the Philosophy of Life which conceived of lived social life as a continuous stream (see Chap. 8). Accordingly, in Simmel's work, style of life refers to a quality inherent in said stream, a modus or tonality typical for a certain kind of life, such as that in the metropolis. This idea, however, is quite different from the notion that style is something carried by distinctive symbols or products. The second predominant form of the concept of lifestyle in the research literature is the contemporary sibling of Simmel's understanding of lifestyle as a feature of episodes of lived life: a matter of identity, socio-cultural milieu, consumption, and aesthetic preferences. However, most authors using the term in this sense are concerned with the style of very long stretches of lived life, such as a lifespan. In contrast, freeskiers focus on the style of much, much shorter episodes of lived life, namely a freeride line or a freestyle performance. In other words, the word 'style' in freestyle skiing does not refer to a lifestyle; and the freeskiing lifestyle (the brands, the music, the fashion, etc.) might be important to many freeskiers but is not the heart and soul of the stylistic practice. But let me first assess what one might call the question of symbols.

As I noted, freeskiers use clothing, skis, brands, gear, and verbal expressions which are quite distinctive from that of 'normal' skiers. In almost all cases, one is easily able to tell a freeskier apart from all other visitors of a ski resort based on outward appearance alone. Accordingly, it seems quite obvious to define freeskiing style as being inherent to or carried by all those specific material or non-material objects that freeskiers regularly possess and use. Furthermore, I have also mentioned in the last chapter that freeskiers know the different types and brands of equipment quite well, and that they have a fine-tuned sense for spotting whether someone is only a mere 'wannabe' trying to fake his freeskiing expertise by wearing an assortment of fashionable freeski gear without actually being able to ride lines or perform tricks or being otherwise well-acquainted to the scene. Nevertheless, from a practice perspective, reducing Style to a code of symbols would be misleading. The nature and forms of the freeskiers' passion for gear makes this point quite clear: Things like skis surely contain a purely symbolic layer—in fact, they are literally coated with a so-called top-sheet whose sole purpose is to provide a canvas displaying the brand and product name, the technological perks hidden under the ski's skin, and other pleasing or attractive images and graphics. There is no question that this symbolic layer reflects the freeskiers' attention to style, and that it serves in part to position its owner symbolically by expressing e.g. his or her taste or liking of a certain brand. In his ethnography of the German freeski-culture, Geisler (2003: 78–82) accordingly cites the graphic design of skis as a perfect example of the role of style in freeskiing: By displaying symbols from the subcultural "pool of symbols," the skis help to express the riders' community membership and position them within the scene, for example as a freestyler or freerider. And indeed, skis are routinely turned into 170 × 20 cm billboards of symbolic extravaganza by skiers and ski companies alike,[9] showcasing anything from naked models to pseudo ghetto-battle-rap spray tags to 14th century medieval church paintings to pictures of old-school snowboarders instead of skiers (thus symbolically reclaiming their rebel status). Yet as these examples also indicate, there is no such thing as a 'the' meaning of 'a' symbol. Pious paintings and pictures of snowboarding are not in themselves symbols of freeskiing or freeskiing knowledge in any true sense; it is only within a very specific context of freeskiing that they can become pretty cool showcases of someone's intricate familiarity with and belonging to the freeskiing family. In other words: Symbolic meaning is in, from, and of the context it transpires in; and thus symbols, when taken for themselves, do not establish or express anything—like, say, identity, membership, or knowledge. From a practice perspective, symbolic 'content' in itself is simply nondescript or arbitrary. For freeskiers, there is probably no question that wearing skis with snowboarding images or a spooky artwork can be really, really stylish—but there is no point in saying that the style is somehow in the content of these images. Do snowboarding images or medieval art 'objectify' what freeskiers 'know' about style or freeskiing? How? This is not to say that the freeski manufacturers could print just about anything on their skiers to make them look cool. But it is only in the midst of other skis, images, designs, and performances that the design can evoke style or function as an element-in-conduct-of-belonging. Expressed in theoretical terms: What one might call symbols are figurations that must stand out of a background in order to make sense; and thus the theoretical vocabulary of symbol use and symbolic language and symbolic knowledge or memory can be misleading in suggesting that what something is or means should somehow be thought of as encapsulated in that strange thing, the symbol. In my view, talk of symbols always immediately raises the question: But what exactly *is* the symbol in this very case? Is the picture of snowboarding a symbol for freeskiing style? Surely not. Rather, in this case the style seems to stem from the fact that the image is printed on a ski—against the background of being printed on a freeski the snowboarding image is stylish. So the ski is the symbol, then? But if so, what is the image? Both ski and image, one can conclude, carry something into the context of lived life; and it is only in any concrete, situational context that symbolic meaning can arise— without there being any guarantee that it does. (How stylish is the snowboarding picture on a ski in a pitch-black room?) This perspective leads to a key point about skis and style: If style is something that becomes intelligible only in a specific situation, then one must acknowledge that skis obviously bring much more into a freeskiing situation than just a colourful topsheet: skis are of course instrumental

---

[9] The skiers use this canvas quite actively themselves, decorating it with stickers symbolizing certain affiliations with brands or locations such as their {homespot}, carefully combined to convey personal creativity and symbolic self-description (see Woermann 2010 for details).

for performing freeskiing Style (as Geisler [2003: 79] mentions only in passing). And as I have shown, skis influence and prefigure stylish skiing in very specific ways, some of which the ski developers purposefully tried to engineer into the materiality of the ski. In conclusion, by taking skis to be symbols, one will fail to grasp their pivotal role in the production of freeskiing's Style. More generally speaking, while I have defended the view that the elements which are amalgamated into practical conduct have enduring qualities in and of themselves, I have also argued that they cannot become visibly or intelligible 'just as they are' without becoming subject to the specific logic or constraints of a form of amalgamation. Conceptualized as such, one can expect elements such as material products to prefigure practical conduct in a specific way sufficiently reliably. However, by way of definition, I conceive style as a feature of concrete conduct rather than elements itself—and symbols are necessarily elements.

5 Style of Life or Style of Conduct?

I now turn to the second way in which one could draw on the lifestyle sport literature and harness the notion of lifestyle to understand Style. I have already noted that in theoretical terms, my view and the lifestyle research perspective match in so far as style is considered as a feature of episodes of lived life; while disagreement reigns on the question of how long the expanses considered should adequately be. The divergence between these points of view, it follows, is empirical (or possibly methodological) rather than theoretical in nature. The basic argument that needs consideration, in other words, is that the way in which participants perform lifestyle sports is an effect or function or reflection of their lifestyle more generally. To begin with, there are prominent some voices within the literature on contemporary lifestyle sports which have criticized the idea that these sports or subcultures can be thoroughly understood through the lens of lifestyle. Wheaton (2003, 2007), for example, has argued that the athletes' *commitment* rather than their style or skill are crucial for their belonging, status, and identity within a lifestyle sport scene; and Donnelly (2006), in turn, pointed out that most studies focus unduly on the especially visible and vocal core participants only, thus neglecting the majority of the less able. In other words: What one could term the lifestyle-aspects in the widest sense—identity, status, belonging, clothing or brand preferences—are *not* necessarily intricately connected to the concrete athletic practice. In a similar vein, authors have since long emphasized that the actual experience of conducting the sporting practice (however badly or well) needs to be distinguished from the social effects and dynamics surrounding it (Celsi/Rose/Leigh 1993; Dant/Wheaton 2007; Ferrell/Milovanovic/Lyng 2001; Stranger 1999; Sydnor 2003; Willig 2008; Wheaton/Thrope 2021)—and so have I. Furthermore, I suggest that the seemingly endless controversies about authenticity, the mass media, the mainstream, commodification, commercialization, or co-optation are also an expression of the same fundamental divide: the difference between lifestyle and the style of concrete bodily conduct. More specifically, I hold that the freeskiers' understanding of, and sense for, Style is concerned with and directed at a fundamentally different phenomenon than issues of clothing, music, gender, identity, and so forth. To be sure: There is no question that important connections exist, for example in that being able to demonstrate stylish tricks is important for one's reputation, status, and eventually identity. After all, as I will detail in chapters ten and eleven, (sub)cultural practices like freeskiing have histories over the course of which they have been shaped by institutions, ideologies, and other structures ordering the availability of resources; as well as media of various forms promoting their popularity. The conditions of their emergence are thus carried forth in the stylistic conventions of the dominant forms of legitimate, normal, or reputable performance, for example in the militarist discipline and marching order of traditional ski mountaineering. But what the history of skiing also demonstrates formidably is the considerable flexibility of (mediated) links between practices and lifestyle formations and ideologies. At various points in time, skiing has been found to convincingly express royalist nationalism, fascist brotherhood, middle-class masculinity, countercultural rebellion, and hyper-individualist self-realization (Fry 2006). The coupling between lifestyle and style of conduct must therefore been both loose enough to allow for such flexibility, and strong enough to mobilise the commitment and legitimacy it commanded throughout this history. This seems possible because, on the one hand, style is a central and near-permanent concern for practitioners of fragile practices, but on the other, the coupling to lifestyles or ideologies that style realizes is *not* the driver of, or reason for, this care for style. This fact is empirically expressed in avid practitioner's disdain for anyone overly devoted to lifestyle expression rather than stylish skiing and becomes visible in their everyday interactions.

When freeskiers talk about the style of a trick or video sequence or a particular rider, they talk about something else than the mere fact that they 'belong to' freeskiing in general, or that some kind of doing freeskiing is visible in them. Consider this small exchange that took place while we were sitting in a chairlift next to a funpark and saw someone perform a pretty impressive 720 Misty at the large kicker:

Phil: "Whoa!" (Everyone turns his head to follow the rider on his way down to the second kicker. He performs a really nice Misty.)

Phil: "Whoa!"

Fred: "That is Bene. Goin' for it. And the G [clothing] combo just looks crap."

Tom: "Way back I still used to think [the combo] looks quite cool."

Phil: "Yeah, but that was when nobody but [international pro-rider] Harlaut was wearing it."[R][10]

---

[10] „Das ist der Bene. Da heizt er wieder. Die G-Combo sieht auch noch scheiße aus." – „Früher fand ich sah die ja noch ganz cool aus." – „Ja, aber als nur der Harlaut die fuhr."

On the one hand, this exchange clearly demonstrates that although the riders do pay attention to how someone dresses and know the current fashion trends within the subculture very well—so well that they know which 'star' had worn which piece of clothing first, much like celebrity aficionados know which actress was wearing that pink Prada dress on that red carpet event already a year ago. But on the other hand, the riders' sharp critique was a mere afterthought to their immediate, emotionally expressed enthusiasm and respect for the stylishness of the trick itself, which is evidently a completely different thing: The trick had Style despite the rider wearing ridiculously exaggerated, super-baggy clothing with attached faked golden chains. In conversations and texts in freeski magazines, one regularly finds references to what is called the {G-style} or Gangster Style (with an ironic, often also slightly negative connotation). Yet having or pretending to have G-Style pertains to many aspects of one's visible persona, but notably not the tricks themselves: It is a matter of clothing (wearing extremely 'baggy' pants, t-shirts, and jackets in a kind of pseudo 'ghetto'-style), music preference (rap music), brand association (using or being sponsored by brands that are seen to have an {urban}- or {bling}-look), ways of talking (bragging; using [pseudo-] American slang expressions such as "What up, bro?"—Tyrolean accents notwithstanding), and gestures used in interaction (elaborate 'handshakes,' cool poses stricken during conversation). But interestingly, there is no G-Style of doing tricks,[11] no way of throwing 720s to complement the G-persona, and no set of grabs associated with the overall image of being a G or some other identity or lifestyle.

Accordingly, I suggest that in what the freeskiers call Style, one has a different phenomenon at hand which is connected to, and relevant for, but not equal to phenomena like a shared lifestyle, a favourite style of clothing or the personal style of someone. I will show that freeskiing Style is to be found in the organization of details of an episode of bodily conduct in that by looking at someone performing stylish freeskiing live or in the media, a freeskier will be able to see Style as a quality inherent to her way of doing it. Based on this observation, I furthermore argue, *style* (in small letters) can be described as a feature of bodily conduct of social practices per se. I will conceptualize it as a specific type of understanding (the ability to observe and produce a certain style) chiasmically tied to a quality inherent in a certain episode of unfolding of a practice, and I seek to show that it can play a key role in accounting for the stabilization, dissemination, and evolution of a certain practice in that it is able to orient practitioners' current conduct. In doing so, I seek to find what I deem a more adequate formulation for the relation of lifestyle sport subcultures and the wider society—a more moderate position reluctant to make bold claims about subjugation and control. Some authors have drawn on practice thought to argue that (socioeconomic or power-) structures of capitalist society at large are reflected and reproduced in the intricate details of performing lifestyle sport practices, that is, in their style (Kay/Laberge 2002; Schmidt 2002, 2006, 2012; Thorpe 2011). While I consider such observations to

---

[11] And also not of riding lines, since 'Gs' are generally expected in the park, not the backcountry.

be well-founded, I will criticize both the scale and scope of their argument as well as its theoretical underpinnings throughout my sketching out what I consider a more viable alternative view. At the core of my arguing lies my scepticism towards a close coupling between lifestyle and the style of conduct of a particular practice. Notably, despite the prominence of the term 'lifestyle sport,' surprisingly few authors have actually sought to establish a systematic, two-way connection between lifestyle on the one hand, and sport practices on the other. While few fail to note that the sport influences and dominates the participants' lifestyle, we do not often learn about how the lifestyle is reflected (or even dominates) the sport practices—safe for the aspects of gender and race, but then 'lifestyle' is not necessarily and adequate label for these categories. There are, to be sure, many studies that seek to track the influence of socioeconomic status or class disposition on *choosing* a sport, but these do not consider if or how one's everyday style of life might bear upon the style of actually *doing* the sport (Bourdieu 1978, 1984; M. Collins 2004; Stempel 2005; White/Wilson 1999). A few notable exception can be found in lifestyle sport research, maybe in part because the local, fluid, and mediatized nature of style is explicit to these subcultures (Booth 2003; Buckingham 2009; M. Stern 2009; Woermann 2012a). Booth (2003), for example, claims when writing on the style of surfing:

> "When surfers dance, they translate a host of philosophies, cultural tastes, values, and perceptions into movement. For many younger surfers, their dancing reflects their interpretation of contemporary urban life. (…) For the abrasive generation of surfers, then, style means spontaneity, individualism, self-expression, competitiveness, profanity, nihilism, and general social dissatisfaction." (Booth 2003: 321)

But while providing a fascinating recount of the development of surfing 'worlds' or 'cultures' from the uptight middle-class sporting clubs of Australian lifesavers via the spiritualistic soul-surfers of the seventies to contemporary professional competition, Booth does not actually show *how* philosophies or values turn into bodily movement. Like too many works on lifestyle sports, he builds almost exclusively on accounts and descriptions provided by observers and commentators of the sport, rather than attending to the everyday routine, practical problems, and immediate experiences of performing the sport. When subcultural media practices link macro-level lifestyles to embodied performances, as Buckingham (2009) and others rightly argue, then understanding this link requires original empirical and theoretical work that spans all three of these layers. And crucially, this original research cannot be replaced by merely analysing the practitioner's own representations regarding this link. While there is no shortage of beautiful prose and strong opinion (usually distinctively elitist) emanating from every better known lifestyle sport subculture, this onslaught of books, magazine editorials, or DVD-feature interviews cannot be treated as an adequate representation of the athletic practice or the state of 'the sport' per se. Instead, I hold that such documents have to be taken as a phenomenon in its own right that fulfils very specific functions (selling books and satisfying sponsors among them) rather than providing a window on concrete conduct or 'actual' sentiments. The overwhelming majority of voices represented in such meta-commentaries are those of professional athletes, editors or producers of special-interest media, and marketing managers. But all three inhabit a very specific and exclusive position within the scene; and for all three, standing out in, and leaving a mark on, the media landscape of the subculture is a key factor of their career (Coates/Clayton/Humberstone 2010; Nelson 2010). In sum, I do not see how the mediated texts and sound-bites produced within the special-interest media can provide a sufficient basis for claims such as that movements express things like "profanity, nihilism, and general social dissatisfaction." (Booth 2003: 321) One symptom showing that such emic accounts of lifestyle sports might be unsuitable as a basis for a sociological examination of the sport or scene per se is the fact that seemingly inevitably, these accounts at some point turn into laments about the pitiful degeneration of the sport, its spirit, the environment, the younger generation's skill, and so forth—a decline of civilization of truly Spenglerian dimensions. In the case of skiing, I will show in chapter ten, such credos have been voiced at least since the beginning of the last century, and remained popular ever since (see e.g. Lunn 1949). There seems to be something about the spirit of (lifestyle) sports that makes them perpetually being lost without ever causing them to disappear. To be sure, the sentiment seems to be so pervasive across not just lifestyle sport, but sport per se, that there must be something to it—but it remains to be seen just what exactly that is. In any event, I believe that some scepticism is due towards studies of the style of lifestyle sports which reproduce such narratives of decline by taking them to be factual statements about the practice's style per se—and Booth's (2003) account of the "abrasive generation" taking over surfing is a case in point.

6 Towards Defining Style: Seeing versus Talking

I should stress that, conceived in the way just laid out, the notion of style circumscribes a phenomenon that is related to, but different from those phenomena which prominent proponents of practice thought have described under the same name. Although this is a bit unfortunate, I still chose to stick to the term; first because Style is *the* central folk term and quintessential in freeskiers' eyes, and second because I consider my use of the term as a more detailed specification rather than a complete redefinition of the notions of style to be found in Wittgenstein and Heidegger in particular. Some mayor alternative uses of the term in practice theory are as follows: In Heidegger, a style characterizes a whole epoch of a culture and becomes epitomized in a true piece of art or a quintessential site, such as the Greek temple (H. L. Dreyfus 2007); in Wittgenstein, style is an aspect of linguistic performance in particular and lived life in general that lies beyond its propositional, formal content but "infuses expression with life" (Stengel 2004: 616) and is thus of ethical value (Frank 1992; Stengel 2004); Bourdieu (1984: 50) treats style as "a mode of representation expressing the mode of perception and thought that is proper to a (...) class or class fraction"; and Schatzki (2002: 153–154) briefly characterizes style as "a manner of carrying on" that is typical for certain regional cultures or social worlds, but not necessarily confined to a single one (unlike in Heidegger). What these terminologies share, in other words, is the notion that a style is a way or tonality of doing that can be found across a relatively large realm of moments of conduct, for example those conducted within a certain culture (Heidegger, Schatzki), or by a certain person (Wittgenstein). In my use, in contrast, style first and foremost refers to a specific episode of conduct in a concrete situation and is tied to a certain practice. Importantly, I do embrace the idea that what can be called a field of practices (Hui 2017)—such as freeskiing—can be characterized by what amounts to a common style; and likewise, freeskiers frequently refer to the individual style of a person. Nevertheless, I hold that these descriptions only make sense in so far as one can characterize the style inherent in specific moments of conduct meaningfully in a way that is sufficiently open (or vague) to capture a very large number of other moments which are similar in this respect. For example, one can say that conduct is aggressive or calm (like, interestingly, a piece of art); and while this characterization can be an accurate and non-arbitrary description of an enormous number of doings, people can judge relatively clearly and easily[12] whether or not something was done aggressively or calmly. In any such case, however, just what was calm or aggressive about an episode will have to be found in the details of what took place in any concrete instance in question. Therefore, I argue that while style can be described as typical for or belonging to a certain epoch or culture or person, it is nevertheless something that, whenever it appears, must appear in the concrete details of concrete conduct. A person's style, for example, is something of that person not because it is printed across his forehead, so to speak, but exclusively because it is manifest in an enormous number of concrete moments of conduct we understood as actions of said person—but inevitably not in all of them. Conclusively, there might well be some general stylistic features that unify more or less all instances of performing freeskiing stylishly—but if so, they would be accordingly broad in nature. Likewise, one might find certain similarities shared across very large realms of practices, such as those comprising a whole lifestyle. In contrast, if one considers a smaller set of performances—such as the performances of a specific grab by a single rider in the last year—it seems reasonable to expect to find them sharing stylistic features that are much more specific in nature in that they exhibit more complicated figural coherences across certain details of aspects.

Regarding the question of whether the general lifestyle or other, more specific details of conduct matter for freeskiing, as e.g. Booth (2003) seems to suggest: I did not find any evidence that such general coherences (like, say, a rebellious 'punk-attitude') were something that freeskiers were drawn to or would attend or orient to throughout their daily conduct. This does not mean, of course, that they do not exist or can have no role in explaining freeskiing's dissemination or attractiveness. But it does mean that, if one attempts to understand freeskiing and its

---

[12] Notably, I am not saying the freeskiers can necessarily agree easily; at this point, I am just observing that they can usually produce a confident judgment straight away.

6 Towards Defining Style: Seeing Versus Talking

evolution on the basis of routine, situated conduct and the experiences and necessities it produces, lifestyle alone is not a useful category. What freeskiers really care about, I hold, are the similarities and differences in the details of conduct's style—details such as those discussed in this very typical exchange between two riders during their lunch break on a sunny day in a funpark.

A: "Patrick Hollhaus, you know. He is stylin' pretty phat."

B: "Definitely. He has this super easy style."

A: "He also has really nice 9er. Forward-9er, like."

B: "Hmmh. [...] The grab that he just did, that's the same that [famous freestyle pro TJ] Schiller is also doing all the time..."

A: "Yes."

B: "...somehow pulling [the ski] through like this." [He mimics the grab by looking over his right shoulder behind his back, twisting his upper torso around and stretches his right arm down towards his right heel.]

A: "Yes."

B: "I just saw him [Hollhaus] doing this one for the first time. [literally: I saw this (grab) on him for the first time.] It looks so PHAT."

(1,2 s)

B: "Yeah, what's so phat about this pulled-through grab is just that in principle, he is rotating away practically automatically because of it."

A: "Yes."

B: "Looks so phat." [R][13]

What becomes evident is how freeskiers recognize and remember the details of someone's style with an astounding precision and can expect each other to do so as well: In the above exchange, both A and B are easily able to agree that one specific personal way (Patrick Hollhaus') of combining a certain grab—for which they do not even seem to have a name—with a certain type of trick (the forward-9) is pretty similar to another riders' (TJ Schiller's) known personal way of combining this grab with this kind of trick, which they know from videos. This exemplifies the point made by one informant (in an interview) I quoted above: He explained that style fascinates him because he can discern 3000 different versions of the same trick performed by 3000 different people. While there is no question that he was speaking metaphorically with regard to the number, it is crucial to note that he was *not* talking about so-and-so many different attempts of doing the trick

---

[13] „A: Der Patrick Hollhaus, ey. Der stylt schon ziemlich geil. – B: Auf jeden Fall. Hat nen superlässigen Stil. – A: Der hat auch echt schöne 9er. Vorwärts-9er, so. – B: Hmmh. [...] Den Grab den der grad gesprungen ist, das ist der den der Schiller auch so häufig springt... – A: Ja. – B: ... irgendwie so durchgezogen... – A: Ja. – B: ... den hab ich bei ihm jetzt auch das erste Mal gesehen. Das sieht so GEIL aus. – B: Ja, das Geile an diesem durchgezogenen Grab ist halt dass, dass der im Prinzip fast automatisch dadurch wegdreht... – A: Ja. – B: Schaut so geil aus."

being completely different, implying that no moment is like the other. Instead, he was expressing that a) there is a collection of performances which share the feature of being performances of the same trick, and that b) within this group one can discern subgroups of versions of this trick which are tied to different athletes. Surely, he would acknowledge that there are also slight differences between each and every concrete performance of every trick, but he was entirely sure that one can nevertheless immediately spot their definitive similarities. And indeed: What fascinates freeskiers in watching endless repetitions of a core repertoire of not more than a dozen tricks performed by the top athletes in more or less all top competitions and on every DVD during a season (or the handful of less difficult 'standard' tricks you see in an average funpark every single day) are the subtle differences between these different personal versions of the tricks (Fig. 6.3).

Freeskiing's Style, in other words, is something that is visible across the details of a movement, and also across the elements of a trick: the Style of a stylish Switch Double Cork 1080 Japan is inherent in the overall performance, not in a single trick itself (Fig. 6.3). Style, in other words, is a key aspect of the scenic intelligibility of bodily movement (Büscher 2005b; Jayyusi 1988). Expressed in the terminology I introduced: against the background of performing a Switch Double Cork 1080 Japan, Style becomes visible—or: what makes the Switch Double Cork 1080 Japan really beautiful is that its aspects become visible against a background of Style, of the smoothness and ease of the rider's conduct. Conceptualized as such, my understanding of style is rooted in Wittgenstein, who frames the style of language as being "that aspect of propositional language that precisely exceeds the propositional." (Stengel 2004: 616) Or, in the same vein, with Garfinkel and Sachs, I could say that the style of talking is the reason why "in the particulars of his speech a speaker, (…) [is] meaning something different than he can say in so many words" (Garfinkel/Sacks 1970: 344)—only that freeskiers let their performances speak.[14]

The relation between ways of talking about Style and seeing Style, between describing it in words or judging it according to a point scale and being fascinated or emotionally moved by it from bodily and situatedly watching freeskiing performances or visual media, is a core topic of this work. I stress that by making this distinction between *talking* and *seeing*, I am implementing what I consider a pivotal implication of a practice perspective: Since the same practices can rest on different recombinations of elements, types of events or types of social processes should not be distinguished prima facie according to the different media or situational set-ups involved. Therefore, I do not consider images and texts equivocally as media representations and thus opposed to witnessing 'live' events, especially not in the sense that one should be somehow considered a weaker or—much worse—less real version of the actual thing. Seeing a video of a jump is as

---

[14] Some have read this quote as simply implying that speaking has certain non-verbal components, which could mean that they are simply a tacit vocabulary of inherently meaningful symbols that need to be decoded side-by-side with the words spoken. It will become clear later that I deem this interpretation misleading.

6 Towards Defining Style: Seeing Versus Talking

Fig. 6.3 Showing, seeing, and filming Style in the park

much a situated event as seeing it happening unmediatedly; and while there are surely important differences between the two (to which I will attend later), they also share many important features. More specifically, my treatment differs from most other discussion of the role of media for (consumption) practices in that I do not so much separate between 'live' and mediated in-praxis encounters with Style, but between dimensions of conduct, and especially between predominantly visual or non-visual practices.[15] Style as something seen, it follows, circulates within

---

[15] More precisely: Practices whose conduct is predominantly oriented to and by the visual dimension of the multi-dimensional phenomenal field, *and* which are understood to be ways of seeing or watching by freeskiers. This does not imply that certain configuration patterns in other dimensions are not important towards accomplishing the understood visual end: For example, freeskiers might hold that music is a key part of freeski movies and an indispensable prerequisite to fully enjoying them. Still, I would consider watching freeski movies a practice of seeing, the inevitable synaesthesia of their conduct in praxis notwithstanding.

the freeskiing subculture carried by a number of different practices of seeing and performing. Its reproduction, dissemination, and evolution is thus an effect of the interplay of said practices. This kind of 'social life' of style is a classic topic of sociological treatments of style, especially with regard to either arts or lifestyle and consumption. Most importantly, authors have asked how the structure of a certain style-oriented realm within society (such as the art market, consumer society, or social classes in general) impact on the evolution and distribution of styles; and how style, in turn, reflects or reproduces these structures. How do such accounts compare to the situation in freeskiing? Towards an answer, let me first sketch out if and how style might be socially determined or negotiated within freeskiing.

7 Style in the Media

I have argued that 'knowing about Style,' or the practice of seeing Style, makes up a crucial part of a freeskier's daily conduct and in doing so helps to forge what freeskiers call "the freeski family." But the fact that certain preferences and emotionally felt stances towards certain visible details of freeskiing performances are shared and dispersed across spectating crowds should not be mistaken for a description of some unilateral consensus-finding procedure in matters of Style. Although I do suggest that freeskiers share a broad general and largely implicit understanding of Style, not all freeskiers have an equal say on the question which performances are to be considered of particularly good Style. A rider's Style can be described or marked as superior in several ways apart from the day-to-day conversations, and these ways have an impact on the career, income, fame, or image of a rider, be it on a local or global scale (Fig. 6.4). What is more, such verbal or symbolic qualifications differ in their impact depending on their origin, in that statements made by more experienced and successful riders yield more attention, or that different magazines or movie production are deemed more influential and knowledgeable. The most important formats of judging style are: a) contests in which riders' Style is judged, rankings are published, and prizes awarded; b) reports and interviews published in freeski magazines and webzines; c) opinions and arguments discussed in online forums or on blogs; and d) support from sponsors which is often mentioned in a)–c) and becomes visible through sponsor badges worn by the rider or in advertisements, on team-websites, and the like.

Echoing the role of (social) media-induced status hierarchies prevalent in all lifestyle sports (Gilchrist/Wheaton 2013), these formats are interdependent and often mutually enforcing in that attention and success in one forum yields a similar reaction in another, e.g. in that a rise in fame in online media garners the interest of sponsors, or having won a prestigious sponsor helps towards being invited to large contests. But the fact that a rider is ascribed Style and status in these formats (that I will call media) does not imply that this Style and status is unilaterally produced by these instances or unidirectionally assigned to or withdrawn from a rider. Notably, from a practice perspective, saying and seeing that a trick or

7 Style in the Media

Fig. 6.4 In praise of Style: Award ceremony at a freestyle contest in Austria. Competitors, judges and spectators stand in a circle to form an arena and applaud the winners

rider has a lot of Style are not the same thing, and thus discrepancies between the two are neither unexpected nor necessarily (but possibly) understood as conflicts, power struggles, or fractures of some kind (Schmidt/Weigelin/Brümmer/Laube/Schäfer 2022). A description of a rider in a freeskiing magazine that mentions the titles he won or the sponsors he received cannot itself invoke his having Style, just like a comment uttered in the park that a trick just performed was looking sketchy. Without exception, Style must be seen to be 'known,' and thus freeskiers might consider a rider to be lacking Style despite all the media attention, sponsor support, or competitions he has won—in fact, they frequently do. Consequentially, verbal or symbolic descriptions (e.g. prizes awarded), judgements, or statements about the Style of a specific run or a rider are being usually coupled with opportunities for seeing said Style with your own eyes whenever possible: On a contest, judges honour or dismiss what everyone else has seen as well; in printed advertisings, sponsors show their support for a rider by presenting an image of his or her pursuits; and in magazines or movies, spoken or written words about Style hardly ever appear without accompanying images showing what is talked about—while images frequently appear without verbal descriptions. Indeed, the freeskiers I observed and talked to confirmed the finding Wheaton and Beal (2003) reported about windsurfers and skateboarders: Especially the more experienced participants become less and less interested in the written texts in special-interest magazines (not to speak of the frequently ridiculed 'trash-talk' interview-snippets often found in freeski movies), but focus fully on the many images—which interestingly implies that advertisings are effectively approached in the same manner as editorial content. Notably, it seems that this relation is inverse to that found in other sports: In sailing, for example, more experienced practitioners usually read more 'technical' or 'thoughtful' magazines that use long texts and few pictures to discuss technological issues in detail or retell complex (historical) stories or abstract ideas. But in freeskiing (and snowboarding), publications that are deemed to have more substance, and are preferred by more seasoned readers, often produce opulent, coffee-table-book-style "photo issues" that let the images speak for themselves. Likewise, Tom told me that he quit reading most of the texts in the leading German freeski magazine; but he still eagerly awaits every new issue to see who is being pictured and which tricks are presented. "The texts are always the same anyways," [M][16] he explained, but went on that there is always something to learn from the images.

Nevertheless, both mediated and unmediated ways of describing and judging Style, rather than providing its direct visibility, have important consequences for individual riders, the structure of the scene as a whole, and the commonly held implicit understandings of seeing Style. For one, there are various indirect influences, for example in that certain tricks and riders considered worthy by contest judges, media editors, or team managers will be more widely visible on events or in the media; or in that said riders receive financial and infrastructural support to advance their skill and visibility. Additionally, there is of course also a certain direct influence in that the 'accounts' from judges or well-respected brands or media outlets can 'prime' or influence onlookers' seeing of Style, for example by pointing out certain aspects or motivating positive expectations. This influence is generally accumulated in a relatively small 'Style-elite' that produces the formal and informal non-visual accounts and also organizes opportunities of seeing Style, such as events or movies. As in many other (lifestyle) sports, experience, seniority, and personal achievements are important factors contributing to someone being enabled to act as a judge, team manager, or magazine editor—but effectively, he will be measured against the overall ability he demonstrated in all matters of judging, managing, and editing by those who nominate or hire him (see Hitzler/Pfadenhauer 2004; M. Stern 2009). The editor of a freeski magazine, for example, will quite likely have a well-developed sense for Style so that he is able to pick cover-shots for the magazine in such a way that both members of the Style-elite and the 'general public' of the freeskiing world find them interesting and stylish; but in the end of the day, he is being paid for selling copies and advertising space as well as managing the publication process. Thus, influential cover-shots are selected and judged accordingly via organisational procedures not only oriented by freeskiing Style [I]. In effect, both accounts of Style and dissemination media

---

[16] „Die Texte sind eh immer gleich."

for Style evolve along trajectories other than those intrinsic to seeing Style itself. Based on this finding, how can one adequately describe the social role of style? As I mentioned, a broad coalition of authors points to issues of power, distinction, and identity to explain why and how style is socially mediated and fulfils social functions. I will critically discuss these in the following section, because my specific arguments concerning seeing and the nature of social practices lead me to argue for an alternative view.

8 Cultures of Style? Contra the Praxeological Perspective on Style

My theoretical decision to consider style in lifestyle sports not as a general marker of a way of life, but as a pivotal aspect of the details of local, embodied conduct is shared by several authors who have been conducting detailed empirical work on different lifestyle sports (Booth 2003; Buckingham 2009; M. Stern 2009, 2010; Snyder 2012; Kidder 2012). While all agree on the pivotal role of visual (social) media for subcultural appeal, tacit learning, and evolution of style, different theoretical frameworks are being harnessed to theorize the manifest differences between global or hegemonic style and local or individual performance. In tune with the practitioners' self-representation, most read the uniqueness of situated performances as intentional expressions of individualism, transgression, resistance, or creativity. Studies that employ the perspective of (some variant of) Wittgensteinian practice theory, however, will necessarily come to see this difference between mediated form and manifest performance as an inevitable feature of lived social order rather than a particular subcultural gesture. Maybe the most detailed and theoretically systematic work of this kind is Martin Stern's (2009) book "Stil-Kulturen" which belongs to a strand of fruitful practice theoretical discussions of sport cultures written primarily by German sociologists. Stern presents a comparative study of three lifestyle-sports: snowboarding, paragliding, and free-climbing. To capture the dynamic and structure of what he labels "the new sports," he emphasizes the importance of style as the decisive feature of such sport communities and seeks to grasp the way in which style permeates the details of conduct as well as the images produced and consumed. Like this work, Stern draws on Wittgenstein's notion of language games and image philosophy of the image paints an empirical picture that is similar to the one presented here, even though it focuses on questions of identity both empirically and theoretically. However, Sterns work also exemplifies the 'classic' sociological view on style in both its strengths and weaknesses. Particularly, it seeks to equate a Wittgensteinian practice perspective with Bourdieu's habitus-field theory in a manner that is popular especially in German sociology (Alkemeyer/Brümmer 2016; Gebauer/Alkemeyer/Flick 2004; Gebauer 2009). As I will detail in chapter ten, this perspective has its roots in a one of two conflicting, but well-established readings of Wittgenstein's writings on "forms of life." This reading informs a strand of practice theory focused on macro-social patterns of practice performances which can be fluently linked to Bourdieusian praxeology. It should be noted, however, that Schatzki made a careful argument to reject this reading and the notion of social practices developed on this basis. The effects of such philosophical disagreements at the root of different strands of contemporary practice theory come to light quite clearly when applied to the concept of style. Building on Bourdieu but also Foucault and Simmel, Stern (2009) seeks to link subcultural style to the socioeconomic background of participants, the general societal discourse, and the nature of communities per se. In doing so, his arguments appear to be guided more by the polished (mediated) self-representations circulating in the scene rather than the practitioner's immediate experience and concerns. In part, this might well be an effect of his choice of empirical methods, which centre on discursive analysis of interviews and documents. In his conclusions, Stern joins what one might call the mainstream consensus of critical perspectives on lifestyle sports. The consensus is that lifestyle sports are not just pure freedom and fun, but actually require discipline, adhere to formalities, erect hierarchies, contain power structures, and are not inherently authentic (see especially Beal/Wilson 2004; Thorpe 2008, 2010; Wheaton/Beal 2003). Having criticized this position above, Stern's work thus offers me an opportunity to sketch out more specifically in which ways a phenopractice theoretical account of lifestyle sport is compatible with these arguments, and at which point such a situation-focused discussion deviates.

Stern is keen to show how the mechanism of style reflects more general developments prevalent in wider society, such as a self-dramatization of the contemporary subjects and an increasing panopticism. Echoing Reckwitz' (2006b) diagnosis that contemporary "subject-practices" favour ways of self-presentation and self-reflection on the basis of the ideal of the "creative subject," he (2009: 257–260) emphasizes what he calls the "theatricality" of lifestyle sports and underlines how they are organized by "choreographic principles" of self-presentation. Bodily movements are no longer employed to reach 'absolute,' quantifiable goals (as in winning a race) but become performances that consist of bodily "poses" and "micro-gestures." (M. Stern 2009: 67–71, 2010) Crucially, what Stern (2009: 260) calls theatricality does not only describe a way of outward behaviour, but also refers to a specific modus of perception and observation: other members of the sport community are judged with regard to the credibility or authenticity of their choreographies. Consequently, Stern's findings match mine in another important aspect: He also points to the importance of images and media technology for lifestyle sport cultures in general, and the observation of style in particular. However, in line with a strand of practice theoretical works that retain a focus on subjectivation but still seek to de-centre the subject theoretically (cf. Alkemeyer/Buschmann 2017), he describes the internet as an "arena of self-presentation" in which individuals showcase their stylized selves and where standards of style are not only shared but also eagerly policed and sanctioned (2009: 189–193). However, this discussion on the community's constraining influence and power to police relies on a background narrative of individual freedom and non-conformity that is itself culturally contingent. The social cohesion and control that Stern emphasizes, and the Foucauldian "micro-physics of power" of "biopolitic regimes" he sees at work in the subculture, constitute a notable phenomenon found by the researcher against the background assumption that people are 'normally' or 'authentically' not inherently enmeshed into social cohesion, but free from control and power. A practice theoretical perspective (such as mine) that asks how a community becomes and remains discernibly reproduced in the first place, however, will see style adherence and routinized reproductions as preconditions to what community members see as expressions of freedom primarily in contrast to a perceived mainstream. In addition to following an implicit narrative of individuality, Stern shares another characteristic feature of critical studies of sport subcultures when he emphasizes the historical novelty of this phenomenon (see e.g. Kidder 2012). He argues that only the technological developments of video technology and the internet after the turn of the millennium have made the specific and central role of images and imagery possible (2009: 227). In the final empirical chapter, I will show that the opposite is true at least in the case of skiing. Images and videos have played a pivotal role for the evolution and dissemination of skiing at least since the 1930s; and the fact that it is scenic in a special way has always been crucial to the nature and form of this sport.

Comparing the theoretical concept of style developed here with Stern's account in "Stil-Kulturen," one finds a two-fold fragmentism in his theorization of style: On the one hand, style is treated as a sum of distinct symbols, independent tokens of meaning which—although being recombined and mixed in various ways in everyday use—are nevertheless self-contained 'bits' of meaning. On the other hand, the (sub-)culture in question is conceptualized as a congregation of individual actors making use of that repository of symbols. As discussed, both notions are not compatible with key assumptions of phenopractice thought as outlined in this work. This becomes especially clear vis-à-vis an observation that lies at the core of Sterns (2009, 2010) study of bodily style: the role of micro-gestures. What separates contemporary lifestyle-sports from their more traditional counterparts—e.g. free climbing from rock climbing—, Stern argues, is that they adhere to a "logic of fragmentation" (2009: 71–79). Both live performances and media representations are organized in such a way that they make visible singular moves or grabs, which are essentially "gestural citations" (2009: 186) that are made to stand out of the natural stream of ongoing conduct. In Stern's account, snowboarders' grabs are paradigmatic examples of such defining micro-gestures in that they are performative reproductions of freeze-frame effects from movies or pictures: Snowboarders try to hold these grabs while flying through the air (in the same manner as freeskiers) in what Stern takes to be a case of life imitating art, so to speak, because the performance mimics the aesthetics of still images (2009: 169–167). In essence, he suggests, demonstrating style means performing what he calls "movement-images" (Bewegungsbilder): Repeating gestures that belong to the 'code' by striking certain poses, not only during athletic performance, but also in everyday life (2009: 182–186). In this way, the body is almost literally turned into a statue, or better a screen displaying the very same meaningful microgestures which are also found in the media representations dominating the sport scenes. Showcasing a meaningful microgesture, striking a culture-specific pose, the reader is to conclude, works much in the same way a brand logo on a t-shirt works: It cites an item out of a repository of symbols, only with the added advantage that it can claim heightened authenticity of the truth of the body. For all its logical coherence, there are two problems with this account of style. The first one is empirical in nature, and the second theoretical. To begin with the former, compared to Stern's descriptions of the image practices of the German-speaking snowboarding culture, my own observations of the German-speaking freeskiing culture—that overlaps to a considerable extend with the former in terms of people, places, brands, events, and media use—yielded a slightly different picture with regard to the supposed aesthetics or logic of fragmentation. In contrast to Stern, I emphasize the fragility and physical danger of performances to be a central theme which in turn meant that characteristics of flow, ease, and smoothness are of extraordinary importance to practitioners. For this reasons, I will argue that style is a quality of either tricks or lines which are a fragile movements rather than static figures or symbols (see also Braune 2021, Kidder 2012). In the same vein, while Stern argues that photos which show the performance of a single grab (thus producing the freeze-frame effect) are paradigmatic for snowboarding images (2009: 173–174), it needs to be pointed out that both freeskiers and snowboarders frequently undertake considerable technical effort to produce still pictures showing a whole movement *sequence* by taking many pictures in rapid succession during a jump and then digitally combining them into a single image. The notion that style in sport subcultures follows an "aesthetic of fragmentation," or is a repertoire of static figures, in other words, is difficult to uphold in that at least freeskiers' (and arguably snowboarders') media do not only exhibit the static forms and genres Stern focuses on, but also see style in flow and movement. As I will show through an analysis of judging practices at freeski competitions, community members are often concerned that the appreciation of style is *lost* if judges focus on whether a certain figure or gesture has been shown—for them, style is what happens despite the 'mechanical' reproduction of bodily gestures.

More important this empirical aspects are the theoretical questions produced by conceptualizing style as a vocabulary of symbols or a repository of inherently meaningful bits of code. Notably, Stern (2009) is clearly aware of one central issue this notion entails: The fact that no concrete performance of a gesture in lived life can be an exact reproduction of the symbolic gesture in question. His solution of this problem mirrors that provided by a large number of authors writing about matters of sport and style: Using gestures of style, he argues, functions like a Wittgensteinian language-game (M. Stern 2009: 187 fn39). I believe that Wittgenstein's (2009) argument about language games—that the meaning of a word is not inherent in the word per se, but in its use in everyday talk—is indeed of crucial importance for the problem at hand. Stern's use of the argument, however, relies on a particular interpretation of Wittgenstein's argument that requires critical examination. As I have indicated, two of the cornerstones of Wittgenstein's late philosophy—the language game and the problem of rule-following—have been interpreted in diverging ways by different authors within contemporary practice thought, and in particular by authors aligning with either Bourdieu or Schatzki. The problem is a vexed one, but for now it suffices to say that some authors hold that one can adequately explain an endless number of unique situated performances as expressions or instances of a limited number of gestures which form a symbolic repertoire of style by characterizing said repertoire as a tacit form of a language game 'spoken' by the athletes' bodies. The concrete performances of a gesture, Stern seems to claim in particular, do not have to be strictly identical in form to be performances of the same gesture; it suffices that they display what Wittgenstein called family-resemblance (M. Stern 2009: 187 fn39). Cultural theories of the social have of course since long held that the social production of such identity-in-difference is possible (see Reckwitz 2002a), the crucial question, however, is *how* one explains this possibility. Note that, while for most social theories who argue on the basis of subjective meaning, the problem is one of interpretation: how does the observer manage to spot sameness? The supposition here, however, is that sameness is itself dormant in what Wittgenstein called a Technik (technique) in his famous argument about language-games:

> "To understand a language means to have mastered a technique." (Wittgenstein 2009: 87, § 199)

This raises two questions: First, whether or not this supposition of inherent sameness is actually the core point that Wittgenstein intended to make about the use of language and rules. This question I will need to leave for later scrutiny (see the excursus below). And second, how one explains the postulated sameness of the body's ways. Here, Stern (2009: 187–188) loosely points to Bourdieu's (1990) "logic of practice" and states with Wittgenstein that meaning is to be found in use rather than in any abstract system of form or logic: Gestures become "charged with meaning" by being reiterated in social contexts, and by virtue of being tacit bodily performances, two separate performances still carry inherent sameness (2009: 187). In my view, Stern and other following this line of argumentation (Alkemeyer/Brümmer 2016, Alkemeyer/Buschmann 2017) do not sufficiently lay out precisely how it can be argued that reiterations of a gesture can be reiterations despite differences-in-detail in the first place, but merely points to the fact that gestures are bodily, and apparently the body can somehow ensure that two different performances are still 'actually' repetitions of the same. What is more, such an explanation is made an additionally delicate matter by the fact that with regard to style, one needs to account not only for repetition, but also for innovation or evolution as well since subcultural styles are continuously evolving and changing. Interestingly, Stern (2009: 205–215) does not invoke Bourdieu to explain how such change comes about (although he mentions him at other points) but instead relies on Nelson Goodman's philosophy of style in arts as a "way of worldmaking" (2001). At the core, Goodman's theory is similar to Bourdieu's in that he rejects both 'pure' positivism and phenomenalism or phenomenology (see Putnam 1979), but nevertheless holds that numerous 'worlds' of style coexist across the physical world (like Bourdieu's fields). According to Goodman, said worlds are constituted by intersubjectively reproduced symbol systems in that artists' (or actors' more generally) ways of expression and perception come to fit within them: Regularities in expressions and pattern perception complement one another in praxis, but cannot necessarily be expressed in words or other formal languages. At least in the way Stern rephrases him, Goodman thus provides a relatively basic version of a practice theory in that style is not intentionally produced, or is only a framework of interpretation, but is constitutive for and reproduced within a certain realm (or world) of events that are moments of stylistic conduct. Notably, this account differs from Bourdieu's in that it does not attempt to tie the different 'worlds,' as well as actor's capacity of producing and perceiving style, to the general socio-economic structure. What is more, Stern emphasizes that order 'in the world' precedes and causes the actor's ability to perceive them: The actor's perception becomes re-organized in such a way that she becomes attuned to the prevalent patterns (M. Stern 2009: 210–212). How does this happen? Stern's argument at this point is in line with my own findings: What one could call attunement to the perception of style happens by and within the practice of observing stylish conduct, either live or in images or videos. Building on Goodman's philosophy of style, he suggests that style invokes a particular "form of perception" in that the images circulated, for example on the internet, shape how participants observe. And since live performance and images are different formats with a different 'visual logic,' they reinforce and cross-influence the respective ways of seeing. Importantly for Stern, this means that images shape what counts as an adequate performance that needs to be achieved in praxis—in effect, participants are subjected to a subtle "tyranny" of images demanding and enforcing bodily discipline (2009: 225–226). Notably, Stern extracts the term tyranny from a quote by Wittgenstein in what I consider a misleading way, as I will discuss in Chap. 8. He then uses the term to connect Goodman, Wittgenstein, and Foucault: Since the lifestyle athletes above all observe themselves in the pictures and videos they produce, he characterizes this mediatized self-observation through the lens of style as invoking new "forms of self-relations" (Formen von Selbstverhältnissen) which—unlike traditional forms like writing diaries or expressing political statements—are implicit and carry a distinct tone of playfulness (M. Stern 2009: 252–255). This playfulness, however, as well as the lack of formal regulation and organizations, is misleading: The new forms of self-relations in the modus of style, he argues, are to be understood as Foucauldian "techniques of the self," as a form of disciplining one's own body in order to be admitted into the community of style (2009: 224–226). Style itself, he concludes, functions in the fashion of Simmel's notion of honour: as an individual and voluntary obligation to self-regulation (2009: 249–252).

The upshot of this praxeological (rather than phenopractical) notion of style, I hold, is twofold: First the argument that adherence to style has social functions such as distinction and status-demonstration, or fostering belonging and a sense of community, works independent of the actual content of what is considered stylish. The social function can be fulfilled by arbitrarily chosen forms of meaning (an argument that has been with regard to modern art in particular). In the case of freeskiing, creativity, individuality, or authenticity could still be expressed and/or gained by microgestures adapted from the Smurfs rather than the HipHop-culture; and at the centre of one's self-presentation could be piety instead of coolness. As I have argued with regard to the design of skis, this is an effect of conceptualizing style as a repository of distinct symbolic forms. Second, in describing how individuals work on their "self-relation" until they are eventually socialized into the community of individuals that sport subcultures allegedly are, the praxeological theorization of styles remains at least open to, if not tied to, an individualistic ontology. Stern for example, although explicitly building on Bourdieu's praxeology and describing the acquisition of the bodily skills necessary to express style as the formation of a habitus (2009: 134–137), backs off from the anti-subjective aspects of the habitus-field theory towards the end of the book. Since the embodied habitus is by definition sub-conscious and shielded from individual reflection and direct formation (instead expressing the overall structure of the field), Stern's emphasis on "self-thematization" and self-optimization would produce a contradiction. The solution he proposes is that image-practices provide the missing link between the implicit and subconscious bodily skills on the one side, and the "explicit self" as the subject of self-reflection and -management on the other (M. Stern 2009: 252–255). In effect, Stern seems to pivot from a strictly praxeological towards what I have called a pragmatist version of practice thought (for lack of a better term): practices are effectively taken to be tacit, bodily techniques—and thus one might read practice theory as applicable only to a specific type of activity that stands in contrast to the intellectual work of conscious reflection. The work of Alois Hahn, to which he refers, is a particularly clear example: Hahn (2009) seeks to connect Luhmann, Gehlen, and Bourdieu by arguing that the bodily habitus is effectively a system running 'underneath' the level of higher consciousness which a) relieves it of part of the burden of interpreting the world and b) constitutes a separate form of embodied memory. Despite its invocation of Bourdieu, in other words, this perspective is thoroughly rooted in the basic premises of the sociology of knowledge and the mind–body dichotomy, especially in that it distinguishes knowledge *of* the body from knowledge *about* the body (see Keller/Meuser 2011a). While 'pragmatist practice theory' such as that implied by Stern seeks to overcome such body-mind dualism, it keeps inviting it back in by simultaneously holding on to subjectivity or subtle forms of theoretical individualism. Note for example that Stern's core argument can be read as aligned with classic Schutzian theory of action (which in turn should not be over-simplified into blatant individualist mentalism): The micro-gestures Stern describes could be identified as instances of applying what Schutz and Luckmann (1973: 108–111) called habitual knowledge, routinized and unproblematic elements of our knowledge which are always on hand for the experienced practitioner and which over time sediment from situation-dependent, purposefully learned means-to-ends to bodily skills no longer consciously noticed but applied unquestioningly. In this way, Stern's (2009) account of style at times reads much like Geisler's (2003: 78–88) explicitly

Schutzian account of the freeskiing subculture: Purposeful actors strive to display their belonging to a community of individuals by making use of symbols in a knowledgeable and systematic way. The main difference between gestures and 'pieces of knowledge' or 'bits of information' would then be the mere fact that these lifestyle symbols are tacit gestures made with the body which are normally 'hidden in' the body in the form of tacit knowledge that needs to be teased out at times and/or stored in images collected for this purpose. Embodied knowledge, in other words, is a theoretical concept that can be weaved fluently into both individualist and non-individualist (practice) ontologies of the social. If style is conceptualized as a form of embodied knowledge, then using said style to explain how subcultural practices hang together can pull the explanation back into the realm of individualist ontologies despite working within the vernacular of practice theory. For my project of developing a strictly social ontology of phenopractices, a closer look at the concept of embodied knowledge is therefore necessary.

9 Is Style Embodied?

In sociological studies of sport in general and lifestyle sports in particular, the concept of embodied knowledge is both powerful and pervasive—and rightly so. Indeed, I do not want to suggest that accounts of style in lifestyle sports like those offered by Stern are inadequate or illogical. Quite to the contrary, they can help to produce relatively complete and convincing portrays of such scenes or subcultures. But in doing so, I believe, authors are profiting from their privilege of being social scientists by neglecting much of the complexity and variety of insights that other disciplines have collected about the body, and instead oversimplify its workings without sufficient justification. At the core, they imply that one simply 'has' one way of doing things that is written into one's body: a technique. This, however, arguably means to reify the body into a reliable machine. As my discussion of the body-on-the-move suggests, it is correct to assume that our body 'does' many thinks independent of our conscious awareness, and often in a surprisingly competent way. This observation alone, however, does not warrant turning the body into a black box, while simultaneously idealizing its capabilities. More to the point, I hold that this position is only justified if one subscribes to a sociology of knowledge or action that systematically defines and restricts its interest to subjective and/or conscious meaning. A rich and detailed literature has laid out how sport participation and sport communities can be studied and explained on the basis of subjective and conscious experience alone (e.g. T. Bucher 2000; Hitzler/T. Bucher/Niederbacher 2005; Honer 1995), and has also developed a complementing notion of style (Soeffner 1995). From this perspective, it is entirely justified to neglect exactly how the body subconsciously does what it does when reproducing stylish gestures, keeping balance, or training movement patterns, since the sole question is and how it features in consciousness. But once Pandora's body-box is opened

9 Is Style Embodied?

by the social theorist, his or her explanations need to account for a much greater range of phenomena and findings. Most importantly, as I showed with regard to the bodily background of vision, there are several levels of the body, different systems working side-by-side and sometimes against each other. Their coordination or alignment, I argued, cannot be undertaken by the body itself, but must be done in practice. But how?

I suggest that the recent practice theory literature on (lifestyle) sport does not attempt to explain in sufficient detail *how* the regularity of bodily conduct is achieved despite the bodies' possibly conflict-inducing pluralism. From my perspective, this means that just like in many, if not all praxeological accounts of practice theory, the fact that something is done bodily (such as performing a gesture or identifying taste or playing a game) is thus treated as providing a sufficient explanation of identity-in-difference because evidently, obviously, somehow our bodies-in-use can tacitly and intuitively produce sameness. To be sure, I have spent a considerable amount of pages detailing the related and similar argument that understandings are carried across repeated unfoldings of social practices; and I have likewise detailed how bodily processes play a pivotal role in doing so. However, I suggest that my account was crucially different in that it a) laid out the intricate details of underlying bodily processes and systems in much detail whereas Stern (as well as authors such as Wacquant) seem to suggest that by flip-flopping between mediated images and bodily praxis, practitioners can somehow reproduce identity-in-difference (cf. M. Stern 2009: 252–255).[17] b) Crucially, and arguably because I have looked at the body's wondrous workings in much more detail, I do not claim that in 'the' body, we have found the one formidable instance that can remedy indexicality and can reliably turn difference into sameness. Indeed, if arguing from a practice perspective, one cannot consider the body to be a single unit in the first place (see Mol 2002). Consequentially, it is necessary to de-centre the body and develop an understanding of circulating elements in which none of the elements can be said to individually carry the logic of practice. Most importantly, this difference in perspective also implies a different understanding of style. The main thrust of the phenopractical argument about style is this: I argue that style itself should not be reduced to an output produced by bodily performances (or images and similar works) but acknowledged as a *resource* or tool in its own right. I hold that the content of style is of functional value in that being able to observe and achieve style is not just a means of communicating status or belonging, but is a tool that helps manage, even survive doing something like a lifestyle sport. Arguably, this crucial role of style, and more specifically of micro-gestures as theorized by Stern, becomes evident when closer attention is paid to the individual experience of struggle and failure that characterizes the actual doing of lifestyle sports: the joy and the fear, the feelings of fragility and exposure, and most importantly, the insecurity whether or not you

---

[17] Other proponents of praxeological perspectives, however, have made much more specific suggestions in this regard, which I will discuss later.

are doing it right.[18] Put in theoretical terms, what I am advocating for is to take a Heideggerian perspective on embodied action and perception that centres on the notion of skilled coping in response to the inherent indeterminacy of situated conduct. As detailed in chapter four, such a perspective complicates the view of the body as well as embodied or tacit knowing, especially if we are to think of style as something that is apprehended and performed bodily. One way to develop such a perspective is to question the concept 'body technique' that plays an central role for theories of embodiment. The acquisition of a style of bodily conduct is frequently portrayed in the sociological literature by drawing on Marcel Mauss' (1973) famous observation that American women had a different way of walking than French women. Mauss emphasized that such "techniques of the body" are acquired by imitation over time, and thus held that said techniques can be defined as being "traditional" (1973: 75). But as critics have pointed out, Mauss' account of the body as "man's first (...) technical object" (1973: 75) can easily lead to an overly simplified perspective, mistaking the body as a passive object that can and needs to be influenced and formed (Lyon 1997).[19] I argue that in building on Mauss, Stern's (2009: 22–24) Foucauldian description of self-fashioning and self-control commits the same mistake. Effectively, Stern portrays the body as an object of social control and manipulation into which one's individual history of socialization and athletic training becomes inscribed. Stored in the body in this way, this learning history can later be read off by observing the style of one's bodily conduct. Conceptualizes style as something that is *in* bodily techniques, and thus effectively in the body means to extend a stream of literature on sport (sub-)cultures which equates three different theoretical notions that are better kept apart: bodily techniques (in the sense of Mauss), habitus (in the sense of Bourdieu, not Mauss) and style. Throughout the coming chapters I will detail the differences between praxeological and phenopractical approaches to style in general and lifestyle sports in particular. For now I will focus only on the relation between technique and style, leaving the question of the intermediate habitus aside (see Chap. 9). My argument is that style is a much more complex and powerful feature of social conduct than just a way of doing a body technique which expresses one's prior history or experience of repeating and training said technique. At the root of the two different conceptualizations of style lie two alternate readings of Wittgenstein's philosophy. I will argue that praxeology links Wittgenstein's critique of a mentalist notion of rule-following with the trope of bodily techniques

---

[18] From my perspective, Stern's work highlights that only sustained and thorough immersion into specific communities of practice enables one to grasp the intricate details of conduct to a degree that allows adequate theoretical understanding. Maybe because he undertook a comparative study, Stern did not really had the opportunity to observe the action 'from within' since—as he notes (2009: 37 fn10)—he did not actually gain anything but most basic skills in snowboarding, and none in para-gliding.

[19] To be sure, Mauss acknowledges that the body can resist and does not always do what it is supposed to—but nevertheless, the shaping of the body's techniques is portrayed as a one-way street and something that, all in all, reliably works if one shows persistence.

in a problematic manner; and in doing so reproduces a misconception of embodied learning, namely a unidimensional simplification of the acquisition of bodily techniques as sedimentation qua repetition. Drawing on an alternative (well-established) reading of Wittgenstein's anti-mentalism and combining it with a recent research on the plural ways of bodily learning, will form the basis for detailing a phenopractical alternative.

Excursus: (Mis)readings of Practice Theory and their Roots in Wittgenstein on Techniques and Rules

> My impression is that the reception and critique of practice theory in sociology-at-large has to an unduly and unhelpfully large extent focused on the mind-body question in the widest sense; and I might add that this is especially true for German sociology. One particular problem emerges from critic's frequent reduction of practice thought to the notion of skill or embodied knowledge, because this does not do justice to practice theory in the wake of Wittgenstein and Heidegger and has allowed some to brush aside some of its insights all too hastily (cf. Bongaerts 2007, 2008; Nassehi 2009: 219–226; Schulz-Schaeffer 2010). One common response (e.g. Stock 2011) has been to point out that practice theory additionally includes important insights regarding the social role of technology or materiality that have been prominently discussed in science and technology studies, particularly those forwarded by ANT. This line of thought fits in nicely with Reckwitz' (2002a, 2002b, 2006c) highly influential account of practice theory, which emphasizes the systematic inclusion of materiality as the key development in contemporary practice thought. But although both the treatment of the bodily and the material dimension of social life are, of course, two key facets of practice thought, I think that critics like Rammert (2007a, 2007b) or Schulz-Schaeffer (2004, 2010) have a point when they argue that these two aspects alone can also just as well be integrated into a 'classic' theory of action by adding a pragmatist and technological twist to it. The paradigms of embodied knowledge and social material alone, in other words, do not suffice to pinpoint the conceptual position the theory of social practices claims to hold—at least if one refers to the version of practice thought brought forward by Schatzki and colleagues. To be sure: Proponents of practice thought (like Reckwitz) by no means explicitly attempt to simplify the theory in this way; but the public debate more often than not shrinks it down to these two issues (in addition to those works just mentioned, see for example the positions collected in Hörning/Reuter 2004). A key reason for this lies in the fact that practice theory is, authors agree in unison, more of a family of theories rather than a single standpoint. But on the other hand, the overwhelming majority of authors refer directly and explicitly to the work of Ted Schatzki as a reference point—but then fail to take note that he neither

discusses subconscious routines or embodied knowledge at any length, nor conceptualizes practices as material. In other words: What makes many materialistic-corporeal reductions of practice theory (written by both critics and proponents) additionally problematic is the fact that they first announce to make an argument that extends to the work of Schatzki, but then follow up by primarily or exclusively discussing Bourdieu and/or pragmatist philosophy (cf. Bongaerts 2007, 2008; Schmidt/Volbers 2011a; Schulz-Schaeffer 2004, 2010). For one, boiling either Bourdieu's praxeology or pragmatist philosophy down to the trope of embodied knowledge is in itself a problematic manoeuvre (as Hörning 2004 shows with regard to pragmatism; and Saake 2004 for praxeology). But more importantly, Schatzki's position deviates in many ways from said positions—not to mention that he criticized Bourdieu's praxeology at article-length twice (1987, 1997) and dedicated a full chapter in his "Social Practices" to the same matter. Specifically, I hold that the concept of action (as crucially different from activity; see Schatzki 2010b: xv) that Schatzki's notion of doings had always implied (see especially Schatzki 2010), and sets his thought apart—not only from Schutzian sociology of action, Bourdieusian praxeology, and strands of pragmatist sociology (e.g. as developed by Srubar 2007a, 2008), but also from most of the concepts circulating within those theoretical 'turns' frequently portrayed as similar or equivalent to practice theory, such as the body turn (Bockrath/Boschert/Franke 2007; Gugutzer 2006; Keller/Meuser 2011b; Schroer 2005) or the performative turn (Fischer-Lichte 2004; Fischer-Lichte/Risi/Roselt 2004; Schmidt 2002). While a more detailed dissection of what Schatzki (2010b: xv) calls the action-accomplishment ambiguity will have to wait until the next chapter, it seems useful to point out the origin of the confusion I criticize. After all, I surely do not wish to claim that the connections that are drawn between theories of embodied knowledge, praxeology, and Schatzki are entirely unjustified or bare any substance. Rather, I believe that it is often overlook how different authors make very different use of their common philosophical point of reference, in this case Wittgenstein.

I hold that the notion 'technique' (together with 'rule') is the heart of most of the disagreements, misunderstandings, and misrepresentations clouding the theoretical position that a theory of social practices has to offer for the sociological discourse. More specifically, I suggest that the relation between what Schatzki calls a "Wittgensteinian approach to the social" and either science and technology studies or pragmatist (or praxeological) theories of the social remain somewhat blurred as long as the specific use that Wittgenstein makes of the notion 'Technik' (or technique) is not being carved out in detail. Not only can the German term *Technik* mean both technique and technology, depending on the context (see Rammert 1998; Schulz-Schaeffer 2000 for different uses in German social theory); but additionally, it acquires a specific third meaning within Wittgenstein's late philosophical work. In short, I suggest that many authors have interchangeably taken Technik to stand for material technology (especially within STS) or technique in the sense of routinized bodily movement patterns (especially in [French] pragmatic theories and [German] sociology of action), while relatively few have managed to preserve the conceptual idea (arguably) prevalent in the *Philosophical Investigations*—and those who do usually avoid the term techniques and speak of practices instead. But in Wittgenstein's writing, the term 'Soziale Praktiken' (social practices) does not appear, and 'Praxis' is used only seldom (but famously in § 202), while he frequently speaks of Techniken and Gebrauch (forms of use).[20] Thus, it is not immediately evident why the social theory derived from his thought is a 'practice theory' rather than a 'technique theory.' The reason why practice theorists use 'practice' rather than 'technique' can be located in their specific treatment of the notion of language games and the problem of rule-following which is of crucial importance for Wittgenstein's late philosophy, and thus contemporary practice theory. Within science and technology studies, however, the problem of rule following has been discussed extensively and was arguably pivotal for the advancement of contemporary practice thought within this field (see Bloor 1992, 2001; Lynch 1992a, 1992b, 2001; D. Stern 2002, Schmidt 2022). The heart of the problem can be shown by juxtaposing two pivotal sentences from the *Investigations*:

> "To follow a rule, to make a report, to give an order, to play a game of chess are customs (usages [German: Gebräuche], institutions)." (Wittgenstein 2009: 87, § 199; original emphasis).

And, on the same page:

> "That's why 'following a rule' is a practice. And to think one is following a rule is not to follow a rule. And that's why it's not possible to follow a rule 'privately'; otherwise, thinking one was following a rule would be the same thing as following it." (Wittgenstein 2009: 87 f, § 202; original emphasis).

Read in conjunction, one could conclude that Wittgenstein is suggesting that all conduct that appears to be guided by rules, i.e. that is regular, is thusly not by virtue of being guided by some mental script, but because human lived life itself is inherently orderly in that it consists of recurrent ways of doings. But while this point is quite clear, it remains opaque whether the terms customs, practices, and Gebräuche simply denote the same basic thing: techniques of doing regular conduct. Very broadly, this is the position of those I collect under the loose terms pragmatic and praxeological version of practice thought; they understand practices as something that can be aptly explained by tacit, embodied knowledge or the habitus,

---

[20] And he actually objected to translating "Praxis des Spiels" as "the practice of the game" and instead preferred "the way the game is played." (Hacker/Schulte 2009: xiv).

respectively. In effect, this position adheres to what is commonly referred to as the philosophical position of rule-scepticism (e.g. Bloor 2001; D. Stern 2002): Explicit rules, as well as any explicit description produced in social life at large, are fundamentally severed from the actual order of lived conduct in such a way that they neither adequately describe, nor cause said order. As Bourdieu (1977) put it, the practice has its own logic that is fundamentally different from rational or logical logic and which cannot be adequately expressed in theoretical models or rule-like postulates. Notably, pragmatic and praxeological versions of practice thought share this understanding with some proponents of 'postmodern' performative accounts (see e.g. Law 2004: 53). In effect, explicit rules are considered as resources for ex-post rationalizations while the question if and how regimes of ex-post rationalization come to shape conduct pre-rationalization remains vaguely answered at best (cf. Schmidt 2022). Instead, the discussions keep reverting to the point that situated accomplishments or embodied techniques are all that is needed to explain the regularity and thus intelligibility of social life. The phenopractice perspective, in contrast, would argue that embodied techniques are intertwined with embodied experience, the orientation and prefiguration of which might offer a clue to how rule-following can be more than just "retroactive correlation" (Schmidt 2022). This view is rooted in a second, alternative position on rule-following which is summarized nicely by Bloor (2001) in pointing out that Wittgenstein included the term "institution" as a proxy for social customs and rule following for a reason. A rule is a social institution,[21] he argues, which is made up of *both* the explicit expression of the rule *and* the regular conduct which are connected in a very specific relationship—a relationship that is not an addendum to, but the very essence of the social. In short, it is argued that Wittgenstein shows that the content or meaning of a rule is to be found in *both* rule following and rule interpretation, that is, the specific constellations of social order that arise from their dynamic co-constitution in lived life. In my view, Schatzki's definition of the social practice as a nexus of doings *and* sayings carrying understandings effectively expresses this concept. Notably, Schatzki uses the term 'rule' only within the expression "explicit rule" and thus only to refer to one half of the duality of rule following and rule interpretation, while he avoids using the term rule-governed because it frequently causes confusions and misunderstandings in his view (1996: 50 f.). Thus it becomes clear that, while rules often play a distinct role within social practices rather than being effectively irrelevant, they neither determine practical conduct in any sense of the word. As I noted, I describe the way in which rules instead help towards the accomplishment of practical conduct with the term instruction

---

[21] Note that his use of the term 'institutions' differs from that but Berger and Luckmann (1966).

which I borrow from ethnomethodology. More specifically, I will later argue that what Schatzki terms rules and defines as "formulations interjected into social life for the purpose of orienting and determining the course of activity" (2002: 80) actually encompasses a category of entities into which images or videos can fall as well.

In any event, this so-called anti-sceptical reading of the discussion of rule following is at the heart of both Schatzki's account of social practices and—as especially Michael Lynch (1992a, 1992b, 1993, 1997, 2001, 2009) has emphasized time and again—ethnomethodology. Especially in the reception of practice theory in German sociology, this point is, in my view, all too frequently overlooked. Schatzki's expression "nexus of doings and sayings" is effectively reduced to "doings," which are in turn equated to actions conceptualized in the traditional individualist fashion, as something that needs to be selected before it can be done (for two clear examples see Bongaerts 2007; Schulz-Schaeffer 2010). For one, discussing a theory that clearly and explicitly distinguishes between doings and actions (e.g. Schatzki 2002: 96) by boldly presupposing their identity *and* then mid-way redefining what they should 'really' mean is arguably problematic. But more importantly, what is much too often lost in the debate is that Schatzki frames the social as a nexus and *not* as (regular) doings—or a pile thereof. To conclude, what stands in between those who reduce the notion of social practices to regularity carried by bodily techniques and those who emphasize that social practices encompass doings *and* sayings—that is, explicit formulations, accounts, rules, and so forth—is not a disagreement about the fact that certain bodily movements or reactions are reliable or regular; but whether or not that is all there is to regular human live and social order at large. This divergence, to be sure, is also what I (inter alia) intend to express with distinguishing individual from social ontologies.

10 The Learning Body and Neural Pluralism

When testing a ski, riders avoid skiing the same model for too long because otherwise they will adapt their riding to the demands of the ski, which is just the opposite to what they intend find out: How well the ski is adapted to their own riding. This sentiment reflects an experience we all know, namely that practice makes perfection. The more we repeat a certain bodily movement, the more it becomes our second nature, a part of us. By way of repetition, the body 'picks up' techniques. This concept is not only immediately plausible and part of our everyday understanding of learning and training, but it is also at the heart of most accounts of learning within sociological theories of action and knowledge (see chapter seven). To be sure, few authors fail to mention that the body is seldom as docile as we would want it to be, or that we often struggle to really 'get' a movement and need persistence and patience until we 'have' it. Still, this observation does not draw into question the basic mechanism; quite to the contrary, it only seems to confirm it: Most accomplishments are difficult at the beginning, but if a feat is only repeat often enough, our body-thing will eventually work smoothly. True, many authors also share my argument that our perception of our body is often polyvalent, and that our control over our body is all but complete and perfect. But again, this finding is often also seen as confirming the basic idea that we only need to make our body do what it should do for a couple of times, and then it will start to repeat it on its own. This reliable mechanism of sedimentation or inscription seems to be the perfect powerful counterbalance to the fleeting and inconsistent content of consciousness: intentions, emotions, and situations might vary each time anew, but the body will faithfully trot on into one direction. I disagree. There is no such thing as 'the body'—at least when we talk about bodily functions rather than our experience or observations-in-practice. Looking at vision alone, one will find a rich array of different systems or (neural) processes that operate independently and sometimes antagonistically, yet side-by-side. One is confronted with the same kind of "neural pluralism" (Ennen 2003) when asking on the basis of which processes we are able to repeat a movement sequence. Nothing would be further from the truth than suggesting that every repetition of a movement sequence is brought about like all the others; or that every repetition automatically leads 'the body' to 'memorize' this very movement. To be sure, neuroscientists do indeed identify mechanisms that are responsible for what is called procedural sequence learning, the learning and improvement of bodily movement and reaction patterns by repetition per se (and notably, this function is described as independent from conscious attention; see Ennen 2003; Graybiel 1995, 1998). But these processes are by no means universal in that we automatically (and involuntary) learn every movement pattern we conduct, or in that all kinds of bodily techniques can be learned via procedural repetition. 'Picking up' a movement or a way of moving from a social context can take inherently different forms: Some movements (like yawning) we emulate involuntarily, spontaneously, and preconsciously when we seem them (even a newborn does that less than an hour after birth; see Jacob/Jeannerod 2003: 234); some we indeed memorize by tacitly repeating the same movement over and over (cf. Foucault's famous docile bodies; see Nissen/Bullemer 1987 and Prinz 2014, 2020); some movements we already 'rehearse' just by *seeing* others doing them (Pellegrino/Fadiga/ Fogassi/Gallese/G. Rizzolatti 1992); others are inherently tied to affective or emotional states that need to be reached before 'learning' can even begin (think sex or violence; see Lyon 1997); again others we pick up via coordinating interactions (like dancing or Goodwin's [2000] instructed vision); and some need to be instructed verbally or accompanied by certain conscious acts (such as trying to remember what the teacher told you). Acquiring a bodily technique, in other words, is much, much more multifaceted than simply doing something a few times until it 'sinks in' and 'the body' will continue doing it on its own. There is no question that this kind of tacit sequence learning is one important form of skill acquisition, but it is by no means the only way (see also H. L. Dreyfus/S. E.

Dreyfus 1986). Therefore, I suggest, it is highly problematic to use just one format of movement acquisition as the bedrock of a general theory of learning a bodily technique. But this is arguably just what different strands of sociological theory do, each promoting a different 'universal' format—and the pluralism of our bodies' ways seems to offer a good explanation why they all have good reasons to believe that they are right: because to some extent, they are. First, most versions of pragmatism hold that bodily skills are automatically acquired by way of repeating, and thus reject all unduly 'intellectualized' alternative accounts. Second, a broad group of theorists builds on a similar unidimensional picture of bodily learning by arguing that, because of this automatic and expectable effect of repetition, one needs to focus the analysis on what happens before this sedimentation can set in: The first few times, they suggest, conscious planning and intending the action and/or the interaction it is embedded in (e.g. between teacher and student) are crucial for shaping what we do, before the body 'learns' from action as intended consciousness,[22] so to speak (e.g. Knoblauch 2010). A third example of a unidimensional approach to embodied learning are the attempts to conceptualizing the acquisition of embodied skills via what is called the mirror system, or our capacity to learn or rehearse a movement (subconsciously) by watching others move (Lizardo 2007; Schmidt 2008). These different theoretical approaches, I will show over the course of the next chapters, have some truth to them in that they describe mechanisms that are indeed at work when we acquire the bodily skill dimension of a practice. But their common flaw is that they insist on a one-size-fits-all solution: They propose an theory of action and learning on the assumption that all repetition means acquisition, or that all bodily actions are first consciously preconceived and later routinely reproduced, or that all our embodied skills have been picked up subconsciously from our environment—or at least, that these are the dominant and most interesting phenomena we need to focus on. In this work, I try to take a different path. I work on the assumption that we acquire the different *aspects* of a bodily technique in different ways, often simultaneously, and not necessarily in an orderly and efficient manner. As the fragility of skiing makes clear, some things need proper planning and focused attention, while others simply happen 'automatically' and are best left alone. Keeping balance on skis is learned either 'intuitively' and quickly, or never. Learning to 'see with your knees' takes time and

---

[22] To avoid misunderstandings: The notion of sedimentation in Schutz describes the sedimentation of certain 'bits' of knowledge within our stock of knowledge: acts that we originally perceived as problematic and had to learn, i.e. approach in a conscious and purposeful manner, over time become more and more unproblematic and natural to us and can eventually be tackled 'en bloc' (monothetically) and thus move to the margins of awareness (Schutz/T. Luckmann 1973: 108–111). In itself, this account does not say anything about how 'the body' might learn or not; it only describes our lifeworldly experience that it does. But in doing so, it nevertheless operates on the assumption that the body 'underneath' subjective consciousness has very reliable and schematic ways of learning. For example, when Schutz and Luckmann state that useful knowledge never fails the Idealization of "I can always do it again." I will discuss the notion of sedimentation in more detail in Chap. 8.

routine but happens tacitly and 'automatically.' Rotating your hip needs to be explained by an instructor and observed actively by the student before it 'sediments.' Skiing in a smooth and stylish manner, finally, is (arguably) learned predominantly via watching others ski—live or on video. Neuroscientists have no trouble explaining each of these cases—but what they, in turn, tend to overlook that if we want to learn seeing with our knees immediately, or try keeping our balance by thinking hard about it, or expect that we get the hip rotation from watching the videos, things go terribly wrong. For this reason (and others), conducting a practice means not just performing a bodily technique; and accomplishing a conduct is not simply having a skill. And for this reason, I hold that it is wrong that we simply 'get' a style of riding in a linear, automatic process; or, likewise, that a community bound by style can simply emerge because people 'stick around long enough.' Style as a background to knowing (things like skis or other gear) and as a dimension of communality is not just a dividend of dutifully repeating some conduct, or an indicator of the time and resources one has spent practicing. In contrast, in order to properly understand the social function of style, one needs to keep in mind the fact that each moment of conduct is an instance of *coping*, of overcoming and managing the alignment of the various co-occurring bodily processes responsible for producing smooth movements.

Here, one finds the deeper reason why my account of freeskiing does not follow the classic lines of ethnographic representation that is structured along the lines of gaining access to, acquiring familiarity with, and undergoing apprenticeship in a certain subculture or community of practice. Conducting a practice to some extend always means accomplishing something new and hone one's skills, and therefore every concrete doing could also be called 'learning doing' (Shove/Pantzar/Watson 2012: 69–70; Wenger 1999). Skill acquisition or learning are thus not just clearly demarcated fields of inquiry, but also lenses for observation and strategies of representation. Especially when underwriting an (ethnographic) narrative, however, they are also inherently dangerous, because all too easily they conjure the image of a style-rulebook to be memorized, or a canon of style to be digested. Without a doubt, ways of learning skills or acquiring competences feature prominently among the topics frequently and fruitfully embraced from a practice perspective (Lave 1988, Lave & Wenger 1991); and I agree that a) this topic holds important insights into the process and logic of what we call learning and that b) every theory of social practices requires an adequate understanding of their dissemination. Further, most practice-minded authors acknowledge—to varying degrees—the important reservations against such connotations of learning or acquisition that have been voiced in practice thought: The inherently implicit or latent nature of much of the knowledge to be gained; the role of rules as incomplete descriptions or a-posteriori justifications rather than programs of behaviour; and the 'epistemological' and 'performative' component of every skill-set that enwraps every conduct into a forgiving padding of collaborative remedy of indexicalities. But, as Fox (2006; see also Hester/Francis 2000) correctly argues, if we pay close attention to these insights taken together, still speaking of learning can be somewhat misleading. The crucial problem is this: The subtext of learning or acquisition found so frequently in studies of practices implies a dichotomy of learner and content to be learned. The assumption that such content exists—the 'logic' of a field, a set of site-specific understandings, a sense for the game—rests on a social ontology, a postulate that something lies above, beyond, between, behind, or across the concrete situations, events, or likewise entities that form a realm. Referring to the learner, in contrast, points to an individualist ontology; the belief that people or humans are to be encountered in said field. A phenopractice-theoretical account seeks to draw neither of the two into question. What it does scrutinize critically, though, is the assumption that the latter should be seen as the *container* of the former, as if the pragmatic toolbox individuals carry around with them could be ever be voluminous enough to hold something like a culture, or at least large chunks thereof (cf. Swidler 1986; Vaisey 2009).

Excursus: Bourdieu's Individualistic Reading of Language Games

I have already hinted at the fact that I side with Schatzki (1987, 1996: 136–167, 1997) in his critique of Bourdieu, and thus consider praxeology to forward an anthropological and individualistic concept of social practices that reifies embodied skills or dispositions as being developed under social conditions (and thus allegedly reflecting social macro relations), but not as actually conceptualizing them to be social in nature in a strict sense. On this basis, however, it seems somewhat surprising that many (including myself) describe Bourdieu's habitus-field theory as a practice theory in the first place. Having introduced the problem of rule-following, I will therefore now take the opportunity to sketch out what Bourdieu made of Wittgenstein's argument and why his notion of practices is so crucially different from mine. In order to illustrate my argument, consider Wacquant's (2005) ethnography of a boxing club that has become a key reference point for the practice theory literature on sports and is often considered an exemplary empirical case-study of those theoretical principles Bourdieu and Wacquant (1992) formulated earlier. In undertaking what he calls a "carnal sociology," Wacquant portrays the gym as a "civilizing machine" producing boxing bodies. In exemplary fashion, the concept of cultural capital comes to life in the form of the boxer's *bodily* capital as the collaboratively exercised discipline, battle-hardenedness, and finesse of the daily training practices become 'inscribed' into the body and can subsequently be 'put to market' in competitions in order to pay off as fame or prize money. These practices, in turn, are carried by the material and spatial order of the gym, the collaborative emotion managements of its members, the explicit and implicit rules and wisdoms of the trade, and so forth. In this way, the notions of habitus and field can be used quite effectively to formulate a powerful, but also quite classic "ethnographic realism" (as Hoffman/Fine 2005: 151 put it) of the boxing gym and its roles, rituals, and artefacts. In Wacquant's

(2005) account, the boxers' visibly masterful moves document embodied skills funnelled into them in the course of the daily exercises, an important aspect of which are the watchful eyes of the trainer and the co-participants. In this way, he holds, the pugilists' capacities are "the product of a collective organization" which is "not thought out and willed as such by anyone" but a result of "the embodied expectations and demands of the occupants (...) of the gym" (Wacquant 2004: 149)—essentially, it is bodies training bodies. In line with Bourdieu, who adopted the notion of the habitus from Mauss and explicitly sought to conserve his basic argument (e.g. Bourdieu 1977: 97), Wacquant accordingly points to Mauss when he qualifies his study as an "anthropology of boxing as 'biologico-sociological phenomenon'" (2004: 149). But on the other hand, just after referring to Mauss in the introduction, he also invokes Wittgenstein in a passing, but informative way. Boxing is a "language game," Wacquant notes, and thus it "is born and persists only in and through *the group* that it defines in turn through a circular process." (2004: 17; my emphasis) In my view, this short nod to Wittgenstein exemplifies the divergence within sociological readings of the philosophical term 'language game' which have arguably strayed quite far from the path followed by Wittgenstein (Schatzki 1996: 94–95; D. Stern 2002). Let me briefly retrace the steps do see where—inter alia—Schatzki and Bourdieu parted ways.

Wittgenstein himself is not concerned with groups of people; he is inquiring into the nature of language and intelligibility per se. His project is, in other words, to convey insights into the most general nature social life. The *Philosophical Investigations*, however, are not formulated as a series of dry, precise postulates (as the *Tractatus* was). Instead, Wittgenstein ponders and tries, advances and retreats as he poses questions, suggests answers, rejects them, then points to a different answer, only to finally reject the very question (Cerbone 1994; Gebauer 2009). Wittgenstein's attempt to capture and agitate his reader in this way has borne rich fruit among scholars in the latter half of the last century—but it also left them in deep disagreement which about Wittgenstein it is that they have read (Bloor 1992; D. Stern 2002, 2003). More importantly, his style of writing had another side-effect: Key to the sociological interpretation of his work was that his writing in the first person and giving everyday examples seems to have invited the impression that his theoretical perspective effectively amounts to a philosophical anthropology (for a book-length treatment of Wittgenstein's [supposed] anthropology, see Gebauer 2009). Read in this way, the *Investigations* seem indeed to be a kind of "imaginary ethnography," as Lynch (1992a) and also Gebauer (2009: 236) suggest. Especially if equipped with a theoretical background in structural anthropology, an avid ethnographer like Bourdieu is not only prone to such a reading, but equally inclined to link the members of the 'ethnos' chronicled by Wittgenstein to the language-games they are playing. Indeed, Bourdieu (1977: 29) explicitly presents Wittgenstein's famous paragraphs on rule-following (Wittgenstein 2009: § 89) as summarizing the *questions* that "structural anthropology and (…) all intellectualism" supposedly evaded. But arguably, it is not Wittgenstein that Bourdieu turns to in search for an answer. Instead, he invokes Wittgenstein only to argue that empirical regularities which exist in social practices cannot be traced back to "known and recognized" rules. He thus proclaims: "One is entitled to posit an 'implicit guidance' (…) in order to account for a practice objectively governed by rules unknown to the agents" as long as one unearths "the mechanisms producing this conformity" rather than turning to the "consciousness of the individual agents" for explanations (Bourdieu 1977: 29).

These mechanisms, as I have shown, are processes forging dispositions that inscribe society's class relations into the individual body; rather than situated ways of talking and doing. In effect, Bourdieu reframes Wittgenstein's notion of language games—the idea that the effective meaning of language lies in the practical ways of its use—by conceptualizing them as games played by and thus coupled to a group of people—in most cases: a social class—understood as an agglomeration of equally primed bodies. As a result, he reads the Wittgensteinian notion that 'rule-following expresses conditions of life' as meaning that possessing a 'sense for the game' or "sense practique" is a result of, and signal for, a certain socio-economic position within society as a whole (Bourdieu 1977). One key upshot of this reading is that not only all verbal accounts, rational explanations, or formal accounts practitioners make about their conduct, but also all conscious understandings or thoughts they have are to be seen first and foremost as expressions of practitioners' belief in the 'illusio' of the game, in its realness, relevance, and authentic existence independent from overall social relations. Thus, they are effects of the "implicit guidance" of the macro mechanisms underlying the game played (e.g. Bourdieu 1996). Bourdieu has argued that his concepts builds on only "minimal anthropological postulates" (see also Bongaerts 2011), but they are anthropological nevertheless: Although he does not speak of actors—but of agents—and emphasizes that it is not individual choice or volition that determines lived life, he nevertheless puts forward a kind of 'second order anthropology' in that a) the 'containers' carrying the structuring mechanisms of social life are individual bodies (and thus provisions need to be made how that happens), and especially in that b) the relations these mechanisms are expressing and perpetuating are (socio-economic) relations *between individual people*. Metaphorically speaking, Bourdieu draws his grand tableau of the social world in pointillist technique: The motifs he elaborate on do not pertain to single dots but the larger scheme of things, but nevertheless each figure he sketches out is in essence an agglomeration of individual points. The conditions of life, the shape of lived social life, in other words, are given by the constellation of status positions of 'whole' humans within the social whole.

Notably, the very possibility of expressing, or even consciously being aware of, one's own belonging to a certain 'ethos' (or class) is accordingly warranted or withheld by the invisible framework of the language game played. The methodological effect is that the philosophical-political a-prioris inscribed into the theory reign supreme: Your informants or respondents deny abiding by the principles you attribute to them?—E voilà, that just proves that they are adhering so devoutly to the rules 'objectively governing' their practice that they cannot even know or acknowledge their very existence. And though the social scientist cannot fully express them either, since he is bound to language games as well, he can uncover the "mechanisms" this particular practice is governed by (and which are, by and large, the same as in all other practices he has studied thus far and will ever study). Accordingly, the extensive reliance on the non-verbal methods of statistics in Bourdieu's work (but also his interest in ethnographic photography) yields from the aspiration to get around the pitfalls of language games and the push through the illusio clouding everyday conduct in order to get straight to the macro causes of conformity. It is in this same sense that a number of authors have used ethnographic methods to inquire into forms of 'forging bodies'—especially in lifestyle sport settings—in order to evidence the dominion of objective social macro relations in the silent truthfulness of the details of bodily conduct, thus repeating the equation of game and social class in a more literal sense (Alkemeyer/Schmidt 2004; Alkemeyer/Brümmer 2016; Gebauer/Alkemeyer/Flick 2004; Schmidt 2002, 2006, 2012; M. Stern 2009). And while their topics and methods are similar to Wacquant's (2004), they draw more explicitly and extensively on Wittgenstein, following Wittgensteinian philosopher Gunther Gebauer's (1999, 2008) proposal to treat sports as language games. While I will treat their works in more detail in chapter nine, it suffices for now to note that their position requires following Bourdieu and remaining within the conceptual framework of structural anthropology—objective relations between large groups of people within society determine individual conduct—, and to read the notion that language games "express conditions of life" as pertaining to general socio-economic living-conditions. This position thus stands in contrast to authors like Schatzki, who take said conditions of life to mean "how things stand" (1996: 22) for someone *momentarily* and situatedly, and not on the scale of class relations and hegemonic powers.

Moreover, these examples point to a general and more abstract theoretical point to be made: Determining or expressing the meaning or character of practices through *dichotomies* is highly problematic. In Bourdieu's praxeology, the logic of all practices, and effectively all social patterns (spatial orders, lines of reasoning, modes of power), are theorized to be rooted in oppositions such as wet/dry in the case of the Kabylian society (Bourdieu 1990), or asceticism/hedonism in the case of contemporary sport (Bourdieu 1984: 219), all of which ultimately express oppositions of class or power. Crucially, these dichotomies are not just descriptive categories applied by the researcher, but are portrayed as *causally* underlying the patterns of practice—testament to the roots of his thinking in structural anthropology. But as Schatzki (1997) argues, the assumption that practices are driven or governed by underlying oppositions is difficult to sustain theoretically. At the core, what is in question is the nature or format of meaning that social practices express: Bourdieu upholds a classical Saussurean conception of meaning as composed of elementary oppositional differences. But as I discussed in Chap. 2, a more strictly Wittgensteinian practice perspective rejects such a 'mathematical' definition of meaning (e.g. in the sense of Spencer-Brown 1971) and replaces it with a multi-elementary figural constellation or 'hanging-together' (Schatzki 2002). This fundamental shift has its origin in diverging interpretations of the shared observation that an infinitive number of concrete events can fulfil the conditions of an explicit rule. The irredeemable problem for bivalent conceptions of meaning stems from the fact that descriptions within binary logic are always inherently ambiguous or contingent: How to say whether a certain attempt of a trick was sketchy or not, or if something concrete is tasteful or not? One trajectory of thought that stretches from Husserl to Luhmann solves this problem by separating bivalent meaning and polyvalent events, confining each to different realms. If, however, one takes up Wittgenstein's account of rule-following, and understands certain events themselves as moments of a social practice (as being of an order that cannot be adequately expressed in the strict bivalent positions of language or logic), then the logical conclusion must be that the meanings of social practices must be conceptualized as polyvalent (but by no means arbitrary)—at least as far as I can see. By insisting that practices themselves carry the social order (and thus meaning), but conceptualizing said order as a series of bivalent oppositions, Bourdieu's account of social practices thus remains inherently problematic. In my view, Bourdieu tries to circumvent this inconsistency by conceptualizing the habitus as an 'observation program,' as an epistemological disposition so to speak. Indeed, as long as the oppositions the habitus carries only come into effect in patterns of observation, the above problem does not occur, since events could even be entirely chaotic and would still be interpreted in oppositional schemas.[23] But as soon as the habitus is described as bringing about practices which are themselves carrying *objective* structures—in other words, as soon as praxeology is read as a social ontology of the social—discrepancies erupt.

As the case of style in freeskiing shows, this abstract inconsistency within the theory translates directly into problems vis-à-vis concrete empirical data. What are the oppositions that are so deeply embedded into the practices of seeing the beauty of a 1080 Double Cork? As I have shown, style can indeed only be observed in situ and in praxis—but this does not mean that it is just a chimera. What is more, the binary conception of meaning found in the emphasis of dichotomies in Bourdieu's praxeology are closely related to a fundamental a-priori assumption about the social mechanisms implanted into the "implicit guidance" at force in all social practice: The assumption that lived social life always produces winners and losers, dominators and dominated; and this both in simple, ritualized interactions, and over the course of life-spans. In other words, the notion that the 'game fields' the members of a certain ethos gather on are *fields of conflict* on which resources for strategic action and tactics are both the tools of the belligerent trade and the prize to be won, is central to the theory. Indeed, Bourdieu envisions social life as "a race of all against all" (H. L. Dreyfus/Rabinow 1999: 88). As Rabinow and Dreyfus (1999) argue, this perpetual and all-encompassing competition is the *ontological* claim Bourdieu's theory rests on, a claim that not only implies the respective field as a totality as well as the 'racers' as individual subjects, but also a basic pattern of its organization that is both Darwinist and belligerent (see also Saake 2004, Nicolini 2012: 59–66). Notably, this postulate stands side-by-side with the presupposition that a field's mechanism is simultaneously hidden in its illusio and uncoverable by the methods of the social scientist since "the illusio is an illusion or 'diversion' only for someone who perceives the game from the outside, form the scholastic standpoint of an impartial spectator." (Bourdieu 2000: 151) In this way, Rabinow and Dreyfus conclude, Bourdieu claims that he (or the critical social scientist in general) can "stand outside the habitus and its illusio, and demonstrate the working of social injustice" (1999: 92)—even though, as Wacquant (2009) convincingly argues, acquiring a field's habitus is an essential prerequisite to studying it. To be fair,

---

[23] One might speculate that some authors do indeed read and apply his concepts in this way. In effect, Bourdieuian praxeology would join the ranks of the sociology of knowledge, albeit emphasizing the (class-related) conformity of stocks of knowledge and their correlation with 'objective' socioeconomic conditions—without being able to underscore the alleged objectivity then necessarily drawn from contingently patterned observation. See Knoblauch (2003) for the possibility to read Bourdieu as complementary to social constructivism.

> Bourdieu was most explicit about his own positionality within the social fields he was studying and made frequent efforts of to make this position as well as its practical prerequisites visible and explicit. However, one important implication of his taking language games as being tied to a group of people inhabiting a definitive position within society is what has been called his "hermeneutics of suspicion," the conviction that while his talk is as good or bad as anyone's within the field of science, at least he openly admits and duly reflects on his hidden 'true' origins—leading to his claims of exclusively offering a "reflexive sociology" (Bourdieu/Wacquant 1992) equipped with superior "epistemic reflexivity" (Wacquant 2005). Taking into account the fundamental role of philosophical a-prioris for all social thought, however, emphasizing such a reflexivity means just repeating the ontological claim that this inherent co-constitution exists, as does the methodological principle to accept a broad spectrum of empirical data (including highly subjective and personal narratives from interviews) as expressions of the respective habitus and thus automatically of the studied field as well (Saake 2004). In other words, I fully agree that *every* sociological observation that develops and relies on a social theory of observation is necessarily self-referential to some extent, and that all empirical and theoretical work should make this fact explicit—but I am not quite convinced that repeatedly reminding ourselves of this unavoidable condition of (not just sociological, but indeed any communicative) work warrants proudly wearing the badge of reflexivity as a testament to unmatched academic virtue (see Lynch 2000). That the reflexivity of social thought must specifically consist in introspection into the thinker's biography and social class is, after all, in itself a postulate taking much for granted—such as thinkers and classes, or fields and their habitus.

11 Storing and Transporting Style

But if it is not humans, you might ask, what is the container that freeskiing's Style is housed in, neatly folded up and stored away for the short snowless summer to arrive and take over the Krimml and the hearts and minds of those who roam there? Why does it not melt away with the kicker-lines on the glaciers in July, or leave the scene as the first generation of freeskiers vacates the stage, taking their fading memories along as they move to the lowlands to get real and raise kids? Bodily skills surely need to be an important part of the answer. Notably, however, equating skills with practitioners or members of the scene only holds insofar as they would need to be *current* practitioners or members, as aging athletes cease to perform at some point. More importantly, performances require some form of observation or recognition in order to be *social* performances. Thus, they require the respective observation skills; as well as stages or arenas, equipment, judging, sayings, courage, the joys of watching and achieving, and so forth. To some degree, their specificity for freeskiing might be dispensable, for example, any makeshift kicker and sufficiently stable ski might do well enough—if, that is, they can be made up for in some other element, for example if practitioners are especially gifted and motivated. In my view, this very relative *redundancy* of the elements of a practice demonstrates clearly that such a practice can never be reduced to or housed in a single element alone—be it an account, a mind, a body, or a tool. The 'container' of style, in other words, is of course the practice itself, in that the congregation of elements into a figural coherence can make a moment of said style stand out. And just like I deem it difficult to ascribe semantic accounts a principally superior position in this relation, I do not seem how and why the body should be seen as the central, the 'actual' carrier. Sure, one can also 'hammer' with a stone, but this does not warrant saying that it is really the body that houses hammering—just ask a carpenter. In effect, I argue that both a historical or 'macro' perspective and a close inspection of situated accomplishments lead to the same conclusion: Meaningful order arises from constellations. From arguing that the figural shape of concrete doing is always accomplished multimodally and multidimensionally (and almost always collaboratively in some sense), in other words, it follows that reductions to one dimension becomes futile.

And now, finally, I can reaffirm and defend my claim that phenopractice theory needs to build on a social ontology of the social: Because style *is* something other than the sum of the details assembled towards its expression. Just like paint and canvas do not just add up to an image, just like a lived human body is quite clearly something other than an accumulation of biological tissue, freeskiing's style is something other than the skills-cum-tools-cum-sayings-cum-images of its' practitioners. And hopefully it thus becomes clearer that a social ontology does not actually deny or replace an individualistic ontology per se, because all but certain religious ontologies assume that things exist alongside each other. What it questions are simply individualistic ontologies *of the social*, or non-social ontologies of the social more generally; ideas that the social does not exist, but is 'merely' performed, said, known, done, imagined, perceived, or the like. To make the same argument coming from a different direction: I hold that the key flaw of accounts treating style as symbol repositories employed to signal status and identity is that they neglect the sites within which style can become only visible or observable in the first place. Thus, they are easily led to ignore the decisively constructive role such sites play for the existence of style, as well as the constraints and limits they impose on it. In the case of lifestyle sport—and here I agree with Beal and Wilson (2004) or Stern (2009)—the two crucial types of sites within which style can transpire are a) embodied, local, interactively framed and spectated performances in sites I will call arenas (such as the skate parks, breaking waves, or the liminal space of skysurfers' soaring [Sydnor 2003]); as well as b) media-in-observation. By examining the details of the concrete situated work of opening up these two kinds of sites, I hope to shed more light on the prerequisites and mechanisms that provide for the observability of style. How, I will ask, are freeskiers able to do what they do; and how does their doing become intelligible as an expression of Style? Let us begin the journey with a visit to the funpark.

Chapter 7
Emotion and Space—The Arena

1 Introduction: "It's Really Strange When Nobody is Looking"

It is already quite late as we reach the snowpark on the last day of the season, but the park is still vacated, probably due to the grey sky. It feels weird to see the park completely empty and silent. Sure, this is only the second, smaller park which lies in a quieter corner of this large ski resort which also offers the larger, internationally known Penken Park with its huge {pro line} of kickers that are reshaped throughout the day by a professional team. Still, hardly ever have I seen this park completely vacated, with no kids undertaking some feeble attempts at the mini-kicker, and no snowboarder hanging around and taking a break in the old deck chairs at the entrance, hoping to watch some action. Not today. The kickers seem freshly shaped, and although the sun is not shining brightly and it is surprisingly chilly, it should still be a good day to do some training runs. But no one seems to have taken the opportunity yet. Suddenly, shortly before we reach the park entrance, Tom stops.

> Me: "What are you doing?"
>
> Tom: "Speedcheck." [M][1]

I see. I ride ahead, down towards the large kicker to make sure that there is nobody standing or sitting in the way. I lift my pole in the air to signal Tom he is good to go. He straight-lines down into the park, freeskier style: His head bend down, arms behind his back, holding his hands with the poles behind his bottom. This

---

[1] „Was machste?"—„Nen Speedcheck."

© The Author(s), under exclusive license to Springer-Verlag GmbH, DE, part of Springer Nature 2024
N. Woermann, *Seeing Style*, Beiträge zur Praxeologie / Contributions to Praxeology, https://doi.org/10.1007/978-3-662-69182-3_7

Fig. 7.1 A medium-sized kicker. 1. In-run; 2. transition; 3. kicker; 4. flat; 5. Landing

way, nobody will mistake you for a lame downhill-skier (arms stretched out to the front, poles tucked under the arms). He speeds into the in-run and towards the transition of the large kicker, a ramp made of snow about 3 meters high (Fig. 7.1).

Just at the foot of the ramp, Tom turns his skis 90° and begins to brake. Snow is spraying into the air as he slides up the ramp, slowly loosing speed. Exactly at the edge of the kicker, he comes to a stop. Standing still for a moment, he looks down into the landing a few meters below him. Then he turns and skis back down the ramp of the kicker. We meet down at the ski-lift. "So?" I ask. "Felt actually pretty well in terms of speed," [M][2] he answers. Still, he seems visibly uneasy. In freestyle skiing, you never want to be the first one to try a newly shaped kicker in the morning. The snow can be 'faster' or 'slower' than you expected, making you jump too far or too short. The landing could be much harder than it looks, with ice underneath. The landing could have a strange angle, causing you to crash if you are not prepared. To be sure, a crash could always happen anyways, regardless of

---

[2] „Hat sich eigentlich gut angefühlt vom Speed her."

1 Introduction: "It's Really Strange When Nobody is Looking"

whether you are the first to jump or not. Still, being the first one today, in combination with the empty park, seems to really take its toll on Tom. We enter the lift and fall silent. Tom seems a little absent-minded. About half-way up, he breaks the silence.

> Tom: "Ah shit! I actually want to jump [over] this kicker!" [M][3]

He has been pondering it ever since we arrived. Should he do it? Everything should be fine; he knows the park, he knows this kicker and used it many times, he even personally knows the shaper that takes care of it. He is feeling fit and well, and he is not planning to try some fancy new stuff. There should be no problem. But there is one: "Don't be first, don't be first!" [M][4] For one, there are the 'technical' reasons: When you see someone else jump, you can already estimate if the snow is slow or fast today, or if the landing seems to be sketchy, and so on. But there is more: When you are standing there above the in-run, looking down onto the kicker, and try to prepare for being catapulted into the air at considerable speed, trying to keep your balance and orientation as you fly, and then manage to land safely on the hard surface of the snow—at this very moment, when you need to be calm and confident, it helps enormously if you can watch someone go and do it right in front of you. If he can do that, so can you. But today, no-one is going to be there to go first—no-one but Tom himself. If he manages to muster the motivation. After a few more moments in silence, I try something.

> Me: "Nothing ventured, nothing gained." I say with an undertone of irony.
> Tom laughs dryly. "Well…" he says sceptically.
>
> (short silence)
>
> Me: "Hmm, well, but if you just go for a straight jump first there is not too much that could happen. … or you just crash."
>
> Tom (laconically): "Exactly. Or you win a Tomahawk [a bad crash]."
>
> (short silence)
>
> Me: "But you can't really hurt yourself when you only go straight, can you?"
> Tom: "Well ok, that's right. (pauses) Ok, so I try it." [M][5]

We arrive at the top of the lift and ski down to the park. We had hoped that someone might have arrived by now. To no avail. Tom is visibly unhappy. "Somehow it's really strange when nobody is watching" he tells me [M].[6] He still hesitates

---

[3] „Ah Scheiße! Ich will diesen Kicker eigentlich springen!"

[4] „Nicht der Erste sein, nicht der Erste sein!"

[5] „Wer nicht wagt der nicht gewinnt."—„Naja."—„Hmm, naja, aber wenn du ihn erstmal nur straight springst kann doch eigentlich nicht so viel passieren. …oder man mault sich halt."—„Aber richtig verletzen kann man sich nicht wenn man nur straight springt, oder?"—„Naja, stimmt schon. (Pause.) Also, dann versuch ichs mal."

[6] „Wenn gar keiner guckt ist 's irgendwie komisch."

to give the kicker a try, and we idle around a bit longer. Still, nobody else shows up. Finally, he is ready to go for it. I ski down to the kicker again to make sure the landing is clear. Tom does his jump, but his attempt is somewhat half-hearted. He does not seem to be very happy with the result. I ask whether the shape is not ok. No, no, he assures me. That is not the problem. Jumping in an empty park just does not seem to make sense. Soon, we leave.

2 The Need for Teleoaffectivity

Conventional wisdom would suggest that freeskiing is a solo sport: not only something done individually rather than in a team, but also a formidable expression of individuality and the postmodern triumph of subjectivity. During my fieldwork in funparks in Germany, Austria, and Switzerland, however, I have made an interesting observation than challenges this widely held view: Not only is there a considerable amount of interaction and subtle cooperation going on among freeskiers in a funpark—the patterns of which I will describe and interpret in this chapter— but I am even convinced that freeskiers *like* to wait in queues. On the slope above every kicker, there is usually a small queue, a group of skiers waiting to jump one after another. And these queues can almost always be observed, no matter how empty or full the park is (see Fig. 7.2). When entering the lift and skiing down to

Fig. 7.2 Freeskiers and snowboarders watching and performing in a crowded funpark in the Stubaital

2 The Need for Teleoaffectivity

an empty kicker, freeskiers will wait for their colleagues to catch up—in fact, they will often wait for complete strangers to catch up. To me, this subtle fact seems remarkable: Who, after all, enjoys standing in line? And it is really the line per se that the freeskiers seek to create, they are not trying to socialize in any traditional sense. Once the others have arrived, they will not strike up a conversation or conduct some other clearly visible interaction, but they will simply wait a few seconds, and then start leaving for the kicker, more or less in the order in which they have arrived. The purpose of this chapter is to answer a simple question: Why?

For every freeskier I spoke to, the presence of friends, colleagues, or at least someone in the funpark where they are training is quite important; yet this interesting prerequisite also seems so commonplace that it is seldom discussed among them. If nobody is watching one's performance, and oneself cannot watch others perform, it seems, freeskiing does not really work, or is not quite the fun it should be—although the riders cannot really say why this is the case. They do, however, explicitly describe and pursue a related collective task that gives testament to the functional role of co-participants for conducting the supposedly solo-sport freeskiing: "pushing" ("Pushen" in German). In order to achieve your best and increase your skill, they told me, "It's really important that the others are pushing you." [I][7] Pushing describes the collective management of emotions among riders; a collaborative mechanism through which the fear or hesitation they might feel can be overcome or remedied. Being the first in a line of waiting colleagues, I argue, is one very basic form of 'being pushed.' Likewise, it was an act of pushing when I was teasing or poking Tom in the lift by mentioning the 'obvious' fact that he will not hurt himself from a simple straight jump. To be sure, it is not something I would have done during the early phases of my fieldwork; but it was part of the everyday routine of talking and interacting among riders to which I became more and more used to. Applied in a measured and sensible way, it is not an expression of rivalry or thinly veiled antagonism; but quite to the contrary it is an important and systematically applied part of the tricks of the trade of freestyle skiing. Testament to the inherently situated and interactive nature of most emotional states, pushing forms an important part of my argument that accomplishing freeskiing Style is an irremediably social practice: Performing and seeing Style does not only depend on acquiring an adequate understanding of what style is, it is not just an 'interpretative task' to be learned from others; it also necessitates a befitting *teleological structure* to be in place—literally in place, not just in 'hearts and minds.' And just like the fourth chapter argued that understandings are not carried in individuals and/or objects, but across situations of conducting the same practice; I seek to argue that teleological structures—i.e. emotional-laden orientations towards certain ends or goals—need to be situationally and interactively accomplished, and are thus carried across situations of conducting the same practice von (cf. Wedelstaedt/Meyer 2017). Rather than being persistent properties of individuals,

---

[7] „Ganz wichtig ist, dass die Anderen dich pushen."

they need to happen to individuals, one might say. The argument in this chapter has two parts: First, I will survey the importance of emotions and moods for accomplishing freeski performances and trace out what I consider to be their inherently situated nature. Second, on this basis I will provide a practice-based account of spaces as sites within which style can become manifest in the course of an artful praxis that weaves together performance and observation. In doing so, I seek to establish the plausibility of two important implications of the phenopractice perspective: That both supposedly 'inner' or 'deep' phenomena like moods or emotions, and supposedly neutral or detached meta-dimensions like space manifest in situatedly and practically established social sites.

3 Emotional Energy

In the eyes of the freeskiers, success in their sport rests on two basic pillars: The number of days in the snow you can manage to spend, and the motivation and drive you can muster. Sure, talent or systematic training can play an important role as well, riders will reply if asked; but more than anything, they hold that skill comes with experience, and experience emerges from pushing the envelope day after day. A key prerequisite for this is a diligent management of one's emotions (e.g. Hochschild 1979), and the most important tool for this task is to carry the visceral euphoria and sense of control gained from one successful jump over to the next. Immediately after safely landing a jump, I always felt a rush of adrenaline and the urge to go right back up and do it again—a feeling, however, that does not last very long by itself. If I had to spend much time waiting for the chairlift, getting back up and waiting in the queue, my heartfelt euphoria had usually vanished, and I had to remind myself of the positive experience I had a mere ten or fifteen minutes ago. One important reason why freeskiers prefer larger funparks that have several obstacles in a row and a fast lift to bring them back up is not just the fact that they are able to do more attempts per day, but that this makes it easier to keep the momentum once they are one an emotional 'winning spree.' Accordingly, a key quality of a successful rider is his ability to quickly overcome the frustration caused by a crash or near-crash, and attempt the same trick again despite the pain and the fear he might feel. Indeed, freestyle skiing is "all in the head"[8] as riders say: Speeding backwards onto a ramp in order to fly fifteen meters through the air while completing complex rotations requires guts and aplomb, but also calmness and self-control. It is not only that every jump attempted means a considerable risk taken, but also that some of the greatest dangers originate from becoming aware of the danger and subsequent hesitation: On a large kicker, jumping too short and crashing into the so-called flat is especially prone to cause injuries; yet while one is speeding towards it, one often feels an urge to slow down to

---

[8] „Ne reine Kopfsache".

make the jump less violent—giving in to such an urge it is highly dangerous. In the same vein, when attempting a rotation, one needs to muster an impulse strong enough to cause a spin of full 360° (or multiples of 180°) in order to be able to land safely, while a half-hearted attempt is prone to cause a feared crash called the "Tomahawk:" landing in a 90° angle towards the direction of movement, so that the skis edges literally stop the skier in his tracks and sent the head smashing into the hard snow. Just like jibbing on a box, jumping over a kicker requires artful management of emotions and overcoming long-established gut-feelings; partly because it does not align well with our usual routines of pragmatic vision. Unlike a freerider preparing a turn, a freestyler cannot 'look into' spinning multiple rotations in the same manner. To be sure, the visual apparatus still guides his bodily movements, but this requires twisting the head in order to initiate a rotation in the air. As advanced freestylers capable of performing multiple rotations unanimously report, not be able to look into the direction in which one is rapidly moving during a jump, and nevertheless being able to control the 'flight' is the most demanding aspect of complex tricks. In contrast, once riders are able to see the landing again by looking over their shoulder while still being in the midst of the last rotation, they consider the jump itself as practically over and focus on the upcoming landing. Accordingly, the specific challenge of jumping rests in trusting oneself as much as the kicker in order to be able to let go the visual control over one's movement (seeing where one is going) at least for a brief moment. "Fear is always a part of it," [I][9] a rider assured me.

Accordingly, freeskiers' widely shared 'folk wisdom' holds that you should not stop training after crashing under any circumstances as long as you are still physically able to do another jump, and a rider will always try to 'take home' a successful final jump from the day—because to some extent, this will be the jump setting the mood for his first attempt the next morning. At the beginning of each day of training, riders start with 'getting into jumping' ("Einspringen") by trying some easier tricks at first, often only a straight jump (see Fig. 7.3 for the layout of a typical funpark). To some extent, they do this in order to warm up and test the current condition of the kicker. But 'technical' reasons are only of limited importance: The actual warming-up in the form of stretching exercises is already completed when the first jump is tackled; and after a long lunchbreak in the middle of the day, which would normally require warming up once again, approaching jumping as carefully and wearily as in the morning does not seem to be necessary. In a similar vein, it is indeed important to know the current condition of each kicker, but they also vary throughout the day and between different obstacles—yet still, the riders seem never as careful and diligent as they are when they take up training in the morning. Therefore, the core reason for the special attention given the initial jump is to be found somewhere else: getting the first one right lays the necessary emotional and motivational foundation for all further performance. "I learn during the

---

[9] *„Der Schiß gehört immer mit dazu."*

Fig. 7.3 The Penken Park seen from the opposite hillside. The park lift runs diagonally from the bottom center to the top left. Next to the lift the three large kickers of the pro line can be seen, as well as the medium line to the right of it. Towards the borders of the park, the blue boxes and rails are visible

first jump if a day is going well," [I][10] Tom explains—and notably, he explicitly speaks about a day already underway, not only about the future hours lying still ahead of him. And indeed, since one great jump is the best preparation for another great jump, the positive drive one can gather during the initial jump can carry a rider through the whole day. In turn, it is very hard to overcome the bad feeling resulting from an initial jump gone wrong. This is even true for important contests: When I accompanied a group of riders to the season's finals of a well-known freestyle competition, one of the female riders almost crashed during her warm-up jump. Frustrated, she declared defeat before the competition had even begun: "I am all about attitude, and that's it for today." [M][11] She ended up last.

I suggest that the significance of 'first jumps' suggests that what I call a practitioner's emotional drive and the intentional ends it is related to (e.g. feeling strong enough to try a difficult trick) are build up sequentially across situations rather than within individuals or situations. I share this sentiment with Randall Collins' (2004) theory of what he calls interaction ritual chains, which is based on detailed examinations of situations of focused interactions much like those I observed in the funpark and the Krimml. Collins assigns the phenomenon of motivation or drive a key theoretical role towards explaining social order in general. While I am sceptical that one can develop a complete theory of the social on the basis of

---

[10] „Ob der Tag läuft, merke ich beim ersten Sprung."

[11] Literally: "I am a mental kind of person"—„Ich bin da ein Kopfmensch, dass wird heut nix mehr."

emotions and rituals alone (which he sometimes attempts to do); it seems clear that the basic arguments of his theory match my empirical observations, as well as the freeskier's own view, quite well: The euphoria and confidence gained from one successful jump seems to 'fuel' the rider towards tackling the next one; and every trick successfully learned can be used as a resource towards learning further tricks in that the rider can get himself 'fired up' with unproblematic parts of his repertoire before trying to push his boundaries. However, one could easily be lead to think that the simple equation "each successful jump or line = motivation for the next jump or line" implies a psychological or individualist trivialization of the complex interplay taking place within the funpark. Collins (2004), in contrast, argues for a situation-centred view on social order that takes its starting point in two streams of thought I have built on as well: ethnomethodology and scientific findings on the social role of emotions. Therefore, I stress that his theory is only plausible and consistent in that it is a *social* theory, since what he calls emotional energy results from the collectively achieved meaning and relevance of what he considers ritualized conduct. In Collins' account, only the other participants' performances turn a mere instance of routinized and regular doing into taking part in a ritual that can yield emotional energy.[12] Collins' arguments, I hold, support my point that emotional drive is dependent on and enmeshed into situated accomplishments, but also build up and carried across situations. Expressed in the terms I will develop in this chapter: The other participants' presence and position turns the kicker line into a site exhibiting feasible paths of action, and only the specific emotional situation they systematically help to create provides the background against which the practitioners gain the sense that doing a certain a certain trick is possible for them right here and right now. In other words: It provides the background that makes a trick actionable (cf. v. Wedelstaedt/Meyer 2017).[13]

Excursus: Interaction Ritual Chains

> The phenopractice perspective based on a social ontology of the social shares a key basic premise with Collin's vision of microsociology: that social live is essentially an aggregation of situations rather than individuals

---

[12] Notably, Collins explicitly seeks to extent the explanatory power of his theory to activities conducted in the absence of others, but emphasizes that the relevancy of an activity as perceived by a practitioner is always derived from its social nature, and that the physical absence of others is frequently compensated by an imagined presence (R. Collins 2004: 345). In other words: Even when being alone, social actors can be expected to act *as if* they were part of an interaction. In my view, while such an assumption holds in many cases, distinguishing between integrated and dispersed practices (as Schatzki 1996 does) can provide a more coherent notion of the relation of conduct in isolation or co-presence.

[13] I will explain my use of the term 'action' in the next chapter.

(R. Collins 1981). Indeed, Schatzki (1996: 199) explicitly embraces Collins' basic framework (Giddens 1984: 139–141 also makes a similar move), especially since he as well emphasizes the importance of chains of action as a way in which different social practices relate and hang together. This similarity is not surprising, since Collins' work is informed by the two streams of thought and research that this work rests on as well: ethnomethodological inquiry into situated, sequentially accomplished situational order one the one; and scientific findings on the role of emotions for both action and perception on the other hand (cf. R. Collins 2004: 104 f.). I will therefore briefly survey how his findings support some of my arguments and in which ways his theory shares convictions with a practice perspective; before sketching out why I also deem it subject to the more extensive critique I spell out against Bourdieuian versions of practice thought. Collins' conviction is that what he calls "emotional energy" functions as the fuel for our social life. Building on Goffman's (1967) concept of the interaction ritual as the fundamental form of everyday interaction, Collins portrays humans as "emotional energy seekers" (2004: 373) wandering from one ritualized encounter on to the next in search of experiencing positive feelings of either solidarity or dominance in order to gain the necessary momentum for further emotional success. If someone manages to exit a social situation with a heightened stock of emotional energy, he has gained an advantage he can use in the following situation: Able to muster higher self-esteem, motivation, and charisma, he is more likely to dominate the consecutive situation as well and yield another rich emotional harvest. On the basis of this rather simple model, Collins argues, social inequalities, class structures, and power relations can be explained as cumulated effects of situated stratification and their emotional effects (R. Collins 2004: 258–262). Towards covering the macro level of social theory, Collins fuses his concept with Bourdieu's notion of individual accumulation of capital of various sorts, adding what could be dubbed 'emotional capital' (2004: 169). In doing so, however, he also picks up on the frequently voiced critique that Bourdieu's account is unduly static, and suggests that the concept of emotional energy can remedy this shortcoming by functioning as an intervening variable within the link between an actors' cultural or material capital and the status gain he actually manages to get (R. Collins 2004: 132): Whether or not one's structurally imposed head-start in terms of economic, cultural, or social capital truly leads to advantages and privileges, he argues, depends on the logic of the concrete situation; and therefore the social sciences should undertake analyses of micro-situations rather than macro-structures (R. Collins 2004: 132 fn22). The direction of Collin's argument, in other words, is exactly opposite to that of Bourdieu: Instead of treating an individual's position within the overall 'field' of society as the causal force behind particular practical actions, he seeks to portray the social macro-structure as resulting from the accumulation of the myriad single situations of lived social life (R. Collins 1981)—situations that are not tightly coupled by a reliable automaton akin to the sturdy habitus, but rather loosely interlinked into chains of actions through emotional energy. Nevertheless, because of the way he is building on Bourdieu, Collins faces the same problems I have identified with Bourdieu's account: His theory remains effectively glued to an individualist ontology in that, although social stratification is not conceptualized as the overall dominance of one class over another, but a mere situational dominance of persons (R. Collins 2004: 258), a) social order is nevertheless understood as a stratified constellation of individual positions, and b) the individual is in effect rendered to be the carrier and reproducer of said positional order. Similar revampings of the habitus-field theory have been voiced once again by other authors, but this time undergirded by (selected) findings from neurosciences (see Cerulo 2010; DiMaggio 1997), maybe most notably in the version of Omar Lizardo (2007, 2009; Lizardo/Strand 2010). From a phenopractice perspective, Collins' theory seems advantageous to his younger cognition-focused soulmates in that he acknowledges that a theory of situated actions needs to consider the importance of the situation itself rather than almost exclusively relying on the wondrous powers of the "cognitive architecture of the actor" (Lizardo/Strand 2010). One important beneficial effect is that this leads Collins to recognize the importance of mass media-technology for altering the resources available within specific situations (although he only mentions "conversational resources" [R. Collins 1981: 999]). Instead of effectively 'skipping' the actual site of the social, as Lizardo does by assuming that "symbolic" resources flow directly between individuals without bothering how their use might be conditioned situationally instead of "the financescapes and the technoscapes that undergird the current global order." (Lizardo 2008: 29) But although Collins' theory therefore seems more in line with the findings and arguments I collected so far, I still deem it deeply problematic in that it suggests that one single theoretical model suffices to grasp the inherent order of each and every situation: the social conflict. Just like in Bourdieu's writings, social live effectively becomes a perpetual struggle for resources—a claim that I deem not only difficult to uphold empirically, but that also carries two problematic theoretical consequences. First, it presupposes a particular kind of a rational actor, a witty strategist of social life and war, and a diligent, bookkeeping trader carefully selecting the rituals he engages in so as to maximize the expected return on his investment in emotional energy (see Baehr 2005; Rössel 1999). And second, it implies that all relevancies or constraints of a concrete situation are effectively seen as depending on the single definition of the situation that the actor consciously or unconsciously relies on (R. Collins 1981: 996–997)—a view already voiced by Circourel (1973) in his cognitive reading of ethnomethodology and picked up by Lizardo. Yet as I argued, as long as the selection of a ritual or the definition of the situation at hand is understood as an individual act, it does not quite matter whether one conceptualizes this formidable ability as conscious interpretation, embodied knowledge, low-level cognition, structures' structuring, or rational choice—in all versions, one turns social practices into building blocks ready to hand rather than sites of the social. Such accounts of practice theory will always be vulnerable to critiques which seek to reify the social actor as laying these bricks according to a grand master-plan (e.g. Schulz-Schaeffer 2009, 2010). In sum, while Collins' theory describes important aspects of the daily shifts in the freeskiers' 'emotional budgets,' from a phenopractice perspective his account suffers from the fact that a) social order is conceptualized as a constellation of strategically investing individuals; and that b) he builds on Goffman's notion of the ritual which I criticize further below. Needless to say, I suggest that both the individuals' strategies and the rituals taking place are best integrated into a single notion: social practices.

4 Visual and Verbal Pushing

The argument that the material and spatial set-up of the funpark per se does not constitute a site where enthusiastic and skilful freestyle skiing action can happen, but that instead the other freeskiers' presence and fine-tuned interactions are necessary for this, can best be evidenced by taking a closer look at the phenomenon the freeskiers call pushing. Pushing has two dimensions: On the one hand, it is a tacit effect of skiing together, a motivation arising from seeing the others perform and achieve, as well as being seen by them; and on the other hand, it is a conversational practice, a form of (typically masculine) banter and subtle challenge continuously played out over the course of a day in the park or backcountry. The first, tacit dimension of pushing is distinctively visual in nature; and the crucial function of the funpark (besides offering the material environment necessary for freestyle) is the systematic production of such motivating visibility through a spatial-practical congregation I call arena. Notably, it is not just the case that seeing freestyle tricks happening infuses riders with a general, vague sense that throwing tricks is cool and that they want to do the same. But more to the point, just like peeking down into a couloir one is about to drop in implies a different way of seeing than just gazing down like a tourist knowing he will walk back to the gondola in a minute, seeing someone {stomping} a trick right in front of you provides a much more direct, visceral sense of the momentum of the moment, the affordances present, and the chance you are ready to grasp. Talking about the first flip (or somersault) that he had finally dared to try immediately after he saw others perform them, a rider explained:

"You just see that this is possible here and now and then you want [to do] that as well." [R]¹⁴

For some riders and with regard to some tricks like flips, momentarily mustering the dash and motivation to try them is a bigger challenge than the actual athletic difficulty of the movement. Therefore, the accomplishment of flips is understood by the riders primarily as the ability to 'snatch' the right moment. This became clear when, skiing down to the queue in front of the park lift one day, Tom and I met an old skiing buddy of his. This friend immediately started to tell him enthusiastically:

"Where have you been yesterday? It was fliptime here, man!" [M]¹⁵

Notably, it would not be generally uncharacteristic, or considered braggish, for the rider to recount his 'sticking' a new trick for the first time in the form of a personal achievement, e.g. by saying 'I finally stomped my first flip yesterday!' But instead, this rider effectively told us about a 'magic moment' that happened in the park and which several participants had shared. Indeed, he went on to say that several others {sticked} their first flip as well on this same special day, and seemed to have no doubt that Tom would have managed a flip as well had he only be there. Tom was quite sorry to have missed the chance, and thus seemed to think so as well. Although 'fliptime' is not a term regularly used by freeskiers, it was readily understood by Tom and me, since it captured a sentiment of shared euphoria, a felicitous combination of conditions and moods in which attempts to flip were bound to succeed. In part, these conditions were qualities of the kicker and the weather: the speed of the in-run, the shape of the kicker and the {pop} it provided (the upward impulse 'shooting' the rider up into the air), the snow quality of the landing, and so forth. Just like the lines in a face, such 'environmental' conditions are subject to changes over the course of a day, but they can also be relatively stable if a weather situation lasts. Yet although the 'objective' conditions were just as favourable that day as on the day before, that was not sufficient to warrant that it would be 'fliptime' again today. In contrary, since several riders did not show up, and others wanted to take it a bit slower to recover from the challenges of the day before,¹⁶ it was quite clear that the specific combination of motivation, determination, and achievement would not take place once more today. And just like a rider does not 'have' a trick after he has done it once or twice, having been able to dare a trick once does not mean that the barrier is broken and the feat can be repeated any time. To the contrary, as far as I could observe, every freeskier knows a trick or two (or a certain difficult line or deep drop) that he has managed to do at some point without being sure he will ever go that far again. More generally

---

¹⁴ „Dann siehst du einfach, dass das hier und heute möglich ist und dann willst du das auch."
¹⁵ „Wo warst du gestern? Hier war Fliptime, Alter!"
¹⁶ All riders need to carefully monitor and manage the stress they put on their body and especially certain parts such as their knees, back, or thumb (which frequently gets hurt during crashes). Thus after any 'big day' one can be expected to take it a bit slower.

spoken, just like acquiring a bodily skill is not a linear process of 'filling' competency 'into' the body bit by bit, (quite literally) having seen an opportunity for an accomplishment once does mean one now necessarily 'has' the teleological structure of this experience. What is more, since the teleological framework that is such an essential aspect of a 'fliptime' needs to be established situationally and cooperatively, it might as well happen again. Thus, in parting Tom's friend suggested optimistically:

> "Why don't you come with us next week. Maybe it will be fliptime for you, too!" [M][17]

While it cannot be expected with full confidence, in other words, it seems likely that this group of riders will 'make it happen' for Tom as well—and if it works, it will be the fliptime *for* him; neither something he just does, nor a chance he could or could not use. This quote is also a good example of the second dimension of pushing: the explicit and active practice of talking each other into achieving a trick. Throughout the friendly conversations freeskiers hold about their own past achievements and future goals, the details of technique and technology, and other's skill and style, they try to motivate each other time and again by assuring the feasibility of a trick, or downplaying a danger or difficulty. When riders are discussing how to do a certain trick, you often hear utterances such as:

> "Once you have got the 7er, you just need to go only half a rotation further." [R][18] or:

> "Actually that [trick] is just almost the same as the Flatspin." [R][19]

To some extent, comments like these are only 'technical' assessments on the basis of the riders' experience. But from my observation, they clearly leaned towards the optimistic and were meant to encourage at least as much as they were meant to inform. In much the same vein, other riders commented on my own jumps that they had witnessed:

> "That really looked quite ok already. Now you just have to give yourself a spin, actually. [Literally: 'throw yourself around']" [M][20]

I took such comments to be simultaneously honest assessments that were meant to encourage, and to be subtle demands for more, indications that I had the skill and just needed the guts—all while downplaying the task that lay in front of me: The first attempt to do a 360 usually involves some hefty crash.[21] Similar forms of subtle challenges or demands noted in passing make up a major part of verbally

---

[17] *„Komm doch nächste Woche mit. Vielleicht ist dann für dich ja auch Fliptime!"*

[18] *„Wenn du den 7er geschafft hast musst du doch nur noch ne halbe Drehung weiter."*

[19] *„Eigentlich ist das doch fast das Gleiche wie der Flatspin."*

[20] *„Das sah doch echt schon mal ganz gut aus. Jetzt musste dich doch nur noch rumwerfen eigentlich."*

[21] I actually never mastered the threshold: After being hospitalized from trying to jib on a box, I followed my informants' suggestion that I was too old to try 360s and focused on freeriding instead of freestyle (as far as jumps were involved).

pushing among the freeskiers—not surprisingly, given that they are mostly male and between about 16 and 28. I should stress that such verbal challenges almost always take the form of a friendly banter 'between mates'; and that the tonality and aggressiveness differs depending on the group in question: Younger 'park kids' would sometimes question each other more overtly and directly, combined with some exaggeration of their own skills and fearlessness; while older skiers (many of them now focusing on freeriding and no longer freestyle) would be more subtle and respectful, leaving more opportunities for 'saving your face.' In turn, female freeskiers (which I could not observe as extensively and systematically as their male colleagues) were involved in conversational pushing in quite similar ways. However, I got the impression that pushing remarks directed at or coming from them were being enwrapped into an extra layer of irony or subtleness, since gender roles can add much force to teasing or banters.

In other words, riders are careful not to go too far when teasing and challenging each other—for two reasons: For one, they need to strike a delicate balance between pushing enough and not pushing too far. Since freeskiing is a fragile conduct and dangerous crashes happen all the time, skiers need to restrain, warn, and cool down themselves and each other just as much as they need to motivate and push. There is no point in talking your friend into attempting something that will send him to the hospital—he ends up there often enough anyways. The second reason is a related point: Freeskiing is a lifestyle sport, and thus there is no official or formal hierarchy (for example in that a trainer selects those who need to sit on the bench during a match) and no overt and definite mechanism that continuously determines winners and losers (for example in that a tennis game can only end when one player has won). Instead, the notion that freeskiing means 'hanging out' with your friends on the mountain while having fun is a core part of freeskiers' self-image. Accordingly, since enjoying yourself is in itself a kind of overarching normative end, being extensively frustrated, aggressive, or loosing your cool implies defeat in a certain way. More precisely said, doing freeskiing in a funpark invokes implicit, yet tangible forms of inclusion and status differentiation; forms that replace the scores, team jerseys, and red cards formally organizing other sports and games with more flexible and situationally contingent procedures. Nevertheless, overcoming challenges, winning duels, and working one's way up to a status or into a group plays an important part and fulfils an important function apart from matters of symbolic distinction and identity display sociologists tend to focus on: motivating and pushing participants. In other words, the subtle, ongoing, and ritualistic competitions taking place in the funpark are not primarily an end itself, but rather a mechanism for producing certain essential and effective teleological and emotional conditions necessary towards achieving freeskiers basic ends: stylish tricks.

5 Drive, Attunement, and Mood

In my view, Tom's lack of drive to undertake freestyle in an empty park despite the fact that the conditions were 'technically' perfect and although he is an experienced and skilled freeskier provides evidence for my claim that emotional drive is as much a necessary condition to undertake freeskiing as a perception of a current state of normality. Notably, I do not argue that it would be entirely impossible for Tom to conduct *some* freestyle moves right away: Kicker, visibility, ski equipment, and bodily skills were all available or ready at hand; thus he was arguably not *unable*, but *not driven*[22] to perform some tricks. He could maybe muster some motivation on his own in order to be able to train for an hour or two if he had to (but he would probably do so by thinking about an upcoming competition or a similar social interaction); just like he can to some degree and for some moments compensate the lack of a properly shaped box and jib on a handrail instead, or ski relatively well with a broken ski. But just like the skill he supposedly 'has' in his body can only 'be' there because on countless other days, the box was perfect and the ski just fine; 'his' craving for skill, 'his' being pumped to go for it, 'his' feeling that he can make something happen here today is in every concrete case only there for him because other freeskiers are there *with* him as well, or—in limited and suboptimal cases—have been there, will be there, could be there, and should be there with him right now. In other words, just like material objects and practical understandings, teleological structures are a 'commons' shared by those present, and not a feature of an individual. Notably, this also implies that I treat drive as a situated condition, a momentary status accomplished in the midst of the flow of conduct; in contrast to Collins (2004), who considers emotional energy to be a substance that can be stored in the handy canister that is the individual. I stress that I do not mean to say that freeskiers' emotions usually directly cause, dictate, or govern their doings, as many sociological treatments of emotions seem to suggest; but I am rather referring to what Schatzki (2010b: 125–127) called "emotional sense," the phenomenon that something only makes sense (seems feasible, attractive, necessary, and just right) to someone given a certain emotional or affective state.

The fact that I treat not ability per se but drive, in combination with ability, as a fundamental condition that must be situationally accomplished in order for social meaning or order to be consistently and sustainably reproduced, marks a

---

[22] I am not entirely satisfied with my choice of words here: One might as well say that he was 'unwilling' or 'not sufficiently motivated,' but I want to avoid connotations of a 'free will' or discoverable monolithic motives causing his actions—I have criticised Husserl's account of vision and eyeball movement as voluntaristic for doing so. I thus use the term 'driven' to indicate that the activity must be directed or oriented in the sense of 'throwing oneself into it'; but I emphasize that this is neither a causal effect of ends 'stored' in the individual, nor do I imply these ends are subsequently 'really' met.

key difference between the phenopractice-theoretical perspective I develop in this work and other positions in social theory I have discussed. This insistence on teleology as an irreplaceable catalyst for, or additive to, competence (or knowledge) and material equipment—which I share with Schatzki—has its roots in building on (a certain reading of) the philosophy of Wittgenstein and Heidegger. More specifically, siding with Luckner (2008: 55), I hold that both pragmatism and the 'classic' sociology of action focus unduly on matters of ability or skill, thus treating ends and motivations as separate from both perception and activity—tasks, ends, motivations, wishes, or problems are generally taken to be given by social roles, past experiences, or rational optimization.[23] In contrast, the practice perspective I embrace argues that for an action to be performed, it must first make sense to the practitioner to perform it—a condition called practical intelligibility (see Chaps. 8 and 9). Importantly, just like intelligibility in general, such practical intelligibility is a contextual phenomenon that transpires in concrete situations and is an effect of a concrete phenomenal field. Likewise, Schatzki's Heideggerian theory of social practices differs from other accounts of social practices through his treating emotional drive as a feature of situational conduct, and thus effects of practices, rather than independent states of individuals (and is thus one of the mayor ways in which my position is close to his): For Heidegger, emotions and specifically moods are "not merely 'subjective' or 'psychic' phenomena but an irreducible pre-theoretical background, relative to which the world and the manner in which we are situated within it is *disclosed* or rendered intelligible" (Ratcliffe 2002: 287; original emphasis). In Schatzki's version of practice theory, this fundamental role of moods is reflected in the notion that practitioners become attuned to an understanding by conducting the practice to which this understanding belongs—'getting' an understanding in praxis depends on its being undergirded by a certain mood (Heidegger: Stimmung), an emotional framework, one might say, only within which the right and wrong things can be right and wrong the way they are. Notably, what is lost in the English translation 'attunement' is that Heidegger's original term Befindlichkeit does not only describe a momentary mood in the German, but also stems from the verb 'befinden,' which means being positioned in a certain spot (at home, to the left of the church, etc.). Attunement, in other words, is an inherently local phenomenon (see also Brümmer/Alkemeyer 2017; v. Wedelstaedt/Meyer 2017). Importantly, according to the terminology employed here, an understanding is a bundle of doings which amount to *both* performing and recognizing a certain practice. In other words, saying that freeskiers become attuned to the signature understandings of freestyle skiing in the funpark is a statement that refers to both the observation and the athletic performance of freeski tricks. Indeed, my point is that the funpark is a key site of the freeskiing subculture precisely because both performance and observation take place in this realm. Here, one finds the empirical motivation for my embracing

---

[23] I will discuss the more specific position of Schutzian action theory in the next chapter.

the relatively abstract theoretical idea that both observation and performance of a conduct should be treated as part and parcel of one meaningful whole: Because in a funpark, doing and seeing are not only mutually dependent, but actually coalesce as freeskiers simultaneously form cast and audience of their playful action. In doing so, I will seek to show, they open up not just a visible space, but a visual site within which freeskiing's Style can take place in such a way that freeskiers become attuned, and eventually emotionally driven to perform their dangerous feats.

6 Enter the Arena—Seeing Seeing

The funpark offers a spectacle[24] in the truest sense of the word: It is not just that there are spectacular moves to be seen; but every freeskier attending is a spectator as much as an inspector, visibly watching the others while trying to get an idea about himself from seeing the others watch him. The pivotal role of seeing for the practices of freestyle skiing becomes evident by a close observation of the daily training routine in a funpark. Although being organized in an informal, rather casual way, training freestyle in a park is clearly structured spatially and temporally. The image of a solo freestyler jumping over singular ramps is misleading, as the park is constantly filled with other freeskiers as well as "tourists", as mainstream skiers are usually called. Standing or sitting and watching by the side of the obstacles, other skiers form an audience which closely observes almost every jump undertaken. Freestylers usually approach a kicker in a group and then jump one after another in intervals of about 30 seconds, and thus the interaction in the park gains a distinctive rhythm, a repetitive pattern of watching jumps that binds all freestylers into a supple common cadence. As the following screenshots from a video of two freeskiers having a chat while observing the funpark shows, whenever somebody is about to jump over a kicker, with great consistency almost anybody present in the park will shortly pause any ongoing interaction and turn his or her head towards the kicker in order to scrutinize the action taking place there—regardless of whether someone can be expected to perform spectacularly or not.

---

[24] I use the term 'spectacle' to allude to the co-production of the spectacular through spectating, and to underscore that the spectator is as much an effect of the spectacle as vice versa. I do not wish to imply that I side with Debord's dismissive use of the term in his bemoaning of the "Society of the Spectacle" (1983)—in fact, my understanding of the arena comes much closer to the positive alternative to the passive, fake spectacle he suggests: the interactive "festival." The reason for my divergent use of the term lies in the "ocularphobia" Debord shares with many French intellectuals, as Jay argues elegantly (1994: 416–434).

6   Enter the Arena—Seeing Seeing   275

Sec.		Description
0.00		Talking to colleagues. In the background, a rider gets ready to go (circled red).
0.48		Informed by the colleagues' shift of attention to the kicker, the rider starts to turn to see what is happening. In the background, a rider is approaching the kicker.
1.20		Focusing the kicker where the action is about to happen.
2.44		Gathering himself to witness this potentially important event, the rider is adjusting his goggle to see better. (The performing rider is hidden behind the kicker).

Sec.		Description
4.48		Attentively watching the performance of the trick. The visceral attention is visible in the bodily posture
5.88–6.42		The rider has 'stomped' the trick. The spectators applauds briefly with his ski-poles while commenting on the performance ("Ni:ce. He made it clean."[R][25]), before…

---

[25] „Schö:n. Hat er sauber g'macht."

7 Visual Space: The Arena as a Stylescape   277

Sec.		Description
6.72		*… returning his attention to the conversation with his colleagues.*

What these interactions show, I argue, is that the funpark functions as a kind of stage, or better, as what I call an *arena* that produces (and is produced by) visibilities, and more specifically: visible style. Unlike in a linearly organized theatre stage, where the audience is looking only at the performers, the play in an arena happens in the round, and thus the audience watches the performances *against the backdrop* of other parts of the audience—the reaction of the audience is thus a crucial part of the 'program' one is watching. I define an arena as a site of the social devoted to the local and interactive production of visible style. I will show how the cooperative conduct taking place at the funpark establishes a nexus of doings and sayings mutually oriented by and to style through the situated interplay of scenic conduct of performing, spectating, and talking style. Taken together, the praxis taking place and making place in the arena entrains persons' emotions and bodily skills and forms a key locus in which freeskiing is instructedly and instructably observable accomplished in that freeski style is expressed, reproduced, disseminated, contested, and reproduced. The visual arena assembled in the funpark epitomizes the various other types of arenas freeskiers assemble in seemingly any locale they can muster and in which they find snow and possibilities to produce visibility: for example makeshift kicker built in someone's backyard, rail sessions held in derelict underpasses or in front of iconic museums in Munich, jib contests held in indoor skiing halls in northern Germany in mid-July, or massive 'super kicker' purposed-built for international tournaments big enough to make riders fly more than 50 far and 30 meters high. In all these locales, attending freeskiers will position themselves similarly to the patterns I will describe with regard to the funpark and operate the same kind of 'system of gazes' inducing the viscerally felt realm of fatefulness and interpersonal reciprocity.

7 Visual Space: The Arena as a Stylescape

A first indicator that the space in the funpark is a fine-tuned visual field rather than just a relatively empty snow-covered expanse, is the emotional reaction from freeskiers to what they perceive as violations of their turf. "They just ski right through—they can't do that!" [M][26] a freestyler exclaims agitatedly as we watch a group of 'tourists' meander through the park in amateurish stem-turns. In the same vein, Tom told me how the only thing that should really be improved about the Penken Park would be a clear separation between "normal skiers" and freeskiers. But in fact, the park is already quite clearly demarcated from the rest of the ski resort by a bright orange fence all around its perimeter. Since the last two seasons, one additionally enters it through a huge inflated gate emblazoned with the "Vans Penken Park"-logo—not a physical obstacle (there are no doors in its arch), but a clear and effective symbolic barrier. Accordingly, most tourists move rather wearily around the park; curiously prying at the strange skiers and snowboarders with their colourful baggy clothes, doing these incredible maniac stunts on these dangerous ramps. Others, however, just use the ski lift next to the park as a convenient help to cross from one side of the ski resort to the other, short-cutting through the funpark on the way. To some extent, the freeskiers' anger has quite straightforward 'technical' reasons, because uninformed skiers sometimes venture into the landing zones of the large kickers and stand or even sit where the rider charging down onto the kicker cannot see them, and thus risk a brutal crash. Policing a kicker by making sure that landings are clear is thus an important and permanent task fulfilled cooperatively by the freeskiers standing in the vicinity of the kicker, in that those standing below or by the side signal those getting ready to jump that it is good to go. But this overly 'rational' motive, I believe, is not the only driving force behind the freeskiers' frequent calls for spatial exclusivity. This is suggested by the fact that the short-cutting, typically more skilled ski-'tourists' earn actually more wrath on behalf of the freestylers than the less able skiers entering the park to take a look, since the latter are at least duly impressed, while the former seem almost provocative in their disinterestedness. More specifically, I argue that those skiers who come to enjoy and awe at least to some extend take part in the establishing of the arena that is the funpark, because by being spectators, they contribute to the spectacle taking place through the duality of watching and performing. In contrasts to what Edensor (2010) argues in his notable analysis of walking styles, the spatial organisation or interactive coordination of body movement is not only and not primarily rooted in temporal (or rhythmical) order while (walking or skiing) styles are merely an indicator of variety or resistance (in Lefebvre's sense). Instead, spatial and temporal orders are an effect of the expression and appreciation of visible style.

The spatial order of the funpark is produced and upheld silently by what Jean-Claude Kaufmann (1996) described as a "system of gazes" in his detailed study of the schemes of social control enmeshing the practice of topless sunbathing on French beaches. The gaze, he shows, is the key instrument with which the beach-goers communicate approval or indignation swiftly, silently, and subtly, so that they are able to establish and police a socio-spatial order for managing the delicate

---

[26] „Die fahren hier einfach durch, das geht gar nicht!"

matter that is the bare female breast. The 'vocabulary' of gazing that everyone can be expected to intuitively understand is composed of the length, intensity, and frequency of gazes; as well as the accompanying mimics in combination with the spatial position and social role of the gazing person—topless women can 'catch' men staring, mothers can earn disapproving looks for not keeping their children's' staring at bay, elder men are held to higher standards than younger ones, and so forth. The pressing problem that requires such elaborate treatment, Kaufmann argues in the tradition of Elias, does not just stem from the 'fact' that bare breasts produce (male) attention and erotic interest: Surely, beachgoers of both sexes are morally required to refrain from certain overtly explicit acts such as staring or stirring arousal, but spatial segregation (special nude bathing zones) or textile covers would provide easy solutions. It is also not just the tension that arises between these moral and (pseudo-) biological 'facts,' and the relatively recent general understanding that the beach is a public place of leisure and that topless sunbathing is a normal and natural conduct every free citizen is entitled to engage in as she (or he) pleases. Instead, what makes matters so delicate, he skilfully carves out, is that 'officially,' there is supposed to be no problem in the first place in that the beach is an innocent place of tolerance and relaxation where everyone minds his or her own business (Kaufmann 1996: 151). Overtly evident uneasiness about other's behaviour, in other words, could imply that one is both a reactionary, uptight moralist *and* is having lewd second thoughts about a perfectly normal and uneventful situation. What is more, only because there is 'officially' nothing to be ashamed about in the practice of sunbathing topless or lying next to someone bathing topless, it is possible to single out those who overstep the line of normal conduct and should be ashamed of themselves. It follows that in order to be able to sanction those who show of their feminine opulence to an unacceptable extend, or pay attention to other's perfectly normal nudity in an unduly manner, the uneventfulness and normality of bare breasts must first be situatedly accomplished in praxis, for example by visibly neither looking at, nor anxiously away from, the exposed bust when dispassionately catching glimpse of one's coincidentally and uninterestingly half-naked neighbours while routinely looking about the beach (Kaufmann 1996: 256). In effect, the gazes immaterially but visibly structuring the beach become a system in that they are both informing and informed, thus reciprocally conditioning and conditioned by the social site—or dare I say: clearing—within which the bare female breast comes to light.

8 The Kicker as a Visual Arena

Despite the difference in content and physical setting, the behaviour of the riders waiting in the line above a kicker exhibits the same basic principles which create a system of gazes in Kaufmann's sense: As a video-analysis of their 'doing queuing' reveals, they very consistently look towards the kicker below where the action takes place and only briefly give up this orientation of sight and body when either a) very clearly attending to themselves, for example checking and preparing their equipment (like the second snowboarder from the left in the picture), or by b) briefly turning to a friend standing next to them to exchange some comments (Fig. 7.4). Most of the chatting that goes on, however, is done without looking at each other; just as it is common for people seeking to be visibly busy with—to speak with Garfinkel—staffing the "local population cohort" of a queue as a "local phenomenon of order" (Garfinkel 2002: 215–216; Garfinkel/E. Livingston 2003). Furthermore, they almost always avoid obviously mustering other participants they do not know once they have joined the queue, which would amount to a kind of aggression.

Blending into the queue, in other words, requires a number of 'egoistic' and purposeful actions: Making skilful adjustments to the changing formation of positionings of riders; conducting subtle, yet clearly indicative manoeuvres such as blocking someone's path or claiming an exposed spot at the front of the queue; and so forth. But throughout doing this, none of the riders seems overtly preoccupied with these ends and tasks in that their gaze is wandering off only briefly and seemingly unwillingly, but mostly remains glued to the only "congregationally relevant business at hand" (Garfinkel/E. Livingston 2003: 22), the business taking place at the kicker below. Adhering to the unwritten laws of 'civil inattention'

Fig. 7.4 The queue atop of the pro line of kickers in the Penken Park: Participants to not orient to each other, but to the kicker or their own

8 The Kicker as a Visual Arena 281

(Goffman 1963: 83), approving and deploring gazes and subtle gestures enforce a fine-tuned social stratification in the park that separates those who know how to behave from those who do not. Not only does it part the true masters of skill from the ambitioned regulars, and in turn those regulars from the mere beginners; but it also allocates places and thus social *positions* to participants to watch legitimately without performing stylish manoeuvres; particularly photographers, friends of well-established locals, or injured riders. (Ethnographers are of course not expected to appear, but they are assigned to one of the latter categories quite easily.) Notably, when I speak of positions in an arena, I use the term to capture the fact that a position is simultaneously a spatial placement within a concrete, momentary congregation of people; a position in a social hierarchy or the local analogue of a Bourdieuian field; and a position in Schatzki's sense, i.e. a theoretical term ("where an entity fits in a nexus") that grounds his entire concept of meaning, sites, and practices (2002: 19). In the local system of order edified by seeing and watching seeing, the placement of persons relative to the kicker (or other obstacles) not only identifies their 'role' and assigns participants a field of vision, but it also constructs segregated spaces within the originally homogenous expanse of snow. Relative to those persons that clearly have a business being near the kicker—for example because they wait in line to jump—all others gain their specific positions by looking and being looked at: The scenic intelligibility of bodily movement (Büscher 2005b, 2006; C. Goodwin 2007; v. Wedelstaedt/Meyer 2017) provides that their posture, stance, line of sight, and field of vision serve as markers of position, skill, and status—but simultaneously, they also determine what and how well these participants see, impose direct bodily, optical conditions, and possibilities of gaining or losing sight of the freeskiers' style. In the arena, in other words, an abstract philosophical argument made by Merleau-Ponty comes to live, namely that it is the very visibility of vision that allows us to see a world from within,[27] in an instance of being-in-the-world (see Carman 2008: 122–127): Vision and position are co-constituted and interwoven so that the arena as a social site is formed and performed.

Frequently, riders accompany their friends on their rounds in a line without always performing tricks themselves. Especially regular local riders capable of tackling the largest kickers in the pro line tend to draw company, often riders of lesser skill that split their time in the park between trying their best at the medium line and hanging out 'with the pros' (Fig. 7.5). This does not necessarily make them wannabes in the freeskiers' eyes since a lack of skill is by far not the only reason for watching rather than performing in the park. For one, riders frequently sustain larger or smaller injuries of some sort (such as a twitched thumb) that forces them to refrain from jumping; or they accompany their peers to take pictures or videos. What is more, motivation is a key prerequisite for trying the dangerous, straining, and sometimes frustrating tricks of freestyle again

---

[27] "To say that the body is seeing, curiously, is to say nothing other than: it is visible [in the act of looking]." (Merleau-Ponty 1968: 273).

Fig. 7.5 Hanging out in the park

and again, day after day (more on this below). As motivation and energy ebbs and flows throughout the day, riders often take a break before attempting another try, or might have given up for today altogether; and in both cases they often opt to leisurely check out the pro line instead of sitting down at the restaurant at the bottom of the park. Most importantly, watching others perform is a key part of doing freestyle, and even the most skilled riders in the park (some of which are known internationally) will not usually spend the whole day performing their best tricks, but rather engage in some 'meet and greet' with old friends or eye up and coming competitors. What is more, the distinction between hanging out and performing tricks is not as clear-cut as one might think, because riders will often queue up in the line and jump over the first kicker without really attempting a trick, showing only a simple straight jump. Again, this might serve different purposes, either functioning as a trial, preparation, or motivation for subsequent 'real' attempts to perform more difficult tricks, or just as a placebo that enables riders to hang out at the pro line without seriously risking their bones. All in all, spectating instead of performing in the arena can take various legitimate forms and is at times practiced by freeskiers of all skills and standings. That said, the status ascribed to, and respect expressed towards, a rider does of course depend primarily on his skill in performing Style, and to some extend also on the commitment shown in trying to improve one's personal Style (see Wheaton 2000b). Those found to be predominantly interested in hanging out rather than improving, or those frequently failing to muster the motivation to really push their style forward do over time earn some eerie looks or disapproving comments. Such reactions should not be mistaken to be nothing but status games or gestures of power and distinction; and although they are to some extent, they are also part of the collective efforts to manage motivation and emotions such as fear and frustration. And exactly because spectating and dismissing or de-valuating spectating can take different forms and functions, I argue, the freeskiers manning the arena are keeping a close eye on everybody in the vicinity of the kicker lines and react sensibly to those who do not belong there. While most other spectator sports such as soccer or (ski) racing are of course affected by the presence of spectators, they arguably do not require it to work—unlike freestyle skiing, which's functioning depends on an audience that displays some expertise in spectating style and assembling an arena.

Excursus: Foucault, Power, and Phenopractices

> To some extent, the combination of silent and verbal pushing turns the funpark into a "panoptic machine" in the sense of Foucault (1977: 217), a space in which the hegemony of vision reigns over bodies disciplined into conforming with the vivisecting gaze (Foucault 1976). Yet while the funpark is without a doubt subject to some of the aspects of visual regimes Foucault detailed, even at first glance it simultaneously provides a notable counter-example to the strictly hegemonic institutions like the prison or the clinic as portrayed by him: First, its participants employ its normative or teleological powers systematically and relatively freely towards pursuing their own pleasure—moving in and out of the park and in and out of queues and lines, they subvert themselves strategically and temporarily rather than either being subverted or resisting actively. And second, the park demonstrates how reciprocal vision also produces emotional entrainment and a sense of community rather than necessarily being a form of power exerted from one unto the other (and back). To be sure, these two observations do not per se inhibit a classic Foucauldian analysis but would rather make such an enterprise all the more interesting, exploring the deliberate cross-surveillance of consumers in their quest for producing and acquiring embodied subject positions (see for a related project Reckwitz 2006b and Prinz 2014). In other words, I do not wish to deny that the arena is to some extend hegemonic

and that one *could* frame the riders' mutual scrutinizing as a form of power play in the sense of Foucault's writings on power and discipline (Schmidt 2022; Stern 2009). But as Giddens (1984: 157) rightly points out, at least in these writings "Foucault's bodies do not have faces" in that they do not engage in *collaborative* face work in Goffman's (1971a) sense, perpetually, systematically, and subtly allowing each other to slip out of overtly strict and effectively impossible conformity. Importantly, as Foucault's work developed through different phases, his position on phenomenology arguably changes, and his notion of power evolves. As with other 'grand theories,' the (in-)compatibility of his thought with the phenopractice perspective depends on the aspects one wishes to emphasize, and the conceptual extensions one deems necessary and compatible. For example, if one follows later Foucault and defines the exercise of power as "a set of actions upon other actions" (1982: 219), one would need to conceptualize the rider's wandering gazes as actions, which seems incompatible with the account of action and activity I will develop in the following chapter. What is more, when Foucault (1982) conceptualizes governing as "to structure the possible field of action of others," he restricts most of his discussion—not unlike Bourdieu—on what I have called prefiguration. Developing a distinctly Foucauldian practice perspective on seeing would therefore require drawing selectively on certain parts of his brought oeuvre and extending it with more distinctly phenomenological thought (as proposed by Prinz 2014). In contrast, I will argue in this chapter that—in addition to prefiguration—orientation as a second key concept is necessary to grasp the specific nature of lived social life (see for a similar argument Schatzki 2002: 45, 225). Above all, however, I refrained from developing a more distinctively Foucauldian perspective on practice thought (Reckwitz 2002b, 2008 develops such an option) because I deem his account of vision inherently problematic. Foucault primarily identified sight as the mayor tool employed since Enlightenment to underscore hegemonic claims to rational or scientific truth; and since he considered knowledge a form of power, he framed the gaze as a tool of domination through categorization, normalization, and surveillance (see Jay 1994: 384–416). Consequentially, in most of his writings on the subject, he rejected the notion of embodied vision both as part of an ontology and as a starting point for a phenomenology of perception and being, particularly as formulated by Merleau-Ponty (Jay 1994: 414).

However, my approach to Foucault of reading him primarily as a discourse theorist aiming to overcome phenomenology as a whole is complemented by a more imaginative approach by Reckwitz and colleagues that build on Foucault's writings on the dispositive and his later works that engage with Merleau-Ponty in a more appreciative manner. With regard to vision in particular, notable examples of a practice-minded re-reading Knorr Cetina's (1999: 248) concept of "viscourses" as an extension of discourses, and especially Sophia Prinz' (2014) detailed proposal for a Foucauldian practice theory of seeing. In her work, the concept of orderliness invoked by embodied perception is used to defend Foucault against the charge of "hopeless subjectivism" (Habermas 1985). For Prinz, de-centring the subject by theorizing practices means moving away from a reading of Foucault fully centred on subjective freedom and creative resistance as the engine of liberatory transgression and political challenging of established orders, and towards a position that acknowledges the formative role of embodied routines on perception and creative expression. The underlying ontology within which Prinz argues therefore reproduces the classic duality of "the constitutive interrelation between the outer social orders on the one, and the individual body on the other side." (Prinz 2016) This becomes especially clear in the core theoretical notion of "incorporation" or "internalisation". As I have argued in chapter five, this concept requires careful scrutiny because it can easily be read as a form of programming of the body as a reliably reproduction engine of regular symbolic forms or orders. The inevitable indexicalities that occur in ever situated reproduction are in this view 'explained away' as evidence of a capacity for improvisation or creativity of the lived body as a "perceiving-acting quasi-subject" (Prinz 2016: 188 fn 18) in the wake of Merleau-Ponty.

At his point, the phenopractice perspective tries to offer a more fine-grained picture that, first, opens the blackbox of the body and embraces neural pluralism to distinguish parallel processes (in particular those of epistemic vision vs. pragmatic vision), and, second, emphasizes the constitution of order by the situation itself as the unfolding of a practice that orients and prefigures. With regard to the details of the visual process, for example, the phenopractice perspective draws on Gestalt thinking to conceptualize seeing as the standing out of a Gestalt from the background-foreground structure of a phenomenal field of a practice itself, whereas Prinz (2016: 189) reads Merleau-Ponty's writings on Gestalt-seeing and motor intentionality as a "learned apperceptive syntax" to argue that the subject "must actively bracket part of the visual field." Prinz' "Praxis of Seeing" and phenopractice theory ask similar questions and discuss many of the same classic arguments regarding the phenomenology of vision, but where I aimed for a more radically social ontology of the social, Prinz concludes that "in the end, the perceiving subject needs to be understood as a culturally formed but nevertheless active instance" (2016: 195; my translation).

9 Position and Posture

Skilfully spectating requires following the same basic patterns adhered to by riders queuing above a kicker; it means fitting in by being visibly primarily occupied with seeing style. Above all, this orientation to style is expressed in the position, perspective, and stance taken towards the action at the kicker, as illustrated in Fig. 7.6.

Experienced spectators overwhelmingly position themselves relative to a kicker line in a uniform manner, in spots that 'make sense' within the logic of the arena. When a spectator accompanies a rider for a "round" in the kicker line, they will typically ride the lift up together and then possibly have a short chat right behind

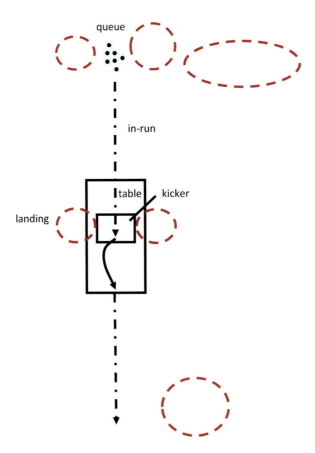

Fig. 7.6 Schematic sketch of the first kicker of the pro line in the Penken Park. Skilful spectators are usually found exclusively in the circled areas

the entrance of the park. After skiing down to the in-run of the pro line 'together' (relatively close to each other), the spectator will stand some meters apart from the group that forms the queue for the kicker; close enough to be able to talk (although actual talking does not necessarily happen) but still clearly detached. What is more, spectators will often stand slightly above the queue or on the same level to the left or right, but not much below the group. Although there is always plenty of space available further down below, to the left and right of the in-run, skilled spectators are almost never found there. Instead, if they do not wait at the top of the in-run until 'their' rider is taking his turn, they will either be standing next to the kicker (on the table immediately next to it or some meters to the side), or they wait a good twenty or thirty meters below the kicker by the side of the slope (see sketch). The logic behind this positioning pattern is only in part dictated by matters of safety or the practical needs of the performers: Standing directly in the in-run or—much worse—the landing would indeed hinder or endanger those riders who jump, but this does not explain why spectators avoid what undiscerning spectators frequently do, which is standing to the left or right of the in-or out-run. These positions, I suggest, are instead avoided by freeskiers because they do not suit the practical purposes of seeing style very well. From the perspective that they invoke, one cannot see the complete trajectory of a jump, because either the transition and the initial phase, or the later phase and the landing remain hidden behind the large kicker and table. Only by looking from further away and above or below, one can easily inspect all critical phases of a jump; while the position directly on or next to the table provides a close-up look on the details of a trick and is thus frequently used by photo- or videographers. Therefore, sticking to the 'traditional' positioning patterns entails a performative element in that it signals experience and a shared interest in style in a setting where (relative) strangers need to cooperate to some extend; but it is also plainly useful for seeing style. To be sure, I do not suggest that these positions are really the only 'technically' feasible choice for watching freestyle. Instead, I argue that every position implies a certain perspective—one that is both visual *and* (more or less) informed—on the performances in the kicker line, and that these perspectives in turn imply a certain bodily *and* emotional stance towards style (see C. Goodwin 2007). In other words, the embodied "architecture for perception" (C. Goodwin 2000b) of the funpark that I call arena is not 'just' a symbolic framework in the sense that a) a very different constellation of positions and perspectives could produce the same effect (e.g. in the sense that wives 'need' to be seated to the right of their husbands in some cultures, or to the left in others, or opposite from them in still others, and so forth), and b) the freeskiers take up these positions because they have memorized a certain 'proper' formation they now consciously try to reproduce (like trying to find a 'good' church-bench to sit in at a good friends' wedding—not too far in the front where the family 'must' sit, but not too far back to appear disinterested). It is not just that the position in physical space has an obvious, direct influence on one's line of sight and thus the 'content' of this sight; but that at a very basal level, our visual perception is being co-constituted by those co-present in the same situation. We are not simply guided in our awareness in that we try to 'read' their gaze orientation in order to scrutinize what they seem to consider interesting, but vision scientists argue that other's visual orientation to an object causes "intentional imposition," that is, it alters the way it is neutrally processed, e.g. in terms of its familiarity or affording actions (Becchio/Bertone/Castiello 2008; Schlicht 2010: 5). For example, seeing someone grabbing an object causes our pragmatic visual system to become active, thus supposedly treating it as a grab-able object—but the same effect also occurs if the other is merely looking at the object while being in a bodily position to grab it. Of course, this specific case differs quite a lot from the precise situation in the funpark; and as always one needs to be careful about precisely what it is that one can conclude from mere measurable brain-cell activations. But while I will later attend to the more specific processes involved in seeing others perform familiar movement patterns, I nevertheless believe it is important to note that conscious visual attention is not the only dimension of embodied vision that can be situatedly and interactively influenced—and arguably organized. Someone's embodied stance towards a feature of a situation, it would follow, does not just express his or her relation towards said feature—as ethnomethodologists' like Goodwin have observed—, but also co-defines what we see and *how* we see it—it alters the teleoaffective structure of our seeing in that situation (Brümmer/Alkemeyer 2017). In sum, when the freeskiers require those attending the funpark to fit in properly, this describes quite literally a spatial precondition. Belonging and creating a sense of community, is not just a question of symbolic interaction, of performing or displaying the *right* kind of things such as sporting the right clothing brand. It is also a phenomenological question, in that it requires a specific 'feeling' to be able to 'go with the flow' of the place and the crowd. And this flow is not just one of outward appearances, but one of *tuning in* to the 'vibe' of the arena, of grasping the sense of feasibility of the extraordinary, the confidence of allowing oneself to be exposed to the fragility and (possibly) danger of public performing, of standing out from the crowd as a modus of (or on the basis of) belonging and blending in. When a freeskier enters a funpark, for example, he will first blend in by joining a queue, by looking like, and standing close to, and *being with* the other freeskiers; and only then, in a second step, he will disengage spatially from the queue and ski down to the obstacle to engage with it, while the others will engage with his performing a trick by watching closely. In this way, the arena becomes what Heidegger (1962: 141) terms a *Spielraum* (translated as leeway, but literally meaning a play-room); a room to play in, and a room in which a play is being staged and spectated (see also Woermann 2018).

Described in this way, arenas exhibit many phenomena typically highlighted by sociological theories centring on the notion of the ritual, e.g. mutual awareness, symbolically loaded interaction, emotional entrainment, and community-forging by participation. To a considerable extent, one might therefore explain what is going on in the Penken Park solely on the basis of these theories. For example, one might wonder whether one could not just as well conceptualize it as a stage in Goffman's (1959) sense, as the site established by interaction rituals. But while I deem the notion of the ritual to some extend applicable to what I described as an arena, I do not consider it to be theoretically satisfactory. I hold that the notion of the ritual poses an obstacle to adequately capture the situated production of emotional states and coordinated orientation of conduct in that it has lead authors (not necessarily Goffman) to deduct a number of assumptions that are either individualistic, unduly static, or both. At the core, the phenopractical notion of style and the interplay of prefiguration and orientation as situated accomplishments that I outline in this work can be read as an attempt to formulate a more viable alternative to social thought grounded in ritual theory that preserves its valuable insights while avoiding its pitfalls.

Excursus: Why the Arena is not a Ritual

> An account of social practices that stresses the situated nature of social order, as well as the importance of interaction and co-presence for teleoaffectivity or emotions builds on a different sociological tradition apart from the phenomenological line of thinking I have predominantly been discussing so far: ritual theory, particularly in the wake of Durkheim and Goffman. But although the topic of this chapter, as well as the arguments I am making here, are indebted to their thought, I argue that what happens in an arena such as the funpark is not adequately grasped by the term ritual. In defence of this claim, let me sketch out the parallels and disagreements between my account and 'Goffmanian' ritual theory in particular. To begin with, the sociological inquiry into processes of interaction is to some degree always rooted in Durkheim's (1965) classic argument that symbolic performances within ritualized interaction create emotional bonds and forge communities that adhere to shared rules with respect to dealing with 'sacred' objects. Indeed, several of Durkheim's main topics feature prominently in the Penken Park and subsequently in my theoretical account as well: the symbolic value of certain performances, the emotional reaction to things gone right and wrong, the sense of community and belonging this creates, and the coordination of orientations that the participants realize momentarily and seek to reproduce in the future. What is more, by drawing on authors such as Collins (2004) and Kaufmann (1996), I also indirectly build on Goffman's reformulation of Durkheim's (1965) notion of collective effervescence in face of the sacred into a sociology of everyday encounters organized as interaction rituals (Goffman 1967). Notably, in his description of the interaction order, Goffman (1974, 1983) provides an alternative to an overtly static understanding of social rituals. Indeed, especially if one employs an ethnomethodological reading of his notion of the interaction order as a realm of order in its own right and "a reality sui generis" (A. W. Rawls

1987), his deep insights into face work, socially enticed emotions, and the subtle mechanisms of everyday encounters can support and inform many of the issues I have raised. In doing so, however, one would neglect what Knoblauch (1994: 14–15; my translation) describes as Goffman's "brilliant ambiguity" that characterizes an account of social order oscillating "between strategy and ritual" in that it postulates the existence of individual actors as strategic thinkers in addition to the self-contained structure of the situation. Moreover, as Giddens (1987: 115) shows, Goffman is "above all a theorist of co-presence" rather than of social practices per se, since the general prevalence of the interactive processes he describes in other realms of society remains somewhat unclear. In effect, Goffman's work can be read as spelling out two different conceptualizations of social order in interactions: A narrower concept of interaction as performance of rituals which equates social order with regularity; and a broader concept of the interaction order as a bounded realm defined by the participants' perceptible (and thus possibly merely performative) adherence to common rules of conduct. Although the former concept is dominant in his earlier work on the presentation of self, and the latter is emphasized in his later works, I hold that it is not quite clear whether he abandoned the former or remained faithful to it (as R. Collins 2004: 22–25; and Schegloff 1988 suggest): If social interaction is conceived of as having a regular 'core' (as being 'truly' organized in the form of a basic, static pattern that remains equal across different situations of the same kind), it will also fulfil the latter definition as well (but not the other way around). And since Goffman did not strive to write a single 'grand theory,' but continually discusses concrete examples and small cases of everyday conduct (Knoblauch 1994), much of his work can be, and has been, read either way. In any event, for the sake of this discussion, I will discern the two notions of ritual (as employed by a number of authors, including Goffman) and interaction order (as his distinctive model) separately and leave it to the reader whether one of the two has been wrongly associated with the 'true' Goffman by those authors claiming to build on him (such as Collins, Alexander, or Giddens).

I identify four intertwined problematic postulates underlying sociological concepts of rituals which yield problems that befall the account of Goffman and those building on him, but also other authors drawing more directly on Durkheim, such as Jeffrey Alexander and his "cultural pragmatics" (2004). While not all postulates are present in all accounts, I believe that they are often tacitly implied as well as theoretically related to one another. They are: First, a single definition of the situation; second, near-ubiquitous and unavoidable conflict; third, individual actors with given strategic interests; and fourth, regularity (i.e. inherent sameness) of conduct. The first underlying postulate is that the effect of a successful a ritual is understood as being the participants' sharing of a "single definition of the situation" (Goffman 1959:

254). In other words, in order for the beneficial effects of the ritual (such as emotional entrainment) to take place, participants' perception and action needs to be synchronized. In theoretical terms, this view is an effect of the presupposition that there is a 'natural,' inherent, and sustained gap between the perception and feelings of individuals which is temporarily bridged while the sharing of the ritual lasts. The difference between people's cognitive or conscious states, one could say, is overcome in the unity of the ritual; and thus the ritual as a single unit must be presupposed lest there would be nothing left that is shared. This condition, that participants need to see and feel and value more or less the same, has been taken to be evident in the empirical phenomenon of focused interaction, to a large extend on the basis of studying the interactive organization of vision and gaze (see also R. Collins 2004: Chap. 2; Kendon 1990). To be sure, proponents of ritual theory of course acknowledge that the ideal condition of a single, shared ritual is not always met in that participants' orientations can misalign and different 'scripts' or 'frames' are pursued—but the crucial point is that they render such misalignments as *failings* of the ritual and thus as problems that need to be solved. Alexander (2004), for example, aims to explain human history from pagan shamans to Reagan's presidential addresses as a series of social performances that either fail or succeed, depending on whether the audience's "background representations" and the social drama's "foreground script" match (or not), so that the performance becomes "fused" or not. In a similar vein, Goffman's (1955, 1967) theory of role-taking and self argues on the premise that 'inward' and currently actualized 'outward' identities produced by the current social script must match to enable the participant to "safe his face" and avoid negative emotions (see for a related concept of emotions Hochschild 1983); as does his emphasis on "keying" and "bracketing" in his later work on frame analysis as vital mechanisms that ensure the mutual alignment of frames of perception as a basis for sharing one frame of activity.[28]

The second problem I identify is a direct consequence (and evidence) of the presupposition that rituals are either mutually followed or otherwise fail: The emphasis on conflicts and domination that Goffman shares with Bourdieu and Collins, and which is rooted in the notion that, if participants

---

[28] Certainly, Goffman's later work on frame analysis (1974) softens the claim that situations necessarily have a single, public order; and it can be read as much closer to Schatzki's notion of a teleological structure of social sites. However, while Goffman accounts for situations which go well although or even because participants operate side-by-side within different frames, he nevertheless primarily emphasizes the aligning and synchronizing of participants' frames through what he calls keying. Likewise, as his discussion of bracketing suggests, misalignments of frames (such as taking a drama for real) frequently invoke a "breaking of frame" which is portrayed as generally problematic, e.g. in that it needs to be remedied and overcome.

cannot establish a single definition of the situation and follow a shared ritual, they will try or even need to establish mutual adherence by force. Goffman's discussion of ritualized conflicts over spatial "territories of the self" (1971a) arguably provides a paradigmatic example. Comparing human interaction to the territorial behaviour of animals, he portrays ritualized conflicts as almost inevitable, as definitive in the sense that territory is either won or lost, and as 'automatically' drawing the present participants in—in his view, shying away from a spatial conflict is already a form of taking part in the ritual, in that one acknowledges the other's dominance. Once the fight is on, so to speak, you cannot get out unaffected. He seems to imply a kind of 'all-or-nothing-situationalism' that takes both the situational order and the direction and effect of rituals as determined and unequivocal—the definitiveness of which, I must stress, is countered and balanced by the divergent subjective interpretations and aims individuals might hold. The concrete social order of everyday interaction is then understood as the effect of the combinations and contradictions of both levels or aspects, that is, of individual cognition or intention on the one side, and the ritual's strict order on the other. In the case of spatial territories, for example, the actual ordering that ensues in lived life can be an effect of the participants' strategies of avoiding being drawn into ritualized conflicts that enforce the production of winners and losers (e.g. Goffman 1971a: 57–59; see also J. Lee 2009). However, framing the freeskiers' playful interaction as a series of conflicts that either occur or are avoided is problematic, because it overlooks the *functional* role of playful banter for what I called pushing. More generally speaking, I suggest that the notion of ritualized interaction is somewhat binary, in that emotional entrainment and mutual orientation either occur unequivocally if the ritual takes place, or do not happen at all if it does not. Again, I stress that I refer to the interaction order which—at least in some readings of Goffman's theory (see Eberle 2000b)—is not necessarily considered as equivalent to subject interpretations of or thoughts about a situation. But subjective consciousness notwithstanding, the ritual's meaning is either taking place 'out there' in the situation[29] or not—and so is the ritual. From the perspective taken in this work, the upshot of these considerations is that the notion 'ritual' can grasp the coordination of conduct within a situation (and thus the sharing of experiences and emotions that ensues) only to an insufficient extent: Since a ritual is either performed, not performed, or avoided, this concept allows only to assume the a) equivalence (ritual), b) complete independence (no ritual), or c) weak and undetermined relationality (via the mutual avoidance of engaging in a ritual) of the teleoaffective structure

---

[29] See also my discussion of the 'publicness' of social order in practices in the methodological appendix.

unfolding in the situation. What is more, it remains unclear precisely how rituals are related to one another (other than through sequentiality, i.e. rituals requiring response rituals), that is, whether a situation can be governed by two or more simultaneously performed and co-dependent rituals, the mutual relation of which is organized or carried by the rituals themselves. Instead, the individual subject as a strategic actor steps back onto the stage at this point; choosing, starting, ending, and managing rituals and their succession or relation. In most cases, in other words, it still depends on the actor whether and which interactions become focused, which emotions shared, and which communal bonds forged (see Knoblauch 1994 on Goffman's dualism). From a theoretical point of view, however, I can see no reason why it should be necessary to conceptualize a ritual as encompassing the whole social order of an (interactive) situation in order to uphold the claim that participant's conduct is coordinated, and that emotions are shared. Rather, it seems to me that this postulate is an effect of the third problem I perceive in Goffman's notion of the ritual: Ritual theorists frequently conceptualize social communities (or whole societies) as groups of people bound together by, or defined by, carrying out a certain ritual; and accordingly the substance of the interaction order is conceived of as a congregation of actors whose perpetual distinctiveness is taken for granted, and who carry individual and pre-given strategic interests. In contrast, by avoiding the juxtaposition of individuals and situational orders, and invoking a notion of social practices, one can account for a variety of modes of coordination of conduct, orientation, and teleoaffective structuring between practices in the form of *orchestration* (cf. Schatzki 1996: 185–192) without having to assume that their unity or identity must be realized in commonality, lest in a single practice.[30] In this vein, my notion of the arena is designed to capture how different situationally concurring practices co-establish a 'working' social site as a congregation by sharing some, but not all elements (such as spatial orders or emotions).

This connects to the fourth, more abstract problem that I notice in the concept of the ritual: At least in the writings of some authors, the performance of a ritual is to be understood as a piece of interaction that shares certain regular and defining features with other social situations; and therefore ritual theory frames social order as a regularity. For example, in an extensive discussion of various uses of the term 'ritual' in social theory since

---

[30] Notably, Goffman's arguably more refined notion of the interaction order (1983) allows for such an understanding as well, since it defines situations via the participants' perceptible adherence to common rules of conduct, which is arguably something else than a shared teleoaffective orientation. Conceived as such, participants could thus adhere to shared rules while conducting different practices with different inherent teleological ends and nevertheless proceed orchestratedly, but not in regularity. But if so, it is still questionable whether rules alone can adequately circumscribe the participants' mutual orchestration (see below).

Durkheim, Randall Collins (2004: 17) argues that every performance of a ritual must constitute "a repetition of what went before" in order to unfold its powers of social cohesion—and accordingly, if repetitions cease to take place, so does the existence of the sacred the ritual carried. Goffman, similarly, does not provide an explicit definition of rituals in this sense, but employs expressions that seem to imply such a reading, e.g. the formulation that a "ritual is a conventionalized, perfunctory act" (1971a: 62). Other proponents of ritual theories are more explicit in this regard, e.g. Alexander (2004) suggests that for rituals to be successful, performances must conform to what he terms "scripts" or "systems of collective representations." I should stress that I do not wish to paint ritual theorists as structuralists in disguise in that they imply that one overarching (e.g. subconscious) symbolic structure organizes all conduct. To the contrary, they usually allow for a variety of explanations of how the accomplishment of a ritual can be accounted for; such as strategic action, common socialization, and so forth. But although some readily assure that rituals are flexible to some extent (e.g. R. Collins 2004: 43), social life is nevertheless understood as ritualistic by virtue of exhibiting certain definitive sequential structures which turn them into the performance of the ritual that they supposedly are (and thus they can fail). My argument against this position comes in different versions and is accordingly restated in this work in different forms. One is the postulate that neither bodily conduct nor language-in-use are inherently regular on behalf of some intrinsic quality of their own. In chapter eight, I will for example counter propositions that our bodies 'automatically' and subconsciously mirror other's conduct. Another, more general way of rejecting this idea is to follows Schatzki's (2002: 57–58) argument that order per se is not necessarily regularity, but is better described as a relational structure that contains positions and thus carries meaning—a conceptualization that conceives meaning not as sameness, but as similarity. In the same vein, my discussion of gestalt-thinking emphasized that a gestalt as a figural coherence arising from a background is not to be equated with a static pattern of said background itself; a notion I likewise tried to capture by arguing that an understanding is carried across, not in singular moments of praxis.

In sum, I hold that ritual theories in the wake of Goffman point to a fundamental dimension of social order: the situated production of affectivities and social positions by adherence to meaningful patterns of orchestrated conduct. However, I do not believe that this form of social order alone can suffice to explain *all* general forms and processes of sociality, especially since the model would be unduly static if rituals are conceived as inherently regular and representing the total order inherent in the whole situation. Arguably for this reason, ritual theorists—including Goffman— usually imply further sources or carriers of social order to be part of the picture, most notably strategic actors or other 'social animals.' This latter

> assumption, however, is one that needs to be avoided if it is a social rather than individual ontology of social order than one is aiming for. Therefore, I hold that important tropes such as co-presence, focused attention, and collectively felt emotions should be carefully uprooted and repotted into a theory of social practices. More specifically, it seems to me that ritual-type arguments are particularly helpful towards providing insight into the collective and situated determination of what Schatzki called practical intelligibility, that is, what makes sense to do (seems adequate, positive, normal, expectable, etc.) in a certain situation. I believe that the central provision that each performance of a ritual has the *effect* of a (successful) sharing of a mutual belief, emotion or—as Alexander (2004) formulates—a "shared understanding of intention and content" can be read as expressing just this idea, particularly because such sharing is not an antecedent, but comes to bear on participants in the midst of conduct. In contrast, however, I deem the ritual perspective unsuited to explain practical understanding (as opposed to practical intelligibility), i.e. by virtue of what a certain conduct is what it is; which is why, I believe, ritual theories tend to rely on either structuralism or individual knowledge in these matters.

10 Space and Spacing

Let me now carry these insights regarding the emotional drive and the positioning of the freeskiers over towards a phenopractice-based discussion of space. The main theme of this chapter is the suggestion that one of the two most important types of sites within which lifestyle sports' style can transpire are 'materialized' arenas in which the sporting practices are performed and spectated. The crucial difference between arenas and the other predominant type of sites—media-in-use—, I hold, lies not in visceral co-presence alone, but in the fact that situational order is carried to a substantial degree by spatiality. In other words, it is a site in which style *takes place*. As a close observation of the Penken Park has shown, space perforates bodies and bodies perforate space in a stable constellation carried by continuously unfolding practices of seeing and being seen. In my view, this situation would be inadequately captured by social theories of space that place monolithic bodies *in* planar space, rather than acknowledging their mutual production in concrete praxis (see e.g. Brümmer/Alkemeyer 2017). Critiques and alternatives to such a static and geometric conception of social space are legion (see Löw 2001 for an overview), and many have seconded Lefebvre's (2007: 75, 286) notion that the visual dimension often takes a dominating role in what he termed the social production of space (Edensor 2010). In this part, I will review some social theories of space that seem to align well with my empirical findings in order to carve out an account of spatiality as effected by the unfolding of social practices in sites—and as I have consistently done thus far, I will focus on the visual dimension.

Let me begin with the notion of space that one can draw from the interaction-ritual perspective. In the work of Goffman (especially 1963), space is essentially conceptualized as a field of territories, as divided into realms established by and bound to ritualized practices of marking and defending, as well as respecting or contesting, territories. Spatial order is therefore understood as a feature of what Goffman calls the interaction order, of situations established via interaction by virtue of the participants' perceptible adherence to common rules of conduct. In Goffman's terms: "the behaviour of an individual while in a situation is guided by social values or norms concerning involvement" (1963: 193) under the premise that "the situation being that entity in which the individual's regulation of involvement is perceptible" (1963: 196). Notably, this definition does not imply that individual behaviour itself is necessarily rule-governed, but only that for social situations to occur, behaviour must be *perceivably* regulated or rule-bound. Therefore, space is framed by Goffman as what Schatzki (2002: 145) terms a "bounded realm," a domain of activity whose content is perceivably defined and governed by certain rules or constraints. In other words, this view would imply that the different positions around the kicker line are defined by the things that a skier standing there should and must not do. At first sight, this seems to be a pretty accurate description: Depending on their position, spectators acquire certain roles according to which they must perform, and are granted, status. But if so, why does Schatzki (2002: 146) reject concepts that posit bounded realms or domains of action, and seeks to replace it with the notion of social sites? His reasons are relatively abstract and theoretical, but at the core they can be summarized as such: A bounded realm is defined by enablement and constraint; that is, if understood as Goffmanian territories, the positions around the kicker are what they are by virtue of the limitations and entitlements they put on the person standing there. Limitations and possibilities of action alone, however, do not suffice to explain action and thus the taking of positions—and indeed, Goffman presupposes the existence of actors with strategic interest (see the excursus above). But if so, then the spatial order as 'done' by the participants is first and foremost an effect or expression of said interests, and *not* in itself established and defined by the rules governing the enablement and constraint. What is more, as Wittgenstein showed, rules per se cannot precisely circumscribe all events or situations that would accord to the rule; and thus a set of rules (however detailed) can neither fully predetermine concrete conduct, nor does it contain a concise description or definition of how the participants will *use* the rules, i.e.: which spatial positions they will take. The territories established in an interaction order, it follows, can well be defined as realms of rule-use, but the order housed in the rules-in-use is neither inherent in the explicit rules, nor in the use itself (since one has named no category according to which a doing conforms to the rules or not). In sum, if one aims to grasp the spatial order in the park *as* a social order in itself rather than as an indeterminable effect of opposing and hidden interests of actors coalescing with rules-in-use, describing them as bounded realms or territories established by accordance to rules does not suffice. Instead, I suggest examining the interplay of position and perspective in more detail as an empirical basis for complementing the aspect of constraint—in my terms: prefiguration—with the aspect of orientation. In other words, the teleological endpoints of conduct which one might (mis-)take to be individual strategic interest will be framed as aspects of social practices rather than properties of individuals—and the phenopractical notion of style will be pivotal to anchor this framework.

In search of an alternative to defining space ex negative—as realm of constraint—Martina Löw (2001, 2008) has developed a theoretical perspective that is seeking to grasp the kind of "atmospheric potency of spaces" (2008: 27) that in my case permeates the funpark as a mechanism of inclusion and exclusion. In line with my suggestion that the emotional and symbolic field of gravity of the funpark is carried by a combination of its material objects or material structure with the doings of the freeskiers, she describes space as a dimension of the social brought about by the "relational ordering of living entities and social goods" (2008: 35; emphasis removed). More specifically, she distinguishes two processes through which space is established: First, "spacing" or the positioning of people and goods in spatial relations to each other; and second, "synthesis," connecting them into a framework through perception. In this vein, she links to Heidegger and suggests that places gain a potentiality which can induce feelings or "tune" people (Löw 2008: 44). Quoting philosopher Gernot Böhme (1995: 35), she further holds that the atmosphere of a place forms "the common reality of the perceiver and the perceived" (Löw 2008: 44) and adds that this shared reality is produced by participants through what she calls "staging work" (2008: 45). My findings from the Penken Park fit the notion that spatial inclusion and exclusion are organized through atmospheres arising from practices of 'staging' the kicker line quite well, and her argument that not positioning alone, but positioning in combination with situated ways of perceiving positional constellations constitute a social space, is an important one indeed. However, it also raises the fundamental question just how this perceiving space should be understood theoretically. From the perspective on visual perception developed thus far, Löw's take on "the perceptual activity of the constituting agent" (2008: 41) is inadequate, in that is ultimately based on what I called the volitionism and fragmentarism of a Husserlian account of "thing and space" that I criticized earlier.[31] Thus, I hold that the mutual co-constitution of physically creating and perceiving spatial relations among persons and things should not be understood as a flip-flopping process of cause and effect between

---

[31] Although Löw builds on Giddens theory of structuration as a mutual conditionality of action and structure, she clings on to a dualistic individualism that separates 'inside' conditions of action and 'outside' effects in the world, which is why she sees "a need to expand Giddens' theory" in order to account for "structuring phenomena that (…) are situated externally." (2008: 32 f.) Should one choose to read Giddens as a theorist of practices (and what else should he be?) one can only wonder: externally of what? Accordingly, I second Schroer (2006: 175) who attested that Löw develops a voluntaristic conception of space.

'physical' states and 'mental' interpretation, and the 'physical' reacting. Instead, I suggest that perception itself is an aspect of the socio-spatial arrangement, not just in that space is necessarily always a space-as-perceived-in-practice, but in that perceiving any spatial realm as a social realm means to take notice of it as a socially ordered *and observable* expanse. Few authors fail to note the importance of the distinction between public and private for characterizing the social character of spaces, but in my view, the criterion of observability this distinction entails should be considered as a situational quality whose validity and relevance is situationally and practically accomplished. In other words, I hold that a space like the funpark has a distinctly social dimension that goes beyond the 'basic sociality' of all social conduct, and which is rooted in the visibility of vision. In practice thought, the relative negligence of reciprocal forms of seeing are most clear in the otherwise very interesting and promising conceptualizations of space on the basis of visibility which centre on the topos of the landscape.

11 Landscape and Taskscape

Several authors (especially within human geography) have traced the phenomenological constitution of space along the lines laid by Merleau-Ponty and arrived at conceptions amiable to or explicitly embracing practice thought—most notably Ingold's (2000, 2007) works on dwelling, perception, and skill (Thrift 2007 developed a related position). Rooted in Merleau-Ponty's thought on the constitutive role of perspective and horizon (2000: 262–266), Ingold emphasizes how bodily moving through the environment practically constitutes spaces, and that our active, perceptual engagement in the world amounts to a form of dwelling in Heidegger's sense (2009, 2011). The idea that space, taken as a social dimension, arises as an effect of practices of moving about while and towards perceiving the physical world is central to a practice-based view of spatial formations, and it also implies what Ingold (1993, 2000) called the "temporalization" of lived space, the notion that social space is intertwined with the temporal patterns of the recurrent conduct that constitutes it as realms of dwelling. Schatzki (2006a, 2009, 2010b) followed this Heideggerian line of thought (but see Schatzki 2010b: 203–204 for his critique of Ingold) and formulated his more abstract and more universal conceptualization of social space and time as the "timespace" of activity.

While both Ingold and Schatzki predominantly focus their ideas on the relation between the individual observer and the surrounding world that is epitomized by discussions of gazing at landscapes (see also Büscher 2006; Cook/Edensor 2017; Wylie 2006), my concept of the arena locates the dyadic relation of vision and space that was already discussed by Lefebvre on a different level: interaction. Or to be precise: It treats spatiality as carried by co-oriented conduct of complementary practices, especially those of seeing and being seen. Therefore, the theoretical notions of landscape and arena differ in that the former can be constituted by the unfolding of a single practice (as e.g. in Edensor 2010), while the latter is carried in the reciprocity of at least two visual practices which complement and orient each other, in this case watching freestyle tricks and performing freestyle tricks. In my view, this notion does not only provide a specific framework to grasp the collaborative production of performed visibilities, but it also sheds light on the functional importance of the thick fabric that is woven by the visible orientations of several co-present practitioners—a visual fabric arguably not yet sufficiently discussed by the practice-minded accounts of space. The reason for this relative silence on reciprocal seeing lies arguably in the philosophical roots from which Schatzki and Ingold develop their notions of the landscape. Building on Heidegger, both stress the teleological character of social space, that is, they argue that space is essentially constituted by the 'path of action' or task currently given. However, Heidegger chose to study Being with regard to being human (or Dasein) and therefore focused on the individuals' forms of being, while "sociality is treated of *only* as a feature of individual life" (Schatzki 2007: 233; original emphasis). This seems particularly true of Heidegger's use of visual metaphors such as 'clearing' or 'unconcealment' and his focus on individual sight in order to obtain "a universal term for characterizing any access to entities or Being" (Heidegger 1962: 187; see also W. McNeill 1999; Protevi 1998). Consequentially, Schatzki and Ingold discuss seen space primarily as a dimension of a singular, often individually conducted practice of seeing (although both in principle acknowledge the co-constitution of social realms by several co-occurring activities, of course). In other words, their discussions focus on the type of seeing I described with regard to reading a face in the Krimml, but they have relatively few things to say about seeing in the funpark, about seeing others' seeing. Ingold (2000: 198–199), for example, employs the felicitous phrase "taskscape" to characterize a surround produced by a teleological orientation that is based on interactivity or reciprocally oriented conduct, and contrasts taskscapes with landscapes, that is, an environment perceived in unidirectional activity. But curiously, he then goes on to say that "the landscape seems to be what we *see* around us, whereas the taskscape is what we *hear*." (Ingold 2000: 199; original emphasis) This surprising correlation stems from his conviction that "to be seen, a thing need to do nothing itself," (Ingold 2000: 199)[32] while interactivity is always characterized by reciprocal reactions to the mutual assumption that one is being observed. Similarly, Schatzki (2010b: 100) defines landscapes as "a portion of the world around receding from the immediate setting of action that can be taken in—scrutinized, gazed at, examined, etc.—as an expanse," explicitly noting the constitutive importance of the line of sight (2010: 98). In his account, landscapes are distinguished from the immediate surroundings rendered by paths of action, and described as more distant "portions of the wider world" that are nevertheless relevant for action (Schatzki 2010b: 98). He sees their relevance for his theory in their ability to coordinate dispersed

---

[32] He later came to a different conclusion reading the instrumental or objectifying character of sight (Ingold 2000: 287), but he does not seem to have drawn conclusions from this for his notions taskscape and landscape.

activities, in that the timespaces of different concurring practices overlap in the mutual orientation to shared landscapes, thus emphasizing that they align activities without requiring activities to be oriented by one another (2010: 103).[33]

My observations in the Penken Park reveal that a schematic differentiation between gazing at landscapes as passive objects and a the task-oriented 'looking into' immediate paths of conduct is in danger of missing an important format of social vision: What takes place in the arena is not just a coordination of activities characterized by different ends and tasks in the sense of mutual 'giving way'—of avoiding hindering one another—and it is also not a collaboration driven by mutually shared ends or tasks. Instead, it is a collaboration happening across co-conducting several distinct activities that have quite different, at times oppositional immediate ends and tasks which create a tension that needs to be kept in balance: Spectating and performing depend on each other and are mutually oriented to the production of visible style, but they not necessarily complement one another. More specifically, performing and spectating overlap within the arena in that especially those who are 'just looking' need to do so visibly and in a certain way, since the other freeskiers do not accept just anyone's attendance and value only some, but not all forms of interest. A competent spectator in the arena thus needs to accomplish a somewhat paradoxical task: He must 'visibly blend in,' that is, he must care, but not care too much about the others, or rather he must care about them only in respect to a particular dimension: Style. The freestylers in the park reject both skiers that do not show sufficient interest in their performances, and those who are visibly inexperienced and are thus too obviously excited, or appear insecure in trying too hard to look cool. A skilful spectator, in contrast, will position himself and organize his watching in such a way that he clearly focuses on the Style of the tricks without interrupting the flow of conduct. Expressed in Heideggerian (1962: 138–139) terms, the spectators' involvement in the production of style (in my sense) necessitates both orientation (Ausrichtung) and 'distance' (Ent-fernung; literally de-distancing), i.e. the *overcoming* of (physical) distance in the activity of spectating itself (rather than by way of engaging in a different activity, e.g. walking closer). In everyday words: watching the tricks so closely that one is being touched by their beauty, even absorbed by it. In this way, the spatiality inherent in the activity of 'doing Style' itself (not the material spatiality of the funpark as a place) is accomplished, and thus the park becomes an arena, the site of the spectacle. In Heidegger's own words:

> "Dasein is essentially spatial in the way of dis-tance, dealings always proceed in a 'world-around' [Umwelt] that in each case is distant from it in a particular leeway [Spielraum—literally: playscape or room to play]." (Heidegger 1962: 141)

---

[33] He discusses directly reciprocal forms of interaction in shared spaces with regard to the notion of the ritual, seeking to defend that even within ritualistic exchange, activity is still fundamentally teleological (Schatzki 2010b: 130–153). He does not, however, turn to the complex contraction of visible teleologies I discuss here.

The term Spielraum, of course, is a most adequate description for what I call the arena; particularly because it carries a threefold connotation: First, it describes the opening up of the space in which the freestylers' playfulness can unfold; second, it expresses the staging of a play (in the sense of the German Schauspiel; literally 'watch-play'); and third, it points to the fact that the performers need sufficient leeway for their doings (since the German 'Spiel' can be used as a technical term in the same way than the English 'play,' i.e. describing clearance or slack). In my view, this last aspect is especially important to note if one tries to spell out a coherent theoretical account which takes situationally established order as the sole (or at least foremost) frame or plenum within which intelligibility and observability can transpire: This perspective implies that in a location such as the funpark, numerous practices are being conducted a) side-by-side and b) to some extent in an overlapping fashion in that they share certain elements—such as the material arrangements—but also understandings. However, such a view would run into trouble if it was to insist that only two 'extreme' forms of relatedness of practices are thinkable; i.e. that such practices either directly share elements or are entirely isolated: The overall order of the funpark, the intricate logistical 'machinery' organizing the staging of the spectacle via positions, paths, and lines of sight, would remain out of sight.

12 Commonality and Orchestration

I believe it is paramount to acknowledge that with the phenopractice-theoretical terminology laid out thus far, it is possible to circumscribe a level of local order which emanates not from one singular practice, but rather from several co-conducted practices in conjunction. The argument I have in mind is best captured by Schatzki's distinction between the *commonality* of elements and the *orchestration* of practices (1996: 186–190). In a case of commonality, "the same understanding, rule, or component of teleoaffectivity governs different people's behaviour" (1996: 186), whereas in orchestration, different practices composed of different elements prefigure conduct nonindependently, that is, through patterns of cross-relevance or co-dependence.[34] Without such a basic concept, I argue, many essential phenomena of social order or relation could not be grasped from a practice perspective, for example organizations or markets. Further, without such a concept, one would be forced to account for the apparent meta-organization of the most everyday social phenomena such as street traffic through what I consider problematic notions such as a general publicness of all social practices, as Schmidt and Volbers (2011a, 2011b) suggested (see the appendix for a discussion). Effectively, they declare all

---

[34] In Schatzki, understandings, rules, and teleoaffective structures are the only elements of practices. Since I additionally consider material objects and spatial arrangements as elements of practices, commonality is an even more pervasive phenomenon than in Schatzki's account.

social conduct to be publicly visible, attended to, and thus shared, because they seem to believe that alternatively, one would need to imply the complete isolation of all episodes of practical conduct from one another. But both of these extreme positions, it seems clear to me, can hardly be aligned with our empirical experiences in the social world.

I emphasize that from a phenopractical perspective orchestration must not mean a kind of 'invisible hand' ordering the social world, some invisible mechanism of coordination which nobody but the sociologist can see (fortunate as he is). In other words, in trying to capture any kind of meta-phenomenon or process, there is always the danger of reifying social orders or structures as self-evident, self-sufficient, and self-sustaining. For this reason, I have placed so much emphasis on observability, that is, the question if and how the relevance of alleged 'superstructures' manifests directly in concrete situations. In this vein, the example of the arena is meant to show how such orchestration can take place in a very concrete and locally bounded format: In this case, while some elements of practices are being shared, in that the park's visitors mutual orient towards the performance of style and share certain understandings, there is also orchestration taking place, in that the *different* practices conducted enable one another, most clearly in that spectating and performing presuppose one another. Indeed, the notion of the arena is meant to highlight just this: that the performances 'on stage' are being seen against the background of others' seeing. To use a felicitous phrase by Michael Lynch from a different, but related context: "It is as though the logical machinery needs to be screwed to the floor before its operation can be effective." (Lynch 2001: 146) Notably, I do not believe that this situation is adequately described by saying that the participants attend to or focus on one another, a situation that has garnered much debate in social theory, for example under the labels of intersubjectivity or double contingency. Is it not rather the case that spectators seek to ensure that the others *do not* attend to themselves or other spectators, but instead become fully attuned to the current performance? Let me try to clarify this specific constellation by expressing it using the terms "landscape" and "taskscape" as developed by Ingold (and similarly, Schatzki): One could say that the rider performing a trick requires a certain socially organized situational background in order to accomplish his art, a landscape of spectators, if you wish. After all, he must fully focus on the kicker and the trick he is trying to 'stick,' and cannot allow letting the explicit idea that he is being scrutinized by those he would like to impress occupy his mind— but nevertheless, he also requires the feeling of 'standing in the limelight' in order to be pushed to do his best, instead of giving in to the nagging fear of crashing. Therefore, he will not begin some form of direct interaction or communication with the attendees of the arena, for example by looking straight at them, or by looking around to ensure all eyes are on him; but he does need to feel the right atmosphere, the certainty that the machinery for producing the visibility of style is in place. The fellow riders and spectators, in other words, should not feature in his taskscape, in the immediate path of action he focuses on; but they should form the social landscape surrounding it, the wider realm adequately embedding the present teleological framework. In turn, the same could be said about skilfully spectating in the arena: The cool and experienced observer should not be unduly impressed by, or disproportionately engaged with, what he sees in the kicker line (unless he happens to witness a truly spectacular event); and he should not be unduly bothered with the others' noticing his presence and the impression he gives. Therefore, he, too, will look at the scenery in the way one looks at a landscape—enjoying the sight but keeping a distance—, while avoiding interacting directly with most of the riders, thus avoiding to pull them directly into his taskscape, for example by approaching them as if he would like to strike up a conversation. Both spectators and performers, in other words, will need to blend smoothly into the background of each other's conduct, and will avoid standing out of this background constellation of the arena—unless they seek to perform publicly visible Style.

Such a mutual orientation to a certain style, I argue, is one particularly important form of coordination of practices. In itself, it does neither imply that practitioners attend or orient directly to one another, nor that the commonalities between their conduct (such as the shared space) are the only or primordial source of their orderly relatedness. In the final part of this work, I will build on this notion of orientation to style to address the coordination and interrelation of spatially and temporally more dispersed practices, such as those forming the freeskiing subculture across the globe. At the root of the phenopractice theory attempt to capture these phenomena, however, lies the conviction that coordination via orientation must be in each instance be realized in situ, for example by trying to see style. This is not to say that commonality does not play an important role, for example via the global sharing of certain understandings of (freeskiing) style. Prior and in addition to such commonality, however, coordination must take place as well. Both the situated nature of moods or emotional drive, and the fine-tuned orchestration of the different practices taking place in the arena, however, do not only point to the fact that conduct must be mutually aligned and coordinated in some way. They also foreshadow another key topic which separates a Heideggerian account of practice theory in the wake of Schatzki from a number of other versions: The importance of action. Drive and coordination, I have emphasized, are background phenomena; they enable certain conduct to unfold. Jumping over an 8-meter kicker or speeding down the steep face of a mountain, however, cannot in their entirety be explained on the basis of routines, mutually established situational order, and emotional drive. Rather, they require a very specific, yet very pervasive format of conduct, namely being in action. Further, while I described both moods such as being driven and local set-ups like the arena as states lasting or enduring for certain episodes of time, action differs in that it exhibits a different temporal structure: it advances continuously towards a certain future. Therefore, the next chapter will look at action and its temporality in more detail, before the orientating function of style can be conceptualized more thoroughly on this basis.

Chapter 8
Time and Action—Flow

1 Introduction: On Riding

> "...'for the pleasure of being so purely played' by gravity and snow." (La Chapelle 1984: 159)

Why skiing? Why do so many people—not only freeskiers—dedicate considerable time and resources to this strange way of moving? Why do they even risk their life for it? From a sociological point of view, there are of course the benefits of belonging to a group, gaining status, and engaging in identity play. Indeed, skiers can prove their character, display their manhood, or mingle with peers. Yet, very similar social processes can be identified with regard to pretty much any other sport as well. If considered as a subculture of consumption or consumer tribe (Cova/Kozinets/Shankar 2007; Schouten/McAlexander 1995; Wheaton 2003), freeskiing shares a number of characteristics with many other subcultures or tribes; and in many ways, the ski industry is not different from other leisure goods industries. Still, everything that is to be said about the freeskiing community, the freeski industry, the freeski films and photographs and homepages and brands and contests needs to be understood in relation to the core or aim of it all: skiing itself. What does it mean to ski? What is so special about it? For me, the experience of skiing stems at the core from a specific mode of being: *riding*. In fact, the German term *Fahren* captures my sentiment even better, being much richer in connotations and conveying a more universal sense of *going*. On a general level, riding something—be it a horse, a car, or a wave—is special because it is not just a way of moving and thus a practice that provides continuously changing perceptions, such as views on the surroundings. Additionally and crucially, it is at the same time a practice that oscillates between aspects of active control and passive experience; it is a process into which one can intervene, but which cannot ever be thoroughly commanded at will. The joy of riding down steep slopes covered in deep powder,

I would argue, stems at least partly from this peculiar dialectic: Exposing oneself to sliding and thus to external, potentially harmful forces; but nevertheless being able to handle these forces just fair enough. Riding thus means to be passenger and helmsman at the same time: One is transported, one is at the receiving end of the experience of riding; yet at the same time one needs to steer the human-vehicle-hybrid in a suitable way. Mastering steering a ride always remains fragile conduct in need of foresighted nudges where small impulses can have large impacts.

The strange practice of riding things like freeride lines, waves, or cars is special because it is characterized by a complex, overlapping temporal structure: On the one hand, a rider is constantly, but with varying degrees of awareness and focus, engaged in monitoring and predicting where her body-vehicle will take her and what she needs to do to keep it on track. But on the other hand, she also needs to react to changing circumstances and adapt continuously. Both foresight and feedback play a key role—or rather something we would describe as such in hindsight—but neither can happen in isolation because both need to melt into the ongoing stream of the ride without much chance for reflection and reattempt. In order to ride, one above all needs to keep up the flow of riding, which is why learning to ride primarily happens *within* riding. Even first timers (on skis, bikes, or in cars) cannot receive much preparation, but need to learn through failing their first attempts; and many of us will remember the special moment of driving a car or (maybe) riding a bike for the first time: Suddenly we are snapped into having this thing going as it has us going with it. Furthermore, when riding goes wrong, it seldom does so abruptly, but usually in a series of small deviations or imbalances that all too quickly accumulate and escalate into a crash. On close inspection, one can observe that indeed throughout riding, the rider needs to correct such deviations continuously and perpetually, yet most of it will happen subconsciously with growing expertise—and of course, different forms of riding in different circumstances need varying levels of guiding interventions.

Compared to other forms of riding, freeriding on skis is particularly fragile, both because powder snow itself is fragile so that a minute movement can escalate into a huge avalanche, and because freeskiers continuously try to push themselves to the limit of what they are able to control athletically. Fundamentally, it is this *fragility* of freeskiing that makes it a fruitful topic of investigation from a phenopractice-based perspective: The routine of any freeskier almost always remains on the verge of breakdown; requiring constant focus, adaption, apprenticeship, and skilful recombination of a number of resources both social and material. Fragile practices are—I want to argue—more transparent with regard to the complex presuppositions that make them possible. Even more important, they bring to the fore how any doing of them really consists in constant *improvisation*, in ongoing, semi-confident getting-it-just-right-just-a-bit-longer over the course of what Garfinkel (2002: 92) called "each another next first time." To understand the practice of riding a ski, I will argue in this chapter, one needs to grasp a crucial dimension: the flow of conduct. Vice versa: Understanding the Flow of freeskiing (with a capital F to signal an emic category, like Style), can enhance our concept of temporality and the flow of conduct per se—a topic that seems of critical for a theoretical view that stresses the continuous unfolding of social order and the processual figuring out of meaning. Further, it is this fragility of conduct, and the sentiment of exposure that it stirs, which I described as fundamental to the 'magic' of being 'out there' in the rock-clad face of the Krimml. This sentiment, I want to suggest, is the empirical correlate of what Heidegger (1962) termed *thrownness* (Geworfen-sein), a fundamental modus of acting in a world always already preceding me (see Fell/Cumming 1990). Yet, riding down a mountain face means more than just being thrown into something alone. Naturally, being in the midst of riding also means going somewhere, or rather being towards something—and what is more, it is dominated by a sense of doing-this-just-here-and-just-now. For Heidegger, this threefold nature is the thrown-acting-projecting structure of being-in-the-world. Therefore, one could argue that riding practices are not really special at all; that they are instead only especially clear examples of the fragile, multimodal riding on the flow of the social unfolding that we perpetually engage in. The rider, one could say, is the *viator mundi* par excellence, the wayfarer that medieval thought had considered the quintessential modus of human existence for centuries until the Renaissance ideal of the ever-constructive homo faber took over (Ladner 1967). If so, what can be learned about practices of riding could provide insights about doing practices per se. It is in this hope in which I am writing this chapter.

2 Flow: The Temporal Order of Riding

Why do freeriders value big turns? In classic alpine skiing, after all, skiers are supposed to achieve turns that are as *small* and as swift as possible. As I will show, this difference is not just an arbitrary attempt to be different in some way. Instead, it is the result of a very different way of skiing which makes use of different material, terrain, and body techniques.[1] Yet at the core, this difference comes down to a difference in the flow of riding, and the way the skier needs to be in control of this flow, and thus of the riding as a whole. Many Alpine skiers, who prefer the classic 'dipsy-doodle' short-turn technique and consider the freeriders' Big Turns a disgrace, lambast that freeriders avoid short turns because they are not skilled and fit enough to master them. My personal account of riding, in contrast, suggest that it is just the other way around: What challenged me was trying to do longer turns without losing the control and balance the shorter terms offered. Indeed, as far as I could observe, every skilled freerider seemed perfectly capable of performing short turns in deep powder and would occasionally do so if the terrain made it necessary. Yet everyone also agreed that skiing wide, open, high-speed turns in

---

[1] "But if so, how did this different way of skiing come about?" one might ask. In Chap. 9, I will provide an answer. In one word: Alaska.

a controlled and smooth manner is much more challenging, because it does not entail the kind of immediate control or grip on the movement that short turns provide. In any event, skiing is a sport that is quite difficult to learn, and for those who have learned to master its basic ways, it remains a constant challenge. Why, then, is skiing so difficult, and why is it even more difficult to ski big turns in fresh powder? The challenge, I hold, is primarily a temporal one. In chapter four, I have argued with Merleau-Ponty that seeing is thoroughly embedded into practices, in that practical conduct is always inter alia realized through movement, which in turn must usually be informed by what I called seeing in flux. More specifically, what is crucial in the case of skiing is the interplay of epistemic and pragmatic vision, for example by visually recognizing landmarks for orientation while preparing smooth movements by also inspecting the surface of the snow in front of the rider. If one understands seeing in flux, as well as riding, as interwoven aspects or dimensions of one practice, however, one also needs to take notice of the temporal dimension of this process of interweaving or amalgamation. On close inspection, it becomes clear that two accomplishments overlap within each moment of riding: While I look forward in order to plan the beginning of the next turn some thirty meters or more away, I am skiing through the present turn and need to keep an eye on what is right in front of me. Speaking in the terms of vision science, visuomotor and epistemic perception, or pragmatic and conceptual seeing, need to happen side-by-side. Skiing, in other words, must happen as a continuous unfolding. On the other hand, however, skiers segment their riding into *turns* when they talk about it, plan it, and—I would say—also when they intend it. Skiing down the face presents itself to me as taking one turn *after* the other and thus coming down step by step and bit by bit. If an important part of the 'work' of making a turn consists in spotting the path of the turn and preparing the bodily ways of taking it, then that means that I am always engaged in (at least) 'making' *two* turns at the same time. The parallel accomplishments of visuomotor and epistemic perception (and the ways of moving they are bound to) are not organized in sequential blocks, but instead overlap, leaning onto each other—the layers of doing riding are not ordered like ||||| but more like /////. The difficulty of learning to ride would then stem from the fact that both accomplishments can hardly be separated and thus learned one after the other. Beginning skiers spend much time anxiously staring down the slopes they are supposed to master, looking for an easy way out of their predicament. Even worse, when they finally decide to get going, they make a single turn—and then stop again, looking for a way to continue. 'Actual' skiing, however, necessarily consists of smoothly interrelating turns. One could even say: Normal skiing happens only in between a turn that starts a ride and the one that stops it, as both of these differ quite a lot from normal turns—kinetically, physiognomically, and mentally. One essential necessity which the beginning skier struggles to learn, I hold, is to achieve visual anticipation as embedded into riding—the riding, so to speak, needs to include a certain future in a sensible way.

3 The Action-Present

If I say that on close observation, part of the making of one turn happens simultaneously with part of making the next, yet at the same time for the skier turns simply happen one after the other, the need arises to specify a notion of the present that can encompass this duality. Ontologically speaking, between observing the beginning of my next turn as an area of snow a few meters in front of me and the physical act of turning the tips of my skis into that turn, some time (maybe a second, maybe less) will pass. If I want to uphold the idea that practical action happens in the present, I will need to expand the timeframe which I call present to encompass both of these ontological instances. I thus arrive at a notion of the here and now that Donald Schön (1983: 62) called the *action-present*: "The zone of time in which action can still make a difference to the situation." The action-present, it needs to be noted, is a quality *of* the practice *for* the practitioner. To him or her, the unfolding of a stretch of praxis is only partially accessible, as there is much that cannot be done any longer, and much that cannot be done yet. As I ski, I need to focus on the here and now; pondering the stupid mistake I just made two turns ago does not help me, and neither does worrying about the difficult part of the line waiting for me down below. Saying that the present happening of riding is always oriented towards and partly filled up by the next step thus means that the action-present of riding is tilted toward and expands into the immediate ontological future: I need to find a smooth beginning of, a good entrance into the next turn now for that turn to succeed, yet I can still do something (but not everything) about the skiing my legs are doing just now. Bodily movement, as much as meaning, is always coming from something and proceeding towards something (as Heidegger emphasized) and it gains its character (or causes the difference it does cause by being somehow) by the way it interrelates those states. Theoretically, it can well be argued that every meaningful event perishes in the same instance in which it begins, reducing it to an infinitesimally small point in time that carries meaning or makes a difference only by way of its interrelatedness to other events (Luhmann 1995a). For the practitioner engaged in a practice, however, the phenomenal field of the practice necessarily offers an action-present, a window of present possibility of making some form of difference. As I have argued in chapter four, the phenomenological field of freeriding is predominantly a visual field in that I can see the mountain environment clear and sharp, while my experience of the body is somewhat diffuse and indirect. As a result of my physical movement, the action-present of the ride expands into the immediate ontological future a little further than in 'slower' practices, because I see what is coming at me and where I am going just now as I orient my bodily movement into that experientially present ontological future. Yet this visual presence is to a large degree different from the bodily presence of the skiing movements my body performs just now—a presence I do not see apart from the tips of my skis reaching into my visual field, but instead feel my body doing. Again, I stress that I characterized the rider as a helmsman-passenger of his body having only limited command of or access to the bodily movements already underway. Body parts, after all, are masses subject to inertia and dynamics of their own, and once I am halfway into swinging a strong punch, I cannot wilfully stop my fist immediately, but can only slow it down or alter its course. The action-present as the zone of time during which I can still make a difference has therefore already started to fade away as my muscle movements have just got underway—at least if one understands the "I" to be a conscious practitioner enwrapped in an unfolding praxis. For the same reason, the peculiar experience of 'seeing myself down the slope' emerges: As I focus on the slope ahead of me (both visually and consciously), I am *visually engaged* in the future aspect of the present, my legs are 'wrapping up' the passing, almost past aspects of it.

But why do I describe this particular arrangement as the *action*-present? Practice theories, after all, are frequently positioned as antagonists to sociological theories of action, particularly those based on Weber and Schutz (cf. Reckwitz 2002a). Having made a long and complex case for the notion of conduct and riding, why do I revert to speaking of action at this point? Because I believe that the term 'action' is still the best way to circumscribe a very specific, yet pervasive phenomenon: The fact that in many cases, practitioners have a clear sense of doing something for the sake of something; of being in the midst of carrying out a certain action. I am convinced that in order to understand the specific character of riding-in-flow, it is essential to not do away with the idea that the practitioner, by virtue of being immersed in the phenomenal field of the practice currently unfolding, is in the process of acting towards something. More specifically, in order to be able to accomplish a state of riding, the rider needs a sense of where he is going; and this sense must necessarily include the sentiment *that* he is not just on the go but going, and that he is going *somewhere* it makes sense to go just now. I stress that in contrast to most 'classic' theories of action, I do not believe that this fact alone in any sense determines or even necessitates a certain outcome or effect in terms of real-world events. My being in the state of skiing towards a rock and me ending up at the rock sometime later, in other words, are first and foremost to very distinct states that might surely relate in certain ways, but are neither identical nor necessarily causally related in any strict sense. The reason why I am interested in the state of being in action is because I hold that many orderly social situations cannot be adequately grasped if the specific nature and effects of this state or mode of being is neglected—but I also see no reason why one would need to consider orders, situations, or experiences as determined or governed by said state (not to speak of its content).

4 Action from a Phenopractice Perspective

The basic approach to action as implied by the kind of practice perspective I outlined thus far is quite straightforward: To be in action means to experience a mode of being-towards against a certain contextual background established by the unfolding of a practice; and experiences are effects, not antecedences, of practices. This way of framing action is of course related to the sentiment of exposure I described above, and Heidegger's notion of being-in-the-world to which I linked it. Most proponents of practice thought refrain from using or specifying a concept of action, although many of them arguably sketch out similar sentiments under different names. Among the theorists of practice, in contrast, Schatzki's position stands out in that especially in his later works, he discusses the concept of action at length (especially Schatzki 2010b). More specifically, his concept of action is rooted in a complex philosophical account of time that combines the phenomenological analyses of temporality by Bergson and Heidegger. In a nutshell, he argues that on the one hand, the world is unfolding in a continuous flow; and thus human activity unfolds within a separation-less continuum. But activity, on the other hand, necessarily takes place in the form of episodes, certain lengths of time. Importantly, for Schatzki an action is something that happens to or befalls the actor, rather than simply happening because of the actor. A key effect is that Schatzki (much like Schutz) draws a distinction between action as a completed accomplishment and activity as a happening or event.

> "The event of performing an action is (...) the event of performing the action that makes sense to the person (whom the event befalls) to perform. The action's making sense is how the actor is immersed in the event that befalls him." (Schatzki 2010b: 222 fn9)

Rephrased in phenopractical terms, what I called being in action is accordingly a certain experience that is (inter alia) characterized by the fact that something 'stands out' as making sense to do. I stress that I conceptualized the experience of a practitioner-in-conduct of a practice as an effect of the phenomenal field of the self-same practice. Therefore, experiencing performing an action is likewise an effect of the phenomenal field. This is not to say that performing an action is nothing but an experience, but I emphasize that being in action, or having a sense of action, requires a certain experience amiable to this state of things. This point is crucial for a phenopractical approach to action, because contrary to our everyday impression that action is an almost unconditional and entirely unproblematic mundane state of the world, I hold that very specific prerequisites must be met in order to enable us to experience being in action. The structure of social situations, as well as the format of many practices, in turn, above all reflects this fundamental necessity, long before things like bodily capabilities or social relations can come into view. This idea has two key consequences: On the one hand, I share with a number of authors who discuss the phenomenology of action (H. M. Collins/Kusch 1995; Gallagher 2007; Pacherie 2008; Smith 1992) the sentiment that being in action presupposes a certain kind of experience. Answers to the question of how we experience what we do while we do it, they argue, are not to be conflated into a phenomenology of the body (or the lived body) per se, because in addition to just being aware of our bodily movements, actions are special in that we are also aware of our will (or intention) to act in this way. In other words, while acknowledging the definitive role intentions have for action, they try to undertake phenomenological studies of something Husserl just presupposed: the intention to act. On the other hand, however, while they focus on the question how we experience success and control of action, I want to stress a different kind of experiential predisposition that being-in-action requires: Something needs to make sense for us to do. I hope that my prior account of seeing affordances, figuring out meaningful coherences, the inherent normativity of the phenomenal field, and the complex prerequisites of intelligibility and understanding has been able to convince my reader that the precondition that something must make sense to do is not as easily met as one might think—especially not if it has to occur in flux. More specifically, the upshot of the phenopractical conceptualization of meaning as occurring in figural coherences (or congregations of field elements), and of experience as tied to enduring episodes, is quite grave given that phenomena like the flow of conduct, but also physical movement happen concurrently, in continuous unfolding. Likewise, if one focuses the discussion of the prerequisites of things making sense for us to do to the visual dimension—and my subsequent example will hopefully demonstrate why this can be a fruitful line of inquiry—one finds a related predicament in the juxtaposition of epistemic and pragmatic seeing: while the former arguably produces the out-standing of gestalts as meaningful states, the latter is inherently tied to the concurring unfolding of bodily movement. At the heart of the vexed problem of what precisely it means to achieve a flow of conduct, I thus argue, lays the finding (or postulate) that intelligibility is a state that needs to be accomplished, or that, to speak with Schatzki, meaning transpires in a site, in a Heideggerian clearing. In Schatzki's philosophy of action, this sentiment translates into the juxtaposition of the continuous unfolding of lived life and objective time on the one, and episodic or segment-like activities on the other side (which he develops by contrasting Bergsonian flowing with Heideggerian happening). The specificities of the argument left aside, the upshot of his concept that is important for now is the idea that a) being in action happens in a succession of episodes—of doing one thing after the other—rather than in a segment-less perpetual stream of details (as for example Giddens 1984 assumes) and that b) this being in action provides the practitioner with a sense of temporality in that every doing is a "doing-from-toward," in that it implies one is 'coming from' somewhere as well as proceeding toward something (Schatzki 2010b: 195).

5 Flow in Minds and Markets

Notably, while Schatzki presents a general account of action per se, riding with flow arguably has some more distinctive features. Specifically, I see some resemblance with the prominent psychological concept of flow developed by Csikszentmihalyi (1990). He describes 'flow' as a mental state of deep immersion into an activity over a prolonged time in which the skilful actor is fully focused on the continually evolving task and thus 'forgets everything around him.' While the concept was later adapted to a very broad range of 'applications' such as group work or personality training, much of Csikszentmihalyi's original research was done with (action) sports participants, and therefore not surprisingly, the core concept shows a number of parallels to the flow in riding I described (see M. Csikszentmihalyi/I. S. Csikszentmihalyi 1988; M. Csikszentmihalyi/Nakamura 2002). Notably, while the concept is based on evolutionary psychology and thus builds on different, individualistic a-priories, it nevertheless emphasizes the role of the situation and the task at hand—in addition to topics like personality traits or types, which can be ignored here. The key aspects of the flow state which Csikszentmihalyi sketches out are: a clear goal of the activity, a high level of challenge that is matched by an equally high level of skill by the practitioner, and the flow of the activity itself, that is, a continuous stream of new challenges or tasks. From a phenopractice theory perspective, one would conclude that the immersion into or absorption by the task itself is not the key issue, while the smooth transition from one immediate challenge or goal—which in itself 'captures' the practitioner due to its immediacy—to the next is at the heart of the phenomenon. Here, it is important to note that Csikszentmihalyi emphasized how the state of flow occurs exclusively or at least primarily in highly structured and sequential activities, with the effect that the practitioner cannot and does not have to "decide" where to focus her attention next. Instead, in river rafting as much as in performing a surgery or in a well-designed computer game, this succession happens 'automatically,' and according to Csikszentmihalyi, this is the key reason why the practitioner achieves a kind of transcendental state (M. Csikszentmihalyi/I. S. Csikszentmihalyi 1988: 30–33). This position aligns quite well with a phenopractice perspective, especially in that what I called practical intelligibility—what makes sense for an actor to do—is not described as a mental decision, planning, or act of will, but rather as a smooth interweaving of situational affordance, directedness of the current conduct, and the engagement of the practitioner. Conclusively, I believe that in order for a state of flow to occur, it is less the skill level with regard to the core task per se, and even less the personality traits of the practitioner which are key (as the psychologists expectably argue), but rather her capability to 'bridge the gap' between the sequential episodes of being fully attentive to a single goal. Personality, transcendence, motivation, harmony, and the like, I believe, become observable only reflexively, as an outcome rather than an antecedent of achieving the situated flow of conduct.

Excursus: The Sociology of Flow

> In the sociological literature, the term 'flow' appears not too frequently but regularly, and in somewhat different ways. It is usually used to describe two different phenomena, and it is not by accident that my use of the term relates to both: First, flow is often related to the mobility and movement of goods, people, or information; often on a global or transnational scale

(e.g. Urry 2000, 2007). Second, at least since Bergson, the flow of time has been a prominent topic for phenomenologists and sociologists building on German life philosophy, especially Elias. By building on Schatzki's notion of timespaces, both dimensions will coalesce in my account of flow. More importantly, from considering all unfolding of human conduct as inherently situated and order as transpiring in sites, it follows that both temporal and spatial flow, in so far as they are qualities or dimensions of unfolding, need to be understood as occurring in, and as an effect of, sites as well. As far as I can see, this distinctly Heideggerian notion has thus been discussed only once in sociological theory: Karin Knorr Cetina has describes financial markets as "flow markets," "flow reality," or "flowworlds" (2003, 2004; Knorr Cetina/Preda 2007) Her argument is that for a trader 'hooked up' to the screen of a trading terminal, the market constitutes a site that is constantly in flux as new information, new deals, and new offers arrive concurrently.

"The new is 'presenced' as-things-happen and vanishes (...) as newer things come to pass. This sort of reality is inherently temporal, which is what I shall also indicate by 'flow'." (Knorr Cetina 2004: 43).

My discussion of flow shares these basic ideas, and much like the global foreign exchange market, the southern face of the Krimml is surely a site that requires coping. Most important for me, however, is an aspect that Knorr Cetina mentions almost in passing: She describes flows as "composed of streams and sub-streams of transactional episodes within which unfolds the multiplicity of events." (Knorr Cetina/Preda 2007: 132) The flow of the market, in other words, is not a natural consequence of the flow of world time, but it needs to be assembled from a large number of distinct episodes of events (the 1-on-1 transactions between traders which, in aggregate, form the whole of the market).[2] In contrast to the case at hand here, however, Knorr Cetina argues that the market's flow is a) produced by a technological "flow architecture"—the global data networks, trading screens, and communication or coordination systems such as the price 'ticker'—and b) brought about by a large number of market participants in conjunction. I take this as supporting my point that flow is not simply given, but must be systematically and artfully accomplished; but I also suggest that my case of a 'lone rider' provides an insightful contrast to her example of an high-tech, highly interactive, globally dispersed flow; and whether equivalents of the key phenomena I called orientation and crucial points could be found with regard to financial markets or flow architectures in general poses an interesting point of study.

---

[2] Knorr Cetina does not elaborate much on the issue of episodes and events, and sometimes she appears to presuppose the flow as simply given, e.g. when she writes about the market as a "timeworld" or argues that the market's "content itself is processual—a 'melt' of material that is continually in flux." (Knorr Cetina 2004: 40).

5 Flow in Minds and Markets

Vis-à-vis the established sociological theories of action, the notion that action unfolds almost 'automatically' and carries its own timespace might seem either naïve, or incredibly abstract, or both. Before substantiating it with an empirical example, however, let me briefly point out that its conceptual roots are actually quite close to those of other well-known accounts of action in sociology. The origin of this basic line of reasoning about action, it might be apparent, lies in Husserl's basic phenomenological argument about the temporality of consciousness and experience: that both past and future must constitute themselves in the 'thick present' of consciousness (as retentions and protentions), which is itself a perpetual stream of meaning (Husserl 1991b). Both past and future, so to speak, must take place somewhere, and this somewhere is the present. The reason why this idea matters for conceptualizing action is that action can best be understood or defined as related to a certain future state, something that is acted towards. Accordingly, this future should be inherent in the state or modus of action, however conceived. One of the most prominent sociological accounts of action—that by Alfred Schutz—builds on this precise idea:

> "Living in my acting-in-progress I am directed toward the state of affairs to be brought about by this acting." (Schutz 1945: 538)

In addition, however, an act, in that it has been brought about by action, seems not to be related to the future, but instead to the past; or rather: the presence of the past. For Schutz, getting a grasp on action as something that has been done likewise requires assessing this present past:

> I may, so to speak, step out of the ongoing flux and look by a reflective glance at the acts performed in previous processes of acting. (Schutz 1945: 538)

For now, the sole point I want to make is that in Schutz (as in Husserl), the meaning of all acting arises in the form of a certain past and future as constituted or taking place in the present. The very same assumption, however, grounds Heidegger's discussion of time and thus the account of action which Schatzki derives from it: Both past and future must take place in the present to be meaningful, and acting gains meaning in the form of certain pasts and futures that turn this instance of acting into what it is. The fundamental difference between Husserl and Heidegger—and in a similar manner between Schutz and Schatzki—is the locus in which the present takes place: In Husserl, it resides in consciousness, which determines our experience of being and acting; while in Heidegger, it takes place more literally, by opening a site of being in the world itself (see Dostal 1993 for the similarity of temporality in Husserl and Heidegger). Holding fast a past and laying down a future, accordingly, is either conceptualized as something happening amid the stream of consciousness or amid the unfolding of practices, the opening of sites—and in both cases, the theorist is confronted with the task of explaining how the lasting of the present moment (containing a past and future) can be understood in the face of, and in relation to, the ever-advancing stream of the world. It remains to be seen how exactly the answers are designed, and what arguments can be made pro and contra placing the present in consciousness or in a site, respectively. But the point I can hold fast for now is, that for a practitioner to experience being in action, a certain past and future must be present—and this, I argue, turns her present into an action-present. Further, the question of flow, one can conclude, is the question of how we manage to 'hop' from one action-present to the next without tripping and falling over. In order to get an idea how this might work in practice, let us take a short ride on skis one last time.

6 Taking a Turn in the Krimml

> "If you're skiing down, that's where you want to be looking. Not where you've been. Where you going. Look where you're going." (Kerig 2008a: 107)

Carving through the powder towards the rock near the bowl I want to drop into, I focus my attention on one turn after the other. I live from one turn to the next, each rising like the sun in the morning and then moving gradually towards its zenith while I bask in its bright light. I do not *do* turns but, as skiers aptly say, I *take* turns. I achieve them, it seems to me, bit by bit; in a process that one could liken to taking a sip from a full glass of water: stretching out the arm, grabbing, lifting it—routinized, yet careful not to spill anything—, slightly tilting the glass against the acceleration caused by being pulled towards the lips, the head moving towards the incoming glass, arm and torso almost embracing it, then slowing down both glass and mouth and making them meet in one fluent sweep. Although the turns I take in the Krimml are not physically there to be grabbed, I nevertheless have the impression that I indeed physically take them: From the moment I start to cut into them with the tip of my inward ski, they are a phenomenal entity that is clearly there. Sometimes, skiers will talk about having "missed" a turn when they accidently go too far and turn a few meters further on—a dangerous mistake in the backcountry where wide, symmetric turns have to fit neatly in between narrow rock openings. Again, the expression 'missing a turn' aptly describes the experience: You go past something that you should have gone through, like a car-driver missing an exit and intuitively turning his head for a brief moment to stare in disbelief at the 'thing' he just missed. Likewise, although the geographical spot where the turn 'lies' is just a patch of white within a homogenous snow surface, it briefly becomes a sort of definite object for me as a rider; it is now something I must get. I fixate the spot, orienting body and mind towards this goal. I aim at it, draw near, then lean into the turn. But while that is being done, how does the next turn become a turn to take? Through vision. Coming out of the last turn, I look for the next, and then—as far I can tell—I fixate a spot that seems to make sense for taking a turn there. Sometimes, I stare at such spots in the snow so attentively that even now, months or years later, I can vividly remember the details of the snow surface I was looking at—not necessarily spots where something important happened, just detailed images of a small strip of ice and slush on a particular slope that I still remember for some reason I do not know. Thus, speeding down the face in the Krimml, I 'grab' certain spots with my eyes, and I hold on to them while I approach so that they orient my ride while I orient to them. The different, overlapping aspects of feeling my skiing going just about well—the balance, the pressure under my skis, and so on—are thus taken care of by me with an eye on the upcoming turn, and it is into this 'soundscape', this ongoing concerto of things-going-good that I speak silently as I remind myself to take longer turns and more speed. "Play it less safe. Go for more." And how do I achieve taking such bigger, faster turns?—Or rather: how does it feel that I am doing this? By visually 'aiming' at turns that are further away, further down, thus sending myself on a steeper path down, gathering more speed. A last, nice long turn to the left, and I fly past the rock and into the bowl.

7   Seeing as Steering: Crucial Points

In chapter four, I have described seeing in flux during freeriding as a combination of 'scanning' the landscape in order to recognize landmarks, and inspecting the snow right in front of the rider as part of the preparation of movement through a form of embodied apprehension. There is, however, a crucial third function or aspect of seeing in flux I have omitted thus far: The seeing *directs* my ride. During riding the line, the rider is not only looking at landmarks and the snow, and no longer is he looking at the line he had figured out earlier, but he needs to see the line that he is *in*, he needs to see the trajectory extending down the slope. But in seeing himself down the slope, the rider's his gaze not only informs, but also directs his bodily movements: If one fixates a certain spot during riding, this is where the ride will go almost naturally, an effect carried by preconscious routines of pragmatic vision. In my view, the rider's visual steering technique matches a concept described by Arnold Gehlen in his anthropological writings on vision and action, the so-called *crucial points* or Knotenpunkte:

> "A movement becomes perfect and usable only after the working out of certain crucial points on which the whole movement depends and on which the consciousness of the movement concentrates. (…) The perfected movement focuses only on the 'crucial points' (Knotenpunkte) and allows the in-between phases to run their course automatically." (Gehlen 1988: 176 f.)

This notion captures quite well how the rider is "seeing himself down the mountain" by focusing on one turn after the other, on segment after segment of the line. What is more, the fact that the riding 'runs its course automatically' in between the different turns can be explained quite well by contemporary vision science, since this same steering effect of vision can also be observed within many other ways of moving. For example, when learning to cliff-dive, one is instructed: "When you jump off the cliff, fixate the spot in the water where you want to land, and your body will do the rest." From the perspective of neuroscience, this instruction has a correlate in our gaze orientation which is organized on the basis of so-called deictic perceptual-motor strategies, in that fixating or 'tracking' one (or very few) objects in the visual field provides 'anchor points' for coordinating further conduct (Ballard/Hayhoe/Pook/Rao 1997; Berthoz 2000: 181–185; Pylyshyn 2000). Thus, humans as well as animals fixate objects they try to grab or trajectories they follow, and then use this gaze fixation to control and fine-tune their own movements in regard to that object or path. Catching a ball while running, for example, happens through first, fixating the ball—which is itself accomplished via a complex coordination of movements of the head, the eyeballs, and the ocular lenses—, and second, observing, on the basis of that gaze fixation, the speed and direction of the ball as well as the moving and balancing of the body.[3] The visual routines underlying these capabilities make up an important part of what I earlier termed pragmatic vision: They are instances of 'vision for action' and thus inherently tied to a certain teleological end. At first sight, it might thus look like we have discovered a wonderfully simple and elegant way to explain how our consciousness stays in complete control of our bodily movements: After recognizing a landmark on the basis of our prior experience, we fixate it and then initiate our moving towards it. If we look closer, however, the situation is more complicated and provides less justification for celebrating the independence and power of consciousness in bringing about action. Crucially, the fact that anchor points are picked up and handled by pragmatic vision when they orient our movement implies that they do not themselves enter our conscious awareness, just like we are not aware of all the complex bodily processes underlying our movements per se. Instead, the pragmatic seeing of anchors or deictic points is to a large degree a matter of bottom-up seeing (see Chap. 3), that is, certain things stick out of the visual field and are almost inevitably attended to by the visual system (Pylyshyn 2000, 2001). In most situations, this is both sufficient and unproblematic: If we walk across a room, for example, it does not quite matter exactly which points our visual system uses to make sure we do not get lost on the way—in fact, we would probably get in trouble if we had to attend to such things all the time. In some situations, however, we do need to interfere into the preconscious workings of pragmatic visual routines, and 'steering by seeing' is a good example. Notably, neuroscientists emphasize that our consciousness does not actually directly interfere with pragmatic vision in such cases; but that consciously we can only 'manipulate' its proceeding indirectly. One example is the way we look for something in a room or on a list: we purposefully let our gaze wander across the room from one end to the other, or down the list, rather than simply looking *at* the room or at the list (Pylyshyn 2000, 2001). In this way, a series of visual fields is created which are pre-structured in such a way that our preconscious routines of pattern recognition can work best. Such fruitful cooperation, however, is not the only way in which conscious epistemic and preconscious pragmatic seeing can relate—they can also get in each

---

[3] Of course, the observation of the body's balance and movement does not happen via the visual alone, yet primarily so whenever possible.

other's way. A classic example is the case of small children learning to grasp an object: Until a certain age, they frequently fail to grasp it because that would necessitate them to fixate the object to direct their hand towards it; but instead they unwillingly focus on their own hand once it 'suddenly' appears in their field of vision, and thus the movement stops. Gehlen (1988: 174) called our ability to overcome such problems "the extraordinary human characteristic of a relieved[4] sense of sight which is no longer caught up in secondary stimuli" that distract the actor from the "smooth execution of efficient movements." *Not* to inadvertently steer pragmatic vision via the visual attention of epistemic vision, in other words, is a capability even more fundamental to successful skiing than being able to do so on purpose. Especially in learning new forms of riding such as riding a bike or motorcycle, or learning ice-skating or skiing, beginners sometimes crash into something without any apparent reason; strangely veering off and slamming into the one single tree standing next to the slope or street. The mechanism is a similar one: Suddenly realizing they might be about to lose course and crash, they preconsciously focus on those elements in the visual field that stick out and seem most dangerous. But while normally this is a good idea in order to figure out what obstacles to avoid (or prepare for impact in case it should occur), they inadvertently steer themselves right into it. Such difficulties clearly seem to be related to the unfamiliar way of moving and its distinct body-world mechanics, as well as the speed in which things happen on a bike or on skis as opposed to, say, walking. Managing or aligning pragmatic and epistemic vision is, in other words, not something that is simply given, but needs to be accomplished—and it is something that is crucial for establishing the flow of riding.

In my view, these observations indicate an important distinction: The crucial points Gehlen describes are something other than the neuroscientists' anchor points. While they *also* function as anchor points, they are neither only subconsciously established deictic pointers, nor only consciously focused spots, but an artful combination of both. In order to be perceived by us *as* functioning crucial points, the smooth performance of the movement must be successfully put underway. For this to happen, however, the overlapping functions of seeing must be coordinated and initiated somehow, and the prospect of taking a specific turn must be accessible to the rider in some way. Crucial points, in other words, are so important because they are *conscious* phenomena in that they—in Gehlen's (1988: 177) words—"represent the whole movement" to the practitioner, as well as orienting *subconscious* pragmatic processes. As I have shown in the second chapter, within formulating a line, descriptions of terrain features are treated as automatically implying riding through or over that feature—e.g., seeing a bowl open up in front of one and riding into a bowl becomes the same thing. Such a description seems perfectly natural to a freerider because it parallels the modus

---

[4]The translation of the German original of "befreit" as "relieved" in this sentence seems a bit unfortunate; "liberated" or "freed" might be regarded as more suitable (literal) alternatives.

of perception he inhabits during riding. In order to ride with what freeskiers call Flow, a freerider needs to be able to tackle the basic challenge of riding through deep powder swiftly and smoothly without paying too much attention to the very segment—such as a big turn or a short couloir—he has already begun riding. Only then he can spend the few seconds of that passage navigating to and preparing for the next section, so that segment after segment can melt into one another to form the smooth Flow of high-speed riding freeskiers long for. Described in phenopractice-theoretical terms, crucial points thus appear in and stand out of the phenomenal field of the practice, and as such they are conscious phenomena that can be followed up. In other words, they are similar to the normatively 'keyed' appearances of certain elements in the phenomenal field, for example the cornices in the Krimml that look inherently threatening, or a skier's sketchy riding that makes an uneasy sight for other freeskiers (see next chapter). Accordingly, crucial points are a kind of liminal object between conscious and unconscious bodily routines; they are the way in which motor intentionality appears in the visual field (or rather: the visual dimension of the phenomenal field) and thus couple epistemic and pragmatic vision. As such, they ultimately help to achieve linking conscious awareness of and attention to an epistemically discerned object on the one hand and preconscious routines of body motility on the other—a link that works in both directions to some extent: Sometimes, we can realize we are 'not going to make it' (and will e.g. crash into something) before it actually happens, but *after* our body has already undertook some emergency preparations of its own.

In so far as they are phenomena we consciously perceive, crucial points can be subjected to phenomenological analysis. In my view, Merleau-Ponty's (1964) description of abstract movement provides such an analysis, although he did not specifically refer to crucial points (Kojima 2002; Protevi 1998). In addition to concrete movements involving the direct manipulation of an object (such as grabbing it), he argued, we also routinely undertake movements which are not guided or oriented by physical structures, but by 'imaginative' orders, for example when we see an arrow and turn our head into the direction it signifies—that is, *away* from the arrow itself.

> "Abstract movement carves out from the interior of that thick world [monde plein] in which concrete movement took place a zone of reflection and subjectivity; it superimposes on physical space a virtual or human space." (Merleau-Ponty 1964: 128)

This notion, I believe, describes the phenomenological aspect of the phenomenon of crucial points quite well. When I am 'seeing myself down the slope' by establishing one crucial point after the other, a virtual path seems to emerge which guides me down the face once it is established. Notably, the argument is neither that the 'actual' perception of the environment is being replaced with an 'imagined' virtual space, and nor is Merleau-Ponty describing a subconscious process such as pragmatic vision. As Protevi (1998: 220–222) shows, Merleau-Ponty conceptualized the relation between our conscious visual experience and subconscious embodied sight (what I call pragmatic vision) not as Hegelian Aufhebung or sublation, but qualified it as a "Fundierung," a founding of the former in the latter; in that it does not eliminate or 'overwrite' this prior embodied apprehension, but rather expresses it in so far as it is rooted in it.[5] In Merleau-Ponty's Phenomenology of Perception, one finds an insightful account of how physical and 'virtual' space relate and coalesce in this process. In one example, he describes how we can see whether we can safely drive a car through a narrow gate *without* actually comparing the width of the car with the opening. In the hope that the reader can follow and understand this car-based example more intuitively on the basis of personal experience, I will use it rather than the less familiar freeriding for a short discussion. Merleau-Ponty concludes that in driving through the narrow gate:

> "The car [has] ceased to be [an] object with a size and a volume which is established by comparison with other objects. [It has] become [a] potentiality of volume, the demand for a certain amount of free space." (Merleau-Ponty 2002: 165; cf. Kojima 2002: 102)

The car is meaningful as a potentiality, and if the gate becomes visible during, and relevant for, the practice of driving it, an affordance emerges as the aspects of 'space-to-be-filled by the car' and 'space-to-be-filled in the gate' converge. As a result, within the flow of driving, a crucial point is formed: the spot we 'aim' at to get through the gate. More precisely, it seems to me that I experience this point not as a specific point in space (like a dot sprayed on the ground), but more like a 'sweet spot,' as they say in golf or tennis, as a position where I intend to be *with* the whole car-in-movement. This spot is somewhere in front of the gate, since I will be sure that everything fits slightly *before* the car front actually enters the gate. Likewise, well before the majority of the car's length, or what I experience to be its 'long end' has actually passed through, I will re-accelerate into the free space that is physically behind the gate, but now lying in front of me. It should be clear that the specific form of this impression that I gain as the driver (which is completely different from that of relaxed passengers) results from the specifics of my visual field (e.g. how well I can see the edges of the bonnet from my position) and the dimensions and movement 'patterns' of the car. Accordingly, I can only drive the car by orienting to crucial points because I am offered this 'window' onto the structured details of the unfolding situation while driving-and-looking, and therefore we might consider this experiential 'scape' as part of the driving which would not be (or be the same) without it. Let me try to use the details of this example to examine the relation to the concepts of action again: It is the crucial point towards and through which I drive; I approach it and in the process I try to understand whether I as the 'driver-car' (cf. Dant 2004) will fit into the gate's opening.

---

[5] In contrast to my account, Protevi (1998: 220) further suggests that the "seeing of sight itself" can be adequately grasped as a relation of Fundierung rather than Aufheben; so that consequently, insight is to be understood as based on a sedimentation of sight. From my perspective, this notion is flawed because it neglects the multimodality and multisensory nature of all conduct, which implies that attending to singular aspects of conduct (such as sight) is an act of sublation (Aufhebung) rather than a mere reversal or tracing-back of a Fundierung.

In doing this, I do not first 'stand back,' then scrutinize the size of the opening, then estimate and calculate whether it is wide enough, and then go ahead—at least in most cases. Instead, I am driving 'in regard to' or 'with an eye on' the crucial point which I can feel my journey gravitate towards. This crucial point is thus given only within the 'thickness' of the current situation of driving; it is not an objective, calculable ideal because it depends not only on the dimension of car and gate, but also my bodily position as induced by the seat and my ways of sitting, the car's shape as seen by me and my way of seeing, my familiarity with car and gate, the current light and weather conditions, my current mood and confidence, the grip of the tyres as experienced by me during the journey on the slippery road, and more.

8 The Organization of Practical Intelligibility

Now it should become apparent why I have chosen to discuss crucial points in a chapter on temporality and flow: It would indeed be misleading to suggest that our preconscious motor routines and the more complex workings of our body are completely out of our reach (as many praxeological accounts arguably do), since we are almost always able to manage our bodily ways in highly competent and quite versatile ways the visual curial points are just one powerful example of. But, I argue, one needs to pay close attention to the specific way in which this indirect-yet-reliable link between conscious awareness, motor intention, and body movement is established: The crucial point functions as a shared *point* of reference between what neuroscientists describe as separate neural systems or pathways, a point simultaneously being 'anchored' at a physical object in the environment, and as such it enables an effective two-way coordination. This situation, I argue, is very different in nature from the classic phenomenological conceptualization of meaning as a continuous *stream*. Sure enough, the riding itself unfolds continuously, just like neurons supposedly fire continuously as well; but only because the crucial point endures as a singular 'thing' for a short while, it can serve to orient the ride, my awareness, the motor-sensory routines, and so forth. It seems quite clear to me that each existence of a crucial point is episodic and binary in character: I spot it, move towards it, and pass it. I can hardly imagine that there can be more than one crucial point at a time (a question phenomenologists would need to answer), and I am very sure that it does not move along with me as I ride down the slope. For a limited, but considerable amount of time (both 'physical' and perceived), it lasts; and then it is suddenly gone. The continuous processing or 'streaming along with the world' of the various aspects of the amalgam of the unfolding riding, in other words, might well venture on on its own; but within a clearly discernible segment of time and space, various aspects of my riding happen with regard to or oriented towards this one crucial point—until it is replaced with the next. In my view, this situation is not adequately characterized as an endless

8 The Organization of Practical Intelligibility

becoming or uninterrupted stream, but as what Heidegger called the opening of a clearing, the establishment of a delimited temporal and spatial realm within which order of a certain kind can emerge—for example riding that goes well or not so well (something it can do only with regard to a certain something).

In sum, I argue that crucial points are one powerful example of how the unfolding of social practices enables and organizes ongoing conduct by opening up sensible paths of action: The turns into which the riding of the line becomes segmented are not simply a kind of 'mental map' that equips the rider with a sense of orientation or direction; but by invoking (and being in turn accomplished with the help of) crucial points which are 'alive in the practitioners world' in that they orient a number of embodied, visceral, and/or conscious processes or routines in a meaningful way. In my view, said crucial points are not adequately described as acts of consciousness, mental simulations, intentional states, or physical locations alone, because to some degree they are all of that. They are manifold in character because their very function is to mutually orient a number of disparate, inherently different, yet concurrent processes or systems in such a way that very different levels of relationality or dependency can be aligned: the physical movement of rider, equipment, and snow; the kinetic dynamics of the skiing muscles and body parts; the subconscious routines of pragmatic vision as a key means to inform the initiation and control of body motion; the conscious experience of riding-towards something in a sensible manner, which is in turn connected to emotional states that can hinder or foster the riding (confidence, joy, fear); and probably more. When I hold that phenopractices are responsible for the taking place of crucial points, I do so because the orderly alignment that I just described is only meaningful or orderly in this way by virtue of (or: if it is understood as) being aspects of the unfolding of said practice—as parts of doing freeriding, they make sense together. Where it not for the ordering that is the unfolding of the phenopractice, the spot in the snow would of course still be a spot in the snow slowly hardening into ice, and the ski would still be a material thing on which physical forces bear, and the visual routines enabling the rider to keep balance would still be active—but only as aspects of riding a line, they become co-dependent or co-relevant, mutually oriented, and aligned in a certain way. The orderly relations that their hanging-together entail, I believe, are not adequately or usefully described by saying that only if observed as such, they are co-dependent or orderly; or that (as systems) they only are related in that they are now 'considered' relevant to one another by one another. Instead, because they are amalgamated into an episode of riding into that very next turn, they become what they are: a skied-on slope, a floating ski, a successfully keeping the balance. The endpoint of the turn is thus pivotal for establishing the kind of orderliness that constitutes the conduct of riding by orienting it—and it does so not just because the skier consciously *intends* or plans to ride there, but also because he literally sees the spot, and because the physical movement taking place is the skiing of a curve by virtue of reaching-but-circumventing that spot, and because the visuomotor coordination is a coordination rather than a confusion with regard to that spot, and so forth. In this sense, I conclude, taking a turn at a crucial point functioning as the teleological endpoint can be aptly described as what Schatzki calls a place-path array that constitutes or opens up the site within which the action of skiing takes place.

> "Teleology underpins the spatiality—the place-path layouts—through which people live. A place is a place to perform some action, whereas a path is a way between places. Place-path arrays are a type of space fundamentally tied to—following from and determining—human activity." (Schatzki 2010b: 147)

In my reading, the turn as an 'object' thus defines what Schatzki calls the spatiality of a setting, the spatial order of "places and paths" that emerges from being organized in order to *do* something—such as walking home or taking a turn. In this way, the spatiality of action works together with the future-dimension of temporality, and is thus termed a teleological phenomenon by Schatzki (2006a, 2009, 2010b). For him, temporality and spatiality are properties of actions as independent units, not of the world in general, and thus constitute what he calls activity timespaces. For my present purposes it will not be necessary to track down the full implication of this reading of spatiality, timespaces, and its relation to what he calls objective space-time.[6] What is essential, however, is to stress the fact that it is *within* riding, by (physically and consciously) coming out of one turn towards entering into the next turn that it *makes sense* for a rider to ride towards that next spot down there to turn into the couloir and avoid that rock. What is more, it does not only make sense to the rider to take that particular turn, but as a teleological endpoint, it also makes sense *of* his current riding. The practical intelligibility of that turn-point—its making sense—is thus a key aspect of the riding as a whole; and the fact that it does stand out to the rider as something sensible to do, I reiterate, is not only something that happens because the rider has a certain knowledge, or freely chooses to apply a certain interpretation framework. It is, for example, also dependent on the simple necessity of being able to visually see the point which can serve as a teleological endpoint turning the riding into what it is: In bad weather it would not have made sense; and likewise it can also only make sense because the skier has a certain body posture and line of sight during seeing; and his ski pole will often serve as a kind of visual-kinetic aid in that he first points to the turning point with it and then later picks it into the snow at just about this point, a movement which also 'automatically' coordinates his torso and shoulder movement in a certain useful way (and thus skiing around a small rock might not make sense solemnly because you cannot pick your pole into it). Finally, I emphasize that crucial points are only one format in which practical intelligibility can transpire; and arguably one that lends itself particularly well to providing

---

[6] In short, a difference between his account and mine arises from the fact that for Schatzki, practices are only anchored by physical arrangements, while I consider material elements as part of practices. In consequence, I would have a different take on what Schatzki describes as the process in which "social life amalgamates activity timespace and objective timespace." (Schatzki 2009: 38).

an example, because it marvellously connects movement, seeing, and the cultural significance of the social thing that is the freeride line. Since the Style of a line to a considerable extend depends on the number and kind of turns a rider takes (since it is not actually freeriding if there are no Big Turns) as well as the way they are fitfully, harmoniously, and creatively placed into and among the physical features of the mountain face. Practical intelligibility, in other words, although being a phenomenon bearing on or happening towards the practitioner in conduct of the practice, can also become visible to others observing the conduct (cf. Mondada 2012)—or even those observing only its outcome, such as the track in the snow or a video of the ride. This consideration, however, also brings us back to the issue of flow; since above all, a freeride line has Style when the riding had Flow. Having emphasized that riding skis happens in episodes of orientation to crucial points, and thus allows seeing-as-steering as a crucial means to accomplish the astonishing mastery of skiing that freeriders exhibit, I will need to explain how my notion of flow can be aligned with the theoretical concept just laid out.

9 Stream and Flow

In order to convey a clear idea of my notion of flow, a clarification is due. I apply the term 'flow' in a different sense than philosophers of life in general, and Bergson, Giddens, and Schatzki in particular. In a nutshell, I insist that the flow of conduct is a situated accomplishment and thus a phenomenon that can be lost (in the sense of Garfinkel 2002, see next chapter). Additionally, I call the basal sequentiality of lived life, the continuous unfolding of the social and physical world, the *stream* of praxis.[7] In a way, I thus complicate already twisted matters a bit further, because I drive a wedge between two contested conceptualizations of the temporality of social practice: that either both the social world and momentary experience/activity flow (e.g. Giddens 1984); or that only the world flows while experience/activity is segmented into distinct episodes (Schatzki 2010b). Having argued that meaning is a figural constellation of enduring elements that lasts not infinitesimally short, I side with Schatzki, but add that within these episodes, the phenomenal experience of a flow of *conduct* (not of the world) must be procedurally accomplished for smooth activity to occur.[8] Therefore, I reformulate the term 'flow' in such a way that it covers only this newfound midground between the two positions, and call stream what Bergson, Giddens, and

---

[7] To be sure, my understanding of stream is not the same as Husserl's. But then it is also somewhat close in that what is a stream of experience in a distinct realm in his account is experience transpiring in the stream of concurrent praxis in mine.

[8] Strictly speaking, I do not deviate from Schatzki's Heideggerian account, in that I only specify a certain modus of what he calls timespace because I am concerned with the phenomenology of temporality rather than its general structure, as he is (Schatzki 2010b: 119).

Schatzki called flow. Why did I not simply leave things as they are, and introduce a new term? The reason is the same as in my use of the term style: I understand my discussion as a piece of theoretical ethnography (see Kalthoff/Hirschauer/Lindemann 2008), that is, I use a 'folk term,' a concept that is alive in my informants' world and employ it as a theoretical trope. Since I aim to develop a coherent and abstract theoretical account of (the visual dimension of) pheno practices, I subject this term to a theoretical discussion and use it in constellations that differ greatly from the freeskiers' talk and thought. Nevertheless, my use is grounded in my participant observation, in that in addition to theoretical-logical coherence, cultural adequacy[9] serves as a second, counter-balancing criterion against which I critically assess my use. In other words: I strive to instil the term with abstract meaning in such a way that it still expresses what the freeskiers call Flow, albeit in more complicated wording.

Let me briefly sketch out how and why my account of flow deviates from Schatzki's (2010) in that it discusses a specific modus of experiencing temporality (or what Schatzki calls activity timespace), instead of restricting myself to acknowledging the basal being on the move Heidegger (1962: 427) spoke about as characterizing happening (or Dasein). As I noted, Schatzki (2009, 2010b: 187–200) contrasts Bergsonian flowing with Heideggerian happening: In his terms, "performances (…) happen. Happening, however, differs from flowing." (2010b: 195) While human life per se can be described as a flow, as a continuous succession, he writes (2010b: 113) that performances, on the other hand, are always segmented, because they are directed towards, or attending to, specific things or objectives. In order to be performances of actions, he argues, they must exhibit a structure of 'coming from' (the motivation) and 'going towards' (the teleology or being for the sake of an end)—the tri-part temporality that Heidegger described.

> "The future is teleology and the past motivation. The present is acting itself. The temporality of activity is, thus, motivatedly acting teleologically." (Schatzki 2009: 38)

Accordingly, Schatzki frames what I described as being 'in the zone' of the action-present as a prerequisite to being able to act. And since, first, performing actions itself produces the experience of being on the move (or, in Heidegger [1962: 427], it is characterized by being on the move in that "Dasein stretches along"); and, second, in most moments of lived live some kind of action seems to be going on, one might be lead to think that both actions and the world unfold in a segment-less continuum (although this is not the case). In broad terms I agree with Schatzki in these matters, although I do not touch upon the topic of motivation in

---

[9] See the theoretical appendix for my use of the term adequacy and a phenopractice-minded discussion of the methodological principle of meaning adequacy.

the same way. What I add to this account, however, is the notion of flow as something to be achieved *across* the succession of actions, across the successive opening of different temporal-spatial sites. To be sure, flow as I conceptualize it differs fundamentally from the streaming of the world per se, since it only concerns a relatively small number of action-episodes, for example those which together comprise a freeride line. While I agree that all being in action necessitates a sense of past-present-future, I am also convinced that some conduct also requires a sense of flow. In other words: Flow needs to be made to happen. And flow can be lost. But if I consider it such a central phenomenon, why does it not feature in Schatzki's account? The deeper reason, I believe, is that Schatzki aims to unveil the structure of activity in general, and is thus interested in its phenomenology only insofar as it helps towards this end.

> "My account, however, neither presents activity *as* its performers experience it nor articulates the experience *of* that activity. Rather, it describes the structure of activity itself, which is *accessible* through the experience that is a feature of that activity." (Schatzki 2010b: 119; original emphasis)

Since Schatzki holds that (what he calls) practical intelligibility *structures* (what he calls) experiential acting, phenomenal experience is relevant to his description, but it is not an end in itself. For one, my account differs from this approach in that I am interested in the phenomenal experience of riding for the sake of itself. What is more, however, I suggest that the fragility of freeskiing demonstrates that my deeper inquiry into the phenomenology of flow is also necessary to provide a purely structural description in the sense of Schatzki, since intelligibly having or loosing flow does also structure activity in important ways. Most importantly, this is true of bodily movement, which in turn does not get much attention in Schatzki's works (which are centring on understandings, teleoaffectivity, and rules instead): Since, on the one hand, the body has inertia and bodily movement must carry an impulse; and since, on the other, both understandings and activity are constituted by bodily doing, the succession and overlapping of actions that Schatzki (2010b: 113–114) describes is not as unproblematic as he seems to assume. The experience of temporality, in other words, does not only influence our experienced activity because it equips it with a sense of past-present-future (turning it into a "doing-from-toward" [Schatzki 2010b: 195]); but also because *some* practices require the accomplishment of flow in order to be experienced and done *as* a performance of that very practice—the Flow of freeriding is a prime example.

I described how, in order to produce a flow of riding, a skier thus needs to achieve a continuous succession of spotting, assessing, and aiming which in turn is embedded into a corresponding stream of bodily movement in which eyeball movement, turning the head, and steering the skis have converged. Importantly, this seeing is 'in flux' because it happens *within* a continuous movement and is firmly intertwined with it, so that not only are both seeing and moving conflated in my conscious experience; but also, both are mutually interdependent parts of the coordinated repertoire of my body. This becomes especially evident whenever I am faced with a difficulty in seeing, because in this moment, I cannot continue riding as well. If I see a spot of snow that looks strange, something that I cannot readily evaluate, I hesitate 'mentally' as much as bodily and start to slow down my ride, sometimes to a complete stop. Stopping the flow of my ride is thus the immediate consequence of a stuttering in the flow of seeing and recognizing the terrain. Crucially, such moments of ambiguity of vision have a strong *emotional* effect: I feel doubtful, uneasy, and urged to find a better position and posture that offers a better sight. Such feelings illustrate the normative dimension of bodily perception that Merleau-Ponty emphasizes: "The felt rightness and wrongness of the different postures and positions" (Carman 2005: 70) which are a direct result of the continuous bodily work of securing reassuring and coherent perceptions. As I will try to show, the emotional dimension of phenopractices plays a key role in establishing the social order evident in freeskiing practices per se, because it is both private—intimately interwoven with the bodily actions of the practitioner and experienced immediately and forcefully—*and* public—observable in the rider's bodily posture and flow of movement, as well as an effect of commonly visible features of the environment. Therefore, Flow receives much attention from freeskiers and is regarded as *the* key measure of style in freeriding (not quite as much in freestyle); which does not mean that the dying down of the Flow of riding is something that does not frequently happen, or equates to crashing (and thus to ceasing to ski). Momentary slowing down can be very frequently observed in rides even at pro level, especially when riders approach cliff drops where assessing the quality of the landing zone is especially vital (in the truest sense of the word), yet at the same time especially difficult. I therefore argue that this typical practice of hesitating because of difficult vision is a *social* practice in that there exists a social norm within the subculture which proscribes stopping during the ride, and thus systematically hinders the riders from hesitating—and seeing—too much. In other words: the aesthetic norm of keeping a continuous flow throughout the run implements a specific style of perception by regulating the outwardly visible bodily behaviour. By trying to make their ride look a certain way (i.e. seamlessly flowing), the riders are made to see in a certain way (i.e. somewhat cursory and not over-cautious), which in turn makes them *feel* a certain way (i.e. confident). In sum, while the Flow of riding does not directly bear on the basic temporal or teleological structure of the episodes of acting, it is nevertheless a key feature of freeskiing action. In addition, the notion of flow just described might also help to make the abstract theorization of activity as carrying its own temporality (which ceases together with the activity) more readily transferable to empirical observations. Finally, since achieving flow can be a crucial necessity for achieving a certain conduct, or conducting it in a certain style, socially organizing or controlling for flow can be an important form of collective management of practical intelligibility more generally.

10 Look Where You're Going: The Collective Management of Action

In a chapter titled "No-fall Zone" in his autobiographical recollection[10] of producing a movie about freeriding and extreme skiing in the French Alps, long-time professional skier William A. Kerig (2008a) describes how a young freeskier is taught what is called the Anselme turn, a very short, pressed turn used by ski mountaineers on hard snow in extremely steep terrain. This skiing technique does not exhibit a stylish Flow in the freeskiers' eyes, because quite to the opposite, its function is to enable the skier to perform a full stop after every single turn in order to prevent falling as surely as possible. (The terrain where the turn is commonly used is called no-fall zone for a reason.) Still, since being a form of riding skis, the technique demands a specific flow of movement to connect turns smoothly—a flow that is 'on the edge,' that pushes the skier forward continuously but can be brought to a full stop at almost any instant. Trying to achieve very short turns in an unusual fashion, the young learner has trouble acquiring the new bodily technique: time and again he ends up twisting his skis, causing him to fall. Struggling to concentrate on the error, he is intently looking down onto his skis to prevent them from twisting. At this point, his teacher—the freeski 'legend' Glen Plake—steps in to instruct him:

> "If you're skiing down, that's where you want to be looking. Not where you've been. Where you going. Look where you're going." (Kerig 2008a: 107)

After this intervention, things work a bit better; but still, the young freeskier called Kye still struggles and nearly falls over. Plake steps in again.

> "Right there, Plake says. It's right there.
> Kye looks at him as if to say, Where?
> It's right in front of you, says Plake. You can do this.
> Kye tries again, and again.
> Just take it, says Plake. It's yours.
> And then something happens, a surprising suppleness. (…) The hill relents; gravity becomes a lubricant." (Kerig 2008a: 108 f.)

---

[10] One can, of course, question the methodological adequacy of the data I am using here (a book written to be enjoyed and sold), and one should. There are two points that have convinced me to include this excerpt nevertheless: First, to draw the conclusions I am drawing from it, one does not necessarily have to take this description to be a fully detailed and accurate transcription of 'naturally occurring data' (which would obviously still be an account anyways). In my view, one can as well take it as a document of how a very experienced skier retells the detail of learning extreme skiing to what he explicitly expects to be an audience of fellow experienced skiers (Kerig 2008b). In other words, the text describes what is interesting, realistic, and remarkable about seeing someone learning seeing for the sake of skiing in the eyes of experienced skiers—it is something that they care about. Second, in the movie itself, the scene described is briefly visible, although unfortunately the audio track has been replaced with music and the scene is cut several times (Kerig 2008b, 2009).

Kye, the learner, achieved what I called amalgamation, aligning (among other things) the details of body movements such as balance and edge pressure with his gaze in a suitable way—and suddenly, the different phases of the turn interlink to produce the flow of riding. Towards demonstrating that the organization of the visual order unfolding towards the practitioner can happen interactively within a situation in a quest to enable practical intelligibility, I want to emphasize that vision plays a central role in this excerpt in several ways: First, Kerig makes clear that "looking where you going" was elemental for the eventual accomplishment of the Anselme turns. Second, for the helpful intervention of Plake to be possible, it was crucial that Kye was *visibly* looking at the wrong spot. Third, as part of their instructive exchange, Kye is "giving a look" as a means of communication. Fourth, Plake was able to observe that Kye was nearly "there," that, although Kye himself did not realize it, most of the movements of his body already interlinked well. Fifth, Plake did not simply say "You can do this," but employed a notable expression instead: "It's right in front of you." He is, in other words, turning what *he* saw right in front of himself—that Kye should be able to do the Anselme turn because most of the necessary 'bits' are already visibly 'there' in his movement—into something that is right in front of Kye; into something Kye can "take" as it lies right in front of his eyes. Although the specific choice and use of words, one can conclude, did arguably make an important difference of the situation, what took place was to a large extent an instruction of seeing on the basis of different ways of seeing; an interactively and situatedly achieved reorganization of epistemic and pragmatic vision on the basis of the scenic intelligibility of Kye's ways of seeing and the "exhibitable analysability" (Garfinkel 2002: 192) of their unfortunate relation to his ways of moving. And far from being simply some kind of elaborate performance to establish mutual awareness and symbolic belonging (or the like), Kerig suggests that this reorganization was pivotal to 'provide' Kye with the skill of turning sensibly. Notably, I do not want to suggest that vision or the visual system 'really' is the 'body part' that accomplishes the majority of conduct that forms the practice of making an Anselme turn. To the contrary, an experienced skier can make a few normal turns with his eyes closed (or in dense fog), as long as he knows that he will not run into something. Once a skier 'has' the technique, in other words, vision is not inevitably necessary for the performance of the turn as a single entity—it is 'only' essential for linking several turns into a flowing movement; and thus it is essential to enable skiing as a form of riding in difficult conditions. But when trying to accomplish a single turn (especially if it is for the first time), the situation is quite different. Here, vision works as a crucial orienting point for the movement itself, in that gaze fixation as part of pragmatic vision provides the moving body with an essential reference point. But moreover, this anchoring vision has a second key function in that it serves as a sort of 'access point' to the practice—both for the practitioner and his observer (cf. Mondada 2012). Looking the right way seemed to orient the skier's conscious doing in an important way, allowing him to focus as he should and not get his thoughts or fears or misguiding aspirations in the way of the unfolding of his body's abilities.

The visibility of the details of Kye's movements, together with the visibility of Kye's gaze, enabled the experienced observer to see their misalignment: Not only was the student hindering his visual system to engage in the necessary pragmatic vision and provide the necessary proprioception to help adequate movements to form, but he was also misdirecting his visual attention and thus probably his attention per se, so that, instead of forming crucial points along which to unfold the movement, he was attending to something else—maybe worrying about what might happen, or trying to steer his limbs 'by force', by way of direct movement. Rather than motivating abstract movements, rather than beginning in the right way and then let his sensori-motor system assemble the full turn as he goes along, Kye probably tried to invoke what Merleau-Ponty called concrete movements such as turning the hip the right way. But as an isolated movement, the hip turning was misaligned, it was maybe not preceded by the preparatory swing of the arm and turn of the shoulder that produce centrifugal force and shift the skier's centre of gravity so that the weight of his upper body no longer pushed the hip down, preventing it from moving freely without causing him to lose balance. The dilemma of learning, this perspective implies, is that focusing his attention on the hip alone will keep the skier from aligning the other complementary bodily elements of the practice—but when he does not at all attend to such details of moving while moving, and instead focuses on nothing but abstract crucial points, the rider will likewise fail, since cannot adequately 'keep in check' what his body was doing in detail. In such a case, 'looking where he wants to go' and using the crucial point as the reference of his momentarily conduct, the only thing the skier realizes in retrospect is that he missed the crucial point, making a turn that was too big, as well as nearly losing his balance. In order to overcome certain mistakes, in other words, reflection is necessary—but reflection requires attention to detail to an extent that in turn inhibits accomplishing the flow of movement. In contrast, a teacher looking 'from the outside' is able to focus his attention on the visible details of the movement and, by way of epistemic vision, compare it to how it should look. As a ski instructor observing students, for example, I could focus precisely on how somebody moved her inner ski during carved turns and ignore most other details for the time being—a recipe for disaster if the students were trying to do this themselves while skiing. But by cooperating to accomplish a kind of 'distributed visual cognition,' learner and instructor can 'get the learner's skiing going' in a way neither could do individually.

I presented the above exchange between Kye and Plake—instead of related, but less clear examples from my own fieldwork—because it makes the significant aspect that I want to add to the existing literature very clear. As I discussed, ethnomethodologists like Goodwin (2000b) have conducted many detailed studies showing how the visibility of vision is used by instructors or speakers to direct attention *towards* something. In the case of learning the Anselme turn, one can observe the opposite: A teacher directing the student's attention *away* from a concrete point of interest, because this point is an isolated bodily move that must be *out* of focus, and instead in what I called para-attention, to enable the pre- or subconscious routines of moving to unfold. It follows that a) the organization of the visual field is a crucial prerequisite to achieve the flow of riding; b) this organization of the visual field *of* the individual practitioner is an interactive accomplishment *by* those people present, and thus achieved situatedly, not by individual will per se; and c) said organization is not a one-way street in that specific aspects are pointed out, but a form of management that also includes purposeful hindering certain visual-bodily routines to 'kick in.' The reason that gaze orientation is crucial for achieving routine in amalgamation in this way stems from the fact that visual attention and conscious attention are tightly coupled—as our dual use of the verb 'to focus' reflects (Cavanagh 2011; Coulter/Parsons 1990; Pylyshyn 2001). The visibility of attention this coupling implies is the bedrock of what arguably ranks among the most basic, rapid, and powerful means or dimensions of orchestrating situational social order: Humans are extraordinarily good at estimating if and what somebody is focusing visually. We can immediately see, for example, whether somebody is looking us straight into the eyes, whether she is fixating at a spot just a few inches away from our head, or whether she is looking into our direction, but 'through us,' not contracting her lens to bring our contours into foveal vision (Jacob/Jeannerod 2003: 242–246). As my examination of the freeskier's interaction in a funpark has revealed, these basic visual routines provide the key means by which complex visual-spatial-social orders can be erected, order which simultaneously fulfil a number of essential functions such as providing social roles or positions, enabling a collective management of emotions and teleoaffective ends, producing feelings of we-ness or community, fostering visual learning, and honing a sense for style. Yet it would be entirely misleading to consider vision solemnly as a means employed towards 'higher' ends, such as social roles or identities. It is not only that within a situation (or an interaction ritual, if you wish) spatial and social position are one—because they implicate seeing and being seeing. But instead, Kye's troubles, and Plake's help in solving them, point to a core argument of this work: Because the visual dimension of lived life comprises epistemic and pragmatic seeing—two very different, immensely important, and co-dependent-but-not-equal ways of seeing that are the backbone of so many essential 'building blocks' of human conduct such as moving, interacting, recognizing, or learning (at least for those of us who can see)—their alignment, observation, coordination, disentangling, prefiguration-in-isolation-from-another, and realignment is a pivotal prerequisite for achieving the flow of human life. My thesis is that, just like we can individually be very versed at using language but cannot quite learn (let alone evolve) language on our own, we are relatively helpless when we try to acquire skills of seeing on our own, because it requires a peculiar form of switching back and forth between attending-to-while-relying-on pragmatic and epistemic vision. Before small children start to speak their first words, they have already spent at least a year developing the most basal ways of practical understanding and use them to interfere into the world around them: moving towards or grasping; attending to something;

recognizing objects or 'tools'; understanding basic emotions, social relations, and action intentions; observing and evoking other's attention; and so forth—and in all of these human essentials, vision is of foremost importance (Jacob/Jeannerod 2003). Notably, the two visual systems do not only carry these abilities, but they are equally indispensable for 'acquiring' them, something that happens mostly pre-consciously and without the interference of language or reflection—e.g., less than an hour after their birth, babies spontaneously mimic basic movement patterns of their parents (such as protruding the tongue; Jacob/Jeannerod 2003: 234). Much like the basic routines of visual cognition 'impose' seeing a gestalt figure in a certain background 'on us' in that looking-at and recognizing are 'hard-wired' or pre-consciously coupled to some (!) extent, seeing and performing certain movements are equally strictly coupled. And just like epistemic visual cognition can happen at various levels (from the most basic synthesis of contrasting receptions in single cells to relatively specialized, slow, and arguably 'avoidable' routines such as seeing the protruding of the Necker Cube), pragmatic and motor vision have different levels as well, some spontaneous and almost inevitable (such as ducking down when others do, or involuntarily copying yawning), and others more complex and indirect (see chapter eight). Because these ways of seeing are so 'deep' in the body, because they are so basal and relatively independent and isolated from free will, reflection, and language use, authors in philosophy (Searle 1983), psychology (Giacomo Rizzolatti/Sinigaglia/F. Anderson 2008; Stamenov/Gallese 2002), and sociology (Lizardo/Strand 2010) have argued that they are the well from which most social order springs forth, that they their abilities, independence, and self-sufficiency explains our individual abilities, independence, and self-sufficiency. But here comes the decisive point: I believe that in doing so, they tend to overcompensate for prior over-intellectualised accounts of perception and action by instead turning practitioners into acting minds and walking sensori-motor systems. For this reason, my phenopractice argument works exactly the other way around: *Because* these visual systems or routines deep 'in' us do not themselves orient to or automatically align with higher-order (long-term, abstract) ends or projects, they need to be skilfully managed, nudging them into one direction and barring them from running off into another; and *because* they remain profoundly out of reach of our direct conscious attention and wilful control (as Husserl would have it), this management of vision needs to happen *in the situation* rather than in us. Here, I believe, one finds the deeper reason why social order and practical conduct in almost all moments of life is in part organized via screens and curtains, gaze orientations and sunglasses, stages and confrontations, perspectives and positions, frames and colours, rules of privacy and the immorality of exposure, signposts and spotlights, shamefully downcast eyes and stern looks, performative gestures and subtle body postures—and above all: visible styles of doing this or that.

11 A Schutzian Account of Flow

To conclude: Freeriding is a skilful activity, happens in the action-present, and requires the situation to be (visually) organized in such a way that it makes sense to the practitioner to perform certain actions. If this is the description of freeskiing that phenopractice theory produces, then how does it differ from the established theories of action available in sociology, apart from its emphasis of the visual order of situations? More specifically, I already suggested that Alfred Schutz' theory of action[11] builds on a concept of temporality that shares many important features with Schatzki's account. But then what is all the fuss about—why not stick with the well-established theories? Or, twisting the question around: How can I claim that the account of phenopractices I have given so far bears parallels to Schutz? After all, I rejected some of Husserl's core postulates concerning kinaesthesia and bodily movement, and instead drew heavily on Merleau-Ponty and Garfinkel. But then, as I will show, Schutz deviates from Husserl in just those aspects I criticized; and some have suggested that Schutz' theory can and should be enhanced by introducing insights from Merleau-Ponty (Bongaerts 2003, 2007, 2008), while others have shown that ethnomethodology can well be read en pair with Schutzian life-world sociology (Eberle 1984, 2008). So, where exactly do I draw the line? For the remainder of this chapter, I will attend to these significant questions. In my view, formulating a concise notion of action and activity is one of the most pressing issues for contemporary practice theory, although less so because the interests and arguments of those using the theory are necessarily directly addressing actions—in fact, I think most of their stipulating insights stem from the fact that they do not. Instead, I believe that an answer to the question of action is essential for clarifying and defending the stance of the practice perspective vis a vis individualist ontologies, especially those inherent in theories of action or knowledge as well as—in my view—praxeology. A good way to do so, I hope, is to contrast and compare the notions of action in Schutz and Schatzki. Not only do I consider the two to be the most precise, elaborate, and versatile accounts of action available; but they also bear several important resemblances. Finally,

---

[11] I use the term "sociology of action" or "sociology of the lifeworld" instead of the denomination that is more common in the Anglo-Saxon discourse, namely "phenomenological sociology," to make clear that building on phenomenology does not automatically imply or define its specific position. Practice theory, in particular, is of course rooted in phenomenological thought as well, albeit that of a different 'generation' of phenomenologists. Instead, the term "sociology of action" expresses that it is the particular (Weberian) concept of action which forms the theoretical hallmark of this approach, is closer to the original German term Handlungssoziologie, and avoids confusing it with the American tradition of phenomenological sociology that differs in some respects. What this wording does not express, unfortunately, is that action is at the same time a term featuring prominently in some strands of practice theory as well—especially in Schatzki's—, but is used in a somewhat different sense.

while such a comparative discussion might seem a bit alien to a chapter on flow, I hold that it is de facto necessary to consider the two in precisely this context for two reasons: First, a specific philosophical notion of temporality is at the heart of both positions; and second, their most crucial differences arise specifically with regard to the question how new actions are initiated or chosen. These differences cannot, I must stress, be found in the crude and misleading straw man-versions of the two positions into which they are regrettably sometimes made: Neither does Schutz suggest that all conduct abides to a meticulous, consciously preconceived mental plan, nor does Schatzki propose some sort of thinly-veiled behaviourism. Instead, both agree that actions are characterized by specific teleological ends, but that nevertheless, their precise outcome cannot be fully fixed in advanced, and that reasons cited for an action are ex-post rationalizations.

12 Projecting and Grasping Actions

Let me begin by rephrasing the challenge of achieving Flow in freeriding with the help of seeing-in-flux in the terms of Schutzian theory. To learn visual anticipation and thus better skiing, one needs to establish some form of "feedback-flow," that is, one needs to be able to draw the connection between the quality of the surface one is just skiing on and what one just saw in this surface a moment ago. In other words: In order to ski smoothly, one needs to train skills for anticipatory observation—but to do so, one needs to engage in reflexive observation. Metaphorically speaking, the eager student of skiing needs to ask himself while riding: "Do the anticipations that I just had match the experience I am having now, and what does that imply for my current anticipation as opposed to the anticipation I should be having just now?" Framed in classical phenomenological terms, 'reading' the snow in front of the skier requires a continuous readjustment of the current protention according to the experienced difference between the retention of a foregone protention and the current perception. It should be obvious that this process is too complex and needs to happen too fast to be reflected consciously in its entirety. Nevertheless, some conscious reflection and interference is indispensable for mastering, even surviving, the challenges and dangers that skiing exposes the rider to, as a day out in the Krimml demonstrates: For example, as Tom and I made our way across the ridge before reaching the drop-in, I saw patches of polished, hard snow the stiff wind had created during the night before, and I reminded myself to look out for the chutes further down into which the soft, deep snow had been blown, since on their edges the snow quality will abruptly change from hard to soft. It is not only that, without being able to spot such subtle tell-tales, learning to ski well is much more difficult, if not impossible. Additionally, I also believe that the continuing fascination and challenge that freeriding offers to even the most adept skiers stems in part from the fact that this process of adaption to and learning about the mountain and the snow never comes to an end: Every ride is unique, and every time a rider drops into a new line, he will need to feel anew 'how things are,' assessing the possible and trying to adapt accordingly. And already a few meters further down, in the shadow, where the wind was not so strong, where the slope is less steep, where the exposition is more southwardly, where the small avalanche went off last year, things will be different again. The specific challenge of riding, to conclude, consist in integrating the explicit 'knowledge' (in the sense of rules, statements, sayings, etc.) about, and experiences gained from, freeskiing and the mountain wilderness into the current riding; and further, in that looking ahead to the immediate future and reflecting on the current now are two different processes that need to be aligned so that learning and coping can occur. How to combine so many different necessities, how to align these separate processes? The answer, according to Schutz: by assigning different matters different levels of relevance in consciousness on the basis of our subjective stock of knowledge. Further, the initiation of action and the way in which one action makes sense to perform over another is primarily conceptualized as consciously choosing among paths of action (see especially Schutz 1962, 1972). Does that imply that each turn I take comes to be seen as a decision I make, one alternative chosen instead of several others considered before? Quite clearly, this notion would stand in contrast to much of what I have said so far about riding and being thrown into riding; and it also seems to suggest an intellectualization of what is an inherently bodily process. But while Reckwitz, for example, considers Schutz' theory the "prototype of a mentalist 'subjectivism'" (2002a: 247), it must also be noted that at least in his later texts, Schutz does leave quite some room for motor automatisms and situationally invoked, so-called "passive awareness" (1945). In other words, a more detailed discussion of Schutz' account of action is due, in part because one needs to ask whether we should consider the taking of a single turn as a preconceived course of action in Schutz' sense—and if not, how else one can account for taking a turn within the framework of his theory. But to begin, I need to sketch out the reasons why Schutz describes choosing between different courses of actions as "rehearsing my future in my imagination" (1945: 539) prior to the actual activity.

At the root of this conception lies Schutz' adaption of Husserl's distinction between open and problematic alternatives, taken from the latter's elaboration of how predicative judgements arise from the pre-predicative sphere. According to Schutz (1962: 79–82)—and whether Husserl meant things in exactly this way is not important here—Husserl held that our attending to an object in what he considered the 'outer world' carries a number of protentions or expectations—the horizon of potentiality that every meaningful event implicitly contains. Upon sequentially 'exploring' the object (e.g. the saccades scanning a rectangle), they will usually be fulfilled bit by bit, each time also crossing out alternatives (e.g. realizing that it is not a pentagram). In some cases, however, things will not go as smooth, and doubt will arise: the identity becomes questionable in some aspect, and the subject is not entirely sure which one of two options is true (e.g. one is hesitating whether it is an even-sided square or only a rectangle). According to Husserl (in Schutz), something peculiar happens: The subject will *oscillate* between the two options, intending first to the one, then to the other. Strictly said: The subject is not actually in doubt; but rather sure about one thing for a very

12 Projecting and Grasping Actions

short moment, and then sure about another right afterwards, before it flips back to the first option.[12] The reason for this notion is the strict framework of intentionality that Husserl relies on: each intentional 'ray of awareness' must be directed towards exactly one object, its content. Let me, before I continue with the explanation, briefly point out that this concept is arguably an effect of what I called the particularistic notion of meaning that Husserl holds, in that he (as well as Schutz and Luhmann) ties meaning to identity or strict regularity. This notion stands in contrast to gestalt thinking, and especially Gurwitsch (1970, 1979: 249–250) criticized Husserl for treating a synthesis of several elements—such as a synthesis of several acts into one—as nothing but the sum of the elements, rather an inherently ordered entity of its own right, a gestalt (see Arvidson 2006: 209–212). On similar grounds, Schatzki invokes Wittgenstein—who in turn also built on gestalt thinking in this point—to argue that intentionality is not regularity (2010a: 13), and more generally conceptualizes meaning on the basis of similarity rather than identity (2002: 57–59). The upshot of this will be, of course, a different take on the problem of choice. In any event, Husserl develops the idea of doubt as inevitably escalating into an oscillation between antagonistic possibilities and concludes that such situations provide us with what he calls problematic alternatives, clearly demarcated options to choose between. Importantly, he contrasts such problematic alternatives to the so-called open alternatives we are usually confronted with: the normal horizons of possibilities given in any sequence of acts. Far from providing definitive options, open alternatives are an open frame of possibilities within which no option bears particular weight and all are "equally possible" (Schutz 1962: 81). Crucially, Schutz introduces this Husserlian distinction into his discussion of decision-making, which is based on Bergson's treatment of choice and time as a flow (Schutz 1962, 1972). For Schutz (1967: 70), the key issue is "the tension between living experience within the [Bergsonian] flow of duration and reflection on the experience thus lived through, in other words, the tension between life and thought." Projecting and conduction actions, in other words,

---

[12] It should be noted that later on, in the Structures of the Life-World, Schutz denies that doubtful situations invoke an oscillation like Husserl suggested (Schutz/T. Luckmann 1973: 208). Instead, he argues that in such cases, "particularized subthematizations (…) are in the foreground of attentiveness in 'comparisons' between the main theme and the two interpretational schemata." (Schutz/T. Luckmann 1973: 208) This description is of course interesting in its similarity to the background/foreground-concept I have used—and indeed, it stems from Schutz' adaption of Gurwitsch work "The Field of Consciousness" (1964) which led him to talk about the "thematic field" in the Structures (Schutz/T. Luckmann 1973: 188, 195). However, his use of the field-notion still follows the basic logic of the sequentiality of conscious acts, in that he contrast the thematic field with "the horizon of the actually present flow of experience"—and notably, it is in this flowing horizon rather than in the background of the field where he positions "the consciousness of the motor process of walking." (Schutz/T. Luckmann 1973: 188) But even if conceptualized as such, I believe that oscillation will nevertheless occur if a) several elements appear in this flowing horizon that seem to demand attention and foregrounding in the field, or b) the "main theme" of the thematic field itself is drawn into question.

happen in two different 'time zones,' and the specific problem of choosing among projects of actions arises from this duality.

In order to clarify this problem, Schutz (1962: 83–84) introduces a notable distinction between two different modes of choosing: Making a decision between "*objects within reach*" and ready to be grasped on the one hand; and *projecting future courses of action* on the other. In the first case, "man finds himself placed among more or less well-defined problematic alternatives," namely, the objects and their enduring qualities. In this case, "a unified field of true alternatives" that both "coexist in simultaneity in outer time" serves as the basis of the actor's choosing (1962: 83–84). For Schutz, the fact that both objects exist independently of the decider in objective time is pivotal, because it makes the situation relatively unproblematic: The actor will "oscillate between A and B as between two equally available possibilities" (1962: 83), maybe being inclined to take A at first, then leaning towards B, but then taking A. Fortunately for Schutz, because of the specific temporal structure of the situation, this oscillation is not per se problematic: According to Bergson's juxtaposition of inner durée and the outer flow (read in my terms: stream) of the world, while the pondering of alternatives takes time, the two objects remain the same. While the actor can, of course, not keep oscillating forever, he can take his time nevertheless, because the options to choose among will neither vanish nor change. This situation, however, is crucially different in the second case, the case of choosing among projects of actions.

In the case of projecting actions, or choosing among possible future courses of action rather than objects immediately available, "anything that will later stand to choice in the way of alternative has to be produced by me." (Schutz 1962: 84) Therefore, if choosing itself was supposed to be an act of consciousness, then projecting-and-choosing must constitute some kind of higher-order act, since the different projects of action that needed comparing must first themselves be preconceived on the basis of *several* acts of consciousness. Making a choice between projects of action thus requires first 'going over' the possible options one after another to figure out what kind of an outcome they will probably yield, and then compare or judge the different optional outcomes so construed. But if each act of consciousness is supposed to be directed at only and exactly one object, how is this possible? Towards an answer, one has to take another look at Husserl, especially to his concept of synthesis. I have shown in chapter three that a key issue with Husserl's conception of vision is that he treats minimal saccadic eye movements as essentially functioning in the same way as walking around a house to see its back—as movements initiated in the expectation of a sensation. Behind this notion is the concept of synthesis, the idea that consciousness can 'objectivate,' i.e. intend in a single act, what was originally a series of separate acts of intention (in this case tied to sensations; see Arvidson 2006; Natanson 1979). The rectangle that I showed in chapter three, for example, is initially 'assembled' in a series of saccades each tied to conscious acts, but can hitherto be grasped as a single object in that the content of the different 'steps' become synthesized. Its overall meaning thus arises from a "monothetic glance" over the "polythetic" stream of sensations. This concept of synthesis of polythetic into monothetic acts was, in turn, of essential importance to Schutz, both to grasp the constitution of meaning in general (particularly Schutz 1967: 67–68; see Eberle 1984: 27–29; Wagner 1984; Heiskala 2011), and to explain how we choose among different projects of action in particular (Schutz 1962; see Eberle 2000c, 2010). In the latter case, it allows the pondering actor to synthesize the different acts concerning the different aspects of each possible action into a single unit: his projection of the outcome of choosing that action (modo futuro exacti). To speak with Schutz, "projection is retrospection anticipated in phantasy." (1962: 87) In effect, the actor produces discrete, clearly defined options (the imagined outcomes) among which to choose—and therefore, he is now confronted with problematic alternatives instead of entirely open alternatives. So far so good, one might say, because up until now we seem to have a classic account of rational choice at hand: the actor projects future states and weights them according to their expected 'costs and benefits' (cf. Eberle 2000c). But according to Schutz, this is not the case, because due to the temporal structure of the situation, a dilemma occurs: As I have shown, the actor will start oscillating between the possible choices in order to weight one against the other, and time will pass while this happens. But unlike the physical objects standing in front of him, the choices themselves to not 'stand still.' Rather, they will—as Schutz says—"grow older" together with the actor, because they are flesh of his own flesh, so to speak: as with every other act of consciousness, the actor will gain additional knowledge every time he 'thinks through' one of the alternatives. Returning to the other options with his newfound insight, he now sees them from a different angle. And once he has considered them according to it, he will have gained another insight, necessitating him to return to the others once again; and so forth. Again, Schutz does not assume that this flip-flopping will go on forever,[13] since evidently, we do act at some point; but the key conclusion is that the clearly demarcated problematic alternatives we first assumed to be constructed are not actually stable entities at all, but evolve over the course of making the decision. But crucially, Schutz continues, this "wavering of alternatives" (1967: 69) ceases once the choice is made: In reflection (at least in the natural attitude), the act will be grasped as a monothetic intentional act and thus "the action, once completed, is a unity from original project to execution" in our experience (Schutz 1967: 69). Against economists' conceptions of rational choice, he argues that it is only *in retrospect* that an actor has the impression that he chose between clearly demarcated alternatives (Eberle 2000c, 2010). This notion is rooted in the idea of synthesis mentioned above, the conviction that "all actions occur within open possibilities and (…) problematic possibilities are restricted to past acts" (Schutz 1962: 87). Our 'live' experience of the immediate present, in other words, is always polythetic and carries an inherently indeterminate future of open possibilities; while

---

[13] Luhmann (1995b, 2000b), in contrast, draws this conclusion: decisions cannot actually be decided in any strict sense; but rather, the meaning-making process of the system simply 'moves on' and references one of the options considered as having been decided.

our subsequent reflection on it is usually monothetic (if we proceed in the attitude of everyday life) and should it include past possibilities, they will be considered as having been problematic possibilities, sets of clearly defined options among which we chose. What is more, these monothetic reproductions of the past serve as the basis of typification, so that the subjective stock of knowledge is permanently 'updated' according to these idealized readings of past reality. And it is on this knowledge, in turn, on which the actor will base her assumptions about the practicability of actions in future situations: These retrospectively established because-motives will serve to "orient" the in-order-to motives governing the relevance-structures of action and perception in situations the actor considers being of similar kind (see also Weigert 1975).

But if subjective prior knowledge is the basis on which all situations in which actions occur are being defined by the actor, how exactly does grasping an object in reach differ from projecting future actions? Indeed, as Eberle (1988: 89–90) has pointed out, this differentiation seems somewhat arbitrary, since it is difficult to imagine any object which is *not* woven into some form of action-context.[14] In order to consider the consequences of this notion, Eberle gives the example of choosing between having a coffee or a beer either if a) reading a cafe's menu or if b) both are standing within reach right in front of oneself. He concludes:

> "You cannot really claim that the decisive difference lies in the fact that in the first case [imagining drinking while reading the menu] I have grown older while the decision process in inner time had lasted and thus every action alternative—drinking coffee or beer—would be different whenever I attend to it once more." (Eberle 1988: 90; my translation)

Is it not rather the full richness of experience that makes a crucial difference, he asks, the sight and smell and colour? Eberle concludes that Schutz' argument about choosing between projects of actions bears primarily on situations that exhibit a certain complexity and temporal "spread" of the projections to be made, while the distinction between deciding about objects immediately present versus about those situationally absent seems to be pointing into a different direction (Eberle 1988: 90). Unfortunately, Eberle does not pursue this thought further, but effectively seems to conclude that every decision should be understood as having the form of a projection, only that these projections can differ greatly in type or scope, ranging from those regarding the immediate situation to very abstract thinking. Indeed, this is basically the solution Schutz himself embraced as well when discerning the different elements of the stock of knowledge (Schutz/T. Luckmann 1973): the difference between grasping an object within reach and projecting future actions is not taken up again in his work. Schutz apparently considered the case settled.

---

[14]This, of course, is also a fundamental postulate of Heideggerian thought: Objects always appear in a 'Zeugzusammenhang,' within a site characterized by the paths of action it entails (see Chap. 4).

13 Sedimentation and the Body

Having completed this small tour of Schutz' account of initiating action, I can now turn towards assessing it in light of the empirical findings and theoretical considerations presented thus far. In the course of this I will need to reopen the case of projecting vs. grasping actions. But to begin with, let me ask what kind of an image would ensue if one would describe skiing with flow in terms of projecting actions in Schutz' sense? As I described above, the basic challenge of seeing while riding a line can well be framed as the need to align the dual process of protention and retention, interpreting the snow surface ahead in such a way that a suitable expectation can be formed according to which the details of the riding will be adjusted. The ability, in turn, would then require a process of learning which would be conceptualized as being based on retention, or (more or less) constant reflection on the experiences just made in order to fine-tune one's understanding of or knowledge about skiing. In Schutzian terminology, this process would be described as sedimentation of 'bits' of knowledge into our stock of knowledge—aspects of the act of skiing are perceived as problematic, thus singled out in awareness, and can therefore be approached in a conscious and purposeful manner, for example by what I clumsily described as 'telling myself' to relax my knees before hitting a bump. Over time, such small acts will seem more and more unproblematic or natural, until they can finally be tackled 'en bloc' (monothetically) with all the other things to be done during skiing: While I might have once struggled to keep my skis parallel in deep powder, I no longer ever think about doing that and instead simply 'tell' myself: two big turns and then drop left into that bowl. The 'bits' of knowledge, one would conclude, have moved to the margins of awareness when we apply them (Schutz/T. Luckmann 1973: 108–111). Schutz himself did not discuss bodily movements similar to that of skiing at any length, but a number of authors have suggested that learning bodily skills can adequately described as Schutzian sedimentation. Knoblauch (2003, 2010), for example, has used the example of learning to drive a car to argue that what one might otherwise call habituation or acquiring bodily competencies is best understood in terms of sedimentation: Sequences like the shifting gears need attention and planning at first, but will be available "en bloc" later, reduced to the margins of attention. Kastl (2004, 2007), however, has attacked this idea, criticizing that the conscious planning and attending, just like the verbal explanations of the driving instructor, cannot directly 'diffuse' into the body, but are just one way of preparing situational conditions in which the body learns 'on its own.' Thus, describing bodily learning in terms of conscious planning would amount to a confusion of categories. But is Kastl right? Towards an answer, one needs to take a closer look on how exactly conscious experiences, knowledge, and bodily conduct are related in Schutzian theory.

We have seen that sedimentation describes a process in which the content of conscious reflections is added to the subjective stock of knowledge. But according to Schutz, how do consciousness and knowledge relate to what I have called bodily routines? The most explicit discussion of bodily skills that Schutz provides is found in his article "On Multiple Realities," that is, in his later work (Schutz 1945). Here, Schutz discerns conduct (of which voluntary action is a subtype)—"subjectively meaningful experiences emanating from our spontaneous life"—from what he calls "involuntary spontaneity." (1945: 536) This latter category covers many of those bodily workings that practice theorists frequently focus on, such as "the mere physiological reflexes, such as the knee jerk, the contraction of the pupil, blinking, blushing; moreover certain passive reactions provoked by what Leibnitz calls the surf of indiscernible and confused small perceptions; furthermore my gait, my facial expressions, my mood." (1945: 535) All of them "belong to the category of essentially actual experiences, that is, they exist merely in the actuality of being experienced and cannot be grasped by a reflective attitude," which separates them from conduct, which does undergo reflection and can thus alter the subjective stock of knowledge (Schutz 1945: 536). Accordingly, many of the bodily processes such as visual routines which I discussed cannot effect sedimentation of knowledge—or rather, as the case of crucial points show, only those aspects that rise to awareness will, while the large rest remains bound to the perpetual shadow of the subconscious. It is important to note that in making this assumption, Schutz deviates from Husserl (as he mentions in 1945: 536 fn6), since for Husserl, every act of consciousness can be grasped in reflection, and thus he does not postulate a distinction between "essentially actual experiences" and conduct. As I have demonstrated in chapter three, this assumption is crucial for Husserl's account of perception and its relation to movement, particularly in the case of eyeball movement. He argued that saccades, like all perceived movement, cause kinaesthesia, which in turn happens necessarily in the modus of "I can" and therefore enables consciousness to develop reliable expectations about changes in the visual field in relation to eyeball movement (Drummond 1979; Mattens 2010). In effect, not only the sensory content received from the environment (the image appearances in vision), but also the kinaesthetic appearances are considered as basally *constitutive* for our perception of space and movement (Husserl 1973: 176), and therefore they necessarily accompany *every* act of conscious visual perception of a thing in space, even in case of minimal saccades.

Excursus: Action and the Body in Husserl

Since Schutz' discussion of action, conduct, and essentially actual experiences builds closely on Husserl's account of bodily action, but then deviates in an important aspect; and since Husserl's account of the body is essential for both his and Schutz' notion of temporality, let me briefly summarize his approach. As discussed, Husserl has been criticized by Merleau-Ponty (among others) for trying to 'purify' intentional perception from bodily qualities. Repeating the same critique with regard to action would not make much sense, since action is quite obviously something bodily—a fact Husserl could have hardly neglected. Nevertheless, Husserl's account of action follows the same conceptual outline Merleau-Ponty criticized: In principle, he defines the body as an ontological thing in the region of Nature, strictly separated from the intentional subject in the region of Consciousness (Arvidson 2006; Dodd 1997; Rang 1990; Smith 2007). In order to explain intentional action, however, Husserl needed to conceptualize how both spheres relate or intertwine in some way; and in order to be able to keep up his separation of consciousness and 'objectual' body, Husserl introduces the Leib or lived body as a separate instance spanning both regions—a unity-in-difference caught in between (Dodd 1997; Summa 2011; Zahavi 1994). The effect of this move, I believe, is quite important: Subsequently, what would have been a phenomenological study of the process of action per se becomes a phenomenology of the lived body as a (partly physical) thing separate from the world it moves through. For decades to come, phenomenologists therefore arguably ended up studying the body when they set out to study action (Smith 1992): They focused on what Husserl called kinaesthesia, the experience of the movement of one's own body. But crucially, in doing so every movement is treated as a datum in itself and thus as a given fact. Husserl pondered but explicitly rejected the expression "kinaesthetic meaning," because for him, movement does not contain a projection and thus no intentional content, but is only given as a datum ex post facto (Mattens 2010: 171). Husserl was well aware of the *temporal shift* this implies (and so is Schutz), as movements of the lived body are thus exclusively treated as already having been caused.[15] Since the body itself cannot produce meaning, Husserl develops a concept of action which confines the crucial element of meaning projection—that the body was denied carrying—to the realm of consciousness. And since this separation of prior initiation and later sensing of bodily movement can hardly be accounted for by spatial separation (e.g. between mind and body) alone, he points to the temporal separation of the two spheres instead, distinguishing the inner durée of consciousness and the cosmic time within which the physical body moves. As I already mentioned with regard to perception, accusing Husserl's theory of sticking to a strict Cartesian dualism (a mind-body separation) is therefore indeed not really justified (see Gurwitsch 1970). More adequately, one can say that his concept is thoroughly Kantian—a characterization he embraced himself (Mohanty 1996)—both in the separation of 'raw' sensation and intentional consciousness, and the introduction of a transcendental ego (or

---

[15] And accordingly, the only attempt of aligning the neuroscientific distinction between dorsal and ventral visual processing (i.e. pragmatic and epistemic vision) with Husserlian phenomenology that I am aware of suggests to treat them as "spatial and temporal processing," respectively (Madary 2011: 423). Nevertheless, I believe that Madary's argument that dorsal processing *can* "contribute something" to conscious perception does not quite answer the key question of how this form of perception *itself* can be characterized in Husserlian terms, e.g. to explain why it does *not always* contribute to consciousness, and just what it is that it does when it does not.

> subject) to explain the analogy of (ap-)perception of separate individuals (Dostal 1993; Mohanty 1996; Rodemeyer 2006). Very crudely said, introducing a temporal divide is Husserl's key move to formulate an anti-Cartesian, yet Kantian view the role of the body in action. On this basis, Husserl can acknowledge the existence of routinized bodily actions and 'instincts,' but nevertheless focus squarely on volition as the "tipping point" of all creative, 'primary' actions, and treat all other 'secondary actions' as empirically caused by and thus retraceable to acts of will (Vongehr 2010). In consequence, he saw a "phenomenology of volition" as the fundament to a phenomenology of action, and very much in line with Kant, subsequently concentrated on ethics as the problem of intending 'the right thing' (Vongehr 2010). For these reasons, Husserl's treatment of how precisely our awareness of ongoing action is structured remains essentially fragmented, as he separates volition, kinaesthesia, and the perception of the environment not only conceptually, but also temporally (Smith 1992). The temporalization of perception Husserl introduces thus amounts to a temporal rift between the initiation and the perception of the effects of action—a rift which makes it difficult to grasp what one I called the "action-present."[16]

Schutz' deviation from Husserl's assumption that even the most minimal bodily movements are both perceived and wilfully intended, one can conclude, does on the one hand save him from some of the criticism that has been directed at Husserl's account (inter alia by me); but on the other, it implies that he will have to provide an alternative account which is both internally coherent and still compatible with all the other philosophical a-prioris he draws from Husserl. Since, although Schutz seems to embrace Husserl's 'active' reading of basic perception when he uses formulations such as: "by active apperception, our mind singles out certain features from the perceptional field" (1945: 534), it must be stressed that unlike in Husserl, such 'active' perception does not concern all sensory experiences. Instead, Schutz distinguishes between active and passive attention (1945: 538), and only the former comprises "the activities of mind which Husserl calls the activities of intentionality" (1945: 561). But that is not all. Schutz goes a step further and declares the content of passive attention, as well as the underlying bodily functions, to be subjectively *meaningless*:

---

[16]This becomes most clear in Luhmann's conception of time, because arguably, Luhmann provides the most stringent continuation of the line of the Kantian aspects of the thought of Husserl (Luhmann 1995a; Nassehi 2009): According to Luhmann (1997: 52), any meaningful event vanishes in the same instance it begins.

"As long as I live in my acts, directed toward the objects of these acts, the acts do not have any meaning. They become meaningful if I grasp them as well-circumscribed experiences of the past and, therefore, in retrospection." (Schutz 1945: 535)

In effect, Schutz (1945: 540) adds, the "self which performed the past acts is no longer the undivided total self, but rather a partial self." The implication of this passage seems to be quite drastic: In contrast to much of what I have written, and in sharp contrast to all proponents of practice theory, Schutz seems to deny that bodily skills or routines are even relevant for social inquiry at all—at first glance. This, in turn, would suggest that such skills cannot be 'activated' or used by way of projecting action. At a second glance, one will realize that while Schutz' distinction is sharp, it is not quite as extreme as one might think. To see why, it first helps to take a look at why Schutz introduces it in the first place. The reason, I believe, lies in the fact that in comparison to earlier works, the role and capability of the body is broadened and strengthened in this specific article "On Multiple Realities," in that Schutz acknowledges the importance of embodied routines and various bodily automatisms (or what he calls the realm of conduct). But this enhanced conception of the body also requires him to defend the core assumption that social action can be (only) adequately explained by studying the subjective experience of the actor (Eberle 2009, 2010). Having acknowledged that the subject does neither become aware of all bodily doings, nor preconceives them in their full detail, this methodological postulate would be violated if he was to conclude that bodily movement itself can be inherently meaningful. By defining that subjective meaning can arise only in reflection, however, acknowledging subconscious routines becomes unproblematic, since they can—and arguably frequently do—remain under the radar of reflection, and thus their particular meaning in each case is still determined based on subjective knowledge alone. Still, together with acknowledging the basic importance of bodily routines, Schutz provides some room in his theory to house them: Between the realms of purposeful action and of essentially actual experiences, he placed the realm of conduct, which comprises any bodily doing 'registered' in reflection that the actor does not consider as action. Many aspects of my skiing, for example, fall squarely into this category, since I do retrospectively realize that they happened. In fact, all my ethnographic data must by definition fall either into this category or that of purposeful action, since I took notice of it in some way—if one supposes that I approached my days out in the Krimml in the natural attitude, which is only partly true since I was of course eager to collect data and reflected on my doings in an analytic stance. In the category of conduct, in other words, there is room for some of the phenomena practice theory is interested in; and Bongaerts (2007, 2008) has suggested that social practices as a whole can be considered as belonging to it. From my perspective, however, this suggestion is misleading in that it is based on a questionable notion of practices as routinized or inherently regular bodily conduct (see Chap. 9).

Nevertheless, it is important to note that many practice-based critiques of Schutzian thought attack it on the basis of a false or imprecise allegation, namely that it would suggest that purposeful intentions on behalf of the actor fully determine what the actor does. Expressed in the terms introduced by Schatzki, such critiques assume that Schutz would suggest that the means-end structure of projected action bears on practical understandings ("Knowing how to X"), that is, that people move their body a) because, and b) in just that manner which they intend to. But Schutz does not. In terms of claim a), it needs to be said that one of the core projects of his whole work was arguably to develop a methodology of the social sciences with which to overcome the postulate of causal explanation favoured by Weber and contemporary economists like von Mises (Eberle 2009, 2010). The social scientists, he argued, should not even attempt to provide causal explanations; but must rather strive to uncover the subjective orientation of the actor from which his actions sprang forth (see especially Schutz 1953, 1954). This latter point also relates to claim b): The Schutzian sociologist is simply not in the business of explaining why and what exactly bodies did what they allegedly did when they did it. Instead, he is (simply put) in the business of understanding or explaining what the actor 'consciously intended to do throughout doing what he did.' If, for example, Schatzki (2010b: 117–118) argues that action is inherently undetermined because he defines action not on the basis of purposes but effects, then his account of action is fully compatible with Schutz' in this regard, since he is not trying to unearth the determinations of doings in the sense of ontological, determined, physical-world events.

That said, on the other hand, the postulate that social scientists should study the typifications that lead to the actor's subjective orientation, and subsequently his plans and projects of acting does of course imply that there is something useful to be found in these typifications towards explaining regularities in past and future action. More precisely, it seems to me that two quite different conclusions can be drawn from this postulate—and it is unfortunately not always quite clear which one a particular text or author seems to imply when building on Schutz. First, one could say that while the subjective orientation and the underlying action project do not always match the precise outcome, they are nevertheless highly influential and thus a kind of robust predictor of what will happen. After all, Schutz does claim that action is motivated by in-order-to motives, although then wraps this claim in the conditions that a) we cannot precisely know in-order-to motives ex post facto, but only their 'beautiful sister,' the because-motives, and b) have to acknowledge the fact than things do not always transpire as intended. Second, one could say that the precise motives bearing on particular actions do not matter for the kind of question that one intends to answer. Questions of identity, worldview, or subjective knowledge (depending on the definition, of course), for example, can well be answered based on the assumption that one can gain proper access to the stock of knowledge (and its process of constitution) that a subject carries away from a situation; without necessarily needing to impose any assumption at all about what happened in that situation, and why. From my perspective, however, this latter position seems both humble and fragile, in that it can arguably very easily slip into imply a relatively stable, near-causal relation between motives and outcomes of action, namely in all cases in which a kind of socialization into a group or the learning of some practice is observed. After all, the mere accumulation of adequate knowledge per se cannot explain how adequate skills or patterns of conduct emerge, but they are arguably necessary to explain that learning or socialization did take place—unless one subscribes to a radical constructivism of Luhmannian kind.

In sum, I hold that Schutz' brief discussion of passive attention and bodily conduct amid his extensive and very detailed discussion of knowledge and action leaves room to take different stances on the relation between bodily routines and consciousness. While Schutz does not claim that both are related in strict coupling, it seems to me that many Schutzian authors implicitly or explicitly assume what I call a strict homology between both: that we know what we can and we can what we know. But on the basis of what I have argued thus far, one does not have to deduct this assumption from Schutz' texts. Accordingly, one could nevertheless argue that Schutz' account of projecting actions is compatible with Schatzki's account of action as well as a certain version of practice theory more generally (just as Bongaerts 2008 argues). But I believe that important reservations remain. In a nutshell, the argument which I develop will be that, while Schutz' account produces a compatible but somewhat limited conception of practical understandings (in Schatzki's words, explaining how actors come to be able to "know how to do X" and "know how to identify X-ing"), it provides a misleading notion of practical intelligibility, that is, by virtue of what it makes sense to an actor to do X in the first place.

14 The Problems of Projecting

The first problem I see in Schutz' account of projecting and sedimentation is the scope of social phenomena it can harness explanatory power for. This is the problem typically emphasized by praxeological critiques of this approach: Should there be pervasive social phenomena which happen based on bodily skills or routines acquired *and* applied 'under the radar' of conscious experience, they would be missed entirely; and should only their acquisition 'slip through' unbeknownst to the individual, they would not feature as the systematic phenomenon in her consciousness—and thus in the researcher's findings which they actually are (Heiskala 2011; Kastl 2001, 2004; Lizardo 2009, 2011; Schmidt 2008). The standard case usually cited is that of taste: The order inherent in people's choosing and judging art, food, clothing, and so forth which is carried by the habituated routines of their daily life escapes analysis because it is simply not in itself meaningful according to Schutz' definition its ex-post interpretations or rationalizations by the subject notwithstanding, since these cannot in any way reflect the underlying order (Kastl 2004; Lizardo 2009). It needs to be noted that this argument is directed at the explanatory scope and methodology of the Lebenswelt approach, but that it cannot undermine the coherence of the theory per se.

The second and related problem is that it seems to me that, from how it is conceptualized by Schutz, the realm of conduct can contain bodily workings of quite different nature: While they are all reflexively seen as 'involuntary spontaneity' pragmatically relevant to the current experience, some of them might stem from sedimentation, that is, originally needed to be devised in advance to be accomplished; while others have always been noticed if at all, then as conduct (breathing is probably a good example). By lumping together "habitual, traditional, [and] affectual (…) automatic activities," Schutz (1945: 536) is thus conflating relatively different phenomena. This is not per se incoherent since he is exclusively concerned with the structure of subjective knowledge, but it potentially implies a methodological problem: When studying conduct, the Schutzian social scientist can never be quite sure which aspects of conduct have been intentionally enacted at some earlier point, and which ones have not—unless he is able to observe the whole learning process from its beginning. This distinction, however, is quite important for Schutz' account of projecting action: Only conduct reflexively considered as voluntarily undertaken will be used to project future actions, and thus only the sedimented parts of conduct qualify for this task (see below). On that note, it should also be mentioned that the opposite process of a 'top-down' sedimentation from full awareness to marginal awareness is equally possible: aspects hitherto unnoticed could rise to awareness and thus enter the realm of conduct 'bottom-up,' potentially rising even further and be considered also devised in advance. On close inspection, learning a bodily technique arguably consist to quite a large extent of such 'upstir'-type of learning in that we need to realize things 'our body already knows.' Skiing provides a number of such examples: I earlier mentioned an exercise in which students were made to realize how their hip rotates during the turn with the help of ski-poles, and in the seventies ski instruction saw a boom of methods that aimed at "discovering your inner skier" based on the argument that small kids can ski quite well after barely any instruction at all (Fry 2006a: 117–120). My point here is not that these examples cannot be explained with Schutzian theory—in fact, the example of the hip rotation first unnoticed, then brought to attention and purposefully 'controlled,' and finally considered unproblematic again can be described by it very well (including the fact that the hip is of course never quite under direct control). The point is that a) the concept of sedimentation captures only one phase of this 'bottom-up to top-down' learning, and that b) it opens up a relatively broad spectrum of differences between individuals who all 'have' them same bodily skills but 'know' about them in very different ways, in that one man's essentially actual experience is the other man's habituated knowledge (cf. Schutz/T. Luckmann 1973: 108–111). Understanding these skills on the basis of the typifications underlying each man's subjective experience is accordingly challenging, since it varies from complete ignorance to complete familiarity. This point is of course related to the first line of criticism I mentioned, and among the reasons why for example Garfinkel (1967: 118) deviated from Schutz to include "seen but unnoticed features" of (inter-) actions into his frame of relevance. Finally, my third point is that c) content 'stirred up' cannot be projected prior to action in a strict sense, since it is by definition unbeknown to the subject which needs to either 'poke around' for or be instructed about it. Again, this still leaves the Schutzian theory watertight in that it does not 'actually' have to be preconceivedly lifted to be considered reliably expectable conduct in retrospect; but it seems to suggest that the model of projecting actions makes it difficult to capture what Garfinkel calls "local pedagogies of instructably reproducible achievements" (2002: 158)—how did the inventor of the 'inner skiing'-method convince fellow ski instructors to pay him to train them how to teach their students how to discover and unleash the skiing abilities *they already have*? In relation to this latter point, it should further be noted that a number of authors have developed phenomenological analyses of skill acquisition and learning that differ substantially from the sedimentation view. First, some have built on Merleau-Ponty's discussion of the formation of the body schema, as well as on Heidegger's notion of coping, to argue that skill acquisition and the reproduction of forms of conduct is neither a goal-directed activity, nor grounded in mental representations per se (H. L. Dreyfus 1996, 2008; M. Reuter 1999; Rouse 2000; Wrathall/Malpas 2000)—a claim that can be additionally supported by findings from experimental neurosciences (Ennen 2003). Second, others have undertaken to develop a phenomenology of action (rather than the body-in-movement) in a stricter sense which distinguishes different degrees in the experience of agency (H. M. Collins/Kusch 1995; Gallagher 2007; Pacherie 1997, 1999, 2008; Smith 1992) and/or different levels of intentionality (Becchio/Bertone 2004; Haggard 2005; Pacherie 2003, 2006; Schlicht 2008), thus undercutting the strict dualism in Schutz (meaning/no meaning; intention/no intention).

The third and arguably most important problem that I see arises from the fact that Schutz seems to paint the body as a kind of faithful passenger of consciousness; and the question of whether what I called the assumption of strict homology between knowledge and 'body knowledge,' while not explicitly suggested by Schutz, is not nevertheless logically implied by his theory. To be sure, in itself, his account does not say anything about how 'the body' might learn or not, it only describes our lifeworldly experience that the body does what it does. But in doing so, I suggest, Schutz nevertheless operates on the assumption that the body 'underneath' subjective consciousness somehow seems to be able to comply with the needs or expectations of consciousness. More specifically, Schutz and Luckmann state that those elements of habitual knowledge they call useful knowledge—highly routinized skills such as "talking, (…) smoking, (…) or frying eggs"—are defined by the fact that "the Idealization of 'I can always do it again' cannot miscarry" with regard to them (1973: 107). To be sure, an idealization is technically still an idealization, even if it "cannot miscarry." Thus, Schutz and Luckmann are, strictly speaking, making an argument about the 'expectations' underlying or build into the relevance structure of the subjective experience of bodily workings, rather than said workings themselves. Nevertheless, I hold, this understanding still implies that both our consciousness in general, and the actor's subjective experience in the situation in particular *are* structured in (not exact, but relatively tight) accordance with the capabilities of the body—and not the other way around: The status or form of habitual knowledge reflects the fact that the body does reliably equip the actor with the skills composing it without problems in all but the most uncommon and disastrous situations.

"It is important to stress this unquestionableness [of 'automatized' skills] vigorously." (Schutz/T. Luckmann 1973: 108)

And indeed, the reliability of this fact is of crucial importance for Schutz' overall conception of action: Second only to the most basic elements of our stock of knowledge (those providing for the temporal and spatial limitation of every situation and the basic structure of experience), habitual knowledge is conceptualized as the foundation which carries any kind of "higher" purposeful action-project, and thus also any kind of more abstract knowledge of the world (Schutz/T. Luckmann 1973: 99–111). This point can hardly be stressed enough: If the body would not be able to provide reliably for the unproblematic availability of skills like "riding, talking, or frying eggs" *on the basis of* our initially undertaking them in the format of a means-end structure, then—according to the model—human life including the accumulation of individual knowledge would basically be impossible. (Well, we could maybe do without unthinkingly frying eggs, but having to ponder prior to talking how talking itself works would be too much.) Since, would we not 'come to know' about these capabilities of our body in situations which enable us to consider them as initiated and controlled by us by virtue of acting, there would be no habitual knowledge about them. Put differently: The position that the social scientist can understand individual conduct and, in the end, social order on the basis of reconstructing the intentional projects or means-end structures that were relevant or predominant in conducting a certain action builds on the premise that the experienced unquestionable reliability of bodily skills (by virtue of which skills are available as skills in the stock of knowledge) is learned or acquired exclusively in the course of conduct that has been reflexively understood to be a means-end type of activity. As I have noted above, a number of phenomenologists have argued that this premise does not hold, because we do not, or not exclusively, experience bodily skills as means to an end during their acquisition, neither in the immediate moment nor reflexively. As with all things purely phenomenological, I do not claim to be in the position to give a confident answer to the question how we really, truly, always experience such things. My argument, instead, is a different one.

Let me try to be clear: In contrast to what some critics such as Kastl (2004, 2007) suggest, the problem is *not* whether or not habituated skills are 'really' being habituated because of being trained or acquired within a means-end framework; since from a Schutzian perspective, it suffices that the individual 'believes' (concludes from reflection) throughout the moments of acquisition that his body's doings transpired the way they did by virtue of him acting purposefully in a certain way. To use an example from freestyle skiing: If a freestyler is learning a certain trick and manages to rotate his body in the right way for the first time, and if, at the time he managed to do the jump for the first time, he happened to turn his head to one side with some momentum in order to initiate the rotation (which is what freestylers do), then he will probably associate rotating and head-turning in the future, and over time, the rotation will be understood by or known to the skier as a habituated skill that can be 'grasped' or 'switched on' by turning the head (which, again, is what freestylers do). Whether or not the head-turning 'actually' has any effect on the initiation of the rotation or not is entirely irrelevant, the argument goes, as long as both transpire in the skier's experience together frequently and reliably enough to solidify the 'mental' connection. Again, I hold that this line of argumentation is theoretically watertight. The theorist can decide that all we care about is conscious experience—tout court. But the question that I want to ask is this: What kind of a body, consciousness, and situations of learning need to be implied for this assumption to hold? The key issue, I believe, is what I term the Schutzian means-end restriction: the assumption that when learning a skill, we experience bodily capabilities necessarily in the frame of conduct (and especially action), that is, as initiated by our purposefully acting towards a certain end (including conduct which was not consciously devised in advance but nevertheless experienced as 'meaningful spontaneity'), and will thus over time consider said capabilities as means-on-hand via habitual knowledge. In my view, this assumption does not actually make an inference about practical understandings themselves, despite possible claims to the contrary.

Instead, I argue, this restriction is problematic because *it bears on practical intelligibility*, on "what makes sense to someone to do." (Schatzki 2010b: 120) My argument is that in order for something to make sense for someone to do—in order to stand out as a viable path of action or as an action affordance—it must appear feasible or actionable—the actor must be at least relatively sure that she is not forcing inevitable disaster by doing it, and she must be able to fathom it as at least vaguely realistically doable. But according to Schutz, paths of action only make sense to someone exclusively in the form of in-order-to motives, that is, in a means-end format. In his view, this is not only true for more complex undertakings oriented towards 'higher-order ends,' but especially and emphatically it is true for habituated knowledge, the knowledge concerning those little things we do 'on the side' of attending to more serious issues. Skills as represented in habitual knowledge, he writes, "are unquestionably 'means to an end' in the realization of open plans of acts." (Schutz/T. Luckmann 1973: 108) Plainly said: Only those doings we can think about as means to an end can make sense for us to do.

I believe that an impoverished image of practical intelligibility results from this means-end restriction. Why should we not be able to find actionable undertakings to be meaningful in other forms than as means to bring about a specific preconceived future state? Notably, I am not referring to the question whether or not action must be planned or motivated rationally, since Schutz allows for a variety of motives in this regard (Eberle 2000c). Rather, it is Schutz (1945: 539) much more basic postulate that it is only and exclusively "reference to the preceding project that makes (…) acting (…) meaningful." To be sure, since I do not fancy myself capable of performing a proper eidetic reduction, I cannot rule out the possibility that Schutz is entirely right. But it seems to me that especially when we undertake to explain how we understand the immediate actionable future on the basis of our past experiences alone, a more versatile field comes to light. A classic topic of study in this regard is improvisation in arts and especially music (Figueroa-Dreher 2008; W. Gibson 2006; Pressing 1988; Sudnow 1978): The assumption that all actions require a preconceived future state seems to violate the observation of creative and/or spontaneous production of variations of pre-existing tunes and themes, especially because the latter nevertheless requires the availability of highly routinized skills of playing as well as non-arbitrary, artful invention oriented by the 'known' tunes. Figueroa-Dreher (2008) has made a suggestion to introduce the findings from studies of improvisation into Schutzian theory and thus extend it by adding an element of improvisation or 'impulse' to its concept of action. But while the categories or processes she describes as being responsible for this element mirror those I have focused on—especially 'the situation' and motor programmes—, it seems to me that they remain a kind of alien appendage to the theory, two residual categories (in the sense of Parsons) that explain what should have never happened in the first place according to the theory. In an interesting inversion of what I called pragmatistic and praxeological theories which use the body and/or material settings to explain ubiquitous regularity, the body now becomes a reliable well of creativity and spontaneity, like a younger brother of the 'real' actor that has somehow sneaked in to catch a free ride and mess things up a bit. Again, I think both views are correct to some extent, since in some ways, our bodies are reliable reproduction machines, and in others, we can bring them to actually surprise ourselves. Take, for example the cognitive psychologists' findings about newborn babies spontaneously repeating their parents facial gestures less than an hour after birth (Jacob/Jeannerod 2003: 234). While Schutz' account is convincing in that it describes how the baby *first* automatically imitates its parents and *later* learns to do so purposefully by linking the retrospectively gained understanding on the meaning of, e.g., smiling with the kinaesthesia accompanying doing smiling; it seems less straightforward to explain how the baby after a few months learns to *not* repeat all facial gestures it sees. Does this happen on the basis of habituated knowledge as well? But if so, can the suppression of such sensori-motor automatisms be adequately circumscribed as sedimentation of a means-end pattern? This would imply that we constantly and routinely pursue myriad ends of the form 'suppress-this-to-avoid-that.' But if we alternately decide that the suppressing is not meaningful, an important step in the development of the baby towards being an able member of our society would simply disappear from our analysis. Again, I do not suggest that it is inadequate to assume that grown up adults simply take these things for granted. The question is whether being-taken-for-granted within means-end schemas captures well enough how we make ourselves do (and learn) things. While we cannot and must not consciously plan and control all abilities of our bodies, we do have a number of quite reliable ways to bring them about. Therefore, should one not consider these ways of bringing about to have exactly that central importance which Schutz considers conscious planning to have? More specifically, if—as I argued in the last chapter—there are many different modi or pathways of acquiring bodily skills, only one of which is purposeful and planned action, why should such crucial differences invariably go amiss as we build up our stock of experiences since everything becomes idealized into the means-end scheme? Do we not 'know' all sorts of tricks and treats to make our body do what it should do, and does this not imply that we do *not* plan and undertake our actions *exclusively* on the assumption of having a faithful tool ready to hand, but according to various 'trick-and-treat-assumptions'? I believe that the Heideggerian philosopher of technology Andreas Luckner (2008: 54–57) is right when he argues that Schutz paints a "technomorph" picture of experiencing or intending action, and that this restriction is problematic in that, especially in the realm of everyday bodily conduct, we usually only attend to something in moments of breakdown, i.e. when something does *not* work. Our understanding of something (such as a bodily doing or posture) being a means towards achieving something, in other words, frequently arises from our noticing it in the context of impending failure or breakdown (H. L. Dreyfus 1979; Ennen 2003). But if so, then, according to Schutz, the only way we can relate to future action would be in the form of 'imagining' problems that needs solution and deducting which 'action-tools' we need to solve them.

15 Reprise: Projecting, Deciding, and the Flow of Conduct

At last, let me now return to the initial question: Is engaging in or choosing an action better understood in terms of grasping something that is situationally present, or instead as a time-consuming process of projecting actions or "rehearsing my future action in imagination" (Schutz 1945: 539)? Phenopractice theory offers a answer that is twofold: On the one hand, I believe that there is something like pondering future actions or imagining what one will do, and maybe trying to discern the most attractive alternative. As my discussion of reading a mountain face has shown, I do not believe that such phenomena are exclusively a mental phenomenon, and that they can be adequately grasped without taking into account the situated body. Nevertheless, I believe that Schutz account of projecting actions can be read as compatible with my account of phenopractical conduct—with the caveat that activity does not transpire the way it might have been projected, of course. But on the other hand, this still leaves the key question entirely open: Should one consider projecting, rather than grasping actions, as the decisive, if not sole way to initiate or pick actions? I do not think so. In fact, I think that Schutz himself provides us powerful reasons to believe that it does not. I fully agree with his analysis that initiating actions by way of projecting is inherently difficult, while picking up one object out of two standing right in front of us is something we can do pretty swiftly and pretty well. Actually, I also agree with the more strict conclusion which Luhmann (1996b, 2000b, 2005) drew from Schutz' considerations: If deciding is conceptualized as sequential, time-consuming elaboration of distinct entities (or forms) which alter as time passes by (for whatever reason, but especially if the process of deciding itself affects the options to be decided about), then decision-making is a paradox and one can say with Heinz von Foerster: "Only those questions which are in principle undecidable, *we* can decide" (von Foerster 2003: 293; original emphasis). Both Schutz and Luhmann have developed elaborate accounts of how explicable reasons for, and legitimate justifications of, decisions emerge ex post factum, in reflection or communication (as have Garfinkel 1967: 114; and Mills 1940). Accordingly, the fact that we think and talk about taking decisions does not mean that we actually take them—there is no problem to account theoretically for the empirical observation that we experience and talk about decisions and decision making without having to imply that the processes or phenomena these terms are applied to are themselves best understood via the theoretical concept of decision making or choosing. I see no reason why choosing among projects of actions—and thus projecting action—must be a pervasive and highly frequent phenomenon of lived life as Schutz seems to suggest.[17] Instead, I believe that in what he describes as grasping objects within reach, we have a much more pervasive and frequently appearing phenomenon of everyday life. However, I also see no reason why one should abolish the phenomenon of pondering, projecting, and choosing actions altogether. Sometimes, we do get locked into a weird spiral of oscillating between evaluating or simply admiring the prospects of two alternative paths of conduct, and we hesitate and struggle as something in us seems to drag into one direction, and something else into another. And if this happens, I argue, *we lose the flow of conduct*. We stop and stare, we pause and think, we stutter and search for the right word. Here, one finds the reason why I suggest considering *riding* as a quintessential modus of going through our every day. Because we not only keep going along the lines of one single action once we are underway (and sometimes stop talking only because of outside intervention), but we also smoothly morph from one activity into the next, much like a freerider taking turn after turn. Sometimes the flow gets lost: We step into a crowded, warm, noisy bar, arriving from a swift walk through the quiet, cold night outside; and we need to recollect, gather ourselves, orient, find our friends, switch the mood, get out of the coat, make sure we do not look dishevelled, cease pondering the problem that accompanied us on the way here, and get ready to dive into the talking and laughing. Like a freerider needs to open up the line he is about to drop in, we need to pick up the thread of a conversation—but like the rider zooming down the mountain face, losing the flow once we have it can quickly escalate in a moment of breakdown, and thus most of our riding the waves of lived life seems to be organized in such a way that we do not. I do not believe that tropes like habit or routine suffice to adequately capture this situation. Sure, as I have shown with regard to the normativity of the phenomenal field, habits, routines, reflexes, automatisms, techniques and the like are important because they leave room for us to attend to other aspects simultaneously, and especially to prepare consecutive orientations. But this also means that in isolation, they do not offer answers to how we keep up the flow over the course of stopping and starting various routines in overlapping sequences.

---

[17] Notably, I reject the notion of decision-making per se rather than only a specific notion of it. For example, I likewise reject the idea that a large part of our cultural life can be aptly described via a theory of "hot decision making" produced by a habitus, as Lizardo and Strand (2010) suggest.

Conscious planning per se, I hold, does not provide us with an adequate explanation of how this happens. Instead, I hold, this phenomenon needs to be accounted for by a situational order that provides practical intelligibility suitable to this task—a concept which, in turn, requires a suitable notion of temporality.

16 Schutz and Schatzki: The Givenness of Order and the Temporal Rift

I began my comparison of action in Schutz and Schatzki on the note that both share important similarities, among them a similar notion of the (known) past and future as taking place in the present. As a last step in my analysis, it now remains to be shown how both nevertheless differ in their account of temporality, and how these philosophical a-prioris turn out to be pivotal for their overall notion of initiating or picking paths of action. I have already noted that a key parallel between Schatzki and Schutz is that for both, acting-in-progress is determined teleologically, i.e. defined or characterized by a certain teleological end, but will be understood as determined by causal factors in retrospect (Schatzki 2006a: 161; Schutz/T. Luckmann 1973: 213–214). Indeed, Schatzki (2010b: 115) himself points out that his account of the teleological character of action resembles Schutz' notion of 'because' and 'in-order-to' motives in that:

> "The determination of activity is its making sense to a person, *given* this and that state of affairs, to perform a particular action *for the sake of* this or that way of being." (Schatzki 2010b: 115; original emphasis)

To avoid misunderstandings, let me point out right away that a) Schatzki's notion of something "making sense to a person" nevertheless differs fundamentally from Schutz' in that in Schatzki, meaning transpires in a site and not in subjective consciousness, and that b) he describes the teleological endpoint of an action as a way of being rather than a state of affairs. So much for the differences, the ramifications of and reasons for I just discussed. The key similarity, however, is that for both Schatzki and Schutz, current activity (or what Schutz [1945: 538] calls "living in my acting-in-progress") is oriented by a certain 'future direction,' while past states of affairs determine the situation in light of which the activity is pursued. I have detailed, Schutz holds that the reflexively established because-motives of past actions shape the relevance structure of current activity by way of the subjective stock of knowledge. The pivotal point of his argument is the temporal spread he introduces between the past and the future co-determining a path of action: While the future orienting the current activity is a present future ("Living in my acting-in-progress I am directed toward the state of affairs to be brought about by this acting." [1945: 538]), the past motivating the current activity is not a present past (the past of this action, the "where I am coming from") but a past past (the past reflections on a past sedimented in my stock of knowledge)—to be precise: a past future (the recollection of what must have motivated action) constructed in the past. The action-present, in other words, is characterized by the past 'past future' and the present future; and the temporal gap between the two is opened by the rift between inner and outer time installed by Husserl. Further, I have shown that in order to bridge this gap, Schutz conceptualizes subjective knowledge as a memory carrying the past into the present, which in turn requires him to insist that all determinations of action stemming from the past must fit through the loophole of knowledge.[18] From a phenopractice perspective, this restriction evidently has a number of problematic consequences. In my view, however, this should not obliterate the fact that practice thought shares (what I take to be) Schutz' reason to introduce this gap in the first place: the insight that current activity carries a particular present past, that it is characterized by a distinctive 'version' of the past currently relevant which is not equal to the totality of the past of the world. The action-present, one could say, must be unplugged from the all-encompassing maelstrom that is the total past of world and life. Building on Bergson and Husserl, it was clear for Schutz that this un-plugging must be realized by first tying action to the individual and then envisioning the individual to rise out of the stream of the world and segment the past while hovering above the current. In effect, the past of the present becomes a subjective past injected into the current situation by the subject—and, on a side note, this past is still a total past in the sense that it expresses the subject's complete history (its "biographical situation"). The alternative that Schatzki suggest is both more simple and more abstract: Building on Heidegger, he holds that the present past is unplugged from the total past by virtue of taking place (Heidegger would say: by temporalizing itself) in the action-present. The relevant past is thus tied to or an effect of the action rather than the subject in that it is transpiring in or being available within the current site of activity.

Notably, this Heideggerian understanding of a relevant past presenting itself is not entirely absent from Schutz' later work as well. According to Schutz and Luckmann, the skills and 'useful knowledge' must be "*continually* 'ready to grasp'" (1973: 108; original emphasis) in *every* situation for us to be able to understand and act in the situation. What is more, Schutz and Luckmann actually employ the Heideggerian terms "vorhanden" and "zuhanden" in discussing habitual knowledge—but they do so in a somewhat peculiar fashion and effectively express the precise opposite position from Heidegger: Schutz and Luckmann assert that habitual knowledge is "present-at-hand [vorhanden] in situations, not simply ready-to-hand [zuhanden] from case to case" (Schutz/T. Luckmann 1973: 108; my translation).[19]

---

[18] He acknowledges material or objectified determinants as well, but holds that by virtue of being intentionally designed and built, they can only 'carry' intentions (or past past futures) that have gone through this loophole already (Schutz 1967: 134; see W. Gibson 2006).

[19] I translated vorhanden and zuhanden in the same way as in the rest of my text for reasons of clarity. But notably, in the original English edition of the *Structures*, they are translated almost exactly the other way around: vorhanden [at hand] becomes "on hand" and zuhanden [ready-to-hand] becomes "at hand." According to the translators, this use of the terms correlates to Schutz own use (Schutz/T. Luckmann 1973: xxxii, 105 fn10). It is difficult to understand the exact

The precise use that Schutz makes of Heidegger would surely be worthy of closer study, but at a glance, it seems to me that, while Schutz was drawn to Heidegger's intuition that 'living in my acting-in-progress' unfolds against the backdrop, and thus in marginalized presence, of a certain past, he insisted on the subject being not just the active epicentre, but the source of each situation. Thus Schutz was unwilling to suggest that habituated skills could be ready-to-hand by themselves, or in the form of something brought about by the situation or site itself, and instead emphasized that they must be *made* present by the subject (via consciousness), thus calling them present-at-hand. In doing so, however, he is arguably blurring the very point of Heidegger's distinction: that there can be no ubiquitous and permanent presence-at-hand of a large number of entities such as the many, many elements of habituated knowledge Schutz presupposes (talking, walking, smoking, frying eggs…). To be sure, Schutz positions these elements at the margins of awareness and thus frames them not entirely unlike Heidegger's readiness-to-hand; but he ties presence in a situation to awareness rather than existence. The effect of this becomes especially clear with regard to tools or material objects: He provides what I would term an epistemology rather than an ontology of tools.

Excursus: Schutz and Heidegger

> Could one not simply say that Schutz acknowledges both grasping and projecting actions as relevant phenomena, but decides to focus on projection, so that his account can be smoothly complemented with a Heideggerian account of grasping? After all, Schutz recurrently refers to Heidegger's phenomenology in his late writings and shares—as I have shown—certain basic convictions regarding teleology with Heidegger. Indeed, Srubar (2007a, 2007b) has argued just that: Schutz, he holds, not only read Heidegger's Being and Time, but also adapted several key notions of his thinking and built them into his late writings (especially "Multiple Realities"): particularly Being-in-the-world, thrownness, and the fundamental fear of death. Yet Srubar (2007a: 35) also emphasizes that Schutz remained firm in his building on Husserl as the bedrock to his conceptualization of the social and of action and that consequentially, he considered thrownness and our fundamental fear of death as *anthropological* facts of subjective life—as a subjective experience rather than an ontic form of Being (Srubar 2007a: 216). But with this being the case, I believe it is problematic (or at least not straightforward) to assert, as Srubar does (2007a: 196 f.), that Schutz

---

reasons for this crucial change, but in my view it is most reasonable to conclude that Schutz does simply not agree with Heidegger's idea and uses the terms somewhat independent of their original context.

achieves a "unification" of the positions of Scheler and Heidegger in his definition of the pragmatic motive in his late works. First, because this effectively means to consider Heidegger's work as commensurate with philosophical anthropology, when in fact Heidegger himself rejected anthropology (and humanism) as "the doctrine of man" (1977: 133) which idealizes the then-contemporary upsurge of technocratic modernity, "the calculating, planning, and moulding of all things" into the equivalent of individual capabilities (1977: 135). In fact, the reasons that Heidegger gives for rejecting anthropology almost sound like being directed straight at Schutz: What troubles him is that "whatever is, is considered to be in being only to the degree and to the extent that it is taken into and referred back to [man's subjective] life, i.e., is lived out, and becomes life-experience" (Heidegger 1977: 134). Indeed, Heidegger's philosophy has arguably been motivated as much by perceived shortcomings in Scheler's work as by shortcomings in Husserl's (Schalow 1991). Second, a unification of Scheler and Heidegger by Schutz seems problematic because it would imply that all three—Schutz, Scheler, and Heidegger—concur in their reliance on one common ontology. Philosophical works are, of course, always open to different readings. Maybe it is quite possible to develop an explicitly Heideggerian perspective on Schutz late work (see Kockelmans 1979)—indeed this idea seems somewhat tempting—, but I am sceptical whether such a reading can also be extended to the early Schutz because, as Srubar (2007b) shows, that would require an individualistic pragmatist position. The inquiry into the question of whether or not Schutz' conception of the pragmatic motive does not already represent a thoroughly Heideggerian understanding of action—so that there is no need to juxtapose his sociology of action (or knowledge) and practice theory—therefore leads us strait back to the original point: A site ontology implies a non-technomorph concept of action and thus rejects the notion that action is determined by individual or subjective volition, or has necessarily a means-end structure.

The similarities and discrepancies between Schutz and Heidegger just described, I suggest, allow me to describe more precisely which philosophical underpinnings drove Schutz to basically abandoning his own sentiment that picking paths of action could function like grasping an object within reach, and to fully focusing on projecting in his later works instead. As I noted at the beginning of my discussion of Schutz' account of action, his thinking is rooted in Husserl's distinction between open and problematic alternatives. Against economists' and rational-choice models of decision making, Schutz argued that future actions are not given to us in the form of clearly outlined problematic alternatives, but rather as nearly formless open alternatives out of which discernible paths of action (represented by their final states) in the form of problematic alternatives need to be 'lifted' by the subject (1962: 79–85). The basic idea underlying both Schutz' and Schatzki's theory of action is Husserl's postulate that the meaning or function of (intended) objects does not stem from their form alone or the basic fact that they are either given or not, but also from their way of givenness or Gegebenheitsweise (see Smith/McIntyre 1982: 132). In Schutz, this idea translated into the notion that the role or meaning of each element of a situation is governed by the relevance structure currently employed (delineated from the subjective stock of knowledge). Husserl further held that the way of givenness of objects transpires exclusively in the realm of phenomena, that is, in consciousness; which allowed him to argue that real-world objects and objects in consciousness are closely correlated (the constancy hypothesis, see Rang 1990), while experience is nevertheless subjective (and thus mental representations are never simply true or false as Cartesians would hold). The point here is that the givenness of real-world objects in subjective consciousness is not per se deemed problematic—the question is not that we see the thing in front of us, but how we see it. In my view, Schutz' (1962: 83) brief description of choosing among objects within reach mirrors this view, in that the situated availability of the objects, their being-within-reach itself, seems unproblematic, in contrast to "the principally problematic possibilities of conflicting preferences." Heidegger, however, deemed it necessary to go beyond an enquiry of ways of givenness and return to the more fundamental question of how the givenness of objects is *ontologically* possible in the first place—a radical move not unlike Luhmann's extension of Husserl (1996b), only that the latter sought to answer the question via epistemology rather than ontology. How does it happen that a thing is given to us *as* a single thing, he asked, thus being sceptical towards Husserl's postulate that every 'ray of awareness' singles out and circumscribes a discrete element.[20] In effect, what was the way of givenness of objects in the realm of the phenomena in Husserl becomes the disclosure of things in the clearing or the site in Heidegger (see Tugendhat 1970: 184–185). Importantly, the upshot of this is that Heidegger would actually agree with Schutz that to the actor pondering which one to grasp, the two objects within reach pose problematic alternatives instead of open alternatives in Husserl's sense—because otherwise the actor would not care and thus not attend to them in the first place.

> "In the language of Heidegger's phenomenology, (..) the only possibilities about which the ego cares are the problematic [alternatives]." (Jordan 2000: 64)

Crucially, for Heidegger such basal care depends on the situated objects themselves (by their being un-ready-to-hand) and cannot be delineated from the actor's relevance structure. As Garfinkel put it, the "immediate in-hand intelligibility of a world 'not yet' reflected upon" (2002: 153) must be already in place (literally)

---

[20] It becomes apparent that although my account of Heidegger might sometimes sound like a form of naïve realism, he is actually more sceptical about the limits and prerequisites of perception and knowledge than Schutz is.

in order to motivate the actors engagement; or, to speak with Gibson (1986), the objects must afford grasping in order for the grasping to evoke the conflicting preferences Schutz discusses. In other words, before practical pondering and practical grasping of the objects can take place, their practical intelligibility must be provided for—and as Schutz (1945) discussion of *passive* awareness arguably shows, like Heidegger he did not quite share Husserl's (or Luhmann's) idealistic confidence that said intelligibility is entirely the actor's work. For Schutz, however, this did not imply that there must be some more fundamental or pre-existing *order* which ground our gearing into the world (which could e.g. be explained by social practices), but instead, it only means that 'living in our acts,' we act into an open horizon of open possibilities. And the reason for this conviction, to return to my main topic, is his notion of temporality. Since if we ask: By virtue of what is the future—as Schutz tells us—a horizon of open, non-distinct, formless possibilities? Because it is not yet underway. Because for Schutz, so to speak, the world and its objective time is frozen in the moment of taking a choice; it is like a still image of a movie whose ending we do not know. Metaphorically speaking: Schutz' actor is writing his autobiography, never knowing what should happen to the right of the blinking cursor. And as he hesitates, pondering what to write next, *nothing happens*, the cursor stands still, and the page remains blank beyond its threshold. Not so in Schatzki. In his account, the words on the page are the beginning of a sentence, a part of a story that is already unfolding. His point is not just that there are only so many ways in which such a half-born sentence can be continued meaningfully (Schatzki 1996: 160); and also not so much that typing is entangled with keyboards and screens and page limitations and deadlines in some ways (Schatzki 2010c). Instead it is that, while nothing predetermines just how the sentence will end before it has been written down in full (Schatzki 2002: 232), the beginning of the sentence, at any moment, is a beginning of a sentence nevertheless: It is by virtue of being part of a sentence that the words are meaningful *as part of* a congregation of words, for example in being grammatically right or wrong (to use Wittgenstein's term). But. Are. They. Not. Still. Single. Words. Nevertheless? It does not look like they are, you see? Even if they are meant to stand alone, fully self-contained. Autopoietic. Because in doing so, they are still an expression of, and thus meaningful because of, that peculiar something I mentioned before: style.

17 Consequences: From Flow to Style

I provided a discussion of the vexed problem of action, practical intelligibility, and flow, because I deem it essential for gaining an adequate understanding of stylish conduct and the role of style more generally. Under the means-end assumption, one would need to assume that the freeskiers use their habituated skills or bodily techniques as means to achieve the end of demonstrating Style. But as I argued in chapter six, such an account of techniques as distinct tools used to produce certain distinct symbols (such as gestures) would be misleading. As one can now see, it is

17 Consequences: From Flow to Style

equally inadequate to portray style as an end in the sense of a concept, a distinct state of the world that one intends to produce. Freeskiers, I hold, do not and cannot have a precise blueprint in their head that allows them to preconceive just what exactly they 'want' to do. Dropping down into a couloir in the face of the Krimml en route to a stylish line, they have no precise idea just what it is they are going to do to make their run stylish. To be sure: They do have a certain plan about where to ski and which drop to try, but these points only determine the course of their line, but not the flow and style of their riding. On the other hand, however, I hold that it would be equally misleading to assert (in a praxeological manner) that the Style they will perform is only an entirely unintended byproduct of their generally going skiing, in the sense that they cannot help but express their freeskiing habitus wherever and however they ski. Doing Style does not happen by accident but is a specific *mode* of acting: The riders, I argue, do strive towards skiing stylishly, but that does not mean they undertake to realize clearly preconceived ends, neither 'in reality' nor in reflection (much like improvising musicians, see Figueroa-Dreher 2008; Sudnow 1978). As Dreyfus (1991: 93) put it, "activity can be purposive without the actor having in mind a purpose." More precisely, what the freeskiers strive to reach is not a predefined goal or symbolic expression, but a state of *being*; a kind of "being in the zone" as they might put it, a modus of acting-and-feeling (Heidegger: um-willen). And one mayor way to achieve this, I seek to argue in the following chapter, is by orienting to and acting oriented by style.

Chapter 9
Understanding and Media—Seeing Style

1 Introduction: Of Beauty and Repulsion

"To this day, I have never seen a person who could charge a line so aggressively, so in control, so commanding, and still keep a smooth feel to it, like Billy did. His style reminded me of the absolute control of Kent Kreitler, the creativity of Eric Hjorleifson, and the aggression of Seth Morrison, all packaged in the fluidity and anti-ego of Brant Moles. Everything looked so easy! It seemed like he and the mountains were old friends, just playing with each other." (user "Dustin" on Billy Poole Memorial Fund 2008)

From my fieldnotes, international snow sport trade fair ISPO, Munich, 16.2.10.

Later in the afternoon, I stroll along the halls with Pit and Jean, a Swiss freeski-pro, enjoying the buzz of the huge trade fair with industry professionals from around the globe. We casually take a look at the new gear and clothing collections coming out next fall, but the trade fair booths themselves are nearly as interesting: Many showcase marvellous freeski images printed on huge posters and show the newest team videos on large screens. As we pass by the booth of a well-known German ski-glove brand with a long tradition, Jean stops short. "Ehhh!" he cringes, his face expressing disgust. "That's ugly! That's so Oldschool! I hate that!" He points at a large poster in the middle of the booth (shown in Fig. 9.1). At first glance, it simply shows a freestyle skier in action, performing some spectacular inverted arial. Apart from the questionable choice of the colour of his clothing, one might wonder, what is wrong with it? But Jean is right: This is a classic case of a conservative brand trying to jump on the bandwagon without having a clue what freeskiing is all about. The problem with this image is that it does not show a contemporary, New School-style flip, but a somersault or what Oldschool freestyle skiers call an Eddie loop: The skier's body is stretched out and tense, like a gymnast at the parallel bars. Instead of grabbing his skis, the arms are stretched out to the side; the whole posture expressing what gymnasts would call body tension and verve. But freeskiers see hectic stiffness, uptight officiousness, and pretentious acrobatics trying to hide the fact that the skier will all too quickly lose control if the kicker is not absolutely perfectly groomed. In short: There is no Style in this picture at all. Putting it into such a prominent place is simply wrong. Jean feels uneasy just from looking at it. "Pew!" he mutters as he shakes his head in disbelieve. "Let's go."

Fig. 9.1 Detail of an advertising by a brand that is trying to be cool, but instead showing "horrible" Style

What does it mean to see Style? Why do freeskiers get so emotional about it? And if style is first and foremost a quality of bodily conduct, what does it mean to say that an image has Style? Because style is a pivotal concept for phenopractice theory, these questions are not simply empirically interesting, but theoretically crucial. Both the strictly situated perspective and the complexities of Gestalt thinking and neural pluralism mean that a simple concept of mental pattern identification does not conform with core assumptions of the proposed theory position. Yet, that both face-to-face encounters and suitable media can afford style apprehension and learning is empirically and theoretically without question. Indeed, a core assumption of this work is that the interactive and mediatized 'seeing' of style forms a key way in which the circulation of practice elements, and thus the recruitment to and dissemination of practices happens in a mediatized society. Therefore, this chapter will present a revised conceptualization of understanding and media from a phenopractice perspective—beginning, as always, with an observation of freeskiers and practical concerns, rather than abstract aesthetics. When Freestylers spectate other freeskiers perform, I have shown, they do not simply watch them showing symbolic gestures that are then 'read' or identified. When looking for Style, freeskiers do not simply try to find out which moves the other performs, but instead, they want to see *how* the other is doing; something that they look for in the details of the movement. But with regard to this understanding, the discussion of temporality which I presented in the last chapter bears a highly important implication: Such an operation, I argue, entails a crucial transformation in that it requires that the observed details of conduct which unfold sequentially are being grasped 'en bloc,' as one 'thing' or unit. The style of one's writing, for example, must be a quality of the writing, of a certain length of text—but at the same time, it must somehow emanate from the flow of the words, for it is housed in their relatedness rather than in the words themselves. Thus, in describing or assessing such style, something happens that one could call entification: the flow of words becomes an entity having a certain quality. Further, if the text was a poem, it would make quite a difference whether one reads it of the page, have someone unskilled read it out loud, or hear it being recited by an actor. Likewise, if we read it ourselves, we will (usually) quickly realize that this is a poem and start to read it differently, we will start to 'recite' it to ourselves, either aloud or silently. The style of the poem, it seems, only comes forth if it is approached from a certain angle, if it is put into practice in a certain way. But nevertheless, it still makes sense to talk of the style *of* that poem, rather than the style of the reading, since even if it is read out in a clumsy way, we could listen, write down the words, and then recite it skilfully to bring out the rhythm of the verses. We can, in other words, transform it from one medium into another, for example to store the poem for hundreds of years or send it across the globe in a split-second; and only in some of its mediated forms, the poem's style can be grasped. In a nutshell, this chapter argues that something similar happens when freeskiers see Style in a continuously unfolding line or trick, or when they record them on video or in a picture, and then look at it on screen. In order to explain how this happens, and to develop an account of style that takes these points into consideration, I will combine the empirical and theoretical insights generated so far with certain neuroscientific findings about visual routines, as well as the sociological and philosophical discussion they have triggered, particularly arguments made that have been about instructed action by ethnomethodology and the philosophy and sociology of art. In doing so, I aim to sketch out a more concise answer to a key theoretical question: What does it mean to understand or become attuned to a style?

2 Face Recognition and Style Recognition

I conceptualize style as a figural gestalt visible in a certain episode of conduct. Although freeskiers ascribe Style to individual persons and treat it as an expression of subject-hood, style must be procedurally achieved, rather than being a given quality of someone or something—or rather: It is only in, through, or (to use Garfinkel's expression) 'over the ground of' situated conduct that style can manifest itself and appear as a momentary state. One interesting way to see why I tie style to the overall conduct, rather than describing it e.g. as something expressed in singular gestures, words, or symbols, is to pay attention to the fact that the freeskier's interactions, reciprocal observation, and mutual care which take place in the funpark all happen while their faces are masked (Fig. 9.2). Freeskiers 'hide' not only their eyes, but a large part of their face behind skiing goggles, facial expressions are not an aspect of freeskiing style (and are usually

Fig. 9.2 Masking the face in style

simply not visible for spectators). Riders in a funpark, seldomly look at each other's face, because they are either queuing at a kicker or lift, watching someone perform, or sit or stand in a ski lift. What is somewhat surprising about this fact is that in most other areas of human life, watching other's facial expressions, and especially their eyes, is *the* principal mode of perceiving and sharing other's emotions and intentions, as well as gaining a sense of community and bonding—not the least in leisure, games, and sports (Gladwell 2005; C. Goodwin 2007; C. Goodwin/M. H. Goodwin 2001; Kendon 1990). Indeed, visual routines arising in response to facial expressions are so ubiquitous and basic that neuroscientists have suggested a specific brain system to be in place that is wholly dedicated to such visual "mindreading," as they call it (Becchio/Bertone 2004; Jacob 2008; Jacob/Jeannerod 2003: 242–246; Newen/Bartels 2007)—thus confirming Wittgenstein's postulate that mental states must be visible in outward behaviour. Yet freeskiers rob themselves purposefully of opportunities to see each other's face. To some extent, this is a side-effect of the specific conditions of the mountain environment and the spatial layout of lifts and parks. But particularly the ski goggle as an iconic part of freeskiing equipment demonstrates that 'de-facing' is a desirable part of the freeskiing culture: While ski goggles might have 'originally' covered a much larger area of the face than sunglasses for technical reasons only, freeskiers routinely enhance this effect by using (more expensive) versions with reflective coating, or add bandanas to mask their face completely. What is more, they often wear them in situations where normal sunglasses would do as well, like having lunch or relaxing. Surely, on the one hand the uses of goggles has a purely symbolic function in that they distinguish the riders from other skiers who seem

Fig. 9.3 A freeskier proudly wearing his goggle while 'tourists' wear sunglasses (in the background)

anxious to wear 'ugly' and 'impractical' goggles only if forced to do so in bad weather, and otherwise prefer sunglasses—a means of distinction epitomized by the freeskiers' custom of wearing a ski goggle around the neck or arm in bars and nightclubs, even on the dance floor (Fig. 9.3). But on the other hand, I hold that much like masks at a carnival, goggles also have a more direct or pragmatic effect of transforming the possibilities and routines of watching and being watched, the patterns of interaction they are linked with, and the emotional routines these are enmeshed into. Because, despite being largely unable to benefit from visual routines of face recognition when interacting with other wearing goggles and bandanas, freeskiers are evidently nevertheless able to identify each other, interact, and share emotions. I deem this point worth noting because it shows that it would be misleading to conceptualize face-to-face interaction as a direct, situation-independent link from subject to subject or mind to mind, as a kind of 'pure' sociality taking place in an empty bubble. To the contrary, I agree with authors arguing that 'reading' and/or sharing other's intentions and emotions always happens by taking into account a broader picture extending to the bodily position, posture, and stance expressed—in other words: the overall style of bodily conduct. Consequentially, I am also deeply sceptical towards arguments or experiments suggesting that 'anthropomorphic' (e.g. face-like) shapes, drawings, or objects automatically and miraculously impose emotional effects analogous or even comparable to those gained in situated interaction (cf. Aggarwal/McGill 2007; Landwehr/McGill/Herrmann 2011; Windhager et al. 2008). In contradiction to such idealizations of 'the human,' neuroscientists have found that the neural systems or visual routines carrying the recognition of faces and facial expressions are the same that are responsible for other forms of recognition of figures and shapes, for example in that birdwatchers identify types of bird in the same way we all spot the growing anger in a friends' face (Gauthier/Behrmann/Tarr 2011; Gauthier/Skudlarski/Gore/A. W. Anderson 2000; Gauthier/P. Williams/Tarr/Tanaka 1998).[1] Given such findings about the neural underpinnings of the accumulation of visual expertise (see also Tarr/Cheng 2003), my claim that freeskiers literally *see* identities, feel emotions, and gain a sense of community by watching the style in others' performances of bodily tricks seems much less far-fetched: In a certain way, seeing a smoothly done 720 Japan is indeed like meeting an old friend.

I should stress, however, that such deep-rooted visual routines, as well as the emotional regimes they are connected to, must be honed over an extended period of time, and that they cannot be equated to 'understanding' or learning abstract conceptual knowledge. Therefore, one the one hand they are 'deep skills' that are embodied, fine-tuned, and largely pre-conscious and thus cannot be adequately formulated in abstract, 'logical' expressions or replaced with schematic or mechanistic solutions. Seeing style, in other words, is not something that can be put into mathematical formulas, done by a robot, or emulated by artificial intelligence (see H. L. Dreyfus 1979; H. L. Dreyfus/S. E. Dreyfus 1986). But on the other hand, these characteristics neither warrant framing them as part of a pre-given, super-natural 'human condition,' nor as inscribed so deeply into us during childhood that we can never quite escape their powers (like a habitus). Instead, I hold that the routines for seeing freeskiing style are built up over a few years—but not decades, nor weeks—over the course of what Lave and Wenger (1991) call "legitimate peripheral participation," that is, spectating together with others. Conceptualized as such, visual routines for seeing style can be linked to the so-called enactive approach to social cognition in neuroscience, a framework of findings suggesting that empathy and intersubjective intentionality (i.e. orienting towards other's feelings and interests, or acting in a 'we-mode') are closely connected to *motor* intentionality and the so-called mirror neurons in the brain, so that the dominant computational paradigm is to be replaced with an inherently embodied and situated view (Hutto 2006; Giacomo Rizzolatti/Sinigaglia/F. Anderson 2008; Schlicht 2010; Sinigaglia 2009). To be sure, social thought must tread lightly when trying to embrace highly specific experimental findings that are themselves heavy with presuppositions about methods, measures, 'the mind,' and sociality at large. What is more, positions within cognitive neurosciences and the philosophy of mind are all but unequivocal. But before looking into these findings—and open questions—in more detail, it suffices to point out that seeing others move seems to be at the neural root of many more complex social emotions and formations unfolding in shared situations. Against this

---

[1] I should note that these findings build to some extent on fMRI-data rather than interactive experiments and thus in part fall into the category of studies trying to match 'activated' brain areas with abstract 'cognitive' tasks which I criticized earlier. The basic argument of the study, however, still holds in face of the basic experimental finding alone (minus the fMRI data).

background, I hold, the emotional and social power of looking at abstract movement figures and seeing the style and identity of fellow freeskiers can be better understood. Once the visual and teleoaffective routines are in place (in the strict sense of the word), they appear to be an intuitive and almost natural ability: They render freeskiers capable of reading tricks like others read faces, recognizing acquaintances in an instant, spotting most subtle notes of trouble, and being deeply touched and moved by moments of seeing unfathomable beauty.

3 The Mirror System

The question of what exactly happens when we see others perform a movement is of great interest to practice theory, because it suggests that bodily ways of doing, rather than mental acts of interpretation, ought to be treated as the meaning-generating (or even inherently meaningful) 'building blocks,' or rather carriers, of social order. The main argument of hermeneutic, rationalist, 'verstehende,' and related subjectivist methodologies (as well as methodological individualism) has always been that a) subjective consciousness is the crucial 'point of passage' through which embodied knowledge or skills must pass before they can bear on individual action, that b) its ways of working conclusively defines what actors can and/or will do, and that c) it is thus the realm whose workings social inquiry must uncover. (A similar argument can be about explicit discourse or communication.) If, however, one could for example show how practical skills can undergo a tacit-to-tacit transmission, this critique could be refuted (and Turner [2001], for example, rejects practice theory precisely on the basis that one cannot sufficiently explain such transmission). Notably, such 'visual contagion' would need to happen with regard to the final meaning of bodily movements (i.e. directed episodes of movement), rather than isolated details. The question, in other words, is: What happens when we see others act, that is, when we see them performing a movement that has a teleological endpoint? In the debate within the literature of the practice turn, this question has become of considerable importance, primarily because some have argued that certain findings from neuroscience can provide scientific explanations for some central claims of praxeology, specifically Bourdieu's notions 'habitus' and 'mimesis' (Lizardo 2007; Lizardo/Strand 2010; Reckwitz 2000b; Schmidt 2008; S. P. Turner 2007). I should note that I will survey the debate that unfolded not so much with regard to the question whether findings from neuroscience prove Bourdieu right or wrong (since I do not draw on his concepts for other reasons), but with regard to the explanations it might yield for a phenopractice-theoretical account of seeing and doing, which differs from both the critics and the defendants of Bourdieu. Moreover, it is worth repeating that scientific findings based on 'exact' data collection in the laboratory can never replace a theory of the social as a whole, and thus while the social theorist can (and should) try to account plausibly for such findings just like they should try to account for freeskiers behaving oddly in the funpark, experiments with macaque monkeys or fMRI results cannot shoulder the burden of taking theoretical decisions. Sometimes (especially in the exchange between Lizardo [2007] and Turner [2007]) authors seem to imply that cognitive neuroscience can provide the 'ultimate weapon' against competing theoretical positions—yet all that sociology can gain from it is inspiration, not absolution.

To begin with, it is not necessarily surprising that athletes develop fine-tuned visual observation skills that are crucial for succeeding in the sport they conduct almost every day. Professional basketball players, for example, can predict quite well whether a player throwing a free shot will hit the basket or not, just from looking at a video of the player's bodily movements prior to the ball actually leaving his hands (Aglioti/Cesari/Romani/Urgesi 2008). What is more, it also not surprising that non-playing experts like coaches are nowhere near as good in predicting; presumably since when watching from the sideline, they do not need to react within fractions of seconds when they sense that an opponent is going to hit or miss (and thus need to jump in to stop the ball or not). In this sense, one could simply say that freeskiers spot more interesting details when watching others perform freestyle, and thus freeski movies are more entertaining for them, just like watching any sport is more interesting when you can tell whether someone is doing well but unlucky, whether the game is close or not, etc. Yet in an experimental study by Aglioti et al., (2008) this kind of visual expertise was not what made the difference between expert players and expert observers—indeed, the expert observers were hardly better at predicting free shots than novice observers. Instead, what the authors tried to argue was that the players are so much better at predicting because they are regularly *performing the movement* of throwing a free shot themselves: that what matters is not visual expertise, but motor expertise. Their study belongs to a stream of literature evidencing the existence of a so-called mirror system (or mirror neurons) in the brain which is 'triggered' or 'activated' *both* when we watch an action being performed *and* when we perform the same action ourselves (Cross/Hamilton/Grafton 2006; Gallese/Goldman 1998; Jacob/Jeannerod 2003: 228–242; Stamenov/Gallese 2002). Since the first discovery of this effect in monkeys four decades ago (Pellegrino/Fadiga/Fogassi/Gallese/G. Rizzolatti 1992), a host of works has demonstrated the same process in humans and other animals, and the basic facticity of the phenomenon (i.e. the activation of said region by either watching or doing) seems most widely accepted in the scientific community. However, both neuroscientists and philosophers of mind are in deep disagreement about the range of human capabilities that can be explained as being an effect of the mirror system. Few question the idea that seeing a simple action being performed can work as a kind of 'dry rehearsal' that helps us to keep the movement being a part of 'our' movement repertoire (Jacob/Jeannerod 2003: 226–234). But for others, this discovery has far-reaching consequences in that it can actually explain the spread of language (e.g. because we 'shadow' the movements of mouth and lips in a kind of 'inner motor monologue' alongside the speaker; see Marslen-Wilson 1985; Skoyles 2000), but also feelings of empathy or 'social cognition' more generally (Cerulo 2010; Gallagher

2005; Jacob/Jeannerod 2005; Malle/Moses/Baldwin 2003; Schlicht 2010). The latter thesis is especially significant for social thought, but also entails the most far-reaching conclusions drawn from experimental studies of the functions of the mirror system. Its proponents (especially Gallese) formulate a "simulation theory of mind," arguing—crudely said—that the brain continuously simulates behaviour as we watch others act, and in doing so shares the motor *intentions* expressed in the actions, and therefore "a multiplicity of states that include actions, sensations and emotions," which effectively amounts to "an implicit, prereflexive form of understanding" (Gallese 2003a) more basic than language-mediated understanding and empathy (Becchio/Bertone 2004; Gallese 2003a, 2003b; Gallese/Goldman 1998; Gallese/Lakoff 2005; Stamenov/Gallese 2002). It is on the basis of this theory (or rather by treating it more like an irrefutable scientific discovery than a theory), that some authors in sociology, most notably Lizardo, have suggested that mirror neurons provide the neurological underpinnings of Bourdieu's habitus and explain his notion of mimesis (Lizardo 2007, 2009, 2011; Lizardo/Strand 2010; see for the German discussion Schmidt 2008, 2009; Schmidt/Volbers 2011b). If true, their argument would indeed imply far-reaching reconsiderations for many aspects of the sociology of interaction, culture, and style. The question is: How convincing is their argument?

Before looking at the arguments in more detail, I suggest, one needs to keep their broader background in mind: The studies Gallese and colleagues draw on largely make inferences from fMRI-experiments in which the "firing" of neurons in certain areas of the brain is measured while the subjects are lying in a huge machine and are shown images or videos, or are asked to *imagine* or *prepare for* certain imagined movements. The brain areas 'mapped' as more active than others are in turn 'associated' with certain brain functions; and on this basis it is inferred that they serve the same task. These 'tasks,' moreover, are treated by the neuroscientists as exemplars of relatively clear-cut groups of mundane actions, such as 'seeing an object being grasped' or 'planning to grasp an object' (e.g. Jacob/Jeannerod 2003: 70–71). Finally, measured activations of brain areas are treated as something "the mind does," which—depending on the text in question—swiftly turns into something "we all do," and further transforms into something "actors subconsciously do." Needless to say, every step in this long chain of generalizing associations is inherently problematic; especially from a perspective emphasizing the role of situational order for human conduct, and with regard to Wittgenstein's argument that 'mental states' or conditions of the brain simply fall into an entirely different category than 'things we do' (Bennett/Hacker 2003). Reasons to be sceptical are thus plentiful, especially when far-reaching conclusions or general theories are being deducted from such studies. On the other hand, I have argued that insights of this kind can and should inform social theory, if taken in digestible doses and with an eye to the concrete circumstances and methods of the studies in question. In this vein, I stress that studies like that by Aglioti et al. (2008) are concerned with a similar topic and situational set-up than the one I studied in detail (athletes watching videos of 'their' sport); conform with my overall concept of situated seeing; and in this work they are thus being placed in an empirical and theoretical context, rather than forming the sole pillar of an abstract theoretical argument (such as the 'class habitus'-thesis). With this important reservation in mind, let me turn to the sociological arguments made about the mirror system.

Excursus: Do Mirror Neurons Verify Praxeology?

The claim that the discovery of the mirror system strongly supports or even verifies Bourdieu's praxeological perspective has not only garnered considerable attention, but also drawn fierce criticism. Most notable in this regard is the exchange between a long-standing critic of practice theory per se, Stephen Turner (2001, 2007), and Omar Lizardo (2007, 2009). Since their topic and lines of reasoning directly touch upon my own considerations, the arguments of both of them demand close study—although they ultimately both go against the grain of the position I defend in this work.

The central claim of Bourdieu's (1990: 73 f.) praxeology is that bodily skills and thus "the essential part of the *modus operandi* that defines practical mastery is transmitted through practice, in the practical state, without rising to the level of discourse." Practice theory so conceived, in other words, needs a concept of purposive, directed action in order to avoid the pitfalls of mere behaviouralism, but at the same time seeks to avoid the problematic notion that well worked-out ends precede and steer practical conduct, especially in the sense that actors follow mental models or consciously reflected and relational strategies (Lizardo 2007: 335). For Bourdieu (1990: 62), of course, "the habitus contains the solution to the paradoxes of objective meaning without subjective intention." But in his influential critique of theories of social practice, Stephen Turner (1994) argued that said theories ultimately claim that actors proceed according to a "tacit rulebook" (S. P. Turner 2001), a set of subconscious mental concepts governing conduct—but without being able to provide an adequate theoretical explanation how tacit knowledge spreads from one person to the next. In effect, Turner (1997) concluded that tacit knowledge is treated as both explanans and explanandum in what he deems practice theorists' "causally ludicrous" attempt to explain for the regularity of human conduct by its very regularity. (I will return to Turner's arguments later.) More recent neuroscientific findings seem to provide Bourdieu's defendants with strong arguments to counter Turner's weighty attack. Drawing heavily on Gallese's (2003a, 2003b; Gallese/Goldman 1998; Gallese/Lakoff 2005; Stamenov/Gallese 2002) interpretations of the mirror system, Lizardo (2007, 2009) argued that thanks to their discovery, this line of critique has become futile: Both the direct 'tacit-to-tacit' transmission of embodied knowledge, and the general sameness of the courses of actions of a collective (e.g. a class) which shares a certain position in a field and thus a habitus, he holds, can now be explained by "empirically verifiable hypotheses." (2007: 320; emphasis removed) In his view, the upshot of the mirror system activity is that the observation of action implies action simulation, and that said simulation in turn equates to "the practical learning, comprehension and representation of the action." (Lizardo 2007: 334) What is more, over time it would accumulate into to what Bourdieu called the formation of a habitus (or at least its expressive part), a collection of bodily dispositions involuntarily and automatically picked up from our everyday surround:

> "By virtue of being part of a given social world, humans will be exposed to countless acts of practical teaching and will be the subject of practical learning during the course of their everyday existence." (Lizardo 2007: 335).

A crucial aspect of this understanding, in other words, is Gallese's (2003a: 521) rather strong claim that practice transmission via observation from co-presence is "automatic, unconscious, and pre-reflexive," which corresponds to Bourdieu's account in which the appropriation of the (class) habitus through mimesis is usually inevitable and automatic, as well as reflecting the general conditions of life of a group rather than individually unique biographies and wilfully conducted learning.[2] In a response to Lizardo, Turner objected to this reading of the function and impact of the mirror system, arguing that "a mechanism that produces sameness simply by exposure is simply beyond plausibility" (2007: 366) because it would effectively rid us of all the labour that is usually necessary for acquiring bodily skills. He cites the example of learning to swing a baseball bat: Even though everyone can do a crude 'natural swing' straight after having seen someone swing, a very long and systematic process of coaching and learning is necessary to become an able player—which is thus everything but an 'automatic' and 'subconscious' process. Precisely because it seems to be the case that the mirror system is more or less permanently involved in our everyday conduct, one might say, it is also quite clear that it must be far too basic or primitive to account for the complexities of social learning. Take, for example, the case of smiling: Smiling and smiling back is a thoroughly social-bodily-emotional doing that often happens pre-reflexive or intuitive, but can also cover a whole range of complex communicative or symbolic forms or functions, e.g. by being derisive, visibly purposefully fake (as to sarcastically express: "very funny"), a comic performance of a it-would-be-funny-if-it-wasn't-so-sad-smile, and so forth. What is more, a number of studies have shown that moving the facial muscles to smile is in a way hard-wired

---

[2] Bourdieu arguably changed his position on the question whether a habitus is shared by a whole class or smaller subgroups within different subfields of society (Schatzki 1997: 305 fn10), and contemporary authors tend to stress that the habitus is a flexible rather than deterministic concept (e.g. Hilgers 2009; Wacquant 2005b). Still, the idea that one's everyday life (and especially upbringing) will inevitably be reflected in every habitus in such a way that it reproduces the order of the field it belongs to without the actors necessarily noticing is central to the model.

to our emotional states in that we can (to some extend) feel better from making ourselves smile—rather than just the other way around—, which is also part of the explanation why joy is contagious to some extent, or 'out there in the situation.' At the core, mimicking other's facial expressions is a very basal bodily ability: New-born babies can emulate their parents' opening their mouth and protruding their tongue a mere 42 minutes after their birth (Jacob/Jeannerod 2003: 234). Seeing and repeating basic bodily movements, it thus seems fair to say, is a part of the bodily 'starter-kit' we already have ready-to-hand as we are thrown into this world.

If one would assess this 'exchange' of gestures between parent and newborn in terms of the classic phenomenological account of body-movement and kinaesthesia as I presented it in chapter three, one could be led to consider it a relatively complex succession of interpretation and wilful action: The facial expression must be 'read' as intentionally and directed at the baby, the kinaesthesia of doing something similar must be intended by the 40-minute old, and the action must be performed. Quite clearly, this would be too much to expect from a newborn. To be sure, hardly any author from within the sociology of action or knowledge would argue for such an explanation. Alfred Schutz (1945: 535), for example, explicitly describes facial expressions as "involuntary spontaneity" rather than action and would suggest that *after* the baby reacted, some kind of reflection would kick in, e.g. in that once the parents smile happily and praise the baby, it will (sooner or later) begin to realize that *itself* did something towards the parents (see chapter eight for an extensive discussion of Schutz). In other words, far from begin a refutation of theories of conscious, experiential learning, and thus of phenomenological accounts of body movement, the very existence of a prereflexive or preconscious ability to mimic movements is a prerequisite to establish their very plausibility—this, at least, is the argument which Turner (2007) makes to refute Lizardo. In his view, "the idea of simulation shifts the emphasis to the individual, who uses himself or herself as a model and means of understanding others." (S. P. Turner 2007: 367) Accordingly, Turner (2007: 356) concludes that "mirror neurons (…) are just another nail in the coffin of Bourdieu's conception of practices." From my perspective, however, a more nuanced view is due. As David Stern (2000: 55) points out, Turner's rejection of attempts to explain behaviour by referring to hidden inner categories bears striking resemblance to Wittgenstein's very own critique of mental objects or states (as well as that by Heidegger). A Wittgensteinian account of social practices that lives up to the title, in other words, will be from the start constructed as a reaction to the very problem Turner 'discovers' in practice thought. And the way it (arguably) achieves this without having to fall back on interpretative individualism—as Turner does—is to deny that practices are 'objects' or pieces of knowledge stored in, expressible by, and shared among individuals in the first place. Instead, as we have seen, it is argued that in order to be recurrent, practices do not *have to be* substantial, in order to be mobile, they do not *have to be* expressible (especially not in words alone), and in order to be socially dispersed, they do not *have to be* shared, that is, housed in individuals in fully identical form. In short, I believe that Turner's arguments work well—both against Bourdieu and against himself. Practice theory does not actually need to make the assumption that bodily techniques can undergo tacit-to-tacit transmission; and thus proving or disproving it's "empirical verifiable" existence does not prove or disprove practice thought.

The basic tacit transmission of practical knowledge, however, is only one part of the argument Lizardo seeks to make. Its function would be to underwrite Bourdieu's claim that tacit skill-dispositions can be conceptualized as an embodied capacity reflecting the socioeconomic background or position of each individual actor, especially in terms of the inherited class dispositions (the habitus). While this is in itself already a relatively strong claim, it covers only a part of Bourdieu's overall model. Namely, unconscious mirroring of certain movement patterns would imply a certain rigidity of social styles of conduct and would position each individual within a certain imaginary chart of 'the' society; but it would also only bear on the expressive 'side' of the habitus, the way we do things when we do them. However, the capacities Bourdieu ascribes the habitus go much further in that it is furthermore understood to a) entail socially 'keyed' perception; and b) turn members of society into 'strategic actors' perpetually trying to defend and better their position (Hilgers 2009; Wacquant 2005b). In order to address these aspects as well, Lizardo makes an even stronger claim about the mirror system, namely that seeing others perform does not only equip us with basic skills and styles of doing, but what Bourdieu called a "feel for the game." We gain, he argues, not only a capacity to respond properly without thinking in immediate situations, but we even routinely engage in "unconscious strategizing" (Lizardo 2007: 336); 'instinctively' following long-term paths towards securing and bettering our (social) capital. This claim, it should be clear, is much bolder than the basic assumption that we might subconsciously acquire certain subtle gestures or a certain style of conducting certain practices (in that we might walk like our parents do, etc.). At the core, it amounts to the claim that what the mirror system picks up are *not* just the details of behaviour or body movement per se, but instead their teleological endpoints or intentional content:

> "*Such unconscious strategizing (...) is in fact a real, routine, neurophysiologically instantiated process grounded in the embodied cognitive ability to 'read-off' goals and purposes from other actors from the direct,* 'subpersonal' attunement and coordination of motor schemes across agents, *without ever resorting to conscious deliberation about goals and purposes.*" (Lizardo 2007: 337; original emphasis).

Again, it is apparent that Lizardo has a certain tendency to generalize his postulates about the functions and effects of what scientists initially described to be a highly specialized neural system. What is more, he even claims that the process is both entirely cut off from consciousness, and ubiquitous, and perpetual, so that "any social setting that acts directly on the body for a given collective will necessarily result in the sharing of similar 'practical presuppositions' about the world." (Lizardo 2007: 343) This generalization, I argue, is not just an unfortunate over-reach, but instead a necessary part of his argument, since as soon as Lizardo would acknowledge that consciousness is involved in selecting the situations from which we learn (e.g. by directing attention), individual dispositions would depend on conscious decisions, rather than being imposed on us by society in their entirety.[3] What to make of these arguments in light of the scientific findings they build on? Lizardo's claim that we subconsciously 'copy' the intentional content of movements we watch others perform is derived from Gallese's (2003a) 'strong version' of the so-called motor simulation theory (see Berthoz 2000): When we observe actions, this theory holds, we engage in a subconscious mental simulation, that is, our mind 'lives through' the action in much the same way as the actor herself does. Notably, the bodily movements referred to in this theory are not only (or not even) 'large' whole-body movements. Instead, some authors argue that since facial expressions, for example, are understood to be tightly coupled to emotions and moods, we can 'read of' and subconsciously copy other's feelings via this inter-face (in the truest sense of the word) (Becchio/Bertone 2004; Gallese 2003b; Gallese/Goldman 1998). Lizardo, however, focuses his account primarily on the topic of purposeful action. He claims that by watching *sequences* of action (rather than momentarily conditions such as moods), we can subconsciously 'get' their teleological structure and simulate them bodily.[4] In effect, merely watching an action equates to "a level of understanding" (2007: 333) which, he argues, conveys us the kind of background understanding practice theorists consider to carry our skills (cf. H. L. Dreyfus 1991; D. Stern 2000):

> "[T]hese implicit acts of embodied simulation are precisely the source of the background pre-understandings and hidden presupposition that are the subject of practice theory." (Lizardo 2007: 333 f.)

---

[3] Arguably, Bourdieu does not even make such a strong claim, at least not in his later works—but Lizardo does.

[4] As I mentioned in Chap. 3, neuroscientists argue that this 'simulation' is not simply mental, but involves nerve endings and (very small) muscles in the whole body (see Berthoz 2000; Berthoz/Petit 2008).

This is a weighty claim, and very significant in the context of the Dreyfus-Taylor-Schatzki strand of practice theory, since understanding (or background understanding) is a central term for it. What is more, my own discussion of human action centres on the distinction between understanding and intelligibility (which I adapt from Schatzki). Therefore, one needs to take a good look at what precisely it is that Lizardo treat as understanding. In his own words: "sameness of practical contents" of mental processes (2007: 334). As we have seen, in doing so he is responding to Turner's critique, which focuses on the problem of sameness—at the core the classic Kantian (or Cartesian) argument that individual ideas never precisely match worldly phenomena. Schematically speaking, Lizardo presupposes the inherent sameness of bodily behaviour, and then holds that it can be accounted for by the mirror system, in that said system allows not just for emulating behaviour, but also for sharing and transmitting motor intentions. Understanding an action from watching it, in other words, for him entails that the regularity inherent in the movement a) stems from, or is at least strictly coupled to, (subconscious) mental content of the performer, and is b) copied by the observer. In sum, performer and observer share a practical understanding by virtue of carrying the *same* mental content. Turner, in contrast, insists on the inherent difference-in-detail of everyone's overt bodily behaviour as evidencing the irredeemably uniqueness of each individual's mental content, and thus needs to explain why there is at least *some* uniformity in behaviour at all. Here, the mirror system becomes relevant for Turner as well, because it can account for uniformity without harming his overall argument that prior "simulative hypotheses" cause our actions (S. P. Turner 2007: 368).

In sum, it becomes evident how the mind/world- or individual/situation-dichotomy forces both authors into making extreme arguments: Either, there is sameness of mental content (which sounds a lot like mistaking a human for a computer disk); or, there is no strict coherence at all. What makes this situation almost ironic is that neither of the two would actually claim that the very bodily movement they seek to explain—and which is the only thing they can observe (since neither of them engages in phenomenology)—is *ever* precisely identical or (almost) *ever* entirely uncommon or one-of-a-kind. I do not quite see how this situation per se poses either a problem of sameness or of strict uniqueness and individuality. Instead—at least from my perspective—both Lizardo and Turner are each chased into their corner because they insist that there must be one single hidden apparatus in charge of the outward behaviour that they see. Further, both its regularity and its contingency, they seem to believe, must be traced back to this single apparatus as the sole producer and carrier of understanding. If not, if the observable similarity of outward behaviour would be accounted for by the interplay of the mirror system with consciousness and situational

> features rather than some conscious or unconscious, learned or unlearned over mind, we could no longer tie understandings to subjects roaming around the world. This, of course, is exactly what I try to recommend. Let me continue by showing how I see mirror neurons fitting into this picture.

4   Basal Understandings versus Action Understandings

A core 'move' of practice theory, I have detailed in chapter five, is that an understanding describes a *bundle* of reciprocal or befitting doings (and sayings), something-that-can-be-done-in-such-a-way-that-others-can-understand-it where this 'understanding-it' describes a doing, an outward behaviour rather than a mental condition. Further, the mirror system model holds that we can spontaneously and preconsciously mimic others' movements or gestures on the basis of this relatively isolated neural system. For example, when someone smiles at us, we might spontaneously or routinely smile back. In Schatzki's terminology, the person smiling back in this simple exchange is expressing an understanding: She 'is knowing'[5] how to identify smiling directed at her; and she 'is knowing' how to respond properly, namely by smiling back, and she observably 'is knowing' how smiling is adequately performed. I suggest calling this a *basal understanding*, and I stress that it does neither involve a teleological end nor a conscious intention, since the behaviour is spontaneous in this case. In Schatzki's terminology, this episode of smiling would be termed a dispersed practice (1996: 91–98), one that does not entail anything else than the understanding per se, especially no additional purposeful ends, rules, and so forth.[6] In many cases, smiling can of course be enmeshed into teleoaffective structures or rule-frameworks; for example when we smile to get someone's attention, or when employees are being ordered to smile at every single customer they meet. Crucially, however, from a practice perspective, this difference is not necessarily a virtue of the smiling itself and must not necessarily be expressed by it. In the case of someone smiling for a purpose rather than as a spontaneous reaction, one could speak of an action understanding—knowing how to smile towards a certain end, so to speak. In my view, praxeologist authors

---

[5] I use this formulation as a reference to Schatzki's formulation "knowing how to X" (2002: 77). I stress that he writes "knowing," which is an observable capacity that becomes manifest (or expressed) in certain situations, and not a mental state.

[6] I should mention two points: First, one should of course say that smiling does have an affective component, but not necessarily a teleoaffective structure, i.e. emotions or moods conditioned by certain ends (being happy about something vs. just being in a happy mood). Second, dispersed practices are not by definition always without teleoaffective structures or rules (Schatzki 2002: 88)—Schatzki only says they often do. For this reason, I speak of basal understandings or basal practices rather than dispersed practices.

like Lizardo effectively reduce all understandings to basal understandings. In some cases, this is plausible: When Japanese people smile in the typical Japanese fashion; this is arguably an expression of a basal understanding in that they 'automatically' do so and have been doing so since a very young age. What this perspective misses are cases in which, for example, an actor plays a Japanese character and thus purposefully smiles in that way, or in which a foreign guest tries to follow the Japanese customs more or less successfully. For many theorists of action as well as authors such as Turner, in contrast, it seems that all smiling would amount to an action understanding, being tied to conscious intention, purpose, or rule-observation.[7] Conclusively, it seems to be a sensible idea to argue for the possibility to acknowledge the existence of both basal and action understandings—a view that also matches the argument I raised in the prior chapter: that very different pathways of learning exist side-by-side.

Therefore, I suggest that the crucial implication of the existence of the mirror system (taken for granted it does function in the form it has been described by experimental neuroscience) is not that it 'proves' the supremacy of either conscious or subconscious learning, or the predominance of conceptual versus non-conceptual content in shaping social life, but rather that *learning itself* is a problematic concept if it is supposed to describe how something is put into the individual which provides for said individual to henceforth undertake a certain action every now and then (and especially when he is supposed to do so). In other words, I embrace the ethnomethodological critique of the trope 'learning' (Fox 2006; Hester/Francis 2000; Macbeth 2000), since neither tacit nor explicit knowledge held by individuals can adequately circumscribe thanks to which situation we are able to say and see that people have learned something. To be sure, the body's human capacity of producing reciprocal outward behaviour must be part of an adequate description; and so does an account of how the routines helping towards this might be acquired—but by no means can such an account alone pass as a complete description or explanation. A good case for this claim is made by Turner (2007: 361) himself when he notes that, while people might make 'use' of mirror neurons when imitating others' behaviour, "what they imitate is nevertheless determined by what they can perceive as imitable." By virtue of what, we accordingly need to ask, something can be perceived as imitable? Can we say that we have anything close to a complete list of the prerequisites by citing "the individual's learning history," as Turner does (2007: 361)? Arguably, the 42-minute old baby that was able to smile back at its parents in an experiment must be an individual in Turner's sense. If so, its 42-minute long learning 'history' can hardly provide a useful clue

---

[7]To avoid misunderstandings: action understandings a la Schatzki differ greatly from actions in a Weberian or Schutzian sense. My point here is rather that from Schatzki's perspective, sociological action theories can only grasp (conduct effecting from) action understandings, but neglect or cannot adequately account for their basal counterparts.

to how it perceived the gesture as imitable.[8] Consequentially, accounting for perceivable imitability in this case would probably involve some reference about how tongue protruding makes itself stand out and invites or even triggers returning the favour. Likewise, one should probably consider the situational background against which this standing-out can happen; e.g. the reciprocally looking in the eyes, the subtle coordination and mutual alignments and entrainments between mother and baby. But if all these aspects are so crucially important in this case, why can we suddenly ignore them all once an average adult is involved? An action understanding, I therefore stress, is still an understanding: the basis of its meaningfulness is laid in situated doing, the precise causal roots of which cannot be part of the definition of the understanding per se. In other words: An action understanding differs from a basal understanding in that it the doing might be oriented to teleological ends, or in that explicable rules bear on the conduct, but the situated performance itself is never causally and entirely predetermined by either.

Thus far, despite the different definition, the reader might think that my account of two forms of understanding still looks very similar to the classic sociological distinction between purposeful action and involuntary behaviour. The see with more clarity where I locate the crucial difference, we need to take into account the way in which neuroscientists explain the co-existence of both ways of understanding. How can we explain that we sometimes do spontaneously return a smile, and sometimes we do not? Interestingly, there are some patients with mental illness who compulsively imitate other's behaviour. This has led scientists to argue that in a 'normal' persons' brain, there is an inhibitory mechanisms at work which "normally pre-empts the execution of actions whose plans may be automatically triggered by the observation of others' actions in normal subjects." (Jacob/Jeannerod 2003: 232) In other words, while one neural system perpetually 'strives' to mimic other's movements, another usually keeps it under control.[9] As we all know, this does not always work: A comedian playing a sketch, for example, might 'fall out of role' and join the laughter of his audience. On this basis, Jacob and Jeannerod (2003: 231) distinguish between mimicry, which might be spontaneous or even accidental, and imitation, the purposeful copying of someone else. But while they use this distinction to support Searle's notion of acting being determined by prior

---

[8] This case also provides an interesting example for the discussion of Schutz' notion of action (see Chap. 8): According to him, the baby could (potentially) reflexively come to understand its own tongue protruding as an action in retrospect, which, in combining the understanding of 'sticking out my tongue' with the kinesthesia produced by the movement would then provide it with the future ability to smile willingly, i.e. purposefully. This explanation, however, does not describe a) by virtue of what the baby stuck out its tongue, b) by virtue of what it perceived the gesture as imitable (here, Schutz would probably point to anthropology for explanations), and c) by virtue of what precisely it will at some point in the future *cease* to inadvertently repeat such gestures.

[9] Note that a neural system does of course not 'do' anything in the same sense in which humans do things. I am merely retelling the neuroscientists argument at this point, and I am thus using their language.

intentions, I believe that the finding they describe actually has a different implication: I argue that repressing 'natural' mimicry is better described as a *state* rather than an act, and likewise is watching-intently-in-order-to-emulate. Take, for example, a parent trying to educate his child and thus making an effort to look stern and not be lured into being soft by the child's sweet smile. It would be misleading to say that the parent watches the smiling, identifies it epistemically, and then "decides" to suppress smiling back and instead continues to scold the kid. Further, suppressing or not suppressing mimicry is itself a process or state that does not entail or process the content of what would be either emulated or not. To the contrary, it must be triggered by something else, which could potentially be a conclusion drawn from an interpretation of parts of the observed behaviour in question; but it could just as well be part of e.g. getting oneself into the mood of being a strict parent, including stern looks and an imposing posture.

In sum, I argue that the primary conclusion to be drawn from the 'discovery' of the mirror system is that for conduct to express an action understanding, it must be observed as imitable; and that this is something not determined by subjective knowledge or intention alone, but instead dependent on a certain way of observing it (in the sense of a situated doing). Put in a different way, even the magic of mirror neurons does not allow one to evade the essential question of this work, the question of intelligibility: How do we come to 'see' an episode of conduct *as something*, as a 'thing' or 'chunk' with a certain quality? And in this point, I suggest, lies the root of the importance of seeing style. I have already assessed and rejected the idea that conduct expressing style does so by employing symbolic gestures which belong to a (relatively) fixed 'symbolic vocabulary.' As we can see now, there is indeed something about stylish conduct that makes it special, and this something is not 'merely symbolic' in that it would be either a) a exchangeable form whose only role is to communicate some content, or b) transitive, i.e. defineable or explicable through a set of static symbols, formulas, or definitions. Instead, I argue, the origin of the importance of style lies in a much more profane goal than expressing belonging to a community, or engaging in postmodern sign and/or identity play: avoiding to break one's neck.

5 Sketchiness

The vital challenge the freeskiers in the funpark face, I argue, is that they need to discern whether or not someone else's performance is worth imitating. As I showed in chapter six, in order to really 'push his limits,' the freeskier needs to overcome his fears and reluctances and allow himself to be carried away by euphoric moments such as the "flip time" during which a whole group of friends suddenly manages a difficult trick for the first time. What happens in these moments, in other words, is at least in part the mimicry of seen movements with the help of the mirror system: The rider sees someone do a trick right before him, and then he 'just' goes for it as well. On the downside, this important 'mimicry-function' of the body can become very dangerous when it lures riders into trying tricks they should better not attempt (yet). They must, for example, be able to see whether their friend who just 'stomped' a flip for the first time was simply lucky to make it despite his making several small mistakes or despite the current difficult conditions, or if he is a great role-model worth imitating. In order to see the significance and function of style, I hold, one needs to link the distinction between basal and action understandings, and the question of how we come to observe someone's visible behaviour as an expression of one or the other back to the difference between epistemic and pragmatic vision. As Jacob and Jeannerod (Jacob/Jeannerod 2003: 232–233) report, experiments have shown that it depends on the situational setting, and especially on the currently given purpose, how an observed movement will be processed mentally: If subjects watch a movement in order to identify it (or rather: have been asked to do so by the experimenter), they engage in epistemic vision; while pragmatic processing becomes active only if they have been instructed to emulated the movement themselves (e.g. repeat a gesture). The key point is that only in the former case one would need to be able to grasp the goal or teleological end of in the movement. This seems plausible: It is quite a difference whether one is asked to watch and repeat a random, goal-less movement, or if one is asked to identify and describe a random movement. For mere mimicry, not being able to grasp the pragmatic goal (e.g. grabbing an object) is not problematic, as long as one can still mimic the pattern itself—e.g. one can repeat a ritual gesture from a foreign culture without getting its purpose or sense. On the other hand, identifying a movement without being able to grasp its intended end is problematic, since one can only really identify it as being random (and maybe name superficial aspects such as the body parts used). Incidentally, the task of discerning random and non-random aspects of someone's movements is just what freeskier do when they watch freestyle tricks and try to learn from them. And the difference between uncommon but 'useful' (or maybe purposeful) ways of doing a trick, and uncommon but random or 'bad' ways is exactly the difference between style and sketchiness. I stress that, to adequately grasp how and why freeskiers watch others perform freeski moves, one needs to keep both ways of seeing in sight: On the one hand, pragmatic vision is vital for freestylers to be able to mimic the tricks they watch others perform. Arguably, what is crucial here is less the basic structure of the movement itself (e.g. in that 'spinning around twice' is a concept we do not need to watch to understand it), but rather the many small details of the performance, such as the way the rider manages to produce the maximum rotation-impulse without losing his balance. On the other hand, I argue that epistemic vision is necessary to discern good and bad performances: The freeskiers need some way of learning whom they can trust (as they would put it), i.e. from whom they can learn by emulating him or her—and again, it would not suffice if the riders were only able to distinguish obvious crashes from clear success; but rather, they need to be able to 'get' *epistemically* which performances exhibit a certain *pragmatic* quality, something only pragmatic vision can pick up—in this case the mirror system 'extracting' very subtle patterns of body movements (with Merleau-Ponty 2002 one could maybe say: a body schema). In my view,

5 Sketchiness 383

this point is highly significant. On a basic level, it provides a better understanding of the 'deep' seeing that the freeskiers in the arena around the kicker engage in. Arguably, they do not simply try to identify a trick in acts of epistemic seeing; but they watch the action as athletes seeking to learn and improve their own skills, and thus engage in pragmatic seeing as well. This would imply that the attunement to Style I described differs from the mere watching of uninitiated tourists not merely on some symbolic level, or in that the 'tourists' do not have much explicable 'fact knowledge' about freestyle skiing or have not seen it very often. Rather, the difference is the same as in the study of basketball players and basketball coaches watching free shots mentioned earlier: The riders, just like the players, engage in a different practice of seeing not just consciously, but on a deeper, a neural and visceral level. Further, this difference is not necessarily one of relevancies[10] or factual knowledge, since at least the basketball coaches surely know and care a lot about free shots—still they do not see them in the same way. And this difference, I argue, is ultimately at the heart of the importance of style.

Consequentially, the normativity governing visual style in the freeskiing subculture should not be reduced to an invocation of effectively arbitrary aesthetic ideals, to a series of fashion fads where black is the new white or where the very contingency of style is attractive because it's rationally unjustifiable impediments allow practitioners to demonstrate their distance from necessities (as a Bourdieusian reading would have it). To be sure, when I described at the beginning of this chapter how a freeskier reacted very strongly to a poster showing "wrong" style, it was not only the image per se that he reacted to, but also the symbolic frame it was embedded into (a large brand displaying it in a prominent position, something only a very stylish picture would deserve). But while certain instances of possibly random aesthetic rules surely exist, I believe that at the core, seeing style is an instance of what I called normative para-attention in chapter three: the normative, emotion-laden back-ground scanning that makes up a vital part of embodied routines of perception—and in a high-risk context like freeskiing, 'vital' is meant literally. In other words, freestylers emotionally dislike sketchiness because they *see* the impediment crash in the details of the images. The poster that so infuriated the freeskier (see the first page of this chapter) showed a skier who performed a backflip in an Oldschool fashion, without doing any grab. From a Newschool freestyler's perspective, grabs are not only a matter of symbolic distinction; they also provide the rider with much-needed stability during the jump. In contrast, a flip without a grab is a disaster waiting to happen—at least if one is trained as a Newschool rider, jumps over kickers made for Newschool jumps, and uses Newschool ski equipment. Merleau-Ponty noted how our embodied vision provides us not with neutral images, but with a sense for the fragile states of the world around:

[10] Depending on the use of the term, see my comments on Schutz in chapter eight.

"A wooden wheel is not, for sight, the same thing as a wheel bearing load. A body at rest because no force is being exerted upon it is again for sight not the same thing as a body in which opposing forces are in equilibrium". (Merleau-Ponty 2002: 60)

In this sense, seeing sketchiness in a trick means seeing an impending crash—at least if this seeing is enmeshed in the wider nexus of freeski practices. If freeskiers, as I argued, rely on clues about the manageability of current conditions for a certain trick that they gain from the close observation of co-participants, sketchiness becomes a crucial red flag for imminent danger and the need for greater care. For example, if a freeskier concludes that it is "flip-time"; that right here, right now, the conditions of snow, weather, and the kicker are favourable for 'sticking' your first backflip, he cannot simply rely on the fact that one or two riders have just managed the flip without crashing badly. Instead, he must be able to *see* that these attempts did also work out really well, that the successful attempts where neither the result of luckily avoiding near disaster, nor that it was only the riders' prowess at keeping balance despite a most unfortunate situation. Mistaking sketchiness for stylishness, in other words, can sometimes cause a freeskier to break his neck. What is more, I showed that vision and bodily movement are tightly intertwined not only on a pre-conscious, pre-conceptual level; but also in our conscious perception in that, to speak with Merleau-Ponty (1969: 256), I perceive my bodily movement as "the natural consequence and the maturation of my vision." Moving about in the world, however, always entails at least some degree of exposure; and when we watch others perform dangerous manoeuvres, this sight grips us quite literally, often in that we tense our bodies. More generally, our visual perception frequently carries a normative undertone such as a sense of urgency or uneasiness. Notably, I do not only say that freeskiers become attuned to the stylish performances when they spectate in the park because they frequently react emotionally and viscerally when they seem someone crash or get hurt—something we usually all do, an experience that can even include a kind of 'phantom-pain.' But I also point out that while the freeskiers' visceral and emotional reaction to seeing bad style is surely not identical in nature to seeing a crash, it is also not too different: sometimes, freeskiers are cringing in disdain, even disgust when they see something severely out of place; and frequently, they get angry about it. Such sharp rejection of images or performances missing Style, I argue, can hardly be adequately characterized as a cognitive valuation of symbolic items according to learned coda, but is instead an expression of a deeper care for Style—a care that is to some extent rooted in the fact that a sense for Style is an important means for a freestyler to take care of himself.

6 Understanding Style and its Roots in Epistemic and Pragmatic Seeing

How can this notion of style be framed in the terminology of a phenopractice theory rooted (in part) in Heideggerian thought? If we were to stick to the concepts developed by Schatzki, style equates to what he briefly discusses under the label *sensitized understanding*: a certain way of conducting a well-understood doing specific for a particular "domain of life" (or field of practices) that has become "sensitized to the particular way the activity runs on there." (Schatzki 1996: 100) Notably, sensitized understandings are thus special versions of understandings belonging to more general, relatively basic practices such as walking or talking which Schatzki calls dispersed practices (1996: 91–98). When these basic practices become enmeshed into more complex and more specific practices (which he calls integrative), he suggests, then they become 'keyed' or sensitized in some way, e.g. in that professors talk different than lovers. Take, for example, the 'baggy' skiing style which freestyle skiers routinely use and value (bending their knees, leaning slightly backwards, skis relative far apart), while traditional-minded ski instructors find it childish or simply repulsive. Apparently unbeknownst to some ski instructors I talked to, technically this way of riding makes sense for two reasons: First, this posture provides maximum stability and the optimal impulse when jumping jump off a kicker or onto a box; and second, the fact that their bindings are mounted at the true centre of the freestyle ski (to make rotating much easier and more stable) forces them to adapt their bodily position in order to still be able to turn smoothly on a slope.[11] In my view, it is only 'on top' of these two points that the sensitized 'baggy' style of skiing also gains symbolic value and thus helps to distinguish freeskiers from tourists or, depending on whom you ask, those who ski properly from crazy kids unable to even ski properly but still performing dangerous and inappropriate stunts. If style is a sensitized understanding, in other words, then this term must not simply describe some superficial aesthetic gloss, but a more thorough transformation basic practices undergo in order to fit into the respective field of practices (cf. Hui 2017).[12] This transformation, I suggest, can be described with the two notions orientation and prefiguration which I introduced in chapters four and six. In the case of the 'baggy'-style of skiing, pragmatic sensibility and symbolic value overlap in that having a low point of gravity during jumping is considered cool and lowers the risk of crashing. How can this 'sensitized' style of skiing be invoked? When a freestyler skis in a baggy posture, he might either do so intently, reminding himself to stay low during the in-run; or this might be brought about by certain elements of the practice, e.g. his body might follow the affordances of the skis, the positive emotions of feeling cool might have been firmly

---

[11] Standard ski have their bindings mounted slightly backwards of the centre. Simply put, the freestyler need to forcefully bend the back half of their skis every time they turn in order not to get stuck; and they do this by leaning backwards when initiating the turn—something that ski instructors spend ages to stop their students from doing (for different reasons) when instructing them.

[12] Schatzki does not elaborate his term at any length; it is only mentioned once in his first book on practice theory and not returned to later. In fact, it seems to me that the distinction between dispersed and integrative practices that is fairly central in Social Practices shifts out of focus over time (it is not mentioned in the latest book on Timespace, but that might also be due to the topic.).

linked to this posture, or his pre-conscious 'muscle memory' might become active whenever the training routine kicks in (see Brümmer 2009). In the latter case, the style is the partial effect of certain prefigurations, which might happen 'under the radar,' i.e. without being purposefully expressed in the practice. In contrast, conduct is oriented to a style when it is organized towards the expression of that style. Notably, by orientation, I do not mean a conscious orientation of an actor. While orientation usually requires the active involvement of the practitioner purposefully trying to achieve stylish conduct, it nevertheless happens across the particularities of conduct and the contingencies of situations. In this vein, I emphasize that a sensitized understanding, like any understanding, is not just a scheme of interpretation, but describes a capacity for doing something, or more precisely the nexus of performing and recognizing that something. In other words, saying that a performance visibly has style—i.e. expresses a sensitized understanding—describes first and foremost a quality which is inherent in the performance itself, but nevertheless can only be appreciated by someone capable of doing so. This links to a key point: When I argue that stylish conduct is conduct which is observably worthwhile to imitate, i.e. worthy of inspecting it pragmatically and trying to learn some tricks of the trade from it, this is *not* the same as saying that the observer has concluded that this conduct was consciously intended in just this way. For the movement to be worthy emulating, it must simply be 'good.' If, for example, a freeskier notices someone perform a trick in a really {clean} and smooth way, there must something about the way how this guy does the trick that makes him not lose his balance. It does not matter whether or not he knows that he does that, or why he does that; all that the spectating rider cares about is that it works. In the face of classic action theories, this point marks a decisive divergence: if seeing-to-copy is a different neural routine than seeing-to-identify-as-worth-copying, than this means that both routines (or neural systems) do not need to share any content (conceptual or otherwise), they only need to refer to the same 'thing' in the situation. Here lies one of the reasons why I consider the notion of two different ways of seeing carried by two distinct neural systems so important: It does not only provide the theorist with the flexibility to account differently for different phenomena (say, a baby protruding its tongue versus someone reading a book); but it also implies that epistemic and pragmatic seeing must be coordinated or aligned in some clever way, because—simply said—one visual system cannot see what the other can see. Recognizing style, I thus argue, means seeing epistemically that there is something to see pragmatically—but the identified epistemic detail must be something other than the details made sense of pragmatically.

7 Regularity versus Similarity

Therefore, I further suggest that the dual format of seeing, or the dual visual meaning inherent in stylish conduct (or media), might also shed some further light on another relatively abstract but essential theoretical postulate I adapted from Schatzki: The argument that not regularity, but similarity is the basis of meaning; i.e. that "the doings and sayings that compose a practice need not be regular." (Schatzki 2002: 74) As we have seen, this argument is inter alia important because on its basis, Schatzki (2002: 74 fn20) acknowledges Turner's main argument against practice theories—that regular patterns of behaviour cannot be explained by shared tacit knowledge—but then adds that it does not apply to his own version, since he does not suggest that practical conduct is inherently regular. I have argued that it is logically necessary for Schatzki to build on this premise, and I have tried to sketch out a notion of meaning able to comply with this concept. Nevertheless, it inevitably raises questions. Most importantly, if it should turn out that the claim, that similarity is sufficient to define meaning in the end rests only on the human ability to treat similar things as identical, then one would effectively end up with a kind of 'subjectivism plus': There might well be order inherent in the world, one could argue in this case, but if it still always depends on the individual to make sense of disorder when push comes to shove, then we neither need, nor can guarantee for, the social world's inherent orderliness in our theory. Accordingly, I believe that a foremost task for phenopractice thought is to flesh out its account of social order-in-similarity. By virtue of what, it needs to be asked, can lived conduct be described as orderly if it is neither interpretation nor inherent regularity that accounts for said conduct having orderly effects? One way to answer this problem, I suggest, is to argue that the same conduct can be observable or intelligible in different ways or 'dimensions'; and thus while it might sometimes lack intelligibility in one, it can still be 'carried forth' in another. More specifically, one might argue that what most practice-minded authors actually refer to when they employ the term 'regularity' describes an epistemological quality: something that must be conceptionally observable in the sense that via epistemic, conscious, and usually explicable observation and discussion, one can make a logical argument showing or proving its regularity.[13] Whether or not one follows this reading, my suggestion is that if one can see a certain movement (or situation more generally) in two fundamentally different ways, this implies that the identifying detail that turns the seen movement into what it is would be *different* in each of the two cases.

Let me point out that my account of seeing style entails two seemingly opposing ideas: On the one hand, I emphasize that seeing style is a visceral and embodied doing which must happen in person—style is something that discloses itself only for or towards specific spectators, it is only 'there' when it is situatedly seen. On the other hand, I oppose the idea that the social phenomenon I call freeskiing's Style—just like any style of conduct indeed—is a kind of 'dark matter' belonging to a parallel dimension of the social universe where bodies tacitly express something, and other bodies tacitly pick up their brother's messages without any of us

---

[13] On the other hand, my sentiment is that practice theorists who argue for a basic regularity of human conduct tend to mystify their account by insisting there is *invisible* regularity to be found in the world (see H. L. Dreyfus/Rabinow 1999).

ever being aware or attending to it. In contrast, there is no question that freeskiers can talk about Style, that they can relatively easily find a consensus about whether a trick or line had some Style or not, and that—consequentially—seeing Style is at least strictly coupled to a conscious epistemic processing routine. I therefore argue that style functions in roughly the same way as the crucial points I discussed in the last chapter: While stylish conduct can be epistemically identified or figured out to be stylish, it will also be 'sophisticated' or 'interesting' when looked at pragmatically (i.e. processed non-consciously with regard to motor patterns). This idea, I believe, has not yet been expressed in this way in social theory. Consequentially, it is not always easy to explain and has a number of important theoretical implications. I believe that the best way to figure out what I am trying to suggest is to examine the different ways in which freeskiers approach Style and how they try to align and organize these ways. Stylish conduct, one could say, can be encountered or dealt with by them in a number of different 'dimensions' such as emotional reactions or gut feeling, talk, scoring lists, images or videos, and so forth. My aim is not just to show that there are these different dimensions or aspects, but rather how the freeskiers manage to map them back onto *the same thing* (i.e. an episode of conduct) and how, from doing so, they gain crucial resources that ultimately enable them to do the crazy stunts they are able to do. One of the most interesting cases in which the different faces of freeskiing Style collide, and need to be aligned, are the practices of judging Style on freeski competitions.

8   Judging: Contests and the Anti-Competitive Ethos

To get to the 'heart' of Style, to understand what it is that visible style is made of, the freeskiing world offers a straightforward ethnographic strategy: Ask those who must know by definition, namely judges at contests who are given the task to assess and rate the Style expressed by different athletes within the 'same' situational conditions (Fig. 9.4). Three judges sit next to each other at the bottom of the kicker line, taking notes. The head coach in the centre records the final results in an excel sheet. Confirming insights from the fruitful line of research at the intersection of practice theory and valuation studies that emphasizes the tacit dimension of the embodiment of the valuation process (Schmidt et al. 2022), freestyle judges can hardly spell out explicit criteria to measure visible Style against—while at the same time insisting that they are routinely able to see them, and award points or rankings accordingly. In particular, they are sure that they can discern Style independently of the "technical difficulty" of the trick and can thus make out superior performances of less spectacular, dangerous, or 'mechanically difficult' tricks. As one judge told me:

8 Judging: Contests and the Anti-Competitive Ethos

Fig. 9.4 Judging style at a freeski contest in Weißensee, Austria

"One time, for example, there were a couple of guys who'd throw totally wild tricks, but it just looked crappy. And then there was this one [guy] taking part that had some easier stuff, but really, really beautifully done and in the end he won, just because we [judges] said: 'Pew, we think it's cool. It's more worthy.'" [I][14]

Although disagreements between judges occur frequently, and although contests increasingly become professionally organized and globally marketed events, a definite rulebook or precise rating system for judging Style is still not in place. An experienced rider that has judged at several contests summed the challenge up:

---

[14] „Da gab's zum Beispiel mal ein paar Jungs, die haben total wilde Tricks gemacht aber es sah halt einfach Scheiße aus. Und es ist da halt einer mitgefahren, der hatte etwas leichtere Sachen, aber richtig richtig schön gemacht und er hat dann hinterher gewonnen, einfach weil wir gesagt haben ‚Puhh. Finden wir cool. Ist mehr wert.'"

"There are so many different directions of movement [e.g. axis of rotation, N.W.], and then on top of that there are the double flips. How do you want to sort that out? Should a Switch Fourteen-forty be more difficult than a Kangaroo-Flip, or, pew... Who determines that? (...) So he who does it more stylishly should just win." [I][15]

Over the years and at different tournaments, several different attempts have been made to develop clear and consistent notation and rating schemes, but the different systems are incoherent and were often short lived. One well-known contest series held in the German-speaking part of the Alps uses 5-point scales, while another uses a 100-point scale; some award points in different criteria and then add them up, while others use only one overall score; and during one competition series, the scales used at different tour-stops were not even compatible with each other. To some extent, such confusions simply reflect the fact that freeskiing is not centrally organized and formally controlled by a governing body such as the International Skiing Federation FIS, and thus no internationally binding 'laws' of judging have been written down. Yet this absence of regulation is not a coincidence, and neither is it due to the fact that freeskiing is still a relatively new sport. Both historically and in the freeskiers' own understanding, freeskiing was and still is a movement against a 'technocratic' approach to skiing imposed and regulated by large organizations like the FIS. While freeskiers and the FIS disagree on many fundamental matters such as how skiing should be taught, or what comprises proper skiing in the first place, the pivotal moment of conflict and divergence was (and still is) the rules according to which contests should be held and judged (see Anthony 2011; Geisler 2003: 45–47). In simplified terms, Newschool freestyle broke apart from so-called Oldschool freestyle—which had been practiced since the early 1970s—because the skiers held that the FIS-rules for judging freestyle (which is an Olympic sport) kept the athletes from unfolding their individual creativity and killed their Style by enforcing static, dull, and uninspired repetitions of ever the same figures. A key issue, for example, was the ban on inverted jumps imposed on FIS-events for reasons of safety (Fry 2006a: 219–234, 2006b; Lund/Miller 1998a), which led athletes to try to circumvent the rule by performing the off-axis rotations that are still the hallmark of Newschool freestyle today (Moseley 2002)— but these were soon forbidden as well.[16] To some extent, freeskiers have drawn the conclusion that formal competitions are per se incompatible with the accomplishment of Style, since an expression of individual creativity cannot be better or worse (Geisler 2003: 56–59), a sentiment regularly voiced within lifestyle sports (Beal/Weidman 2003; M. Stern 2009; Wheaton 2003, 2004b). For this reason, the

---

[15] „Es gibt so viele unterschiedliche Bewegungsrichtungen und dann gibts die Doubleflips noch dazu. Wie willst du das einsortieren? Soll ein Switch fourteen-forty schwieriger sein als nen Kangoroo-Flip oder, puh.... Wer macht das fest? (...) Soll halt der gewinnen, ders stylischer macht."

[16] In chapter eleven, I will look in some more detail at the various revolutions and movements that have reinvented skiing five or six times since its emergence, and argue that their dynamic depended on different forms of coordination of style such as organizations (e.g. writing rules for instruction and competition) or visual media (e.g. fixating and disseminating a certain style).

judging manual of the Freeride World Tour, by far the most professional and well-known series of international freeride (not freestyle) competition begins with the somewhat paradoxical statement:

> "By definition, the term freeride is contradictory to the word competition." (Freeride World Tour 2011: § 1)

To be sure, the introduction continues by saying: "Though for some riders, freeride and competition fit together. (…) Therefore, we need judges" (Freeride World Tour 2011: § 1). But the statement seems remarkable nonetheless; being the equivalent of the IOC or FIFA stating that by definition, Olympics or the Soccer World Cup should not be competitive. It points to an inherent tension, if not contradiction within the general conceptual understandings that frame freeskiing competitions and the judging of Style. What makes this observation significant is that from a sociological viewpoint adhering to symbolism, one is led to argue that style is whatever the dominant social institutions observe as and declare to be style. But the freeskiers fear just the opposite: That the institutionalized judgment of and communication about Style will gloss over and hide, rather than reward and promote, good Style. One can, of course, considers this to be a purely 'political' claim, or as a move to ensure symbolic distinction—one group of (younger) self-declared experts trying to wrestle the interpretive dominance from another group of well-installed professional experts. From this perspective, a number of authors within the sociology of sport have sought to uncover the contradictions and sub-surface hegemonial forces lurking behind lifestyle sport's narratives of equality, freedom, and friendship, especially by pointing out that inclusion also implies exclusion or even 'symbolic violence' (see e.g. Atencio/Beal/Wilson 2009; Edensor/Richards 2007; Frohlick 2005; Thorpe 2010; Wheaton 2000a, 2004a). In contrast, it is not my aim to unmask the skiers' 'false consciousness' in a similar manner, since I am not convinced that freeskiing should be read as an identity project in the first place. Instead, I suggest that a sociological analyst should not be too quick in dismissing the freeskiers' universally stated reason for rejecting over-formalized competitions. If we assume that contests are not only, or not primarily, important because they help produce identities—such as winners and losers—, but because they provide mutual orientation or coordination in terms of Style, thus effectively functioning as a school of seeing Style (as well as giving opportunities to socialize and bond as a community), then the rejection of FIS-ruled competitions and judging would be less a question of politics and expert power but instead a question about procedural details: Which format of competition and which process of judging are best capable to tease out and highlight the identifying details of great Style and transform them into ranking placements? In my view, the various judging formats and scoring systems that are currently being tried out in the freeskiing world, as well as the many fine-tuned details of the judging procedure at the Freeride World Tour which I will now present, both testament that freeskiers are very sensible towards not only the fact that Style must be grasped via a combination of different observation and description practices, but also that these very practices, by virtue of the influence important contest can have on the development of the sport as a whole, will effect back onto the freeskiing Style circulating globally. With regard to freestyle skiing, for example, freeskiers are concerned that too many contests implement a 'spin-to-win' logic according to which so-called 'technical' tricks with many rotations lead to the highest scores, even if they are inferior in terms of Style. In the long run, this would lead to a race towards ever-more difficult technical tricks, but a loss in the level of Style athletes can demonstrate. As my discussion of the long-term evolution of skiing practices in the two final chapters will show, I believe that freeskiers have every reason to fear such a development: Competitions, as well as other media of dissemination, I will argue, are pivotal in shaping the development of a practice and the subculture around it. Here, we find the deeper reason that the judging manual of the FWT is so diplomatic and careful in explaining that 'real' freeriding can happen on a contest *despite* its being judged and scored. Likewise, the process of judging is prescribed in such detail because the judges must take great care not to lose sight of the actual Style of riding currently performed while trying to come up with their scores.

9 The Instructed Flow of Judging

For advanced freeskiers, taking part in a contest is a regular feature of their sport; and if they gather experience and remain active in the scene as they grow older than, say, 22, they will sooner or later be asked to judge at some small contest (Fig. 9.5). During my fieldwork, I observed about a dozen contests and interviewed several of my informants about their experiences of judging. During a contest, it is possible to observe the judges relatively well since they usually sit next to the crowed watching the spectacle and can sometimes be overheard talking. Since, for the sake of my argument, I am interested in the procedural details rather than the experience of judging, I will use the judging manual from the Freeride World Tour as my empirical example in the following part. The instructions for judging contained in the manual circumscribe the systematic procedures that carry the practical accomplishment of seeing and judging Style in some fascinating detail and are thus worthy being quoted at some length. It needs to be said, however, that a) the precise procedure applied differs in some details from one contest to the next, for example in that different rating scales are used, and b) that such a manual is a specific kind of ethnographic document that must not be confused with an accurate ethnographic account of the judges' precise doings. Thus, while the manual cannot in any sense represent the observable detail of the artful embodied accomplishment of 'doing judging at the Freeride World Tour,' it is one key element of this practice that prefigures and orients the judges conduct in several important ways. Particularly, it reveals how their interactive judging methods are situated in a fine-tuned spatial-material-optical arrangement structuring and synchronizing the embodied, emotional, and intellectual work of producing Style scores (cf. Weigelin 2022). On the basis of the ethnomethodological dictum that

Fig. 9.5 A funpark during a contest as the judges see it from their booth

instructions need to be read by those following them as descriptions of their work which's adequacy must be accountably produced (see Chap. 4), the manual can be read as providing an insightful account of some 'outstanding' general features of the judges' situated work– features that need to be situatedly and performatively made to stand out of the judges' visible conduct over the course of said conduct, that is. While the procedures to follow at the World Tour differ in some aspects from those judging processes I witnessed during my fieldwork, they link up and support my findings from said fieldwork, as well as reaffirming the adequacy of a number of empirical and theoretical arguments concerning practices of seeing and seeing style made thus far (Fig. 9.5).

The first and most basic insight to be gained from the manual arguably supports a general argument I seek to make regarding style in this chapter: While there are different aspects to every observed performance, and different ways to approach, observe, and think about Style, these aspects are not necessarily all epistemic in quality so that they can be expressed and rated separately and symmetrically in order to subsequentially being added up again. On the one hand, the manual defines five different qualities or categories of worth that need to be considered: 1) the creativity, difficulty, and beauty of the line; 2) the fluidity of riding; the riders' control; 3) the quality of jumps; and 4) whether or not crashes occurred, how they were handled, and how they impacted the other categories. Based on this list, one would expect the judges to rate each category separately, or that different judges concentrate on different aspects. But this is not case. Instead, it is emphasized that only the overall impression of the ride can and must count. The tour's judging system uses "overall impression scores, given mostly by former riders respected by the new active generation, based essentially on emotions rather than mechanical descriptions." (Freeride World Tour 2011: § 1) The reason for letting every judge determine the overall impression rather than scoring every aspect separately (line, fluidity, control, jumps, crashes), the introduction explains, is that neither letting different judges focus on a single criteria, nor asking all judges to rate all criteria, led to universally accepted results. If read as a description of past judges' situated work, this statement confirms my argument that figuring out different aspects from the same phenomenal field yields different overall gestalts rather than different 'pieces' of the same thing that can be smoothly reassembled: Even though the judges were right about the individual characteristics, it proved impossible to put the 'big picture' back together in an adequate way. The manual continues by arguing:

> "The fact is, the criteria are linked together. Splitting these elements is more confusing than convenient. A judge has to ask himself at all times how fast, how big and how in control a rider is compared to how steep, how exposed and in what snow conditions the action is happening to make up his mind. A split criteria structured mind is key to good overall impression judging." (Freeride World Tour 2011: § 1; original emphasis)

This explanation is illuminating in that it shows how different legitimation strategies are combined although they would usually be seen as contradictory. At first, the manual had emphasized that Style is essentially a quality that can only show up in the "overall impression made" and is most aptly reflected in the emotional reaction of the judges. But now "the mind" of the judges is introduced as a source of authority and the locus of fair decision making: Although the visible or public judging procedure does no longer systematically separate and evaluate the different dimensions, one can rest assured that a systematic structure is still in place—it has only been relocated to the "split criteria structured mind." The cognitive metaphor, in other words, is used as a placebo for those features of conduct that are no longer visibly evident from the judges' conduct itself (e.g. in that every judge writes down different ratings for each criteria and the adds them up), but can nevertheless be proclaimed to be relevant and accountably governing conduct since the judges can always give testimony of their going diligently through all criteria *in their mind*—a claim that cannot be refuted just because one could not see them do this (cf. Weigelin 2022).

The further detailed rules of conduct then evidence how the manual seeks to organize the judging in such a way as to ensure the production of observable-and-reportable results (in the form of scores) that are adequate for all *practical* purposes. In other words, it does not actually prescribe ends or tasks such as fairness or accuracy at lengths, but instead emphasizes practical matters such as the "Fluidity of the Event" (§ 3.5) and introduces a range of measures to ensure that judging happens swiftly and routinely—in part by actually *discouraging* judges to try to be very accurate. Notably, the process is very strictly timed (see below), leaving exactly 60 seconds for judging a run which often lasts several minutes. Further, towards the end of the contest some time is reserved to conduct 'quality management,' but the manual instructs the judges *not* to try to be very precise:

9 The Instructed Flow of Judging

> "*§ 2.5 Validation:*
> At the end of the contest, the judges will get the overall results and ranking. They have 20 minutes to validate these results and are allowed to change scores if obvious mistakes have happen. This is not the time to discuss if a rider should have been 5th or 6th but to check if someone who should have been ranked around 5th is somehow ending up 13th."
> (Freeride World Tour 2011: § 2.5)

Given that the World Tour is a highly professional competition among the world elite of riders who take great risks and train for years in order to be able to take part; and given that only four main events consisting of one or two runs must suffice to determine the annual champion, it seems somewhat surprising that an official rule-book determines that judges should not "discuss if a rider should have been 5th or 6th." After all, this difference could be decisive for the whole career of an athlete, and e.g. cause him to loose or gain an important sponsor. However, I argue that it does not document irresponsibility or a lack of interest in fair judgment on behalf of the organizing committee, but rather points to a general sentiment reflected throughout the manual and the procedure it regulates: that verbal expressions in general, and conversations in particular, are inadequate to capture and assess freeriding style; that judgments need to be produced relatively spontaneous; and that while practices of reflecting on one's own and other's scores is necessary and beneficial to some extent, it must be tightly restricted. It seems that practices such as arguing, pondering, reassessing, doubting, or rationalizing need to be kept at bay at all times during judging, since they harbour the potential to overgrow the judging process by invoking self-perpetuating discussions, instil indecisiveness and insecurity into the judges, and distract them from grasping and articulating that all-important 'gut feeling' that guides them best in picking the true winner. Interestingly, I will try to show, this happens by keeping up the *flow* of judging in a team. Various measures from time restrictions to performative procedures to decision-making hierarchies are prescribed by the manual in order to 'keep the judging going,' which above all means to keep to judges from pondering and discussing too much. The most important ones, according to the manual, are the following four: consistency, synchronization, calibration, and silence. Let me discuss them step by step.

First, the various measures prescribed and the material tools used are all employed towards establishing, regulating, and keeping this flow of judgment which seems key for achieving scores that conform to the most important practical purpose: the consistency of scores.

> "*§ 3.3 Consistency:*
> The most important quality for a judge is his ability to remain focused for many hours in order to give every rider the same chances and a consistent level of judging." (Freeride World Tour 2011: § 3.3)

On a basic level, this rule simply describes a basal prerequisite that must be fulfilled so that judging of any kind can work: The individual results produced must be consistent, that is, if taken in sum, they must show coherence, the condition of which is that the results must appear to have been produced in equal conditions, against an equal background. In some cases, this requires exactness to be procedurally produced, for example in that measures used and scales applied are 'precise' (as defined by the context). In the case of judging freeskiing, in contrast, consistency is achieved by establishing a rhythmic flow of swift and largely tacit decision-making which is distinctively emotional and 'intuitive' in character. Producing accuracy and consistency, in other words, requires certain bodily and 'mental' routines to take place undisturbed by alternative practices often associated with making judgments, such as rationalizing or debating. All further principles and procedures which the manual postulates can be read to work towards this end.

Second, a key element to gain a flow of judging as well as consistency is the synchronization of the position and perspective of the different judges over the course of their seeing. As the spatial organization of the funpark as an arena made clear, the spatial position of a spectator, her optical perspective on the matter of interest, and her viscerally-emotional stance towards this matter are tightly linked (C. Goodwin 2007; C. Goodwin/M. H. Goodwin 2001). Since seeing Style is necessarily a conduct oriented to and by emotions, for example in that a line must be a joy to watch in order to have Style, the position and perspective of judges provide a valuable resource towards producing consistent scores. While the manual fails to mention explicitly that the judges share a small booth throughout their work, its rules do imply that judges sit directly adjacent to each other. A number of additional rules describe the use of technological tools for spectating, and these rules foreshadow the core argument of the following chapter: That tools and media for seeing have a profound impact on ways of seeing in general, and thus on the form and evolution of visible styles in particular.

> "§ 2.7 Viewing Equipment:
> Judges will use binoculars, a TV screen or their bare eyes to judge. It is important that all judges use the same viewing system to avoid conflicts. If judges use binoculars, they should all have the same power." (Freeride World Tour 2011: § 2.7)

The third pivotal measure is the 'calibration' of the judges' judging, the procedural production of a local, temporary, and shared normality or standard. Testament to the inherently sequential nature of situated seeing I described in the first chapter, several rules are in place that aim to ensure that judges 'get into' judging together and become entrained with regard to the expectations and mood with which they will approach judging a line. As I have argued, 'getting' an understanding necessitates attunement, and as such it is dependent not only on the situational setting, but also the mood and stance with which one approaches that what is to be understood. More specifically, the judges need to 'get on a mutual level' in terms of their critical stance so that they will look for similar things in a good (or bad run). This alignment of attunements happens in two phases:

> First, "judges must prepare themselves (…). They should check the face and analyze possible lines and imagine what could be a very hard or safe line on the face." (Freeride World Tour 2011: § 2.3)

> Then, "the head judge will make sure that all judges agree on the score of the first rider down and could open a discussion if opinions differ. If the first rider has a terrible run, this scaling of all the judges will wait until the first 'normal' run. All other runs from that day will be judged according to the first calibration." (Freeride World Tour 2011: § 2.3)

Needless to say, the fact that the first run was "terrible" or instead "normal" and therefore should or should not be used as a basis for "scaling the judges" must become evident from the details of the witnessed performance and this evidence must be cooperatively and situatedly produced.

Notably, this scaling has to be accomplished within the interactive praxis of observation and judgment, because in freeriding, many of the alternative common strategies of equalization that employ material arrangements and technological tools towards this end do not work. In most traditional sports, such 'scaling' happens by regulating and standardizing the material equipment used and the environment within which the sport is conducted in that playing fields, balls, race cars, obstacles, and similar material arrangements are more or less exactly equal. Consequently, e.g. performing a perfect somersault on the parallel bars is considered equally difficult in any given gym, and thus the judges' ratings do not need to be adapted in a similar manner. On the other hand, it seems to me that this particular rule is also testament to the fact that freeriding does not (yet) have professional judges who can be legitimately expected to a) adhere to a universal, clear understanding what a good or bad performance is and b) do so consistently on any given day. In a way, one could even say that because freeriding judges do not consider it part of their professional ethos that it is out of the question that they must first 'tune in' with the others before the scores they produce in the next hours become comparable, they have the opportunity to systematically produce the local coherence of their judging by 'scaling' themselves first.

A fourth key goal set by the judging manual is the systematic restriction and avoidance of talk which I already mentioned. While it seems on the one hand clear that talking is both necessary and helpful for producing scores in a flow, it is on the other hand clear that the manuals' authors deem speech inadequate to represent Style or reflect on it in a way useful for the task at hand. Further, one apparently needs to avoid the self-propelling dynamics of disagreements and pondering it could cause (see also J. Lee 2009). Three resources are employed towards these ends: the social hierarchy, material tools and a specific workplace settings, and a temporal synchronization of the judging conduct. To begin with the first, the head judge is empowered and expected to cut of discussions and enforce the conformity of decisions:

> "§ 3.4 Discussions:
> Discussions between judges should be kept to the strict minimum. The head judge is allowed to speak to individual judges or have all judges take part in a discussion if needed. (…) If a judge missed an action because he lost the rider for a couple of seconds with his binoculars, he is allowed to ask the head judge what he just missed." (Freeride World Tour 2011: § 3.4)

Especially this last rule shows, I suggest, that the judges would not only be distracted from the 'actual' work of judging if they were to discuss about what they see, but rather that it needs to be avoided that someone describes in words *what there is* to be seen. From a phenopractice perspective, the reason for this is not only that the phenomenon in question—the Style to be seen—would be lost in the words; but also that describing or talking about the spectacle would instruct the other judges to see specific things in the current view. As I will discuss in some more detail below, I suggest that talking about visible conduct offer a certain framework to organize the visible, for example a certain relevance pattern in that certain things would be made to stand out, while other fall into the background. Second, judges are required to use specific judging sheets and sit in a certain spatial formation so that a kind of 'distributed cognition' can take place on the basis of this visual-material set-up (see Chap. 1). If one supposes that these rules have not been developed incidentally, but are the result of nearly two decades of trying to develop a reliably functioning procedure of judging Style in freeride competitions (see next chapter), it is fascinating to see which details of conduct seem to be instrumental in allowing the production of coherent judging.

> "§ 2.1 Judging sheets
> On the judge sheets, next to the riders name is a graduated line from 0 to 10 with marks every tenth, giving judges a scale of 100 different possible scores. The judges will mark their score with a colour pen on the line. These graduated lines are placed on the judging sheet vertically to help a judge who wants to give a 5.4 fine tune his judgement by quickly comparing to other closely related scores." (Freeride World Tour 2011: § 2.1)
>
> "The head judge has to check that all judges are working separately and not comparing scores." (Freeride World Tour 2011: § 3.4)

Judging, I have shown, is essentially the work of producing differences, of comparing one state of things with another. Importantly, such states must be attended to sequentially, for example in that the judge has to look back and forth from his sheet and the run he is looking at, and thus try to treat each of them 'en bloc' in that he needs to consider the 'overall impression of the ride.' The current score and the performance he can see, however, are not the only things worth comparing in order to produce a judgement. A comparison that the judging sheet is designed to afford, maybe even enforce (since the adjacent ratings can hardly be ignored), is that with the prior judgements made. In contrast, both the seating of the judges (next to each other) versus that of the head judge (behind them), as well as the explicit ban of comparing scores (in rule 3.4) are implemented in order to keep the judges from making comparisons among each other. More particularly, the specifically designed worksheets produce what Goodwin (1994) described as a "heterotopia" in his discussion archaeologists' colour-scales, and while the judging booth and seating order erects a specific 'architecture for perception' notably different from that of an arena, in that an *asymmetric* visibility of the ongoing pondering of scores is systematically produced since the head judge can use the scenic intelligibility of the judges' conduct while they themselves are barred on relying on this resource to produce agreement with their colleagues. Again, it is worth noting how fragile the practice of seeing Style seems to be: even a mere glance over to the others seems to be enough to throw the judges out of their 'deep seeing' or full focus on the inherent details of possibly stylish conduct unfolding before their eyes. This aspect becomes even clearer vis-à-vis the third method of restricting talk and enhancing the flow of judgement installed by the manual, namely the temporal synchronization and compression of the three judges' conduct. Again, this longer segment of the manual is worth quoting, because even better than being a folk-description of the practice of judging, it is a folk-prescription, so to speak: It unveils the identifying details of the conduct by telling us how it must be done.

"§ 2.4. One Minute Of Judging

0–10 seconds
The first 10 seconds are used by each judge to decide around what score he is aiming, (4 to 5, or 6 to 7). Judges are asked to place the point of their pen on the judging scale around the mark they wish to give. The head judge sees right away whether all the judges agree on the run they saw or not. If two judges are together and one disagrees, the head judge can ask this judge to rethink his score. If the head judge's own opinion was close to the two judges who agree, he will ask the third judge to bring his score closer to the others. If the head judge's own opinion was close to the judge who stands alone, he could either leave it the way it is or get the three judges into a discussion about the run.

11–55 seconds
Without reaction from the head judge, the judge can go on with fine-tuning his judgement with confidence, knowing the other judges have about the same score. The judge will first mark the spot on his graduated line, then fill up his comment box, then compare this run with past close scores and finally mark his final score in the score box.

55–60 seconds
The head judge communicates the scores to the competition administrator."

(Freeride World Tour 2011: § 2.4)

Judging a line as described in this excerpt happens through a series of clearly different and independent practices which each seem to follow their own logic, can potentially produce contradictory results, and must therefore be carefully managed and aligned. Interestingly, verbal discussion is treated as a kind of measure of last resort which is supposed to happen within less than ten seconds—arguably an unrealistically short period of time. (As far as I know, there is no 'super-head' judge to supervise the head-judge on this matter.) Instead, if things go smoothly, the procedure is designed to instil confidence into the judges regarding their planned score, who can then use the rest of the time to "fine-tune" their opinion. In sum, producing a coherent judging score happens by flip-flopping between different practices and different levels of observation: watching the ride, making a first decision, comparing it with the scores of the prior rides, being asked to rethink the score, discussing with the other judges, fine-tuning the score, and justifying it in writing. In fact, the brief description I just gave glosses over an enormous amount of important details (some of which I noted earlier) which need to be aligned to make these practices possible. There are, in my view, two key conclusions to draw from observing this complex and ingenious procedure: On the one hand, determining the quality of visible Style is not a verbal negotiation, not a homogenous consensus-finding, but neither a simple top-down exercise of expert power. Rather, the 'mental' and the verbal, the tacit and the performative aspects of doing judging are juxtaposed and recombined together with different media or forms of expression: pointing at scores, discussing, marking, and writing. In lieu of what I argued about Style not being simply an arbitrary symbolic vocabulary, I hold that this observation supports the notion that different ways of seeing and expressing the seen must be combined, or woven into a nexus, in order to produce one coherent understanding of how good or bad this particular witnessed ride was. Consequentially, seeing and judging Style is not simply a speech act or a construction process in that one communicative act simply fixes what the judges have seen. On the other hand, while it is surely an embodied and somewhat intuitive process, I believe that this example of decision-making also goes against the grain of praxeological accounts of decision-making which describe it as *nothing but* an intuitive and inevitable manifestation of someone's habitus. As we have seen, Bourdieu's conceptualization of deciding about styles basically implies that one's embodied dispositions immediately produce a valuation which is 'enforced' upon the conscious actor, particularly through moods or emotions. Likewise, Lizardo and Strand (2010: 219) have argued that if cultural sociologists would only start to study "fast, 'hot' cognitive-emotive judgments of right/wrong, like/dislike, propriety/impropriety 'online' and 'on the fly,'" then they would find how clearly structured the outcomes are, and how persistently they are imposed by our habitus. I stress that my point is not simply that the observations I just presented refute this idea, but rather that while such 'hot judgements' surely exist and can play an important role for answering questions of taste and style, they do not simply overpower the people on which they bear (usually, at least); but that they can be carefully managed and arranged by them in order to be actually able to produce exactly the coherence and stability of decisions Lizardo and Strand seem to take as given. More to the point, my case demonstrates how quite different situational set-ups function as 'media' of the social precisely because they are systematically juxtaposed and recombined as practitioners purposefully switch from situatedly provisioned and managed 'gut feeling' or tacit, 'hot' decision-making, to explicit verbal justification, and back. In this case, this happens by alternating between overt debate or 'enacted confrontation' in the discussion phase and 'automatized' coordination or consensus-production by virtue of routinely calculating the average score points from originally disparate or mismatching decisions. Conclusively, intelligibility does arise in the organized situation and is not miraculously manufactured by the (subconscious) neural ghost in the machine—at least not in such a fashion that it fits. Lizardo and Strand are right that regularity does not arise from meticulous invocation of logically coherent rules or rationales per se, but it does not arise from gut feeling or embodied disposition alone either. Further, contrary to their assurance that the situation is not needed to "offload cognitive work (…) towards (…) the environment in which the actor is embedded" (Lizardo/Strand 2010: 223), situated order is crucial to capture and preserve the 'intuitive' aspect of hot decision making—e.g. in that the judges only have to point at the scale rather than write something down or explain themselves. Likewise, the situational order is important particularly because the judgements need to be 'hot' and swift in order to 'work out': As the rules imply, the judges' confidence of making a legitimate choice is an important factor that allows them to trust their own gut feelings, since they can assume that their decisions are accountable (in Garfinkel's sense) as long as the head judge overseeing their proposals does not step in.

10 Juxtaposing Media

In sum, I suggest that the judging procedure instructed in the judging manual testaments how different observation practices do not simply direct attention to different details of a witnessed performance, but rather invoke different perspectives, different ways of observing which cause different figural gestalts to be seen. In the terminology I proposed, one could say that the different ways of seeing that the judges combine and juxtapose amount to different aspects to be sublated—lifted out and simultaneously idealized or glossed. In contrast to constructivist theories, however, I stress that, because the phenopractice perspective takes the given 'object' of inquiry to be a constellation of stable elements in a phenomenal field, such an operation can be 'rolled back' in a certain way: Surely, after observing the observers 'know' more than before, i.e. their procedure is sequential in that prior steps influence later ones. But on the other hand, my perspective suggests that one can nevertheless let one aspect 'sink back' into the background and reassess the whole from a different angle. At the core, this notion is—I believe—an effect of gestalt thinking: The idea that one can see either one or the other gestalt of a ambiguous figure (such as Wittgenstein's duck-rabbit) implies that the prior seeing of the first figure *does not* prefigure or 'key' the seeing of the second, which is instead seen despite the fact that the same image looked very different just a second ago. In contrast, constructivist (as well as constructionist) theory typically emphasizes the sequentiality of observation, in that every step or operation in an observation or interpretation is taken to be path-dependent and thus ultimately happening in the shadow of the very first move. I take the judging process just analysed to provide a somewhat different picture: While there is no doubt that the overall procedure is sequential in character, and that prior activities (e.g. the individual first assessment) bear on subsequent ones (e.g. the concluding discussions), I also suggest that the different ways of observing and assessing the run (or indeed any 'social thing') each figure out different aspects independently and in distinct episodes. In my view, the pivotal point is that in each episode, different resources (being composed of different elements) are employed, such as different ways of seeing (different mental routines) which each invoke different prefigurations. I deem two kinds of elements crucial in this regard: First, the embodied routines (e.g. what amounts to pragmatic seeing and 'gut feeling' vs. epistemic identification and conscious deliberation), and second, what I will call the different media of expression: the pointing at a scale, writing down descriptive bullet points, or having a discussion. These media, I should explain, mark a notable difference between the practices of observing episodes of conduct I am discussing now, and the general practices of observation dealt with in chapter four. In the latter case, I considered qualities of elements 'baked' into amalgamated practices and the question was how single elements could be made to stand out against the conduct they are part of. Here, I am concerned with qualities of something that needs to be practically 'entified' into a circumscribable unit from which an aspect can thus stand out—and the description of this situation is complicated by the fact that the 'unification' and the sublimation happen in one step, within one phenopractice. Talking about a performance in order to justify a certain score, for example, at once recasts the performance and puts it into a certain light.[17] And the way this happens depends on the media in question: Some things are better said than calculated; seeing the teleological end of a movement via pragmatic vision in a static picture is not impossible, but difficult; and so forth. As I have shown, the artful combination, juxtaposition, and realignment of the practices employing these media provide the judges with the flexibility and versatility, but also the accountability and restrictiveness which their difficult task demands. In the following parts of this chapter, I will now pick out some of these media of observation or deliberation and assess in some more detail how their invocation provides the practitioners with a different grasp on the slice of the world in front of them—in this case, visible practices of freeskiing. More to the point, I will ask how Style appears, can be grasped, but also slips away again in some of the key media which freeskiers work with. I will begin my discussion with what most social thinkers take to be the most powerful and most complex social medium (although they usually employ this term differently than I do): language. After that, I will then turn to the predominant medium in freeskiing, namely visual images and videos.

My use of the term 'medium' has an important caveat: By no means do I suggest that the order or style of the conduct being observed with its help will be somehow 'shock-frozen' and stored or preserved in said medium. With regard to the matter of style, I have already rejected the idea that style is a symbolic vocabulary that can be broken down into singular pieces; and below I will present a very different (and more complex) ethnomethodological account of how something like a video can 'contain' visible style, and how the practice of seeing style in said video can best be described. I thus reiterate that what I call media are practices (or bundles thereof) such as talking, pointing out, or watching a video. Further, it is with reservation that I will discuss how freeskiers talk about freestyle tricks. In doing so, I will not even touch upon the question whether language can 'represent' the tricks or their Style in any strict sense of the word—I have already made clear my position on this matter. Rather, just like in the case of the ski's flex, I will ask what speaking about tricks *does for* other phenopractices concerning the skiing performance in question, namely identifying and performing a trick. The conduct of these practices, I have postulated, primarily requires intelligibility and understanding to take place, both in that a doing must be intelligible as the doing of a practice, and in that conduct performed in the form of action requires practical intelligibility, i.e. an action to make sense to do to the action. Therefore, I will try to sketch out how and what language makes intelligible with regard to freeski

---

[17] In my view, this situation is not fundamentally different depending on whether or not the conduct in question is still ongoing, in that every observation-in-practice of any conduct needs to 'install its presence' in the current phenomenal field. Retelling the past or explaining a movie that is currently running does not differ in principle (but of course in detail).

performances, first towards understanding them, and second towards performing the actions they consist in. To be sure, speaking about something is of course itself conducted through doings and sayings; yet my focus here is not how the speaking itself becomes understandable as the saying of a particular something, but rather how the intelligibility it provides enables or prefigures further doings.

Let me begin with an excerpt from a conversation between two riders—Pete an Jo—who are sitting in a chairlift next to the funpark and watch someone perform a freestyle trick (a so-called 720) that nearly ends in a crash. While the rider is rotating twice around his horizontal axis, his rotation becomes an off-axis spiralling that almost makes him loose control. While it seems clear that this performance was bad in terms of Style and control, things are complicated by the fact that there exists a trick called a Misty which consists in purposefully performing exactly the kind of off-axis rotation that just happened. The subsequent brief exchange is thus informative in that first, it points to a very common task freeskiers (and freeski judges) face: determining precisely which trick it was they have just seen. As I described, a broad variety of tricks exist, many of which come in several versions and each of which can be combined with a number of different grabs. And while one does not need to know the name of a trick to watch it or enjoy its style; one does need words to talk about, judge, or learn a trick (e.g. so that other can provide suggestions and support; or that one can simply know what it is that one has learned). The second point this exchange aptly demonstrates is thus the basic fact that in this case, seeing and talking about a trick are two different practices, each of which refers to the same conduct, but has its own object. But if so, how do seeing and talking relate?

> Pete (hastily): Uhuhuhuhuh! Uh! (2s) That was a Misty 7, was it?
> Jo: Yep. But I think the Misty-part was not really planned.
> Pete: No::, I think not. Roy does Switch Misty 10s. THAT looks crass! Completely tweaked, and, and (.) ehhm nosegrab." [R][18]

From my perspective, what is notable here is how there is first an intuitive emotional reaction produced by the embodied seeing of the performance of the trick which for a long time looked like it would end in a crash. This moment of seeing Style has arguably had all the characteristics of situated seeing I described earlier, and it seems quite clear that it was a manifestation of the embodied observation skill of Pete, who reacts spontaneously and almost instinctively. Next, there is a break, a moment of silence. And only now Pete begins to put into words what he had just witnessed. In my view, he is not exactly offering a re-interpretation of the immediate past, but instead he is working out what was going on: a Misty that was not actually a Misty. With Wittgenstein, one could say: the meaning of a word is in the use of the word, and thus talking and seen conduct together help to carry

---

[18] *Pete (schnell): „Uhuhuhuhuh! Uh! (2 s) Das war ein Misty 7, oder?"—Jo: „Ja. Aber ich glaub das Misty war nicht ganz so geplant."—Pete: „Ne:, ich glaub nich. Der Roy springt Switch Misty-10. DAS sieht krass aus! Komplett getweakt und, und (.) äh Nosegrab."*

forth the understanding of what a Misty is. They do so by offering a certain way of looking at the current situation (being a performance of a Misty) which can thus be further qualified should the need arise. Likewise, calling the jump a Misty provides the opportunity to link to the next topic of this small snippet of talk, namely a counter-example of a good Misty which can serve to reaffirm what a real Misty is—again without forcing the speaker to put into words what it actually is that makes a Misty and Misty. In other words, continuously juxtaposing spoken words and witnessed events in this way provides a way for the freeskiers to deliberate the meaning of events in light of the 'social things' that are the known freestyle tricks without ever coming close to needing to define or list or explicate all definitive particulars of concrete events or abstract entities. Instead, the spoken word "Misty" is wedged in between the principle it seeks to express (what I clumsily described as an off-axis rotation and which would be so much easier to grasp from a picture) and the full concretes of the performance it is directed at. Presented like this, however, it seems that all words employed are entirely disconnected from the events they are applied to. This view would be misleading, since I have suggested that words or phrases—if put into practice—do provide for the structuring or ordering of conduct. In order to assess the role of language more thoroughly, one first needs to look at the practice they are being 'mapped onto' in this case: If words are used by freeskiers to describe details of a certain trick, how do these details become relevant and describe-able in the first place? Seeing and talking about a trick, in other words, need to be observed side-by-side in order to see how both open up different levels of aspects in different-but-related ways which in sum allow for the fact that the meaning of a word can be carried by using it to mean just 'that what can be seen here or there.'

11 Seeing a Trick as Gestalt-Seeing

What does it mean to see an acrobatic performance on skis as a freestyle trick, as a unit that has a certain name (or two) and can further have certain qualities on the basis of being that something, e.g. a particularly good or stylish performance of said trick. Harnessing the theoretical considerations about human vision laid out so far, it seems safe to say that seeing and discerning a certain trick means seeing a gestalt, a figure arising from the details of a specific performance. To be precise: In order to discern a certain trick, freeskiers need to see not just one, but several gestalts. To be able to grasp and judge a certain performance such as a specific jump, they need to segment each performance into certain elements that can be kept apart although being aspects of a single fluent episode of conduct that hardly lasted longer than three seconds overall. In order to underpin this claim, let me begin by taking a look at how freeskiers discern tricks and trick-combinations verbally. A Switch Double Cork 1080 Japan, for example, contains a description of the basic trick, plus a series of qualifiers: a 1080°-rotation around the horizontal

Fig. 9.6 A switch 1080 Double Cork with a Mute grab. (by Zach Seward, licensed under CC 2.0)

axis (three full rotations) combined with a double cork or two rotations[19] around the vertical axis (so that a diagonal overall rotation results—one that looks like a corkscrew) which was begun riding switch (backwards) and was coupled with a Japan grab, i.e. grabbing a ski behind the binding with one hand and pulling it towards one's back by bending the knees.

Each of these different terms, in other words, describes a certain movement pattern that has been visible simultaneously with the others within the self-same episode of activity (the jump, as illustrated in Fig. 9.6). The horizontal rotations, for example, lasted *while* the vertical rotations where performed; as did the Japan grab. In other words, the different parts of the jump that the verbal description lists are aspects visible within one overall movement, aspects which could themselves be described as composed of smaller units, e.g. in that a Japan grab is a figure compiled by certain positions of the hands (one at the ski, the other stretched out into the air), the skis, the corpus, and so forth. What is more, these names are describing certain definite, lasting constellations or bodily figures such as 'the'

---

[19] These are not actually full vertical rotations bur rather elliptic, off-axis rotations in that the head is never actually the lowest point of the body. I spare this detail here to make things not even more complicated. The off-axis rotation is itself the result of an interesting historical development: In (Oldschool) freestyle competitions held by the FIS such as the Olympics, inverted tricks are banned for safety reasons. The off-axis rotation (initially called a Diner Roll) was developed in order to bypass this rule in that it is not a 'real' vertical rotation. It's performance was allowed after legal battles, but not really accepted by the traditionalist FIS judges (Moseley 2002). Off-axis rotations are thus an important formal remnant of the separation of Oldschool and Newschool freestyle.

Japan grab, despite the fact that each jump is necessarily an ongoing stream of movement in which one micro-episode (such as stretching out one arm) blends seamlessly into the next (such as pulling it back to prepare the landing). At this point, I hope, it becomes more clear why I provided such a complex discussion of the procedures of human vision in chapter three: On the basis of the insights considered there, I can now argue that seeing a Japan grab (or for example "that grab which TJ Schiller is doing all the time") is not simply an ex-post, mental interpretation performed by the consciousness of a knowledgeable individual via synthesizing the 'raw data' provided by the eyes into seeing certain forms in an inherently formless medium (such as infinitesimally small and short 'bits' of 'input' from the whole visual field). Instead, there are certain orderly formations of details inherent in the jump itself, formations such as "three horizontal rotations" that seem to stand out 'naturally,' possibly because certain routines of visual cognition are in place that enable us to spot and count rotations 'en bloc.'

What is more, I argue that it is not by accident that these formations stand out visually *and* are easily grasped with a single verbal expression as well. Consider, for example, the 1080 Double Cork: Formally, it would seem more logical to speak about a '1080 horizontal 720 vertical' or something similar. However, it appears quite difficult for us to extract this combination of abstract concepts out of a movement we watch, just as it is relatively difficult to try to picture an object performing a 'simultaneous 1080° horizontal and a 720° vertical rotation' in our head. In contrast, it seems much easier to see or imagine 'two diagonal rotations' or 'a corkscrew-kind of movement.' Talking about the Double Cork, in other words, seems to provide us with what Merleau-Ponty called our best grip on the situation. But then why still call it a 1080 Double Cork? In freeskiing, a Double Cork is always performed as a 1080 (and a triple cork is always a 1240), although theoretically, a 720 would be sufficient to perform two simultaneous vertical rotations and still achieve two diagonal rotations, yet the freeskiers' bodies seem incapable of this. The reasons for this 'fact' are again difficult to put into words, but they are probably perfectly clear either to a freestyler who has already performed a Double Cork, or to a scientist studying the biophysics and kinetics of human movement. In any event, freeskiers refrain from calling the trick a Double Cork (without the 1080) because there is a different terminological logic inherent in the expression Double Cork 1080: Confronted with the task of recognizing and name complex combinations of very rapid successions of movements, the freeskiers organize their naming—and arguably also their seeing—according to the number of horizontal rotations[20]: The basic name of a trick is always the horizontal rotation, e.g. 180, 360, 540, and so forth. Importantly, freeskiers usually also learn to perform the tricks in the same ascending order: They start with 'clean' 180s and 360s, then add different grabs; then proceed to learn 720s, again adding grabs; then learn horizontal rotations (or flips) before combining 720 and flip into a 720 Cork, and so forth. Indeed, freestylers talk and arguably think about

---

[20] With the exception of flips, which consist of vertical rotations only.

their own tricks in just the same modular way. The logics of learning, naming, and visually grasping a trick all share a common basic gestalt. To underpin this claim, let me now look in some more detail how a freeskier manages to conduct the performance of a particular trick. My thesis is that, just like the visually out-standing details and those well circumscribed in language fit nicely and thus allow one another to be meaningful, suitable ways of initiating and controlling the performance of a trick and the trick's verbal description as well overlap in a manner useful for all practical purposes (as ethnomethodologists would say).

12 Talk and Action

I am running the risk of confusing my reader at this point: I have just been discussing the role of media for intelligibility, and now I switch over to action, the topic of the last chapter? To gain some clarity on what I am trying to do here, it might help to recall the argument I made in the first part of this chapter: that in the phenopractice perspective, understandings (the inner core of practices) are defined as bundles of capacities of understandable performing plus understanding performances. Further, I discerned basal and action understandings which can both only take place on the basis of the local achievement of intelligibility. And while basal understandings not necessarily require that it is consciously intelligible that a certain doing should take place (e.g. rapidly readjusting the body posture to avoid slipping and falling), the last chapter has shown how the performance of actions requires said action to make sense to do in the given situation. Thus, what moves into focus now is the question how that kind of intelligibility which action understandings require becomes established—and what, apart from a skilled practitioner, enables this. It is at this point that language enters the picture.

Imagine a freestyle skier knew how to do a 360 (one full rotation), for example, and now aspires to learn a 720 (two rotations). He would think to himself something vaguely akin to: "Ok, just jump and do the same thing, only spin around with more force, and try to be patient until the second rotation is over before you land." That sounds laughably inaccurate and incompetent, you say? Of course it is—how else to tell yourself to do something you have never done before? If I ask you now to stop reading, stand up, and jump into the air to spin around a full 360° before you land—what do you think to yourself before, and in order to, doing that? (Apart from laughing at yourself, that is.) Probably something strangely inaccurate and vaguely incompetent about throwing around your arms and shoulders as hard as you can, something that helps you to 'get a grip' on the myriad things your body will need to do—but that you cannot even think about in any reasonable way. My point is that what this silly exercise requires you to do is to *figure out* a movement sequence, an episode of bodily activity; and the only way to do this is to 'chunk together' a number of details which then provide you with a kind of proxy for a hole complex of particulars. A few of these proxies or crucial points taken together might then allow you to do what you 'want' to do; for example jump up, throw yourself around, and land on your two feet again. Notably, you cannot 'choose' such proxies or crucial points in any way you like. Quite to the opposite, they must fulfil two very specific prerequisites. First, they must be 'knowable' or better already known to you in some way: You can plan to throw your arms around, but you cannot consciously intend to 'perform' the visual-motor routines that allow you to keep track of your swirling around—you cannot quite 'do' stabilize your eyeball during rotation in such a way that you can fixate an element in your visual field for fractions of a second in order to keep track of the direction and speed of your rotation so that you know when you have successfully spun around far enough (see Berthoz 2000). Second, these crucial points must somehow link up in favourable way so that an overall successful movement results. Although you must bend your knees before jumping up, for example, it does not seem to make much sense to focus on the bending, but much more to orient towards the jumping up.

I am not entirely sure whether I was able to put across what I am trying to convey; but in any event, I hold that when trying to perform stylish tricks, freeskiers think and talk in much the same way. Take for example this excerpt from a conversation between Tom and another experienced freestyler. During talking about their recent advances in training, one is telling how, during performing a 720 Cork, he could feel that with a little additional impulse, he could extend the same movement into a 1080 Double Cork, or the same trick with one additional rotation.

> Jo: "If you, so to speak, think during the Corked 7: '5er'"
> Tom: "Yes."
> Jo: "You, so to speak, have to already for the—initiate the 10er, the Double Cork."
> Tom: "Yes."
> Jo: "And I just think: As I was pulling it [the Cork 720] around, I felt a few times like… where I was saying: 'If you would throw over your head one more time…
> Tom: "Yes."
> Jo: "… you would make it.'" [R][21]

I realize that it is quite difficult to understand just what exactly the two are even talking about. But the basic idea is that for a freestyler, every trick feels a certain way, and in order to accomplish a new and more complicated trick, he tries to 'assemble' it on the basis of those tricks, those 'feelings' he already knows. In order to do a Cork 720 (two horizontal and one vertical rotations combined), for example, you have to begin a 720 but then "think" like you would when doing a 5er (a 540° rotation), only that you do not initiate a horizontal rotation (by 'throwing yourself to the side'), but a diagonal rotation (by throwing yourself forward in a tiled angle, as if to roll over your left shoulder). What is more, you initiate these rotations by moving certain body parts you 'know well' how to move—typically

---

[21] „Jo: Wenn du, sozusagen, beim Corked 7 denkst: '5er' – Tom: Ja. – Jo: …, musst du sozusagen dann schon für den – das in den 10er einleiten, den Double Cork. – Tom: Ja. – Jo: Und ich mein halt wie ich den rumgezogen hab, hab ich m paarmal so (..) gemerkt. Wo ich gesagt hab: Wenn du jetzt dein Kopf nochmal rüberwirfst… – Tom: Ja. – Jo: … dann, ähm, haust du ihn raus."

your arms, shoulders, feet, or head—and ignore the others. In the case of the Cork 720, you tilt you head forward and to the left, in a similar way as in taking a header, where you think: "Head forward!" rather than: "Feet up above my head!" Consequently, the more complicated freestyle tricks feel like, and are understood as, combinations of two more basic moves: If you have to think "5er" to do a Cork, then accordingly you have to think "10er" (or "two tilted forward rotations") to perform a Double Cork. Again, it is surely difficult to try and understand what exactly is going on in doing insane multiple rotations with skis on your feet while high up in the air. Still, I hope I am able to convey this key point: If the freeskier were not able to segment the tricks in this way and approach them step-by-step, it would be all but impossible for them to perform them at all. What is more, only because it is possible to segment them in this way, the freestyler Jo is able to have the feeling that he is 'almost there,' that it would take only this little nudge, this one additional tilt of the head to initiate the second rotation. And it is only because he *has* an understanding of the concept '5er' that he can 'think to himself' about adding another 5er at the end of the first—and having the understanding means having the thought-related-to-a-feeling-and-to-something-he-can-do. Furthermore, it is only because of having this understanding of a 5er *and* being able to grasp it in a verbal expression that he can talk about it to Tom. Because Tom intelligibly shares this understanding they can have a meaningful conversation which helps *both* to understand a bit more about doing Double Corks. Tom could, for example, be sceptical about Jo's thinking and point out a flaw or danger. What is more, he might remind Jo of their conversation later on and try to motivate or push him to go ahead and find the courage to attempt a Double Cork in praxis.

Interpreting this situation in the terms of phenopractice theory, I argue that Jo being able to sense that he could almost extend his Cork into a Double Cork constitutes an action affordance. More precisely, its doing so depends on two different factual states. First, it happens in the modus of what Schatzki (2002) calls *practical intelligibility*: the realistic possibility of doing a Double Cork transpires as a contextual phenomenon, in the midst of action, and against the backdrop of competently doing a Cork 720. If the rider would not be in the middle of purposefully conducting a Cork 720, there would be no way he could sense this opportunity for a Double Cork—you and me would be simply in panic and fearing death while swirling around 8 meters up in the air. But since the ongoing action presents itself to the rider as an orderly set of segments (such as phases of a jump he can initiate or which are already complete), states (such as having enough speed or being stable), and crucial points (such as 'tilt your head to spin around'), practical intelligibility can "single out" (Schatzki 2002: 79) something like the opportunity to initiate another diagonal rotation. Notably, the way this opportunity stands out of the phenomenal field of the current moment cannot be adequately described with the terminology of volition or decision, since it is something the practitioner 'receives' or 'picks up' from and amidst the field; but neither can it be thought of independently of the situation of currently-doing-a-Cork-720-and-having-almost-finished-the-rotation. That is, the practical intelligibility cannot transpire independently of or separate from the unfolding of the practice, because the conduct of the practice is the *site* within which the opportunity transpires. However, such an instance of practical intelligibility alone does not suffice to constitute an affordance that is actually actionable. Second, it required what I called a crucial point with which to initiate the action—the tilting of the head as a proxy for initiating what will sufficiently, reliably amount to performing another corked rotation. In Schatzki's (2002: 77) terms, it necessitates a practical understanding—"knowing how to X." As my discussion of performing, feeling, thinking about, and talking about Corks and Double Corks tried to show, having such an actionable practical understanding at that moment up in the air in the midst of a Cork 720 is not something the rider has 'in his head,' but rather depends on and is carried by that nexus, that manifold of overlapping doings and sayings which allow Jo and Tom to feel, "think,"[22] know, name, see, do, and above all understand just what a corked rotation actually, practically is. As I tried to pinpoint when asking you to jump up and swirl around in a silly manner, what must occur across different performances or unfoldings of the same doing is a peculiar alignment of very different necessities or functionalities on very different levels of enablement and constraint: For it is not just that the corked rotation must be something that is smoothly 'knowable' or 'intendable'; it must also be expressible, seeable, remeberable, and doable as well. It must, in other words, be carried in and across a number of doings and sayings hanging together in a nexus. Without other people having 'invented' and popularized the Double Cork, without Jo having seen and read and talked about Double Corks, he would not be able to do or feel like he could do a Double Cork (but at best something with a different name and meaning); and it is entirely possible that he would not even have noticed that (or tried to see if) there is the possibility of adding another rotation just by tilting his head once more would he not have come to understand Double Corks earlier on.

Finally, let me point out that Schatzki insists that practical understanding and practical intelligibility are two pairs of shoes in that you can very well have one without the other. Tom, for example, apparently has a pretty solid understanding of what a Double Cork is[23] and how it is done via tilting the head, but that does not mean that it would make sense for him to do it just now or indeed at any foreseeable moment in the near future (since he is not as competent a freestyler as Jo).

---

[22] On a side note: It is quite interesting how the freeskiers says "think" where a philosopher would say "intend" (see below).

[23] From his second book onwards, Schatzki (2002) makes a distinction between practical understandings—knowing how to do X—and general understandings—knowing something about X. As this example shows, this distinction is somewhat problematic: By knowing how a Cork 720 feels, but not (practically) knowing how to do a Double Cork 1080, does Tom know something specific, practical about the Double Cork, or only something general? Unlike me, the ethnographer, he has a much more specific, 'pragmatic' insight into how a initiating a Cork feels, and initiating the second half of a Double Cork allegedly feels just the same. Notably, I am not disputing that he cannot publicly perform a Double Cork, he is not a 'knowing' practitioner of it. But in the course of the conversation, does he not emerge as a knowing practitioner of *feeling* how it feels when you can dive into a Double Cork just about now?

More precisely: For both Jo and Tom, quite a lot of things have to come together in order for it to make sense to them to 'just do' a second corked rotation; namely they must be flying up in the air and being in the midst of a well-going Cork and still having enough impulse to go for a second rotation this time. Only in the midst of certain situated doings, in other words, it is possible that:

> "Practical understanding (...) executes the actions that practical intelligibility singles out." (Schatzki 2002: 79)

Schatzki is correct, I believe, to argue that practical intelligibility does not determine what people do—feeling that you could throw over your head in order to initiate another rotation does by no means necessarily lead you to actually doing it. Instead, should Jo one day go for it and attempt a 1080 Double Cork, he would do so by virtue of having (currently being attuned to) the practical understanding within which tilting the head and rotating are connected. What is more, most likely this would only be made possible by, and happening against the background of, the 'full package' of the practice that, upon unfolding, constitutes a 1080 Double Cork: The material arrangements of kicker and equipment, the teleoaffective structure that makes doing a 1080 Double Cork a meaningful end that a freestyler like Jo strives for motivatedly (but also fears), the implicit and explicit rules bearing on a freestylers' daily practice (such as: never attempt a new trick if the prior attempts of easier tricks did not go well, always grab your ski poles in such a way that you do not break your thumb when you crash, and so on), as well as the general understanding that a 1080 Double Cork is a difficult, but very respectable and possibly very stylish trick. What is fascinating is how the language does not reflect this order, but is an incremental part of it. Theoretically, the Double Cork would be possible if one could not talk about it—but it would be immensely more difficult. On the other hand, the 'logic' inherent in names such as Switch Double Cork 1080 Japan does not 'float' above the 'actual' order of doing the trick, but is constrained by, aligned with, and interwoven into it. To speak with Wittgenstein:

> "[E]very interpretation [of a rule] hangs in the air together with what it interprets, and cannot give it any support." (Wittgenstein 2009: 86, § 198)

I stress that Wittgenstein does *not* write that the interpretation hangs in the air in isolation—he does not suggest that it is a parallel dimension isolated from the 'real world' or the authentic truth of visceral doings and embodied dispositions. Instead, the prescribed doing as the 'product' of the rule-talking 'hangs up there' together with the words of the rule. It is in this sense that I understand words to be a medium providing for practical intelligibility, not as predefining or even adequately reflecting what precisely it is that makes sense to do; but nevertheless as an indispensable prerequisite for its taking place. And is in this vain, I believe, in which Schatzki emphasizes:

> "When I write of the 'determination' of practical intelligibility I do not mean causally determine in the sense of efficient causality (X makes Y happen). I mean states of affairs and ways of being combining to specify what makes sense to someone to do." (Schatzki 2010b: 120)

13 Intelligibility and Understanding

The distinction between practical understanding and practical intelligibility I just sketched out—building on my account of action presented in the last chapter—is in my view a centrepiece of Schatzki's practice theory and of key importance for theorizing phenopractices. In particular, it fleshes out the distinction between basal understandings and action understandings I introduced at the beginning of this chapter: action understandings are capabilities of performing and recognizing conduct which qualifies as action, i.e. entails the practitioners' being-in-action. The separation of practical understanding and practical intelligibility can in some cases still lead to accounts quite similar to those produced by more traditional distinctions such as that between mind and body; for example if how and why something makes sense for someone to do seems predominantly mental or 'rational' in nature, while the practical understanding necessary for conducting it depends predominantly on bodily routines. Writing down the answer to a simple equation like $2+2=$ might be a good example. However, especially in such cases it needs to be emphasized that the way writing down "4" made sense to the practitioner is not adequately described as "calculating," since "calculating" only points out what the person visibly and understandably did, namely hesitating very briefly and then writing down the number 4. Just how it made sense to the person to do this is not captured by this description, especially since there are many different options: It will probably be quite different for an average adult who is 'not even thinking,' compared to a dutiful 2nd grader, compared to an adult simultaneously having to pass a flight-simulator test, compared to a panic-stricken 2nd grader trying to make an educated guess. What is more, while both the meaning of the "4" (a test is failed, the symbol "4" is not known in this culture, etc.) and the way of making sense will vary depending on the practice currently unfolded, they do not depend on the practice in the same way and can appear in many different combinations.

The general distinction between intelligibility and understanding lies at the core of the phenopractice-theoretical perspective I work out in detail in this text. One important feature is of course the fact that both intelligibility and understanding are not conceptualized as individual actor's deeds, but as transpiring within sites into which humans are embedded, but which are neither controlled or defined by, nor equal to, them. However, the fact that intelligibility and understanding transpire or appear in a site is not theorized to be a simple causal effect or inherent quality of such sites themselves, but rather as the realization (or reproduction) of a certain overarching relationality or coherence called phenopractice. An instance of doing a Misty 7, for example, is the doing of a Misty 7 by virtue of being an exemplar of those social things made possible by (or carried by) the nexus of performing and recognizing Misty 7er; a nexus which needs to be thought of as one social meshwork since unrecognizable performances or unperformable cognitions cannot have social existence (thus escaping social ontology). In Schatzki's (1996: 103 f.) terms: "A doing or saying belongs to a given practice if it expresses components of that practice's organization," especially its understanding, in this case the understanding formed by performing and recognizing Misty 7er. Likewise, intelligibility is bound to and an instantiation of a site or hanging-together in that it is an effect of a phenomenal field; it can only occur amid such a field, across its different elements, and against its background. Furthermore, the distinction between intelligibility and understanding has another important feature. By making this distinction, the phenomenon of human activity or conduct is sliced in a way that differs from other strands of social thought, and particularly from sociological action theories: What a doing is and how it makes sense to a practitioner to do it are understood as separate phenomena; and because they are separate, they do not need to be housed in the subject together. In the classic sociological theories of action at least since Weber, knowing how to do something (or what doing will constitute some deed) and knowing what to do (next) have been pulled together, since the former was understood as a means or tool for fulfilling the latter. In a way, the sticking-together of the two has troubled theories of action ever since, because the meaning of a doing (what it is) is evidently also a societal phenomenon. Schutz' (and others') solution was to multiply the meaning of all doing as being different for different actors (and possibly again different in social realms such as interactions or texts); while structuralist solutions declare not only the identity or meaning of doings to be entirely social, but also its instantiation (why it was done). Phenopractice thought—by making use of Wittgenstein—suggests avoiding the problematic implications of either solution by splitting understanding and intelligibility into two phenomena that are related but different in that they are stemming from an overarching entity—phenopractices. What a doing is transpires on a different plane, so to speak, than why it made sense to do it.[24] In my view, one advantage of this separation is that the relational mesh which makes one phenomenon (or the processes carrying it) possible does not have to exhibit deep structural homology with that carrying the other one. In particular, this means that the epistemological processes or capabilities which are central to identifying action must not play a big role for 'motivating' action as well. Entities or processes which are widely perceived to be essentially different and possibly antagonistic, such as rationality and emotions, impulse and planning, materiality and mentality, or mind and body do not necessarily have to be crammed into the same housing. Neither is there a need to postulate that, while both share uneasy coexistence, one has control or superiority over the other or fully eclipses it, e.g. in that the meaning of acting 'really' only lies in experiencing acting.

The separation of practical understanding and practical intelligibility, in combination with the idea that they manifest in sites, likewise provides the opportunity to move beyond talking about relatively broad philosophical or common-sense categories such as emotions, impulses, or whole body movements. Instead, I tentatively suggest that what we find in such sites are—among other things such as tools—the neuroscientists' much more specific and (crucially) independent,

---

[24] Note that this formulation does not imply nor require temporal succession of the two.

single-issue processes or routines of cognition and motricity. In my view, this is precisely the implication of what I have called *neural pluralism*, the idea that human neural or brain activity comprises a number of independent, single-issue processes which co-occur simultaneously and independently, and therefore their alignment and organization must be achieved within the situation. What makes this sentiment attractive to the phenopractice position is the fact that such routines are understood to be a) partly subconscious, b) independent, and c) need to be aligned or organized in some way to enable the conduct of orderly purposeful activities. These routines can be understood as relatively stable 'elements' that need to be situationally managed and recombined in the right way in order to produce situated order. In this way, two important theoretical prerequisites are being fulfilled: First, the subject-situation demarcation is transcended. E.g., subconscious neural processes are clearly something 'human' and are 'done' by the individual body, but at the same time they can only have meaningful or orderly effects by virtue of being enmeshed into (or carried or 'activated' by) a suitable situational order. Second, although some of these processes can well be thought of as relatively primitive stimulus–response processes—that is, as exhibiting stable regularities—this does not warrant giving up the important argument that all lived order is inherently contingent or indexical. More to the point, I believe that taking a close look at how for example the routines of visual cognition operate can provide much plausibility to Schatzki's basic claim that the intelligibility and orderliness of social conduct is not based on regularity, but similarity. An object or situation, I believe, does not need to be clearly *identified* by an actor in the strict sense, because many of his bodily doings can very well operate on the basis of mere similarity. More importantly, unlike Cartesian understandings of meaning and consciousness, a perspective derived from neural pluralism can easily acknowledge that *some* neural routines might operate on the basis of limited, task-specific internal models, mental maps, or conceptual content without having to conclude that there is a *complete* 'inner world' in light of which human conduct transpires. Instead, conscious, subconscious, and material orders or processes might well be simultaneously at work and jointly responsible, and each of them might well be strictly regular if taken on its own; but it is only in their (contingent) sum that the impression of an overall regularity of social conduct can shine up. The opportunity to embrace neural pluralism arises, I stress, only because such a conception does not necessitate one to over-generalize, idealize, or reify any such process: There is, for example, no need to (and justification for) assuming that 'deciding' for an action has to be ruled or even influenced by the same process underlying how we do actions—as sociological interpretations of neural networks or mirror neurons suggest (Cerulo 2010; Kastl 2004; Lizardo 2009)—just like there is no need to equalize drawing rational or logical conclusions about objects or states of the world with picking a path of action, as rational choice theories would have it.

There is one further implication of the general idea to separate practical intelligibility and practical understanding that I should point out: Distinguishing what a doing is from how it makes sense to the practitioner undercuts the traditional notion of intentionality. In my view, either of the two can be described as an intentional phenomenon—at least to some extent and depending on the notion of intentionality one is inclined to employ (see below). Conclusively, using the term 'intentionality' in the context of the theoretical perspective I laid out is not always helpful, since it can denote a number of different things. For example, practical intelligibility could well be described as invoking the intention to do something, but if so, then this intention would possible have conscious as well as subconscious aspects and would be tied to the current situation. While some theoretical conceptions of collective or situational intentionality align well with this premise, many others do not. What is more, assigning intentionality to practical intelligibility might easily lead one to extend this view to practical understandings as well, since many (but not all) doings are organized towards certain teleological endpoints. But this would harm the very heart of the idea of separating intelligibility and understanding, as well as the key argument of practice theories that the inherent directedness and outcome of practices is *not* necessarily something the practitioner must, or even can be, aware off (e.g. because it co-depends on subconscious routines, material technology, etc.), and that it is neither necessarily this directedness or outcome that lead the practitioner to engage in some conduct (e.g. since he is not aware of them, is lead by emotions, etc.).

Excursus: The (Too) Many Faces of Intentionality

Being based—in varying degrees and not always explicitly—on the philosophy of Wittgenstein, Heidegger, Merleau-Ponty, and Gurwitsch (as well as positions derived from them), theories of social practices are on the one hand deducted from phenomenology, but at the other go against some fundamental assumptions made by its founder Husserl. What unites these four thinkers and those they informed is (inter alia) the fact that the notion of intentionality plays a constitutive role for their respective system of thought. Let me briefly explain why I nevertheless avoid the concept. One conclusion that could be—and often has been—drawn from the shared focus of these thinkers is that practice theories do not question the notion of intentionality per se, but the way intentionality should be conceptualized and/or the realm, locus, or function it should be understood to be housed in, or carried by. However, definitions and uses of the term differ widely among theorists of practice; maybe so widely that using the term can do more harm than good. Just one example: Bourdieu (1977: 79–80; see Gebauer 2000; Marcoulatos 2003 for intentionality in Bourdieu) contrasts what he calls conscious intention ("dear to the phenomenologists") with the "objective intention" inherent in peoples' concrete practical actions, an intention which produces the objective state and factual history of the world. In Giddens (1984: 8–14; see Johnson 1990), in contrast, intentionality is equally characteristic of activity, but here it is not only defined as a conscious purpose or planned outcome held by "the author of an act," but it is also emphasized how actions additionally have unintentional consequences. Accordingly, while both authors are apparently after the same basic idea, one man's objective intentions are the other man's unintentional consequences. Such diversity is surely not coincidental. Rather, it merely reflects the broad range of philosophical takes on intentionality in general (Siewert 2006), and the different positions of the different philosophical 'forefathers' of practice thought in particular. Given that the term is so central to Husserl, it is not surprising that those seeking to continue, but also alter, criticize, or enhance the phenomenological project developed alternative understandings of intentionality.

Let me try to line out the problem I see in the notion of intentionality in very broad sketches: At least since its modern reformulation by Brentano, intentionality describes directedness towards a certain object or state, such as thinking about something or doing something for the sake of something else. These two examples point to what one could call the two opposite poles of the range of phenomena commonly described as intentional, namely a) intentionality as a mental or conscious phenomenon, and b) intentionality as a definitive feature of bodily action (in contrast to involuntary or unpurposeful conduct). For Husserl, the former notion was of course fundamental, expressed in his distinction of noesis and noema—intentional act and intended object—as constitutive for consciousness. Actions understood as bodily activities in the physical world, in contrast, can for Husserl only be intentional by virtue of being intended in consciousness, e.g. by being motivated by a mentally projected goal. This basic understanding still underlies most, but not all conceptions of intentionality. The alternative notion is of course almost equally prominent, and, as we have seen, not entirely absent from Husserl as well (Summa 2011). Still, its core idea is quite different: Here, intentionality describes physical or bodily activity as being directed towards a certain end or goal—and notably, this intentionality can accordingly be located in the movement itself, independent of mental states. I have suggested with regard to the topic of human vision that Husserl's notion of intentionality as being restricted to consciousness arguably forces him to conflate what are phenomena of different complexity and situational dependency: the directedness of the most fundamental bodily acts such as a single saccade is treated in the same way as complex plans or projects. While my critique was only aimed at a specific topic (vision) and a certain period of Husserl's thought, one can we find the same point in the—obviously much more profound and systematic—critique of Husserl by Heidegger, which in turn laid the base for Merleau-Ponty's work:

In this characterization of intentionality as an extant relation between two things extant, a psychical subject and a physical object, the nature as well as the mode of being of intentionality is completely missed. (Heidegger 1982: 60).

Heidegger argued that a) intentionality is not exclusive to mental content (or events) and that b) human beings are related to or rather *in* the world in a more basic, not already intentional way (H. L. Dreyfus 1993; Jordan 2000). It should be clear how this move is pivotal for practice thought, for example as the basis of Bourdieu's and Gidden's distinction between mental consciousness and the directedness inherent in practical conduct (although both build on Wittgenstein in this point, see below). Unfortunately, it also means that we are left with at least three, possible four options with regard to intentionality: Intentional and unintentional conduct, as well as intentional plus possibly unintentional mental processes/events (in the language of neuroscience: non-conceptual content). This Heideggerian take on intentionality is (at least in its basic structure, see Taylor 1995) paralleled by that of Wittgenstein. For Wittgenstein, intentionality is a fundamental aspect of all human activity, and as such it is tightly bound to our fundamental ability to use (in German Gebrauch)—to use the body, things, but also language (Gebauer 2008, 2009: 67–74; Glock 2010b). More precisely, the notion of Gebrauch can be seen as a central concept of Wittgenstein's late philosophy (Gebauer 2001, 2008) much in the way that Schatzki uses the notion of practice: It frames the realm within which our bodily being in the world, our skilful adaptedness to it, the affordances of materialities, as well as the structuring force of language frame our perception of and existence in the world.[25] Accordingly, it has been argued that for Wittgenstein, intentionality is not a quality of acts of consciousness, but of human activity in general—and more precisely: it "lies in the situation." (Gebauer 2008: 46; my translation) From my perspective, the notion of intentionality becomes problematic if it is used in such generalizing terms. In my view, what practice theory argues on the basis of Wittgenstein is, after all, that all conduct is tied to situated order. Describing this situation as: "All conduct is inherently intentional, and so is every situation" does not add anything to the argument. Instead, it opens the door to introduce (almost) mono-causal arguments about some singular or predominant source of intentionality as secretly underlying and effectively explaining all kinds of situated order—for example, as Gebauer (2008) does, in the form of the habitus as the carrier of Bourdieu's "objective intention."

To be sure, I do not suggest that the relation between the different forms or realms of intentionality (conscious/mental, bodily/motor, situated/worldly) has not originally been developed within the frame of coherent and systematic

---

[25] Since Wittgenstein uses the notion of Gebrauch much more frequently than that of Praxis, their precise relation might well worth be a discussion of its own, especially because Gebrauch has a much broader meaning than use in English as it does not carry the same tone of instrumentality, but instead in Wittgenstein's days it was also used as meaning "tradition" (Gebauer 2009: 254 fn30).

philosophical positions—it is only that the shifting of the realms' borders between the different positions have led to the fact that subsequent authors have tied dramatically different phenomena or arguments to intentionality as a kind of convenient proxy. As a case in point, a body-minded position towards Husserl depends on how much one emphasizes the Kantian roots of his thinking and the extent to which his taking the *ego-cogito-cogitatum* as the apodictic starting point for his philosophy is understood as a continuation of Descartes' dualism. While Merleau-Ponty argues along those lines to recommend the phenomenological field as a post-dualist alternative (cf. Toadvine/Embree 2002), the other prominent proponent of a field-theory of meaning, Gurwitsch (who was in turn a teacher of Garfinkel), argues the opposite. According to Gurwitsch (1970: 366), Husserl replaces the Cartesian duality of consciousness and the external world or *res extensa* with the intrinsic duality of consciousness stemming from the noetico-noematic correlation; and Gurwitsch therefore holds that Husserl's notion of intentionality already contains an understanding often ascribed to existential philosophy (Arvidson 1992, 2006; Gurwitsch 1970). In my view, these conflicting readings reflect the relative openness which the term intentionality gains once it refers to bodily action or movement: If intentionality describes bodily activity which gears into the world in a non-arbitrary way, then any factor or process or mechanism coupled to said activity can potentially be seen as carrying or evoking intentionality. If, for example, motor-intentionality is conceptualized in such a way that its content is the endpoint or effect of a certain bodily movement (such as moving the body from point A to point B), then the body can well be described as bearing this content subconsciously and non-conceptually, for example via sequence memory (Ennen 2003; Graybiel 1998). In contrast, however, one can also observe bodily activity, describe it as intentional, and then conclude that by virtue of being intentional, the activity must be tied to some mental process, because one presupposes intentionality is exclusively a mental phenomenon. In effect, the debate goes round in circles. In my view, it is on the basis of this latter line of reasoning that some contemporary discussions of intentionality build on neuroscientific findings to suggest ever-new roots or forms of intentionality, most notably what has been termed shared or situated intentionality and social cognition: Most generally said, one can show that the directions one's actions take are influenced or instantiated by situational order, interaction, or orientation to co-present 'conspecifics'; and more specifically, that neural processes active in (what amounts to being observed as) intentional action are also activated by looking at others act. From this, it is concluded that intentionality is either shared, transmitted, or collective in that the actors switch into a 'we-mode' (Becchio/Bertone 2004; Gallagher 2005; Goldman 2010; Jacob 2008; Pacherie 2003; Schlicht 2010). To be sure: I hold that many of the findings cited in favour of shared or collective intentionality support and enhance my own line of arguments, and like a number of other sociological authors, I build selectively on some of them. But on the other hand, I believe that a good part of what I perceive as the somewhat gridlocked and repetitive debates on whether or not neural processes or brain states themselves suffice to explain either intentionality (see e.g. Searle 1980) and/or consciousness (see e.g. Daniel 2001) in full suffer from an ontological individualism that insists on locating analogues to all relevant intentional or conscious phenomena *inside* the human body, either in the brain or mind alone or—the anti-functionalist or phenomenological position—on some higher level tied to the subject. Hand-in-hand with this problem goes the issue that physical states of the brain are being equated to everyday understandings of mental conditions, often by referring to Searle's (1983, 2000) conception of intentionality (e.g. Jacob/Jeannerod 2003) which suggests to differentiate prior intention—mentally aspiring a precise end—and intention-in-action that is manifest in bodily movement. But as Schatzki (2010b: 155 fn12) points out (echoing the critique by H. L. Dreyfus 1993, 2000: 323–337), Searle violates "phenomenological saliency" because he provides an "ad hominum characterization" in developing a naturalistic, causal link between (allegedly intentional) brain states and (observably intentional) bodily doings. Yet as Wittgenstein argued, this is deeply problematic, since the later necessarily and exclusively describe conditions of lived life expressed in outward behaviour and thus cannot be mapped onto invisible mental states in any coherent way. The same is true, I might add, for more contemporary suggestions to discern even more layers or levels of intentionality on the basis of neuroscientific findings (e.g. by Schlicht 2008). This latter consideration also leads me to my final point regarding intentionality: If one distinguishes different forms, realms, carriers, or kinds of intentionality; and especially if one ties them to neural processes, how can one conceive of their internal relation? Can they co-occur? Can they point into different directions, thus distracting or nullifying each other? Is there an aggregated intentionality e.g. of the overall situation? What happens, for example, when the body 'intends' one thing, and 'the mind' another? In my view, the best conclusion to draw from such a complicated situation is to mimic the likes of Schatzki and Garfinkel and not use the term intentionality to pinpoint a specific element within the theoretical framework. The fact that we often (but, as Wittgenstein and Heidegger argued, not always; see Glock 2010b) think about something specific, and the fact that bodily movement gears into a certain direction and (arguably) needs to be oriented do not, in my view, imply much about their similarity or relatedness in one way or another. This does not mean, however, that intentionality can go entirely unmentioned: First, it is of course necessary to discuss it as a key part of many of the theories I referred to, and second, it is also a frequently used and well-understood folk term of everyday life and as such alive in most practitioners' worlds (see Malle 2004; Malle/Knobe 1997). It is in those two senses only that I use the term intentionality.

14 Attunement and Expression of Style

Up to this point, my discussion of style with the help of the terms understanding, intelligibility, and media has not sufficiently discussed the notion of attunement. Having defined style as a specific kind of understanding, I have relied on Schatzki in formulating that a practitioner of a phenopractice becomes attuned to understandings and thus to style—for example when freeskiers spectate Style in the arena of the funpark. Further, I said that a stylish performance expresses Style, and so does—I can now add—a stylish image or video (see Reckwitz 2000b for a critique of Schatzki's term "expression"). But what exactly does it mean to say that a video clip 'expresses style'? Very well, you might say, so attunement is inherently local and tied to the current mood, position, and stance of its practitioner, and it depends on his observation skills to realize the intelligibility provided by the 'carrier' of style, the video or performance (Brümmer/Alkemeyer 2017). But it is still quite a step from intelligibility—a potentiality—to the taking place of understanding—an event. How can one conceive of this step theoretically? Or, put differently: What kind of a relationship is being described when one says: this video expresses Style? My suggestion will be that the best way to conceptualize this relation can be adapted from the ethnomethodological concept of instructed action, and more particularly, from what Garfinkel (2002: 187–190, 274–276) calls a Lebenswelt pair. I will, in other words, embrace Garfinkel's concept to clarify Schatzki's use of the Heideggerian term 'attunement'; and it should be clear that I do not claim that in doing so I merely apply any of the three notions without making any adaption of my own. Nevertheless, I believe that all three fit together quite neatly, at least within the phenopractical framework of thinking I have tried to sketch out thus far. I will proceed in two steps towards an answer to the questions I formulated: I will first explain what it means to conceptualize the video clip as the first segment of a Lebenswelt pair, and seeing Style as the second segment in Garfinkel's terms. As a second step, I will then show that the Lebenswelt pair provides one with an enhanced notion of what it means to say that the video clip expresses Style.

The video clip I will use in order to answer the question how a video, rather than a live performance, can express style will be taken from freeriding rather than freestyle, since the inherent order of 'logic' of freestyle movements is much more complex to understand and explain. When, for example, I say that a freerider needs to ride towards a certain cliff and this has to happen smoothly, the reader can (hopefully) grasp a lot better what this means as if I say that the freestyler needs to let go of the Mute grab and stretch his torso into a more upright position in order to stop the diagonal rotation of his skis in order to stomp a clean landing; and that this has to happen smoothly. Therefore, I will look at a video clip expressing Style by virtue of documenting a key quality of every freeriding run: the fluidity or flow of riding. Having flow, or riding with ease and style, is a quality highly valued by freeriders and often described by them as the ultimate end towards which they strive: riding extreme lines with flow. As I have shown in the last chapter, this aesthetic imperative is not just an arbitrary choice, but achieving flow is instead intimately coupled with the experiential and visual core of riding. As I have noted, riders automatically slow down or even stop when they cannot see a landmark they are looking for, or when they see a potentially difficult or dangerous spot. In turn, *not* to exhibit such hesitating has become an important measure of the quality of a ride (and the athlete performing it) as it expresses confidence and control. Likewise, the flow or fluidity of one's riding is the second of five key criteria judges assess during freeride competitions (freeride World Tour 2011; [D]). Therefore, my discussion of this video can also be taken as sketching out a more specific theoretical account of the freeride judges' work of 'entifying' an episode of conduct into something that can be judged by figuring out which factual, definitive qualities are being visible in the concurrent stream of details of conduct—in this case, the stylish quality of flow.

> "2. Fluidity:
>
> Is the rider going fast compared to where he is in the face? Is the rider following his line without hesitations? Does he slow down too much or takes unnecessary stops before jumps? Is he lost and searching for his way?" (Freeride World Tour 2011: § 4.1; [D])

What exactly is judged when flow is observed? Since I can unfortunately not explain the matter while we are actually looking at someone riding down a line, let me use a related example from the freeski world instead: A video clip produced by Tom that shows him ski down a line in the Krimml face towards a cliff drop, something he does with style and flow, as the clip testaments—at least if a freeskier watches them (as my informants assert).

The pictures in Fig. 9.7 are stills from a video filmed with the help of a camera attached to Tom's helmet, which were not produced especially for my research, but stem from the routine practice of freeriders filming their pursuits—in fact, these stills stem from a short video clip that was edited and uploaded on YouTube a few weeks after the ride. What do these pictures demonstrate? First, although they do provide some clue to what it could be like riding down a powder face and doing a cliff huck, it is also quite obvious that they are what Harold Garfinkel (2002) called "inadequate analogues" to 'the real thing' of skiing that run. In terms of phenomenal experiences, the viewer of these pictures requires a great deal of imagination when trying to reconstruct the thrill of the speed, the exposure to danger, the chill of the cold wind in the face, the sudden rush of dropping down the cliff, and much more. The second key aspect the spectator is missing from the pictures is the bodily reality of skiing; the turning and steering and tensing and pushing—and as I have argued in concurrence with Merleau-Ponty, this dimension of the practice is by no means just a separate realm, but is closely intertwined with the situated seeing that takes place. What we see in the picture is a dual process of physically approaching the cliff the skier aims at *and* a successive revelation or unfolding of the details of that cliff. The smoothness of the ride that makes this particular clip a piece worthy of being shown to the world is an achievement by the rider which is (in a freerider's view) less susceptible to difficulties connected to motor abilities, but to visual abilities. Skiing down that slope towards the cliff

Fig. 9.7 Still images from a video clip made by Tom with his helmet camera to document his ride in the Krimml, including a cliff-drop. The cliff is visible in the centre of the first image and remains the key landmark towards which both his riding and looking are oriented

per se is quite easy (unlike the subsequent cliff drop). However, the challenge for the rider is that he needs to get into a good spot close enough to the cliff so that he can see how precisely the drop-off looks in terms of the snow, ice, and rocks to be found there (e.g. so that he will not get stuck just before taking of and thus tumble down the cliff headfirst)—but he needs to do so while he keeps on riding towards that cliff, since he is not supposed to stop and needs to keep sufficient speed in order to perform a clean drop (going over the edge to slowly will cause him to hit the bottom of the rock). The rider needs, in other words, to assess the cliff and its current state sufficiently and correctly without losing the Flow of the ride—and on the video, this must be visible in order for the video to document Style. But what precisely is the Flow of a ride? In my answer, I will distinguish between freeskiing's aesthetic category—Flow writ large—and flow as a modus of conduct I discussed in the last chapter.

From the point of view of a detached observer, it seems quite clear what Flow is. The Flow of a ride describes its quality of being an uninterrupted process of smoothly overlapping parts of the ride: a sequence of turns, a drop, a landing, more turns; all smoothly interconnected. But if the Flow is something observed 'from the outside,' how is this observation related to the concrete episode of riding with flow documented in the video? In the following part, I will propose an ethnomethodological reading of this duality of the observed and the performed flow. To begin with, it should be clear that the arguments made during my discussion of seeing a ski's flex in chapter four also bear on the similar case of the Flow of a ride. Seeing the aesthetic Flow of freeriding, much like seeing a line in a face, is above all something that freeskiers do: When watching a freeride video clip, they can see that the ride has Flow, and somebody unacquainted with freeriding cannot. He can, however, be *instructed* to see the Flow for himself, and after a short phase of instruction and inspection, he will quite reliably confirm that this ride has Flow while another might not. In Garfinkel's terms, the phenomenon of Flow has praxeological validity because it is instructably observable, and accountably so. What Garfinkel insists on, however, is that the existence of a phenomenon would not be without these courses of instruction, so the existence of the phenomenon of Flow (the aesthetic category) is inextricably tied to the situated phenopractice of seeing flow (the modus of conduct). A phenomenon that is not reliably reproducible as instructably witnessable, on the other hand, cannot exist as an ordinary occurrence or stable fact (Bjelic 1996; Bjelić/Lynch 1992; Garfinkel/Lynch/E. Livingston 1981). It is important to note the condition applied in this definition: Repeated observability is *not* seen as sufficient for establishing socially normal and known things, but instead the ability to *instruct* its repeated observability reliably. Thus far, the Flow of the ride does not seem to differ from the flex of a ski, a social thing carried across repeated and repeatable situations of seeing it, inter alia made possible by certain enduring qualities of the observed entity. But unlike in the case of the ski, what exactly is the enduring entity in this case? For one, there is of course the video 'conserving' one possible vista of the riding in particular way prefigured by the specificities of the camera, its position and angle, and so forth. As in the case of the flex, I thus hold that while seeing the Flow requires the engagement of a capable see-er, there must also be something about the visible riding that affords seeing Flow. On the other hand, I argued in the last chapter that the flow of conduct describes a certain way of proceeding from one action to the next, that is, a quality of conduct per se. In effect, we are left with not one, but two different entities: the flow of riding, and the sight of Flow of the ride (both to be produced in situ).

If I am to answer the question of how these two are related, I first need to address a crucial matter: The expression 'the Flow of the ride' treats the ride itself as an entity, a clearly demarcated thing. This being-an-entity of the ride, however, is not a state that is simply given in praxis (e.g. by virtue of the rider having ridden), but one that needed to be practically accomplished. In this specific case, one could easily overlook this fact since the video produces the delineation of 'the' ride almost automatically, but the theoretical distinction is important. At a freeride contest, in contrast, the delineation of 'the line' as an object to be judged must be systematically produced by a combination of material arrangements—namely a start and a finish line—and a set of written rules instructing the judges to determine what counts as part of a run and what not (Freeride World Tour 2011; [D]). Only at first glance, the task is trivial: First, there is of course no fixed route to follow, so the run must be anything the skier does in between the start and finish line. Second, stopping and searching for a path to continue is a legitimate part of freeriding (although the Flow will be lost, of course), so 'the run' does not consist exclusively of moments of riding. Third, although speed is encouraged,[26] there is purposefully no time limit set, which would be another mechanism to produce the end of a run (Freeride World Tour 2011: § 4.3; [D]). Fourth, while crashes 'normally' imply that a run is over, there are also "intentional crashes," crashes that do not "compromise the fluidity of this run," purposeful jumps ending with a "landing crash," as well as purposeful jumps that only look like a crash (Freeride World Tour 2011: § 4.1; [D]). The only plain and simple option seems to be that a run is over if a rider looses a ski (Freeride World Tour 2011: § 4.1; [D]). In any actual case and with regard to all these written and unwritten rules and expectably normal things to do, the facticity of the beginning and end of a ride must of course be situatedly and interactively produced by the judges, for example by talking or writing down scores. The purpose of this example was simply to demonstrate that depending on the situation, quite different processes and criteria can come into play that help to 'bundle' the observable details conduct that occurred during a certain stretch of time together and pack it into a delineated something that has happened.

I emphasize this point because in the last chapter, I followed Schatzki in describing the performance of an action as an event, that is, as a demarcated episode with a clear beginning and end. From this, one might erroneously conclude that I am suggesting that all practical conduct or human lived life presents itself to an outside observer as transparently segmented into distinct episodes. This is surely not the case, since I characterize praxis or lived life as continuous unfolding with the stream of the world. Further, I argue that it is within phenomenal fields that figurations can stand out to appear as distinctive entities for certain durations, which implies that their enduring in the foreground is something other than their real-world enduring or change. The upshot of this is that the episodes of conduct the practitioner undertakes are demarcated episodes for said practitioners (such as taking one turn after the other), but not for a different observer engaged in a different (pheno-)practice (e.g. that of watching the skier ski). In a sense I therefore preserve Schutz' notion that delineated acts are 'lifted out of' the perpetual flux of cosmic time by virtue of reflection—or rather: observation—, although I see no reason why this must happen exclusively ex-post and should not apply to the actor living in his acting-in-progress. In a nutshell: It is by virtue of conducting a practice that the details of unfolding praxis form (at least briefly) lasting constellations in a phenomenal field, and thus taking one turn after another

---

[26] And as one would expect based on my discussion of rules and rule-following in Chap. 5, the explicit rule describing this 'encouragement' employs a whole range of ad-hoc and common-sense criteria to describe the delicate fact that, although there is officially no time limit, the rider should behave as if there were one. The rule says: "Judges will simply lower their scores if they feel that a rider spent way too much time on the face." (Freeride World Tour 2011: § 4.3; [D]).

is as much a practical accomplishment as seeing 'a ride' as an entity, or as what Garfinkel (1988; Garfinkel/E. Livingston 2003) calls an 'organizational thing.' And only in the course of such 'entification' of the ride, practical understandings can be brought to bear on it—such as the view that to be stylish, a freeride run must exhibit Flow.

15 Seeing Style in Media: Lebenswelt Pairs

Having clarified this point, I can now proceed to the question how the two entities—the flow of riding-on-film and the sight of Flow of the ride—relate. My suggestion is to describe the flow of the ride and the Flow seen on film by employing the ethnomethodological concept of *Lebenswelt pairs* (Garfinkel 2002: 187–190, 274–276; E. Livingston 1986). This suggestion might be surprising for those familiar with the concept, since it originally describes the relation between written instructions (such as a mathematical proof) and their implementation (such as 'doing' or 'checking' the proof). This, however, is my key point: I argue that the video of the ride should be described as *instructing* the competent viewer to see the Flow, thus providing for the repeated observability of the flow of riding. And this 'getting' the understanding that this ride has Flow is precisely what I would call becoming attuned to this understanding of style. In my view, the concept Lebenswelt pair describes a specific case of the relation between rule and rule-following as understood by Wittgenstein (see Bloor 2001; Lynch 1992a; D. Stern 2002): Neither can the rule precisely prescribe what it means to follow it, nor does rule-following express the rule by virtue of being inherently regular; but instead both work in conjunction to organize conduct in different situations in such a way that rule-conformity exists as a social thing. It is in the same sense, I believe, that Garfinkel describes the Lebenswelt pair as a set of two segments:

> "(a) the-first-segment-of-a-pair that consists of a collection of instructions; and (b) the work, in just any actual case, of following which somehow turns the first segment into a description of the pair." (Garfinkel 2002: 105 f.; original emphasis)

Garfinkel emphasizes the last three words for a good reason: His argument is not simply that the collection of instructions and the situated work of following are two incommensurable alternates constituting one another, for example in that the following is an instance of following by virtue of turning the instruction into an accurate description (or prescription) of following them. Rather, his point is that the specific conjunction of 'instruction' and 'following' constitutes the phenomenon of order in question, a phenomenon that must situatedly achieved (Bjelic 1996; E. Livingston 2006a; Roth 2010). I should thus note that the relation which I describe as being part of a Lebenswelt pair is something other than the general relation that exists between different situated doing of a nexus of a practice. Just like the flex of a ski, the Flow of a ride is established and carried as a social thing across a number of situated accomplishments of observing, showing, proving, or describing it (etc.). Lebenswelt-pairing, in contrast, describes the situated accomplishment of a relation between a meaningful order-in-conduct 'embossed' in an element and that very situated accomplishment, which helps towards the establishment of a nexus of doings able to carry or reproduce the order without itself being equal to it. The video as one segment of a pair, in other words, is a resource helping to make the flow "instructably observable and instructably reproducible in and as the phenomenal field's (…) ordered details of structure" (Garfinkel 2002: 149). The reason why I deem it necessary to describe the relation between the flow of the riding and the Flow on video in such complicated terms is that both need to practically accomplished and that both are not themselves elements of the unfolding phenopractice: Flow is a phenomenon while flow is a modus of conduct, and both are ordered in a complex temporal relation. Let me attempt to shed some light on what I am trying to say.[27]

As a first step towards discerning how the flow of conduct and the Flow that can be seen on video relate, one might try to detail more precisely what the two phenomena in question consist in. To this end, I will follow Garfinkel's suggestion and ask what happens when the phenomenon is lost (Garfinkel 2002: Chap. 4).[28] What does it mean to lose the Flow of a ride? In a first step, one needs to assess which the phenomenal details are in which the flow of this particular ride is witnessable. The smoothly-approaching-the-cliff consists of a combination of myriad miniscule particularities of the movement, such as "starting the turn by steering into the turn by dipping the shovel of the ski into the snow by redistributing body weight to the right foot by shifting posture by turning the torso to the right by swinging the left arm forward and to the right in a forceful but smooth sweep." These particulars in turn are, as I have shown, intrinsically connected to the inspection of the cliff and the steering-by-focusing conducted in the course of seeing in flux. How can one know that these particularities are interwoven in such a way that one can say there is flow? Crucial for an answer is the temporality of this possibility: one can see this Flow only recursively. Only immediately after it was achieved one can say it was achieved, and only immediately after it was lost one can say: "Oh, now he lost it." Why? Because the ride as a smooth ride towards the cliff can only be *this* ride *after* one knows that it is a ride towards the cliff. The cliff, in other words, *orients* the ride in that it is retrospectively and with regard to that cliff that the ride has Flow. The quality of the interconnection of the particulars of the ride that is the Flow of the ride only becomes apparent once one has realized that the ride will lead towards the cliff. If instead the rider was attempting

---

[27] To paraphrase Garfinkel: Should I succeed in telling you what I am trying to tell you, then, at some point into my explanation, you will realize what it is that I have been telling you already long before you knew I was trying to tell it to you. Which, of course, turns this text and your realization into a Lebenswelt pair.

[28] I am aware that my description of losing the flow at this point does not quite fulfil Garfinkel's notion of losing the phenomenon (or rather, only in an even more complicated sense), but I will return to the notion below.

15 Seeing Style in Media: Lebenswelt Pairs 427

to reach the ridge to the left or show a high-speed, straight line, he has failed miserably. The *second* part of the Lebenswelt pair in Garfinkel's sense thus consists in the retrospective activity of seeing the Flow of the ride in the course of the unfolding of its particulars on screen. What is the *first* half of the pair? In an ethnomethodological understanding, this first half is precisely the part which the observer of the pictures shown above cannot see: It is what the rider visibly does—or rather, it is the phenomenal details of the rider's doings that are preserved on the video.[29]

Tom is moving down the slope in such a way that he is prospectively approaching the cliff. He is, in other words, in a very physical sense creating the cliff as the first goal of his ride, lifting it out of the manifold of rocks and lips and bowls over the course of his unfolding journey down. And he is doing this in such a way that retroactively he will have done the approaching in a manner causing it to visibly having Flow. It should be reemphasized what has been said about riding earlier: Riding is a multisensual, multimodal achievement crucially depended on seeing certain things, which in turn can only be accomplished in the course of riding in a manner that enables and bodily achieves seeing. The complexity of this task is enormous: a) spotting and focusing the cliff to steer towards it while b) visually establishing crucial points for each turn to both orient and direct the riding plus c) also inspecting the snow conditions between the current position and the next turn and d) inspecting the cliff while coming closer in order to see better and more—*but* e) not coming closer too fast too quickly since seeing takes time, all while f) making sure that sufficient speed is kept to 'clear' the cliff safely once the moment has come to speed over its edge. All of these are necessary prerequisites to riding this line, but even if taken together, they are not yet the actual thing that is achieving Flow: Achieving Flow is doing all this in such a way so that the visible riding underlying all these activities happens in a consistent, calm, uninterrupted manner. In short, achieving Flow means making freeriding look *easy*, natural. It

---

[29] Note that a very specific form of naturalism underlies this sentiment (see ten Have 2007; Lynch 2002 for the specific ethnomethodological naturalism): there is no question that watching the video is something else than watching the live performance. However, both the practice of watching live and watching from video happens on the basis of phenomenal field details; and some elements of this field—namely the outwardly visual details—are at least structurally homologous. Take, for example, the freeride judges who might use binoculars, but also cameras to watch a run: There surely is a difference between watching the rider with bare eyes from afar, and watching through binoculars, or watching on a screen and with the help of a camera. In each case, the level and kind of visible detail will be different (and the bare eyes will not necessarily provide the 'best grip'). This does not automatically imply, however, that the identifying detail of the Flow will be lost or stand out especially well in any one of those ways of seeing—but this can happen, of course. Evidently, the difference between a judge watching a run 'live' on screen and someone watching the DVD later is fairly small. The point I seek to make is this: In my view, the visual phenomenon in question will always be the visible flow of the ride; and thus there is not a sharp difference between the 'real' ride in all its detail and the 'virtual' representation of the ride on video. The practice of riding will always be different from the practice of watching riding, whatever the medium.

means making the struggle invisible. This cannot be emphasized enough: Riding with Flow means showing that you *have* flow, not that you *do* Flow. It means that you somehow manage to ride this aggressive line down a spectacular face with effortless flow. Having Flow means visibly not just attempting to gain flow, just like being self-conscious means visibly knowingly demonstrating the non-contingency of the inherently contingent unfolding of this very demonstration of self-consciousness. In other words: All the particulars that the rider achieves in order to create flow need to disappear and be conflated into this very phenomenon of Flow, so that they are no longer visible behind its shiny surface of us seeing one smooth thing happening. If this happens, Garfinkel suggests, the Flow of this ride as a social thing is accomplished by seeing it in the video, and thus the second half of the Lebenswelt pair is established. What is more, expressed in Garfinkel's terms, this also means that the original phenomenon is 'lost' in a very specific way (2002: Ch. 4; see A. Rawls 2002: 33–37): The bodily work of skiing-cum-seeing in flux is no longer apparent in the video of the ride precisely because the video is *visibly* meant to show Flow as a social thing—a thing that consists in 'loosing' the contingency of the bodily situated achievement of flow. In watching the video, Flow comes into being by as being instructably observable in the video, and thus by rendering the details of its bodily achievement invisible via seeing the flow of the ride as a given quality. Garfinkel (2002: 97–99, 150–153) provides a very powerful example to illustrate what it means to lose a phenomenon in his sense: the question in his case is not whether someone has flow, but whether he has rhythm. As a demonstration, a person is thus asked to clap to the 'tick-tack' provided by a metronome. In phenopractice terminology, the clapping should thus be hearably oriented by the metronome to provision for the evident fact that this guy has rhythm. The key point is this: If the person will clap perfectly in tune with the metronome, one will no longer hear the metronome as a distinct sound apart from the clapping. Indeed, if the metronome is not too loud, it's 'tick-tack' will be lost entirely. Further, the person doing the clapping cannot wait for the metronome to signal to him that it is time to clap—he must be doing something else in order coordinate his own bodily doings in such a way that at the very moment in which the clapping takes places, the *absence* of the metronome's sound confirms the rhythm the clapping person 'has.'[30] This example, I hope, helps to explain why I distinguish between orientation and prefiguration: There is no point in saying that the metronome hinders or blocks the clapping person from clapping randomly, or from clapping in a different rhythm than that which the metronome 'recommends.'

---

[30] Garfinkel retells this example for a slightly different purpose: In his account, the clapping is additionally recorded on video; and his point is that while the clapping person will not hear the metronome over his own clapping, the (not ethnomethodologically informed) social scientist later analysing the video will hear it and thus conclude that the metronome is the crucial phenomenon to study, since it is responsible for the evident order (the rhythm). I might add: A 'pragmatist' scientist studying nothing but the bodily clapping and ignoring the metronome will commit a different, but equally devastating mistake.

Further, there is no point in saying that either the person or the metronome are the 'real' source of the rhythmic clapping, since it is their situational organization which produces the taking place of rhythmic clapping.

Let me now, as the last step, return to the question of becoming attuned to the understanding of style. In my terms, one could say that the person clapping is 'tuning in' with the beat provided by the metronome, or rather: he is becoming attuned to the understanding of this rhythm. Imagine, for example, that the metronome is not ticking in a four-four time, but a 'more complex' rhythm (to Western ears), e.g. a Latin five-six time: At the beginning, one would need to cope with the challenge of 'getting' that rhythm, and over time there would be some kind of learning process (carried primarily by neural sequence memory, see Graybiel 1995). However, regardless of whether one is concentrating on the metronome, counting mentally to find the rhythm, or just 'going with the flow' to master the clapping: From a phenopractice perspective, what counts is that attunement takes place as soon as the rhythmic clapping is taking place—and specifically this implies that it must be taking place already in order for the 'sinking in' of the bodily routine to even begin. More importantly, while the sounds emitted by the metronome will adhere to a certain 'physical' pattern (and at close observation there will be many sounds, not just the 'tick-tack'), for this tool to function as a metronome, the rhythm it is capable of producing must be heard (or better yet clapped to) *as* a suitable rhythm. Whether or not the Latin five-six time metronome can orient sensible music, for example, depends on the listener's ability to 'share in' to this understanding. Likewise, I argue that it is the 'work' of seeing Style in the visible details of the ride provided by the video which turns the video into something exhibiting or (to use Schatzki's term) expressing Style. More precisely, as Garfinkel (2002: 106; original emphasis) reminds us, this situated work of seeing the Style turns the video into "a description *of the pair*": The video's intelligible Style and the seeing the Style-on-video together make up for the fact that 'this video is stylish.' In this same sense, to conclude, I understand the general situation I seek to describe by saying that a conduct or media content expresses (or has) style.

16 Beautiful Errors

Let me now, in a last step, apply these considerations to the specific aesthetics of freeskiing and the function of freeskiing images and videos. In line with my argument that freeskiing's Style fulfils a practical function beyond its symbolic value, the origin of the images' significance in freeskiing is to be sought in its ability to instruct the (capable) onlooker to see style. Towards making this argument, let me take another look at the notion of sketchiness, the impending loss of control and crashing that freeskiers spot in a non-stylish performance or image. As I have argued, for all its unpleasance and repulsiveness, sketchiness is also a virtue in that it teaches the spectators by negative example. Notably, it would be misleading to say that freeskiers always try to be in perfect control, and by virtue of this achieve Style. Searching for style necessarily means venturing beyond the threshold of security and complete control; it is an attempt of walking the thin line between crashing and merely repeating the perfected. Therefore, seeing sketchiness amounts to a kind of collective border-work towards the impossible. In a truly stylish trick or jump, the crash, the breakdown of flow is visibly 'nearing' or 'faintly presencing' in that it forms the very background against which the beauty of staying in command comes to the fore. In contrast, what freeskiing's masterful aestheticists despise in Oldschool Olympic freestyle acrobatics is its perfectionism, its technocratic insistence that beauty is to be found in conformity, and its blatant supposition that strict repetition is possible and virtuous. What freeskiers at least think they know so much better than the FIS' pretentious advocates-turned-judges—because they know it from their own experience of stomping tricks—is that every freestyler is just "dancing in chains" as Nietzsche (1996: 140) put it; and it is the rattling of these chains that makes music in their ears.

Philosopher of art Alan Singer (1998) has argued that the two classic philosophical stances towards aesthetic judgment, intuitive romanticism (the notion that authentic art touches our inner sense for the sublime) and idealist rationalism (the belief that the quality of a true artwork derives from its proximity to perfect form), are flawed in so far as they remain perfectionist at the core, trying to qualify art in terms of its ability to meet a gold standard, be it authenticity or perfection of form. I hold that in practice thought, these two contrasting stances on aesthetics are exemplified in the Heideggerian and the praxeological approach to art, because both notions bear on either of the two classical positions—and carry a decidedly moral undertone: In Heidegger, we find the former in his assurance that a true piece of art can capture the overall style or true nature of a whole epoch and culture (H. L. Dreyfus 2007; Protevi 1998)[31] but also in his lambasting of technology as severing humans from authentic experience (cf. Adorno 1973). In Bourdieu, the latter returns in the postulate that the value of art is indeterminate and taste is irremediably irrational, so that nothing but our embodied belief in a game's illusio, in its worthiness despite its effective arbitrariness is responsible for our investing capital into it (Bourdieu 1996). The freeskiers themselves share both stances to some extend: Their rejection of overtly 'technical' tricks and their praise of true style, as well as the authentic experience that is to be had in the backcountry untouched by civilization and technology makes them proper Heideggerians. The in-your-face self-mockery that often accompanies their lavish spending of time, resources, and their bodily integrity, as well as the demonstrative carelessness that goes with it, on the other hand, reveals them to be lay praxeologists well aware that they celebrate the arbitrary, the stupid, and the senseless for the heck of it, bathing in the glory of irrationality (and machismo) precisely because it might as well be seen as morally dubious.

---

[31] Compare Ingold's (2000: 201–203) discussion of Bruegel's painting "The harvesters".

Excursus I: A Tyranny of Style? Wittgenstein on Images

The nature and role of images was not only a topic Wittgenstein discussed at some length, but images and human vision in turn provided many of the metaphors and arguments for his late philosophy in general (Heßler/D. Mersch/Richtmeyer 2009; D. Mersch 2006; Richtmeyer 2009; Stengel 2003). Therefore, a concise reading of Wittgenstein's view of images is essential for a phenopractice-minded discussion of images and visual practices. Unfortunately, I believe, much like in the case of language games or rule-following, the interpretations of Wittgenstein tend to go astray. Therefore, I will take a closer look at his philosophy of images; and I will be doing so by taking issue with a particular sociological interpretation of his arguments and their adaption to the very topic I am concerned with as well: the visual practices of lifestyle sports and their emphasis on style. In line with a relatively common sociological interpretation of lifestyle sport subcultures (see Chap. 6), Martin Stern (2009: 202–204) presents Wittgenstein as having argued that the "obligations of style" (Verpflichtung zum Stil) amount to an "absolute, palpable tyranny"—the latter words being a quote from Wittgenstein (available in English in Wittgenstein 2006: 258). This quote is pivotal for Stern, since he returns to the expression several times and uses it to establish a link between Wittgenstein's thought on images and language-games, and Foucault and Bourdieu (Stern 2009: 202–204, 225–226, 269–278). In order to pin down the precise point Stern makes about the influence of style and the effects of images, and in order to detail why and how I detail from some of his conclusions, it is worthy looking at the origin and context of this quote. In his book, Stern cites a specific passage from Wittgenstein twice and at full length. In my view, he is not quite consistent in the way he presents and interprets the passage: The first time, I argue, he takes the quote out of context in a potentially misleading way (2009: 202–204); and while his use of it is more concise the second time (2009: 224–225), he still misinterprets Wittgenstein in an important way. Let me briefly underscore my allegation. At least once, Stern seems to suggest that Wittgenstein himself argued that the "obligations of style" amount to an "absolute, palpable tyranny." But this allegation is rather surprising if one looks at the complete passage in Wittgenstein's work which Stern shortened when he quotes it, since it does not mention neither style nor images:

> "The effect of making men think in accordance with dogmas, perhaps in the form of certain graphic propositions [bildhafte Sätze], will be very peculiar: I am not thinking of these dogmas as determining men's opinions but rather as completely controlling the expression of all opinions. People will live under an absolute, palpable tyranny, though without being able to say they are not free. I think the Catholic Church does something rather like this." (Wittgenstein 2006: 258; original emphasis).

First, it needs to be noted that the quote stems from the "Vermischte Bemerkungen" (Wittgenstein 1984a), a loose collection of autobiographical fragments, aphorisms, and philosophical notes (also published as "Remarks on Culture and Value" in English [Wittgenstein 1984b]) which have not been included in one of the different editions of Wittgenstein's famous "Zettel," the notes written in preparation of his works and lectures. In other words, if the Zettel provide the historical and genealogical background to the mayor works Wittgenstein himself published; then the Bemerkungen provide something of a background to the background. For this reason, the editor in his introduction explicitly warns against reading these largely undated and unsystematic notes out of the context of Wittgenstein's general philosophical arguments (Wittgenstein 1984a: 448). Here is the problem: Stern claims that in the note he cites (no. CV 28–9), Wittgenstein is discussing style in accordance with his later philosophy of images (M. Stern 2009: 203, 202 fn5). But as the detailed discussion of this very note by Hoyt (2007; see also Solum 1987) makes clear, it was written in the context of Wittgenstein's discussion of Christian faith and is part of his critique of the nature of dogmatic thinking. As Hoyt (2007) shows, Wittgenstein was deeply critical of religious dogmas and dogmatic thinking. The reason why he links dogmas to 'graphic propositions' (an expression from Wittgenstein's systematic philosophy) in this quote is because he wants to show "how religious dogmas often function like pictures" (Hoyt 2007: 46)—and *not* how all pictures functions like dogmas, as Stern claims.[32] Wittgenstein saying that dogmas are "*perhaps in the form* of *certain* graphic propositions" (my emphasis), it seems to me, is a far cry from him suggesting that images can erect a "tyranny" of style. Now, if Wittgenstein did not make this point himself, one could of course still argue that what Wittgenstein thought true of Christian dogmas is true of images in lifestyle sports today. Indeed, this is just what Stern suggest when he introduces the passage a second time, stating as his thesis that "images (…) unfold their effect like dogmas" (2009: 225; my translation). If so, one would still need to show why it this proposition is justified, which in my view Stern fails to do. In any event, it is worthy to track down this argument; since if dogmas can be like certain pictures, it would be interesting to suggest that stylish pictures can be like dogmas which are like certain pictures. But what was Wittgenstein trying to say about images and dogmas in the first place?

Wittgenstein makes a very specific philosophical point about the nature of dogmas, namely, "that one struggling under the burden of a dogmatically held picture would suffer a deficit of self-expression rather than a mere restriction on opinions held." (Hoyt 2007: 46) A dogma, Hoyt (2007:

---

[32] "According to Wittgenstein, [images] have an effect like dogmas." (M. Stern 2009: 203; my translation).

46) explains, thus "reflects and reinforces a more fundamental orientation in life." He concludes: "Here and elsewhere, Wittgenstein's metaphor of a guiding picture is far more revealing than the metaphor of a network of interlocking statements." (Hoyt 2007: 49) To understand why this distinction between a guiding picture and delimiting statements (such as proscriptions like the Ten Commandments) is important for Wittgenstein, one needs to look at the broader context of his philosophy. Wittgenstein had argued persistently against the idea that explicit, exact rules can prescribe or determine a person's concrete conduct, since concrete moments of lived life can never exactly match the definitions laid down in any rule. If, therefore, dogmas were simply a list of explicit, definite statements or rules, they would not be as dangerous as Wittgenstein argues they are, because they could not actually predefine the believers' everyday life. Thus, he needs to show that dogmas do *not* function like "a wall setting limits" (as the note continues; Wittgenstein 2006: 258), as a list of prohibitions fencing off certain areas of life or courses of action but invoke their "absolute, palpable tyranny" in a different way. Instead, he suggests, dogmas do so by imposing "a fundamental orientation in life." (Hoyt 2007: 46) Dogmatic faith, Wittgenstein wants to say, does not mean dogmatically adhering to certain laws that prohibit this or that; but adhering to a certain single orientation in expressing oneself. And for this reason alone, he makes the link to "graphic propositions": Images *orient ways of expression* rather than "determining men's opinions." Only in dogmatic belief, however, a single image dominates a whole life and leaves no room for alternative orientations.[33] To conclude: Does it make sense to say that lifestyle sport enthusiasts are dogmatic in terms of style; accepting only one orientation as legitimate in all forms of expression? In light of my own findings, I believe this assertion is unjustified. True, freeskiers treat tricks as a form of expression and judge it according to its orientation to style—and in exactly this sense I embrace Wittgenstein's philosophy of images. But in order to be able to say that this orientation is dogmatic and thus tyrannical, it would need a) to be applied to all moments of expression the skier's life; and b) to allow only one single orienting imaginary endpoint as acceptable. Neither is true: First, Schatzki argues (1996), Wittgenstein's notion of "expression" refers to situational, momentary conditions ("how things are standing"); and I could find no indication that freeskiers are expected to express style in all moments of life. Quite to the contrary, they emphasize how freeskiing is not like their quotidian off-snow existence. Second, as Stern himself argues, style is an expression of

---

[33] Hoyt (2007: 47) cites the example of how Wittgenstein later came to regret that his Tractatus was founded on a single idea—that there is an underlying calculus behind language—which led him to absurd conclusions at times. This idea, then, was a dogmatic orientation.

creativity and personality—and therefore, athletes are expected to demonstrate variability and difference in their orientations.[34] In essence, while I believe that having style can be aptly conceptualized as expressing orientation to a figural ideal in the way an image can, I doubt that lifestyle sports can be adequately described as dogmatic or a case of "absolute, palpable tyranny." More importantly, I also believe that Stern misrepresents the very point Wittgenstein is trying to make when he argues that images contain orientations, but are not "a wall setting limits." In other words, even if lifestyle sport subcultures' fixation on style would be dogmatic, this implies different conclusions than those Stern draws. Let me clarify this point.

I stress that the specific idea of orientation of expressions is central to Wittgenstein's philosophy of images and rule-following; and that it is essential to keep in mind that according to him, neither images nor rules-in-use can be adequately conceptualized as laying down definite ways of thinking or acting. Unfortunately, this is just what Stern does when he concludes: "According to Wittgenstein, images [visual representations] can be understood as a modus of regulating the social" in that images influence a person's style by "pre-structuring" the person's "horizon of possibilities" for action (M. Stern 2009: 203 f.; my translation). This view mirrors the standpoint of most theorists of practices—and especially of Bourdieu—that social practices shape social life by determining the possible actions an actor could pursue at any concrete moment. Schatzki (1997, 2002: 160), in contrast, systematically shows that Wittgenstein's later philosophy actually argues that such views are misguided and that it is misleading to construe the site which practice-in-conduct opens up as a plenum of possibilities. Indeed, Wittgenstein made just that very point in the note on the dogma: Our life is not structured by "a wall setting limits," but by orientations-in-conduct. If practices would provide a mere field of possibilities, one would effectively still be left with a classic account of action, only that these actions would now happen under constrains (which is something all theories of rational and/or subjective action assume anyways). Such a version of practice theory, I hold, pushes the door wide open for all kinds of wilful, output-maximizing, strategic decision-making accounts of actors-in-praxis. And within such an account of the 'actual' freedom of will and action, in turn, it makes most sense to suggest that images propagating style enwall us, delimiting our options for free expression and indeed encage the poor lifestyle-sport

---

[34] See for example this description by a professional freeskier in an anthology of lifestyle sports: "Free-skiing (…) is any individual's expression of glissading. As there are many individuals, there are many expressions ranging from extremely fast skiing, jumping, flying, or whatever you can imagine. Free riders are creative and every day we learn another possibility or new expression." (Kremer 2003: 374).

> enthusiast in a "total institution." (M. Stern 2009: 274) If one chooses to embrace a different account of action, however, one adhering to the idea of oriented coping for example, then the perspective on style changes, and one is poised to ask about its functional role, to see it as an enabling tool rather than a method of control.

A stringent analysis of the function of style, I believe, must try to steer clear of embracing either romanticism or rationalism in any form, precisely because detailing them is part of the descriptive rather than the analytic aspect of ethnographic work. It is in this vein that I deem Singer's (1998) argument against perfectionist notions of aesthetics and his urging us to acknowledge what he calls *the beauty of error* important. Drawing on Nietzsche's philosophy of art and his rejection of perfectionism on the grounds that "when something is perfect we tend to neglect to ask about its evolution" (Nietzsche 1996: 145), Singer postulates that it is only because of its imperfection that a piece of art can convey a 'message.' The meaning (or 'rationality') of the artwork, he suggests, is not expressed by its actual form itself; for example in that a portrait is beautiful because it depicts a beautiful human as realistically as possible (my example). Rather, "from Nietzsche's perspective, the intelligibility of artistic form obtains only in relation to what constrains it" (Singer 1997: 10)—the beauty of the painting lies in the way the human is depicted 'wrongly,' because it brings to the fore and makes us 'stumble upon' an aspect of beauty we had hitherto not really seen when looking at a beautiful face. What is crucial about this notion is that it entails the understanding of beauty as a sequential unfolding, which Singer expresses in his notion of errors as bound to contexts. He writes:

> "My use of the term error references itself most acutely to the relation between a rule and a contingent practice: the situation of its implementation. This relation, a threshold of error, is precisely what guarantees the vitality of aesthetic experience." *And further:*

> "Errors can come to light only within an emergent context of judgment. The emergent context reveals prior conceptions to be inadequate to the intentionality instantiated through their deployment." (Singer 1997: 9 f.)

It might well be that I am doing violence to Singer's ideas (which centre more on subject formation), but based on the thinking I developed so far, I believe that the "context of judgment" providing the beauty-in-error, and thus the very intelligibility of an artworks meaning, is to an important extent provided by the artwork *itself*, or more precisely by the artwork-put-into-praxis. In discussing the visibility of a ski's flex, I cited ethnomethodological studies of peoples' practical and interactive assessment of artworks in museums (Heath/vom Lehn 2004; Heath/Luff/vom Lehn/Yamashita/et al. 2009; vom Lehn/Heath 2007) in order to argue that the ski itself must instruct the potential customer about the visibility of its inherent qualities. The above thoughts from the philosophy of art allow me to pick up this argument and detail it with regard to freeskiing's images: Inherent in these works, one can say with Singer, is a certain 'program,' some final form towards which the work seems to strive, some idea of sublimity and beauty—but the work itself does not quite manage to get there. It fails to deliver, so to speak; it bears seeds but not fruit. Its form gels, but never crystallizes. And the fact that it does not will not simply irritate us, but cause something to stand out, to demand attention by virtue of being what Heidegger (1962: 288) calls un-ready-to-hand—more precisely: It present us with some stubborn detail that needs to be lost (in Gafinkel's sense) in order to be able to see the beauty that is there to see. This detail, to be sure, will only be of relevance for an observer capable of seeing any of the image's specific beauty in the first place. But in the course of such an observer's seeing of the picture, amidst his doing what Garfinkel (2002: 247) felicitously calls "making the reading good over the ground," said note-worthy deviation will occur in that the artwork, so to speak, initially seems to point in to one direction, but then does not end up just exactly there. In my view, what is happening here is that the image is orienting the spectator's seeing in the same way the metronome was orienting the person clapping: by providing something that is a dissonance at first and then needs to be equalled out—and once that has happened, the observer can be sure that he has become attuned to the orienting work. For this reason, freeskiers, just like aficionados of any kind, become interested in ever more subtle details with grooving expertise. Tom, for example, told me that he has become less and less interested in freeride videos and has started to enjoy photographs more. On a DVD, he explained, many of the details of the riding are not clearly visible, both because things happen so fast, and because the resolution of a film (shot from a certain distance) is never as high as that of a really well-made photograph. Even more interestingly, he continued that only in a picture, he can precisely spot the little details of a rider's bodily postures, e.g. the way he holds his pole during a specific phase of the turn. Since I have focused my discussion almost entirely on the topic of seeing style in movement, and since I argued that the style of a conduct emanates from the visible details of a movement pattern, one might expect that only videos and films truly matter for spreading style. After all, where is the movement in a static photograph? But as vision scientists assure us, seeing *implied* body motions from static images is quite possible (Jacob/Jeannerod 2003: 240): We can, for example, see from a photograph that someone has just tripped and is about to fall over in a split-second—and we will quite intuitively look closer to make out what it was that she just tripped over. More importantly, studies have shown that in order to asses implied or impending motions in a photograph, the same neural routines are activated that are also important for bodily moving itself—just like in the case of video, seeing bodily movement and moving overlap as far as the brain is concerned (Kourtzi/Kanwisher 2000; Pavan/Cuturi/Maniglia/Casco/et al. 2011).

As a systematic survey of freeskiing pictorials will reveal, the images that are especially interesting to riders in this sense are those which do not simply depict a very large number of details, but rather exhibit a certain texture or structure from which noteworthy details stand out, and into which they must be made to fit by the spectator's skilful scrutiny. The 'functioning' of visual media I suggest, in other words, bears close resemblance to what Niklas Luhmann called the self-programming of the artwork. When we observe a powerful artwork, he argues, "the work takes control" and enables us to discover "something that no one, not even the artist, has seen before." (Luhmann 2000a: 70) Notably, despite a certain resemblance, this view differs fundamentally from the notion put forward by hermeneutics, i.e. that in the structure of the image itself one can find an order or 'iconic paths' which mirror either the subjective interpretation process or the subjective knowledge of the individuals who will look at, or have composed, the image (Raab 2007, 2008; Schnettler/Pötzsch 2007; Schnettler/Raab 2008). From a (pheno-)practice perspective, neither the image, nor the individual subject or knowledge-bearer is considered to hold any stored meaning, since meaning is understood to be something that transpires only if both—see-er and seen—are thrown into the self-same situation. Thus, there can be no "overlapping" of subjective and objective meaning (cf. Raab 2008: 319), and neither can one "consider social data as manifestations of the protagonists' perception" as proponents of a hermeneutic position suggest (Schnettler/Raab 2008: para. 45). Likewise, Luhmann's basic theoretical postulate, that individual consciousness and communicative system (e.g. the system of arts) are 'worlds apart' or distinctive systems each holding unique views of one another, does of course not conform to the phenopractice position I outlined in this work. Nevertheless, his notion of the self-programming artwork seems interesting in two ways: first, because the relation between Luhmannian systems theory and the practice turn has been subject to fierce debate; and second, because the statement that artworks contain programs seems a surprising one to make for Luhmann, since in his theory, programs are usually understood as qualities of communication systems rather than objects. On the other hand, my discussion of the Lebenswelt pair should have made clear that I take it that the seeing of style happens *to* the observer (who needs to engage in a kind of 'deep spectating' of the image as a prerequisite). But nevertheless, they happen on behalf of the image or artwork, so to speak: It is within the seeing style in freeskiing image that breathtaking beauty discloses itself. And because visual media have this power to evoke attunement, I argue in the following and final chapter, the role of visual media in freeskiing goes further and deeper than providing mere symbolic associations: they are pivotal for the stabilization, dissemination, and evolution of skiing practices.

Excursus II: Luhmann and the Self-programming of the Artwork

Particularly within the German debate, the relation between practice theory and Luhmannian system's theory remains a contested terrain. With regard to ethnomethodology, for example, some authors have argued that ethnomethodology was a kind of half-baked predecessor of systems theory (a view which Luhmann himself expressed, see 1984: 612 fn33); an idea that ethnomethodologists have sharply rejected (Hirschauer/Bergmann 2002; Nassehi/Saake 2002a, 2002b). On the other hand, many important parallels between both positions can hardly be overlooked (cf. Woermann 2011); for example in that both positions conceptualize meaning as transpiring only within certain bounded spheres (sites or systems, respectively) and frame subjects as effects rather than causal sources of social meaning. In this vein, some authors have argued that Luhmannian systems theory could in fact be well understood as a practice theory (Nassehi 2009; W. L. Schneider 2004); and others have suggested that ethnomethodological research methods could be used as a basis for system-theoretical research (Hausendorf 1992; Messmer 2004; W. L. Schneider 2000, 2008). That said, I have also argued (in Chaps. 3 and 8) that very fundamental differences between both approaches remain. An interesting perspective on this debate, I suggest, can be derived from a close study of Luhmann's "Art as a Social System" (2000a). At the core, my sentiment is that, if applied to the case of vision, Luhmann's perspective effectively only captures processes of epistemic vision while neglecting pragmatic vision—and this negligence becomes visible once he turns to the bodily work of perceiving and producing artworks, rather than the other topics of language-centred communication he discusses in his other works. My comments, I might add, are not meant to prove the superiority of practice thought. Rather, I believe they might a) help to further clarify my own position by pointing out similarities and differences; and b) suggest some starting points for further thought about a possible recombination or (independent) evolution of either theory.

In his work on art, Luhmann attends to some of the processual details of embodied perception that he usually glosses over by concentrating on a an abstract model of observing as the drawing of distinctions which he derived from theoretical mathematics (Spencer-Brown 1971). In short, the crucial question with regard to Luhmann is whether or not a system's environment—e.g. what I call the situation a practitioner is in—can prefigure or inform the observer in any strict sense, or whether its influence can never amount to more than "irritation," as Luhmann put it. The hallmark of Luhmann's theory is that all observing systems are completely closed off from their environment in that they are autopoietic—they reproduce themselves entirely on the basis of elements they contain. Since the systems he is interested in are meaning-processing systems such as consciousness, one notable way in which the environment could 'intervene' into the system would be by structuring its relevance—a function which Schutz emphasized. In this context, it is quite interesting that Luhmann writes about the evolution of the style of artworks:

> "It is clear, however, that the struggle with media that impose different kinds of constraints draws attention to the formal correlations that can be realized within these media." (Luhmann 2000a: 228).

The innovation of form such 'struggle' initiates, in other words, happens non-purposefully or non-intentionally. When Luhmann writes that the constraints certain media impose "draw attention," he implies a 'weak' notion of attention, so to speak, since he treats attention as a general condition of observation that frames observation only very loosely: attention is a state of an observer that cannot prefigure the content of the ensuing observation (e.g. Luhmann 2000a: 23). A close look at this notion of attention is necessary because Luhmann relies on it to define what artworks are: What makes a piece of art special, he writes, is that "the work of art does not emerge in the course of being perceived, it deliberately draws attention to itself" (Luhmann 2000a: 68).

I feel that Luhmann's discussion of art stands out of the broad spectrum of his work because it discusses the social nature of the *process* of perception in more detail. To be sure, the notion of observation plays a central role in all parts of his theory, but Luhmann usually relies on an abstract account of observing as drawing distinctions in order to be able to treat both human consciousness and social communication systems symmetrically as 'mechanisms' processing distinctions (see Luhmann 1995a). The effect of this abstract notion is that he largely neglects how sensory perception happens en detail, since social meaning is carried by the distinctions used and not the bodily processes of seeing or hearing. His account of art, however, is different. The strict separation between observer and observed that forms the bedrock of his thought is at least framed in a new way, maybe even undermined at times. At first sight, the case of art seems to be a low-hanging fruit for constructivism since its social nature seems obvious: anything can be art as long as we treat it like art, as long as its 'art-ness' is communicated in some broad sense. But if distinguishing between sacred and profane, or art and non-art is an entirely social operation, where does that leave the artwork itself (see Maanen 2010)? In other words: What does a piece of art itself *do*? Luhmann's (2000a) answer is that observing an artwork as an artwork means to conduct what he calls second-order observation, that is, observing how the artwork (or the artist who produced it) observes (represents, communicates) reality. "What in the world was the artist thinking when he did that?" might be an everyday expression of this abstract idea; and Luhmann emphasises that asking oneself such a question is an effect of acknowledging that a) the artwork could have been done differently (that its form is contingent) and that b) there is something specific the work is 'trying to tell us.' In his terms, in doing so the observer is invoking two distinctions by first treating the artwork as an "utterance"[35] or message, and second by implying that there is information or content to be found in said 'message' (Luhmann 2000a: 24). Finally, if the observer is successful in understanding the artwork by grasping the 'idea behind' the piece—by discerning message and

---

[35] Luhmann uses the term *Mitteilung,* and the common translation 'utterance' seems somewhat unfortunate in that it seems to imply a verbal exchange in a way the German term does not.

information—, the tri-part operation that Luhmann calls communication has been conducted. In this way, Luhmann is able to fashion art as a system of communication that is operative whenever an observer (which includes social systems such as the mass media) 'understands' the principle of an artwork in this way. This, however, has an important consequence which finally brings us back to the topic of this system-theoretical detour: the relation of observer and observed. If art is a self-referentially closed communication system in the above sense, then this implies that the "material embodiment of artworks" is not part of the system of art (Luhmann 2000a: 79). What is more, the artist herself is not part of it either, because she is an observer as well, asking herself how others will observe her work. Therefore, she is performing operations of observation which are different from (producing the) the materiality of the artwork—and which necessarily happen *after* the artwork (or at least the currently relevant detail of it) has already been produced (Luhmann 2000a: 38).

At this point, one has to ask the crucial question once again: What does the artwork do? By arguing that understanding art is an operation conducted by closed systems, Luhmann seems bound to erase the artwork from the equation and embrace an all-out solipsism. But he does not. Instead, one reads: "The work takes control" and enables "discovering something that no one, not even the artist, has seen before." (Luhmann 2000a: 70) The observation of the art does not happen at the sole discretion of the independent observer, but it is *guided* by the artwork in question, because artworks contain what is called their own programme—the criteria according to which the observer will understand the artwork (classically, as being either beautiful, or not). Aptly, Luhmann calls this the self-programming of the artwork, and writes:

> *"In order to observe a work of art adequately, one must recognize how the rules that govern the work's own formal decisions are derived from these decisions."* (Luhmann 2000a: 204).

This statement is remarkable in several ways. First, the notion 'program' is a cornerstone of Luhmann's argument that observing systems are de-coupled from their environment, because programs a) control what something is socially—e.g. whether an act was lawful or unlawful—and are b) strictly different from the objects of observation since they belong to the system, not the environment. The laws governing the judicial interpretation of a case, for example, exist independently from the case itself—and this is what makes law a functionally differentiated, self-referential social system. What Luhmann calls the self-regulation of society, in other words, happens on the basis of these programs. Indeed, Luhmann sometimes writes that these programs "orient" the operations of systems (see Esposito 1999): They e.g. determine what is scientifically true or false, of monetary worth or not, or whether a person is included or excluded. Therefore, I suggest that it has grave consequences if Luhmann remarks almost in passing that artworks are self-programming: He is effectively acknowledging that perception and observation can be guided by the (material) forms of objects, and that social order is thus to be found in the structural details of each separate object itself. Second, this also forces him to attend to the process of bodily perception and—crucially—the work of producing material objects in a different way than he does in most other works. If the artist is a de-coupled observer of the artwork he produces, and if the program governing observation is to be found in the work itself, it follows that the bodily work of perceiving and assembling must be guided by the piece of art—piece and body intertwine. The implications Luhmann draws read like they were written by a staunch theorist of practice:

"In most cases (...) a producer must deploy his body as a primary observer. He must rely on bodily intuition, teasing out the distinctions that matter, and in doing so, he must differentiate unconsciously. His ears and eyes can dispose over what has already occurred and perhaps motivate corrections. The artist's genius is primarily his body." (Luhmann 2000a: 38).

The self-programming of the artwork, in other words, happens through "bodily intuition" and "unconscious differentiation," which are—see the quote at the beginning of this excursus—themselves co-determined by the physical qualities of the media used: situational features and bodily workings intertwine and 'program' paths of perception and observation into objects. What is more, this bodily, pre-conscious "observing activity that guides production" (Luhmann 2000a: 38) clearly has a teleological character—something that the operations of social systems cannot have, as Luhmann never ceases to emphasize. Instead, he holds that all social order emanates from recursive, ex-post observations governed by the programs of social systems. But in this brief account of the artist at work, by trying to explain how the orienting programs found in the artworks themselves have come about in the first place, he seems to acknowledge what might be called the directedness of social practices. This fundamental source of social order, however, remains firmly excluded from what Luhmann considers the realm of the social. He saves his theory from contamination with allegedly naive ideas of situated order by discerning first-order and second-order observation and pointing to the temporal difference between the two. What consciousness and social systems try to see in an artwork, he argues, is only how the artwork—or rather: the bodily routines 'struggling' with the material media as they work out the piece—"observes." In other words: *Because* the bodily workings are inherently structured, and *because* they leave powerful traces in the material world, they themselves must *not* be considered social (only their social 'interpreted versions' are)—for reasons which are in my view to be found only in the self-inflicted restrictions of the theory.

These considerations, finally, enable us to grasp Luhmann's answer to the problem of rule-following and gestalt phenomena more precisely: It is not by accident, I suggest, that the terms "gestalt" (which he equates to a work's form, see Luhmann 2000a: 326 fn57) and "rule" appear much more often in his work on art than they do usually in his writings. When Luhmann writes that the "rules that govern the work's own formal decisions" are to be found through second-order observation, it becomes apparent that he identifies rule-following (for example by bodily producing the gestalt to be found in artworks) and judging whether certain conduct happened according to a rule (for example trying to understand what an artwork is supposed to show) as first- and second-order observation—and concludes that only the latter should be considered social.[36] The result is his radical notion of an over-complex and thus inherently meaningless world in need of constant interpretation. His treatment of art, however, discovers the rule-accordance of the objects of observation in the self-programming of the social artefacts that are artworks to be a *necessary condition* of being able to observe meaning sufficiently reliably. By calling the artwork the medium of the communication system of art, and at the same time acknowledging its inherent structuredness, in other words, Luhmann breaches with his own radical postulate that media are necessarily entirely homogenous, form-less matter—instead, at least in this case they are programmed. As the above quote shows, trying to preserve the idea of a strict separation of observer and observed in the face of these important insights leads to an interesting dualistic view on bodily perception: One the one hand, the body is fashioned as an independent observer marching ahead teleologically—but one the other, "his ears and eyes" seem to act in separation from this independent body-observer as they can only "dispose over what has already occurred" (Luhmann 2000a: 38). The rift between observer and observed, between first- and second-order observation that Luhmann insists on thus goes right through the body, as seeing for action and seeing for interpreting the products of action are described both temporally and almost anatomically distinctive.

One cannot fail to notice that Luhmann does neither explain his subtle differentiation in any detail, nor even attempt to underscore it with scientific (or any other) findings. However, one might try to do just that by building on some of the insights from vision science I discussed in this work, particularly the notion of pragmatic versus semantic seeing, and the two

---

[36] And the insight that an explicit rule can never predetermine its own adequate use is reflected in the fact that programs of systems only provide criteria for retrospective 'judgement,' rather than steering behavior.

separate neural systems underlying each other. This option—although surely in need of much more extensive consideration—seems plausible at least to some extend: Semantic or conceptual seeing must indeed invoke conceptual understandings or distinctions and process them 'internally,' that is, by virtue of operations such as pattern recognition whose outcome cannot be determined or controlled 'from the outside' but must be effectively self-regulated. Luhmann's strict notion of observation, in other words, seems to fit scientists' account of semantic or epistemic vision—at least in broad terms. Examining the extent of this fit and the theoretical implications it might have seems well worth further consideration. But if so, what about its pre-conscious twin, pragmatic seeing? A large part of this work has been dedicated to detailing the many important ways in which these 'pragmatic' aspects of vision contribute to, intertwine with, and make possible social order, practical conduct, even our bare survival in the most general terms. Maybe it would indeed be possible to describe these aspects of lived social life as the kind of first-order sociality Luhmann seems to (vaguely) imply, but vastly underestimates in its importance and finesse. If so, many of Luhmann's important insights and challenging abstractions regarding semantic meaning could be put to good use on such a basis—however, reserving the use of the term 'social' and the sociological imagination to the 'upper floor' of second-order, conceptual sociality alone would appear totally unwarranted. But still, any benevolent re-reading of Luhmann on the basis of the pragmatic-semantic divide within vision would lead to the crucial question of how both levels of vision, how bodily first and conceptual second order observation relate. In my account, I emphasized that the flow of social life is achieved by aligning both modi, and that—broadly speaking—pragmatic seeing prefigures activity, while semantic vision orients it. In Luhmann's account of art, the self-programming of the artwork steps in at just this point: the "prepared perception" they provide is described as what he calls "structural coupling" of individual perception and the system of arts (Luhmann 2000a: 69). Finally, one needs to ask: Is the self-programming of perceivable social objects really an exclusive feature of artworks—or rather a quality of everything perceivable, because perception itself has *social* conditions that need to be fulfilled by the situation? In Luhmann's account, the 'self-programming' of the perceptible world is only paid attention to if something is understood as a piece of art. But as I demonstrated with regard to vision, the ability of perceived environments to guide our conduct and perception into a certain direction is a crucial resource to perform any kind of doing, even walking down the street. For this reason, we systematically look for and attend to affordances, for possibilities to be guided in helpful ways by features of situations—always, not just when we look at a piece of art. For example, this is exactly the function most basic visual routines: a light patch in a dark background draws visual attention and is being focused via a deep-seated bodily routine. When 'designing' our world—for example, placing the key on the table where we will see it later—we attend to such 'programs' of perception certain constellations call forth—and I argued that freeskiing style produces visibilities as well, for both skier and spectator.

Chapter 10
Invention—Emergence and Stabilization

1 Introduction: Alaska, the Motherland

> "Ever since I saw film shots from Alaska for the first time when I was 12 or 13, it was my dream to ski there. A dream that governed my life. (…) Without this incisive experience, my life today would probably look very different." (freeride-pro Stefan Häusl in Polzer 2009: 34; [D])[1]

For freeriders, Alaska is akin to the Holy Land of skiing. The place where their culture emerged and is still practiced in its purest and most refined way. It is a place and practice to yearn for, transported into their hearts, minds, and caravans by countless freeride movies showing magnificent lines in near-vertical couloirs against a stunning backdrop of a glorious sundown over pristine mountain ranges. The best thing Tom and his friends can say about the Krimml is that on good days, some of its couloirs and spines are almost like Alaska. Indeed, when they perform freeriding, in a way they try to let Alaska take place in the Austrian Alps. {Big Mountain} skiing, as the name suggests, was born in the specific terrain and snow conditions of mountains much 'bigger' than those usually found near North America's ski resorts: "Alaska was the place where people and powder came together to reinvent a sport". (Anthony 2011: 69) Because of the extraordinary conditions found there, and because of the extraordinary skiing they demanded and afforded, Alaska impacted the global ski culture both as "location and notion." (Anthony 2011: 64) Alaska is a notion that stands for a specific way of skiing and the spectacular images it produces; a locale and style that can be used to position

---

[1] „Seitdem ich im Alter von 12 oder 13 Jahren das erste Mal Aufnahmen aus Alaska gesehn habe, war es mein Traum dort Ski zu fahren. Ein Traum, der mein Leben bestimmt hat. (...) Ohne dieses einschneidende Erlebnis würde mein Leben heute vielleicht ganz anders aussehen."

oneself, but that also expresses deep emotional attachment. But what exactly was it that this 'magical' place did to skiing? Until now, my account of the practices of freeskiing took it for granted that they are simply given. But now, I believe, it is time to ask: Where do they come from? As far as freeriding is concerned, the answer—in a nutshell—is: Alaska. How did it become the birthplace of a new form of skiing; and how did this process differ from the very invention of modern skiing itself? This chapter sets out to provide some answers.

2 Emergence and Evolution

Over the last two decades, the emergence and evolution of practices has proven to be both a challenging theoretical question (Schatzki 2002, 2010a; Shove/Pantzar/Watson 2012), and a fruitful area of empirical research, especially within the sociology of consumption (Ingram/Shove/Watson 2007; Shove/Pantzar 2005b, 2005b; Warde 2005; Watson/Shove 2008). Theories of practice offer a particularly strong framework for conceptualizing social change without unduly focusing on single actors or reifying unidimensional and unidirectional processes. In addition to accounting for multiple dimensions or aspects that influence practice evolutions, the practice perspective requires tracing trajectory of single practices in their embeddedness in larger constellations or fields of practices as discussed in the second chapter (Shove/Watson/Spurling 2015). However, simply adding ever-more factors will not strengthen but overwhelm the analysis at some point (and I have criticized ANT for inviting such tendencies). Of crucial importance is therefore how the "connective tissue" (Blue/Spurling 2017) between complexes of practices is theorized, and if it allows for both coherence and adequate broadness. I suggest that the notion of style in phenopractice theory allows for precisely such an analysis. Because the vibrant and current discussion of the birth and change of practices have not taken the issue of style into consideration, I will use the remainder of this work to outline some conclusions that can be draw from my insights on style and intelligibility. I believe my perspective might add an interesting twist to the ongoing debate. One key idea this work sketched out is that phenopractices consist of enduring elements which become amalgamated in the local unfolding of a practice in such a way that intelligibility transpires and understandings are carried forward. Further, I emphasized that the mere availability and arrangement of elements, and especially of the body, do not per se suffice to account for the situational orders that need to take place; but that this frequently requires practitioners' conduct, particularly their being-in-action. Style, finally, was identified as a way to 'get a grasp' on a certain episode of conduct which allows said episode to be first managed and coordinated (to a certain extent), and second to be memorized and mobilized (in an indirect way). Armed with this understanding, I will in the two remaining chapters tackle the complex question how phenopractices emerge, spread, and evolve. From what has been said thus far, it should be clear that, while the invention and development of singular elements play an important role, they alone cannot provide a full picture. Instead, the question will be how existing as well as (possibly) new elements come to coalesce in such a way that a new phenopractice emerges, a process that is necessarily tied to the emergence of new style of conduct. It should be clear that from my perspective, the crucial point that needs to be discussed is how the intelligibility or observability of a new phenopractice *as* a new practice first emerges and then becomes stabilized so that it can be 'memorized' and mobilized. Towards this end, this chapter aims to work out the underpinnings and implications of a phenopractice perspective on the evolution of style vis a vis certain episodes from the history of skiing. As recommended by Nicolini (2012), I will zoom in on the change certain details of the basic bodily technique of taking a ski turn have undergone throughout the last century and then gradually zoom out again as I retrace the places, arguments, organizations, and media systems that have coordinated these details by enabling stabilized ways of producing the practical availability of them—and in most cases, this means their visibility.

In this chapter, I will use a range of examples from the history of skiing technique to craft my account of the evolution of style. Due to the nature of the long-term developments I am interested in, the data used in this part of this work differs from those I drew on so far, and the selection of my examples is to some extend motivated by the availability of the kind of detailed written accounts or analyses and images I consider suitable for drawing the broad conclusions I aim at. Without a doubt, the depth and nature of these sources cannot fulfil the high methodological standards with regard to understanding concrete, situated conduct on the basis of prolonged participation that I discussed earlier. However, I do not claim that the data used here could have led to the same kind and depth of insights I propose to have produced so far. Therefore, this final part stands apart from the account of freeskiing I have provided. Strictly speaking, one could say that it does not add anything to my ethnographic account, although it might help to clarify some points. In my view, however, what is more important that this relation works the other way around: My historical account is deeply informed by my ethnographic insight, and I am confident to draw the conclusions that I present on the basis of these findings, i.e. since they seem plausible on their basis. Thus, what I undertake in the following is a re-assessment of the data available through the lens of the position I developed. In doing so, I necessarily imply that certain key characteristics of the conduct of skiing I observed myself have also been features of skiing throughout the last century: the general nature of snow and mountains, the particular challenge of riding, the indirectness of grasping bodily doings, the necessity of flow and failure, and so forth. But to be sure, there is no way I could 'prove' the facticity of said features or other's accounts of earlier skiing, so that 'mere' plausibility and logical coherence of the argument must fill the void potentially left due to this inhibition. Theoretically speaking, however, the phenopractical notion of style, the assumptions about the enduring nature of elements, and the basic idea that experiences are effects of social practices rather than subjective knowledge or learning histories imply that not the inter*subjective* generalizability of findings or experiences is a core methodological issue, but rather something like their inter-*practical* similarity. While the methodological appendix will offer further thoughts on these important let me remark that the following account is arguably and at least to some extent rooted in understanding (in the sense outlined by me) of some of the practices involved, rather than in an understanding of other's recollections or descriptions alone, in that it relies on some of the historical elements of practices which I assess against the background of my own skills of performing, teaching, and observing skiing. If, for example, I look at a picture that was used to teach skiing in the 1960s or try to make sense of the rules prescribed for taking Stem Turns in 1910, then the understandings on which I rely will of course differ from 'the original.' Nevertheless, I believe that it does make quite a difference that I have a practical understanding of teaching and being taught about similar skiing techniques with the help of similar pictures, as well as of performing and instructing taking Stem Turns in accordance with similar rules.[2] Beyond such a level of bringing historical documents to life in a certain way, however, my account is ultimately simply a theoretical consideration of a topic that one could otherwise not discuss on an empirical basis at all.

3 Circulation and Invention

In contrast to most theories of innovation, the practice perspective implies that the elements which are linked up already exist, rather than being the essence of innovation. As Elizabeth Shove and colleagues (2003a, 2007; Shove/Pantzar 2005b, 2007; Shove/Pantzar/Watson 2012; Shove/Watson/Spurling 2015) have argued in a number of studies, elements of new practices are often adopted or imported from other practices or places, and the key moment is the way they become linked, rather than the elements themselves. In more theoretical terms, their point of view stresses that every conduct of a practice is necessarily a local performance of that practice, the product of a situated re-assemblage of the practice's different elements. My take on the emergence, dissemination, and evolution of phenopractices shares many core convictions with the work of Shove and colleagues on this matter, among them the idea that elements of practices circulate on their own and are amalgamated into praxis situatedly. I argue that this idea implies an important difference between everyday accomplishments of the same practice and the first time accomplishment of a new practice, in that the latter can only post eventum attract stabilizing elements such as routinization or explicit rules governing a conduct's being an instance of said new practice. In order to shed light on the concrete and purposeful practices that typically bring about a recombination of elements such as explicit rules and practical understandings, Shove and her collaborators

---

[2] Note that my reliance on the concept of similarity (rather than, e.g., regularity) in making this methodlogical statement is itself a key pillar of the theoretical edifice I am trying to erect.

3 Circulation and Invention 449

have examined a number of interesting cases that reveal important parallels with the phenopractice account I propose (Shove 2003b, 2007; Shove/Pantzar 2007; Shove/Pantzar/Watson 2012; Watson/Shove 2006, 2008). One especially interesting study of the evolution and dissemination of practices is Shove and Pantzar's (2007) study of the emergence of Nordic walking. They describe the 'invention' of Nordic Walking as a fusion of pre-existing elements that had already been in (transnational) circulation, but where recombined by the efforts of different organization such as a Finnish national sports institute and a large sports equipment manufacturer.

> "[I]nventing Nordic walking is a matter of integrating images of fitness and wellbeing, the walking sticks themselves, and the knowledge of how to use them so as to create a new practice." (Shove/Pantzar 2005b: 54)

The different elements, they suggest, can be summarized as belonging to three basic categories which they call skill, stuff, and image—in combination knowing how to do proper Nordic Walking, the essential walking sticks, and the positive public associations constitute the practice. Shove and Pantzar highlight the importance of the institutional contexts for forging these elements together, especially the role of image and national (or Nordic) identity and the emergence of a functioning market system. They show how Nordic walking was introduced to different countries by different organizational actors via different processes and in different version (e.g. as a symbol of classic Finnish virtues, or as a fitness practice for the elderly in the UK) and thus speak of the "local re-invention" of the practice. It does not fully transpire, however, what precisely distinguishes a local re-invention from a local performance—one could speculate that they tie their notion of reinvention to a change in the general understandings aligned with the practice, in that these presumably differ only across, but not within countries. On the other hand, it also becomes quite clear that the different organizations involved did not only (expectably) pursue different goals or strategies (e.g. commercial versus government organizations), but also differed in their view on what precisely Nordic Walking *is* in the first place (e.g. a new sport, a training exercise for athletes, a fitness program). This leads Shove and Pantzar to emphasize that, while organizations produce the elements of a practice, their fusion must be brought about by the consumer him- or herself. What is more, the fact the elements of a practice need to be put into practice for this to happen leads them to conclude that "practices like Nordic walking are always 'homegrown'" (Shove/Pantzar 2005b: 61), and that while elements freely circulate, practices themselves do not. Accordingly, they seem to suggest that practices undergo more or less perpetual evolution, since every reproduction is effectively a local 're-invention.' While I agree with the broad line of their argument, I believe there is an inherent tension between the notion of a practice as a routinized doing and the idea of perpetual change. While it is out of the question that the linking or amalgamation of elements requires the involvement of practitioners, this alone does not quite explain how the practitioners manage to bring about this fusion, especially since the skill or competence for doing Nordic Walking is itself considered an element (and the article unfortunately lacks a description of how the walking is actually learned and taught). I surely agree that elements themselves circulate independently and do not constitute practices on their own, but I also believe that there is more to be said about how the practitioners manage to reassemble them in the right (though always slightly different) ways; and that this point can neither be adequately explained by pointing to the creative powers of human action (since this does not explain how some practices work and others do not; or why some change quickly and others almost never), nor reducing this factors to a single element alone (e.g. by saying that the skill of assembling the practice is the single element responsible for it). It seems that there is something missing in the picture; namely, how practitioners manage to get a grasp what it is they are trying to 're-invent' in the midst of the very situation in which they are doing so—which is something other than the public image of a practice. The practitioners, in other words, need what I would call orientation.

Shove Pantzar, and Watson elaborate on this point in some more detail in their influential Dynamics of Social Practice (2012). In discussing of the emergence of snowboarding for example, (2012: 118) they emphasize the importance of the "ongoing setting and re-setting of conventions and standards" (2012: 103) and argue that "examples of monitoring, recording, calibrating and feedback give a sense of the means by which performances and practices constitute each other" (2012: 105). They add:

> "Finally, systems of classification and standards constitute what Bowker and Star refer to as 'invisible mediators of action' (Bowker/Star 2000). They do so by establishing templates in terms of which performances are compared; by defining what any one enactment is a performance of (this being in part determined by how performance is recorded), and by reconfiguring elements of the practice and the manner in which they are integrated." (Shove/Pantzar/Watson 2012: 105)

It should be apparent that a similar thought has motivated my own research. Practices such as classifying and standardizing are especially clear examples of organized ways of coping with the general problem I have focused my attention on: By virtue of what and over the course of which processes does practical conduct become intelligibly as conduct of a certain practice?[3] However, with regard to the argument of Shove, Pantzar, and Watson, I am still left somewhat unsatisfied with the vocabulary available for and level of detail of observation of the concrete conduct in the course of which a new practice emerges or coalesces. There is arguably a danger of misreading their arguments as implicating something akin to a pragmatist version of speech act theory in which something is what is simply by virtue of being named or defined as such. Names, explicit rules, or general understandings, however, can only be elements of practices, none of which can on its own determine what a practice is. Thus, distinguishing between

---

[3] And for just this reason, ethnomethodologists have a long-standing interest in phenomena of defining, describing, marking, rating judging, or classifying conduct in the widest sense (Garfinkel 2002).

practices-as-performances and practices-as-entities and noting that performances differ in detail since they are subject to local contingencies (see Warde 2005), does not yet explain how practices-as-entities come into being: Performances are what they are by virtue of being performances of that particular practice, and thus the question remains what makes them instances of just that practice. Further, as my account of seeing style in a funpark demonstrated, this problem is not just a matter of abstract logic, but a frequent lived-through problem that needs to be solved by practitioners on an everyday basis. Focusing theory and research on practices whose performance is oriented by style, as phenopractice theory proposes, allows for a more coherent position—but at the cost of leaving practices or practice performances out of the picture that do not express style, or are oriented by style.

Excursus: The Organization of Normality

> Through analysing the dissemination of a number of (particularly resource-intensive) everyday consumption practices such as showering or laundering, Shove (2003b) undertakes a study of "the social organization of normality," focusing on the core question of how the new becomes normal. One key factor she describes are processes of scientific construction of normality, especially via statistical analysis and modelling or laboratory testing, the results of which are then formalized into industrial standards or legal norms, ensuring further dissemination of practices able to match the newfound normality. Normality established through statistical measuring techniques, in other words, reflexively constitutes the very status it officially only seeks to capture and describe; and moreover, innovations are often path-dependent in that subsequent related developments build upon and thus reinforce formalized normalities. For example, once scientists had 'found' the optimal room temperature for normal houses, and once new understandings of normal comfort as including artificially cooled air had spread, houses where increasingly designed to enable easy air-conditioning rather than offer shade and natural ventilation. In this perspective, the sedimentation of normalities in society is on a basic level to be understood as a long-term process similar to what Gehlen (1987) described as the crystallization of forms: over time, certain variations of common practice sediment from being new or deviant, to being known and expected as normal. However, such processes should not be misunderstood as a continuous evolution in the sense of a homogenous flow of ongoing variation and selection, but rather as highly path-dependent trajectories driven by moral understandings and/or technical infrastructures, trajectories that are often influenced, accelerated, or dominated by professional institutions, experts, or commercial interests (Shove 2003b). I should note that my account of the stabilization of phenopractices differs in an important aspect from this general line of thought: I distinguish

> the style of a practice from the normality of conduct of said practice in that I describe normality as an implicit and permanent condition of social conduct that is prevalent unless abnormality is situatedly demonstrated (see appendix). Towards sustaining this condition, failure—or the out-standing of the abnormal—must be (made) possible within practical conduct, which in turn requires that said conduct or unfolding of the practice happens in such a way that its phenomenal field has coherence, something that, I argue, usually happens because the conduct has been oriented to a style. The normalities such as the standard room temperature of 23 °C which Shove (2003b) discusses match this conceptualization in so far that their absence can indeed be situatedly demonstrated, for example by measuring them, but is usually not attended to in everyday conduct since they match commonly held expectations of normality. Where my account differs, however, is how I conceptualized non-attended contextual conditions such as 23 °C in terms of their ontological status. I suggested that background and foreground of a practice do not directly imply each other, e.g. in that a specific phenopractice must be tightly coupled to all its background conditions. Instead, most practical conduct can be achieved against a variety of different backgrounds as long as they can be arranged so as to enable standing out and blending in according to the necessary patterns. Most everyday practices, in other words, can happen within a rather large range of temperatures. Thick business suit simply require certain aligning elements, for example the understanding that wearing lighter suits or shirts only is acceptable as well. In conclusion, conditions such as 23 °C would feature as elements of practices rather than normalities in my account, so that shifting the standards codifying them would not necessarily imply changing the overall style of conduct (although this is an option), but alternatively, a more simple adaption of neighbouring elements would do as well. From this perspective, a pervasive problem of many attempts to instil healthier living or fewer carbon emissions could be that often, a wholesome change of lifestyles is being demanded or aimed at where subtle swapping of elements would already do—usually eating organic food, for example, does not in itself amount to, or must be part of, a whole lifestyle of health and sustainability.

To some extent, most practices seem to undergo a continuous incremental evolution in that some of their elements are being changed or exchanged. Different historical periods or cultures, for example, might attach different general understandings to certain practices; or the technical equipment used might be 'advanced' over time. As freeskiing shows, the style of phenopractices can undergo a similar eventual evolution; and practices are usually surrounded by complementary practices of monitoring, judging, regulating, or improving conduct which also play an important role in disseminating and stabilizing a practice. One way of explaining the emergence of new phenopractices therefore points to such ongoing incremental evolution and argues that over time, new practices crystallize in that what were initially unusual deviations over time stabilize into permanent versions of a practice that develops into a direction away from the original practice (cf. Gehlen 1987). But regardless of whether one holds that a) styles of conduct crystallize as complete wholes over time through repetition; or that b) elements of practices are purposefully produced to be combined into a new practice later, the emergence or invention of a style must in both cases itself be understood as happening of the course of ongoing lived life. Therefore, both an influence of social macrostructures and an evolution of phenopractices must happen in specific social situations; and that the conditions, constraints, or practical workings of said situations must be decisive for the ensuing change. In other words, I hold that the evolution of phenopractices ultimately depends on complex patterns of interrelations of factors in situations of innovation, experimenting, learning, exercising power, marking distinctions, and so forth. I will thus put forward a vocabulary which circumscribes what I see as the specific role of elements and style towards innovating and spreading practices by discussing the unplanned (but not strictly coincidental) birth of a new style of skiing: Big Mountain freeride. To be sure, I agree with Shove and colleagues that the ways and conditions of establishing or breaking such relations can themselves be socially organized to some extent, for example by organizations in charge of rule-making or product development. Indeed, I will make a number of suggestions about how this might happen. But before rushing to discussing such 'organized' and purposeful forms of social evolution, I will discuss a different, arguably not purposeful or organized driver of style evolution, one that possibly escapes sometimes macro-sociological or cultural interpretations because its key protagonist is clearly not human; it is a terrain.

4 Mobility, Access, and Natural Laboratories

Seeing, working out, and choosing a line is a situated process of interaction and communication, I argued, and an important part of freeride skiing because the terrain always co-determines the kind of skiing that will happen, for example the speed or the radius of turns. However, local or 'micro' decision-making is not the only social process that can be found to determine the terrain for and thus style of skiing. A clear example of a social macro process which is not a form of communication or an exchange of symbols but has always been central to the growth and development of skiing is the development of modes of *transport*. An important step for the local stabilization of the newborn practice of Alpine skiing, for example, was that in 1899 the authorities permitted the transport of skis on trams in Vienna; and in the following years special rates for skiers on local trains were introduced (Allen 2008: 12). In the following decade, the growth of ski tourism and railway transport in the Alps became closely intertwined: Special trains for skiers left from place as far away as London, and the new goal of developing ski tourism in poor mountain villages became a factor in the planning and construction of railway lines (Allen 2007: 86–88). From a cultural-theory perspective, one might argue that these developments demonstrate how the new practice of skiing had been successfully aligned with the predominant ideas of the time (e.g. manly heroism, conquest of nature, conspicuous leisure) and thus garnered wide support; and with a focus on power and class hegemony, one might add that a small elite had successfully established a new, highly exclusive way of keeping the emerging urban middle class at a distance both symbolically *and* geographically by retreating to exclusive mountain resorts—and even secured government support for transport or university ski clubs by declaring an elite pastime a public good (see Coleman 2004). Both views surely grasp an aspect of the macro-scale development of the meanings or images associated with the new sport and help explain its dissemination and consolidation. However, I suggest that they tell only part of the story in that they effectively erase the particulars of skiing from the equation: Had the elite taken up mountain-top Hula-Hoop, the argument would remain basically the same. From a practice perspective, a different image emerges. The expansion of transport systems available for skiers, it implies, is not just an expression of much more general transformation of meanings 'in society' (whatever that means), but also had very thorough effects on the nature and style of skiing itself. If so, then these effects might go some way to explain why skiing and not mountain-top Hula-Hoop (or any other random symbolically 'loaded' leisure practice) garnered the support and success it did; thus not rendering above explanations obsolete, but adding to a more complete picture. Let me try to sketch out what the phenopractice perspective might add to such a picture in the particular case of transport.

Not only technically, but also in skier's own understanding, skiing is essentially one large system of movement to, up, down, and away from mountains. In freeskiing, this is demonstrated by the so-called {travel-sequences}, a stable feature of today's freeski films (both professional and amateur) in which the travelling from and to resorts and ski spots around the world is symbolically celebrated. In this vein, Anthony (2011: 69) writes looking back on his decades-long professional skiing career: "To ski was to travel, and to travel was to ski."[4] It becomes apparent why the history of skiing and skiing style is intimately intertwined with the development of transportation systems: The fundamental importance of the Arlberg for early alpine skiing stems to considerable extend from the fact that it lay en route a mayor transnational train service between Vienna and Zurich that crosses through the Arlberg Tunnel and briefly stopped at high altitude at the small village of St. Anton, thus appearing on the map of the (frequently British) upper-class, especially in Winter, when travel on road passes came to a complete

---

[4] As a phenomenon, skiing thus falls squarely into the emerging realm of the sociological studies of mobilities (Urry 2000, 2007; Urry/Sheller 2004)—a perspective that can well be combined with practice thought (Büscher/Urry 2009; Sheller/Urry 2016).

stop (Lund 1995). In consequence, the Arlberg technique of skiing developed and popularized here befitted the steep mountains and differed greatly from the Norwegian style from the Telemark region (Nohl 2005). Similarly, the first and second boom of skiing in the US build on the emergence of designated "ski trains" (and later the Interstate Highway System) that provided affordable and effective transportation from the large cities into the mountainous hinterlands—and the change in the scape and scope of the ski segment in turn fuelled many important innovations in ski technique, equipment, and style (Fry 2006a: 13–14; 57–59). A third example of the interdependence of transport systems (routes, times, prices) and skiing style which I will consider in more detail is provided by the big mountain-style of freeriding Tom and his friends (including myself) undertake in the Krimml; a style of skiing that was born in Alaska (Anthony 2011: 51–69). As I described, one essential element of freeriding that distinguishes it from traditional ski mountaineering is the stance towards, and use of, altimeters the skiers make. In ski touring, skiers focus on making economic use of every altimeter they ski down by trying to squeeze in as many turns as possible; an emotionally pursued end linked to the viscerally felt and lived understanding that they paid in sweat and labour for gaining each altimeter when ascending on foot. Freeriders, in contrast, 'spend' altimeters lavishly, engaging in Veblenian perspicuous consumption of vertical feet (Fry 2006c). Two crucial parts of the framework within which their alternative emotional-moral logic of thrill—as an alternative to the ski-mountaineers' ethos of discipline—emerged and became popularized by powerful media images had their roots in transport systems: For one, the use of helicopters dramatically changed the amount of vertical distance that could be skied in a single day, causing an enormous inflation within the symbolic and motivational economy of altimeters as getting back up to the drop-in became a matter of minutes (Fry 2006c: 13).[5] Second, much like the Arlberg's steeper and more exposed peaks had led to important adoptions in ski technique and technology a century earlier, Alaska both required and invited similar innovation when it became the latest "last frontier" of skiing to be made accessible to larger numbers of skiers from the early nineties onwards (Anthony 2011: 51–69; Dawson 1998: 101–109; Obernhaus 2008: 44:00). Arguably it was primarily because of dropping prices in airline travel (driven by the emergence of low-cost carriers) that Alaska could be considered "easy to reach and relatively close to home for Americans" (Anthony 2011: 64); and the ensuing commercial success of heli-skiing led operators to develop the first "fat" ski models that allowed skiers to handle the enormous snow masses found there (Fry 2006c; Obernhaus 2008: 47:50). But notably, it would be simplistic to assume that since a certain terrain requires a certain ski technology and technique, skiing style is just an effect of environmental necessities. In my view, practice theory's notion that practices

---

[5] Still, heli-skiing operators usually charge more if a certain amount of vertical feet has been 'spent' on a day of skiing, therefore skiing (almost) straight lines—as freeride pros do—is nevertheless a sure sign of elite spending power—in their case provided for by film sponsors.

and the material arrangements that host them constitute each other (e.g. Schatzki 2010a: 10) should not be misread as implying that both have a causal effect in that the prevalence of one will breed the other, as some uses of Bourdieu's terms habitat and habitus seems to suppose (cf. Alkemeyer/Schmidt 2004; Schmidt 2006). Precisely speaking, saying that skiing and line constitute each other and by virtue of this radiated style negates granting any of the two some kind of ontological priority; and indeed the sheer persistence of mountains' terrain features did not suffice to stabilize the bundling of wide ski and big turns that characterizes Big Mountain skiing. As it seems to be the case with many other equipment innovations in skiing, the purely technological solution of building wider skis to allow floating on powder snow, rather than 'plowing' through it, had already appeared and re-appeared in Europe several times in different places and circumstances without ever gaining stable circulation. What is more, the popularity of wide skis in Europe today demonstrates that there are few direct or necessary effects of the terrain features on the equipment used, because they are not necessarily beneficial given the conditions typically found in the Alps. Several ski developers I interviewed stressed the fact that snow and terrain conditions in the Alps are different from the US. For example, the French founder of a 'core' brand of freeride ski explained that his vision had been to build "a brand with skis that technically could fit well with the snow that we have now in Europe" [I]. Said snow is often much harder, and routes frequently lead through narrow, steep couloirs rather than the wide, open flanks to be found in the US and especially Alaska; and therefore, European brands tend to sell skis that are considerable less wide, as well as stiffer [I]. Thus, as our trips to the Krimml show, the Alps might not always *invite* the big turns epitomized by Alaska, but they surely *afford* them—if the capable skier is able to spot the right lines. And as the second chapter detailed, seeing Big Mountain lines where ski mountaineers had earlier only seen opportunities for classic short turns requires a certain constellation of equipment, technique, and understandings of style to be already in place. In other words, transportation to and within Alaska was crucial for the emergence and popularization of wide skis and the Big Mountain style; but once its images, understandings, and tools had spread globally to landscapes that provide affordances for skiing in a style that is intelligibly Big Mountain, its practical relevance became merely symbolic. Today, heli-skiing in Alaska is still considered *the* iconic and paradigmatic way to do freeriding[6] and remains a dream for most European freeriders—but if access to Alaska would vanish tomorrow, Big Mountain technology and technique would surely not cease to exist. As Anthony (2011: 64) writes, the influence of Alaska on the global ski culture stems from it being both "location and notion"—but today, it is the notion, the idea of Alaska-style skiing that is key.

---

[6] For example, when a European freeski crew was finally able to present a scene shot in Alaska in their latest movie, they were being acknowledged as finally showing "real" Big Mountain skiing [D].

5 Orientation and Prefiguration

How can this specific relationship between the factors or structures of the social world (e.g. transport systems) and the style of a practice (e.g. Big Mountain freeride) be expressed in the terms of phenopractice theory? In my view, a situated unfolding of a practice can be said to be related to the wider social context or social environment in three different ways. First, there are the *contingencies* of the immediate context of happening. As I discussed at length, what makes a concrete 'slice of social life' an instance of a particular practice is inter alia the fact that it frames many of the details occurring—and, maybe even more important, the details potentially occurring—as local contingencies, unavoidable indexicality, or the inevitable and perfectly uneventful clutter of everyday doing best dutifully ignored. Most of the possible or 'factual' instances of relatedness, in other words, are not of the essence for any given practice in question; and because this is the fact, both sufficiently stable social conduct and endless sociological theorizing and disagreement are possible.[7] More important for an analysis of the dispersion and evolution of social practices are thus the second and third form of relatedness: those whose relevance is a feature of the practice itself. As part and parcel of a practice, and thus as a prerequisite to the possibility of its conduct, they are testament to the fundamental fact that human praxis is inherently social, perpetually preceded by and dependent upon social life en gros. Building on my findings so far, I suggest distinguishing two broad forms of relatedness—but I should add that depending on the case at hand, it might be necessary (and will surely be possible) to add a number of further forms or sub-forms.[8] But for the sake of clarity, allow me to try to make do with only two: *prefiguration* and *orientation*. Prefiguration, being the second form of relation of practice and wider social life, has already been discussed vis-à-vis the material dimension of social practices. At the core, the conviction is that elements of practices can travel or be disseminated, for example through physical movement. When assembled into a figurational coherence in concrete happening, they prefigure conduct in important ways one might describe as enabling or disabling certain aspects of conduct, and thus pointing or leading to a certain way of doing (which must not be coherent with a sought-after style). Prefiguration is thus an effect of what I called the ontological duration of elements, the fact that a ski moulded in a factory in China flexes in a certain way when skied in the Krimml two years later. By linking prefiguration to

---

[7] For reasons of clarity I should add that I suggested that such relations or indexical details are not necessarily arbitrary or over-complex; and that I opposed the notion that it must be possible to draw a sharp border between the relevant or necessary background of outstanding aspects of a practice, and completely unnecessary or fully ignored happenings of the world—who decides which part of the world is unnecessary, anyways?

[8] Schatzki, for example, discusses a much longer list of contexts and cross-relations of practices and social sites (Schatzki 2002: ch. 4).

the circulation of elements, I further imply that material elements are by no means the only carriers of prefiguration—rather, they only offered a convenient option to introduce the concept. Explicit rules are one important example of non-material elements of practices that can prefigure conduct, e.g. in that the rule that a slalom skier has to pass through all gates 'channels' many aspects of his skiing into a certain direction, but without directly determining the shape of his skis or his bodily technique. Prefiguration, in other words, is a 'nudge towards' a certain figurational coherence. It has concrete effects, but these are by definition particular: prefigurations are not predeterminations of the whole but only concern a certain aspect (or a few of them). A ski with a centrally mounted binding, for example, prefigures skiing to some extent, for example in that its width makes skiing in soft powder easier and skiing on hard-pack more difficult, or vice versa. In contrast, the style of a freestyle trick done on these skis is different in that it concerns the overall figuration arising from the details, only some of which are being prefigured by elements such as the ski. Double flips, for example, have been performed on race skis, and a versatile and skilled skier might still do proper short turns on twin-tips, presenting a classically elegant, upright posture. For this reason, I deem it important to distinguish prefiguration from *orientation*, which describes the *overall* conduct as being organized towards becoming attuned to style by either performing or observing it. Notably, orientation must not be (but frequently is) an effect of a conscious goal; and it can take a number of forms. Most importantly for the case at hand, a phenopractice is oriented to a style if it is organized towards achieving said style, although it always does so across the particularities of conduct and the contingencies of situations. Thus, elementary prefiguration is one important means towards achieving visibly smooth orientation, but taken alone, it can never suffice. An explicit rule, for example, can be an element of a practice, and thus a moment of prefiguration of conduct. However, the rule alone does not fully determine or capture all details of conduct, and not explicitly or consciously following that rule might still amount to conducting the same practice: different combinations of elements can amount to the conduct of the same practice. Therefore, prefiguration is not orientation.

6 New Ways of Seeing

In theoretical terms, one could thus say that as a notion, Alaska still *orients* the freeriding happening in the Alps and elsewhere. However, as a physical environment, it was the birthplace of a new skiing style because it invoked what Schatzki (2010a: 10) calls "[material] arrangement-anchored place-path arrays" that influenced several dimensions of skiing conduct directly—it *prefigured* skiing there: Without using helicopters and super-wide skies, skiing would have been not impossible, but inherently difficult. In a similar way, taking the iconic big turns celebrated in countless freeski films and pictorials is not just a performance, but also a strategy used by riders to deal with the specific dangers of the snow and terrain found in Alaska: Because the snow is relatively wet, it sticks to even very steep mountain faces, which makes them 'ride-able,' but also particularly fragile and avalanche-prone (Obernhaus 2008: 44:00–47:00). When riders speed almost straight down along the top of so-called spines (small ridges running vertically down a face), they do so to avoid avalanches as well as the inevitable {slough} (loose snow trailing down a face cut loose by a fast skier that is dangerous because it can take your sight), which both slide down in between but not on top of spines (see EpicSki Community 2009; [D]). When freeriders assure that "Speed is your friend" [M], this is also especially true for skiing in such conditions: As many ski movies' spectacular scenes testament, professional freeriders can escape the avalanches they trigger by simply outrunning them—skiing extremely fast and straight down. The specific challenges of skiing Alaska, in other words, provided the conditions within which heli-skiing, wide skis, and big turns did not remain isolated experiments, but were repeated, refined, and finally routinized. According to the phenopractice perspective developed in this work, the most significant of the phenomenal reconfigurations the specific challenges of Alaska invoked were the new *ways of seeing* skiing that emerged both in terms of perspective and aesthetics. They arguably have their roots in the fact that helicopters do not just provide effective means of transport but also make excellent observation platforms—which is why they are frequently used for tasks such as search-and-rescue missions, TV coverage, or crime surveillance. In freeriding, helicopters changed *both* the views their companions gained on the skiing action, and the view the skiers themselves gained on the mountain slopes. Phenopractice theory implies that both aspects have a very significant impact on the emergence and dissemination of a certain style of conduct. To begin with the first transformation of perspective: the circulation of visual media content is often fundamental for the diffusion of a style. The spectacular images produced via heli-skiing played a pivotal role both for the rapid growth of the ski industry in Alaska and the global success of the techniques and technologies associated with it (Anthony 2011: 51–69). As I will show with regard to several other skiing styles, this success depended on the practical visibility of virtues such as beauty, skilfulness, or creativity within the images of skiing. If one compares the typical images (or videos) depicting classic short-turn powder-skiing with those of freeride Big Turns, it becomes obvious that in the latter case, the camera must be located much further away from the skier in order for the skill of the ride to become visible, since it lies in the length and 'straightness' of the turns, the speed achieved, and the overall flow and symmetry of the line as a whole. The beauty of Oldschool figure eights, in contrast, can only be seen on closer inspection, since its beauty lies in the symmetry of the details of the many short turns—and accordingly, the images a shot from a much closer distance.[9] The on-screen visibility of the aesthetic qualities of the different styles, in other words,

---

[9]To be sure, some pictures can be found where 'Oldschool' powder-skiing can be seen from large distance; but if so, the actual short turns can no longer be discriminated and blur into one straight line—the beauty of symmetry that ski mountaineers value so much is gone.

is inherently tied to the angle and positioning of the camera. As many freeride movies document—albeit in an aestheticized fashion—helicopters have become an essential tool for professional freeriders to read faces and spot new lines. Notably, when circling a mountain looking for affordances to ride, freeriders eye the slopes from a different angle than those who remain on the ground (or peek from airplanes): they (mostly) see the whole mountain side at once, from top to bottom. As I described, it is crucial for riders to gain what they call a good visual on a face before riding; and that in 'Oldschool' powder skiing, a slope is divided into several shorter stretches, each of which is first inspected and then skied in a series of steps separated by a short break. In other words, one important innovation of Big Mountain-style freeride is to view the whole mountain-side as one unit[10] ideally to be skied in one take—and such a view requires a certain perspective, a 'helicopter view' in the truest sense of the word. Again, gaining such a perspective is by no means impossible without helicopters; and freeriders not fortunate enough to have them available sometimes laboriously climb the mountain opposite of the face they intend to ride only to acquire a similar vista and then climb down again. But for the idea that one run should equal one continuous movement down one face from top to bottom to become normalized, the practical visibility of such a new type of line was a key prerequisite—and the view from the helicopter reliably provided this practical visibility as a *by-product* of other ends and projects. In my view, this point is very significant because it provides an example of how non-purposefully or institutionally organized, planned, or managed innovation of social practices through the invocation of a new orientation can take place—in this case governed via the visual domain. The evident, practical visibility of the coherence of a Big Mountain face as being one integrated whole comprising the whole mountain-side from drop-in to out-run can well be *instructedly* observable in places like the Krimml. That is, given certain ends, projects, or tasks as well as certain tools and some effort to gain a good perspective, its practical visibility can be (cooperatively) accomplished; and therefore, it can form part of the normal background of details against which a freeride line can stand out in the conduct of seeing lines. Without these specific ends, projects, or tasks, however, a face's coherence is not likely practically evident when crossing mountains like the Alps on foot—it does not 'stare you in the eyes' as it does when you fly in a helicopter. One crucial effect of heli-skiing in Alaska, in other words, was that it produced such practical visibilities *prior* to the availability of respective instructions, ends, understandings, and the like. The prefigurations invoked by the terrain, in other

---

[10]This transformed understanding of mountains is also evident in the folk terms of German-speaking freeriders: Unlike ski-tourers, they speak of [faces] and thus adopt the language of climbers. Therefore, the expression has its origin in a fundamental development in climbing (and Alpine sports more generally.): Instead of focusing on mountain *peaks* as goals to conquer, climbers started to single out certain (steep) *stretches* of a mountain-side as the true object of their sport (see T. Bucher 2000; Robinson 2004; T. Williams/P. Donnelly 1985). In other words, the meaning of success or skill in climbing changed from '*somehow* reaching a peak' to 'crossing a terrain *in a certain style*.'.

words, lead to the stabilization of patterns of orientations of a new style of skiing over the course of skiers' sustained coping with them. The explicit rules, embodied routines, and practical understandings that are the hallmarks of freeride today were not miraculously thought up in a lone mind or systematically assembled in an engineer's workshop or marketing department; they consecutively emerged *after* the concrete praxis of what was later called freeride was already well underway. The 'social role' of mobility and access, one can conclude, predominantly stems from the fact that certain locales or environments prefigure conduct in such a way that in a gestalt-effect, certain aspects 'naturally' stand out and demand attention, and that certain ways of doing become more likely or befitting without being necessarily purposefully (or intentionally in a classic sense) pursued at the beginning. In doing so, they might function as a kind of 'natural' laboratory (in the sense of Knorr Cetina 1995) in that they provide for certain reconfigurations of the phenomenal field of ongoing praxis that motivate, enable, and orient methodical manipulations of tools, states, and techniques towards establishing new practical coherences (see Schatzki 2010a: 14 for a similar thought). In effect, I thus argue that the study of the long-term, macro-scale evolution of phenopractices must pay close attention to the situational specificities of the practical conduct in question. In the spirit of Karin Knorr Cetina's (1988: 22) call for "methodological situationalism" that demands "that descriptively adequate accounts of large-scale social phenomena be grounded in statements about actual social behaviour in concrete situations," I call for a 'theoretical situationalism' with regard to social change that requires that adequate accounts of large-scale social changes need to be grounded in statements about the details of social conduct in concrete situations. One important implication of this perspective is a general scepticism towards explanations which account for the emergence of very specific styles, practices, or trends by pointing to very general and large-scale social relations or transformations (cf. my critique of the use of the term 'lifestyle' in chapter five)—particularly if they are voiced from a practice perspective. To be sure, I do not suggest that such relations cannot play a role, and some of the evolutions of media systems and markets I will discuss in the following chapter could as well be considered large-scale transformations. But the question that needs asking is whether and how such influence manifests in the details of situated conduct itself—and here, I believe, many of the accounts currently available run into problems.

Excursus: Lifestyle Sports, Job Markets, and the Habitus

One particularly interesting version of the general claim that the evolution of (subcultural) style reflects macro structures or power relations has been voiced predominantly in the German debate: By drawing on Caillois' (1961) theory of play, an anthropological reading of Wittgenstein (see Gebauer 2008, 2009) and Bourdieu's notion of habitus, it is argued that sport or lifestyle activities tend to "train" as well as "show, emphasize and dramatize" (Alkemeyer/Schmidt 2004: 575; my translation) a very specific habitus (which is equated to bodily skills and embodied knowledge) that serves the need of predominant forms of waged labour. Alkemeyer and Schmidt (2004), for example, compare gymnastics and BMX-biking in order to demonstrate that both carry antagonistic "dispositions" of the relation of bodily routines and artefacts that can be linked to different forms of labour. Gymnastics, they hold, carries a "disposition of formation" in which the body becomes "subverted" to machines and the principles of industrial production; while BMX is characterized by a "disposition of implication" in that "body and technology complement each other" and merge into a sensible whole (Alkemeyer/Schmidt 2004: 577; my translation). Such homologies, they further suggest, help to "produce and naturalize" social inequalities in that they become prerequisites for the employability of individuals (2004: 577), an argument they seek to underscore by arguing that computer programmer's frequent participation in computer games prepares and enhances their bodily skills of using said computers. Let me first asses the latter claim. It should be noted that the authors do not explicitly suggest that the homology between sport (the type of sophisticated computer gaming they describe is increasingly called "e-sports"; see Jonasson/Thiborg 2010) and forms of labour is causal in nature, or that agents choose their sport strategically in order to better their position on the job market—unlike Bourdieu, as we have seen. The (re-)production and naturalization of inequalities in the fine details of using artefacts in the different sports they diagnose, however, do amount to a mutual co-constitution of what they call "culture-specific styles of use" and social macrostructures (Alkemeyer/Schmidt 2004: 577); and it is in this sense that they describe the training of work-related bodily routines as an "important latent meaning" of e-sports (2004: 575).[11] In my view, their examples demonstrate that one needs to be careful about assessments of just how 'deep' such stylistic homologies really go. In other words, I am not quite convinced that the bodily skills honed in sport are really of pragmatic relevance when it comes to office work. For one, we do not learn how BMX skills might come in handy when typing away in your cubicle. And in the case of the ego-shooter, the pragmatic relevance of the highly developed fine motor skills that are central to such games (i.e. aiming via moving the computer mouse in an extremely rapid fashion) for typing computer code and fulfilling other managerial work seems somewhat far-fetched. Rapidly typing with all ten fingers is arguably

---

[11] More explicitly, in another text Alkemeyer describes the "forms of subjectivation" inherent in motorcycle-riding as a "precursor" of the contemporary "dismantling of social security." (2004: 38; my translation).

the specific bodily routine that can boost a programmer's productivity—but it is surely a *different* routine than using a computer mouse in e-sport fashion. On the other hand, it seems plausible that a more general affinity to computer technology developed while gaming as a teenager, along with social ties or role-models, can play an important role for future programmers' interests and career-paths. As I have argued, similar 'chains of contagion' can be observed in freeskiing, for example when one of my informants 'inherited' his fascination from an older brother and later studied marketing as part of striving for a career in the ski industry. By focusing fully on the bodily dimension of practices and striving to demonstrate the unique and predominant role of embodied routines, however, Alkemeyer, Schmidt, and colleagues overlook or ignore such more plausible routes of influence which take into account the different elements of a practice more fully.

To be fair: The direct pragmatic relevance of certain bodily routines is not the only aspect of a labour-sport homology suggested; arguably even more important are the parallels on the more abstract level of one's self-relation or body-image. The core argument of Alkemeyer and Schmidt is that the style of object use found in gymnastic and BMX is oppositional, and that this opposition is homogenous to the object-body relation found in the factory and the contemporary office, respectively. But in the case of BMX, it seems possible that the authors seem to fall prey to the athletes' verbal, or the movements' aesthetic, narrative of playful freedom and unconstrained self-expression. Can we really say that gymnastics' parallel bars "subvert," "fixate, regulate, school and discipline" (2004: 573) the body and its 'owner,' while moving on the BMX-bike is "easy, smooth, and casual" and "akin to dancing" (2004: 572)? As Alkemeyer and Schmidt (2004) mention only in passing, learning the bike tricks also requires enormous discipline, as well as extended subversion to both riders' critical gaze and the bike's merciless bodily punishment of mistakes. Further, what they do not note is that in turn, classic gymnastics also values performances that are akin to dancing, express ease and smoothness, and can very well celebrate the symbolic unification of body and tool, as in the case of the gymwheel or the use of balls and cones. What is more, one would expect that the 'logic' of industrial labour is epitomized by amorphous masses of workers and de-individualization, while today's offices demand teamwork—but gymnastics surely puts the expressive self of the individual on the stage, while BMX' performances arguably hide team collaboration in the same way freeskiing does. In conclusion, the assumption of a synchronous evolution of the organization of activities from a factory model towards an office model seems difficult to uphold. Moreover, if there is indeed symmetry between 'the' discipline of 'the' work in 'the' factory at 'the' time of gymnastics' height of popularity, and the discipline demonstrated at the parallel bars, then this would amount to a symbolic homology: a similar performance of what counted as discipline at the time (or looks like discipline if assessed today). Judging from my findings from skiing, such symbolic homologies between the general zeitgeist and a subcultural repertoire of style seem both plausible and pervasive across various subcultures. What seems questionable, however, is whether the existence of such more popular themes of performance across various practices at a given time warrants claims that they affect society at large.

Put in theoretical terms, the question is whether a certain style can be conceptualized as being in effect across wider stretches of society. In my view, such is the core claim made by Alkemeyer, Schmidt, and colleagues—but does it align with the concept of style I developed in this work? By arguing that its endogenous style is the 'essence' of freeskiing practices, and that its patterns correlate to practical necessities and functions of the immediate accomplishment of conduct (so that style becomes a tool for being a 'better,' e.g. more controlled, skier), I have put forward a different understanding. Note that this understanding does not per se deny the possibility of a homology between social macrostructures and the details of style, but could even be read as supporting the thesis that certain patterns 'picked up' in one realm can proof helpful in others—but if so, then only in the sense that when humans roam about different fields, they acquire (become attuned to) certain bodily routines or patterns of speaking and judging. What they cannot 'carry over,' however, is style per se as it is bound to specific sites rather than individuals. Consequently, the meaningful order assembled with the help (or hindrance) of said embodied residuals cannot be causally or linearly effected by other fields. Practical conduct in one field can at best be *prefigured* by elements from another—like kickers and other obstacles from snowboarding pre-configured freeskiing to some extend—but they cannot, as Bourdieu claims, *express* objective conditions (what ever that is) prevalent in other fields. What is more, the 'logic' of each field remains autochthonous, since it is bound to particular practical necessities—it is not either symbiotic or oppositional, but in most cases it is just different. Finally, I should emphasize that I am referring to the functions and necessities of the *details* of immediate practical conduct. One persistent problem of Bourdieuian accounts, however, is that they generalize life conditions and practical necessities of concrete conduct to a grossly exaggerated extent when they characterize 'the practices' of 'the dominant class' as being of a certain disposition (see Reay 2004). Expressed in the terms developed in this work, it can be concluded that Bourdieu's account of the habitus is problematic because it does not distinguish prefiguration and orientation. On the one hand, the embodied dispositions reflecting one's "personal history" or socioeconomic background surely prefigure conduct in important ways. However, this does not imply that a certain form of doing necessarily ensues—and I am also sceptical whether it does have a specific effect with heightened statistical frequency, as Bourdieu implies when studying class habitus by statistical means. On the other hand, Bourdieu holds that orientations towards style—which he calls taste—are also an inherent part of a habitus. In this way, ontologically stable but particular, effects on conduct become more mixed up with more general, but only potentially instructive, orienting patterns of coherences. In effect, the notion of habitus flip-flops between an epistemological and an ontological reading: taste is what people like and almost intuitively perceive as fitful; it is thus a scheme of aspiration of interpretation that can be invoked somewhat independently from actual occurrences or factual states. But at the same time, the habitus is invoked as a stable effecting factor for concrete conduct. In the former case, the habitus absorbs eventual discrepancies in that something can be taken *as* tasteful; but in the latter something *is* the effect of a taste, thus there can be no discrepancy between taste and conduct. Dissolving this contradiction, however, is only possible if a theory of observation is invoked, which is why the habitus seems to align well with notions of subjective of knowledge—but this in turn leaves the supposed *ontological* nature of the social in limbo.

7 From Orientation to Innovation

How can a 'theoretical situationalism' as I proposed it provide useful explanations of the emergence, diffusion, and evolution of social practices? If Alaska functioned as a kind of 'natural laboratory,' what about man-made laboratories? Should I wish to argue that the emergence of a new style—indeed of all new styles—is always and exclusively the outcome of a felicitous fusion of elements and contexts in some random corner of the world? To be sure, I do not. As my analysis of the development of single elements of a practice—skis in this case—already foreshadowed, the evolution of a practice is an inherently social process many parts of which are carried by specific purposes and are characterized by a systematic process of figuring out suitable solutions. However, I have also demonstrated that a) attending to or knowing about aspects of a practice requires said aspects to stand out against the background of conduct, something that is made possible by orienting to a certain style; and that b) the visibility of style must be systematically produced with the help of 'resources' such as collaboration, talk, or material set-ups which are themselves only possible to accomplish under the condition of an existing style. Consequently, the way I described them, workshops for ski prototyping or funparks in which incremental advances along the overall trajectory of a certain style are laboriously achieved every now and then cannot usually be considered the sites where dramatic innovations are made and practices are born. In order for workshops or funparks to have the same effect Alaska arguably had, something other has to happen, namely that conduct prefigured by certain existing elements (and possibly oriented by an established style) intelligibly shows a different, new style that is instructably (that is, repeatedly and expectably), *but not yet instructedly* available, and can thus henceforth orient future conduct.

Only on this basis, I argue, organized social processes of innovation and dissemination can be adequately discussed. I stress that describing such processes as organized or purposeful does not imply that their actual outcome was somehow predetermined or anticipated precisely. I only mean to express that some set of goals, agenda, or organizational rationale played an important part throughout the process, without this being a statement about their content or success. Precisely that 'inventing' a phenopractice or a style is not something that can be done by following a single fixed plan is, after all, what makes the phenomenon interesting. Since the process always concerns a number of different elements, several different organizations, markets, and forces are usually interchangeably at play, particularly as far as modern consumption practices are concerned. As I noted, Shove and Pantzar (2005b) descried with regard to Nordic Walking how different organizations held different views about the practice they effectively developed and promoted together, and concluded that it is the consumer who fuses their output into coherent conduct. While this is surely true to some extent, I suggest that it is the practice and not just the practitioner which is relatively independent from such organizations. That is, there must be some mechanism of coordination in place that aligns the 'output' to a sufficient extend before the consumer even gets involved, and which helps to orient the practices constituting the organizations in such a way that they align in a suitable manner (see also Schatzki 2005). More to the point, my argument is that both the evolution and the circulation of elements differs in important respects from the evolution and diffusion of style, since elements have enduring qualities which can stand out, style needs to be observed in episodes of unfolding conduct *as* a quality of that conduct. For this reason, I have argued, style requires media to be observable and differs from elements in that it orients, rather than prefigures, conduct. The following account of the 'invention' of modern skiing and its subsequent development is designed to show precisely this: While the availability of the key elements of skiing (such as ski, accessible mountains, and adventurous sportsmen with sufficient time and resources) was of course a fundamental prerequisite for skiing to emerge, its history is first and foremost one of media in my broad definition: of ways or formats of making skiing observable, understandable, instructable, and optimize-able. For this reason, instruction techniques, competition formats, and teaching principles arguable played a pivotal role—just as they did for the subsequent evolution and revolution of skiing practices.

8 Inventing Problems, Finding Solutions: How Skiing was Born

The precise moment of birth of modern alpine skiing is a subject of seemingly endless arguments among scholars and aficionados (see Allen 2007 for details). Early forms of skiing have appeared on the globe thousands of years ago, in that moving on snow with the help of skis has been a means of transportation used in mountainous regions, for example in Scandinavia or by mailmen and miners in the US before the turn of the century (Allen 2007; Benson 1977). Although such practices resembled contemporary snow-sliding in certain ways, they were also fundamentally different from the modern sport of alpine skiing. This fundamental difference, I should emphasize, is not just an effect of elementary discrepancies, of the fact that the tools used and movements made during skiing looked quite different than they do today. To the contrary, some basic principles and functions still remain the same: two skis, poles, boots, bindings, sliding, turning, and so forth. Some of these core elements have been invented, forgotten, and reinvented in different place throughout the world, before a number of more long-lasting innovations were made in the Norwegian region of Telemarken in the second half of the 19th century (Allen 2007; Lund 1996a). In my view, the various technical inventions—like the first bindings stemming from this period—were not in themselves *the* crucial moment of birth. Instead, the fundamental difference lay in the way they related, namely in the fact that the new collage of elements which emerged in Norway showed a completely different picture that was organized according to very different principles from those governing earlier skiing-for-transport. What emerged was a modern sport: a leisure practice, a play-like activity in the sense of Caillois (1961), and something that could be done competitively. Still, I suggest that the Norwegian development of what is today know as Telemark or free-heel skiing did not yet amount to the practice of alpine skiing because it was not yet clearly marked by the fundamental notion that characterizes this modern sport: the notion that skiing is at the core about *going down* a hill rather than covering a distance; and thus the understanding that the sliding movement is an *end* in itself rather than a means (see below). By being fashioned according to these two understandings, the emergence of alpine skiing falls into the broader context of the appearance of modern sports in roughly the same period (Elias/Dunning 1986); and more specifically, it mirrors an important development in alpinism: the metamorphosis of mountaineering or 'somehow reaching a mountain *top*' into climbing or ascending *parts* of a mountain in a very specific way (T. Williams/P. Donnelly 1985). What I consider, modern skiing thus emerged on the basis of the Norwegian tradition of skiing when mountaineers—many of them British or German—began experimenting with Scandinavian technology and technique in the Alps (Fry 2006a: 3–10). In retrospective accounts, the primus inter pares among them was the Austrian Mathias Zdarsky (Allen 2007, 2008; Anthony 2011: 85–87); by many considered "the father of Alpine skiing" (Fig. 10.1).

Fig. 10.1 Matthias Zdarsky, the 'father of modern skiing' demonstrating his single-pole technique. (© brandstaetter images / Austrian Archives (S) / Anonym / picture-alliance)

How do you father a practice? It should be clear that I do not wish to suggest that a single individual can put a practice on the face of the earth. However, I do hold that practitioners' ability to demonstrate respectable pedigree and tell an awe-inspiring foundational myth upon request can be an important success-factor in the dissemination of a practice; thus the supposed parenthood of Zdarsky (and others) is part of the phenomenon rather than the explanation. In other words, one still needs to ask: How does a practice emerge and stabilize in such a way that someone's authorship becomes visible (long) after the fact? In everyday thought, innovation is often equated to technological invention, and in retrospect, the design of a tool or equipment is considered the moment of birth, for example the birth of the automobile. The endless arguments about who the legitimate inventor of modern skiing really was reflect the problems of this thinking. From a practice perspective, it is clear that the sheer existence of the technological or material elements of a practice cannot be equated to its prevalence in lived conduct (Shove/Pantzar 2005b, 2007; Shove/Pantzar/Watson 2012; Suchman/Trigg/Blomberg 2002). Alpine skiing is a case in point: Skis, boots, bindings, and poles had been around for quite some time. And while Zdarsky, reportedly a "formidable gymnast, bodybuilder, inventor, architect, sculptor, and painter" (Lert/Lund 1999: 15), also made an important technical invention—the metal binding—, his success stemmed from the fact that he developed a whole system of interlocking components he called the Lilienfeld Ski Technique (Allen 2008). At the core of the new technique was a routinized movement called a Stem Turn that is still today the first thing every beginner learns: a basic way of breaking and turning by forming an inverted "V" with both skis (holding them apart at the back and nearly touching at the tips). Despite the name, the actual technique of skiing (the bodily way of moving) was but one part of a whole composed of modified, shorter skis, the new "Lilienfeld binding," a system of distinctive manoeuvres (different types of turns for different speeds or terrain), and, crucially, a teaching methodology for skiing— all framed by a hugely successful book (published in 1896 and reprinted in 17 editions) defining and explaining a very specific understanding of skiing. Being based in Lilienfeld close to Vienna, Zdarsky was able to attract part of the capital's elite to the sport, found a ski club, garner support of the authorities, and made tireless efforts to teach skiing for free—to as many as 20,000 people in total (Lert/Lund 1999: 16).

The case of skiing, in other words, confirms many of the findings Shove and Pantzar gained from studying the invention Nordic walking (Shove/Pantzar 2005b): the diffusion and re-appropriation of pre-existing elements, the local reinvention of the practice in different countries, the role of institutional contexts for linking powerful (national) meanings to the practice, and the importance of the mass media for public support and the recruitment of new practitioners. But in my view, these points primarily describe *why* Alpine skiing could be successfully stabilized and spread, but not quite *how* it got there. The list of correlative innovations made by Zdarsky alone does not really explain how the felicitous fusion of Alpine skiing came about. How was Zdarsky able to have all these crucial parts available more or less at the same time, and how come they interlocked so smoothly? Put in more theoretical terms: The pioneers of a practice do not only need to gain novel practical understandings (i.e. How to ski down steep slopes? How to build a binding that is easier to use?), but the things they did also needed to make sense, i.e. they needed to be practically intelligible (Why is it sensible and possible to ski steeper slopes? Why do we need a new type of binding?). What, in other words, *oriented* the practical conduct in the course of which the coherence of skiing became visibly evident?

The emergence of a new practice must happen in the course of ongoing lived life—it must be accomplished in praxis, step by step, and bit by bit. As I have detailed with regard to ski testing and development, the conduct of tinkering and improving must itself be oriented in decisive ways; it must entail the capacity to fail and thus include understandings of, or guidelines for, discerning better and worse. Crucially, I emphasized that practices of testing and developing share this quality with all practical conduct, and particularly with phenopractices such as learning a new bodily technique or judging the adequacy of others' conduct. Therefore, I argue that the work of designers or innovators shares many aspects with the work of a student acquiring a practice or an instructor assisting her: While they cannot have a definite idea how they can achieve what needs to be achieved, they must have a practical understanding how they can determine *that* it has been achieved once it has been achieved. Therefore, I hold that the key part of the Lilienfeld system where the principles of skiing which Zdarsky had formulated and which oriented the work of working out the technique both for the sake of innovating or refining and teaching and learning:

> "Zdarsky had formulated his version of the Stem Turn and the skiing principles that remained the same throughout his life: to achieve no-fall skiing, the ability to handle all terrain, and the skill to manage all obstacles." (Allen 2008: 8)

Only these principles or *rules* of skiing, I suggest, allowed him to develop the different interlocking elements of his technique, because only within this framework, they were observable *as* developments, as parts interlocking adequately with other parts. I can hardly emphasize enough that these rules pose *problems*, not solutions. They are not definitions of skiing in the sense that they list or define the means, elements, or style of skiing. By themselves, they do not give the slightest idea about what a skier actually does when he is skiing, or how a good ski needs to be constructed, or why one should go skiing. Nothing within the principles tells us what it actually is that the terms "skiing," "not falling," "all terrain," or "managing obstacles" describe—just like the expression Switch Double Cork 1080 does not in itself capture just how you do something that justifies calling it a Double Cork while nevertheless being an important resource allowing the freeskiers to organize and understand their doings (see chapter nine). My point is that this is precisely what made these rules valuable towards inventing or learning Alpine skiing, because what the pioneer or beginner needs to work out practically is precisely just what kind of conduct it is that brings these terms to life. They were, so to speak, the first segment of a Lebenswelt pair still waiting to be accomplished in praxis. What made Zdarsky the father of Alpine skiing in other words, was that he not just had solutions; he also had the matching problems. Only because trying to follow his rules amounts to asking adequate how-questions, one might say, attempts became solutions. Just as Wittgenstein argues with regards to rules (see e.g. S. Turner 2001), the principles Zdarsky stated could by no means contain an exhaustive definition of the practice itself, but become meaningful only if put into praxis, against a background of implicit notions and conditions. "The ability to handle all terrain," for example, raises an endless list of questions about what precisely expresses able-ness of "handling" (read: a way of skiing)—and *that* the principle raises these question, I hold, is just what made it important and useful towards working out and establishing the practice of skiing.

Consequentially, I do not wish to suggest that Zdarsky's principles themselves must have remained unaltered to be effective. As my subsequent discussion of the evolution of skiing will make clear, the perpetual deliberations about and reformulations of the orienting rules and understandings of skiing were key parts of its long-term success. Indeed, as the case of freeski style shows, such a lack of definiteness can itself be used as an important resource for keeping a practice 'alive', in that the deliberations of what constitutes able-ness or skill can become an (aestheticized) end in itself. I thus do neither wish to suggest that rules such as these guiding principles contain or represent a practical solution—as if a question would contain its answer—, nor that the genius Zdarsky somehow dreamed up his principles and then the practice's crucial elements (such as the Stem Turn) followed automatically. Both the work of fiddling with the prototype of a new kind of binding—Zdarsky allegedly tried 200 different builds before he saw fit (Allen 2008: 9)—and the work of mastering your first sketchy Stem Turns are practical accomplishments and thus lived improvisations over what the rules seem to imply. In theory, one could think about many different rules that could be used to determine whether a learner's attempts or a new technology are adequate enough; and indeed, several alternative descriptions of and rules for skiing circulated at the time, since Zdarsky's how-to-book was not the only one available (Allen 2007: 126). In fact, in Norway, there was already a full-fledged system of skiing in place, complete with techniques, technology, ski clubs, and competitions—all based on a different principle of skiing, on different rules that apparently oriented this different form of organizations and the invention process of prefigurations (such as material equipment or formats of competition) well enough. Still, Zdarsky's rules prevailed. Why?

9 Teleoaffectivity and Self-Explanation

It is of course difficult, if not impossible, to name definite reasons why Zdarsky's rules became foundational for Alpine skiing. But at the core, I suggest rested on the fact that they were able to link two completely different planes of social order very well: On the one hand, they facilitated what I discuss below as the *deliberation* of a practice, that is, they enabled discussions to be held, rulebooks to be written, and—as I will show—competitions to be held. In doing so, local ways of skiing could be coordinated in such a way that skiing became a stable, global phenomenon that could take place not just at the Arlberg, but also in Alaska. More specifically, I will argue that this became possible because something I term effective *media of coordination* emerged, most notably among them organizations, markets, and competition events. On the other hand, however, Zdarsky's principles also made immediate sense to the individual practitioner doing skiing in a particular situation, that is, they were crucial towards providing practical intelligibility. They did so, I hold, by helping to 'install' a pervasive *teleo-affective structure* within doing Alpine skiing, a "range of prescribed or acceptable ends coordinated with a range of prescribed or acceptable projects and actions to carry out for those ends." (Schatzki 2010a: 14) I want to stress that the ends formulated by Zdarsky are not just abstract goals but intertwine very closely with strong emotional states and viscerally felt achievements or failures on the slopes. This is especially clear with regard to the aim of not falling: for a beginner on skis, the possibility of falling tends to dominate thoughts, feelings, and bodily behaviour.[12] The fear of falling can be paralyzing, just as the euphoria of having made it down a slope without breaking all bones can be overwhelming. Indeed, said fear seems so 'natural' or 'biologically inevitable' that it might seem unwarranted to consider the principle of not-falling an innovation at all. What is at question here, however, is whether falling should be seen as a normal part of good skiing, or whether it should be defined as failing and thus avoided at all costs. In fact, the Norwegian style of skiing did not pay such special attention to falling because it was practiced in less steep terrain and was about endurance rather than safety (Allen 2008); and in contemporary freeride, falling is not necessarily considered a failure either but can be considered as a adequate way of braking (Freeride World Tour 2011)—just like it was common before Zdarsky's technique became predominant (Zehetmayer 2005). What distinguished the stem technique from the many other suggestions about, experiments with, or established traditions of skiing was that it is not just a way of sliding, but also a way of *breaking* sliding, or rather breaking-while-sliding. Several authors argue that the root of its popularity can be found in this fact (Allen 2007, 2008; Lert/Lund 1999; Lund 1996a).

> "The power of Zdarsky's approach lay in that it worked for novices, for klutzes. In particular, it worked for adults who had never skied." (Lert/Lund 1999: 16)

Towards understanding the emergence of (pheno-)practices, I suggest, one needs to take a closer look at processes of trying, learning, and instruction—which are, in turn, ways of coping with the exposure to the unknown and un-controlled, and thus routinely require effective teleo-affective structures to deal with. Throughout this work, I have demonstrated that 'getting' a practice must not be understood as getting the practice into the body, as internalizing certain content, but rather as getting the body in (to the) practice. I thus argue that the 'design' of a practice co-determines the *conditions* of accomplishing said practice, and that whether or not a practice 'opens' itself up easily to a (new) practitioner depends less on the inherent sophistication of the practice's conduct, but more on the practical visibility (or observability) of the current state of things. Riding a ski unleashes a complex interplay of physical forces of acceleration and deceleration of various kinds. Within riding, bodily movements and micro-routines such as balancing and adapting intertwine with the forces of gravity pulling the skier downwards and those

---

[12]The following argument is mainly based on my personal experiences from my work as a ski instructor which took place before the research project that led to this book started. It also matches the description and advice that can be found in any ski-instruction guidebook—as well as the behavior of skiing novices one can observe on any given ski slope.

of the snow surface causing friction and vibrations and dragging and twisting the ski in various directions. The rider herself, however, is not aware of many of the details of her bodily conduct, and the outside observer can also only 'know' or see what is visible or measurable in some way. As a result, methods of teaching and learning skiing are necessarily also ways of making certain details of one's own skiing knowable or visible.

The Stem Turn is a perfect example of a technique that is not only effective for meeting a pragmatic yet invisible end (such as braking), but whose sight is self-explaining: Upon seeing someone forming the figure of a V with his skis, beginners can immediately grasp the abstract concept (bending the knees, lower the point of gravity, canting the skis by turning the knees inwards, and so forth) and start to emulate the technique; and already by looking at their skis, learners themselves can correct themselves and experiment with the angle of the skis and the speed of sliding. What is more, when unfolded into praxis, a stem is both self-evident and self-explaining: At the very first, students are often anxious to do the strange V-position of the skis, but immediately upon forming it, they feel how it brakes the awkward sliding of the skis and stabilizes their body balance. Very soon, skiers do the Stem 'instinctively' whenever they feel in danger of falling—a routine is so persistent that later on, it takes weeks to get ski students to *abandon* the V-stem they learned within a few minutes in order to move on to more subtle techniques. In other words, the imperative end invoked by the not-falling-rule, the highly emotional states induced by viscerally caring about not falling, and the bodily doing of forming an inverted V-figure with the skis become tightly intertwined. The ends determined by a teleo-affective structure, it follows, "need not be conscious goals" (Schatzki 2002: 81) to be pervasive and effective. Nevertheless, the end of not-falling can also be formulated verbally quite easily, and whether or not someone has fallen is visibly and publicly evident in almost all kinds of skiing practice—and both qualities were arguably crucial for its widespread success. In sum, the V-shaped Stem Turn seems so felicitous because it is scenic in a specific way: its visual dimension provides a) the second segment of practical understanding in that both the student and a teacher can know quite easily whether or not the student is doing a stem or not, and b) instructable practical intelligibility in that it suffices that it makes sense to the beginner to 'form a V with the skis' for him to do a stem (the stem does not ab initio need to make 'intuitive' sense as a method for braking or turning). More generally speaking, I argue that for a practice to diffuse widely, its techniques and technologies must be self-evident or self-unfolding in a certain way. More to the point, they must be translatable into a verbal account, image, product design, or similar, which yields quick results once put into practice by an inexperienced practitioner; maybe like a seed that can bear a sprout if—and only if—put into the soil and given water and light. Not coincidentally, such inherent practical intelligibility also implies that a practice falls into the more particular category of phenopractices because it can thus be oriented to a style of conduct.

Skiing instruction is a case in point that allows some insights into the specific conditions that need to be met for such 'self-evidence' to work. In chapter three, I noted how the visibility of certain details of bodily conduct can be situated produced with the help of certain tools, in my example a pair of ski poles tied to learners' hips to signal their hip rotation to them. What I did not elaborate on was the work that turned the strange practice of tying ski poles to one's hips into an exercise in the first place: my own, the ski instructor's work. Just what this work consists of can be read in a study of the acquisition of teaching skills of ski instructors by Duesund and Jespersen (2004). They show that becoming an able ski instructor requires two general types of learning in that the instructor must be able to grasp two things: first, "what makes a successful process"—they call this the *task sense*—and second, "when a person has learned something"—the *achievement sense* (Duesund/Jespersen 2004: 230). Crucially, they do not describe either of the two as a kind of 'speech acts,' that is, as imposing explicit frameworks by dictating goals and postulating achievements. Instead, they frame both as (embodied) observation skills and emphasize the pivotal role of allocating one's attention and grasping relevancies within ongoing conduct. What Duesund and Jespersen (2004) are not very explicit about, yet seem to imply is that the sense for task and achievement must of course also be shared by the students—again as a way of coping with the current situation. Albeit surely conducting different practices, instructor and instructed can only cooperatively accomplish said practices under the condition of the observability of task and achievement. Looking at Zdarsky's three principles, it is evident that they make both task and achievement of skiing clearly observable at any moment of ongoing conduct for both the skiing practitioner and the practitioner of watching skiing (e.g. no-fall skiing). In other words: They allow a practitioner to gain a certain sense for the tasks and achievements determining his current conduct of a phenopractice.

Importantly, Duesund and Jespersen (2004) develop the notions of task sense and achievement sense on the basis of a model of skill acquisition developed by Dreyfus and Dreyfus (1986) which is in turn grounded on Heidegger's notion of coping as a fundamental way of being in the world. In this model, the eventual progression from novice to expert is described as an evolution of skill. Initially, conduct happens somewhat awkwardly on the basis of a set of abstract, context-free rules that point out very specific issues of concern and steps to take, until finally, situational contexts are grasped intuitively and solutions are invoked smoothly and with embodied foresight. Integrated into the phenopractice perspective and terminology, the Dreyfus model implies that, as the practitioner builds up experience, the 'division of labour' among the different elements of the practice shifts, because what is initially achieved instructedly—by the prefigurations arising from aiming to adhere to explicit rules—, is later on covered by bodily routines oriented by an overall style. This process, I argue, is of fundamental importance for the dissemination of a practice, since some elements are much more mobile than others; and especially explicit rules and images (and sounds) can be mediated, that is, duplicated, stored, and distributed in very efficient ways. Notably, the notions of style and orientation that I introduced extend the existing argument that practices are disseminated on the basis of the circulation of elements (Shove/Pantzar 2005b, 2007; Shove/Pantzar/Watson 2012), since the mediatization and circulation of style (providing orientation) and elements (invoking prefigurations) differs in certain important respects. One key argument phenopractice theory seeks to convey is that the interplay of style and elements is crucial for understanding how practices emerge and evolve, because elements themselves neither determine nor necessarily motivate their own amalgamation. Instead, Duesund and Jespersen's (2004) study of task-sense and achievement-sense shows that skill acquisition crucially depends on having a sense of style (and that acquiring a sense of style is the crucial effect of practicing a practice). Thus far, I have therefore underscored my claim that Zdarsky's principles of Alpine skiing played a key role in recruiting practitioners for Alpine skiing and demonstrated that they are effective because they describe a certain style of conduct.

On this basis, I will now turn to the second part of my claim, which is that these original 'rules' of Alpine skiing are not just enacted in emotional and visceral ways by skiers on the slopes, but were also central for enabling deliberations about skiing, that is, discussions about, definitions of, or inquiries into the nature and ways of skiing. Such deliberations, I further need to show, are not actually disagreements that draw into question the very existence of some single doing called skiing, but instead *stabilize* and help to spread the practice, even though they often lead to breaking such explicit rules. This claim is rooted in the call for a theoretical situationalism with regard to change that I outlined above, because it implies that macro processes of coordination of a practice cannot be thought of as producing something (such as elements) that directly determines situated conduct, since such conduct must necessarily overcome local contingencies generalized coordination mechanisms cannot foresee (see Preda 2000, 2006). The phenopractice-theory version of an answer to this problem is the notion of style I have sketched out: The coordination and deliberation of a practice like skiing happens within an overall coherent 'framework' of style in that the various incremental developments of technology and technique that took place over the past century are nevertheless oriented by a common gestalt-figure of skiing. The case for this argument will need to be made over a longer stretch of text in which I discuss the different formats (that I will call media) in which skiing was stabilized and spread while (and not although) being consistently discussed, re-defined, and questioned. The first step towards this argument will be to consider the precise role of Zdarsky's principles for the genesis of Alpine skiing and how they came to bear on the practical, situated ways through which skiing emerged in its modern form.

10 Style and Paradigm Shifts

The account of the early history of Alpine skiing I have been following so far holds some important insights regarding the role and nature of organized forms of standardization, monitoring, normalizing, or classifying that Shove and colleagues have found to be central to the stabilization and diffusion of new practices. Although acknowledging their importance, I suggested that such complementary practices attend to variations within a certain type of conduct and are thus pivotal for understanding incremental change of practices (or lack thereof) such as shifting the normal temperature from 23 to 26 °C. In many cases, a focus on such incremental changes goes hand in hand with the thesis that new practices crystallize over the course of many incremental changes or variations among local performances. I hold that the findings regarding early Alpine skiing imply an important addition to or alternative for this thesis. After all, Zdarsky and his collaborators (and some of his competitors) did not just randomly pile up an impressive number of small changes to the technique and technology of skiing adapted from Norway, and mixed them with adapted versions of other elements, for example from mountaineering. To the contrary, they did so in an ordered manner, within a specific framework epitomized by the three principles I quoted. This situation, I argue, is not aptly described by noting that some kind of variation and selection process took place, but should best be likened to what Kuhn (1962) called a *paradigm shift*. Notably, I do not simply mean to say with a different word that (new) Alpine and (old) Telemark skiing are different practices carrying different understandings and styles. Instead, I seek to emphasize a more specific point that Kuhn made: In his terms, a paradigm is not a set of solutions (read: phenopractices) embraced by a certain community, but rather a set of problems:

> "[A] paradigm is a criterion for choosing problems that, while the paradigm is taken for granted, can be assured to have solutions." (Kuhn 1962: 37)

As I have shown, Zdarsky's principles had just the effect Kuhn describes: They circumscribed a set of problems—skiing all (steep) terrain safely and being able to avoid obstacles—which can be solved by any Alpine skier as long as adequate skill, equipment, and determination are available. Importantly, it does not matter for the paradigm to be effective whether or not solutions are always found or are always of the same type, but instead that the same kind of problem is understood to be solvable under normal conditions. As long as a paradigm is in place, it follows, failure is not only clearly discernible, but also remediable in the sense that it can be seen as attributable to some un-normal local condition or a malfunctioning singular element while it remains out of question that the practice does normally work, that a normal solution exists. In this sense, Kuhn (1962: 35) describes what he calls normal science (science on the basis of a stable paradigm) as puzzle solving—in my words: working out a familiar 'big picture' with the specific pieces at hand. The metaphor of puzzle solving fits the position I have tried to unfold quite well, since puzzle solving, as ethnomethodologists have shown, is a situated accomplishment of 'cognition on the ground' rather than abstract reasoning (E. Livingston 2006a, 2008a; Maynard 2006). It is in this sense that I embrace Kuhn's ideas: that problem solving happens in the course of bodily and situated practical conduct (Bjelic 1996; Bjelić/Lynch 1992; Lave 1988) which entails coping (H. L. Dreyfus 2001, 2008). Although formulas and definitions are of course a central part of scientific work, Kuhn (1962: 45) notes, they need to be seen as part of language games in Wittgenstein's sense, as expressions bound to specific practices or forms of life.[13] Here lies the reason why I am using the term paradigm to help illuminate an important point: a paradigm shift is not contained in explicit principles or rules themselves, but expressed by the work of applying them. Thus, I hold that the importance of Zdarsky's principles did not just lie in the ways of talking they enabled, but in the interplay between talking and doing skiing that ensued in praxis. In other words, what gave these principles their defining role was the trouble that their practical 'application' caused. This effect was nicely demonstrated when Norwegian skiers—who considered themselves as the sole legitimate guardians of skiing at the time—questioned Zdarsky's technique and technology in several articles and books (Allen 2008: 9–10). As accusations went back and forth and tensions rose, a committee was formed to organize a contest that would establish the practical validity of the superiority of one of the alternative ways of skiing (the respective bundles of technique and technology). Just as one would expect if one takes them to follow different paradigms, however, the Norwegians and Zdarsky could not only not find common ground on how proper skiing works, but also not on how one can *find out* if a kind of skiing works: They first settled on holding a public competition, but then could not agree about just what the competitors should do. What came into question were not just the bodily movements aptly performed to ski, or e.g. the superior type of ski binding, but what kinds of doings should be considered part of skiing in the first place. Most pressing among the many issues was whether moving *uphill* is an integral part of skiing, or whether it is a different practice (Allen 2008: 10). In other words, the attempt to practically validate the adequacy of certain details of technology and technique brought one of the most important abstract background ideas of modern alpine skiing into the limelight: Alpine skiing only happens downhill; moving uphill or across plains is an entirely different matter.

11   What is Skiing? The Paradigmatic Understanding of Going Down

Let me briefly discuss how the nature of skiing as a sport and industry is tied to the paradigmatic understanding that skiing happens downhill. The importance of the essential separation between going up and going down can be seen well in the various forms of boundary work surrounding it: For example, the defining feature of ski touring is that moving uphill is considered part of the sport, and thus

---

[13] Instead of referring to Kuhn's paradigm, I could therefore have used Wittgenstein's term "forms of life" in a similar way. But the reception of this notion is somewhat problematic and fuzzy (Gourlay 2006; D. Stern 2002), while the paradigm seems more straightforwardly adaptable to causes of invention and innovation. In any event, I will link the notion back to my general concept of style to make matters clear.

something to be done manually and in a skilful manner. Still, even in this case it is clear that ascending on skis is a different practice that belongs to the same sport, and thus a test of ski touring equipment lists the suitability for going up and going down as different qualities with inherently contradicting needs.[14] In contrast, consider for example other alpine sports like rock climbing or mountaineering, where climbing up and climbing down might be somewhat different, but still clearly: climbing. The freeskiing revolution, to be sure, does not question the essential understanding of skiing being skiing down. But to some extent, freeriders have reopened the negotiations about whether the style of the complementary practice of ascending a mountain should be considered relevant to skiing, and they thus debate the virtues of {hiking} versus using ski-doos or helicopters as a question of "philosophy" (Bickel 2007; [D]). But what is at question for them is the nature of going up per se, not the fact that skiing happens exclusively downhill, which is why hiking or other matters of access cannot express style. More precisely, what divides ski tourers and freeskiers is the understanding that for the former, ascending is an athletic practice. When I joined 'classic' ski tours led by mountain guides at the Arlberg, the speed of moving, as well as participants' fitness was a constant topic of debate and performativity. Ascending had to happen in an ordered, disciplined, and skilled manner, was part of proving oneself, and could afterwards be discussed and remembered in a positive and detailed manner. What freeriders call hiking, in contrast, shares none of these features, although it is 'technically' the same thing. But freeriders consider moving uphill under the term "access," a necessary prelude or obstacle to the real thing—which is why no freerider would ever hike if he could use a lift or gondola instead, something ski tourers frequently do. In doing so, freeskiers also act according to the underlying principle of the ski resort industry, namely the separation between going uphill as a burden taken off the customer as a chargeable service, and going downhill as an enjoyable sport. To be sure, providing uphill transportation is by far not the only service resorts provide, as piste preparation or infrastructure provision makes up a large part of their costs. But in order to function as a business model, clearly demarcated 'blocks' of conduct that can be charged for must be defined. Besides marginal fields such as parking, providing food, or rescuing injured skiers—which may or may not be charged for depending on the resort—providing uphill transportation is the principal moment of roaming about a ski resort that must be paid for by the skier-as-customer. I suggest that one key factor behind the overwhelming success of this business model is that it aligns very well with the core logic of skiing that going up is not a sought-after part of the sport. Interestingly, it was not until about 2010 that this felicitous marriage of commerce and conduct was being challenged: Increasingly, ski tourer started to use groomed pistes rather than

---

[14] For example, weight is universally considered the crucial factor with regard to ascending, while in descending factors like rigidness are important—but more rigid skis are usually heavier.

the 'backcountry' to *ascend* mountain slopes, and only now ski resorts were being forced to point out that using the piste had been part of the contracted service all along (APA 2011; Reindl 2004).[15]

In this sense, I hold that the importance of explicit principles like those put down by Zdarsky stems from the fact that they enable transformations of the meaning of practical conduct in that they proffer an orienting frame, the adequacy or fit of which can subsequently become a topic of disagreement and deliberation. By doing so, they initiate a social process of working out the key aspects that make a practice what it is, such as ends, projects, or tasks carried out in conducting the practice. Notably, at close observation, the notion that Alpine skiing happens exclusively on downhill slopes contradicts Zdarsky's own paradigmatic principle that declared "the ability to handle all terrain" as crucially important for good skiing—his postulate already implies that terrain relevant to skiing is a) snow-covered and b) inclined. This situation hints toward an important aspect in Kuhn's theory that follows from his fashioning science as a language game: paradigms cannot be fully reduced to explicit rules, and therefore they can be binding for a community even though its members do not univocally agree on the explicit rules:

> "[Scientists] can (…) agree in their *identification* of a paradigm without agreeing on, or even attempting to produce, a full *interpretation* or *rationalization* of it. Lack of a standard interpretation or an agreed reduction to rules will not prevent a paradigm from guiding research." (Kuhn 1962: 44; original emphasis)

As my subsequent portray of the development of skiing technique and the accompanying endless quarrels among experts of various kinds will demonstrate, this argument is important in order to be able to grasp something as complex and multi-faceted as the field of skiing as one coherent whole. Among the experts of 'mainstream' Alpine skiing, different interpretations and rationalizations of skiing implying different techniques of riding and instructing abound, yet still it seems sensible to say that they are all concerned with the same basic phenomenon and the challenges it entails—and that freeskiing or snowboarding are a different kind of animal. The crucial prerequisite for a collection of related doings and sayings to be joined into the coherent nexus of a new phenopractice, in other words, is the emergence of frames of *deliberation* within which the different aspects of the "proto-practice" (Shove/Pantzar 2005b: 58) can be cooperatively observed, reconfigured, and redefined towards establishing the praxeological validity of certain modes of intelligibility. Notably, establishing a phenopractice in such ways is inevitably a work of *de-liberation* in the true sense of the word, a systematic reduction of complexity (to speak with Luhmann) or elimination of possibilities

---

[15] As one can imagine, all sorts of interesting problems follow, for example because hikers without skis can traditionally walk around mountainsides for free—in winter and summer. Then, there is the question of justification;, and as it happens all too often, arguments about safety or morality come to the rescue where legal logics are difficult to explain.

and thus: a loss of freedom. Importantly, the codification of explicit rules is but one resource put to work in the process, as are for example the shaping of technological artefacts and the fostering of emotional routines. Taken together, these processes then work towards normalizing—not necessarily defining or codifying—a certain style of conduct that installs the practice in the lived social world. The crucial point here is that, although different forms of working out a practice using different material, visual, semantic, or other resources can be employed, and although definite and complete descriptions cannot be produced, these forms of deliberation are by no means 'soft' or imprecise. Quite to the contrary, they must be organized in such a way that they concern *instructably observable* features of conduct which is able to produce the practical validity of certain principles, which can subsequently be expressed in 'compressed' or abstract formats such as language, formulas, titles, symbols, and so forth. 'Inventing' a phenopractice, I argue, happens in the form of deliberating its paradigmatic principles and thus its style. Deliberation is necessarily a situated accomplishment that, despite all local contingency and inaccessibility of the amalgam of praxis, must produce relatively clear results suitable for moving the process of deliberation forward.

12 Defining Moments: Demonstration and Competition

As the development of ski prototype shows, two key strategies of meeting these criteria are a) producing practical visibility and b) formalizing or institutionalizing ways of remedying local contingencies in the way standardized test methods for experiments in laboratories do. And not by accident, the history of skiing practices can be retold as a succession of such organized practices of deliberation taking place in what I called the natural laboratory that is the mountain. By far the most prominent method of deliberating skiing is holding contests or competitions: organized gatherings that not only reliably produce definite results that can be codified, communicated, or recorded, but do so in a highly visible manner and in a ritualistic format that forms emotional and communal bounds. To be sure, skiing competitions can be a highly routinized enterprise, and most regular events produce not much more than endless rankings of competitors from local ski clubs that only matter for a few people and a few weeks. But a few ski events became defining moments for the sport, because they were able to 'lock in' almost all subsequent conduct of the practice into a certain new paradigmatic frame: Whatever happened afterwards in skiing was very likely to be compared with and measured against the framework that this event made 'official' and relevant. The competition held between the Norwegian heralds of Telemark skiing and the Austrians around Zdarsky was such an event. After the Norwegians had first accepted Zdarsky's challenge to publicly prove the superiority of their methods, but then opposed his demand that the competition was to be held on a downhill-only course at the steep slopes of the Arlberg, they finally sent an 'investigator' in 1905 to what was explicitly a demonstration rather than a contest (Allen 2008: 11). The event, in other words, was by no means clearly regulated or formally planned and endorsed—but nevertheless, it became a defining moment in that Zdarsky was visibly skilfully doing something that was both different from Telemark and adequate in the given terrain. The Norwegian ambassador subsequently rationalized in a public letter: "[S]ince your alpine terrain would be disregarded in Norway, your skiing is bound to have a different character than ours." (cit. in Allen 2008: 11) And a sport newspaper reported:

> "It was a gripping picture to observe two masters as they increased their speed and each doing his own technique." (Allgemeine Sport Zeitung cit. in Allen 2008: 11)

The event thus publicly installed the notion that Alpine skiing was not a failed way to do Telemark skiing (the proper style of which was Norwegian), but a different, independent practice legitimately and demonstrably pursuing different ends by different means. As the quote nicely demonstrates, this effect predominantly rested on the fact that the skilfulness, intentionality, and difference in style of both forms of conduct were clearly *visible*. To be sure, when I say that a single contest defined what skiing meant from then on, I hold that the relevance of that meaning for some conduct must be reproduced within that conduct each time anew, and that the relation made to it can be both in the form of affirmation and deviation. I also suggest, however, that such relevance must not necessarily be explicitly formulated or expressed but is often implicitly embedded into the elements and style of the phenopractice unfolded. As Kuhn (1962: 46) points out, "paradigms could determine normal science without the intervention of discoverable rules," since a community of scientists—or practitioners of skiing, for that matter—can engage in conducting a coherent nexus of doings and sayings without necessarily being able to pin down the organizing principle of this coherence in words or formulas. Freeskiing is a potent example of a community of practitioners adhering to a common paradigm and policing violations of it quite strictly without being able to formulate the defining principle or exact rules governing their conduct. In this vein, I suggest that Dreyfus (2007: 410) is indeed correct when he argues that Kuhn's paradigms are equivalent to Heidegger's notion of style in art in that style gives "things their look and men their outlook on themselves" (Heidegger 1971: 41). What is crucial is the adequacy or validity that becomes situatedly visible, and while discoverable or explicit rules might play an important part in shaping this visibility, they cannot contain its underlying logic in a strict sense. Deliberation, it follows, should not be understood as a circular process in which knowledge is first explicated and then altered, before it is 'put back' into things or texts again (cf. Nonaka 1994), since 'the knowledge'—that is, the principle inherent in the practice—does not necessarily need to move into focus or awareness to be altered.

One important effect of this situation is that coordinative events (or what I call media of coordination more generally) often, if not always, influence the style of a practice because they adhere to a 'logic' of their own; that is, they bring certain aspects to the fore regardless of whether this was intended or not. Just like 'the Norwegians' where effectively overwhelmed by the praxeological validity of the quality of Zdarsky's skiing technique and in that way 'lost' what they did not even wanted to be a competition, Zdarsky's own understanding of skiing was later pushed aside by the powerful logic of formally organized competitive events, namely ski races. For Zdarsky, security, versatility, and control were the guiding principles of proper skiing. But as skiing became a popular (elite) sport, it seemed only 'natural' to many practitioners that ski competitions should be regularly held. Such sport competitions, however, need to comply with quite specific necessities, namely a) producing clear results in terms of winners or losers, b) appearing to be 'reasonably' consistent and fair in doing so, and c) being attractive to participants and audiences alike. Freeskiing itself is the best example of how these requirements can change a practice to such an extent that the practitioners do not accept it anymore—in other words, the defining principles of the sport can get lost among the needs and effects of competitions (depending on what one takes these principles to be). A similar thing happened to Zdarsky: his ideals of security, versatility, and control proved to be difficult to measure in competitions and were soon challenged by races that were only about speed, supported especially by British sportsmen drawn to the appeal of dash and manliness in speedy skiing, most notably by a gentleman called Arnold Lunn (Allen 2008; Hussey 2005). As the history of ski competitions shows, definite and explicitly communicated results force decisions about winning to be highly accountable, and over time lead to a strong need for 'objectified' decision criteria put down in explicit rules—and soon, Zdarsky's ideas about safe and controlled skiing proved difficult to 'measure' and were pushed to the side.

In the following decades, the victory of the racing-paradigm was almost all-encompassing. With the help of the Olympics, ski competitions became almost tantamount to ski races; and the idea to judge the style of skiing to determine an athlete's skill survived only in a marginal corner of the professional skiing circus: in ski jumping and ski flying, where points for style count alongside the distance covered (but it seems to me that the style points are not frequently decisive and do not receive much media attention). It was not until the early seventies that the principle of judging skiing style resurfaced on broader scale when the first freestyle movement started to organize contests—and it took almost another thirty years until the skill of skiing in open, difficult terrain would be judged once again in international freeride competitions on a regular basis—judged according to criteria that match those Zdarsky and other proponents of *Stilgemäßes Laufen* (riding with style) had developed a full century earlier. Additionally, the dominance of the racing paradigm was strengthened by the fact that a strong link between skiing-as-covering-distance and nationality was being forged that went on to dominate the global ski scene for more than half a century. This link was epitomized by the hugely popular expeditions of Fridtjof Nansen who crossed Greenland and almost reached the North Pole: the lonely hero conquering empty lands and winning glory for his nation—by moving on skis. This combination was bound to last: To this day, your nation will be eternally proud of you if you move fastest across a distance on skis and win an Olympic medal. Countless expeditions have restaged the heroic act of moving up, down, and across various lands or mountains on skis—and media reports will never, ever fail to mention the nationality of the practitioner. This development, I suggest, points to a possible antagonism between dissemination and deliberation that can (but does not have to) hamper either the distribution or the evolution of the style of a phenopractice: effective media of dissemination are not necessarily effective media of deliberation as well. And since, as I will show, it depends largely on the fit to the predominant media systems which variant of style of a practice will prevail and become widely practiced, the 'fate' of different phenopractices is arguably to a large degree an effect of the changes and dynamics of said media. In order to work towards this argument, let me begin by comparing two very different media that were important for the early development of skiing: first, films as medium of dissemination, and second, language as a medium of deliberation.

13 Media of Dissemination: A Short Visual History of Skiing

If my argument that the dissemination of a phenopractice requires that practitioners learn to observe and orient to a certain style of conduct, and that media play a pivotal role in spreading this skill by circulating instructive content such as images as well as elements of the practice such as understandings is correct, then the technical development of media formats should be expected to leave a mark on almost all practices. Notably, I do not wish to argue that media simply transmit 'information about' phenopractices, and that something like the 'amount of information available' (whatever this could be) is a crucial impact factor. Instead, I suggest that different media formats are capable of transporting different kinds of elements of practices (such as understandings). More specifically, they can instruct practitioners towards acquiring different sorts of understandings and skills of seeing while consuming the media content—and particularly, they are able to instruct them to seeing different styles. On the basis of the available accounts of the history of skiing, I argue that the development and popular success of the different skiing styles was directly dependent on the (visual) media formats available at different points in time. The visual, in other words, is the dimension in which the mediatization of skiing style predominantly took, and still takes, place—and as I have argued, I do not speak of the mediation of style since I do not consider style as an element or form that can be pushed "through" the medium as if it were a tube; but instead, I consider media recordings as elements subjected to local conduct in order to evoke style situatedly. From my perspective, visual media are especially powerful tools to create and disseminate styles of conduct if they are used to record conduct that is intelligibly instructive with regard to the stylistic principles that can be used to learn emulating that very style of conduct.

Throughout the history of skiing and long before the contemporary predominance of the medium. It is in this sense that I hold that the history of skiing is to a large extend a visual history. Within such a visual history, two functions of depictions of skiing stand out: On the one hand, ski films and pictures helped to 'spread the word' about the sport and its beauty, thus disseminating general understandings framing it in a positive light and potentially turning the practice into a means of symbolic distinction and social positioning (see chapter eleven). But on the other hand, I argue that there was a second, arguably even more important function: photos and films spread certain practices of seeing which are in turn intimately intertwined with or necessary for skiing itself. Far from just reflecting symbolic connotations of skiing, I hold, ski films played a much more direct role in the formation and dissemination of skiing technique as a lived and detailed conduct. First, film recordings of skiing techniques have repeatedly proved instrumental for the spread or re-discovery of a technique by highly skilled ski professionals. For example, Picard (2005) reports that the introduction of the then-exotic short-turn or "Wedel"-technique to the US was aided by ski instructors seeing footage of demonstration runs of the style shot at the Arlberg; and in a similar case, a key pioneer of freestyle was inspired by ski movies from the 1920s showing Somersaults (Fry 2006a: 225). Second, films were instrumental in that they did not only serve as a resource for the relatively small crowd of professional propagators, but also reached large audiences of non-skiers. Based on my detailed examination of practices of seeing, the visual dimension of activity, and the pragmatic use of visual media technology, I hold that visual mass media such as movies do not just fuel the diffusion of general understandings about a practice, but also of some of the practical understandings, teleo-affective structures, and bodily routines needed for conducting the depicted practice. In the case of skiing, (extensively) watching ski films can impel the ability to see the style of a skier or the beauty of a mountain, to feel the urge to enjoy skiing or the dangerous challenge posed by dramatic terrain, as well as a 'gut feeling' for sketchy snow conditions or 'an eye for' proportions and distances in mountain terrain (e.g. how large a large rock looks from further away). Some seeing skills necessary for skiing are thus arguably much more widely disseminated than skiing itself, just like the skill of 'knowing' what to look for in a televised soccer match (e.g. discerning dangerous or unusual situations) is probably more widespread than the skill of playing soccer (cf. Brümmer 2019). The wide distribution of such complementary practices is usually a key prerequisite for the sustained stabilization and success of a practice, both because it eases the recruitment of practitioners and because it facilitates public, governmental, or organizational support for, or acceptance of, installing necessary infrastructures for the practice. In the case of skiing, it is quite clear that the popularity and diffusion of the sport beyond the relatively small and exclusive group of upper-class alpinists who had witnessed skiing face-to-face was tightly coupled to the evolution of film technology. It co-occurred with and through the invention of the mountain film by the German Arnold Fanck—which where simultaneously the first widely circulated landscape films and sport films in general (Bogner 1999; Franck 2009; Lund 1993; Rentschler 1990; Seel 1992). Fanck's success was extraordinary, and his films ranked among the most successful movies of the whole decade (Bogner 1999: 5). One classic approach within cultural studies holds that certain details of conduct found in popular works of art or culture express a collective mentality. In this vein, the German mountain films by Arnold Fanck that made the Arlberg and the Arlberg technique of skiing famous during the 1930s have been heavily criticized by Siegfried Krackauer (1947: 257) for reproducing and paving the way for the emerging Nazi heroism and anti-rationality; and indeed Fanck's visualizations of landscapes and athletes were an important inspiration for the later propaganda works of Leni Riefenstahl (whom Fanck had employed as an actress; see Bogner 1999: 3; Rentschler 1990; Seel 1992). Such an approach, however, requires interpreting the films as expressions of suppressed subconscious needs or fantasies (Bogner 1999: 2–6), and thus to speculate about hidden mental conditions and discover hidden messages of the films without taking the practical intelligibility or relevance of either into account. Thus, while I agree that visual documents can provide important clues about the evolution of the style of skiing, I believe it is misleading to consider them as visible reflections of invisible features of individual or social wholes. Instead, I suggest considering their practical relevance for and influence on situated conduct such as aspiring or fantasizing about skiing. Thus, while the political motives and effective ideological impact of Fanck's works are a matter of dispute (Bogner 1999), they undoubtedly gripped their viewers at the time and instilled a longing for powder skiing as they "defined and glamorized the discipline" (Lund/Miller 1998a: 24). Even the young Joseph Goebbels—of all people—was captured and wrote autobiographically[16]:

"That was my yearning: for all the divine solitude and calm of the mountains, for white, virginal snow." (Jospeh Goebbels, cit. in Rentschler 1990: 140)

If such practices of seeing, complete with the longing and daydreaming and even the erotic connotations they entail, were powerfully evoked by Fanck's films, then they would be of fundamental importance for the rapid popularization of skiing which began at the same time (Franck 2009). This importance, I argue, does not just stem from the fact that they promoted the *idea* of the beauty of the mountains in general and the joys of skiing per se, but is instead rooted in their "masterful imagistic immediacy" (Rentschler 1990: 142), in their ability to *instruct* the viewer to see the mountains in an aesthetic framework: as heroic and sublime. As I noted in the second chapter, the ability to see the Alps as aesthetic is an important prerequisite underlying freeskiers' phenopractices of seeing lines, in that it is this framework of understandings that charges them with both emotional attachment and a sense of feasibility. If so, mountain films were an essential factor in the rise of mainstream skiing because they functioned as dry-rehearsals of 'seeing for skiing' and thus spread important complementary practices enabling the actual act of skiing. In other words: A key success factor for modern Alpine skiing practices was the emergence of phenopractices of *filming* skiing. Indeed, Fanck was as much a visual artist as he was an inventor of camera uses, a perpetual tinkerer with

---

[16] To be sure, this quote does of course also testament that Fanck's films resonated with the horrible political figures of the time; and they were subsequentially embraced by the emerging regime.

filming technology who pioneered many techniques still applied today by videographers in general and freeskiers in particular, such as a camera mounted to the skis or to the head of a skier (Franck 2009). His works assembled all the crucially elements of contemporary freeski media for the first time: skiing as a topic of filming, ways of filming, camera angles (such as shooting ski jumps from below), and technological solutions needed to go hand-in-hand to enable his success. In assembling these pieces, he also made the crucial move that evoked the specific aesthetic canon of style governing ski movies still today. Initially, he followed a purely documentary approach, thus treating skiing and mountains as content (Rentschler 1990: 142); but soon, he began to articulate their sublimity in a visual language of its own, most paradigmatically represented by images of clouds slowly engulfing austere peaks—images that seemingly inevitably reappear in probably every single freeski film I have ever seen.

Mainstream mountain films were not only pivotal in that they were able to instruct a wider audience to sense the beauty of the mountains per se, but they were more directly instrumental in that they greatly facilitated and prepared the spread of different styles of skiing in that the audience became accustomed to seeing new styles on screen prior to trying to learn it themselves. In other words: The movies did not only capture the attention and imagination of the people, but by virtue of attending to the film, they became oriented to the style expressed therein. The pioneer of the Arlberg technique Hannes Schneider for example wrote:

> "It would hardly have been possible to make the Arlberg technique so popular throughout the world in so short a time had I not had the opportunity to show what I was able to do in films." (Hannes Schneider, cit. in Lund 1993: 8)

In a similar vein, one of the most iconic and influential figures of skiing technique and instruction was an Austrian named Stefan Kruckenhauser, dubbed the "pope of skiing" for several decades (see below). But albeit being the predominant scholar and evangelist of skiing style of his time, he was not actually a very good skier himself (Nohl 2005: 10)—instead, he was an acclaimed photographer who published several books on landscapes and photography and was featured in several art exhibitions. It was this set of photography skills which proved essential for popularizing and deeply influencing skiing. And arguably not by accident, Kruckenhauser shared this double vocation for skiing technique and visual arts with many of the influential preachers of style that shaped skiing throughout its history: Zdarsky himself had been a painter (Allen 2008). And Otto Lang for example, who founded some of the earliest and most influential ski schools in the US and was a key global evangelist of the classic Arlberg technique, later became a successful movie director at Hollywood (Lund 1995). The influence of the first Hollywood production showing skiing on the subsequent rapid emergence was comparable to that of Fanck in Germany in the 1920s. Skiing slowly emerged in the US during the 1930s, and again the details of its cinematic depictions were crucial:

> "[Lang's] film, more than any other, got across the idea that skiing was a technical sport, not a wild ride down the mountain. It was a perception that badly needed propagating in the U.S. where skiing was popularly seen then as a fringe sport for crazies." (Lund 1995: 34)

In the same vein, several key pioneers of different generations and style of skiing have expressed that seeing a certain movie at a young age was pivotal for creating the devotion, but also the creativity they brought to the sport in the years to come (Lund/Miller 1998a: 25). In the case of Newschool freeskiing, the pivotal film "The Blizzard of Aaahs" in 1988 pioneered the combination of freestyle tricks and Big Mountain lines that has become the hallmark of contemporary freeriding.

> "The Blizzard of Aaahs was the first ski movie coming out after VCRs were widely adopted, so you could watch it over and over again. It brought Chamonix to your living room. It brought Chamonix to you in a much more intimate, personal way." (Obernhaus 2008: 43:54)

The significance of this film, it should be noted, stems from a combination of the 'classic' factors that already made Fanck's films so pivotal for skiing—namely its ability to lead the viewers to become attuned to novel understandings of skiing style—and the fact that such film productions are subject to a very different (market) dynamic than the institutionalized formats of defining and teaching skiing style via ski schools (see below). Ski films, in other words, opened up a novel channel through which notions of style could be circulated; and the kind of skiing that proved amiable to such movies (i.e. drew large audiences) proved quite different from that style which was able to win the endorsement of ski instruction officials. Until the beginning of the 1990s, however, this media channel was primarily one of dissemination: a very small production elite—for almost 40 years there were basically three professional ski film producers in the world—distributed vistas of skiing to a broad audience. Since then, this situation has dramatically changed in that today, large numbers of ski films and videos are being produced *and circulated* by laymen, so that these videos can be seen as responding to one another and effectively amount to a new format of deliberation of what skiing style is (see Woermann 2012a for details). This ability to deliberate style by 'striking up a conversation' about the pros and cons of different styles, so to speak, was for a long time not given with regard to films, but it had been available in the format of photography since about 70 years earlier—and it was always given, of course, in the medium of language.

14 Media of Deliberation: Talking Skiing

The deliberation of a phenoractice happens interchangeably and often simultaneously with regards to various dimensions and elements of it. Some dimensions, such as the design of a ski-binding, prefigure practical conduct directly and at (almost) every moment of conduct, while others seem predominantly useful for orienting the establishment or acquisition of phenopractices—the deliberations about and learning of (emerging or existing) practices—but do not necessarily feature in routine unfoldings of them. The two key dimension of the latter type are the verbal and the visual—at least in the case of skiing, but arguably in almost all phenopractices. Furthermore, the increasing mediatization and digitalization of sport practices creates new media of deliberation particularly in the realm of datafication, algorithmization and self-tracking. I have proposed drawing on the concept of scopic systems (Knorr Cetina 2003, 2005) to grasp the effects of the globalized reflexivity they afford (Woermann 2012a), but will focus here on the more fundamental epistemological and conceptual challenges deliberation media pose (see for example Schmidt 2015 on the case of the datafication of soccer). Before I will treat the visual dimension of the birth of alpine skiing in more detail, let me briefly note that verbal expressions played a role as well. As far as the limited (and of course never fully reliable) written sources tell us, one question took centre stage early on that seems particularly interesting in light of the specific character of riding I have mentioned: Zdarsky and the proponents of speed like Lunn where in disagreement whether skiing should be called *Skifahren* or *Skilaufen*—*riding* or *running* skis (Allen 2007: 99–106, 2008: 13–14). Explaining the importance of the difference in retrospect and in a foreign language is not an easy task, but what was at stake was precisely the question whether skiing should be understood as a fragile, semi-passive conduct (the understanding I emphasized in my own autoethnographic account), or as an unproblematic, controlled act of volition. Therefore, after competitions had proven successful in producing the practical visibility of the superiority or norm-worthiness of Alpine ski technique, technology, and athletes' skill; and efforts were made to repeat and institutionalize competing, not only the content of, but also the proper name for such events was at stake. Having written extensively about skiing and ski instruction, pioneers like Zdarsky and Lunn were apparently well aware of the power of words and the subtleties of language in expressing the unspoken paradigm behind a style of conduct with a befitting term. When Zdarsky developed the slalom discipline, he designated it "Wertungsfahren" or judged riding (Allen 2008: 13–14)—just like today's Freeride World Tour (2011) does. The other organizers, however, were keen on framing skiing as a sport discipline in line with the British emphasis on speed or 'dash' and thus insisted on using the term "Wettlaufen," literally competitive running or racing. This conflict proved to be held but one round in a debate held several times again, for example at the time of the freestyle skiers of the seventies (Fry 2006b). In the twenties, ski-racing pioneer Lunn formulated what is basically the exact opposite of the contemporary freeskiing mantra of style and beauty:

> "The object of a turn is to get round a given obstacle losing as little speed as possible. Therefore, a fast ugly turn is better than a slow pretty turn." (cit. in Hussey 2005: 9)

After some struggle, the term "Ski-Wettfahren" or competitive ski-riding was used; a compromise to some extent, but effectively a victory for Zdarsky and the notion of riding (Allen 2007: 99–106, 2008: 13–14). As things developed, however, his victory did not last. His format of judged races was quickly abandoned and soon forgotten by most, and the term Skirennen or ski race was adapted and became almost synonymous to skiing competitions in general. On the other hand, while Zdarsky's notion of adequate competition vanished almost entirely, the understandings of the practice of skiing he supported remained in circulation. Therefore, the rivalry of understandings of the very nature of skiing was carried on through the following century—and to this day, both rival terms for skiing are used interchangeably in the German: Skifahren and Skilaufen.

In conclusion, establishing or 'fixating' the normalities of skiing happened over the course of a sequential process in which alternative orientation-frameworks of style were (tentatively) invoked and then either kept or discarded. Crucially, this process needs to be understood as happening simultaneously 'top-down' and 'bottom-up' (much like vision), in that it is never clear whether the details of conduct will be adapted so that they fit the principles (e.g. inventing skis for going faster if speed is identified as the key end to pursue), or whether the principles might be reformed to fit persistent features of conduct (e.g. when the notion that skiers must prove that they are able to come to a stop at any moment was dropped as it destroyed the flow of conduct). To be sure, practices such as sports, as well as many everyday undertakings such as household work or car-driving, are an especially clear-cut case where most conduct is non-verbal, while deliberation and instruction are verbal; other doings like practicing law or managing differ in this regard. Still, I argue that one can conclude as a general principle that a) enabling instruction and deliberation is by no means the only role of the verbal or the visual for practical conduct; and that b), nor it is the exclusive dimension with regard to which both can happen. I thus agree with Luhmann (1995a) that language in particular is of outstanding importance for the emergence of social life, because of its functional capacity for facilitating spatially and temporally dispersed deliberation, orientation, and instruction on a high level of both precision and flexibility. Further, I have suggested that a practice perspective over-emphasizing the bodily dimension or the local character of concrete conduct is in danger of misrepresenting and underestimating the exceptional influence language obtains in certain matters, particularly the dissemination and deliberation of practices. On the other hand, it should also be evident that I reject all attempts to reduce the realm of the social to the verbal or semantic; and, consequently, also attempts to diminish the study of social order or meaning to the audible dimension of conduct (as conversation analysis sometimes does). One is easily misled by the (sometimes political) rhetoric en vogue within a scene or subculture, especially if one uses nothing but verbal accounts (often gathered in interviews) to construct grand narratives painting supposed hegemonic superstructures or mysterious societal undercurrents as 'really' driving the evolution of a practice. Assessed from the perspective of phenopractice theory, such accounts grossly overrate the importance of such abstracted vocabularies of motive (Mills 1940), while simultaneously underestimating the *practical* relevance of the subtleties of language as a resource employed towards accomplishing situated conduct. For this reason, the following chapter will take a detailed look at the long-term evolution of skiing styles over the last century by trying to focus not on media *content* such as rules or images, but by examining the different organizational formats within which the different media were enmeshed, and through which they were able to gain situational relevance as well as situatedly produce the observability of different aspects of the different variants of skiing, for example as a sport worth learning or as a technique superior to others.

Excursus: Communication from a Practice Perspective

> Luhmann is among those theorists who emphasize the extraordinary importance of semantics for the possibility of sociality. It should be noted, however, that it would be a misconception to suggest that by naming communication as the one essential social operation, his theory proposes a notion of society as discourse or language-use. But although he focused exuberantly on the semantics of language in his own works, language is by no means defined as the only medium of communication. More specifically, while he employs the term semantics mostly to discuss issues of language, he does at times use phrases like "the semantics of signs" (Luhmann 2000a: 113), indicating that semantics are symbolic, not necessarily language patterns. Let me briefly clarify the relation of his terminology with the one I have developed here: First, it should be noted that his notion of communication does not describe something akin to sending information back and forth (Luhmann 1995a: 143), but denotes a self-referential process within a system that employs what he calls other-reference, that treats a 'bit' of information (meaning processed as being new) as having been sent or meant by someone else. Thus, this notion would in my terms describe a feature of the phenomenal field, a moment (a meaningful figure standing out) of lived conduct framed as expressing an understanding by another person (or social entity more generally). However, what would be usually described as communication in more everyday terms would feature in my concepts in several ways more closely resembling our everyday use: a) I chartered for the possibility that more than one individual can conduct a practice at the same time. For example, I hold that two separate people can engage in a communication practice together, for example when they talk on the phone. (In Luhmann's terms, communication would happen potentially in three separate systems in this scenario; two systems of consciousness and one interaction-system.) b) This does, however, neither imply nor deny that something like information is 'passed' between the two when they talk on the phone. The answer would simply depend on the notion of information one wishes to employ. I must emphasize that a pphenopractice theory as an ontology of the social is not concerned with meaning or features of people that can be considered strictly personal. Just like the physical world is sprinkled with materiality that does not per se matter for or feature in social life, but still has enduring qualities

(unbeknownst to us until practically sublated), bodies or brains or humans might have enduring qualities of any number. c) As far as meaningful practical conduct is concerned, however, a practice perspective is highly interested in modes of circulation of *elements* of practices (see Shove/Pantzar/Watson 2012). The dissemination of explicit rules, for example, could be seen as falling into the domain of communication. Here, the role or impact of different media of communication might be considered; and some insights from Luhmann could surely be embraced in an only slightly reformulated fashion. One should be reminded, however, that the figural order of any practical conduct happens despite and because of an inherent haecceity inter alia caused by the inevitable slight invariances of particulars. Whether or not a rule must be disseminated word-by-word in order to be effective as a rule depends on the particular conduct. Thus, the spread of word-sequences or letter-codes or utterances, and the dissemination of rules or sayings correlate, but are not equal. d) Similar assumptions could be made with regard to the dissemination of understandings or bodily routines: One would need to distinguish the mobility of carriers of elements (such as bodies carrying routines) from the travel of elements themselves (such as material artefacts). For example, I have suggested a certain contagiousness of bodily routines through participation in practices exists, even if these are 'only' practices of seeing. Whether or not the vocabulary of communication or transmission of knowledge or information can be used to capture this situation aptly is not a concern here, but I have refrained from doing so for good reasons. In any event, the acquisition or embossing of routines by or into a body can probably happen in a conscious or unconscious manner, as an end pursued or 'automatically'—the practice perspective can account for a range of options, especially if they concern situated conduct of some kind. (Genetics might be a marginal option as well.) e) Finally and most importantly, none of these points touches upon the dissemination of practices themselves. Taken alone, neither the mere availability of certain elements, nor of discrete features of any elements (and thus individuals or humans) can account for the existence nor unfolding of practices, the persistence and ontological givenness of which is a necessary a priori postulate of the phenopractice perspective. Beyond the circulation of elements, I have made several suggestions how the coherence or alignment of practical conduct can be accounted for, including the notions of orientation, prefiguration, and instruction. I do not suggest that communication is a suitable term to capture this general understanding or these processes.

Chapter 11
Innovation—Coordination and Evolution

1 Introduction: Unfree Skiing?

If freeskiing is free, does that mean that skiing is enslaved? The freeskiers' answer, of course, is yes. As the adage goes, skiing is held in chains by the evil overlord called FIS (Federation International du Ski), but luckily it has broken free.[1] Yet revolution has not been declared for the first time in the world of skiing—instead, this happened about every fifteen to twenty years since the advent of modern skiing from 1880 onwards (Fry 2006a; Lund 1996a; Lund/Miller 1998a). Skiing—its technique, technology, and style—has been challenged, reinvented, reformed, and re-formalized time and again; and rejuvenating the lost soul or joy or ease or truth of skiing ranks high among the favourite promises repeated over the decades (Fry 2006a). But before looking at the dynamics and driving forces behind the evolution, dissemination and reinvention of the practice, one might ask why skiing is getting 'enslaved' time and again in the first place. Why was the spirit of riding, the beauty of the line, the rush of sliding choked by senseless rules and formalizations? Freeskiers emphasize the self-perpetuating logic of bureaucratic organizations and the conservatism of official ruling boards and competition judges—and as I will detail below, I believe their answer is somewhat plausible. More often than not, however, one will get the 'ugly twin' of this explanation, the polemic, pseudo-political shortcut: capitalism's greed is to blame. Heartless global players are raping the innocent soul that is skiing for sheer profit, the account holds, gallantly ignoring the fact that modern skiing itself is all but unthinkable without the backdrop of modern consumer society, and that especially its 'good old days' were a project driven by a rising bourgeoisie's spending power and an urge for

---
[1] As Anthony (2011: 194) suggests, freeskiing can be defined as "anything different from a traditional FIS event".

conspicuous consumption (Allen 2007; Coleman 2004). Interestingly, the anti-capitalist narrative seems to be a favourite among snowboarders, but not as much among freeskiers—and among academics. Lifestyle-sport and its mediascape have been admonished for expressing and reproducing the general reign of unauthentic commercialization proving the "hegemony" (Beal/Weidman 2003; Coates/Clayton/Humberstone 2010) of corporate overlords illegitimately profiting from what is essentially a "monopolistic panopticon" (Rinehart 2003) of "hyper-commodified" (Stranger 2010) "capitalist kitsch" (Kay/Laberge 2003) and "manipulation" (C. Palmer 2004)—not to mention the connected evils of "hypermasculinity" (Huybers-Withers/L. A. Livingston 2010), "imperialism" (Kay/Laberge 2003), "eurocentrism" (Frohlick 2005), "symbolic violence" (Kay/Laberge 2003), and a "white-male backlash" (Kusz 2003). On the other hand, authors have also suggested that subcultures echo a cacophony of voices and can thus alternatively or simultaneously be understood as a sites of "resistance" (Coates/Clayton/Humberstone 2010; Humphreys 2003), "subversion" (Stranger 2010), "struggle" (Nelson 2010), even "revolution" (Wilson 2007) and, eventually, "liberation" (Wilson 2007) from said problematic tendencies. I will not be able to refute the detailed and nuanced arguments behind this handsome collection of buzzwords, and instead formulate a more general theoretical argument in this chapter: In my view, the evolution of skiing and skiing styles primarily reflects the development of media system and technology which in turn impact the organizations and markets that link to them. In other words, I suggest that the skiing world is not a miniature model of 'the society' within which general class or power structures are mirrored. Prior to developing this argument, let me simply point out that purist laments of the abduction and exploitation of skiing in the course of commerce and technology's merciless march are almost as old as modern skiing itself. They could be heard well *before* the scope and scape of the ski industry and ski resorts resembled anything close to the time of the subcultural consumer 'revolutions' from the late seventies onwards. In 1949, when skis were made of wood, skiers usually lodged in simple huts with bunk beds, 'resorts' mostly consisted of one or two short tow-lifts, and a day ticket cost less than 2$ (Fry 2006a: 26), the sociologist, long-time skiing evangelist, and author Arnold Lunn already sang the song of lost community and inspiration, lambasting:

> "Today we struggle in telepheriques and funiculars as crowded as the slums of our megalopolitan civilization, and the surface on which we ski is nearly as hard and quite as artificial as the city pavements which mask the kindly earth." (Lunn 1949: xiv)

The problem of such *grand récits* about power and hegemony, I suggest, is that they imply that some—usually exceptionally vaguely defined—outward force breaks into the realm of skiing (much in the way of a Habermasian colonization of the Lebenswelt) and deforms, crushes, or alienates its essence or true core. The idea, in other words, is that there is something like real and raw skiing which is then commercialized, commodified, monopolized, exploited, enslaved, and so forth. But what could that 'something' be? What is it in skiing that is pre- (or post-) capitalist, non-hierarchical, ungendered, de-racialized, and not symbolic? At

1 Introduction: Unfree Skiing?

the core, skiing's true spirit lost or its egalitarian idyll to be reclaimed must come down to some way of doing skiing, some basic sliding-down-the-mountain of a certain kind. In other words, claiming that skiing is destroyed or abused implies a 'hard core' of the practice of skiing per se—but that core, phenopractice theory would suggest, can be nothing but an imaginary real or authentic *style* of doing skiing. Taken individually, none of skiing's elements define what skiing is. Thus, the isolated fact that equipment is cheap or expensive that slopes are steep or shallow, or that black or white people conduct it does not make or unmake skiing as a practice. Under any given circumstances, the elements of the practice always need to be assembled in a certain way—skiing needs to be done *somehow*, not anyhow. But just how it should be done is a matter of endless controversy, reform, and revolution; a matter that was never and will never be decided once and for all. The vocabulary of returning, reclaiming, or freeing is thus inadequate: Real skiing was never stolen, lost, encaged, or abused because 'real skiing' was never real.

If one follows my argument that capitalism and commodification cannot—despite much rhetoric—be the forces or processes freeskiing can be directed against or a liberation from, then one is in need of a more precise and adequate description of why the freeskiing revolution occurred. Particularly, this requires one to explicate how a subculture-defining style relates to organizations as well as mainstream styles and mainstream media. A good point to start from to develop such a description, I believe, is to ask why the formalization of skiing technique and regulation of ski competition that freeskiers seek to replace (and replace with what is of course simply an new informal formalization and regulation scheme) occurred in the first place. Could we not just all go out and play around in the snow, enjoying the freedom of tempering with gravity, friction, and balance? As John Fry writes in his history of modern skiing, we could not:

> "The early technique pioneers necessarily restricted the promise of boundless freedom. Their job was to clarify and codify the forces involved in turning skis so that tourists could be taught and racers coached. They were idealists, not ideologues, and the skier owes them a debt of gratitude for their strenuous efforts to turn ignorance into knowledge." (Fry 2006a: 92)

Although I suggest that 'ignorance' and 'knowledge' are not the most befitting terms to describe the accomplishment that was necessary, I believe that this statement nicely sums up the basic point of the preceding chapter. The aim of this chapter follows directly from this logic: If the early pioneers of modern skiing needed to codify styles of skiing in order to teach and compete, so did the later pioneers, revolutionaries, and idealists of skiing. What is more, just like I claimed that the emergence of early skiing was less the work of single heroes but rather the outcome of a complex interplay of media of deliberation and dissemination, I will of course claim the same for the subsequent developments that skiing style underwent. Put in a different way, one could also say that this chapter will discuss how freeskiing relates to, or is carried by, the wider social realm. Even though phenopractice theory is focused on the micro-relevancies and practicality of situated conduct as well as the 'internal logic' of the freeskiing universe, it does not need to amount to a sociologically naive neglect of the fact that freeskiing practices are situated in a wider social context. To be sure, a phenopractice perspective, and arguably any practice perspective, remains antithetic to speculating about 'the society' and other social wholes, especially if they are conceptualized as a mass of people. Instead, I suggest that the perspective enabled a more nuanced and coherent understanding of the forms of embedding and relatedness of practices to wider contexts. I will, of course, again focus the scope of the discussion of style on matters of visuality. As my comments on product development and technology implied, a field or subculture like freeskiing is enmeshed into wider contexts such as markets or industries—which are themselves effects of situated practices, or rather: dynamics happening across fields of mutually oriented practices. With regard to style, this chapter will explore such forms of relation or cross-relevance in greater detail. The basic line of inquiry implied by a phenopractice perspective is therefore rooted in the assumption that both coordination and variation of styles are necessary, and that the evolution of a style is first and foremost subject to the prerequisites and dynamics of the coordinative global 'ecosystem' carrying it. On this basis, phenopractice theory can then be used to discern and analyse three mayor types of such coordination mechanisms: first, organizations; second, what I call symbiotic fields; and third, media systems.

2 Organizations: Ski Instruction

The most important and most pervasive form of coordination within which a phenopractice can be stabilized and disseminated is arguably that of organizations (see Shove/Pantzar 2005b). Organizations, I suggest, are especially good at three key things: First, forging stable links between pre-existing elements of a phenopractice; second, organizing audiences for the systematic promotion and especially instruction of a phenopractice; and third, mobilizing resources for stabilizing and spreading a phenopractice by linking it to general understandings that fit the current zeitgeist. In the case of skiing, organizations such as the International Skiing Federation played a key role in helping to define, legitimize, and promote the sport. During the first phase of the evolution skiing, the founding of ski clubs was instrumental for promoting skiing both as a healthy sport and as a military exercise (Allen 2008: 12). By having successfully tied the new practice to generally accepted causes and virtues, and by having established formal organizations and 'special-interest media', Zdarsky and his colleagues-competitors were able to advance the dissemination of skiing through bettering the infrastructure available. Already in 1908, they acquired their own training ground, complete with electric lights and changing rooms nearby (Allen 2008: 12). In the following phase of expansion, the ski clubs and especially the semi-official ski federation and ski instruction administration bodies were key for deepening and strengthening the engagement of governmental organizations within skiing, most importantly in that a) soldiers were equipped and trained as skiers, and b) universities and other government agencies started to further systematize, legitimize, and regulate ski instruction as a form of physical education. From the 1920s until the early 1960s, nationality and official status were the two crucial sources of authority and expertise within the skiing world. Notably, this was not only a symbolic relation, but was also reflected directly in the predominant skiing style of the time: "There was something in ski technique that attracted (…) an authoritarian strain of thinking." (Fry 2006a: 100) This influence is palpable still today in the heroic ethos of ascetic endurance, discipline, and authoritarianism prevalent in 'classic' ski mountaineering, and especially its emphasis on parallel and marching-style rhythmic movements. From a phenopractice perspective, such cultural frameworks are not just schemes of interpretation or visible in the overall picture of a craft, but instead condensate in the minute details of conduct since they are carried by discrete elements of the practice. Ski mountaineering, in other words, does not just generally express the abstract ideas of military machismo, but carries forth important elements of military *practice* in an almost unaltered fashion. This might be a direct effect of the historical context emerging from the fact that practical conduct is necessarily accomplished in a 'pragmatic' manner, that is, on the basis of those elements which are within easy reach. Just like ski equipment was at the time made out of leather and wood since these materials were widely available, it is hardly surprising that the forms of instruction and organization of skiing together were adopted from the military's bodily routines and understandings almost all men (supposedly) already possessed at the time.

Further, the national ski organizations were pivotal drivers behind the first wave of differentiation of skiing styles; namely the 'nationalization' of ways of skiing. Ever since there had been a clash of 'Norwegian' and 'Austrian' ways of skiing at the beginning of the century (see Allen 2007, 2008), styles of skiing had been understood as expressions of, and belonging to, national identities; and nation-states regulated ski instruction and sponsored athlete's participation in competitions. Skiers at the time were sharply divided in their adherence to national styles of skiing such as the "French Method" or the "New official Austrian Ski System." (Fry 2006a: 94–102) The understanding that the proper legitimization of a skiing style must come from the authority of state and nation is epitomized by the Austrian "Bundessportheim" (literally: federal sport home) in St. Christof at the Arlberg, the national institution for advancing, regulating, and instructing skiing and ski teaching methods which used to be part of the ministry of education and honed a highly hierarchical logic of expertise (Nohl 2005). Still today, skiers and instructors in Austria strictly distinguish between those who are "only" ski-teachers carrying an official license from the national ski federation ÖSV, and those who are "Staatliche" (staatlich geprüfte) or governmentally certified ski instructors.[2]

---

[2]To complete the conjunction of the authority of place and state: This pyramid of unshakeable belief in bureaucratic correctness is sometimes seen as crowned by the title of *Tyrolean* governmentally certified ski instructor, since St. Christof and St. Anton at the Arlberg, the "cradle of alpine skiing", lies in Tyrol where the 'real' mountain people come from.

Notably, Austrian ski teachers where not only local authorities, but had a worldwide influence, especially in the US. A prime example is Hannes Schneider, an icon of no-nonsense skiing from the 1930s to 1950s and the prime evangelist of the Arlberg Technique. He opened the first modern ski-school in St. Anton, later emigrated to the US, trained the 10th Mountain Division that was established during the Second World War, and organized ski classes in the spirit and style he had been imbued with when serving as a drill instructor at the Austrian Imperial Army between 1911 and 1918 (Fry 2006a: 108–110; Lund 2005). In doing so, his legacy exemplifies how, first, a certain style of skiing and instructing skiing spread in tandem, as a set of co-dependent phenopractices; and second, that this global expansion was carried by a meshwork of organizations: ski schools as commercial companies, ski schooling bodies as semi-official coordinative agents, and various military institutions as multipliers, for example in that many American ski resorts or ski schools were founded or expanded by veterans from the 10th Mountain Division (Moll 2009). One key effect of these schools was that each functioned as a 'local hub' at which the practice was represented, upheld, and evangelized. In the 1950's "having the best teaching method became an important marketing tool for ski areas" (Nohl 2005: 10)—an important factor of success that reappeared in almost exactly the same fashion 50 years later, when almost all ski areas built funparks in the hope of attracting younger audiences, arguably a crucial step for the dissemination of freestyle snowboarding and freestyle skiing.

Not only did organizations provide the economic and material background that allowed people to make a living as professional skiers, that is, ski instructors, mountain guides, and so forth; but arguably most important was that they instantiated systematically organized frames of deliberation of the sport's style and methods: instruction manuals were written, course systems designed, and instructors' qualification levels defined. Further, these mediated ways of observing, describing, thinking about, and testing skiing were on the one hand unified and stabilized—for example in that national organizations still today each publish their own official instruction manual of proper skiing—, but on the other, organizations also established levels of meta-coordination through which competing style-systems of skiing and ski instruction could be compared against each other. The most important meta-organization of this kind is Interski, the international congress of ski instruction bodies, which provides another formidable example of the kind of 'theoretical situationalism' phenopractice theory suggests to be crucial for understanding the deliberation and dissemination of the style of a practice. At a biennially event, ski instruction experts and officials from around the globe (i.e. mainly Europe and the US) gather to promote and debate their different approaches to ski instruction. However, especially in the 1950s to 1970s, these events were not simply scientific conferences at which academic rigour was supposed to validate and legitimize the superiority of different skiing methods. Instead, the evangelists of style staged carefully orchestrated elaborate shows with dozens of trained performers in order to produce the praxeological validity of their methods and the visibility of their superiority (Fig. 11.1; Nohl 2005: 11–12). In this way, the global standards of

2 Organizations: Ski Instruction

Fig. 11.1 Two identically dressed ski instructors demonstrate the correct shoulder angulations for the Wedel-technique. (by Franz Hoppichler; from the collection of Verein Tiroler Skigeschichte)

proper skiing could be opened to debate, recalibrated, and then fixed again within the span of a few days.

Much like in the case of the early ski races, the key effect of these events was that skiing styles that were to spread globally must have been able to pass through this 'needle's eye': Rather than 'simply' being a practical way to master skiing on the slope or teach a beginner, they first and foremost needed to 'work' when demonstrated properly. A good example is the advent of the Reverse Shoulder Technique which is at the heart of the Austrian 'Wedeln'-technique still very popular today: This technique had been practiced locally at the Arlberg for several decades and was already described in ski instruction books in the 1920s, but "the inability to properly demonstrate and document the technique through film and sequence photography doomed [it] to official rejection" (Nohl 2005: 9). This changed only when a professor Kruckenhauser was able to a) harness the institutional resources and legitimacy of the Austrian Bundessportheim (the government's skiing technique research and education institution) in order to promote the technique and b) developed new ways of performing and photographing the turning technique that made it look easy, precisely defined, and professional (Fry 2006a: 96–100; Nohl 2005). Kruckenhauser invented a new technique of producing image sequences clearly demonstrating the conjecture of a move—before the advent of today's rapid-sequence photography. To this end, he took "a single image of several superbly trained instructors, all dressed alike and each demonstrating a different phase of the turn." (Nohl 2005: 12) Notably, Kruckenhauser himself was neither known to be a good skier, nor used 'his' own technique, nor did he ever actually invent it. However, he systematically observed and filmed skilled skiers and 'condensed' the new technique from the visual data he had collected (Nohl 2005: 10–11). Put in idealized way, Wedeln was thus developed, deliberated, and disseminated almost solemnly via the visual dimension: certain figural principles were extracted or made to stand out from bodily movement routines and then mediatized. In the form of images and staged performances, they circulated globally and were deliberated on the Interski congresses, before being 'injected' back into skiing bodies around the world—or at least, this was the idea.

Notably, the observability of certain features of conduct produced in such a way is in principle an accomplishment specific to that practice, and thus does not necessarily also 'work' within other practices, such as those of a skier trying to learn Wedeln, or a scientist trying to observe the conduct through the lens of his science in order to 'optimize' or explain it. Further, one important effect on phenopractices is that within organizations, sensitized understandings can develop that become effectively de-coupled from the wider social realm (cf. Schatzki 2005, 2006b)—in other words, what makes sense on Interski congresses must not make sense in other circumstances. Accordingly, the history of organized skiing instruction is ripe with conflicts, failures, and theoretical ideas never quite understood by the skiers on the slopes. Despite more than a century of research into the kinetics, physics, and biomechanics of skiing, its scholars remain divided—not just on the question of the optimal way of skiing, but on the question of how skiing actually *works*. For example, it is perfectly clear for an engineer that a ski can carve—that is, cut into the slope rather than drift—but from a mathematical point of view, carving is a myth (Kassat 2009), and from a historical viewpoint, Zdarsky already introduced a kind of carving in the early 20th century that was later forgotten (Zehetmayer 2005). In the same vein, it is clear from the viewpoint of biomechanics that a ski is not actively turned by the skier, but by the slope (via the friction it causes; Kassat 2000, 2009). But as Zehetmayer (2005) shows in a detailed study of a century of ski instruction manuals and methods, most of the history of ski instruction was effectively an endless debate about the question how skiers should actively turn the ski (e.g. by rotating or counter-rotating the upper body, by bending the knees, and so on) although this does not 'actually' work.[3] Time and again, he argues, skiing technique ended up in various blind alleys while producing ever-new types of stems with ever new names (see also Fry 2006a: 92–107). The reason for this predicament—which proved quite useful and profitable for the various evangelists of the newest techniques as well as for ski schools—Zehetmayer holds, is that although photographs and films have been used extensively to demonstrate the details of skiing by all of them, one cannot see precisely enough just what the demonstrator is doing in detail.

> "Here we find a phenomenon that reappears time and again throughout the history of skiing technique: Looking at others [skiing], you only see what you want to see, or rather, you are blind towards facts that do not fit into your own system." (Ulrich cit. in Zehetmayer 2005: 37; my translation)

---

[3] That is, the skies turn because of canting it and moving one's centre of gravity, while pushing it into any direction does only hinder smooth riding.

In effect, since a) writing about ski turns, b) looking at images meant to demonstrate a technique, and c) doing a turn on the slopes are fundamentally different practices, it is not necessarily surprising that the techniques most suitable for one practice are suboptimal for another. More specifically, selling books on 'revolutionary' ski methods, or becoming a successful academic in sport science requires discovering new techniques or principles whose superiority can be made visibly evident on the pages of a book, or in academic presentations and writing, respectively. What exactly skiers did when coping with situational contingencies, the intractability of their body, and the abstract tasks imposed by the rules of the newest skiing method is quite another thing—and it is quite possible that skiers do the 'right' movements when failing productively in following 'wrong' methods.

Therefore, the history of skiing is not only a testament to the effectiveness of organizations when it comes to stabilizing and disseminating a practice; it also clearly shows the weaknesses of, and problems caused by, organizational forms of coordination. First and foremost, the skiing organizations and federations proved not very successful at initiating and coping with change. For one, they tend to be very conservative, hierarchical, and dogmatic with regard to the style of skiing and the methods of teaching they accept, and thus they have been bypassed both by marketplace developments such as independent ski-schools, and by consumer-driven (re-)evolutions of styles, for example in snowboarding or freeskiing. Second, while they were very successful in forging vital links between military-inspired discipline, commercially organized but scientifically legitimized ski instruction, and the nation and its institutions, they have never been able to emancipate themselves from these links and have thus been directly affected by the loss of image, importance, and influence on everyday practices that entities like nations-states or the military have suffered. Most importantly, from the late fifties onwards, the link between nation and style crumbled: the most successful How-to-Ski book in the US was no longer called "The French Way" or "The Official Austrian Method," but had the title "Ski like Stein," named after Eric Stein, an iconic personality still today lauded for his unique and personal rather than national skiing style (Fry 2006a: 225). One important factor in this transition was arguably the long-lasting struggle that divided the Olympic committee for more than a decade and came to an end in 1974 (Fry 2006a: 150–159): the eventual abolition of the rule that only amateurs were allowed to compete in the Olympics, and the immense influx of sponsoring and commercialization that followed. When the nation-state and governmental regulation began to lose much of their unquestioned authority, strategies of legitimization and ways of speaking about skiing shifted: the late Sixties and early Seventies brought the idea of creative self-expression and unique individuality onto the slopes.

Teaching methods such as "positive previsualization" and instruction manuals such as "Inner Skiing" now emphasized very different aspects of skiing that seemed fit the current zeitgeist (Fry 2006a: 116). Skiing was being reinvented, and most importantly, ski instruction was de-verbalized. Children's 'natural' ability to learn skiing despite not understanding verbal instructions and avoiding discipline provided the visible evidence for the practical validity of the fact that "preconceived ideas about the right way to ski" only inhibit skill acquisition (Fry 2006a: 117). To some extent, ski instructors thus started to focus on what I described as pre-conscious processes of pragmatic vision, as well as the role of motivation and flow for accomplishing riding. But as the detailed observations of the multi-modal character of skiing presented in this work should make clear, "inner" and "outer" skiing cannot replace each other and are each surely not more true or authentic than the other. Ridding skiing of preconceived ideas would make it impossible altogether, and silencing instruction lessons proved immensely difficult as well—after a few years, the boom of inner skiing was over (Fry 2006a: 119–120). Still, it arguably left a mark on ski instruction and the influence of the ski schooling bodies, since they had officially embraced a radically different understanding of skiing style as individual. The 'discovery' that children can teach themselves to ski went hand-in-hand with the notion that "hidden within each of us is a talent, an individual style of skiing." (Fry 2006a: 119) Style, in other words, needed to be teased out of the skier's body, rather than embossed into it. An understanding fundamental to contemporary freeskiing had sneaked into the formalized accounts of disciplined skiing. How did it happen? As I argued, the structures and logics of rule-making organizations are necessarily somewhat hermetic and unable to instigate fundamental change. The impulse must come from the outside, but an outside that is acknowledge as relevant and legitimate within the organizations. The rebellious zeitgeist, however, was outright antithetical to the whole concept of governing skiing in all its details, and thus Interski could have hardly embraced it. Still today, customer demand is not a concept that the official heralds of safe and sound skiing officially acknowledge, in part because they are governmental and academic organizations which by definition should not bow to the wishes of laymen who cannot always know what is good for them. Instead, the source of the vital rejuvenation of ski instruction had been ski racing. The new psychological techniques that soon swept mainstream skiing had originated in racing, and the results they produced could muster the full moral authority of winning (Fry 2006a: 116).

3 Symbiotic Fields: Ski Racing

The sustained success and ongoing evolution of skiing, I want to argue, is to a great extend due to the fact that ski racing (more precisely: formally organized and internationally visible forms of competition) has functioned as a mechanism of coordination and variation. While the official organizations such as ski instruction bodies or the FIS, have proven effective but conservative, ski racing has proven essential in that it provided legitimation for many disruptive innovations. For example, for several decades the success of a new equipment technology depended on its adaption in race skiing (Fry 2006a: 77–80). Initially, both average and professional skiers were reluctant to switch to breakthrough novelties such as the metal or fibreglass ski, plastic ski boots, or alloy ski poles—instruction bodies, racing teams, and mainstream consumers united in conservatism. Only after top athletes served as pioneers and succeeded in international competitions when using the new equipment, the innovations' positive effect became a 'fact' one could barely ignore: Adaption trickled down from competing racers trying to stay level in the technological arms race to instruction bodies bowing to the professional expertise of racers and their coaches' quasi-scientific knowledge, and further to the eager 'power-users' among skiers seeking to profit from state-of-the-art equipment both practically and symbolically. The special importance of ski racing, in other words, yields from a) its international visibility enabling global coordination and b) its apparent ability to provide non-ambiguous 'hard facts' produced by a purified, almost scientific rationale: win or lose, faster or slower. The authority of winning that ski races provide thus enabled the race circuit to provide adjustments for the wider skiing universe, making it a mechanism of coordination and deliberation of standards or ideals. Yet while winning per se is unambiguous, reasons for success are of course always open to debate. In consequence, professional racing has both a stabilizing function—do not question what works for the pros, since they obviously know—*and* opens the field of skiing to innovation, albeit usually in weak doses. Borrowing a term from systems biology, one could say that the mainstream market and the specialized subfield are linked in symbiotic co-existence: The subfield coordinates the mainstream practice, so that organizational hierarchies, explicit rules, and the normal set-up of equipment are not continuously called into question within mainstream skiing itself, and thus the organizations-market nexus is being stabilized. From a phenopractice perspective, this *inhibition* of change is crucial for said nexus to work. Although the current public discourse—as well as much of the literature in marketing—emphatically praises the value of never-ending (technological) innovation, trendsetting, and perpetual change, I suggest that both bureaucratic organizations and commercial enterprises can only cope with change in reduced doses. Large investments in ski resorts, product development, or international competitions all require relatively stable long-term planning; as does the recruitment of professional expert practitioners to a practice. Professional careers, brand building, as well as the accumulation of personal status or fame all take relatively long and thus depend on the sustainable existence of organizations, markets, and media outlets. For mainstream practitioners to be recruited to and kept fascinated by a phenopractice—especially one that is as expensive, intensive, and dangerous as skiing—, in turn, the existence of images, role-models, equipment, and much more is necessary (Shove/Pantzar 2005b, 2007; Shove/Pantzar/Watson 2012)—and these require relatively stable styles. Additionally, the average practitioner going skiing for a week or two every year cannot re-purchase new equipment and different clothing every year, and as the case of carving shows, re-learning a new style of skiing even once in a lifetime is a challenge most skiers avoid. To sum up, investors, companies, organizational bodies, professional athletes and industry professionals, media planners, average practitioners and aspiring beginners all depend on the overall stability of the style of a phenopractice—and in the case of skiing, they have all been reluctant or unable to follow certain innovations or trends in technique, technology, or fashion.

This need for stability alone, however, does not in itself seem to necessitate the development of a symbiotic relationship with a detached symbiotic field. By my definition, fields of phenopractice can organize the routinization of conduct and the normalization of phenomenal conditions, since the stable routines, understandings, and (usually) explicit rules are a precondition for phenopractices to exist. Many mundane practices such as walking down the street seem to remain much more stable than skiing did so far, and arguably they do so because no symbiotic field has emerged—at least, until Nordic Walking entered the stage, and if one assumes that racewalking does not orient mundane walking.[4] The practice of skiing, however, must re-attract participants from the cities back to the mountains after every summer anew (lately, indoor ski halls help this task), and the ski industry needs to collect relatively high and recurrent spending from consumers to make the necessary investments. Arguably, an eventual evolution of style is crucial for this and similar fields of consumption practice not to lose its attractiveness: a stagnation of style causes an absence of exciting novelty and thus few chances for aspiring newcomers to gain success and status relatively easy. As freeskiing makes very clear, optimism and enthusiasm are important resources for a self-sustaining scene and industry to emerge both on the slopes and in trade fair halls. Freeskiing's precarious economy caused by uncurbed enthusiasm, and the many bankruptcies of overoptimistic ski resorts and equipment brands during the 1980s, however, also serve as reminders that fields need to find and sustain a delicate balance between stability and change, between optimism and reluctance, between creativity and conservatism. Expressed in theoretical terms, what needs to take place is an evolution of the style rather than just uncoordinated waves of changes in single elements of a phenopractice (such as new products or places), which always threaten the routine accomplishment of amalgamation and flow. Symbiotic fields seem to be especially helpful to achieve such a sustainable evolution, because they 'offer' re-vitalizing new orientations, but they do so without de-stabilizing the whole field and practice. In a way, the task of variation and selection of styles is being 'outsourced' to them from the main field. The largely homogenous field of tennis, for example, provides an interesting case compared to skiing: Having emerged about the same time in similar circumstances, both sports also shared a boom-time during the seventies and eighties—and several important brands and innovators such as Howard Head who revolutionized the design of both skis and tennis racquets (Fry 2006a: 78). From the eventual demise in attractiveness and market size both sports suffered in the late eighties or mid-nineties respectively, however, skiing seems to have recovered much more successfully, arguably because of the successive advent of freestyle, snowboarding (to some extent), carving, and freeskiing (Coleman 2004; Fry 2006a; Lund 1996a). Tennis,

---

[4] One could consider whether the mass media or commodity markets could function as generalized symbiotic fields or systems for such everyday practices, in that they offer re-definitions of a style for said practices—an idea that could be spelled out in the terms of Luhmann's thoughts on markets (1999) and mass media (2000c).

3 Symbiotic Fields: Ski Racing 505

in contrast, was never able to reinvent itself in such fundamental and attractive ways, has lost many practitioners, and still seems largely dependent on the classic techniques, rules, and forms of competition.

In the case of carving, ski racing was pivotal for the widespread acceptance of the technique as well as the rejuvenation of the ski market it caused. At first, race skiing coordinated the global skiing style and market by *devaluing* all attempts to change the authoritative ways of skiing and ski-building towards carving and shaped skis; but later it fuelled the universal embracement of carving by effectively all ski manufacturers and ski schooling bodies, thus coordinating through the overwhelming legitimacy provided by winning races (Lund/Pfeiffer 1993; Masia 2005). Notably, it should not be concluded that race and recreational skiing are governed by the same laws or logic, or that all 'style switches' occurring in racing were inevitably copied in mainstream skiing. One mayor development of technique in race skiing, for example, was prompted by the introduction of flexible slalom poles which allow the racer to ski a line much closer to the pole (since the pole retracts when it is hit) and necessitate a different posture and positioning of arms and hands. But while bodily routines, style ideals, talents required, and understandings expressed in race skiing changed "dramatically, (…) the new arms-and-hands slalom technique has had virtually no influence on the way recreational skiers make their turns." (Fry 2006a: 106) Symbiotic fields like race skiing, in other words, should be considered a different field (or subfield) of practice because they are oriented by a different style (and use many different elements). In this regard, they differ from organizations such as companies or media distributors which are well capable to provide innovations in terms of single elements, but arguably not of developing whole new styles. For example, a single company might invent an important new technology, but its widespread acceptance and circulation must usually be aided by distributors, the media, and so forth. Further, other elements such as skills or understandings must often be slightly adapted so that the innovation can fit into the current style.[5] I should emphasize that by saying that a symbiotic field has its own style, it follows that subfield and mainstream cannot share the same style, and that a style cannot be directly imported from either. Instead, the symbiotic field offers an alternative set-up of elements, some of which can then circulate into the main field, but this does not mean that the styles of the two fields become synchronized. Quite to the contrary, it seems that mismatches frequently occur when mainstream customers strive to adopt brands, sayings, or heroes from specialized fields, for example when skill and equipment do not match. As the freeskiers' disdain for tourists and so-called {gapers} shows, participants of subfields are eager to point out that while some elements might be

---

[5] In the same way, I suggest that single media phenomena such as influential books or movies can hardly be said to introduce a new style (and not just a fashion trend or saying) on their own. There are cases, however, where single companies (or the military or church in earlier epochs) were able to introduce and spread a whole bundle of elements at once, for example when the iPad or iPhone stabilized and popularized tools, ways of using, and a certain image of the latter at once—yet still the mass media played an important part in this feat.

shared with the mainstream, the style of conduct remains exclusive (see Wheaton 2000b). For organizations and participants of the mainstream, however, these differences in style are usually not problematic. They are able to profit from the new prefigurations imported into their conduct by adapting subfield-specific elements, but they do so selectively and without being bound by the same high aspirations or strict rules. One might add, however, that the ways of profiting from such imported elements can differ greatly between organizations and practitioners. Again, the case of carving provides an interesting example.

The sweeping success of the carving technique and technology in racing occurred because it enabled faster and thus 'better' skiing—but the subsequent widespread adaption of carving ski in mainstream skiing did not necessarily mean that many people actually started to conduct the very practice of carving at all (Lund/Pfeiffer 1993: 19). Most customers would buy new carving skis that were considerably shorter in length than those skis they had used before, since this was advised by both manufacturers and the ski instructor associations as the international wardens of 'proper' skiing technique and equipment. The reasons for the shortened standard length lay in racing, because it was discovered that optimal speed was gained on skis about twenty or thirty centimetres shorter than classic race skis (Masia 2005). Since manufacturers, ski schools, and advanced skiers all followed the examples set by the professionals in racing, the broad majority of less adept skiers followed suit as well. Subsequentially customers were delighted that these new models were so much easier to turn and control. For example, I myself still vividly remember how I switched from 210 cm metal-plated monstrosities designed for downhill racing to 175 cm slalom carver that weighted about half as much. While my technique these days never came close to anything resembling either downhill or slalom, skiing did become considerably easier and more enjoyable for me. But ironically, this was predominately the effect of the shorter ski length rather than the carving-shape per se. What is more, most skiers continued to ski the now 'old' style they had come to learn, which is still somewhat true even twenty years later (Fry 2006a: 107). Seen through the lens of skiing 'by the book,' that is, the proper way of skiing taught by semi-official ski federations, the average customer thus switched from mediocre, semi-improvised skiing on longer skis made for racing to mediocre, semi-improvised skiing on shorter skis made for race-carving—but the effect for the skier was enormous. As Fry (2006a: 107) notes, more skilled skiers adapted their style to the different skis over time—but only very few ever engaged in race-style carving. In other words, the understandings of, and reasons given for, adapting elements from the highly symbolic and highly visibly contexts of symbiotic fields can differ to a large extend without hindering the dissemination of said elements. Therefore, the symbiosis that takes place works because it is beneficial to the mainstream field (for example when carving revived the industry), but whether or not they help concrete conduct is a different question. For this reason, I suggest that the phenopractice perspective is well-equipped to grasp and explain the specific relationship between symbiotic fields and the dynamics of innovation and change in style that emerge from it. As the case of the carving ski demonstrates, it is one the one hand necessary to consider how elements (material or symbolic) present themselves to the single practitioner during their use, rather than drawing conclusions from 'the discourse' or symbolic macrostructures. But this slice of the world visible through the eye of the practitioner, on the other hand, should not be equated to subjective meaning bound to subjective intentionality, for example if one strives to understand why carving worked: It is perfectly possible that consumers felt they were 'really' carving like the pros with the new skis, yet the possibility of them doing so cannot be traced back to nothing but the social meanings they had internalized, or the implicit skills (or knowledge) that were at work. The positive, emotional experience they had clearly depended on the specific interplay of the material features of the ski and the style of riding they had been taught—and the positive image of these new ski they had (supposedly) internalized had emerged because the same ski fit into the specific arrangement of racing in a particular way. In sum, neither ski designers, nor marketers, nor ski instructors, nor practitioners necessarily ever consciously *intended* or even noticed at the time that carving succeeded for the reasons it (arguably) did, so that explanations which take only these levels of social order into account seem to be bound to jump too short. Public symbolic meanings, ideas held (by different groups of people), bodily skills applied, material effects taking place, and economical forces at work pointed into very different directions; expressing different goals, intentions, logics, knowledges, symbolic orders, rules, and so forth. Attending to any of them in isolation (e.g. by exclusively interviewing developers, analysing business models, or conduction an auto-ethnography of learning skiing) would have yielded internally consistent, yet inherently one-dimensional accounts.

Does this imply that a plausible analysis giving due credit to these different aspects or dimension must necessarily be utterly complex? I do not think so. Instead, a phenopractice theory account of the success of the carving ski seems well-suited to explain many of the inherent tensions and frictions within skiing without having to draw on rather unspecific factors such as corporate power (which can crumble very fast due to market dynamics), or echo problematic authenticity-claims voiced by parties deeply tied up into the logics of specific fields. For example, rather than accusing evil-minded marketers of making false promises and spinning phony stories to lure innocent consumers into buying useless new skis, it seems more adequate to acknowledge how aspiring athletes and equipment developers, entrepreneurs and media producers, ski federation officials and ski instructors' educators all routinely look to those few cases—such as top-level racing or freeski movies—where the aesthetic and pragmatic logic of the specific genres of skiing practices are spelled out in near-perfection. But the understandings that emerge from and are carried in those peak phenopractices—the tools, techniques, norms, standards, rules, brands, or fashions found there—do not necessarily lend themselves well to appropriation and domestication in more mundane, less gifted settings. Or rather: they do lend themselves well, but to the 'wrong' ways of doing, and for unnoticed reasons. And while racing officials might cringe at the sight of mainstream 'pseudo-carving', just like freeskiers do when witnessing 'tourists' complete lack of style, these frictions are side-effects of the necessary independence in terms of style between the two fields; an independence which is vital for the symbiosis to work. Its key advantage, after all, is that just like companies might offer innovations, fail, and vanish without harming the stability of the market per se, symbiotic systems might emerge and fail without causing fundamental problems to the mainstream. Despite their relative independence, they can function as a coordination mechanism and innovation lab for style without de-stabilizing the mainstream: When racing is caught in a deadlock, or developments occurring there seem to endanger the structures of the mainstream field, innovations can be rejected and reliable orientations kept. Even better: A field of practices can even sustain and profit from several alternative symbiotic subfields, and it can shift interest and support from one to the other without risking its overall stability. The first freestyle revolution in skiing in the seventies is a prime example.

4 Media Systems: The First Freestyle Revolution

The long birth, rapid rise, and eventual stagnation of Oldschool freestyle skiing is both of key importance for understanding the nature and context of contemporary freeskiing, and a prime example of the contradicting roles of organizations and media systems for symbiotic fields. But above all, it arguably provides important insights into the nature of rebellion and revolution within consumer culture. Like almost all subcultures of consumption, lifestyle sport cultures are usually thick with heroic talk of resistance, creative breakthroughs, and unheard-of novelties—and freeskiing is surely no exception. Skiing, however, has seen revolutions driven by an enthusiastic, independent, entrepreneurial and rebellious youth re-occurring about every ten to fifteen years at least since the mid-sixties. First came the long-haired, pot-smoking, anti-corporate, undogmatic freestyle skiers; then the long-haired, pot-smoking, anti-corporate, undogmatic snowboarders; and then the freeskiers, also long-haired, pot-smoking, anti-corporate, and undogmatic at first—until they underwent a remarkable (dare I say revolutionary) shift I will discuss later. Not only were all of these supposedly one-of-a-kind revolutions surprisingly similar in many respects, but at least in part, the practices and styles they had allegedly invented were not quite as new as they seemed: Rather than being a sudden outburst of creativity, they had been a long time coming—in the case of the first freestyle revolution, something had been brewing even before Zdarsky made his first turns (Lund/Miller 1998b). In order to understand the long history of freestyle skiing—freestyle being defined here as a ludic approach to skiing, a performance of aesthetic jumps, figures, and tricks (Lund/Miller 1998a)—, let me briefly consider the temporal lifecycle of phenopractices. Elements of practice, I argued, are enduring, able to hold a certain potential for prefiguration for an extended length of time. Practices, in contrast, need to be continuously performed, or otherwise they undergo what Shove and Pantzar (2005a) have called "social fossilization": they die out and leave nothing but material or semantic residues.

Sometimes, Shove and Pantzar add, these residues might be re-integrated into practical conduct again, and in some cases, this might mean that a practice has been dormant rather than dead. This idea, however, poses an important question, since cultural history knows many examples of pseudo-traditions and reinventions of the past, sometimes in the form of whole epochs such as in neo-classic or neo-gothic art. Thus, how to discern revivals of an old practice from a re-appropriation of certain elements (and sometimes the two practices might share nothing but the name or certain symbols)? The answer following from the argument developed in this book must be: according to their style. Style itself, I suggested, cannot be stored for longer periods, since its observability for a practitioner must be practically accomplished. Discerning reinvention and revival, it follows, must be practically accomplished. However, I cautioned against the notion that the conditions of the possibility of such an observation are to be found dependent on or 'in' the observer alone. Thus, two instances of observation might yield different conclusions, for example because they put different understandings into practice: but whether or not old and new style can be found to be the same depends on several other factors, as well as the way they interplay. What is more, I argue that styles have certain *persistence*. To some extent, this is due to the fact that all conduct needs orientation, and thus some tried and tested style that fits will be needed. When a style dies, in other words, it will usually die slowly and be replaced by a somewhat similar way of conduct that fits the various persistent elements of the phenopractice still in place—unless, of course, key elements themselves suddenly go amiss as well. Radical innovation of phenopractices is rare. The persistence of style, however, is arguably not rooted in the unavoidable necessity of orientation alone. Instead, I hold that successful styles are those which can fall in place somewhat automatically; that is, they seem to work *themselves* out to some extent, in that their accomplishment is likely not just due to the nature of the elements integrated, but also due to their 'internal logic', due to the conditions of integration they themselves govern. The origins of Oldschool freestyle skiing are a good example. There seems to be something in doing skiing that invites playful experimenting with the forces of gravity and the possibilities of movement during riding, sliding, and jumping. Indeed, several skiing techniques already involve small hops or jumps (e.g. short powder turns on steep slopes or in moguls), and twisting and turning the extremities in various ways to keep balance and rhythm is an essential aspect of all skiing. The otherness of freestyle that made it rebellious and new is therefore primarily rooted in the understandings and symbolic values associated with it—while all skiing is 'trick-skiing' to some extent, a performance of artful and 'artificial' movements.

Seen from this perspective, it is not the persistence of freestyle that seems astounding, but rather its prolonged absence from the global skiing stage. After all, style-minded trick-jumping was one of the first 'disciplines' of skiing that emerged in Norway decades before Alpine skiing appeared: In Norway, ski jumping of roofs and self-made jumps had been practiced in competitions since the mid-1800s and quickly became a symbol for a nation that had just won independence (Lund/Miller 1998b: 14). In the decades that followed, however, the initial popularity of the idea that jumps should be inventive and playful gave way to the notion that skiing is about covering distances, and the development of the Telemark technique and cross-country races greatly accelerated this trend. While style was still being judged in ski-jumping, it was now supposed to express control and discipline rather than inventiveness; a notion that Zdarsky adopted when he sought to prioritize safety in skiing and held competitions where style was judged according to safety. As I described, however, his ideas soon lost out to the imperative of speed, and races in which distance-per-time was the only dimension to be measured became the uncontested standard. In ski jumping, the priority of distance covered soon came first as well, although the judgment of style remains a (less important) aspect related in competitions still today. This codified and closely regulated style in ski jumping, however, strictly adheres to the logic of usefulness, safety, and control; punishing all deviation from the 'optimal' and perfectly safe flying and landing. In effect, the notion of visible style as an end in itself had not only vanished from all forms of organized competition, official instruction, or media coverage, but was also systematically de-legitimized and criticized by the guardians of correct skiing wherever it appeared (Lund/Miller 1998b). Still, freestyle skiing did not die. From the turn of the century until the 1950s, reports and images of ski-tricks appeared in different media—some of them astoundingly similar to those 'invented' later—, and individual performers reached passing, local fame. Freestyle skiing lingered on undead, occasionally performed by master skiers to amuse and impress the audience (Lund/Miller 1998b: 15). It took until the later Sixties that the situation changed dramatically: Within a few years, thousands attended (Oldschool) freestyle competitions and watched screenings of freestyle ski movies; companies offered scores of specific freestyle-ski models, lucrative sponsorships and international competitions allowed whole teams of freestylers to ski professionally, and many ski schools offered freestyle classes (Fry 2006a: 219–234). Considering the enormous attractiveness it garnered later, it seems somewhat astounding that freestyle skiing had remained unpopular for so long. Portraying the advent of skiing, I have argued that the success of Alpine skiing was due to the fact that a 'full package' had emerged, a bundle of co-dependent technology, technique, instruction method, a book, a ski club, favourable media depictions, and so forth. But if one takes a close look, all of these necessary ingredients were actually already available long before freestyle took off: One of the first picture of a Somersault on skis dates from 1907, a book described trick ski methods in 1929 (and another in 1956), the hugely successful Arnold Fanck ski movie "White Ecstasy" presented trick skiing to the mainstream in 1930, and specifically designed shortened trick-skis were produced during the 1930s (Lund/Miller 1998b: 14–16). Still, despite the considerable skill of some practitioners, all these crucial elements never linked up in a sustainable way, and freestyle tricks remained a marginal phenomenon. From what is known, it seems implausible that practitioners did not have fun, found the practice unbearably difficult to learn, or unacceptably dangerous. In other words, the conduct per se seemed to work just fine. What was missing?

4 Media Systems: The First Freestyle Revolution

In a word: the audience. Based on my findings from contemporary freeskiing, it seems clear that the presence of an audience is a necessary condition to engage routinely and persistently in the performative production of freestyle skiing. More specifically, since the visible style, the figures and tricks performed are the effective end or product of doing freestyle, and since style has to be seen in order to exist as a social thing, it is plausible that freestyle skiing remained marginal because it failed to draw (sufficiently skilful) audiences. This failure had two aversive effects: On the one hand, the pioneering practitioners of ski tricks were lacking important resources that are key for acquiring skills in today's funpark, namely the emotional support, the 'visual acquisition' of tricks through watching others, and the observations of one's own performance 'from the outside.' On the other hand, very few new participants could be recruited to the practice from among the audience. Thus, although skills, tools, understandings, and places for conducting the phenopractice existed and where successfully combined now and then, the dissemination of the necessary practices of seeing the beauty of the performances did not reach a level that allowed economies of scale to occur until the late sixties. What I broadly called a lack of audience for freestyle, in other words, can be better described as a lack of practices of seeing the style of freestyle; and I argue that this was due to both a lack in understanding and opportunity. Let me address the former first. Schatzki (2010a) argues that, for a new practice to be established, two kinds of understandings need to spread: common practical understandings and common general understandings. In the case of freestyle, practical understandings are those that allow an on-looker to 'get' what is going on, to be interested, fascinated, and eventually emotionally touched. As I have shown, these skills are predominantly, if not exclusively, acquired through what Lave and Wenger (1991) called "legitimate peripheral participation," in this case, watching tricks again and again, especially in the presence of others. The lack of practical understanding, it follows, was thus basically an effect of the lack of opportunity to watch freestyle skiing. Towards explaining the scarcity of practical visibility of the art, however, the absence of fitting general understandings seems an important factor—or, more specifically, the absence of fitting and positive associations with doing and watching freestyle. The common descriptions and self-descriptions of the first and second freestyle movements focus exclusively on this aspect: The semi-official bodies of ski instruction and racing had neglected or de-legitimized this form of skiing since it did not conform to their ideology and even threatened their authority. When Arnold Fanck showed trick skiing in one of his films in 1930, for example, it was performed by a "ski clown" (Lund/Miller 1998b: 14), while the lead actors, including movie star Leni Riefenstahl, displayed disciplined and 'proper' skiing. Only after the zeitgeist did no longer firmly embrace the values of discipline, order, and national pride from the Sixties onwards, their tight grip on skiing could be loosened, and the "protean period" (Schatzki 2010a: 16) of Oldschool freestyle skiing dawned. The new ideals of individual freedom and self-expression, spirituality, rebellion, and creativity linked up perfectly with the expressive and eccentric performances now seen on the slopes (Fry 2006a: 219–234, 2006b; Lund/Miller 1998a). The freestyle boom, one might argue, was thus only one symptom of a seismic shift that occurred in skiing per se: style was no longer thought of as belonging to, or an expression of, a nation and its institutions, but rather to individuals and particularly individual stars. Set within this fundamentally changed framework of understandings, the marginality, deviance, creativity, and individuality that could easily be seen in freestyle now provided effective ends or motives for attempting to witness freestyle and immerse oneself into the beauty of this sparsely known art. In this vein, skiing could be well described as following the historical development of what Andreas Reckwitz (2000a, 2012) called "subjectivity practices" (building on Foucault)—practices of 'discovering' and expressing one's personality or subject-hood, for example by diary-writing (especially at the turn of the last century) or through tasteful consumption. During the Sixties, Reckwitz argues convincingly, one could witness the raise of a new kind of ideal subject-hood: the creative subject, a subject which's individuality, likeability, success, and (paradoxically) conformity is evidenced by its creative expression, uniqueness, and aesthetic productivity in the widest sense. While the classic alpinists of the modern era found proof of their true being in the manliness, valour, strength, discipline, and dash of semi-militaristic mountaineering and ski racing, the Seventies, freestylers would thus unleash their true inner self in peaceful and playful dancing with mother nature's elements.

Without a question, what I called the shifting zeitgeist was thus an important factor in the occurrence of the freestyle revolution. However, I believe it would be misleading to portray it simply as an effect of this larger shift, because it was but one factor in the successful dissemination of the practice of seeing freestyle. Specifically, I criticized the notion that the doing of freestyle skiing per se could be seen as somehow directly coupled to 'the society', or that it amounted to direct resistance against macro hegemonies or power structures—neither account fits the indirect and multidimensional relation outlined here. Concluding that general understandings motivate opportunities for seeing, which in turn produce practical understandings, which in turn equals dissemination, I suggest, yields only an incomplete picture. Particularly, such a 'cultural' perspective harbours an implicit individualism and voluntarism suggesting that motivations or ends stemming from general understandings are sufficient for opportunities of conduct to be wilfully arranged. Contrary to this assumption, however, a closer look at the increase in opportunities of seeing freestyle during the sixties produces a more complex picture.

Throughout this chapter, I emphasized that the production of the visibility of a style of skiing was key to its widespread adaption. Particularly, I described two different forms of dispersion of the practical visibility of skiing that were important: On the one hand, the seeing-in-presence that occurred during organized performances (in the context of ski instruction techniques); and on the other, mediatized seeing. Not surprisingly, the rise of freestyle was carried by those same two forms—enabled by circumstances other than the shift of general understandings alone. Regarding staged performances, it should be reiterated that they usually involve a certain amount of organization and preparation in order to work, and that they thus require a certain amount of (financial) resources and collaboration to be organized. For these reasons, regular performative events seem to be held almost necessarily by some kind of formal organization; and in contemporary freeskiing just like in early ski racing, the need for regular competitions turned out to be the key driver for the professionalization and regulation of the nascent scene. In the history of skiing, events like races or technique demonstrations were usually organized by the 'official' ski clubs and federations with the explicit aim of achieving some greater good, such as advancing correct skiing or finding and honouring a nation's greatest skiing son. However, the organizational infrastructure that could have provided highly visible (Oldschool) freestyle skiing events earlier on—as the Olympic committee does today despite the lack of much popular interest—did not do so because it had formed around an alternative style of skiing. Another possibility to sustain regular public freestyle events was apparently tried several times throughout the first half of the century, but never seemed to work sustainably: collecting entrance fees and running freestyle as a form of professional entertainment (Lund/Miller 1998b: 14–16). Speculating about reasons, one could guess that the uninformed public was only drawn by the spectacular appeal of the stunts without being able to grasp and enjoy the finer details of style—something that still seems to be the case with regard to contemporary freeski events, in that mainstream media or mass events held in big cities focus heavily on spectacular flips and big jumps which are not actually of too much interest to 'knowing' members of the freeski scene. The effect of the spectacular, however, vanishes with repetitions, so that maybe, seeing what appeared as the same spectacular thing over and over again did not seem worth the money. In any event, as far as I know, freestyle skiing events have never been able to generate sustainable revenues by collecting entrance fees (and they still do not do so today).

Therefore, it was not until two other forms of organizations started to support such events that Oldschool freestyle skiing could be witnessed live on a larger scale: ski schools and ski equipment manufacturers. The advent of freestyle skiing is thus tightly intertwined with market phenomena, more specifically the increasing competition between independent ski schools, as well as the advent of corporate sponsoring in skiing. The thought that ski schools were instrumental in organizing performative displays of freestyle during the late 1950s and 1960s which prepared the ground for the later boom might appear counterintuitive, since the official and semi-official ski instruction bodies were among the staunchest opponents of all deviations from the proper ways of skiing. But while the European ski schooling system was (and still is) strictly controlled by the government-endorsed and deeply conservative national organizations, ski schools in the US were less strictly regulated. What is more, unlike European schools which still today hardly actively market themselves at all but rely on the respectable look provided by official certification and uniforms, ski schools in the US played an important part in attracting customers to resorts (which usually owned the ski schools and had for some time offered lessons for free; Fry 2006a: 108–124). As the ski industry boomed and new resorts mushroomed, exotic teaching methods and well-known head teachers became important marketing tools for lift operators. The key forefathers of the ski revolution of the late sixties (Doug Pfeiffer, Eric Stein, and

Art Furrer) were all ski-school directors that doubled as PR professionals by gaining media attention and selling books through their inventive skiing tricks (Fry 2006a: 220–226). The first regular audiences of freestyle tricks, in other words, were ski school classes (and bystanders on the slopes). Consequentially, early freestyle was framed according to the logic of ski instruction—it was understood as helping the student to become a more apt, versatile, and secure skier. One of the earliest stories about freestyle that appeared in a ski magazine in 1964, for example, was titled "Acrobatics for Agility" (Lund/Miller 1998b: 17), effectively reviving Zdarsky's classic argument that skiers should practice and prove their secure control of skiing by performing certain tasks or movement figures. In doing so, the forefathers of freestyle build on a classic stance towards freestyle cultivated in the European ski school system until this day—but they also changed its framework in a highly important way because of their different organizational alignments. In Austria, far from being a challenge to the authority of the ski-schooling system, freestyle tricks were at the time used to "assert the authority" of the ski-teacher (Lund/Miller 1998b: 15). This tradition can be traced back to the cradle of disciplined, military-style ski instruction, the Arlberg: Pioneer Hannes Schneider demanded in the 1940s that ski instructors were able to perform a signature move (such as a double pole-plant jump) evidencing their superiority (Lund/Miller 1998b: 15). Within the government-regulated ski-school world, in other words, freestyle moves were co-opted in that they could be performed legitimately because they were portrayed as a preparation for and step-stone towards real skiing, and because they were staged in such a way that they reconfirmed the organized hierarchy of 'ownership' of skiing style (with the head teacher at the top). At least in the ski schools of Germany, Austria, and Switzerland I have observed, this specific approach to all forms of 'free' style is still very much alive today. When I joined a ski class for a day during my fieldwork at the Arlberg, I witnessed how the concept of asserting teaching authority by jumping performatively is routinely practiced. As we stood above a spot where a small jump down a cliff was necessary, our seasoned instructor challenged the apprentice instructor accompanying us to show something special, yelling at him in front of the whole group: "Now show us how it's done. Don't mess this up!" [M].[6]

In the same vein, after decades of neglect, the new 2006 edition of Interski's official German instruction manual for ski teachers contains a section on freeskiing (Deutscher Verband für das Skilehrwesen 2006: 94–105) but emphasizes that freeski style per se is a personal matter which cannot and should not be taught by ski instructors. Style, it follows, cannot be an end in itself, and indeed the freeskiers' concrete conduct in the funpark is not really described as something a self-respecting ski teacher has business with. However, the handbook employs some clever rhetoric in order to be able to suggest some basic freeski moves as part of a serious ski-course without drawing the traditional idea of skiing style into question. Three other respectable ends and tasks of playful freeskiing are

---

[6] „Jetzt zeig uns mal wie's geht. Mach kein' Scheiß!"

named which legitimize addressing aspects of freeskiing and Style as part of serious ski practice, even though the ski students (short-sighted as they are) might not be aware of them: a) motivation (to continue learning 'real' skiing), b) versatility and body-control, and c) safety (Deutscher Verband für das Skilehrwesen 2006: 95–96). Undeniably, all three topics fall squarely into the realm of responsibility of every good ski instructor, and thus freeskiing must neither be neglected, nor does it draw the validity of the traditional goals and proper ways of skiing into question. Notably, this cleverly crafted and somewhat diplomatic account of freeskiing does not mention what is arguably the first and foremost reason why more and more ski schools visit funparks: customer demand. Instead, from the perspective of the ski instructors' professional organization, class participants are not customers of a service industry that have wants or wishes; they are students that need to be motivated—in other words, not just what, but even *that* they want something happens on behalf of the instructor, not the learner. Accordingly, the language and thought of business or marketing is conspicuously absent from a training manual predominantly aimed at future employees of a shrinking and highly competitive industry. Here lies the crucial difference between the 'classic' understanding of a ski school as a branch of an official professional organization like Interski (whose German chapter is the publisher of the handbook), and alternative the market-logic framework embraced by the ski schools in the US after the war. The logic of a book like "Ski like Stein" is a chain of affiliation: style-person-ski school-resort. In effect, the meaning of freestyle took on a hybrid form, as it could be read both ways, as confirming the authority of instruction boards, *and* as expressing individuality. In doing so, freestyle skiing achieved something that had proved essential for the wide dissemination of Alpine skiing about forty years earlier, namely winning the support of well-established organizations on the basis that it came to be seen as directly aligned with the ends orienting the organizations, without itself being an organizational practice, a practice that is nothing but a means to the organizational end. What the military did for Alpine skiing and the nation-state for racing, in other words, US ski school-businesses did for freestyle: providing resources during a critical time of growth after the broad strokes of the phenopractice had been sketched out, but before participation was stable enough for sustaining attendance and circulation of elements. I suggest that towards understanding why such organizational support does or does not occur, the polyvalence or 'multi-connectivity' of the practice's style plays a key role (a sentiment shared by Shove/Pantzar 2005b): Organizations themselves have to navigate between different, sometimes antagonistic ends and demands often upheld by different stakeholders (for example economic ones and question of spirit or authenticity); and the practices must evidently help towards, and not collide with, (more or less) all of them. In the case of freestyle, for example, it was essential that it attracted customers *and* pleased the media *and* was at least acceptable for being a ski school.

Still, the audiences witnessing (and sometimes learning) freestyle tricks performed by entrepreneurial ski-school directors remained clearly limited in scale. Their main effect was to enabled a small 'hard core' of pioneers to develop their skills and develop new tricks. In this way, independent ski-schools provided the primordial ooze from which a new breed of skiing practice sprang forth, a practice that would soon prove highly successful. Arguably most important among the understandings woven into the fabric of moves and looks of early freestyle was the idea that the attention the individual performer gathered could simultaneously be counted as attention for companies, and more specifically: brands. From the early sixties onwards, freestyle pioneers started to perform regularly in ski shows. Crucially, they won ski equipment manufacturers as sponsors (Lund/Miller 1998a: 20)—the essential link was forged which still sustains the freestyle culture today. This transformation of resource supply, I argue, implied a fundamental shift because it meant that the staged practices now had to be oriented towards befitting different practices of seeing: above all, they had to capture spectators' attention rather than being exclusively tailored to appealing to a committee of professional judges. Within the classic understanding, a ski race could be held in complete absence of any spectators apart from the race officials, but now, the number of spectators mattered much more.[7] And while race officials looked for rule-conformity and speed, lay spectators enjoyed seeing style—that is, a performative style of skiing made to be watched. Within the new conditions of an attention economy, the repertoire of freestyle quickly proved to be much more attractive than the sight provided by the classic techniques. The clearest example is provided by the history of the so-called "Ski Masters," a competition first held in 1966 that re-established formalized style competitions decades after those promoted by Zdarsky had been abolished. The contestants had to perform a canon of classic ski school forms such as the Stem Turn or parallel turns, and then had two "free skiing runs" to demonstrate they could link them fluidly, which was judged by points (Lund/Miller 1998b: 18–20). In a nutshell, these contests thus already contained the key elements of today's freeski competitions—the only problem was that they were, as a spectator reported, "painful to observe." (cit. in Fry 2006a: 228) In the same year, however, a racing association had with great success staged an "exhibition skiing" show to draw crowds to the actual race that followed afterwards; and within a few years, the Ski Masters refocused on freestyle and became a regular freestyle competition. Until 1971, it had grown into a spectacle held in Aspen that included a wet-T-Shirt contest, was sponsored by General Motors, and drew thousands of spectators (Fry 2006b; Lund/Miller 1998a)—the 'logic of attention' had transformed the style, format, and elements of what could count as a successful skiing competition. And besides the rapid increase in the attractiveness of live freestyle events that developed under this new logic or orientation framework, it had another, even more important effect: Freestyle soon proved suitable for the

---

[7]To be sure, a similar evolution was well underway in race skiing as well, in that TV audiences and popularity became a key success factor for individual athletes as well as sport disciplines as a whole. However, for most athletes in traditional sports, elegant performances are a bonus at best when it comes to popularity and income—it is winning that really counts.

mediated ways of seeing whose influence grew rapidly at the time—not surprisingly, because their organization and design was "driven by what would look good on TV." (Lund/Miller 1998a: 24).

The single most important factor for the rapid dissemination and development that Oldschool freestyle skiing finally enjoyed in the late 1960s, I argue, was the visual media, namely film and television. On the one hand, they had an indirect effect in that they enabled an independent symbiotic field to emerge and prevail commercially much in the same way they (today) sustain the field of racing: To attract both corporate sponsors and additional spectators and participants, mass media were pivotal, and thus the manifold opportunities for observing freestyle 'live' and as a part of an enthusiastic crowd during organized performances was indirectly dependent on media attention. That freestyle skiing and contemporary freeskiing (and snowboarding) were able to establish themselves as viable and influential alternatives to racing was to a large extend due to the fact that they produce 'better' images, that is, they are in several ways more adequate for being watched and filmed (Fry 2006b, 2009; Lund/Miller 1998a). Notably, I suggest this is only to some extend due to the fact that they match a certain zeitgeist especially well, but rather because of the particular affordances for seeing with enjoyment and captivation they produce for a particular audience. Specifically, they seem capable of serving two separate, potentially contradicting conditions: First, they attract the attention of broad audiences of advertising or 'snippets' of reporting in the mass media and are able to entertain them without requiring a high level of skilful seeing and understanding for it, albeit necessarily only for relatively brief periods of time; and second, they possess a certain 'stickiness' in that they can keep a much smaller, but highly dedicated and experienced audience interested and attentive for years on end. Fulfilling these conditions, in turn, has become a necessity due to the evolution of media economy and technology: The commercial success of ESPN and its influence on sport culture (particularly in the US) as a whole was made possible by the advent of cable TV, and thus a much more diversified TV programmed tailored to entertain very specific segments of viewers (Fry 2006a: 287), an effect that was even enlarged by the advent of VCR and, eventually, web-based video broadcasting.

5 Fit to Media Forms

In conclusion, I argue that mass media play an essential role for the stabilization and diffusion of a phenopractice because they help to circulate important elements: directly, they enable the dissemination of both general and practical understandings (both across oceans and within one group of practitioners); and indirectly, because they foster the commercial exchanges providing the availability of specialized equipment, or the means of living for professional evangelists of a phenopractice. By comparing the success or failure[8] of different forms of skiing in reaching widespread circulation I will now show that the respective fit to the practical and economic demands of certain types of visual media is a key factor. I will, one could say, assess how well different bundles of elements of skiing practice oriented by different styles fared when put to the test of fitting to media forms over the course of the last four decades of skiing history. Fortunately, said history provides several highly interesting and well-comparable test cases. Besides freeriding and racing, at least three other forms of skiing had at some point reached a relative high level of professional organization and media attention, but then faltered and are today marginal at best: extreme skiing, speed skiing, and Powder 8. All five are specific forms of skiing down a mountain according to certain principles: Racing is about minimizing the time needed to follow a predefined course; freeriding about riding beautiful and demanding lines with style and flow; extreme skiing describes riding down the steepest and most difficult terrain possible (Dawson 1998: 15–22; Fry 2006a: 206–210); speed skiing means trying to reach the highest possible speed on skis (Fry 2006a: 210–213); and Powder 8 is a form of powder skiing in which a team of two skiers tries to ride in perfect symmetry and rhythm, producing a track of many interlinked figure 8s (or what German skiers call "Zöpfle") (Fuchsberger 2005; funsporting 2007; skiinfo 2003; Walter 2008; [D]). In all sports, international championships have been held, at least some mainstream media attention was attracted, and highly specialized ski equipment is or was available. All ways of skiing require exceptional skill if pursued at the highest level, all are certainly dangerous and resource-intensive to conduct, but all can be practiced at relatively modest and accessible forms by aspiring amateurs. Still, only two of them could be called a symbiotic field of skiing (in my sense of the term), while extreme and speed skiing are today highly marginalized niche-formats briefly mentioned in the media every few years at best (mostly when either a spectacular record has been set, or a great tragedy occurred), while Powder 8 seems practically extinct. Of course, many reasons could be found for such demise; and I should clearly note that the individual experience the practitioners gain from conduct, as well as a host of practical reasons (such as costs) could have played a pivotal role that have not been documented well enough for me to notice. Still, I point to the fact that at some point in time, a fairly large group of practitioners, organizers, sponsors, and spectators have been drawn to each sport for more than a decade each; and when trying to assess the factors behind the sudden ebb of enthusiasm and interest, the role of the media seems definitely important, if not decisive. For reasons of clarity, I will differentiate between three

---

[8] Success defined as relatively wide-spread diffusion and stable following; specifically in that the respective form of skiing can provide at least some professional athletes or instructors with a living, amounts to a relevant product category served by both mainstream and dedicated brands, and produces relatively regular mass media attention. Without being able to provide the respective data, I suggest that the overall number of more or less regular practitioners of these reflects these factors.

broad categories of diffusion media which a phenopractices' style must match: first, mainstream media such as the large TV networks or news magazines, and the sponsoring of mainstream brands (from non-skiing categories such as cars or soft drinks) they motivate; second, special-interest or subcultural media such as niche magazines and web-based publications, plus the sponsoring from within the ski industry they draw; and third, large events or competitions which attract attention from both types of media, connects and motivates practitioners, and are important sources of income and fame for professional athletes (the practices' evangelists).

To begin with speed-skiing, it seems clear that the concept of skiing faster than 200 km/h makes a spectacular 'news snippet' for mainstream media, and occasionally, newly set records occasionally make headlines. But although it is officially sanctioned (and thus supported) by the FIS and had even been a demonstration sport in the 1992 Olympic Winter Games, a regular race circuit with the potential to sustain professional athletes turned out to be short-lived, so that today, only a very small community (predominantly in France) appears to conduct it regularly (Fry 2006a: 210–213). Yet in theory, it is not clear why Speed Skiing should not be as attractive as Big Wave Surfing or Drag Racing, since just like these two, it surely provides the practitioner with an emotional 'kick,' a consistent challenge, and a rebellious image. I thus argue that a key reason is its lack of fit to visual media formats. Unlike the other two mentioned disciplines, it does not yield media images that are fascinating in their detail, for example because the racer does not visibly move his body at all and appears to be a statue rather than an athlete (Fig. 11.2); and a typical video is usually shot from a great distance and

Fig. 11.2 Speed skiing. Neither the movement, nor the speed, nor the details of doings of the athlete are visible. (Image by Simon Billy, Wikimedia Commons: licensed under CC BY-SA 4.0)

shows not much more than a tiny point zipping straight down a mountain (see e.g. Plueddeman 1994; [D]). Likewise, competitions did not prove as enticing as one might expect, especially because for practical and safety reasons, races do not compete head-to-head but one after another. Neither special interest media nor events, in other words, seem capable of producing practices of observing this way of skiing that are sufficiently interesting in the long run—apart from the number showing the speed reached, each run appears very much alike.

While speed skiing seems to be well-suited to attract mainstream media attention, but failed to appeal to regular media or event consumption, Powder 8 seems to be just the opposite case: While offering an aesthetic view and visible variation in details to the skilful observer, it lacks the spectacular or the controversy that brought speed and extreme skiing into the mainstream media. Powder 8 was a direct predecessor of contemporary freeride in that it emerged as an early form of competitive powder-skiing often aided by helicopters, and for some years, it enjoyed the support of large corporations like Atomic (a mayor ski band) and Red Bull (a key sponsor for many lifestyle sport disciplines) (Fuchsberger 2005; [D]). Annual world championships have been held for more than 25 years (according to Falcon 2003; [D]) and for several years, European championships took place at the Arlberg but have ceased to exist (Fuchsberger 2005; funsporting 2007; [D]). In many ways, Powder 8 contests follow the same pattern as contemporary freeriding competitions, in that riders are judged by eyesight for the "synchronization, technique, turn shape and dynamics" of their riding a line in untouched powder (Falcon 2003; [D]). But while such details of conduct, as well as the overall beauty of a line seem to be practically available for those regularly observing the sport, the images and stories that result do not seem spectacular or immediately captivating at any rate: neither high speeds nor jumps or crashes are involved, but instead riders perform a single figure over and over. I want to emphasize that it would be unwarranted to simply conclude that the sport in itself is necessarily visually boring: For the untrained eye, the tricks that freestyler perform on boxes or rails can sometimes seem similarly repetitive and unspectacular; yet still experienced practitioners are fascinated by the many details they spot within such moves. The same seems true for Figure 8 (see e.g. skiCrystalMtn 2010; [D]). Additionally, the visual learning, as well as the hedonistic enjoyment freeskiers gain from watching videos, seem equally possible with regard to recordings of Powder 8, as does enhancing the videos by adding a soundtrack and slow-motion effects. Still, the style visible in videos or contests was unable to draw a larger following or sustain sponsor support, and arguably, this was due to its inability to invoke awe and long-term aspiration even if performed at the highest level.

The third forms of skiing that has at some point enjoyed considerable success but fell back into the margins of global skiing due to its lack of fit to media of dispersion was extreme skiing. According to Dawson (1998: 19), "traditional extreme skiing was about control on impossible slopes," with 'impossible' predominantly meaning the steepest possible (Fry 2006a: 206–210, 2009). Although it emerged as a form of ski mountaineering, its sole goal lies in accomplishing a specific descent (just like in freeriding) rather than reaching a certain peak or mastering a challenging ascent. Because of these common roots, some authors (like Dawson 1998) equate extreme skiing to the ski mountaineering expeditions conducted today, but in view, these differ considerably, especially in that the route of descent tackled on skis is not at issue (e.g. Frentzen 2008). Extreme skiing became highly popular during the 1970s and 1980s and made use of very specific skiing techniques as well as special equipment that enabled skiing in extremely steep faces and couloirs. As the documentary "Steep" (Obernhaus 2008) demonstrates, it is capable of producing highly spectacular and captivating images; and during its heydays, it garnered not only widespread attention via the mass media, but also a sustained demand for more extensive coverage in special interest media such as movies, books, and magazines (Fry 2009; Kerig 2008a). Despite this once-widespread recognition, the idea to tackle the steepest slope possible today seems as outdated as the equipment and turning techniques that came with it, although some of them are still relevant in ski mountaineering (Kerig 2008a). More specifically, I suggest that extreme skiing has been transformed in freeriding in that the paradigm of steepness has been replaced with the paradigm of style; and thus while today skiers still tackle very steep slopes (yet not as steep as the virtually-vertical 60 degrees and more once achieved), the predominant organizing motive is a very different one—as are the technique and technology. The origin of this important transformation can be pinpointed quite precisely: While matching the demands of mainstream and niche media, extreme skiing in its classic form seemed inadequate for staging competitions. For some years, extreme skiers achieved ever more extreme descents and set ever-new records, but oddly enough, they soon simply ran out of possibilities for finding unskied, almost-vertical rock faces that would still hold snow at all (Obernhaus 2008). When the first "World Extreme Skiing Championships" were held in Valdez, Alaska in 1991, steepness itself could thus no longer be used to determine the winner (although the terrain definitely was steep and dangerous, see Anthony 2011: 181). Despite the name, in other words, the contest was not actually a competition in extreme skiing in the true sense, since it would not be a reaffirmation ritual for the principle of controlling steepness as determining extreme skiing skill. Necessarily, the event had to be about something else instead, and indeed this event would be in retrospect regarded as the moment of birth of a new form of skiing: freeride.

6 The Birth of Modern Freeride

Like several times in the history of skiing before, a scenic event would come to define a new style in that it became a known entity to which one could refer to in order to describe a certain type of skiing. As several chroniclers of the freeride culture assure, Doug Coombs' winning run at this contest helped to define (visually) what freeriders today call style or flow (Anthony 2011: 180–184; Fry 2006a: 209; Obernhaus 2008: 44:00–47:00)—although at closer observation, the winning run by John Hunt in the following year was equally important, as it added the crucial speed definitive for Big Mountain freeriding (Anthony 2011: 182). Today, the idea that skill in 'extreme' forms of skiing becomes expressed in a visibly smooth and elegant style seems self-evident to almost all practitioners. But as the following quote from a description of the style of a well-known veteran of 'classic' extreme skiing shows, it is only the contemporary way of skiing extreme terrain which strongly reflects the particular demands of visual media production. After praising the veteran's classic style for his bodily control, the author notes:

> "But he is not supple. The hard corners of his technique have never been smoothed to please the cameras. He is perfectly functional but inelegant." (Kerig 2008a: 99)

The transition from steepness to style, in other words, invoked a shift of the relevant visible qualities of skiing, so that functionality was no longer sufficient and elegance had become important instead. Notably, it would be misleading to conclude from this transition that mass media attention automatically transforms a phenopractice (as lifestyle sport practitioners sometimes seem to fear), or that the increasing importance of visual media has replaced the pivotal role of scenic events for defining styles of conduct: Extreme skiers had regularly been the subject of ski films or television features, including the veteran skier described in this quote. But the purpose of these films was to document the very possibility of skiing down such extreme inclination; and thus the orienting principle that would need to become visible in the riding was the difficulty of the challenge and the cold-blooded professionalism with which it was tackled. The novelty disseminated from about 1991 onwards was thus arguably not that the riding style had to be organized in such a way to make certain qualities visible, but that "pleasing the cameras" meant "smoothing" one's technique not performing the drama of steepness. On the other hand, the breakthrough and definition of this new camera-pleasing style did nevertheless happen to a large extend at a 'traditional' event, during a face-to-face gathering. Crucially, just like one could not know what proper skiing was before Zdarsky's defining demonstration of what became Alpine skiing (or the Lilienfeld version of it) had taken place, it was not entirely clear what was to be expected of the athletes gathered for the World Extreme Skiing Championships organized in order to promote heli-skiing in the Valdez area. But vis-à-vis the runs of the eventual winner and later freeride-idol Doug Coombs, one could see a way of skiing worth aspiring and rewarding. As a spectator commented, Coombs was riding "stronger, crisper, cleaner, makes it look easy—there was just absolutely no question who had won." (cit. in Obernhaus 2008: 45:42) Far from inducing only a passing moment of fascination, the thusly witnessed performance had a long-lasting effect:

> "Every skier you see today was influenced by Doug Coombs and Jon Hunt, whether they know it or not. Anybody who's on ESPN in the X-games or in a [freeride] film, their skiing was influenced by those guys." (cit. in Anthony 2011: 182)

It is important to note that I do not wish to suggest that a singular, possibly accidental 'magic moment' alone simply defines the style trajectory of whole phenopractices. After all, I suggested that styles of conduct do not change overnight, but need to evolve over the course of repeated conduct oriented by certain factors (I discussed the examples of terrain and technology) before becoming an orienting style in their own right. Thus, what happened in Valdez—or at the Arlberg almost a century earlier, for that matter—was a culmination of a development that crystallized in a certain pivotal moment, namely at a significant public event. The judges at the Valdez contest were looking at a way of powder skiing that had begun to emerge over the prior decade among a small group of ski 'bums' in a resort (Jackson Hole in Wyoming) whose mountains are famous for the steep terrain and heavy snowfalls (Anthony 2011: 164–184). Among them were two professional mountain photographers, and over the course of a decade, the band of skiers had begun to experiment with filming cliff-drops and bigger turns in deep powder in search of spectacular shots (Anthony 2011: 169–170). "Style was very important to us because style defined the guys we admired" one recalled; and since they felt they could not compete with the 'local heroes' of perfected classic Alpine skiing (one of them a Olympic gold medallist), they worked towards their own ways of dealing with the 'extreme' local terrain (Anthony 2011: 169). The conditions they found at the contest in Alaska seemed to fit their ways of skiing exceptionally well: among them, they shared the three first spots (Anthony 2011: 181). Just like the visibly evident superiority of Zdarsky's riding 80 years earlier, Coombs performance helped to define a certain style of skiing as preferable and led to the development of rules, understandings, and ends for a kind of skiing that reproduces the style that had been visible. The framework of practical observation and judgment within which Coomb's (and colleagues') specific way of skiing had been worked out over the course of years, however, had been different: While the classic Extreme skiers still adhered to Zdarsky's understanding that control and prowess are evidenced by not falling, the Jackson Hole skiers relied on the visual details proffered by their cameras. Not coincidently, they soon cultivated the cliff-drop as a new element of the movement repertoire of a skier, and combined it with some of the on-piste freestyle tricks that had been developed in the previous decade: Both drops and tricks produce spectacular images, even though they often end in a crash or a 'hard' landing quite similar to what was hitherto considered falling. Consequently, the judging manual of today's Freeride World Tour distinguishes different kinds of crashes according to the visible details of *how* a rider crashes. For example, judges should ask themselves: "Did the rider lose control in the air or did he just not stick his landing, even though he looked perfectly in position to stick it?" (Freeride World Tour 2011) In other words, just like on camera, what counts towards winning a live event is not what 'actually' happens, but whether it "looked like" it *should* have happened according to the visible flow and style of the riding. This point should be emphasized in order to avoid a common misconception: The role of visual media in contemporary lifestyle sports such as freeskiing differs in important ways from that of earlier times—but *not* because they are a new addition to the sports, or because they are replacing interactions, events, or rituals. Instead, they alter interactions, events, and practices in that they are more fundamentally oriented towards the visibilities recorded and then produced by visual media technology. In my view, the 1991 championships marked an important transformation because the mediated visibility of skiing was no longer a means towards meeting or promoting a certain abstract end of skiing such as speed or steepness (in that it was used to optimize speed or advertise a way of skiing fast), but it became an end in itself—and as such, the adequacy of someone's skiing in accomplishing this end was from then on also be judged through live observation, not just on film.

As a result, contemporary freeskiing, just as its predecessor Oldschool freestyle skiing, offers visibilities that 'work' quite well in the three media formats mainstream, special interest, and event, since they are both spectacular (and potentially controversial) enough for brief mainstream attention and entice skilful observers for extended periods. Within freeskiing, however, freestyle as opposed to freeriding is more adequate for being held as a contest in front of large audiences—testament to the latter's roots in individual filmmaking (Daher 2008; [D]). 'Alaska-style' freeriding is difficult to observe directly and without the help of helicopter-mounted cameras, highly dependent on weather conditions, and—most importantly—oriented by a principle that is antagonistic to the practical necessities the organizers of an event have to cope with: the local site of freeriding, the line-in-a-face, is viewed as something to be produced by the athlete rather than provided in a neutral fashion by the organizing committee, in that *where* someone rides is a part of *how* he rides, since choosing and seeing a line is a key skill in itself. In a freeride contest, contestants are indeed in part judged according to their skill in selecting a line, but they are necessarily heavily constrained in their choice because all contestants must ride within a single face at a given time and date—and accordingly, both competitors and spectators feel that freeride contests produces less elegant, more dangerous, and somewhat 'un-natural' riding. Tom, for example, has considered several times to take part in freeride contests to bolster his standing with his sponsors, but concluded that the restricted conditions would not allow him to properly choose and prepare for his line, and thus perform what he considers good (and reasonably safe) skiing. For similar reasons, several earnest attempts to establish a regular international series of competitions have faltered over the years due to disagreements about the suitable formats and rules among freeriders—and the high costs of holding events in locations deemed adequate for 'real' freeriding, such as Alaska or Siberia. While adequate kickers and half-pipes needed for freestyle can be (and are) erected even in places like downtown London, thus far it seems only one material and spatial 'set-up' has been found in the world that is both adequate for high-level freeriding but also within sufficiently easy reach of spectator crowds: The north face of the Bec des Rosses in Verbier, Switzerland. In conclusion, it seems that the contemporary success and global stabilization of freeskiing is in part due to the flexibility in terms of 'media-fitness' it enjoys due to its being composed of two related-but-different sub-forms, each of which befitting just that media format especially well (events in the case of freestyle, and videos in that of freeriding) which the other seems to cause problems for. This flexibility notwithstanding, I also conclude that for the 'birth' of a completely new style to occur, pivotal events—and thus situated interaction—were key in all the cases I discussed (though I do not rule out the existence of alternative cases on theoretical grounds). Nevertheless, all forms of media can equally impact the particular style of a phenopractice that is being successfully disseminated, not the least because they play a potentially decisive role in providing the economic underpinnings fostering the (professional and lay) conduct of said practice.

7 The Sponsor System

I have argued that the evolution of mass media technology available at different points in time was a key factor determining the success of different styles of skiing at different times. More specifically, I hold that the predominant styles of conduct needed to fit the available media in such a way that the practical visibility of the style needed to be made (visibly) instructively and instructedly observable by the mediated images; and that enabling the production and consumption of such instructive images was a pivotal virtue of the popularized style. Said phenopractices of production and consumption, however, are not accomplishments achieved via embodied skills alone, but also depend on the technological tools available. So far, I described how the emergence of freestyle skiing was not just an effect of changing general understandings, but more specifically of changing practical understandings, some of which need to be developed in the course of seeing freestyle. As I have argued with regard to watching freestyle trick in a funpark, seeing style is itself a skill or technique that must be acquired. More specifically, I suggested that freeskiing images and videos are (or should be) to some extend able to instruct the viewer just what it is that is visible in them. I can now add that this logic works into the other direction as well: Only ways of doing freestyle which enabled or afforded the production of photos and videos that made style instructedly visible could arguably reach widespread dissemination. After all, ski movies were by and large the single most important factor in providing broadly available opportunities for seeing freestyle; both directly, because they enable the seeing itself, and indirectly, because they allowed the sponsorship system supporting professional athletes to work. Therefore, the breakthrough success of freestyle skiing did not only depend on the ascend of a new media infrastructure of, first, cable TV with its special-interest programs (most notably ESPN) tailored to a much more specific and thus knowledgeable audience (Fry 2006a: 287) and, second, video recorders; but it was also an effect of new ways of presenting freestyle moves to the audience and effectively teaching spectators what was there for them to see and enjoy. Initially, freestyle seemed unsuitable for screens because the hallmark of Oldschool as well as Newschool freestyle are complicated jumps that involve multiple rotations on different axes. The prototype of this trick was the so-called Moebius Flip, which had been developed during the mid-Sixties, a somersault with a simultaneous twist. But before becoming a standard move co-defining a whole new Olympic discipline, the complex trick had to be made visible. If witnessed face-to-face, "it appeared so complex that spectators experienced difficulty recalling exactly what they had seen." (Fry 2006a: 226) From 1967 onwards, however, hugely successful ski movies were being produced that pioneered "ways of expressing freestyle's ultimate capacity for beauty, achievement, and adventure" by combining slow-motion sequences, complex cutting techniques, colourful special effects, and extensive use of music into what was a technological as much as an aesthetic innovation (Lund/Miller 1998a: 20). Importantly, the new style of filmmaking was not just spectacular if witnessed in passing and thus guaranteed broad attention, it was also able to capture the viewers for extended periods and unfold the beautiful details to be seen in skiing before her eyes. And unlike the earlier ski movies, it worked on its own, without the need of a narrator: until then, ski movie screenings were almost always accompanied by a narrator (usually the filmmaker himself) who brought the silent images to life and explained what was shown on screen (Fry 2006a: 283). Now, however, filmmakers had not only found new ways of 'telling their story'; but the stories to be told also adapted more and more to their ways. In this way, several elements fell into place which collectively changed both the content and the commercial underpinning of ski movies—and which enabled the rise of a new type of professional skier: the ski film star.

Different types of mass media do not only differ in the format in which they offer content, so that things that work for example in a book do not necessarily work in a movie and vice versa, but they are also enmeshed into different kinds of economies or commercial logics. Until about the mid-1960, skiing appeared on film in basically three formats: either as part of mainstream movie productions, or in TV-coverage of ski racing (primarily of the Winter Olympics), or in special-interest ski-films produced by independent filmmakers who travelled from town to town each autumn to show their new films (see Fry 2006a). In either of these forms, the possibility for the skier to earn enough money from filming alone remained relatively limited (since sponsoring in the Olympics was still forbidden, see Fry 2006a: 150–159). But together with the advent of a new style of skiing, new forms of competitions able to attract and fascinate different audiences, as well as the advances of media technology that lowered the cost of production, enhanced the mobility of the cameramen, offered new ways of cutting and presenting the images, and the new mid-range distribution systems of cable TV and VCR (reaching more people than travelling filmmakers, but more specific segments than mainstream TV), a new link was forged that continues to sustain most of the freeski 'industry' still today: filming and sponsoring became linked. By the end of the decade, the two essential formats of sponsored attention-production I described had been developed. On the one hand, ski manufacturer K2 was financing a "demonstration team" that travelled from resort to resort in a branded campervan accompanied by filmmaker Dick Barrymore to shoot a movie simultaneously promoting the skiers, their style, and the ski brand (and turning both athletes and the filmmaker into icons as well; Barrymore 1997; Lund 1996b; Lund/Miller 1998a). On the other hand, companies sponsored freestyle events and competitions which would then in turn draw media attention. The impact of these developments for contemporary freeskiing can hardly be underestimated: These two media-driven formats continue to form the backbone of the freeski industry that allows professional skiers, filmmakers, photographers, event organizers, team-managers, freelance journalists, and many more to make a (small) living from their passion. More importantly, it has established a system of variation, selection and dissemination of new forms of skiing, new idols and role-models, and new brands which bypasses the traditional skiing 'ecosystem' in its entirety (see Woermann 2012a for details). Independent filmmakers living from sponsorships allow professional athletes to sustain themselves completely independently from the 'classic' links formed during the first three decades of the century, namely the link between national sports organizations, (semi-) official ski instruction bodies, the FIS racing circuit, government-funded sport-sciences, and (at least in Europe) the military (which employs successful athletes as part-time soldiers and is active in ski schooling bodies and research). And while these basic pillars of the skiing world are without a doubt still active and important for the Alpine disciplines today, freeskiing has emerged as an independent symbiotic field of skiing which provides the mainstream with innovation, Style, and adventure in small doses. With the advent of the internet, service such as YouTube, and ever-cheaper and more advanced video technology, the mediated ways of seeing Style available to a broad range of skiers have changed significantly. While this implies a great potential for a further acceleration and diversification of skiing styles, the internet or any other technology per se does not de-couple phenopractices from the wider meshworks of complementary practices they depend on. Freeskiing's 'ecosystem' of Style, sponsorship, and independent media production, in other words, is arguably not less, but more dependent on a great number of organizations (various sponsors, film producers, resorts, 'core' brands, social media companies, and so forth), markets (the 'core' and the mainstream ski market, apparel and gear markets, online advertising, etc.), and ultimately complementary practices from editing videos to printing t-shirts. Seen from this perspective, one might indeed ask if freeskiing really is 'freer' than skiing ever was. This conclusion is of course paradoxical, because the very idea of freestyle and freeride skiing is to move away from the rigid formalization and regulation of skiing Style imposed by professional organizations, ski racing, and ski instruction bodies. And while the freeskiers have surely succeeded in some ways, I hope it has become clear that they cannot (and often do not) hope to break skiing free from all ties and forms of mediation.

8   Authenticity: Skiing and Being

This sentiment brings me back to initial question this chapter began with. What is real skiing? Today, laments about the 'Disneyfication' of the Alps and the loss of the true mountain experience seem as pressing as ever. But as I argued, what separates real from fake, authentic from commodified, unfree from free skiing is essentially a question of style. Against the background of my phenopractice-theoretical account of the emergence, dissemination, and evolution of style of skiing happening through and conditioned by different media formats, let me now try to return to this issue that freeskiers care so deeply about. Does, for example, the 'taming of the wild' that the grooming of slopes and mechanisation of ascending entails destroy the soul of skiing? For many, skiing is about mastering the challenges and dangers of ('real') nature—or as Lunn (1949: xv) put it: to "learn to love the snow as a friend and wrestle with it as an enemy." Conducting a practice, in other words, is equated to using a certain skill; and since the practice is being reconfigured so that technological solutions now contribute aspects hitherto conducted bodily (for example in that the skier does not need to react to countless bumps on a slope since it has been groomed for her), the practice supposedly becomes less 'real.' It is not by accident that this kind of critique is voiced almost without exception by those belonging to the skill-elite of a certain field; and at least to some degree it can indeed be seen as a move to defend their own symbolic superiority by delegitimizing the participation of the less apt (and very often the younger ones) and ward off challenges by up-and-coming competitors (M. Donnelly 2006). Freeskiing itself, to be sure, has been made the aim of such delegitimizing, echoed in statements such as this one about skiing switch (a signature style of riding in contemporary freeriding):

> "Backwards skiing is a generational thing. Only kids do it. The men smile." (Kerig 2008a: 119; [D])

In my view, authors of Bourdieuian accounts of practices tend to adhere to such reasoning when they equate skill and practice. However, not only does it seem unfortunate to reproduce gestures of machismo in social theory; but more importantly, such a reification of the body carries the danger of individualising practice thought and therefore neglecting the fundamental role of situational features such as equipment or the co-presence of skilful colleagues. This type of lament about the loss of authenticity, it thus needs to be noted, necessarily springs forth from a heroic account of a practice that systematically downplays the fact that every 'individual' competence is without exception tightly interwoven into a dense tissue of social prefiguration and cooperation. To paraphrase Lunn, the snow can only be a friend to wrestle with because insulated clothing, highly developed equipment, and warm meals are all silently part of the package.

Still, it seems to me that there is something to the arguments made in the name of authenticity and the lost soul of a practice. After all, I have repeatedly argued against 'flattening' the rich details of lived conduct and treating it only as an effectively non-descript medium of social symbolism or communication. I suggest that the seasoned practitioners voicing these concerns indeed describe an important process worth closer consideration—including some demystification and de-heroization. The phenopractice perspective I outline can be particularly useful for this task of finding a more nuanced description of the problems of 'civilizing' a practice in Spengler's sense. Rather than elevating skill above technology, it invites us to consider the experience a phenopractice provides for the practitioner and acknowledge—as Heidegger did—that by assisting our life, technology also reduces the scope and scale of our actively lived life. To be sure, I believe that Heidegger himself later mystified and heroized lived life and nature, and demonized technology to some extend (Luckner 2008). Thus, I argue for a hopefully more nuanced view that looks as follows: On the one hand, there can be no doubt that zipping up the slopes of the Arlberg in today's high-tech lifts with seat-heating and music for entertainment, instead of hiking uphill through the snow for several hours alters the overall experience of a day out skiing. In discussing several similar cases such as transport systems or ski-building, I agreed with the critics that these are not just superficial developments of marginal aspects but transform the details of conduct quite profoundly. In explaining such impacts, a phenopractice view can provide explanations where theoretical perspectives focusing on subjective experience alone run into problems: since the latter insist that all meaning is essentially subjective, they must trace the change of experience back to subjective knowledge before anything else, so that material technology can at best be said to play an indirect and underspecified role. In contrast, a phenopractice view can grasp the processes behind these transformations very well, for example showing how technological developments change the predominant style of conduct. On the other hand, however, the phenopractice view also highlights the fact that the experience of the practitioner is an effect of the interplay of several elements of the practice, and that changing one or more elements cannot be directly equated to changing the practice as a whole. With regard to the authenticity of skiing, the key elements are of course the understandings and ends or tasks defining what makes certain conduct an instance of doing just this practice: For example, instruction manuals for ski instructors usually suggest that skiing is at the core about experiencing the forces of sliding and "playing with gravity" (Deutscher Verband für das Skilehrwesen 2006), and consequently, perfectly groomed slopes and a warm behind during sitting in a ski lift do not per se hinder this experience. If, in contrast, one adheres to the notion of classical alpinism that 'real' skiing is about exposing oneself to the sublime danger of the mountain—an understanding that is arguably also at the root of climbing (Robinson 2004; T. Williams/P. Donnelly 1985)—, then an expansion of the mechanized or organizationally provided aspects of a practice, and the decrease of experienced, lived-through risk it invokes indeed amounts to the felt (not just claimed) loss of an essential part of skiing. It follows that the authenticity-critique is at the core a disagreement about the style of a practice; more specifically: about changes in the composition of the *background* of a practice. Does real skiing only happen against the background of 'untamed' slopes and hard-earned ascents? What makes the question so difficult is that it is unclear whether or not aspects such as taking grave risks or struggling with ever-changing snow conditions despite being reasonably skilled are only unimportant background aspects blending into normality, or important figurations worth awareness and visibility. It should be clear that there cannot be an adequate answer that is not informed by personal attunement to the understandings of the practices in question. But as this work tried to show, it is neither simply a question of personal interest, nor something shaped by subjective attention and knowledge, nor dictated by a macro-scale discourse. Rather, the very intelligibility of certain aspects *as* significant, out-standing aspects is a result of the specific organization of the situatedly achieved practical conduct taking place—and thus, it is the accomplishment of intelligibility that demands the attention of those trying to provide answers. Whether or not a simple ski track left in the powder snow of the Wilde Krimml at the end of a long, beautiful day is anything that is worth attention, capable of showing beauty, and testament to skill and Style ultimately depends on whether or not one is able to see it as freeskiers do: as a trace of a state of being.

Chapter 12
Summary, Conclusion, and Outlook

This work set out to develop a phenopractice theory perspective on the freeskiing subculture. My aim was twofold: First, to spell out a systematic theoretical account of intelligibility and style that integrates phenomenological thought into a practice theory framework. Working through different aspects of the empirical case, I attempted to extend key arguments from Schatzki and Garfinkel by tracing their philosophical roots in Wittgenstein and Heidegger, as well as integrating selected findings from the state of the art in vision science. My second aim was to clarify and sharpen the argument by working out the commonalities and differences between this account and a number of 'neighbouring' theoretical positions within, and outside of, the so-called practice turn. In this conclusion, I will provide a rejoinder in four parts in order to summarize my findings and trace out the implication of an account of phenopractice theory. In the first part, I will compare the phenopractice perspective on style I developed to the existing views on lifestyle sport subcultures and sketch out what my findings can add to the debate. I will then provide some suggestions on how my line of argumentation might also be fruitfully extended to the contemporary literature on lifestyle, consumption choices, and taste. The second part will take a look at practice theory more generally and subsume the conclusions which I have drawn from comparing the different theoretical positions and alternatives. Here, I will outline some points or problems which will need further future discussion or research in order to develop more clear-cut and coherent views within practice thought. The third part will summarize phenopractice theory in a series of brief statements and seeks to give a compact description of the theoretical terms and core arguments. The final and fourth part will then suggest some open questions and areas of future research.

1 Style and Lifestyle: From Symbol to Tool

In the sociological literature, style is usually treated as a purely symbolic domain: styles of clothing, conduct, consumption, and so forth are portrayed as means of expression or communication, and as markers of social groups or individual positions. The literature on lifestyle sports mirrors this general perspective. Although few studies fail to take note of the importance of the visceral experience of performing the sport, two other topics dominate the discussion of style in lifestyle sports: identity and community. On the one hand, authors emphasize aspects of identity play and expression, distinction, and subject-hood; and on the other, they focus on themes of belonging, hierarchy, and power. The phenopractice theory position taken in this work suggests a fundamentally different perspective on style. It argues, first, that style is ultimately always lived style, a style of conduct (e.g. wearing stylish clothes or visibly performing identity) and therefore must be practically and situatedly accomplished. Second, it suggests that style fulfils practical, non-symbolic functions in that it serves as a resource that helps practitioners achieve basic ends such as learning the sport or avoiding crashes. Third, because it can be mediated, style is essential in that it enables the global dissemination, coordination, and evolution of phenopractices, as well as the subcultures and industries they might spawn. Therefore, while many of the issues predominant in the literature (such as status, gender, or identity-play) proved to have some relevance in freeskiing as well, I argue that by framing style as symbolic, the literature on lifestyle sports overlooks the crucial pragmatic relevance of style for the day-to-day accomplishment of lifestyle sport practices. More generally, phenopractice theory suggests that an emphasis on the symbolic or performative aspect of social life bears the danger of treating symbolic 'content' as effectively arbitrary or fully contingent. Lifestyle sport practices can of course fruitfully be analysed as providing distinction and demonstrating distance from necessity (Bourdieu 1984, 1988) or as enabling communication about the paradoxical relation of the individual and the social system (Bette 2004). But in order for these things to happen in the first place, 'doing lifestyle'—e.g. producing, enjoying, or talking about style—must already be happening. Therefore, a phenopractice perspective cautions that the ways in which such doings happen are predominantly shaped by their immediate necessities, affordances, or qualities rather than by abstract macro-level goals or functions. Consequently, this perspective questions if, by portraying something like freeskiing as a strategy to acquire cultural capital and gain advantageous positions in the global battle for status and jobs, we can learn enough about what it means to ski, why freeskiers do what they do, why the skiing industry developed the way it did, how the media technology impacts on the freeskiing culture, and so on. In short, I argued that style can well be understood as a symbolic code or a medium of communication—but it cannot be *reduced* to this function alone, because this requires treating it as a formless medium, a blank space to be filled at will. In their quest to emphasize the communicative or strategic function of style, authors frequently follow a basic two-step argument: Firstly, they describe the supposed creative playfulness, relaxed ease, and informal authenticity of lifestyle sports and their subcultures; before secondly 'discovering' mechanisms of power, exclusion, capitalism, gender-normativity, class distinction, commercialization, and so forth to be at work within them. In a phenopractice theory view, in doing so, despite their critical stance many authors fall prey to the athletes' verbal and visual narrative of perfection and aestheticism, of unconstrained self-expression and competent symbol-play which turns style into an end in itself, into something chosen or crafted for purely aesthetic or symbolic ends—ends which the sociologist then uncovers to be 'actually' some other social issue. What is lost in this way is that the performance of style is first and foremost a moment of *being* in an openly unfolding but concrete situation framed by pressing needs, powerful moods and emotions, impending dangers, and immediate tasks and problems to be figured out. What is lost, in other words, is the feeble; the insecure; the half-hearted, half-baked and good-enough; the unmotivated and the compromised and the myriad everyday moments hanging somewhere between awkward and stylish. Where is the style in these moments? Is it simply amiss, attempted but not achieved? Style, phenopractice theory argues, is not important despite these ubiquitous moments, but because of them; because it orients and orders and aligns things.

In order to develop phenopractice theory based on a rich and deep empirical case, this work focused on the visual dimension of lifestyle-sport practices, particularly because because style in lifestyle sports predominantly appears in visible performances and visual media. In contrast to a strong tradition in social thought which casts the visual as quintessentially superficial, inauthentic, distanced and/or a means of control and hegemony (Jay 1994), key theoretical arguments were developed based on the fact that vision is fundamentally intertwined with our bodily movement, interaction, immediate goals, and emotions or moods. More specifically, phenopractice theory as outlined here builds on selected findings from experiential neurosciences to argue that the visual dimension of lived life comprises two very different, equally important, and co-dependent-but-not-equal ways of seeing I called epistemic and pragmatic seeing. Further, because these two together form the backbone of so many essential 'building blocks' of human conduct such as moving, interacting, recognizing, or learning (at least for those of us who can see), their alignment, coordination, and disentangling is a pivotal prerequisite for achieving the flow of human life. However, since these visual systems or routines deep 'in' us do not themselves orient to, or automatically align with, higher-order ends or projects, they need to be skilfully managed or coordinated; and because they remain profoundly out of reach of our direct conscious attention and wilful control, this management of vision needs to happen in the situation rather than 'in us.' Here, the phenopractice perspective suggests, we find the deeper reason why social order and practical conduct in almost all moments of life is in part organized via screens, curtains, gaze orientations, stages, perspectives, postures and above all: visible styles of doing this or that. And here, it invites us to argue, we find the reason why media images are so extraordinarily important in lifestyle sports: because they can provide orientation to fragile conduct and thus fulfil a functional role by practically enabling the athletes to understand, reflect on, and organize their own complex artful conduct. Mediatized styles of conduct—and in this case: visual style—can effect, orient, and even 'store and transport' ways of doing, not unlike explicit rules do. However, neither rules nor style, phenopractice theory argues in line with Wittgenstein's influential remarks on rule-following, can predetermine or adequately express concrete conduct. Instead, because they are 'woven into' moments of lived life by the practitioner, they direct or orient his or her conduct—and because they can be recorded and mediated, they can function as a kind of cultural or practice memory, and they can enable (media) systems of coordination. Only on this level, at the end of a long 'assembly line,' they might then appear to be a purely symbolic medium and function as a means of communication or expression of abstract, not pragmatically relevant content. While the contrast between this phenopractice perspective and alternative theories is most clearly prevalent in the literature on lifestyle sports, I suggest that a similar disparity can be found and described with regard to many other aspects of contemporary consumer society, such as lifestyle and consumption choices, or taste, culture, and art. More specifically, I have systematically criticized the praxeological perspective established by Bourdieu which is currently predominant in studies of these broad aspects of everyday life. Extending phenopractice theory insights to these fields seems to be a promising avenue for further research. What is more, this account of style specifically focused on the question of how practices spread and evolve, and sketched out a functional perspective on the role of media. A broad and expanding literature discusses these questions with regard to issues such as consumption choices, sustainable or (un-)healthy ways of living, or social exclusion and discrimination. Issues like lifestyle, fashion, or trends feature prominently in these discussions, but much like in the lifestyle sports literature, they are primarily connected to notions of identity expression or symbolic in- and exclusion. Consequently, the phenopractice perspective outlined here could likely provide some fresh insights and provocative arguments for research into consumption styles, for example if applied to clothing, beauty, and the fashion industry.

2 New Theoretical Perspectives

Moving from the empirical to the theoretical aspects of this work, I will now sketch out what I consider to be the three most important conceptual arguments made that might inspire and advance the debate: first, the rift between 'situationalist' or 'individualist' theories of social practices building on either an anthropological or a Heideggerian reading of Wittgenstein; second, the reformulation of action as split into practical intelligibility and practical understanding; and third, neural pluralism.

Heidegger and Situationalism in Practice Theory

A key aim of this work was to contrast and compare different sociological stances on a number of issues of key relevance to practice thought. One mayor conclusion that can be drawn from this exercise (which can, of course, never be really complete since there is sheer endless supply in alternative theories) is that the frequently cited and often bemoaned variety or disparity among the different sociological (!) positions collected under the label 'practice turn' can (and should) be distinguished with regard to their relation to Heidegger. While it is clear that all theories adequately called practice theories build on, or at least conform to, the basic points of Wittgenstein's arguments on language, mind, and social practices, it has come to light that they often draw on quite different readings of his late philosophy, especially his remarks on rule-following and language games. However, my suggestion is that this difference in the use of Wittgenstein ultimately depends in turn on whether or not the authors build on, and conform to, Heidegger's thought on being, practices, and sites. At the heart of the dispute is the question whether or not there is inherent regularity to human conduct, for example by virtue of tacit knowledge, embodied dispositions, mirror neurons, or a habitus. Authors whose answer is affirmative typically equate social order to regularity and hold that Wittgenstein's basic argument—that explicit rules can never fully predetermine or even describe concrete moments of lived life—simply points to the fact that social orderliness springs forth from a different, subconscious, and tacit entity: the skills or dispositions housed in the body or the individual. In effect, I argued, these theorists still cling on to an individualist ontology (but maybe a social epistemology), and therefore their positions need to be distinguished from those practice theorists who do not equate order with regularity and—following Heidegger's postulate that being is bound to clearings or local sites—embrace what one might call situationalism rather than individualism. Two factors make this distinction important: a) While the importance and implications of Heideggerian thought are clearly present in the (Anglo-American) philosophical discussion on practice theory (especially in the early edited volumes on practice theory by by Schatzki/Knorr Cetina/von Savigny 2001 and Wrathall/Malpas 2000), they have been too often overlooked in subsequent debates in sociology (safe for ethnomethodology). This has not only lead to frequent misconceptions or misrepresentations of the work of both Schatzki and Garfinkel, but has given rise to three predominant versions of practice thought which I criticized for different reasons: First, what (for lack of a better term) I called pragmatist practice theory, which equates practices to bodily techniques operating 'underneath' consciousness, explicit communication, or the like. Second, praxeology; the predominant Bourdieuian account of practices as invoked by an embodied habitus which regularizes not only conduct but also perception, and in doing so reflects and perpetuates macro-social relations. Third, postmodern performative versions of practice theory which do not take social conduct to be inherently regular, but effectively deny orderliness per se and thus cannot move beyond the basic conclusion that all social life consists of contingent performances (making it difficult to account for intelligibility). b) Failing to acknowledge 'the Heidegger option' leads those who rightfully voice phenomenological critiques of practice thought—namely the sentiment that the relevancies and experiences as they present themselves to the practitioner must be the starting point of sociological inquiry and explanations—to an all-out rejection of all its versions and possibilities.

For this reason, I focused my discussion on different forms and factors of observability or intelligibility. The core idea of phenopractice theory as I suggest it is that by tying order, meaning, and even being to situations (sites, clearings), one undercuts the classic tri-part separation of observation, observer, and observed. Consequently, a phenopractice-minded account of meaning, knowledge, or action does not simply offer a new name for meaning, knowing, or doing; it reformulates them as *accomplishments of the relation* between the (act of giving) meaning and the meant, the knower and the known, or the doer and the deed. Maybe one could say that phenopractice theory conceptualizes a real-world, situated semiotic triangle in which referred, referent, and reference only make sense together—and because they only make sense together, there is no point in trying to tear them apart theoretically or methodologically, house them in different realms, declare one to be the foundation of the other, and so forth. What makes this perspective (possibly) 'radical' or different is the stubbornness, so to speak, to refuse to focus on either aspect—on the knower, the known, or the process of knowing (or any two of them)—and explain the other as mere effects or outcomes of it. In this way, I believe, the very overcoming the subjectivism/objectivism-dichotomy which all practice theorists strive for can be adequately accomplished. In my view, the Heideggerian notion that meaning transpires in local sites rather than individual minds or the entire world provides a necessary and adequate framework to achieve this theoretical goal.

Splitting Action into Intelligibility and Understanding

A second important argument of this work is that, despite the frequently voiced notion that practice theories are exclusively concerned with routinized and/or subconscious behaviour, an adequate account of phenopractices cannot do entirely without a concept of action. While it would be misleading to portray all kinds of human conduct as action, or to ascribe all social order to be an effect of purposeful action; being in action is nevertheless a frequent and important way in which people go about their daily lives. Rather than abandoning action, I hold, it is best to follow Schatzki (2010b) who reformulates the concept in terms of the practice-theoretical perspective. Phenopractice theory therefore builds on three core convictions: First, that practices consist of persistent and mobile elements. Second, that all meaning transpires in sites opened up through conducting practices. And third, the separation of action into practical intelligibility and practical understanding.

One can deduct this latter fundamental distinction between practical understanding—how to do something, or rather: which set of doing will constitute a certain action—and practical intelligibility—what makes sense to do for a practitioner in a concrete situation—from a Heideggerian site ontology of the social. Consequentially, neither understanding nor intelligibility are conceptualized in phenopractice theory as something done by, or solemnly dependent on, an individual actor—although neither can they transpire without human involvement in the site. Further, the fact that both take place in a site is not a simple causal effect, or an inherent quality of such sites themselves, but rather brought about by the realization (or reproduction) of an overarching relationality or coherence called phenopractice. In my view, it is crucial to note that both understanding and intelligibility are conceptualized as carried by two different relational meshes or arrangements which are found on two different levels and only fall together in the moment of conduct. On the one hand, understandings are carried by a nexus of doings dispersed across different situations. Simply put, the nucleus of an understanding is a 'pair' of compatible doings—performing X and recognizing X—which together instantiate the social existence of the understood X. The basic reason for this is that unrecognizable performances or un-performable recognitions cannot have social existence, thus escaping social ontology. On the other hand, practical intelligibility is bound to and an instantiation of a site or hanging-together, in that it is an effect of a concrete phenomenal field; and it can only occur amid such a field, across its different elements, and against its background. This separation of levels has several consequences. Most importantly, by distinguishing understanding and intelligibility, the phenomenon of human activity or conduct is split up into three separate, yet related aspects: the capability to do a recognizable ('well-known') doing; the way in which a certain action stands out of a situation as the one to perform; and the experience of being-in-action which the practitioner gains from it. Notably, the latter experience is an effect of conduct and not strictly coupled to understanding or intelligibility (inter alia because action can fail).

In effect, a phenopractical account of action differs in important ways from established notions of action in social thought: What a doing is versus how it makes sense to do it to a practitioner are understood as separate phenomena; and because they are separate, they do not need to be housed in the subject together. In the classic theories of action at least since Weber, knowing how to do something (or what doing will constitute some deed) and knowing what to do (next) have been pulled together, since the former was understood as a means or tool for fulfilling the latter. Arguably, the conflation of the two has troubled sociological theories of action ever since, because the meaning of a doing (what it is) is evidently a societal or macro-phenomenon, while the way something makes sense at a particular moment to someone is best understood as a micro-phenomenon (but not necessarily as a subjective phenomenon). Various solutions to this dilemma have been formulated, but all seem to cause further problems: Schutz' (and others') solution was to multiply the meaning of all doing as being different for different actors (and possibly again different in social realms such as interactions or texts); while structuralist solutions declare not only the identity or meaning of doings entirely social, but also its motivation or making sense (why it was done). Phenopractice theory follows Schatzki and suggests avoiding the problematic implications of either solution by splitting understanding and intelligibility into two phenomena which are related but different in that they are stemming from an overarching entity—social practices. What a doing is transpires on a different plane, so to speak, than why it made sense to do it. In my view, one advantage of this separation is that the relational mesh which makes one phenomenon—or rather the processes carrying it—possible does not have to exhibit deep structural homology with that carrying the other one. In particular, this means that the epistemological processes or capabilities which are central to identifying action must not play a large role for 'motivating' action as well. Entities or processes which are widely perceived to be essentially different and possibly antagonistic, such as rationality and emotions, impulse and planning, materiality and mentality, or mind and body, do not necessarily have to be crammed into the same housing. Neither is there a need to postulate that, while both share uneasy coexistence, one has control or superiority over the other, or fully eclipses it, for example in that the meaning of acting 'really' only lies in experiencing acting.

Neural Pluralism

A third important argument I developed has its roots in the implications of certain advances in neurosciences. Some authors have argued that selected neuroscientific studies support or even prove the philosophical standpoints of Wittgenstein, Heidegger, or Merleau-Ponty. While I have acknowledged the general relevance of certain findings for practice thought, I have also criticized this assessment as a confusion of categories, especially in that neuroscientific data can never prove or disprove phenomenological insights per se. Therefore, I have argued that such findings can provide inspiration for, but not authentication of, sociological theory. Especially in neurosciences and a strand of philosophy, but also among some sociologists, there is a tendency to reify scientific models and measurements in order to suggest that they provide definite descriptions of or answers about human lived life and social orders. To a considerable extent, my discussion of findings from vision science was dedicated to the rejection of such attempts. On the other hand, precisely because I built on Wittgenstein's philosophy of mind which contains a sweeping critique of psychologisms of all sorts, and because I refrained from employing individualistic explanations of social phenomena, I also felt confident to make use of neuroscientific insights to some extent. Particularly, I have argued that the separation of practical understanding and practical intelligibility—in combination with the idea that they manifest in sites—might provide an opportunity to enrich sociological theory by drawing on a number of findings from neurosciences. This could be done by embracing what I have called *neural pluralism*: the idea that human neural or brain activity comprises a number of independent, single-issue processes or routines tied to specific aspects of cognition and motricity. From a phenopractical perspective, a good part of the somewhat gridlocked and repetitive debates on whether or not neural processes or brain states themselves suffice to fully explain either intentionality (see e.g. Searle 1980) and/or consciousness (see e.g. Daniel 2001) suffer from an unreflected ontological individualism that insists on locating analogues to all relevant intentional or conscious phenomena, either inside the human body, in the brain or the mind, or—the anti-functionalist or phenomenological position—on some higher level tied to the subject. At its most basic, neural pluralism transcends these positions by suggesting that different neural processes can co-occur simultaneously; and while they might be self-dependent and housed inside the human in their entirety, their alignment and organization must always be achieved within the situation. What makes this sentiment attractive for a phenopractice theory position out is the fact that such routines are understood to be a) partly subconscious, b) independent, and c) need to be aligned or organized in some way to enable the conduct of orderly purposeful activities. For this reason, they match the social ontology focusing on local sites phenopractice theory takes as a starting point: these routines can be understood as relatively stable 'elements' that need to be situationally managed and recombined in the right way in order to produce situated order. In this way, two important theoretical prerequisites are being fulfilled: First, the subject-situation demarcation is transcended. For example, subconscious neural processes are clearly something 'human' or 'done' by the body, but at the same time they can only have meaningful or orderly effects by virtue of being enmeshed into (or carried or 'activated' by) a suitable situational order. Second, although some of these processes can well be thought of as relatively primitive stimulus–response processes, that is, as exhibiting stable regularities, this does not warrant giving up the important argument that all lived order is inherently contingent or indexical. More to the point, I believe that taking a close look at how for example the routines of visual cognition operate can provide plausibility to Schatzki's basic claim that the intelligibility and orderliness of social conduct is not based on regularity, but on similarity. An object or situation, I believe, does not need to be clearly identified by an actor in the strict sense, because many of his bodily doings can very well operate on the basis of mere similarity. More importantly, unlike Cartesian understandings of meaning and consciousness, a perspective derived from neural pluralism can easily acknowledge that *some* neural routines might operate on the basis of limited, task-specific internal models, mental maps, or conceptual content; without having to conclude that there is a *complete* 'inner world' in light of which human conduct transpires. Instead, conscious, subconscious, and material orders or processes might well be simultaneously at work and jointly responsible, and each of them might well be strictly regular if taken on its own; but it is only in their (contingent) sum that the impression of an overall regularity of social conduct can shine up. Therefore, I stress that only because such a conception does not necessitate one to over-generalize, idealize, or reify any such process, it might be possible to integrate them fruitfully into social thought. There is, for example, no need to (and justification for) assuming that 'deciding' for an action has to be governed or even influenced by the same processes which underlie our management of ongoing actions—as sociological interpretations of mirror neurons suggest (Cerulo 2010; Kastl 2004; Lizardo 2009). I should end with a disclaimer: I believe that by sketching out neural pluralism, I have done nothing more than tentatively suggest what might be a very fruitful future line of thinking and area of investigation. Further, by no means do I suggest that we should try to discern and collect all independent 'functions' of the neural systems to get a 'complete picture.' The exact borders and dependencies between one routine versus another is not of the essence for phenopractice theory. I emphasize that I see this notion as nothing but a framework with which one might be able to integrate selected findings from neurosciences and cognitive psychology into a sociological analysis in order to enrich its scope of explanation. The way I presented them, neither neural pluralism, nor any single cognitive routine (or bundles thereof) can themselves provide answers to sociological questions; and how and which findings one might integrate necessarily depends entirely on the theoretical perspective taken and the empirical case in question. Insights into the nature of the social, in other words, will always remain the exclusive realm of social theory.

3 Phenopractice Theory: Key Axioms

This work set out to develop and suggest for scrutiny a coherent theoretical position that brings a range of phenomenological insights into the fold of practice thought by theorizing phenopractices, that is, practices whose conduct can invoke experiences oriented by style. By treating phenopractices as a class or category of practices, many key insights of general social practice theory have been brought to bear on the specific focus of this theory. What this strategy intentionally left open is the question if there are social practices whose performances do not invoke and require ordered experience, or whose ordering should not be understood to be styled. Based on this approach, the following theoretical assumptions and conclusions of phenopractice theory can be summarized in the briefest possible manner, as axioms. This list intends to provide an overview of the theoretical decisions taken, but not to defend them. I formulate these statements brief and precise so that they can be criticized and refuted; they are in no way intended to provide final answers, but to help taking steps ahead.

1. Phenopractice theory can provide a viable and coherent alternative to other positions in practice-based social thought and sociological theory.

    1.1. It is rooted in a distinct set of philosophical a-priori postulates.

       1.1.1. It builds on a social ontology of the social rather than an individual ontology of the social.
       1.1.2. It takes its roots primarily in the philosophical works of Wittgenstein, Heidegger, and Merleau-Ponty.

3 Phenopractice Theory: Key Axioms

- 1.1.3. It is an adaption of the use that Garfinkel and Schatzki make of these philosophers.
- 1.2. It shares arguments and findings with a number of neighbouring sociological positions, but each of these overlappings is only partial.
- 1.3. It differs from several other strands of practice thought.
    - 1.3.1. It diverges from 'pragmatist' practice thought in that it does neither consider bodily conduct as inherently regular, nor takes social order to be explicable on the basis of bodily techniques or tacit knowledge per se.
    - 1.3.2. In contrast to praxeology it does not conceptualize social order as predominantly invoked by a single instance (such as the habitus) carried by individual bodies; it does not consider embodied dispositions or routines as paralleling and inevitably reproducing social macro relations; and it does not assume that practical conduct is characterized by hidden regularity.
    - 1.3.3. Unlike 'performative' or postmodern practice theory, it holds that elements or entities have ontological existence and that social order reaches beyond entirely contingent performances.
2. Phenopractice theory aligns with findings from neurosciences and cognitive psychology, especially with regard to vision and visual routines.
    - 2.1. Neural pluralism suggests that several embodied neural systems conduct different, embodied, principally independent conceptual, sensory, and sensori-motor routines side-by-side.
    - 2.2. Some routines are conscious, some are not; some concern conceptual content, some do not; some can be purposefully initiated or stopped, some cannot.
    - 2.3. Embodied routines are to some extent interdependent (being housed in the same body), but not mutually oriented, automatically self-organizing, or efficiently optimized for all practical purposes. Instead, they can be antagonistic or unhelpful, and need to be aligned or 'managed'.
    - 2.4. Such alignment cannot happen by direct conscious control alone. It must be organized in the current situation. Social situations provide a number of resources or tools for this.
3. Social life happens in situations.
    - 3.1. Meaning transpires in situations.
        - 3.1.1. Meaning appears in form of gestalts arising from related elements-in-context.
        - 3.1.2. Meaning is an assemblage that can only appear across several elements and is never tied to a single one of them.

- 3.1.3. Meaning is a foreground-background relation.
- 3.1.4. Meaning is a figural coherence standing out from a background.
- 3.1.5. Figural coherences are lasting constellations (however shortly).
- 3.1.6. Figural coherences have gestalt-qualities.
- 3.1.7. Meaning must be accomplished in conduct.

3.2. Social order takes place in situations of conduct.
- 3.2.1. Conduct is always situated.
- 3.2.2. Situations are multidimensional. They are not comprised of or controlled by individuals alone.
- 3.2.3. Situations of conduct are inherently meaningful for practitioners. They contain states of order that precede their perception.
- 3.2.4. Situations contain assemblages of elements with enduring qualities.
- 3.2.5. Situations are opened up by unfolding social practices into current praxis.
- 3.2.6. Unfolding a practice means amalgamating (and thus aligning) its elements in befitting ways.
- 3.2.7. Amalgamated elements show up as aspects of the amalgam of praxis.
- 3.2.8. Not all aspects of a situation must be an element of a currently unfolding practice.
- 3.2.9. Elements cannot be observed in isolation or outside of praxis.
- 3.2.10. Aspects can be made to stand out from suitable backgrounds. Systematically isolating and observing elements in this way amounts to sublating them.

3.3. Social conduct or social order is not regular.
- 3.3.1. Conduct is always contingent by virtue of being situated.
- 3.3.2. Conduct can be similar, but not identical.
- 3.3.3. Order exhibits figural forms. Figural forms can be assembled by different elements, in different manners, and against different backgrounds.
- 3.3.4. The identity or stability of elements does not imply regularity or sameness across different situations, even if the same elements exhibit the same figural coherences.

4. Phenopractices are part of lived social life.

4.1. A phenopractice is a nexus of doings and sayings.

4.2. Doings and saying unfold social practices situatedly by amalgamating their elements in particular ways.

3 Phenopractice Theory: Key Axioms

4.3. Phenopractices have distinct elements. Elements are understandings, teleoaffective structures, media (including rules), bodily routines, and material objects or arrangements.

    4.3.1. Elements have enduring qualities. They can circulate in different ways depending on their type.

    4.3.2. Understandings are abilities to undertake doings belonging to a bundle of doings and sayings that together establish the fact that certain things are going or standing for someone in some way.

        4.3.2.1. Understandings are carried across unfoldings of a social practice and are expressed in the doings and sayings that compose said unfoldings.

        4.3.2.2. Understandings are bundles of both ability and intelligibility or observe-abilities. Knowing how to do something and knowing how to identify said doing together warrant for the identity of an understanding.

        4.3.2.3. Different sets of doings and sayings can express the same understanding.

        4.3.2.4. Understandings are not a mental state, but a condition of lived life or being.

        4.3.2.5. Expressing understandings must happen in situated conduct and thus depends on the contingent accomplishment of situational order.

    4.3.3 Teleoaffective structures are normative ends, projects, or states of things that relate to emotional and motivational states as well as current moods (e.g. feeling anxious about a current state of things).

        4.3.3.1. Teleoaffective structures bear on practitioners in conduct of a practice.

        4.3.3.2. They must be situationally accomplished.

        4.3.3.3. They depend on, and effect back on, certain aspects of phenomenal fields, which therefore often have a normative structure.

        4.3.3.4. Teleoaffective structures invoke relevancies.

    4.3.4. Bodily routines underlie all orderly bodily conduct. Bodily conduct or movement is not inherently regular.

        4.3.4.1. As elements, they do not appear in isolation and cannot be independently observed or controlled.

        4.3.4.2. Bodily movements or doings are necessarily situated aggregations and combinations of bodily routines.

        4.3.4.3. Many, but not all routines can be trained, controlled, and managed in different ways. Only some are acquired and honed by repetition.

        4.3.4.4. If at all, practitioners are aware of bodily states, not the dynamic concurrence of routines.
    4.3.5. Material elements have enduring qualities. If put into practice, they prefigure unfolding in persistent ways.
        4.3.5.1. Material elements frequently form larger material arrangements structuring situations.
        4.3.5.2. They are often physically mobile and often retain characteristics over extended periods of time.
        4.3.5.3. One important prefiguration that material objects can invoke is making certain qualities of their own instructably observable in conduct.
5. A practitioner conducting a phenopractice is enwrapped by a phenomenal field; he or she encounters an experiential scape.
    5.1. Phenomenal fields are effects of unfolding a practice.
    5.2. Phenomenal fields comprise the totality of perceptions given to a practitioner in the course of the unfolding of a practice.
    5.3. Phenomenal fields have a background-foreground structure, i.e. every aspect gains meaning in relation to the other aspects of the field.
    5.4. Meanings and relevancies of entities that shine up in a phenomenal field depend on the field, not on the practitioner (or his interpretation) per se. Because phenomenal fields are effects of conduct, however, the observability of things indirectly depends on skilful practitioners.
6. Conducting a phenopractice frequently requires action on behalf of the practitioner.
    6.1. Carrying out an action is a state of being of a practitioner. It is tied to a certain experience of being-in-action provided by the phenomenal field.
    6.2. Being in action means conducting a practice in such a way that one is having the sense of performing an action towards a certain end and on the basis of a certain initial state.
    6.3. The performance of actions depends on first, practical intelligibility, and second, practical understandings.
        6.3.1. Practical intelligibility singles out which action makes sense to do.
        6.3.2. Practical intelligibility is a feature of situations and must be accomplished in conduct.
        6.3.3. Practical understanding is knowing how to perform a certain action.
        6.3.4. Performing an action means performing those doings and sayings which are understood to amount to the performance of said action.

3 Phenopractice Theory: Key Axioms

6.4. Action takes place in an action-present.

- 6.4.1. The action-present is the zone of time in which action can make a difference to the situation.
- 6.4.2. The action-present takes place for the practitioner-in-action.
- 6.4.3. Each action-present carries a certain future (the teleological endpoint of the action) and a past (the initial motivation status). It has a 'doing-from-toward' structure.
- 6.4.4. Action-present happens within an episode of concurrent world-time. It begins at a distinct moment, lasts, and ceases.
- 6.4.5. Since the performances of actions can overlap, so can action-presents.

7. Performing phenopractices often requires achieving a flow of conduct.

- 7.1. Lived life unfolds within the concurrent temporal stream of the world.
- 7.2. Action happens in episodes or distinct segments (filled out by the action-present).
- 7.3. Flow describes the smooth transition between sequential episodes of actions in that the practitioners' conduct amounts to successive performances of actions without breaks or stuttering.

8. Conduct of phenopractices can be oriented by media.

- 8.1. Media are mediatized explicit rules, orders, instructions, images, videos, formulas, and so on, which can orient conduct.
- 8.2. Conduct is oriented when it establishes a Lebenswelt pair consisting of two segments: first, the orienting medium and second, the conduct.
- 8.3. Within a Lebenswelt pair, the second segment is organized in such a way that it turns the first segment into an expression or description of the pair. Within a pair, conduct would for example qualify as rule-following or adhering to the style visible in a picture.
- 8.4. Media do not control or predefine conduct.
- 8.5. Orientation must be situationally accomplished.

9. Conduct of phenopractices can express style.

- 9.1. Style is not a repository of inherently meaningful symbols.
- 9.2. Style is a way of conducting a practice.
- 9.3. Style must be observed in episodes of life conduct or media representations.
- 9.4. Style must be observed across the details of ongoing conduct or mediatized content.
- 9.5. The style of an episode of lived conduct can be a product of prefigurations by elements (purposefully or not), or of orientation to style.

10. Fields of phenopractice are characterized by shared understandings and a shared style.

   10.1. Style is disseminated via media.
   10.2. Predominant styles often evolve over time.
   10.3. The dissemination and evolution of style depends on the necessities and dynamics of media formats and systems.
   10.4. Fields of phenopractice can rely on symbiotic fields to import elements from such fields or orient to styles developed in such fields.

4 Avenues for Developing Phenopractice Theory

Even if a theoretical project is successful (and this remains to be seen), it is never complete. The most important theoretical developments one could hope for will of course come from the responses of others. Careful critique and well-founded rejection of arguments and ideas are often the most valuable impulses for clarification, reflection, and development. They are a genre of thought that this work has tried to engaged in extensively, and something that any work should be blessed to receive. Beyond such potential future sources of developments, the present work has a number of shortcomings and shallow areas that offer potential for further development. First, while I was able to document many details of the freeskiers' artful everyday accomplishments which produce and reproduce the visible style they crave for, there is arguably more left to be said about a number of issues I touched upon only briefly: the practices of filming and photographing which produce the images whose form and function I described; the role and impact of ever-new media infrastructures; or the inherent dynamic of the freeski industry itself (in contrast to the overall ski industry's dynamic on which I focused). I believe that my observation of the basic processes underlying seeing, style, and style evolution, together with the theoretical terminology I sketched out to describe these phenomena, can provide a bedrock for such further inquiries. Second, I hold that I was able to outline a stringent position on style and highlight its importance for the nature and evolution of social practices. Although I have tackled a number of important theoretical issues as well as their interrelations and my focus on visual style was surely beneficial in this regard, it has naturally also limited the scope of inquiry. My strategy was to delineate a general phenopractice-theoretical perspective from philosophical, scientific, and sociological deliberations of visuality and seeing; and therefore an important further step would be to ensure this account fits well with arguments and findings specific to other dimensions of social life. For example, my discussion of styles of speech and semantics was relatively brief, and styles of writing were left almost entirely out of the picture. Especially because I believe it is misleading to portray social life or social order as divided into separate spheres such as the textual, the haptic, the imagined, the emotional, and so forth, weaving findings regarding these different aspects even more tightly into

4 Avenues for Developing Phenopractice Theory

phenopractice theory will be necessary. Third, because my discussion aims to contrast a 'Heideggerian' perspective from alternative theoretical positions, it glosses over certain disagreements or variations among those different practice theorists building on Heidegger. Most importantly, I focused on Schatzki and Garfinkel because of their high relevance to the sociological discussion (currently in the former, since decades in the latter case) and research methodology (only in the latter case) and aimed to show how their positions are related and complementary. I did not, however, discuss their differences at great depth. Likewise, I only mentioned Hubert Dreyfus and Charles Taylor relatively briefly, although their theories are both predecessors of, and alternative to, Schatzki's position. Bringing them into the picture could likewise enhance the scale and scope of my argument.

Beyond adding depth to areas this work remained shallow on, phenopractice theory could be developed conceptually, by integrating and extending on key concepts of social thought that seem to align with the tentative position I sketched out. A first one is the notion of systems. In this work, I have spoken of neural systems and media systems as lying 'below' and 'above' local sites of unfolding. While I have referred to Luhmannian systems theory primarily as a kind of theoretical alterity, as the foreign Other in contrast to which the identity of a phenopractice position was affirmed, Luhmann's thinking on distinctions, processually upheld system/environment borders, and structural coupling nevertheless undergirds my use of the term system to an important extent. Put differently, if one takes it to be a key idea of practice theory that elements circulate and last while praxis unfolds locally and ceases, then not only unfolding but also circulation are key concepts that needs detailed development. To be sure, many of the foremost thinkers of practice theory have addressed the topic of circulation in their discussions of how practices spread; and I have built on their ideas in chapters ten and eleven. Still, my sentiment is that there is more to be said about this circulation as an abstract phenomenon of its own, maybe as a dynamic process "swimming on the sea of perpetually newly formed and soon dissolved" local unfoldings, as Luhmann (1997: 812; my translation) would have it. Some moves into the direction of systems thinking have been made by the literature on mobilities (Büscher/Urry 2009; Sheller/Urry 2006, 2016; Urry 2000), whose potential for developing practice theory has been highlighted (Hui 2012). On the other hand, my focus on local unfolding was born out of the conviction that one first needs a good grasp on its principles before translocal circulation can be adequately addressed; and the account that resulted differs from those employed in either systems thinking or the mobilities paradigm. Here, a second line of thinking currently evolving promises significant insights, a thinking which—as I understand it—attends to the local presencing of meta dynamics or systems: I mentioned the notion of scopic systems (see Knorr Cetina 2003, 2005, 2009; Knorr Cetina/Preda 2007) only in passing (as well as the emerging literature on phenomena of mediatization more generally); but it connects almost seamlessly to my thoughts on visual media (see also Woermann 2012a). Aligning the work on scopic and mobility systems surely provides further food for thought, especially when taking into account that neural-motor systems are currently also labelled systems (despite substantial differences).

A second task that seems especially attractive for further inquiry would be to fill the canvas framed by what I called neural pluralism with some more detail. Since the inquiry was focused on the visual, the discussion of neural and motor routines was restricted to visual cognition and the visual dimension of movement coordination. As indicated, my suggestion is not to try to cover all routines that are there, but still, taking a broader spectrum into account could a) help to test and possibly adapt the framework of situated rather than (strictly) cognitive coordination of routines; and b) provide additional input towards sketching out my rather coarse framework in some more detail. For example, one could compare different types or kinds of coordination and maybe develop categories vaguely similar to what everyday language calls 'mere thinking,' 'mere doing,' 'teamwork,' and so forth. Likewise, I have explained that routines are often co-dependent and/or antagonistic, but these are of course still very general categories. Again, I do not suggest it is possible or even useful to develop a complete matrix to 'know' which routine hangs together with others in which ways. Instead, discerning different types of dependencies or mutual constraining could add more detail to the phenopractice theory framework, plus it might also help to better understand a third future field of inquiry: how practices are unbundled and rebundled in such a way that certain elements are replaced by others (Shove/Pantzar/Watson 2012).

I have made some tentative comments about this third issue, for example when the discussing 'amalgamate-ability' of certain skis, but I believe there is surely more to say. Empirically, this point relates to questions about technological innovation or the mechanization and automation of certain routines (from IT to drones to households), learning and skill perfection (e.g. replacing forms of coordination, or conscious routines with subconscious routines), as well as changing unhealthy, unsustainable, or unethical aspects of routine conduct. Further, I also believe that a more systematic understanding of the swapping of elements within a practice might aid in developing the methodology and empirical methods underlying the practice-based view in that it we might get a better grasp on how and which elements (such as recorded data) can 'stand in' for others without fundamentally altering the practice conducted.

Appendix: Phenopractice Methodology

1 Theory, Methodology, and Methods in the Practice Turn

Questions about methodology are among the most fiercely debated of all questions in the social sciences. A considerable part of these debates, I believe, is somewhat futile, in that what should really be a discussion about a-priories or ontologies is held in the form of an argument about methodology instead. In my view, a-priories frame theories, and theories imply methodologies. To some extent, one can model theories on the basis of methodologies (i.e. in that one seeks to restrict oneself to theoretical arguments that can be confronted with empirical findings), but this does not mean one has left the fly bottle of one's a-priori. Instead, discussing theories on an empirical basis is arguably even more dependent on a solid ontological basis to fall back on, because empirical work regularly forces authors to decide whether something can be taken for granted (by virtue of an a-priori), or needs to be empirically 'verified,' that is, shown to be defendably the case. Given that, one can undertake a kind of triangulation between theory, methodology, and empirical findings within an a-priori framework in order to establish mutual fit between the three. I cannot claim that the triangle I have sketched in this work is equal-sided. Rather, I have spent most pages working back and forth between the theory and the findings; while my comments regarding the methodological point of view from which I confront and align the two have been relatively brief. This appendix sets out to remedy some of my omissions, but it cannot—I am afraid—do full justice to the work of developing a methodology for phenopractice theory that is still ahead.

Phenopractice theory inherits its methodological challenges from practice theory in the wake of Schatzki. Attempts to delineate a systematic, singular, and stringent methodology from contemporary practice thought in general, and Schatzki's

© The Editor(s) (if applicable) and The Author(s), under exclusive license to Springer-Verlag GmbH, DE, part of Springer Nature 2024
N. Woermann, *Seeing Style*, Beiträge zur Praxeologie / Contributions to Praxeology, https://doi.org/10.1007/978-3-662-69182-3

(and colleagues) position in particular[1] face considerable difficulty (Nicolini 2012, Jonas/Littig/Wroblewski 2017). Authors that have tried can be coarsely divided into two mayor fractions: On the one hand, there are those who adhere to a particular long-standing version of practice theory (such as Foucault, Giddens, Bourdieu, Garfinkel, etc.) and thus rely on the specific methods and methodology that have been established on that basis over decades. At the core, they do not seem to see many reasons to alter what they have been doing since many years, be it incompatible with, or under attack from, other practice theorists' work, or not. On the other hand, there are those who see the position suggested by 'Schatzki et al.' as a genuine novelty worth further development and empirical application. But since Schatzki does not cover epistemology at much length and remains largely silent on methodology, they tend to act as bricoleurs rather than engineers of methodology, so to speak. Maybe most prominent among these works is the volume "Practice theory, work, and organization: An introduction." by Davide Nicolini (2012). Drawing on the broad tableau of practice-minded social thought from Aristotle to Schatzki and efficiently addressing many of the key philosophical and methodological debates I have delved into this work, Nicolini solves most paradoxical and paradigmatic problems pragmatically, that is, by translating them into practical problems facing empirical researchers (particularly in Organization Studies). Pondering, for example, the difficult question whether ethnomethodology is too reductionist while Bourdieu's habitus-field theory is too determinist, he recommends a dialectical research strategy rooted in an a visual metaphor: zooming in and zooming out as a way of empirically and theoretically reframing problems in pursuit of refractions and adumbrations of representations of practice. Emphasizing the importance of coherence with each "package" of theory and method, and therefore ontology and methodology, Nicolini (2012: 239) suggests foregrounding and backgrounding as theoretical metaphors for his approach. There are, in other words, many parallels between his approach and this work. However, where Nicolini is explicitly content with remaining "in search of an eclectic set of sensitizing concepts that allow different features of practices (...) to come to the fore," (2012: 239) my aim was to propose a more systematically integrated version of practice theory that loops the visual methodological metaphors back to a vision-based ontology and epistemology in search of coherence. The result will inevitably be less elegant, more difficult, and especially less practical.

By building on ethnomethodology on the one and the ethnographic research tradition on the other hand, however, phenopractice-minded studies are able to draw on a broad range of specific methodological guidelines, as well as clearly marked points of disagreement. In developing this work, I compared and

---

[1] This discussion was picked up more earnestly at a Symposium on Methodology and Practice Theory at the University of Sheffield on Nov. 5th 2011. However, it also became quite clear that few systematic considerations exist, in that most empirical procedures are derived from specific theoretical standpoints (e.g. discourse analysis), and thus their alignment to an overarching theoretical framework still needs to be worked out.

re-assessed them on the basis of the axioms of phenopractice theory. This appendix therefore has the dual function of documenting the principles of my ethnographic work and discussing some of the methodological issues that concern practice theory in general, and phenopractice theory in particular. While working with and from these theoretical bearing points has proven—I hope—to be very fruitful, their specific combination also raises some challenges when it comes to aligning theory, methodology, and empirical findings. Arguably, both Schatzki and Garfinkel avoid precisely pinning down all three—theory, methodology, and empirics—but focus on only one of them: Schatzki, on the one hand, concentrates on theory and—at least in two of his three books—uses (quite detailed) empirical data to merely "illustrate" his theory and show "its compatibility with the social world." (2002: xvi) He denies, however, that he will be able to present "first rate social investigation" (2002: xvi) in its full form and only acknowledges that he does so "to a limited extent." (Schatzki 2002: xvii) Schatzki's rationale is more a practical reason than a theoretical argument: First, constraints of time and page space; and second, the difficulty of defining or measuring the quality of research done and insights gained (2002: xvii–xviii). Garfinkel, in turn, understood ethnomethodology as a scientific practice rather than a theory, and thus stressed that he was only presenting ways to study empirical phenomena (Garfinkel 1996; Lynch 1999), hence focusing on empirical and methodological questions (with methodologies being empirical phenomena in his view, of course). Both authors, however, do effectively and necessarily cover the third position they seem to circumvent, in that Garfinkel of course makes theoretical arguments, while Schatzki necessarily makes certain methodological assumptions (e.g. see Schatzki 2002: xix–xxi).

Accordingly, the empirical methods I recommend for a phenopractice-theoretical study follow primarily the guidelines of what has been called ethnomethodologically informed ethnography (ten Have 2004, 2007; Heath/Hindmarsh 2002), while I also feel that it is both possible and necessary to align the strict methodological postulates of ethnomethodology with a more systematic (and less 'grounded') theoretical framework derived from Schatzki. As of yet, there is no clear consensus regarding the methodological implications of contemporary practice theory. Instead, a variety of methods have been employed by researchers working within the practice framework; but their precise procedures are usually derived from 'classic' theoretical positions which are today associated with the practice turn, such as discourse or dispositive analysis in the wake of Foucault (Bührmann/W. Schneider 2007; H. Schäfer 2010); or the many works building on praxeology, whose methodology has itself evolved from survey research towards in-depth ethnographical work (see Lizardo 2012 for an overview). Reckwitz (2008) is among those who have suggested that this openness—if not malleability—of the practice approach when it comes to methods should be seen as a particular strength of the program. While I agree that it might yield a great potential for innovation and fresh ideas, it also requires each work to outline its own methodological approach adjusted to the specific 'version' of practice theory it embraced—something that does not always happen. In effect, practice-minded inquiries sometimes end up with entirely incompatible methodologies despite their shared theoretical roots. In the following, I will therefore work towards specifying some methodological principles for phenopractice theory by comparing and contrasting some key methodological arguments that have been derived from the different theoretical standpoints within practice theory. Therefore, this appendix has two parts: First, I will discuss some core methodological issues that have been raised with regard to practice theory and seek to formulate an answer on the basis of the phenopractice theoretical vocabulary I have developed in this work. Having worked out the methodological background of my research methods, I will then in the second part provide an overview of the principles of my empirical work and the ethnographic data I have collected and interpreted.

2 Participation and Observation

The core methodological principle that follows from phenopractice theory is the postulate of methodological situationalism. Arguably the most fundamental a-priori assumption of phenopractice theory is the notion that all meaning transpires in situations. Accordingly, the first and foremost methodological question has to be: Did the empirical work attend to those situations where the phenomenon allegedly studied manifests? Or, in the words of Karin Knorr Cetina:

> "I shall call methodological situationalism the principle which demands that descriptively adequate accounts of large-scale social phenomena be grounded in statements about actual social behaviour in concrete situations." (Knorr Cetina 1988: 22)

This postulate, I believe, provides an adequate foundation for a phenopractice-minded methodology—at least if one brackets the "large-scale" part of the sentence and replaces behaviour for the (more inclusive) term conduct. Further, making statements about concrete situations, I hold, first and foremost requires understanding said situations, and this in turn requires ethnographic study, more particularly participant observation. While I am surely not the first to voice this idea, it has also drawn considerable criticism. At first glance, the practice theoretical postulate that meaning or order are inherent to situations and do not spring forth from subjective interpretation seems to betray a naive empiricism or naturalism implying that all social phenomena are readily available in the concrete situations to anyone who happens to walk to past (e.g. Nassehi 2009: 234). Accordingly, the whole methodological finesse of the ethnographic research tradition, one might think, is simply discharged of through the bold claim that meaning is 'just there.' I hope the discussion of practice thought I presented in this work already made clear that this impression is misleading. Nevertheless, in some respect it is surely true that practice-minded empirical studies are somewhat more forgiving in their ways of treating data (safe for ethnomethodological works, that is). Two points, however, have to be kept in mind: First, I suggest that these studies do so for very specific and coherent theoretical reasons (or at least they should); and second, I also believe that the practice perspective also poses quite strict limitations to the use of certain types of data that are the bread and butter of a healthy majority of social researchers, namely surveys, statistics, and interviews.

Nevertheless, both the criticisms and what might look like the methodological eclecticism of many practice-minded works require a more concise answer to the question: How can participant observation be understood from a phenopractice perspective? An answer requires commenting on two issues: a) participation; and b) observation. On a basic level, point a) has one straightforward solution: participation in a (pheno-)practice necessitates (co-)conducting the practice in a situation of unfolding of said practice. As far as ethnographic research is concerned, I believe that the basic obstacles to, and tried and tested methods for, field access or 'getting in' and 'getting on' as an ethnographer in an unfamiliar field (Gobo 2008: 117–134; Harrington 2003; Wolff 2007) can be applied in just the same way if one operates under a phenopractice perspective (see below for the specificities of the case of freeskiing). Such participation, however, can only yield any kind of insight if there is something to observe, that is, if the situation is intelligible in some way—strictly speaking one is not even participating in the first place if the situation remains entirely opaque. The second half of the term 'participant observation,' however, raises several more complex questions. While every ethnographic research logic necessarily builds on some version of the notion that social phenomena are accessible or graspable through observation, different theoretical positions obviously imply quite different concepts of what observation is (cf. D. B. Lee/Brosziewski 2007). Phenopractice theory emphasizes that observability is a situated accomplishment that transpires only in local and adequately arranged sites of conduct—for example through skilful practices of seeing while reading a mountain face, flexing a ski, or spectating in an arena. In other words, in contrast to authors who argue that practice theory postulates the unproblematic availability or transparency of situated meaning, phenopractice theory insists that the public visibility of practical conduct is necessarily carried or brought about by an organized and systematic production of visual intelligibility, instead of simply being a 'natural fact' of everyday life. The suffix "pheno-" in phenopractice is not only a reference to the phenomenological underpinnings of the proposed version of practice theory, but also meant to signal the fundamental importance of visibility for social order (because the Ancient Greek phaínō means "to bring to light, to make appear"). That I have developed my argument with regard to visibility is therefore not coincidental, but motivated by the fact that it is the visual dimension of social order which is most often (mis-)treated as being, well, obvious. Accordingly, to avoid imposing a simplistic picture, a phenopractice perspective tends to consider even the most 'unproblematic' forms of observability to be the outcome of relatively complex processes. In doing so, it offers a counterpoint to works which imply that visibility of things is simply a given and thus not a phenomenon reflecting the social production of order.

3 Observability: Understandings, Intelligibility, and Publicness

This particular point was taken up by Schmidt and Volbers (2011a; 2011b) and subsequently slightly amended by Schmidt (2017). For both its merits and its problems, a closer look at this argument is due. Schmidt and Volbers' main suggestion is that visibility is an ill-fated concept better replaced with the superior alternative of "publicness." In doing so, the authors follow Bourdieu, who arguably adheres to a long-standing tradition of denigrating vision in French social thought (Jay 1994) and seek to overcome "the problems associated with immediate visibility" (2011a: 17) they diagnose. Notably, Schmidt and Volbers do so although they seem to share my basic understanding of vision and e.g. embrace Goodwin's notion of practices of seeing. However, I am not convinced that trading the notion of visibility or intelligibility more generally for the concept of publicness is very beneficial. More importantly, I do not share the methodological conclusions they draw from this concept, namely that Bourdieu's (1984) 'Distinction' with its large-scale statistical evaluations of 'the' French society provides a methodological role-model for research practice fully in line with the implications of for example Goodwin's notion of practices of seeing. I have attacked Bourdieu's praxeology and the reading of Wittgenstein it is based on at some length throughout this book, and thus there is no need to reiterate theses points here. However, I will briefly discuss the methodological claims made by Schmidt and Volbers under the label of publicness' for two reasons: First, over the last two decades, the claim that a Bourdieuian praxeological approach can underwrite both large-scale survey research *and* intricate ethnographic studies has found many proponents and was arguably a mayor driver of its popularity (Lizardo 2012; Manning 2009; Wacquant 2009). Despite claims to the contrary, however, this claim cannot be properly aligned with, or strengthened by, using arguments from authors such as Schatzki or Goodwin. Instead, I will argue that it is based on a fundamental misconception of intelligibility as a sited phenomenon. Second, clarifying this popular misconception will serve as a helpful avenue towards pinpointing my own understanding of intelligibility, which in turn led to my own methodological approach.

Let me begin by saying that Schmidt and Volbers (2011a) are right when they assure that what they call "the problem of the publicness of social practices" is central to all contemporary strands of practice thought, and that I also share their sentiment that the nature and prerequisites of intelligibility or 'publicness' are not always sufficiently spelled out in the debate. This is unfortunate, because the notion that order or meaning transpires in social situations rather than emerging in realms such as consciousness, language, or the social unconscious is probably the most basic premise of all theories of social practices (Reckwitz 2002a): For example, at the core of Garfinkel's critique of "the worldwide social science movement" and its remaining stuck in what he calls "formal analysis" is the allegation that this 'movement' is trying to bring back order into the alleged chaos of social life while overlooking or ignoring that "there is order in the plenum" (Garfinkel 2002: 142;

see Garfinkel/E. Livingston 2003); that is, for the social scientist to be able to recognize and research anything, he must have been exposed to a phenomena of order in an already orderly situation. Likewise, Giddens (1984: 139–144) seeks to overcome the false dichotomy of structure and agency by pointing out that they necessarily coalesce visibly in concrete situations; and underlying Schatzki's (2002: 135) notion of the site of the social is the Heideggerian idea that meaning is "out there in the practice," as Charles Taylor (1971) put it. This latter formulation, it seems to me, has drawn much attention—and has arguably led to misunderstandings and ill-conceived methodologies. One of these is exemplified by Schmidt and Volbers' argumentation that:

> "If social order and complex cultural formations are constituted publicly in and through practices, as the site hypothesis claims, these acts of constitution cannot be explained by entities that are inherently unobservable and remain purely hypothetical." (Schmidt/Volbers 2011a: 3)

I surely agree that some of its entities must be observable for a practice to be public. This does not, however, necessarily imply that they are always observable, nor that they are observable independently of a certain context. More importantly, I do not see why one should not be able to explain public acts of constitution by unobservable and/or hypothetical entities—apart from the fact that something which is not inherently unobservable can still be unobservable in certain situations. Furthermore, neither do I believe that every theory which conceptualizes "social mechanisms" as "hidden or concealed" is necessarily "intellectualist" in nature, as Bourdieu alleged (Schmidt and Volbers 2011a: 4).[2] Both assumptions are deducted from the fact that social practices are bound to or carried by their situated unfoldings. Since each local doing is 'publicly accessible,' the argument goes, and practices are in the end a sum of related doings, the practices themselves must be public—"site, practices, and events therefore all must be conceptualized as public phenomena." (2011a: 2) The methodological implications of such a reading would be quite grave: The mere presence in any situation of an unfolding of a practice would suffice to 'get' the practice's understanding; and additionally, one could also conclude that all sorts of methods of recording or documenting this 'out-there' would suffice to capture said understandings. In other words: intelligibility and understanding would be conflated. And indeed, Schmidt and Volbers (2011a: 14) define publicness as situationally and "plurally [sic] constituted, shared attention" and formulate: "if alter and ego look at the same object, this constitutes a 'public space'"(2011a: 5). How useful is such a notion of publicness as a basis of a methodology for phenopractice-minded research? I believe that both parts of the definition—'attention' and 'public'—are problematic. First, a key premise of

---

[2] On a side note, the authors recommend Bourdieu's habitus as a remedy to theories that hypothesize about hidden mechanisms as secretly governing all social conduct and/or intellectualize human activity, but unfortunately do not discuss the frequently voiced argument that these very two problems befall the habitus concept as well (Lynch 2001; Schatzki 1997; S. P. Turner 1997, 2007).

phenopractice theory is that the organization of attention plays a critical role in determining the meaning or understanding carried by a social practice. But I also want to point out that attention is a relatively weak and general prerequisite for the production of publicness and shared "practical understanding." (Schmidt/Volbers 2011a: 5) Do we understand everything we attend to? In my view, for example the freeskiers' behaviour in the funpark demonstrates that mere attention does not suffice to establish a shared social site. The complex social order of the arena with its different positioning and skilful ways of orienting and spectating would be missed in its entirety if one would simply say that everyone who attends to the setting in some way—such as the 'tourists' actually hindering the freeskiers' producing Style—shares its central understandings. Because of this, phenopractice theory distinguishes between orientation and understanding: Orienting towards something manifests its intelligibility (the *conditional* possibility!), and thus it is a prerequisite of, rather than equal to, expressing, becoming attuned to, and carrying forth an understanding.[3] For this reason, I suggested that the Heideggerian term 'attunement' is much more suitable than "attention," because it formulates a more specific prerequisite for accomplishing situated understanding. Second, the category 'public' is equally problematic from a phenopractice perspective, because just like attention, it seems to describe a very weak prerequisite that must be met for the researcher to diagnose a shared understanding. For example, Schmidt and Volbers (2011a: 16–17) use the generality of the term to assert the "public character of social structure" of society as a whole; and later in their article, it appears that in a sleight of hand the "public social space" of France becomes an "object" that can be readily grasped by statistical means. This supposed object also "makes itself public in a specific way" by being "empirically condensed" in form of the (actually not too condensed) city of Paris (2011a: 16–17). At this point, Taylor's formulation that understandings are "out there" in the practices has come a long way. The suggestion that a society, as well as a whole city, are to be understood as a) singular objects of b) shared attention which are c) publicly visible in their entirety seems unconvincing. Conceptualized in this way, the "publicness" of human praxis has become a kind of methodological vademecum which ensures that the researcher is free to employ just about any method, since just about anything seems to count as a 'public thing' in public space—including what Schatzki (2002: 68–69) calls pseudocontexts, i.e. groups of individuals such as members of a society, entities which are, he emphasizes, not site arrangements but effects thereof. It is worth mentioning that Schmidt (2017) subsequently seems to reframe his position slightly, but not without further generalizing the claim: "Practice theory considers all components of practices to be public. For these components to be public is for them to be accessible to observation and interpretive perception on the part of participants and observers of practices." (Schmidt 2017: 151) First, practice theory is not a monolith, particularly with regard to conceptions of

---

[3] N.Bb.: "Being oriented by," in contrast, describes an achievement and thus regularly entails that some understanding has been realized.

practice elements and their observability. Second, by equating publicness to accessibility to observation and interpretive perception and maintaining that publicness is a universal feature of all components of a practice, a claim to a universal transparency of practices independent of the limits and performative effects of in-situ observation is being implied. But on which theoretical or empirical basis can we assume universal accessibility? In chapter five, I have developed the concept of sublation to argue for an alternative view that accounts for the performative nature of phenopractices without relying on the "interpretation of participant" as the engine of meaning. In conclusion, one might ask if Taylor's notion of 'out-thereness' necessarily leads to rampant over-generalization and is better abandoned, or if it can be kept at bay? More to the point, how can the borders of the contextual arrangement within which a practice (or practice bundle) unfolds be conceptualized in accordance with the phenopractice theory perspective? In other words: If all meaning transpires locally, where are the borders of the local?

4 Delineating Empirical Phenomena

Discussing Goodwin's (2000a, 2000b) studies of situated seeing in chapter three, I showed that his account operates on the basis of implicit demarcations imposed on situations of co-attendance by the limits of human attention and sensory perception, as well as a relatively close temporal succession of acts of gaze orientation. My argument was that these limits are set too tightly, as well as somewhat arbitrarily. Even in co-presence, people always continue to look 'on their own' for (however brief) episodes after attending to one another. In other words, I argued that the demarcation of the relevant phenomenon (in his case certain professional practices of seeing) cannot be adequately defined with regard to spatial or other dimensions of the situation itself, but must happen with regard to a concrete doing. We find the same sentiment in Schatzki's theoretical writing. He shares the sentiment which arguably caused Schmidt and Volbers' object of study (the public) to 'explode,' namely that the borders of spatial and material arrangements of elements cannot be clearly defined on the basis of their own characteristics (Schatzki 2002: 46). Expressed in phenopractice theory terms: Local situations always have horizons. But unlike Schmidt and Volbers, who seem to take this as a licence to treat e.g. the whole of Paris as one large site of order, Schatzki (2002: 46) draws the conclusion that "the demarcation of specific arrangements is (…) relative to the interests and purposes of the demarcator." Interests and purposes, it needs to be added, are in his view not permanent or inherent qualities of a practitioner, but depend on, and stem from (take place by virtue of), the momentarily doings he is engaged in. This conclusion is very significant in terms of methodology, because it means that, despite the fact that the practice perspective de-centres the subject and does not consider it the relevant 'object' of study, the practitioner is nevertheless the instance *with regard to which*, rather than by virtue of, the objects of study (the practices) transpire, that is, become observable. And for this reason, I argued that although the subjective actor is not considered a 'well of meaning,' it is nevertheless the subjective *point of view* from which the phenomena transpire that phenopractice-minded studies are concerned with. Importantly, I hold that this does not mean that the researcher can study just any phenomenon that in some way unconceals itself to the practitioner—e.g. in that 'the' distinction mechanisms of 'the' society are 'sometimes' and 'in some part' apparent to 'all of us'—but what must be studied is just *the* way in which they present themselves to specific practitioners in specific situations. This postulate raises some important methodological questions—most clearly laid out by those discussing the methodological procedures and principles of ethnomethodology (e.g. ten Have 2002, 2004)—the discussion of which will have to wait briefly. For now, I shall only emphasize that in the phenopractice view, the 'content' of such unconcealment, the meaningful order which becomes apparent is the very phenomenon which needs explanation, the explanandum, but not in itself the explanans, the means by which it can be explained. Hence, the phenopractice perspective does not share Schmidt and Volbers' idea that all entities or factors responsible for it must themselves be directly present in or part of the phenomenon, i.e. the practitioner's experience (and much less her shared attention). Instead of supporting any kind of methodological 'free-for-all' eclecticism, this perspective instead aligns with Schatzki (2002: 135) in his reading of Taylors' formulation that understandings are "out there in the practice." actually. Paying close attention to Schatzki's argument, it becomes apparent how this implies a methodology that is not loose at all, but quite restrictive:

> "In Charles Taylor's phrase, action understandings (...) are 'out there' in public space, accessible in principle to anyone. Individuals come to have understandings of action by becoming attuned to these public understandings." (Schatzki 2002: 135)

First, what Schatzki describes as being 'out there' are practical understandings, *not* (practical) intelligibility. Practical understandings, however, do not determine which doings and sayings someone will engage in, since practical intelligibility is (in his and my view) responsible for that. Therefore, the 'entities' crucial for constituting public practices are not themselves conceptualized as public. Second, as I have discussed (in chapter seven), Schatzki holds that getting attuned to an understanding happens within the performance of an activity itself. Only in this sense are understandings "out there" in the public performance of a practice; and therefore his site ontology does not imply that they are public in the sense that they are open to, or openly visible for, 'the general public' not undertaking the activity in question. In fact, I would argue that it means just the opposite: without ever taking part personally, there can be no attunement nor understanding. For this reason, I have developed a different understanding of the relation between the ('public') performance of a practice and its ('non-public') elements in this work. Phenopractice theory embraces the difficult, yet central assertion that practices can only be said to exist or happen in the form of an ordered whole (a site), and that the meaning or order of a practice cannot be reduced to, encapsulated in, or fully represented by single entities other than the practice itself, such as accounts, rules, or objects. In my view, accepting this premise is fundamental to envisioning phenopractice theory as a non-individualist ontology of the social. But this conviction does not imply that any unfolding of a phenopractice effectively lays bare all of its elements. Instead, I believe that it implies just the opposite: Since I take it for granted that the level of available detail must always be limited for intelligibility to be possible, the elements of a practice can never be available simultaneously in their full detail—and the organization of the availability of details is exactly what I consider the core function which phenopractices fulfil. Maybe one would be going too far by saying that *hiding* certain details is one of the key 'capacities' by virtue of which phenopractices enable intelligibility; but surely it is that of evoking or providing what Heidegger called the Zuhandenheit of things, their being present-to-hand or 'seen but unnoticed' (as Garfinkel put it). Consequently, the ability to capture such situated ordering of elements is the basic methodological prerequisite a study of phenopractices must fulfil.

5 Intelligibility: Can there be an Adequacy Criterion?

If intelligibility (rather than publicness) forms the foundation for methodological principles guiding empirical research from a phenopractice perspective, what kind of quality criteria can be delineated? In other words, how can the researcher ensure the adequacy of the empirical account provided? First, classical guidelines such as avoiding methodological subjectivism, or ensuring sufficient control for intersubjective validity are not building on categories phenopractice theory acknowledges. Instead, the notion of style, the assumptions about the enduring nature of elements, and the basic idea that experiences are effects of phenopractices rather than subjective knowledge or learning histories, imply that not the inter*subjective* generalizability of findings or experiences is a core methodological issue, but rather something like their inter*practical* similarity. Let me try to make a suggestion for judging the adequacy of a phenopractice-based empirical account by drawing a comparison with a very specific requirement for meaning-adequacy that has been developed in the context of ethnographies of the lifeworld (Hitzler/Eberle 2007) and builds on Schutzian social theory. My thinking behind trying to build on this particular concept is as follows: As I have shown in chapter eight, the notion of practical intelligibility in Schatzki fulfils a theoretical function similar to the actors' orientation of meaning (in the pragmatic attitude) in Schutz, in that its relevance structure determines how a situation makes sense to the practitioner. Furthermore, Schatzki emphasized the indeterminacy of actions and denied the idea that practical intelligibility could causally determine conduct. We find the same sentiment in Schutz, who dismissed Weber's call for causal adequacy and identified it as a sub-case of meaning-adequacy. Eberle (2010) has demonstrated that Schutz also softened his own postulate of adequacy of meaning under the influence of then contemporary economic thought, reducing what is demanded from accurate representation of concrete experiences towards calling for mere principal intelligibility of scientific concepts from within a stance of common-sense. If 'softened' in this way, Eberle (1999, 2010) argues, the postulate potentially becomes applicable to the most abstract theoretical constructs fully detached from real-world events. Therefore, he suggests sharpening it again so that it might serve as a reference point towards discerning if scientific work grounded in empirical findings is adequate, or less so. Eberle proposes the following definition:

> "Complete adequacy has been reached if the concrete orientation of meaning of actors has been grasped appropriately. With this, we declare the subjective perspective of the singular actor to be the absolute reference point for social-scientific analyses." (Eberle 1999: 115; my translation)

Could it be possible to emulate this postulate in such a way that phenopractice-oriented work might benefit from it? I believe that this requirement for meaning-adequacy can be transformed if one replaces its grounding in the subjective process of constitution of meaning with a reference to its situated practical accomplishment. As my discussion made clear, every enquiry into empirical features of phenopractices must, in my view, be concerned with meaning as it presents itself to, and from the viewpoint of, a practitioner. This is precisely why I consider ethnographic methods as an obligatory feature of studies of phenopractices. Accordingly, I also hold that a particular notion of adequacy of meaning is still the standard to which an ethnographic description can and should be held—but from a phenopractice perspective, the particular 'typical' meaning to be discussed cannot be subjective, but must rather be situated. My account of (practical) intelligibility shared with a Schutzian view the notion that the relevance structure of any concrete meaningful situation is crucial for the way said situation makes sense for a practitioner; but it differed in that said relevance is not conceptualized as an effect of the subjective knowledge, but rather the standing out or blending in of details brought about by the situational background-foreground arrangement. Accordingly, I suggest to reformulate the postulate of adequacy in that qualitative research arguing from a phenopractice perspective should strive to grasp not "the concrete orientation of meaning of actors," but instead the concrete meaning available *for* actors from the phenomenal field generated by the unfolding of the phenopractices in question. Crucially, just as Eberle (1999, 2010) proposes, such a postulate needs to be understood as an ideal that can never be fully reached but is nevertheless important because the degree of approximation towards it serves as a benchmark of the quality or appropriateness of alternative understandings of the field under study.

At a most basic level, I suggest, an empirical account must present and discuss intelligible features of the situations in question: they must have been observable in the concrete moment, rather than being only imaginable in abstract terms, or observable in data collected about, rather than from, said situation. First and foremost, this implies that the phenomena a sociologist seeks to study will appear and vanish together with the local situations within which they are constituted, and thus the methods employed to this end must be directed at said concrete situated doings—hence the postulate of methodological situationalism. From a phenopractice perspective, methods like surveys or biographic interviews are therefore directed at rather peculiar phenomena: how people fill out surveys, or how they manage to respond properly to the highly unusual situation of having to answer questions about one's 'course of life' coming from a complete stranger. What is more, not only does this phenomenon differ quite dramatically from what the researchers usually claim to be studying; one also needs to ask whether the 'data' produced, the answer sheets and recordings, can tell the researcher much about how the respondents did what they did—i.e. the nature of the situational order which left readable or hearable traces on these media (Garfinkel 1996; Law 2009; Lynch 2002; Pollner 1991).

6 Validation: Ensuring Adequacy

How can one ensure that the adequacy of research findings—conceived as suggested—can be maximized, or does not fall below a critical threshold? In my view, the postulate just formulated implies that several basic methodological guidelines usually informing participant observation apply to phenopractice-minded research as well, most importantly the prerequisite that a) the observer engages in concrete situated conduct, and that b) she has acquired an adequate skill level enabling said participation. Notably, the importance of the ethnographer's basic competency regarding the practice under study is invoked by a different argument than in the Verstehen-tradition: The point is not that he needs to build up a suitable stock of knowledge on the basis of which the ethnography can be written, but rather that without competence, there would be no participation in the first place. In ethnomethodology, this sentiment has led Garfinkel to formulate the so-called unique adequacy criterion (Garfinkel/Wieder 1992): only those who are competent enough to pass as members in a certain setting are able to study it properly. Some have argued that this is a relatively extreme principle which implies that (too) many fields of study remain closed off for the researching sociologist (ten Have 2004: 131), while others view it as not strict enough because mere competence does not equal biographically informed, lifeworldly engagement (Nicolini 2012: 151). In my view, however, this principle should not be read as imposing a hurdle that must be passed in order to be able to claim 'proper' insight. Rather, I believe it is just a matter-of-fact description of the methodological implication of not just ethnomethodology but also phenopractice theory and the notion of intelligibility at its centre. What is more, I do not believe the principle implies one cannot actually study a setting or field which one is not an expert of—it only means one cannot adequately grasp how the things that *only* the expert practitioner conducts make sense to her. As my fieldwork in sites such as the funpark show, many different 'folk practices' can take place at the same time, or concurrently. From a practice perspective in general, studying a culture or community means studying what might be called a field of practices rather than group of people. Therefore, the depth of insight into the field depends on the question, which of the practices of such a field the ethnographer can engage in, and in which not. Usually, by far not all of these specific practices will be so special that a researcher cannot learn them at all. In the case of freeskiing, for example, I was not able to learn any but the more basic freestyle tricks, and I possibly reached an intermediate level in freeriding. What I did learn quite well, however, were other core phenopractices such as discerning, judging, and enjoying freestyle pictures and videos, debating ski technology or freeskiing brands, 'hanging out' and spectating in a funpark, and so on. As ten Have (2007: 146) rightly points out, becoming what Garfinkel calls a member of a certain setting requires first and foremost taking part in it in some ways, but not in all ways. What is more, the most important and often most insightful way of engaging in a setting is as a learner or beginner of (some of) its phenopractices, especially because this often entails learning many important field-specific observation skills—that is, becoming attuned to the field-specific understandings—quite early on.

But how to determine whether or not sufficient skill has been acquired? From a phenopractice theoretical perspective, this can only happen in appropriate situations; namely in situations in which insufficient skill would 'stick out' and could thus be recognized. Accordingly, the sufficiency of the ethnographer's understanding or skill must be found out 'in the field' and in the course of participating in the phenopractices in question. Take, for example, my own ability to see Style in freeskiing images and videos, a skill that was obviously important for my own research. It seems trivial to point out that I needed to look at freeski images in order to acquire it. However, as I described, Style cannot be seen in just any freeskiing picture, a point that some of the ski industry's brand managers sometimes seem to miss. Therefore, I needed to look at stylish images in order to be able to learn to 'get' the Style's 'unconcealment' or intelligibility. In effect, I acquired a sense for Style in the course of participation, by watching freeski DVDs with Tom and the others in his camper van, by reading comments on freeski websites, and by chatting about the newest early-season-edit on someone's Facebook page. At the later stages of my fieldwork, I would quite intuitively see if some advertising poster showed a freeride action that was actually pretty lame since the rider was about to lose his balance; and in order to test and hone my ability to see Style, I would comment on such a case during my fieldwork to see if the others would agree. This brings me to a key point: While I would argue that in this way, one can get a pretty accurate idea of whether one has acquired a certain observation skill or not, this does *not* imply that what one would see at any precise moment will be exactly the same that other practitioners see. What I am describing is the adequacy of the intelligibility, the *possibility* to see or sense something in a certain situation. Thus what I am 'testing' for when tentatively commenting on a picture while being in the field is not whether all my informants see just the same level of style in a certain picture as I do, but rather whether one 'can legitimately,' or 'would normally,' or 'should' see Style in that picture, or not. The way phenopractice theory is designed, this relatively flexible requirement is already sufficient—and precisely because it is, the theory would expect that more or less all skilful practitioners would in *similar* situations at least be able to see Style as well—i.e. it would make sense for them to see it.

Based on this methodological procedure which one might call in-field validation of understandings, I suggest, not only phenopractical skills such as 'seeing Style,' or 'being able to pass as a member' can be tested for sufficiency. Importantly, the same applies to the more general ethnographic descriptions of the field of (pheno-)practices the researcher has studied: from a phenopractice perspective, they are understandings as well; and particularly, they are sayings. Therefore, as far as they are descriptions of (sayings about) pervasive features of the phenopractices in question, they should 'make sense' to the practitioners as well in that hey should seem plausible and not widely off the mark in their view. To use a notion introduced by Circourel (1996, 2007), one could say: they need to have *ecological validity*. What I am suggesting—and what I strove to practice when researching this work—in other words, is conducting a form of 'feedback-interviews' with key informants during which they are asked to comment on the mayor thoughts and insights the researcher has developed. Such interviews, it is clear, must tread a thin line in two ways: First, the informants cannot usually make sense of the abstract theoretical considerations or arguments the ethnographer might have followed. For this reason, I wrote that the ethnographic *descriptions* should be subject to feedback, not the (theory-infused) findings per se. Further, almost necessarily these findings will touch upon points which the informants did not notice or saw in this particular light before; and thus I am only saying that they should seem plausible or sensible to informants. For example, the freeskiers did not pay much attention to the fact that they do not like to perform in a funpark if they are alone; and thus they would not make a detailed argument about the reasons behind this when I asked them. However, what was important to me was the fact that they did neither deny that the phenomenon actually existed (they all agreed they do not usually train when they are alone), nor found my explanations for it implausible or unrealistic. Quite to the contrary, Tom later told me that he had thought about this point and concluded that I was probably right. While such comments are of course enormously helpful, they also link to the second restriction that applies to this kind of validation: One needs to be careful not to inflict one's own (theory-driven) ideas onto the key informants, for example in that they start to pay attention to phenomena which had not actually featured in their experiences during, or understanding of, a certain conduct. For this reason, I undertook such explicit feedback-discussions only towards the end of my fieldwork.

Finally, I should point out that the phenopractice perspective on action stipulates that practical intelligibility is relevant in order to grasp how (and thus possibly why) it made sense for a practitioner to do something. Therefore, if one is not able to grasp the practical intelligibility which manifested in a certain situation and prompted someone to engage in an action—especially because someone else was that particular person in that particular moment—then this does not imply that one is not able to gain *understanding* of the ensuing activity or conduct. In other words: From a phenopractice perspective, a non-participating observer would still be considered to be possibly able to see or identify just what is being done—he would only be barred from explaining *why* the other undertook this particular action. To be sure, gaining such an understanding is itself a doing which requires both certain skills and a suitable situation (i.e. the others' visible conduct must justify seeing what is seen in it). Nevertheless, I emphasize that gaining understanding is much poorer in prerequisites than retracing practical intelligibility. Particularly, it seems to me that research data in the form of recordings or transcriptions can often provide a pretty good understanding of what was being done (e.g. in that one can hear on the tape what was said)[4] but not how it made sense to the doer to (try to) do it (e.g. we can often only speculate on why the speaker wanted to say what we think he wanted to say from hearing him saying something).

7 Generalizability: Average, Typical, or Normal?

Thus far, my discussion of the methodological implications of phenopractice theory has yielded that, in order for an empirical account to be adequate it must be ensured that the phenomena which are described have been intelligible in concrete situations for a skilled practitioner, i.e. a practitioner who would share the understanding of 'emic' practitioners if engaged in similar situation. Still, this leaves open under which conditions such skills (or understandings) should be acquired, and what can count as 'a similar situation.' Here, one is confronted with a basal problem that all kinds of empirical research will encounter: How to make sure that the situations or data 'bits' that are being examined are not special or different from all others in some way? There is, I believe, no ultimate solution to this dilemma. However, certain specific definitions which can provide indications can be developed on the basis of the theoretical postulates invoked. In a phenopractice view, ethnographic data, as well as the ethnographers' capabilities, must be based on what I call normal conduct. Simply said, the researcher must ensure that the cases she describes (apart from those moments in which she claims to describe exceptions) must be instances of what members of the field in question would call "perceivably normal courses of action," to use Garfinkel's (1967: 35) formulation. In other words, I suggest using the concept of *normality* as a benchmark to determine the adequacy of the situations which are in turn treated as manifestations of the phenopractices in question, and whose intelligibility should be adequately captured. I suggest that this concept could be used as a replacement for the two most widely used alternative concepts in this regard: the notions *average* and *typical*, which both do not seem fitfully applicable to a phenopractice perspective (if they are used in the strict sense that they acquire in the methodological discussion in

---

[4] Because a competent listener is able to—to speak with Garfinkel—'make the hearing good over the ground'; not because what is being said is *on* the tape in a strict sense.

sociology). Let me briefly sketch out why, before I go on to suggest how normality might fill their space instead.

The notion of the average is problematic for studying phenopractices in two ways: First, it seems to me that we are simply lacking the methods to produce a statistical average of situations on the basis of the meaning or order as it transpires multi-modally in said situations. How does an 'average' ride in the Krimml feel or look like? How to capture it? Second and more fundamentally, it needs to be emphasized that according to the phenopractice view, lived praxis is not considered to be meaningful by virtue of being regular, but on the basis of similarity. Thus, even if we suppose that we could pin down the average way in which a certain phenomenon manifests in lived life, what this average would reflect would be regularities that can be found in the world (e.g. a word appearing so-and-so often in newspaper articles on a certain topic), but it would not reflect the quality or situation responsible for its own (and other situations) being meaningful (in that in my example, a) the meaning of the word still depends on the context, and b) the same thing could as well be said in different words). A phenopractice, in other words, is understood as being fundamentally different from praxis, and since concrete praxis (in singular or aggregated) is not a 'dirty' version of the practices it unfolds from, polishing it by statistical means will not help. Typicality, on the other hand, when understood as building on the postulate of subjective interpretation and Max Weber's notion of ideal types, aims at reconstructing or modelling the social actor's subjective meaning of and motives for actions, for example in a Schutzian sense (Eberle 1999, 2010; Hitzler/Eberle 2007)—both of which in a phenopractice account come to be seen as carried by practices rather than subjects themselves. Like in the case of the average, while one can speak about typical situations in a meaningful way, in a phenopractice view it is not by virtue of typification in the above sense that situations can be observed as typical. To be sure, to a certain extent the notion 'phenopractice' is not unlike an ideal type in that it describes a kind of 'standard version' of some doing prevalent in the social world, but its being 'standard' is not understood as an ex-post association constructed by a subject, but as an antecedent of any conduct (i.e. of its unfolding)—in other words, as an ontological condition of being. The crucial difference between the "normal" as opposed to the concepts "average" and "typical" therefore lies in where they locate the necessary process of ordering: in the ex-post scientific treatment of data, in the coeval subjective typification undertaken by social actors, or in situational conduct itself. In everyday conduct, it remains flexible to some degree what precisely is normal—in Ashby's (1958) words, assuming normality retains sufficient "requisite variety" in order to be routinely applicable. In other words, the concept of normality seems useful to phenopractice theory precisely because it is both a prerequisite and an accomplishment of phenopractices, and as such it is a criteria that is revisable in any given situation: Practitioners will be able to tell or demonstrate if things are not normal—usually even without any need to ask. If I describe practices of seeing and how, for example, a rider needs to ride closer to a cliff in order to inspect the snow quality, such a general description implicitly refers to a rider exhibiting normal vision. A visually impaired rider would act dramatically different—in fact, skiing seems only possible for the blind by riding on a well-groomed slope directly behind a guide shouting command. More generally speaking, ethnographical descriptions and phenopractice theory-based explanations seem impossible without building on certain assumptions of normality. But what exactly is it that makes a normal situation normal? What does it mean, for example, to say that my account of seeing in freeskiing refers to practitioners commanding normal vision?

8 Conceptualizing Normality

In phenopractice theory terms, normal situations of conduct imply that normal elements are being amalgamated towards achieving said conduct. In this sense, a blind skier is not skiing 'normally' according to e.g. the understanding of Tom and his friends because his not-seeing is 'abnormal,' because it differs in a very significant way from their own capabilities. Accordingly, one could consider elements or things more generally—tools, body parts, and so forth—a plausible candidate for the position of the 'bearer of normality.' Especially if we follow pragmatist or praxeological versions of practice theory, this option seems plausible. Implicit in Schmidt and Volbers' (2011a) discussion, for example, is the idea that the public objects they postulate turn situations into what they are, that is, normal occurrences of something. From the phenopractice perspective, this view is misleading. A key methodological principle following from Heideggerian practice thought is that what I call the normality of a situation which makes it an adequate source of empirical work cannot be tied to any particular element. Elements have certain enduring qualities, but they are by themselves not normal. Rather, it is in normal situations in which their qualities come to be known to us. Take, for example, the case of normal vision: Throughout this work, I described different ways of making use of an entity called "the eye" which might be phenomenologically or consciously not usually present or accessible to me, but still appears to be a stable tool. However, from the phenopractice perspective recommended here, body parts such as the eye cannot come into view as objects separate of phenopractices (cf. Hirschauer 1991; Mol 2002). More to the point, discussing practices of seeing does not actually mean making an argument about the eye, but making an argument about *vision*. In other words, normal vision is a) an assumption or understanding which common social praxis routinely implies, and b) a state of things which's facticity can be tested, conformed, and denied in—and only in—the course of conducting a phenopractice. In everyday conduct, the normality of someone's vision is usually neither tested nor described. Should, however, the need arise to clarify whether someone 'has' normal vision, for example in order to declare him or her visually impaired by law or in need of medical treatment, sufficiently definite knowledge can be established by testing: Normal vision describes the ability to pass a test of normal vision. What is essential for a phenopractice-based view of seeing is the fact that basic examinations of normal visions are local, interactive accomplishments which are crucially dependent on material tools and spatial orderings, and establish by way of talking what nobody can actually see directly: seeing itself. And indeed, normal vision is commonly defined as what is called "20/20 vision": The ability to read a specific line of letters from the distance of 20 feet which the average person would be able to read from 20 feet distance as well. Thus, scientific definitions and explanations of normality are ex-post rationalizations of artful accomplishments of knowing about normality in the form of situated testing.

But if so, how can one conceptualize the normality of the moments of conduct one describes as the object of phenopractice inquiry? A good starting point are studies of interaction such as Goffman's (1971b) work on 'normal appearances.' He shows how the concrete manifestations in social conduct which 'stick out' are *not* instances of the normal, but rather of the abnormal. In other words, the concrete event that occurs in praxis can only be one of abnormality, and only from abnormality's very absence one can routinely imply normality as the implicit and permanent condition of social conduct that is prevalent unless abnormality is situatedly demonstrated. From a phenopractice theoretical viewpoint, it follows that normality is part of the understandings defining a phenopractice, while abnormality is exclusively a quality of praxis. Normality, accordingly, describes a certain set-up of the phenomenal field that befits the teleological structure a practice's normal conduct entails. Further, abnormality is never total, but whenever it occurs, it must be contained via referring to certain aspects as being abnormal (not necessarily, but often through the form of causal explanations). On the one hand, moments of conduct are treated as bundles of normalities by practitioners so that, should something go wrong, the bundle can be unpacked and the problem be singled out.[5] On the other hand, abnormality can be systematically produced in order to single out and manage certain aspects of conduct. As I have discussed, discerning normal from abnormal, success from failure, or rule conformity from mistake is a frequent, if not constant challenge invoked by the fragile phenopractices of freeskiing that lies at the core of freeskiing's aesthetic character: for the individual skier on the move, it manifests as the challenge of maintaining the flow of riding; and conversely, in the intersubjective practices of spectating and judging other's accomplishments, it manifests as the challenge of seeing style. In sum, normality describes a state of order that needs to be 'convincingly' achieved by phenopractical means (in other words, the understanding must be expressed), and therefore, it should not be confused with an ontological state of orderliness per se: Neither is something abnormal necessarily without order, nor must what is taken to be normal by practitioners follow linear structures of causality. It can well be the norm that purely coincidental events happen, e.g. in games of chance such as roulette. A core consequence of this is that an empirical study of normal situations builds

---

[5] This does not imply that the 'real' problem can be isolated or de-amalgamized—but this notion seems nevertheless compatible with the experience that some ways of singling out and solving lead to better results than others.

on the assumption that normality is necessarily and beneficially imprecise, or not 'sharp' in its contours—or rather: if one tries to explicate or define it in a precise manner, be it in everyday conduct or for the sake of scientific description, then—to speak with Garfinkel—it will be lost. What was a clear sense that this current situation is normal or 'good enough for all practical purposes' will suddenly appear a fuzzy, unsatisfactory, or arbitrary concept or assumption.

Dreyfus (1991: 152) provides a nice illustration of this idea with regard to the style of talking: When someone is (overly) mispronouncing a word or name, and someone else corrects him, he usually does so by subtly stressing or even exaggerating certain aspects of saying the word (e.g. stressing a syllable). In other words, he will neither really define explicitly or describe precisely what was wrong, or which particular rule had been broken, nor will he instruct the other about the correct way of speaking *by speaking normally* (since he is over-emphasizing some part of the talking). This point can hardly be stressed enough: The normality of speaking, the orderly and understandable way of saying what the other 'evidently' wanted to say is *not* upheld and reproduced in the regularity of speaking per se. Thus, if Schatzki (2002: 72) writes that "the identity of sayings (…) lies in what is said," or if a phenopractice theory formulates that the meaningfulness of a doing is carried in the lived praxis of the doings composing the practice to which they belong, then this does *not* mean that this meaning is housed in the inherent regularity of 'normal' speaking or doing. Further, these doings and sayings are not only not identical; they also do not even need to exhibit overlapping details (i.e. partial identity): One speaker correcting the other can do so by 'repeating the word and exaggerating the aspect that needs correcting,' or he might as well state a rule, or make fun of the other, or pronounce a *different* word wrongly in the same manner. In all these ways, he would be pointing towards a meaningful detail without ever uttering the actual word in question in a normal, regular way. Thus, if the question is where the 'meaningful form,' the normal way of speaking can be found, what better answer can one give than 'out there' in the sum or cluster or nexus of everyday using, understanding, correcting, and prompting that very word? But does that mean that all these moments of doing share a single distinct overlapping or regular feature or detail? No. Nevertheless, they can be identified as being similar in important ways, can be considered as answering to certain rules or customs of conduct, and so forth.

9 Data, Elements, and Media

What are the methodological consequences of the concept of style in phenopractice theory? Suppose a researcher trying to inquire into styles of speaking or pronunciation has collected an audio or video recording of one speaker correcting the other (e.g. because he is studying inequality and discrimination). There is no question that by having caught this moment on tape, the researcher has gathered something that should help her to learn about style and doing style. But in which way is the style of talking actually *on* the tape? The tradition of conversation analysis suggests that through extremely precise transcription, the minute details of 'doing speaking normally' can be brought to the fore. In a similar way, I have in several cases analysed videos frame-by-frame and used arrows, circles, and blend-over effects to make certain visible details of gestures or postures stand out (cf. Mondada 2012). I did, in other words, follow the suggestion by the proponents of ethnomethodologically informed ethnography (Heath/Hindmarsh 2002; Heath/Luff 1992; Hindmarsh/Heath/Luff 2000) to employ transcriptions (in the widest sense) of recordings to unearth and highlight certain particulars of situated conduct. Yet conversation analysis has often been criticized for tending to employ a kind of naïve empiricism in the sense that the data which it analyses (e.g. transcriptions of turn-taking sequences) are treated as itself being 'hardcopies' of social order, that is, as offering direct access to the meaning-in-structure of the situation (Bogen 1999: 83–120; Potter 2002). Lynch (2002: 535), for example, reminds us that recordings (and especially transcriptions) do not "provide uncontrived or unmediated access to an external world of conversational activities." At least for the ethnomethodologists, he argues, the phenomenon that is being researched (because of being what I have called a 'social thing') is to be found in "naturally organized ordinary activities" and not recorded data per se (see also Potter 2002). Therefore, he argues that recordings can only "serve as exquisitely detailed *reminders* of what we already do, as a matter of course." (Lynch 2002: 535, original emphasis) In doing so, he echoes Garfinkel's critique of ethnographic descriptions (which he called "documented conjectures") which on the one hand emphasized that "a documented argument is essentially (…) an inadequate analog to this local availability" (Garfinkel 2002: 223); but on the other hand acknowledged that data such as recordings can at least convey "a sense of structure" (2002: 221) on the basis of which the researcher can work out what he takes to be the documented phenomenon. The actual work of making sense of data, accordingly, is still the researcher's own work, just like it must be the reader's task to understand a scientific article he is reading (cf. Garfinkel 2002: 219–244). The phenopractice theory notion of understanding I have sketched out, in other words, needs to be applied to the researcher's or reader's practices of inspecting data or theoretical arguments in the same way that they pertain to the freeskiers' seeing Style in an image. This sentiment, however, not only means that the precise meaning an article conveys depends on the understanding as locally performed by the article's 'audience'; and thus no type of data or transcription can in itself carry or fix absolute truths. Notably, this view differs fundamentally from the notion put forward by hermeneutics, i.e. that in the structure of the image itself one can find an order or 'iconic paths' which mirror either the subjective interpretation process or the subjective knowledge of the individuals who look at or have composed such an image. Neither the image, nor the individual subject (mind, knowledge-holder, Anthropos) is considered to hold any inherently meaningful structures and/or stored meaning, since meaning is something that transpires only if they are thrown into the self-same situation. Thus, there can be no "overlapping" of subjective and objective meaning (Raab 2008: 319), and neither can we "consider social data as manifestations of the protagonists' perception" in the sense of subjective meaning-making (Schnettler/Raab 2008: para. 45). Nevertheless, I suggest that from the phenopractice theoretical position contrived here, one can deduct an approach to data in the form of ethnographic documents that differs in fundamental ways from the methodological procedures of ethnomethodology (but see E. Livingston 2006b, 2008a, 2008b). The reason for this lies in the notion of elements, as well as the stance on what delineates the phenomena whose "audiovisuality" (Garfinkel 2002: 223) one is studying (see Chap. 3).

A key point for a methodology derived from phenopractical thought as outlined here is the treatment of elements of practices as well as 'social things' such as 'emic' images, texts, and so forth. In several cases, my empirical account of freeskiing relied on what I called ethnographic documents rather than data recorded first hand in the field, or my ethnographic observations per se; for example in that I used an instruction manual for freeride judges, historical pictures from ski-instruction books, and media representations of disciplines such as speed-skiing. How can their methodological status be framed? First, phenopractice theory suggests that elements are not necessarily directly intelligible in any given situation, and that no single element can on its own determine the meaning transpiring at any moment of lived social life. Therefore, I hold that studying the social, or social phenomena, cannot happen via studying elements or their qualities per se. Instead, I have described in chapter five how elements' identities and qualities can be discerned or made intelligible in phenopractices, and I have defended the idea that they have enduring qualities (which said practices might not necessarily ever 'get'). From this, it follows that definitive descriptions of material or bodily elements provided by other disciplines—such as findings about visual routines—can and probably should be integrated into explanations of social phenomena. In so far as they are not social phenomena in their own right (the elements, not the practices within which they might become observable), methodological considerations of the social sciences do not apply to them. Treating a material object (or a cognitive routine) as an element, in other words, implies that it is not considered as a social phenomenon in its own right, but can instead be invoked as an explanandum towards account for some social phenomena, including the observability of said object.

In contrast, if I use an ethnographic document such as a stylish freeskiing image, I am aiming to study a social phenomenon on the basis of the elements it is usually tied to, in this case: seeing Style. As argued in chapter nine, understanding the stylishness of such an image entails the work of turning the image into the first segment of a Lebenswelt pair. My local and skilful conduct of the practice of seeing Style, in other words, effectively means that I am 're-enacting' an everyday freeskiing practice. And while I have argued that learning to do so can only happen in the company of freeskiers, once established, the procedure can later be repeated while sitting alone at my desk—as long as that my situated doings of watching freeski images on my laptop are alike the freeskiers' mundane conduct (which they arguably are). Notably, classic methodology of qualitative research in the wake of Schutz cautions that only if I approach the work of seeing in a pragmatic motive of everyday life, it would resemble anything close to what the freeskiers do; while approaching it as a scientist invokes a much more detached, analytic stance (Schutz 1953). I believe that this notion raises some interesting question that would deserve further, more thorough discussion than I can offer here. Just some basic points: At the core, I suggest, this sentiment can be translated quite well into phenopractice thought. Surely, two instances of looking at the same image can amount to conducting different practices, depending on the goals (e.g. scientific instead of hedonic), rules (e.g. methodological procedures), or understandings (e.g. theories) involved. Accordingly, the question is: At which point does such an analysis amount to being the conduct of a different phenopractice, as opposed to a tonality or version of the freeskiers' emic practice. An alternative view could maybe also be derived from the argument that practices can overlap, that is, several practices can be conducted at the same time. While it seems not entirely plausible to assert that one can simultaneously enjoy the beauty of an image and observe how one is 'doing enjoying,' it does seem quite plausible in the case of analysing (some aspects of) one's own walking down the street. In fact, as I have shown, learning a sport practice to a considerable extent depends on observing one's own conduct while being in the midst of it. We are indeed all practicing sociologists, as Garfinkel remarked; but unlike he implied, we not only study others' behaviour, but our own bodily doings as well.

This thought also brings me back to the question of elements and objects. I have provided a number of examples of how different objects in general, and different media formats in particular, are systematically being employed as "Heideggerian troublemakers" (Garfinkel 2002: 211) by practitioners in order to study their own or others' conduct: the ski pole tied around the ski students' hips was one case; and the freeride judges using either binoculars, or cameras and screens, or their bare eyes were another. My argument was that they are able to systematically produce the visibility of the phenomenon they are interested in (such as sublating an aspect or element) by alternating between different approaches or 'access paths.' When a social scientist flip-flops between pragmatic and analytic stances in the Schutzian sense, it seems to me, she is potentially doing just the same. In order for her to be able to do so, however, she requires more or less the 'full package' of elements that everyday practitioners employ as well. An interesting 'liminal case' was provided by the historic images of ski instruction I discussed. I argued that I could achieve a degree of understanding of these images that was at least sufficient to make my arguments because I was able to assess them against the background of my own skills of performing, teaching, and observing skiing. While looking at an image from the 1960s probably would amount to gaining (or becoming attuned to) understandings which differ from the understandings held by ski teachers back then, I nevertheless it is justified to assume that I was able to pick up the intelligible order offered by these images in a relatively adequate manner, e.g. I could see their being informative for a 'normal' ski instructor about the body posture required for the Reverse Shoulder Technique. I am, in other words, inferring similarity on the assumption that shoulders, photos, and the basics of ski turns are today more or less the same as they were then, e.g. in that the images' inherent orderliness has endured since then—and I stress that, unlike some sociological accounts of meaning, both similarity and endurance are explicitly part of my theoretical model itself rather than additional assumptions that need to be made only for the sake of methodology. Such claims, of course, cannot be made sensibly in all cases; and delineating their adequacy is a delicate and difficult matter. Can we for example say that we can understand Shakespeare's style today; or do we need to assume that today's background of speaking English is so different from his that what we consider as his style or the beauty of his poems is something other than it used to be? On the other hand, compared to the social scientists' concern that they might miss the true sense or meaning of the data they collect and analyse, the beauty or 'message' of some written texts, pieces of music, or paintings seems to be incredibly durable and universal—if situatedly unfolded in normal ways, that is. Finally, I also believe that in developing the phenopractice-theoretical notion of the Lebenswelt pair, I have sketched out a blueprint of the function or character of *theory*, not only of written empirical accounts: In reading and assessing the presented data or arguments, the reading needs to be made "good over the ground" (Garfinkel 2002: 247) in such a way that the theory 'matches the data,' i.e. so that it can pass as a plausible or adequate description of the theory-data pair.[6]

10 Research Procedure of this Work

The Framework: Ethnomethodologically Informed Ethnography

Based on the considerations just outlined, the empirical research process on which this book is based followed an adapted version of what has been called ethnomethodologically informed ethnography[7] (ten Have 2002, 2004; Heath/Hindmarsh 2002; see also Gobo 2008; Pollner/Emerson 2001). Accordingly, I undertook a 'classic' ethnographic study in that I conducted extended participant observation in order to become a competent member of the freeskiing subculture, but combined it with 'high resolution' research methods such as video (interaction) analysis and analysis of recordings of naturally occurring talk (C. Goodwin 2000b; Heath 2004; Kissmann 2009; Knoblauch/Schnettler/Raab/Soeffner 2006). Since I

---

[6] This point, I believe, makes clear why Garfinkel insists that the first segment is turned into a description of the pair, rather than simply the second segment: Quite clearly theory cannot be an adequate description of praxis, but it can formulate a certain relation to it.

[7] The part this subchapter is meant to give a relatively compact overview over my research procedure. See for a more extensive discussion of the concrete steps of my ethnographic work (e.g. selecting my informants, delineating the different loci to study) the preliminary study (Vorstudie) to this work.

treat meaning as bound to sites, but also sought to compare different forms of situated order and phenopractices, the ethnography was multi-sited (Marcus 1995) in a specific way, namely in that I followed some of freeskiing's 'social things' such as lines, flex, Flow, and Style across the different sites in which they transpire. My work thus shares many of the basic premises of (ethnographic parts of) what Büscher and Urry (2009) call mobile methods, especially because they argue on the basis of Wittgenstein and Merleau-Ponty, and in part recommend ethnomethodologically framed video-analysis (see especially Büscher 2005a; Mondada 2011, 2012). A third, again closely related ethnographic research framework I build on entails a sharp focus on the details of situated interactions into an ethnographic 'background' and has been proposed under the label focused ethnography (Knoblauch 2001, 2002, 2005b) which I have discussed in more detail elsewhere (Woermann 2018). This approach not only builds on ethnomethodological studies of work in general and video interaction analysis of situated interaction in the wake of Goodwin in particular, thus taking a reluctant stance towards conducting interviews (see below), but it shares the conviction that ethnographic research is to be guided by theoretical interests. That said, Knoblauch's stance also differs from the phenopractical approach taken here in two important respects: First, in contrast to the phenopractice perspective, Knoblauch understands ethnography as a study of 'the Other' in a Schutzian sense, that is, of (situation-specific parts of) intersubjective knowledge (Knoblauch 2005b: para. 8). In other words, the question is what precisely one is studying by "analysing the structures and patterns of interaction" (Knoblauch 2005b: para. 28) on the basis of recorded data: a "rich surface" (Edwards 2006) that functions as a kind of gateway to the underlying subjective knowledge lurking under said surface, that is, as a different level of order manifesting in a different realm than subjective experience; or alternatively as the one single level of manifestation of meaningful social order. The second, more important difference lies in the fact that, while I agree that the "strangeness" of the studied field—and much less one created through an artificial "estrangement" of familiar phenomena (Amman/Hirschauer 1997)—is not a definite condition for ethnographic research but rather one resource among several that can be employed to gain ethnographic insight (Knoblauch 2005b: para. 5–9), I was initially a stranger to the field of freeskiing and my findings are to a considerable extent based on the insights gained during the process of establishing my eventual familiarity. In my view, Knoblauch is right to emphasize that ethnographic work must necessarily be rooted in expertise and does inevitably build on our skills to competently manage everyday situations and practices (at least if we do not study very 'exotic' societies). Thus, if we study familiar setting within 'our own' society, long-term field research is neither the single key strategy nor inevitably necessary; and recording and analysing naturally occurring situations can indeed yield very 'deep' insights despite a relative short time spent in the field. Effectively, I hold that parts of my research were indeed focused in just this way, for example in that my observation period of trade fairs was relatively short (8 days in total), were supported by systematic data recording, and profited greatly from my general acquaintance with visiting trade fairs, holding conversations with business people, and inspecting or discussing skiing gear and technology. In contrast, my research in funparks happened over longer stretches of time and entailed a steep learning curve in that I became accustomed to a place I had never once visited before. Towards the end of my project, however, my visits to the park much more resembled the focused visits Knoblauch describes: I relied on my general familiarity with the setting and recorded large amounts of data in relatively short time.

Becoming a Member: Access and Rapport

The basic rationale behind the phenopractice approach is that the phenomena a study seeks to address are either instances of situationally accomplished order, or manifest in moments of concrete conduct. In order to achieve the kind of "thick description of social action" (Sharrock/Button 1991: 170; see also Atkinson/Coffey/Delamont 2003: 114) this approach aims for, however, I considered it indispensable that I first acquired the basic understandings which underlie freeskiing practices—and importantly, this included the practical understandings of freeskiing. In other words: In order to be able to grasp *how* it makes sense for a freerider to drop down into a steep and narrow couloir in the Krimml or jump over a large kicker, I first needed to assure *that* it would make sense for me in the concrete situation of standing on that ridge or atop that kicker. Thus, although the phenopractice perspective lead me to reject the 'radical version' of the unique adequacy requirement (see above), I did deem it fundamental to learn the basics of doing freeskiing myself. As ten Have (2007: 145–146) rightly points out, what thus informed my research was to a lesser degree my actual *being* a member of the freeski world, but predominantly my *becoming* a member, the process of skill acquisition and becoming accustomed during which I 'naturally' became attentive to "practices that have become embodiedly transparent in their familiarity" (Garfinkel 2002: 211) for experienced freeskiers.[8]

I was in a hybrid position in terms of prior acquaintance with, and skills (or understandings) needed in, my field of study: on the one hand I had been only vaguely aware of the freeskiing subculture before starting my research and had not met nor mingled with freeskiers—in freeskiers' eyes I was clearly a 'tourist.' On the other hand, as I indicated throughout the work, I had extensive experience in skiing, a sport which I began learning when I was less than three years old; and in particular, I have occasionally worked as a ski instructor for a German ski tour operator. Without these prior familiarity with the basic practices of skiing, gaining the insights I described would have been all but impossible—for example, my impression is that many of the problematic conclusions which Stern (2009) drew

---

[8] I would not, however, say that I was studying myself not as an individual, but as a member, as ten Have formulates (2007: 146). My aim was to study practices, not myself as a person of any kind—put in Heideggerian fashion, I was interested in my being rather than in the 'what' of my being.

about the Snowboarding culture, and which I criticized, are rooted in the fact that he was not able to snowboard himself and could thus not conduct participant observation in any strict sense (see M. Stern 2009: 37 fn10). Generally, gaining ethnographic access to the freeskiing scene is primarily a challenge of "getting on" rather than of "getting in" as Cassell (1988) put it (see Gobo 2008: 119; Wolff 2007: 340). Places such as a funpark or the Krimml are principally open to anyone on skis or snowboard willing to pay for the lift ticket, but precisely because this is the case, mere presence does not equal meaningful participation in freeskiing. Nevertheless, after I was able to enlist my two first informants via incidental acquaintanceships and had started to 'hang around' with them, bought proper freeskiing gear and clothing, and showed enthusiasm for skiing (e.g. by sleeping in my car on the parking lot of the gondola in order to catch the first ride and untouched powder slopes in the morning), it became relatively easy to acquire further informants via snowball sampling (Gobo 2008: 108; Hammersley/Atkinson 1983: 78 f.). More importantly, especially my key informants showed an enormous openness and willingness to help me with my project, which was generally greeted with some curiosity, but especially sympathy by freeskiers: While earning a good amount of scepticism both in- and outside of academia, no freeskier ever asked me *why* I chose skiing as my topic. Instead, I usually earned some instant respect for "pulling that off," for inventing such an innovative legitimation for going skiing. Despite my initial unfamiliarity with the subculture, I could thus relatively quickly feel as 'one of them,' not simply because of the (at least roughly) shared socio-economic background and age bracket, but because freeskiing is what Wheaton (2000b) called a subculture of commitment: since I shared the freeskier's interest in and fascination with Style, and because I was committed to learning the sport (a project which sent me to the hospital twice). On the downside, however, probably because I was considered by strangers as basically an average (and not very stylish) freeskier with a weird excuse for going skiing, rather than a 'serious academic,' those parts of the freeski world which remain fenced off to all but a few 'elite' freeskiers proved difficult to access for me as well: Although I had initially planned to conduct more extensive participatory research of ski development in workshops, developers remained reluctant to let me in and talk to me. On the one hand, warding off nosy freeskiers of insufficient experience and status seemed to be a routine exercise for them; and on the other hand, when approached in a more 'official' and formal manner, they told me that there was "nothing there" to see and that I better observe some "more professional," larger ski developing workshops [I]. Accordingly, interesting work remains to be done in the field of freeskiing.

Documents versus Recordings

A key methodological question demanding specific answers from a phenopractice perspective is the kind of empirical material that ethnographic research collects, and how the different data formats are used towards making an argument.

As customary for ethnographic research, multiple methods and data of different formats should be combined and juxtaposed in order to work out (or rather figure out) the phenomena in question from different angles (see Woermann 2018). In doing so, ethnographic research work bears fundamental resemblance to some of the phenopractices freeskiers themselves employ; for example when they observe themselves on video and 'interview' others about their opinion in order to find out if they could improve their performance of a certain trick; or when they juxtapose different media of deliberation to figure out which ski to buy; and so forth. That said, it must of course be stressed that making sense of empirical research phenomena is informed by very different (theoretical) understandings, and oriented towards different practical ends (such as writing theory). The collection and use of empirical material should thus be guided by two key distinctions: First, a distinction between ethnographic documents (understood as openly circulating elements of phenopractices) and ethnographic data purposefully produced for the sake of research. And second, a differentiation between the various situations of conduct from which the empirical material stems, i.e. what kind of phenomenon had been manifest in that situation.

Let me begin with this first important distinction between elements of the phenopractices I described—such as freeskiing videos, skis, or texts from freeski magazines—and data which I produced purposefully in the course of my 'doing ethnography,' such as fieldnotes or videos of freeskiers standing in queues (rather than performing tricks). One key difference between a phenopractice approach and the three related approaches ethnomethodologically informed ethnography, mobile ethnography, and focused ethnography (see above) lies in the treatment of ethnographic documents. I did not confine myself to studying the 'public' structures visible in interactions 'caught on tape,' but in that I also built on the insights drawn from my own solitary, practical, in-situ conduct of freeskiing practices vis a vis freeskiing-specific elements (cf. Woermann 2018). Looking at a freeski image, I argued, 'brings it to life' in a certain sense in that I put it into praxis—because I assume that my own routines honed in the field and the images themselves are relatively stable, I effectively suggest that my own becoming attuned to freeskiing's understanding is not exclusively a matter of travelling to mountain tops or to other exotic locations, but can to some extent as well happen in that such elements 'travel' to me and then offer me what is a very similar phenomenal field to that which freeskiers gain when they look at such images at night in their campervan, or at home on the internet. Videos of interaction or recordings of conversation, in contrast, cannot reproduce the original phenomenal fields provided by the phenopractices' conduct they show. Instead, they can be a key help to a) discerning the crucial elements amalgamated in the practice's unfolding (e.g. in that very subtle body reactions or utterings which remained in the background for the practitioners can be made to stand out), and b) function as "exquisitely detailed *reminders*" (Lynch 2002: 535, original emphasis) of the forms and procedures of coordination and alignment through which the situations in question had been organized, for example via lines of sight, posture, position, and so forth. For this reason, I marked all quotes from ethnographic documents as well as all pictures I considered documents (rather than 'documentary' or having been produced purposefully as part of research practice) with a [D].

Interviews and Naturally Occurring Talk

The second differentiation implied by phenopractice theory is one between the different situational origins of data: Because it is held that the meaning of anything is determined by the situated conduct in the midst of which it appears, the 'situational origin' of empirical insights becomes of outmost importance. In this work, I responded to this situation primarily in two ways: First, I signified the origin of all quotes which I presented; and second, I relied only to a limited extent on formal interviews and—whenever possible—did not use them as the only source on any topic, but sought to complement them with data collected in different ways. To the first point: I intend to make transparent the methodological origin from each quote by using a system of abbreviations. In my view, it should be clear that any empirical insight which I paraphrase in my own words without using explicit quotes or other data is an outcome of my aggregating, selecting, and interpreting my field observations, literature readings, or theoretical conceptualizations. A quote or image shown, in contrast, implies a representational quality on a different level. While I cannot reproduce either the full relevant situational context of the production of each quote, nor its exact position within the meaning structure of the block of data itself, I do at least intend to hint towards the fundamental differences that exist between, for example, a quote taken from a formal interview, a professionally edited movie, and a naturally occurring conversation I did not take part in. Throughout this text, employ the following abbreviations: Any statement without explicitly mentioned source is a result gained from my general ethnographic work (which of course mixes fieldwork and scientific reflection) and usually stems from my fieldnotes and memos. Thus, I do not ascribe my fieldnotes an unquestioned representational authority and—safe for the introduction parts of chapter meant to transport a 'general feeling' for the phenomena that will be discussed—I do not quote directly from them, as if reading from a script of what happened. Scientific sources are quoted as it is common practice. If I quote from publicly available material that I consider a field-specific document, such as an article in a freeski magazine, I quote it (author, year, [D]). Quotes from documents without a named author (such as leaflets or ads) carry just a [D]. Apart from this basic distinction, I discern four different types of 'empirical talk' or verbal data according to the situation of their origin: First, formal interviews during which I openly recorded the answers were marked with an [I]. Second, because I frequently relied on informal interviews (see below) during which I could not record, a number of my quotes are from memory, that is, I usually recorded them on a dictaphone a few minutes after the conversation. These are marked with an [M]. I should add that I only used this label when I was reasonably sure that the word or phrase I quote had been uttered quite precisely in this way. In many cases, I would thus record (and later build on) the general remark or statement made during the conversation, as well as a few precise expressions that were used. Writing about a topic, I would accordingly only mark the quasi-verbal expressions with an [M], while the rest would become part of my general ethnographic description, without the 'representative' touch to them. Third, I recorded several hours of naturally occurring conversations among freeskiers, especially during lunch breaks, in ski lifts, or in cars (see below). All parts marked with an [R] are verbatim quotes from these conversations into which I did not interfere (apart from my occasional taking part in them as part of my being a freeskiing member of the situation). Notably, the informants present had earlier given consent to me for doing so and thus they knew that I might be recording. I consider the data collected in this way as helpful towards reconstructing the freeskiers' normal or 'naturally occurring' talk which I had become accustomed to by way of participation (ten Have 2004: 118; Silverman 1993: 201; see also Potter 2002; Lynch 2002; Atkinson/Silverman 1997).

This brings me to the second point: the status of interviews. While ethnomethodologically informed ethnographers differ in that some dismiss them entirely, while others use them to some extent, they all agree that interviews are a "game in its own right" (Atkinson/Coffey 2003: 427), in that they are distinctive social events with their own 'autochthonous' order structure rather than faithful reflections of other events, situations, or factual states; and that thus recordings of naturally occurring talk should be preferred whenever possible (Atkinson/Coffey 2003; Atkinson/Coffey/Delamont 2003: 97–118; Atkinson/Silverman 1997; Dingwall 1997; ten Have 2004). I generally share this view, and for this reason I did not extensively rely on interviews. From a phenopractice theoretical perspective, however, not all kinds of interviews are necessarily as problematic as they are from an ethnomethodological stance. A saying, after all, is considered as a specific type of doing; that is, as an expression of a certain understanding (that what is being said) in a concrete moment of conduct. Accordingly, the 'classic' problem ascribed to interviews that there could be a "gap between the interviewee's declared state and his or her actual state" (Gobo 2008: 192) is not per se an issue from a phenopractice perspective, because it rejects the idea that hidden mental mechanisms or states are part of the social phenomena the analyst is concerned with, e.g. in that they have causal effects on their outcomes (cf. Nicolini 2012: 219–223). Further, seen through a phenopractice theory lens, social order or social phenomena are not considered to be expressible in words in their entirety or in the actual form and structure in which they transpire in lived life, and thus there are no 'high expectations' towards interviews which might subsequentially be disappointed. Instead, I argue that the key question is whether the interviews conducted express understandings that are part of freeskiing practices, or not. And contrary to the strict ethnomethodological position, it could very well be that practices of answering interviews about freeskiing matters share certain understandings (i.e. elements) with talking practices 'natural' to the freeskiing world. Whether or not this is the case, I hold, depends primarily on the situational set-up of the interview, rather than on alleged interests or plans of the interviewee. In my view, there is not necessarily a sharp distinction between 'natural' talk and 'unnatural' interviews, but rather a gradual transition. As I noted, freeskiers chat about freeskiing all day long, for example by retelling past experiences and events, by discussing their preferences or feelings towards certain situations, brands, people, events, products, and so on, and by describing their plans, goals, and dreams. In other words: A good part of what one might inquire about during formal interviews will be openly discussed anyways. Chatting with an informant about how he came to pick up freeskiing, or why he believes it is important to continue training immediately after crashing (if possible) is not necessarily markedly different from interviewing him about exactly these themes. More to the point, skiing entails a great number of 'natural' situations perfectly amiable to conducting short, informal interviews: especially ski lifts and gondolas provide almost perfect conditions for conducting such interviews which come as close to naturally occurring talk as possible. Not only are the respondents fully immersed into 'the skiing experience,' but it is also a frequent custom in ski lifts to have casual chats, even among strangers. When I spent time in a funpark, in other words, I had ample opportunity to strike up conversations with a kind of 'random sample' of freeskiers visiting that park who happened to end up in the ski lift next to me; and I could ask each one of them the same thing over the course of the day, comparing their answers and experimenting with different ways of introducing myself, or commenting on certain topics such as, say, the current state of the kicker in this park. Further, such informal settings have another advantage I deem particularly valuable: the conversation partner does not feel obliged to answer. In a formal interview, respondents will usually 'come up with' some kind of answer, regardless of whether or not this particular issue matters to them in actual conduct, and they will further seek to find a 'respectable' and legitimate answer. In a ski lift, conversations frequently tend to drift along with longer pauses in between sentences, or someone uttering a statement and the other not reacting to it. I thus tried to make use of this custom by 'proposing' points to talk about, rather than asking straightforward questions, thus trying to invite the freeskiers to answer without 'forcing' them to do so. In this way, I believe, I was able to get a good sense of the things that freeskiers take deep interest in, or that they care about. To be sure, such informal interviews need to be accompanied by more formal ones which are both longer and in which I could take the role of an 'official' interviewer in order to ask questions freeskiers do not usually discuss as a part of chatting. For example, fear and frustration where topics which I could only discuss with informants I knew well already and could ask these things 'for the sake of science.' In sum, by alternating between a) listening to, recording, or taking part in casual everyday conversations among freeskiers, b) conducting informal interviews of different types, and c) recording formal, in-depth ethnographic interviews with my informants, I believe I was able to discern relatively well between what I would consider normal sayings and thus elements of practices, versus mere accounts of experiences, views, motivations, moods, etc. invoked by doing freeskiing.

The Data Set

The research presented in this book is based on data collected between September 2008 and October 2011 in the German-speaking freeskiing subculture, focusing on the core members: Informants were between 19 and 27 years old and described themselves as dedicated freeskiers. They had several years of experience, participated in contests, and received some form of sponsorship from one or more companies. Such sponsorships are fairly common in the scene (most athletes do not actually get any monetary support, but instead free gear or support for buying lift tickets, travel to contests, and so on), and they provide a useful criterion to ensure all informants have considerable experience, skill, and standing. In addition to these athletes, I regularly met with and talked to freeski industry professionals, for example an independent importer of a US freeski brand, the owner of a well-known independent ski manufacturer, or freelancing and semi-professional photographers and movie producers. (I also conducted interviews with a broader range of professionals and skiers, see below.)

Participant Observation

Participant observation entailed 49 full days of observation over a time span of 42 months, with field trips lasting from one to ten days. On most occasions, I stayed overnight with my informants, and was therefore able to participate in all their ski-related activities throughout the day and not just the skiing itself, e.g. preparing and repairing gear, watching freeski videos or reading freeski magazines, meeting at night in a bar to talk about the day, travelling from one spot to the next on the hunt for good weather and untouched powder, and so on. I observed the training routine in 11 different funparks; 5 freestyle contests; took part in 18 freeride-trips in 10 different ski areas; and accompanied 6 days of semi-professional video shooting. Additionally, I spent 8 days on 4 international winter sports industry trade fairs in Munich and Zurich, where I focused observation on the interactions at the booths of independent freeskiing gear manufacturers and additionally had the opportunity to formally interview or informally meet and talk to a large number of industry professionals as well as several internationally known 'stars' of the freeski subculture. I wrote about 100 pages of fieldnotes, but since it proved impractical to write on the slopes and drew much attention from freeskiers since it is an unnatural thing to do on a mountain, I recorded most of my observations on a dictaphone that I constantly carried around with me. This method proved very economic for quickly and spontaneously collecting many impressions and ideas, and it worked particularly well in conjunction with the many informal interviews I conducted in ski lifts and whose results I recorded right afterwards (cf. Hammersley/ Atkinson 2007: 157). And while written fieldnotes arguably invite more reflection and precision during writing, audio notes additionally have the advantage of providing a more dense or somewhat more immediate impression of the situation of their origin since they also convey background noise (e.g. from a bustling trade fair versus an isolated mountain range) and certain details of the ethnographer's talk (such as hesitation, enthusiasm, and so forth).

Interviews and Recordings of Naturally Occurring Conversations

In addition to such informal interviews, I conducted 33 formal, in-depth interviews (from 30 minutes to 2 hours) with 21 industry professionals and 12 athletes. Further, I systematically recorded everyday conversations among freeskiers with prior consent (additionally, all my data has of course been anonymized). I collected about 80 recordings between 10 seconds and 20 minutes in length. In total, I collected slightly more than 50 hours of audio material (audio notes, interviews, and conversation recordings combined). Of these, parts of my audio notes and parts of recorded conversations were not transcribed since I did not deem them worthwhile based on the interests, themes, and understandings that emerged over the course of my research (cf. Hammersley/Atkinson 2007: 161).

Video

I shot approximately 4 hours videos of interaction during training in the funpark, focusing on the organization of space, gaze, and stance; and about 1.5 hours of interactions on trade-fairs. Additionally, I carried a photo camera, which I used for capturing short episodes of interaction during freeriding, which proved logistically complicated. Generally, however, taking photos and videos in freeski settings is widely common among freeskiers and therefore does not disturb interactions to any larger degree. Finally, the freeskier's savviness for video technology and the mundanity of such equipment in freeskiing settings provided me the opportunity to experiment with further modes of video data collection: I asked one informant to carry his helmet camera not only during freeriding, but also in the funpark (something riders sometimes do) and keep it running throughout longer stretches of time. In this way, I could collect first-person video material (about 4 h) that not only captures the various casual interactions among riders, but also reproduces the visual field of the rider relatively faithfully. I did not make extensive use of this material in this work, because I believe that it first requires a more systematic methodological discussion and possibly a new transcription format in order to be adequately analysed, and thus poses an opportunity for further work, but I did use it to verify my observations regarding the different lines of sight freeskiers are provided with by virtue of the positions and postures they take up in the funpark.

Photos

Throughout my fieldwork, I additionally used a photo camera to document various aspects of freeskiing practices, taking in total in about 650 pictures. Just like shooting, taking pictures did not draw any special attention, neither on the slopes nor in settings like the trade fair. Unlike the video material, however, I used these images more like a "visual logbook" in order to remind myself of certain details or aspects that caught my attention, and to later be able to convey a better sense of the phenomena to my readers. I did not, in other words, systematically analyse these pictures in a hermeneutic or another analytical procedure, for example to 'find' certain details of conduct I was not previously aware of, but instead used them as a medium for reflecting and reaffirming things I had observed either during conduct or on the videos.

Documents and Media Immersion

I systematically collected field documents, primarily in the form of magazines, promotion and marketing materials, professionally produced videos, skiing books, and online content. My use of these documents can be divided into two main categories: immersion and analysis. To begin with the former, I immersed myself into a broad range of freeski media materials as a background to, and part of, my ethnographic work: I read all issues of the German freeski magazine which appeared during this time (2006–2011), as well as a number of other ski-magazine articles relevant to my topic I could find, collecting notable excerpts and citations covering the emerging focus topics of my research. Further, I watched numerous freeski DVDs, as well as a large number of freeski video clips available online. Essentially, I considered my watching (and learning to enjoy) these videos as part of my fieldwork, as part of becoming a member of the community of Style by gaining an eye for freeskiing's aesthetics. In several conversations with freeskiers and industry professionals, my knowledge of these films proved to be important background acquaintance. Finally, I immersed myself to some extend into the sprawling online content available about freeskiing. I thus followed online discussions (without taking actively part), visited my informants' Facebook photo albums or their team galleries, and read freeskiing blogs. However, I did not conduct a systematic 'netnographic' study of the overall online freeskiing culture (which has, for example, a very active forum community), but instead used these documents to gain a more general understanding of freeskiing. In contrast to these more general immersion techniques which allowed me to hone my sense for Style and stay 'up to date' during the summer months, I also undertook a more systematic analysis of two specific data sets: First, I collected (online) articles, discussions, and documents on the topic of ski flex in order to gain a systematic overview of the different approaches to, understandings of, and opinions towards ski flexes (see Chap. 5). And second, I conducted a systematic content analysis of three freeski movies in order to get a grasp on their basic structure and the 'visual vocabulary' they employ.

References

Adorno, Theodor W. (1973): The jargon of authenticity. London: Routledge & Kegan.
Aggarwal, Pankaj/Ann L. McGill (2007): Is That Car Smiling at Me? Schema Congruity as a Basis for Evaluating Anthropomorphized Products. In: The Journal of Consumer Research 34(4): 468–479.
Aglioti, Salvatore M/Paola Cesari/Michela Romani/Cosimo Urgesi (2008): Action anticipation and motor resonance in elite basketball players. In: Nature Neuroscience 11(9): 1109–1116.
Akrich, Madeleine/Bruno Latour (1992): A summary of a convenient vocabulary for the semiotics of human and nonhuman assemblies. In: Wiebke Bijker/John Law (Eds.): Shaping technology/building society: Studies in sociotechnical change. Boston: MIT Press, pp. 259–264.
Alexander, Jeffrey C. (2004): Cultural Pragmatics: Social Performance Between Ritual and Strategy. In: Sociological Theory 22(4): 527–573.
Alkemeyer, Thomas (2004): Mensch-Maschinen mit zwei Rädern. (Praxis-)Soziologische Betrachtungen zur Aussöhnung von Körper, Technik und Umgebung. In: SportZeiten. Sport in Geschichte, Kultur und Gesellschaft 4(3): 27–40.
Alkemeyer, Thomas (2021): Praxis (und Diskurs). In: Kristina Brümmer/Alexandra Janetzko/Thomas Alkemeyer (Eds.): Ansätze einer Kultursoziologie des Sports. Baden-Baden: Nomos, pp. 19–48.
Alkemeyer, Thomas/Robert Schmidt (2004): Technisierte Körper – verkörperte Technik: Über den praktischen Umgang mit neuen Geräten im Sport. In: Karl-Siegbert Rehberg (Ed.): Soziale Ungleichheit – kulturelle Unterschiede. 32. Kongress der Deutschen Gesellschaft für Soziologie in München 2004. Frankfurt/New York: Campus, pp. 569–578.
Alkemeyer, Thomas/Kathrin Brummer (2016): Körper und informelles Lernen. In: M. Harring/M. D. Witte/T Burger, T. (Eds.): Handbuch informelles Lernen. Interdisziplinäre und internationale Perspektiven. Weinheim/Basel: Beltz Juventa, pp. 493–509.
Alkemeyer, Thomas/Nikolaus Buschmann (2017): Learning in and across practices: Enablement as subjectivation. In: Allison Hui/Theodore Schatzki/Elizabeth Shove (Eds.): The nexus of practices: Connections, constellations, practitioners. Milton Park: Taylor & Francis, pp. 20–35.
Allen, John B. (2007): The culture and sport of skiing: from antiquity to World War II. Amherst: University of Massachusetts Press.
Allen, John B. (2008): Mathias Zdarsky: The father of alpine skiing. In: Skiing Heritage Journal 20(1): 7–14.

Alvarez, María (2010): Kinds of reasons: an essay in the philosophy of action. Oxford: Oxford University Press.
Amman, Klaus/Stefan Hirschauer (1997): Die Befremdung der eigenen Kultur. Ein Programm. In: Stefan Hirschauer/Klaus Amman (Eds.): Die Befremdung der eigenen Kultur. Zur ethnographischen Herausforderung soziologischer Empirie. Frankfurt a. M.: Suhrkamp, pp. 7–52.
Anthony, Leslie (2011): White Planet: A Mad Dash through Modern Global Ski Culture. Vancouver: Greystone Books.
APA (2011): Skigebiet Sternstein wehrt sich mit Anzeige gegen Tourengeher. In: nachrichten.at. http://www.nachrichten.at/oberoesterreich/art4,551701 (accessed August 3, 2011).
Araujo, Luis/Hans Kjellberg/Rob Spencer (2008): Market practices and forms: Introduction to the special issue. In: Marketing Theory 8(1): 5–14.
Armstrong, Richard L./Eric Brun (Eds.) (2008): Snow and Climate: Physical Processes, Surface Energy Exchange and Modeling. Cambridge: Cambridge University Press.
Arvidson, P. Sven (1992): The Field of Consciousness: James and Gurwitsch. In: Transactions of the Charles S. Peirce Society 28(4): 833–856.
Arvidson, P. Sven (2006): Gurwitsch and Husserl on Attention. In: The Sphere of Attention. Dordrecht: Kluwer Academic Publishers, pp. 86–114.
Ashby, W. Ross (1958): Requisite variety and its implications for the control of complex systems. In: Cybernetica 1(2): 83–99.
Atencio, Matthew/Becky Beal/Charlene Wilson (2009): The distinction of risk: urban skateboarding, street habitus and the construction of hierarchical gender relations. In: Qualitative Research in Sport and Exercise 1(1): 3.
Atkinson, Paul/Amanda Coffey (2003): Revisiting the relationship between participant observation and interviewing. In: James A. Holstein/Jaber F. Gubrium (Eds.): Inside interviewing. New Lenses, New Concerns. London: Sage, pp. 415–427.
Atkinson, Paul/Amanda Coffey/Sara Delamont (2003): Key Themes in qualitative research. Continuities and changes. Walnut Creek: Altamira Press.
Atkinson, Paul/David Silverman (1997): Kundera's Immortality: The Interview Society and the Invention of the Self. In: Qualitative Inquiry 3(3): 304–325.
Augé, Marc (1995): Non-places. Introduction to an anthropology of supermodernity. London: Verso.
Baccus, Melinda D. (1986): Multipiece truck wheel accidents and their regulations. In: Harold Garfinkel (Ed.): Ethnomethodological Studies of Work. London: Routledge & Kegan, pp. 20–59.
Baehr, Peter (2005): The sociology of almost everything. In: Canadian Journal of Sociology Online 2005(1).
Ballard, Dana H./Mary M. Hayhoe/Polly K. Pook/Rajesh P. N. Rao (1997): Deictic Codes for the Embodiment of Cognition. In: Behavioral and Brain Sciences 20(04): 723–742.
Barrymore, Dick (1997): Breaking Even. Missoula: Pictorial Histories Publishing.
Barwise, Jon (1989): The situation in logic. Stanford: Center for the Study of Language (CSLI).
Bauman, Zygmunt (2001): Community – Seeking Safety in an Insecure World. Cambridge: Polity Press.
Beal, Becky/Lisa Weidman (2003): Authenticity in the skateboarding world. In: Robert E. Rinehart/Synthia Sydnor (Eds.): To the Extreme. Alternative sports, inside and out. Albany: SUNY Press, pp. 337–352.
Beal, Becky/Charlene Wilson (2004): 'Chicks dig scars' Commercialisation and the transformations of skateboarders' identities. In: Belinda Wheaton (Ed.): Understanding Lifestyle Sport: Consumption, Identity and Difference. London: Routledge, pp. 31–54.
Becchio, Cristina/Cesare Bertone (2004): Wittgenstein running: Neural mechanisms of collective intentionality and we-mode. In: Consciousness and Cognition 13(1): 123–133.
Becchio, Cristina/Cesare Bertone/Umberto Castiello (2008): How the gaze of others influences object processing. In: Trends in Cognitive Sciences 12(7): 254–258.

Behrend, Olaf (2007): Rezension zu Jo Reichertz & Nadia Zaboura: Akteur Gehirn – oder das vermeintliche Ende des handelnden Subjekts. In: Sozialer Sinn 8(1): 159–163.
Bennett, Maxwell R./Peter M. S. Hacker (2003): Philosophical foundations of neuroscience. London: Wiley-Blackwell.
Benson, Jack A. (1977): Before Skiing Was Fun. In: The Western Historical Quarterly 8(4): 431–441.
Berger, Peter L./Thomas Luckmann (1966): The social construction of reality: a treatise in the sociology of knowledge. New York: Doubleday.
Berthoz, Alain (2000): The brain's sense of movement. Cambridge: Harvard University Press.
Berthoz, Alain/Jean-Luc Petit (2008): The Physiology and Phenomenology of Action. 1st ed. Oxford: Oxford University Press.
Bette, Karl-Heinrich (2004): X-treme: Zur Soziologie des Abenteuer- und Risikosports. Bielefeld: Transcript.
Bickel, Alois (2007): Freeride Philosophie. Runter kommen Sie alle. Aber wie kommen Sie rauf? In: skiing (01): 89.
Bijker, Wiebke/John Law (Eds.) (1992): Shaping technology/building society: Studies in sociotechnical change. Boston: MIT Press.
Billy Poole Memorial Fund (2008): Remember Billy. http://billypooleskifoundation.org/share-your-memories-of-billy-poole/ (accessed February 5, 2009).
Bjelić, Dušan I. (1992): The praxiological validity of natural scientific practices as a criterion for identifying their unique social-object character: The case of the 'authentication' of Goethe's morphological theorem. In: Qualitative Sociology 15(3): 221–245.
Bjelić, Dušan I. (1995): An ethnomethodological clarification of Husserl's concepts of "regressive inquiry" and "Galilean physics" by means of discovering praxioms. In: Human Studies 18(2–3): 189–225.
Bjelić, Dušan I. (1996): Lebenswelt structures of Galilean physics: The case of Galileo's pendulum. In: Human Studies 19(4): 409–432.
Bjelić, Dušan I./Michael Lynch (1992): The work of a (scientific) demonstration: Respecifying Newton's and Goethe's theories of prismatic color. In: Graham Watson/Robert M. Seiler (Eds.): Text in context: Contributions to ethnomethodology. London: Sage, pp. 52–78.
Bloomfield, Brian P./Yvonne Latham/Theo Vurdubakis (2009): When is an Affordance? Bodies, Technologies and Action Possibilities. In: Lancaster University Management School Working Paper 36.
Bloor, David (1992): Left and right Wittgensteinians. In: Andrew Pickering (Ed.): Science as practice and culture. Chicago: University Of Chicago Press, pp. 266–282.
Bloor, David (2001): Wittgenstein and the priority of practice. In: Theodore R. Schatzki/Karin Knorr Cetina/Eicke von Savigny (Eds.): The Practice Turn in Contemporary Theory. London: Routledge, pp. 95–106.
Blue, Stanley/Nicola Spurling (2017): Qualities of connective tissue in hospital life. How complexes of practices change. In: Allison Hui/Theodore Schatzki/Elizabeth Shove (Eds.): The nexus of practices: Connections, constellations, practitioners. Milton Park: Taylor & Francis, pp. 24–37.
Bockrath, Franz/Bernhard Boschert/Elk Franke (Eds.) (2007): Körperliche Erkenntnis. Bielefeld: transcript Verlag.
Bogen, David (1999): Order without rules: critical theory and the logic of conversation. Albany: SUNY Press.
Bogner, Thomas (1999): Zur Rekonstruktion filmischer Naturdarstellung am Beispiel einer Fallstudie. Natur im Film „Der heilige Berg" von Dr. Arnold Fanck. Dissertation Thesis, Universität Hamburg.
Böhme, Gernot (1995): Atmosphäre. Essays zur neuen Ästhetik. Frankfurt a. M.: Suhrkamp.
Boltanski, Luc/Laurent Thévenot (2006): On justification: economies of worth. Princton: Princeton University Press.

Bongaerts, Gregor (2003): Eingefleischte Sozialität. Zur Phänomenologie sozialer Praxis. In: Sociologica Internationalis 41: 25–53.
Bongaerts, Gregor (2007): Soziale Praxis und Verhalten-Uberlegungen zum Practice Turn in Social Theory. In: Zeitschrift für Soziologie 36(4): 246.
Bongaerts, Gregor (2008): Verhalten, Handeln, Handlung und soziale Praxis. In: Jürgen Raab et al. (Eds.): Phänomenologie und Soziologie. Theoretische Positionen, aktuelle Problemfelder und empirische Umsetzungen. Wiesbaden: VS Verlag, pp. 223–232.
Bongaerts, Gregor (2011): Vom Sichtbaren und Unsichtbaren sozialer Akteure – Überlegungen zum Akteursbegriff im Rahmen von Bourdieus Theorie der Praxis. In: Nico Lüdtke/Hironori Matsuzaki (Eds.): Akteur – Individuum – Subjekt: Fragen zu "Personalität" und "Sozialität." Wiesbaden: VS Verlag, pp. 149–170.
Booth, Douglas (2003): Expression Sessions. Surfing, Style and Prestige. In: Robert E. Rinehart/ Synthia Sydnor (Eds.): To the Extreme. Alternative Sports, Inside and Out. Albany: SUNY Press, pp. 315–333.
Bourdieu, Pierre (1977): Outline of a theory of practice. Cambridge: Cambridge University Press.
Bourdieu, Pierre (1978): Sport and social class. In: Social Science Information 17: 819–840.
Bourdieu, Pierre (1979): Entwurf einer Theorie der Praxis (auf der ethnologischen Grundlage der kabylischen Gesellschaft). Frankfurt a. M.: Suhrkamp.
Bourdieu, Pierre (1984): Distinction: a social critique of the judgement of taste. Cambridge: Harvard University Press.
Bourdieu, Pierre (1987): Die feinen Unterschiede. Kritik der gesellschaftlichen Urteilskraft. Frankfurt a. M.: Suhrkamp.
Bourdieu, Pierre (1988): Program for a Sociology of Sport. In: Sociology of Sport Journal 5(2): 153–161.
Bourdieu, Pierre (1990): The logic of practice. Stanford: Stanford University Press.
Bourdieu, Pierre (1996): The rules of art: Genesis and structure of the literary field. Stanford: Stanford University Press.
Bourdieu, Pierre (2000): Pascalian meditations. Stanford: Stanford University Press.
Bourdieu, Pierre/Loïc Wacquant (1992): An invitation to reflexive sociology. Chicago: University of Chicago Press.
Bowker, Geoffrey C./Susan Leigh Star (2000): Sorting things out: classification and its consequences. MIT Press.
Le Breton, David (2000): Playing Symbolically with Death in Extreme Sports. In: Body & Society 6(1): 1–11.
Briscoe, Robert (2009): Egocentric Spatial Representation in Action and Perception. In: Philosophy and Phenomenological Research 79(2): 423–460.
Brümmer, Kristina (2009): Praktische Intelligenz – Überlegungen zu einer interdisziplinären Systematisierung. In: Thomas Alkemeyer et al. (Eds.): Ordnung in Bewegung: Choreographien des sozialen. Körper in Sport, Tanz, Arbeit und Bildung. Bielefeld: transcript, pp. 21–50.
Brümmer, Kristina (2019): Coordination in sports teams – ethnographic insights into practices of video analysis in football. In: European Journal for Sport and Society 16.1: 27–43.
Brümmer, Kristina/Thomas Alkemeyer (2017): Practice as a shared accomplishment. Intercorporeal attunement in acrobatics. In: Christian Meyer/Ulrich v. Wedelstaedt (Eds.): Moving Bodies in Interaction–Interacting Bodies in Motion: Intercorporeality, interkinesthesia, and enaction in sports. Amsterdam: John Benjamins, pp. 26–56.
Bucher, Annemarie (2003): Landschaft – zwischen Bild und Begriff. In: Jochen Meyer (Ed.): Trans 11 – transScape. paysage / landschaft / cityscape. Zürich: gta, pp. 12–19.
Bucher, Thomas (2000): Die Härte. Sportkletterer und die Schwierigkeitsgrade. Neuried: Ars Una.
Bührmann, Andrea D/Werner Schneider (2007): More Than Just a Discursive Practice? Conceptual Principles and Methodological Aspects of Dispositif Analysis. In: Forum Qualitative Sozialforschung / Forum: Qualitative Social Research 8(2).

References

Büscher, Monika (2005a): Social Life under the Microscope? In: Sociological Research Online 10(1).
Büscher, Monika (2005b): Interaction in motion: Embodied conduct in emergency teamwork. In: Lorenza Mondada (Ed.): Online Multimedia Proceedings of the 2nd International Society for Gesture Studies Conference "Interacting Bodies", Lyon.
Büscher, Monika (2006): Vision in motion. In: Environment and Planning A 38(2): 281–299.
Büscher, Monika/John Urry (2009): Mobile Methods and the Empirical. In: European Journal of Social Theory 12(1): 99–116.
Burri, Regula Valérie (2008): Bilder als soziale Praxis: Grundlegungen einer Soziologie des Visuellen. In: Zeitschrift für Soziologie 37(4): 342–358.
Caillois, Roger (1961): Man, play, and games. New York: Free Press.
Callon, Michel (1986): Some elements of a sociology of translation: domestication of the scallops and the fishermenof St Brieuc Bay. In: John Law (Ed.): Power, action and belief: a new sociology of knowledge? London: Routledge, pp. 196–223.
Callon, Michel (1991): Techno-economic networks and irreversibility. In: John Law (Ed.): A Sociology of monsters: essays on power, technology, and domination. London: Routledge, pp. 132–161.
Carman, Taylor (1999): The Body in Husserl and Merleau-Ponty. In: Philosophical Topics 27(2): 205–226.
Carman, Taylor (2005): Sensation, Judgment, and the Phenomenal Field. In: Taylor Carman/Mark B. Hansen (Eds.): The Cambridge companion to Merleau-Ponty. Cambridge: Cambridge University Press, pp. 50–73.
Carman, Taylor (2008): Merleau-Ponty. London: Taylor & Francis.
Cassell, Joan (1988): The relationship of observer to observed when studying up. In: Richard G. Burgess (Ed.): Studies in qualitative methodology. Greenwich: JAI Press, pp. 89–108.
Cavanagh, Patrick (2011): Visual cognition. In: Vision Research 51(13): 1538–1551.
Caysa, Volker (2008): Körperliche Erkenntnis als empraktische Körpererinnerung. In: Franz Bockrath/Bernhard Boschert/Elk Franke (Eds.): Körperliche Erkenntnis. Formen reflexiver Erfahrung. Bielefeld: transcript Verlag, pp. 73–85.
Celsi, Richard L./Randall L. Rose/Thomas W. Leigh (1993): An Exploration of High-Risk Leisure Consumption Through Skydiving. In: Journal of Consumer Research 20(1): 1–23.
Cerbone, D. R (1994): Don't look but think: Imaginary scenarios in Wittgenstein's later philosophy. In: Inquiry 37(2): 159–183.
Cerulo, Karen A. (2010): Mining the intersections of cognitive sociology and neuroscience. In: Poetics 38(2): 115–132.
La Chapelle, Dolores (1984): Earth Wisdom. Silverton: Finn Hill Arts.
Chapman, David (1991): Vision, instruction, and action. Boston: MIT Press.
Circourel, Aaron V. (1973): Cognitive sociology. Language and meaning in social interaction. New York: Free Press.
Circourel, Aaron V. (1996): Ecological validity and 'white room effects': The interaction of cognitive and cultural models in the pragmatic analysis of elicited narratives from children. In: Pragmatics & Cognition 4(2): 221–264.
Circourel, Aaron V. (2007): A personal, retrospective view of ecological validity. In: Text & Talk – An Interdisciplinary Journal of Language, Discourse & Communication Studies 27: 735–752.
Clark, Andy (1997): The dynamical challenge. In: Cognitive Science 21(4): 461–481.
Clark, Andy (1998): Embodiment and the Philosophy of Mind. In: Royal Institute of Philosophy Supplements 43: 35–51.
Clark, Andy (1999): Visual awareness and visuomotor action. In: Journal of Consciousness Studies 6(11–12): 1–18.
Clark, Andy/Rick Grush (1999): Towards a Cognitive Robotics. In: Adaptive Behavior 7(1): 5–16.

Coates, E./B. Clayton/B. Humberstone (2010): A battle for control: exchanges of power in the subculture of snowboarding. In: Sport in Society: Cultures, Commerce, Media, Politics 13(7): 1082.

Cochoy, Franck (2009): Driving a Shopping Cart from STS to Business, and the Other Way Round: On the Introduction of Shopping Carts in American Grocery Stores (1936–1959). In: Organization 16(1): 31–55.

Coleman, Annie Gilbert (2004): Ski style: sport and culture in the Rockies. Lawrence: University Press of Kansas.

Collins, Harry M. (2001): What is tacit knowledge? In: Theodore R. Schatzki/Karin Knorr Cetina/Eicke von Savigny (Eds.): The Practice Turn in Contemporary Theory. London: Routledge, pp. 107–119.

Collins, Harry M./Martin Kusch (1995): Two Kinds of Actions: A Phenomenological Study. In: Philosophy and Phenomenological Research 55(4): 799–819.

Collins, Mike (2004): Sport, physical activity and social exclusion. In: Journal of Sports Sciences 22: 727–740.

Collins, Randall (1981): On the Microfoundations of Macrosociology. In: The American Journal of Sociology 86(5): 984–1014.

Collins, Randall (2004): Interaction Ritual Chains. Princeton: Princeton University Press.

Cook, Matthew/Tim Edensor (2017): Cycling through dark space: Apprehending landscape otherwise. In: Mobilities 12.1: 1–19.

Coulter, Jeff (1991): Cognition in an ethnomethodological mode. In: Graham Button (Ed.): Ethnomethodology and the human sciences. Cambridge: Cambridge University Press, pp. 176–195.

Coulter, Jeff/E. D. Parsons (1990): The praxiology of perception: Visual orientations and practical action. In: Inquiry 33(3): 251–272.

Cova, Bernard/Robert V. Kozinets/Avi Shankar (2007): Consumer tribes. Oxford: Elsevier.

Cross, Emily S./Antonia F. de C. Hamilton/Scott T. Grafton (2006): Building a motor simulation de novo: Observation of dance by dancers. In: NeuroImage 31(3): 1257–1267.

Crosset, Thomas/Becky Beal (1997): The Use of "Subculture" and "Subworld" in Ethnographic Works on Sport: A Discussion of Definitional Distinctions. In: Sociology of Sport Journal 14(1): 73–85.

Csikszentmihalyi, Mihaly (1990): Flow: The Psychology of Optimal Experience. New York: Harper & Row.

Csikszentmihalyi, Mihaly/Isabella Selega Csikszentmihalyi (1988): The flow experience and its significance for human psychology. In: Optimal experience: psychological studies of flow in consciousness. Cambridge: Cambridge University Press, pp. 15–35.

Csikszentmihalyi, Mihaly/Jeanne Nakamura (2002): The Concept of Flow. In: C. R. Snyder/Shane J. López (Eds.): Handbook of positive psychology. Oxford: Oxford University Press, pp. 89–92.

Czyzewski, Marek (2003): Reflexivity of Actors Versus Reflexivity of Accounts. In: Michael Lynch/Wes Sharrock (Eds.): Harold Garfinkel. Sage Masters of Modern Social Thought. London: Sage, pp. 201–227.

Daher, Dom (2008): Die geknebelte Freiheit. Warum Freeriden nur schwer als Contest funktioniert. In: skiing – the next level (36): 36.

Daniel, Dennett (2001): Are we explaining consciousness yet? In: Cognition 79(1–2): 221–237.

Dant, Tim (2004): The Driver-car. In: Theory, Culture & Society 21(4–5): 61–79.

Dant, Tim/Belinda Wheaton (2007): Windsurfing. An extreme form of material and embodied interaction? In: Anthropology Today 23(6): 8–12.

Dawson, Louis W. (1998): Wild Snow: A Historical Guide to North American Ski Mountaineering. Golden: American Alpine Club Press.

Debord, Guy (1983): Society of the spectacle. London: Rebel Press.

Deleuze, Gilles/Félix Guattari (1987): A thousand plateaus: capitalism and schizophrenia. Minneapolis: University of Minnesota Press.

References

Deutscher Verband für das Skilehrwesen (2006): Ski-Lehrplan praxis. München: BLV.
DiMaggio, Paul (1997): Culture and Cognition. In: Annual Review of Sociology 23: 263–287.
Dingwall, Robert. (1997): Accounts, interviews and observations. In: Miller G, Dingwall, Robert (Eds.): Context & Method in Qualitative Research. London: Sage: 51–65.
Dodd, James (1997): Idealism and corporeity. An essay on the problem of the body in Husserl's phenomenology. New York: Springer.
Doll, Theodore J. (1993): Preattentive Processing in Visual Search. In: Human Factors and Ergonomics Society Annual Meeting Proceedings 37: 1291–1294.
Donnelly, Michele (2006): Studying Extreme Sports: Beyond the Core Participants. In: Journal of Sport & Social Issues 30(2): 219–224.
Donnelly, Peter/Kevin Young (1988): The Construction and Confirmation of Identity in Sport Subcultures. In: Sociology of Sport Journal 5(3): 223–240.
Dostal, Robert J. (1993): Time and phenomenology in Husserl and Heidegger. In: Charles B. Guignon (Ed.): The Cambridge companion to Heidegger. Cambridge: Cambridge University Press, pp. 141–169.
Dreyfus, Hubert L. (1979): What computers can't do: the limits of artificial intelligence. New York: Harper & Row.
Dreyfus, Hubert L. (1991): Being-in-the-world: a commentary on Heidegger's Being and time, division I. Boston: MIT Press.
Dreyfus, Hubert L. (1993): Heidegger's Critique of Husserl's (and Searle's) Account of Intentionality. In: Social Research 60(1): 1–13.
Dreyfus, Hubert L. (1996): The Current Relevance of Merleau-Ponty's Phenomenology of Embodiment. In: The Electronic Journal of Analytic Philosophy 4(2).
Dreyfus, Hubert L. (2000): Responses. In: Mark A. Wrathall/Jeff Malpas (Eds.): Heidegger, coping, and cognitive science. Essays in Honor of Hubert L. Dreyfus, Volume 2. Boston: MIT Press, pp. 313–350.
Dreyfus, Hubert L. (2001): How Heidegger defends the possibility of a correspondence theory of truth with respect to the entities of natural science. In: Theodore R. Schatzki/Karin Knorr Cetina/Eicke von Savigny (Eds.): The Practice Turn in Contemporary Theory. London: Routledge, pp. 151–162.
Dreyfus, Hubert L. (2007): Heidegger's Ontology of Art. In: Hubert L. Dreyfus/Mark A. Wrathall (Eds.): Oxford: Blackwell, pp. 407–419.
Dreyfus, Hubert L. (2008): Skilled Coping as Higher Intelligibility Heidegger's "Being and Time." Assen: van Gorcum.
Dreyfus, Hubert L./Stuart E. Dreyfus (1986): Mind Over Machine. The power of human intuition and expertise in the era of the computer. New York: Free Press.
Dreyfus, Hubert L./Paul Rabinow (1999): Can there be a science of existential structure and social meaning? In: Richard Shusterman (Ed.): Bourdieu: a critical reader. London: Wiley-Blackwell, pp. 84–93.
Drummond, John J. (1979): On Seeing a Material Thing in Space: The Role of Kinaesthesis in Visual Perception. In: Philosophy and Phenomenological Research 40(1): 19–32.
Drummond, John J. (2009): The Enactive Approach and Perceptual Sense. New York. Manuscript.
Duchowski, Andrew T. (2007): Eye tracking methodology: theory and practice. London: Springer.
Duesund, Liv/Ejgil Jespersen (2004): Skill Acquisition in Ski Instruction and the Skill Model's Application to Treating Anorexia Nervosa. In: Bulletin of Science, Technology and Society 24(3): 225–233.
Durkheim, Emile (1965): The Elementary Forms of Religious Life. New York: Free Press.
Eberle, Thomas S. (1984): Sinnkonstitution in Alltag und Wissenschaft. Bern: Haupt.
Eberle, Thomas S. (1988): Die deskriptive Analyse der Ökonomie durch Alfred Schütz. In: Elisabeth List/Ilja Srubar (Eds.): Alfred Schütz. Neue Beiträge zur Rezeption seines Werkes. Amsterdam: Rodopoi, pp. 69–120.

Eberle, Thomas S. (1999): Sinnadäquanz und Kausaladäquanz bei Max Weber und Alfred Schütz. In: Ronald Hitzler/Jo Reichertz/Norbert Schröer (Eds.): Hermeneutische Wissenssoziologie. Konstanz: UVK, pp. 97–119.
Eberle, Thomas S. (2000a): Lebensweltanalyse und postmoderne Organisationstheorie. In: Lebensweltanalyse und Handlungstheorie. Beiträge zur Verstehenden Soziologie. Konstanz: UVK, pp. 223–252.
Eberle, Thomas S. (2000b): Lebensweltanalyse und Rahmenanalyse. In: Lebensweltanalyse und Handlungstheorie. Beiträge zur Verstehenden Soziologie. Konstanz: UVK, pp. 81–126.
Eberle, Thomas S. (2000c): Lebensweltanalyse und Rational Choice. In: Lebensweltanalyse und Handlungstheorie. Beiträge zur Verstehenden Soziologie. Konstanz: UVK, pp. 127–222.
Eberle, Thomas S. (2008): Phänomenologie und Ethnomethodologie. In: Jürgen Raab et al. (Eds.): Phänomenologie und Soziologie. Wiesbaden: VS, pp. 151–161.
Eberle, Thomas S. (2009): In search for aprioris. Schutz's life-world analysis and Mises's praxeology. In: Hisashi Nasu et al. (Eds.): Alfred Schutz and His Intellectual Partners. Konstanz: UVK, pp. 459–484.
Eberle, Thomas S. (2010): The Phenomenological Life-World Analysis and the Methodology of the Social Sciences. In: *Human* Studies 33(2–3): 123–139.
Edensor, Tim (2010): Walking in rhythms: place, regulation, style and the flow of experience. In: Visual Studies 25:1: 69–79.
Edensor, Tim (2012): From light to dark: Daylight, illumination, and gloom. Minneapolis: University of Minnesota Press.
Edensor, Tim/Sophia Richards (2007): Snowboarders vs Skiers: Contested Choreographies of the Slopes. In: Leisure Studies 26(1): 97–114.
Edwards, Derek (2006): Discourse, cognition and social practices: the rich surface of language and social interaction. In: Discourse Studies 8(1): 41–49.
Elias, Norbert/Eric Dunning (1986): Quest for excitement: sport and leisure in the civilising process. Oxford: Basil Blackwell.
Engler, Martin/Jan Mersch (2006): SnowCard. Lawinen-Risiko-Check: Risikomanagement für: Skitourengeher, Snowboarder, Variantenfahrer, Schneeschuhwanderer. München: Deutscher Alpenverein.
Ennen, Elizabeth (2003): Phenomenological coping skills and the striatal memory system. In: Phenomenology and the Cognitive Sciences 2(4): 299–325.
EpicSki Community (2009): Slough Management. http://www.epicski.com/wiki/slough-management (accessed February 21, 2009).
epicski.com (2007): Ski flex compared. In: epicski.com. http://www.epicski.com/forum/thread/62848/ski-flex-compared (accessed June 22, 2011).
Esposito, Elena (1999): Programm. In: Claudio Baraldi/Giancarlo Corsi/Elena Esposito (Eds.): GLU – Glossar zu Niklas Luhmanns Theorie sozialer Systeme. Frankfurt a. M.: Suhrkamp Taschenbuch Wissenschaft, pp. 139–141.
Falcon, Mike (2003): News Release: 25th Anniversary Powder 8 World Championships. http://www.powder8.com/publicity.asp (accessed August 22, 2011).
Featherstone, Mike/Roger Burrows (1995): Cyberspace/cyberbodies/cyberpunk: cultures of technological embodiment. London: Sage.
Fele, Giolo (2008): The Phenomenal Field: Ethnomethodological Perspectives on Collective Phenomena. In: Human Studies 31(3): 299–322.
Fell, Joseph P/Robert D Cumming (1990): The familiar and the strange: on the limits of praxis in the early Heidegger. In: The Southern Journal of Philosophy 28(S1): 23–41.
Ferrell, Jeff/Dragan Milovanovic/Stephen Lyng (2001): Edgework, Media Practices, and the Elongation of Meaning: A Theoretical Ethnography of the Bridge Day Event. In: Theoretical Criminology 5(2): 177–202.
Figueroa-Dreher, Silvana K (2008): Musikalisches Improvisieren: Die phänomenologische handlungstheorie auf dem Prüfstand. In: Jürgen Raab et al. (Eds.): Phänomenologie und

Soziologie. Theoretische Positionen, aktuelle Problemfelder und empirische Umsetzungen. Wiesbaden: VS Verlag, pp. 389–399.
Fischer-Lichte, Erika (2004): Ästhetik des Performativen. Frankfurt a. M.: Suhrkamp.
Fischer-Lichte, Erika/Clemens Risi/Jens Roselt (2004): Kunst der Aufführung: Aufführung der Kunst. Berlin: Theater der Zeit.
von Foerster, Heinz (2003): Understanding understanding. Essays on cybernetics and cognition. New York: Springer.
Force, William Ryan (2009): Consumption Styles and the Fluid Complexity of Punk Authenticity. In: Symbolic Interaction 32(4): 289–309.
Foucault, Michel (1976): The birth of the clinic: an archaeology of medical perception. London: Routledge.
Foucault, Michel (1977): Discipline and punish: the birth of the prison. New York: Doubleday.
Foucault, Michel (1982): The Subject and Power. In: Hubert L. Dreyfus/Paul Rabinow (Eds.): Michel Foucault: Beyond Structuralism and Hermeneutics. Chicago: Chicago University Press, pp. 208–227.
Fox, Stephen (2006): 'Inquiries of every imaginable kind': ethnomethodology, practical action and the new socially situated learning theory. In: The Sociological Review 54(3): 426–445.
Franck, Matthias (2009): Arnold Fanck. Weisse Hölle – weisser Rausch. Bergfilme und Bergbilder 1909–1939. Zürich: AS-Verlag.
Frank, Manfred (1992): Stil in der Philosophie. Frankfurt a. M.: Reclam.
Franks, David D. (2010): Neurosociology: The Nexus Between Neuroscience and Social Psychology. New York: Springer.
Freeride World Tour (2011): Judging a freeride contest. http://www.freerideworldtour.com/judging.html (accessed August 22, 2011).
Frentzen, Carola (2008): Kritik an Extremexpeditionen: "So was ist reine Dummheit." In: Spiegel Online. http://www.spiegel.de/reise/fernweh/0,1518,569937,00.html (accessed August 20, 2008).
Frers, Lars (2007a): Einhüllende Materialitäten. Eine Phänomenologie des Wahrnehmens und Handelns an Bahnhöfen und Fährterminals. Bielefeld: transcript Verlag.
Frers, Lars (2007b): Perception, Aesthetics, and Envelopment: Encountering Space and Materiality. In: Lars Frers/Lars Meier (Eds.): Encountering urban places: visual and material performances in the city. Aldershot: Ashgate, pp. 25–46.
Frohlick, Susan (2005): 'That playfulness of white masculinity'. In: Tourist Studies 5(2): 175–193.
Fry, John (2006a): The story of modern skiing. Lebanon: University Press of New England.
Fry, John (2006b): How Freestyle Became an Olympic Sport. In: Skiing Heritage Journal 18(1): 29–33.
Fry, John (2006c): Up by air! The adventure-filled golden years of Heli-Skiing. In: Skiing Heritage Journal 18(3): 8–14.
Fry, John (2009): Extreme's father and son. Jim and Shane McConkey's daredevil defined the 50-year evolution of a new kind of skiing. In: Skiing Heritage Journal 21(4): 22–27.
Fuchs, Peter (2005): Die Form des Körpers. In: Markus Schroer (Ed.): Soziologie des Körpers. Frankfurt a. M.: Suhrkamp, pp. 48–72.
Fuchsberger, Franz (2005): Powder 8 online. http://www.powder8.com/ (accessed November 23, 2010).
funsporting (2007): Tiefschnee-EM in St. Anton am Arlberg. http://www.funsporting.de/News/Powder_8_5547/powder_8_5547.html (accessed November 23, 2010).
Gadamer, Hans-Georg (1994): Heidegger's ways. Albany: SUNY Press.
Gallagher, Shaun (2005): Phenomenological Contributions to a Theory of Social Cognition. In: Husserl Studies 21(2): 95–110.
Gallagher, Shaun (2007): Phenomenological and experimental contributions to understanding embodied experience. In: Tom Ziemke/Jordan Zlatev/Roslyn M. Frank (Eds.): Body, Language and Mind, Volume 1: Embodiment. New York: de Gruyter, pp. 271–296.

Gallese, Vittorio (2003a): The Roots of Empathy: The Shared Manifold Hypothesis and the Neural Basis of Intersubjectivity. In: Psychopathology 36: 171–180.
Gallese, Vittorio (2003b): The manifold nature of interpersonal relations: the quest for a common mechanism. In: Philosophical Transactions of the Royal Society of London. Series B: Biological Sciences 358(1431): 517–528.
Gallese, Vittorio/Alvin Goldman (1998): Mirror neurons and the simulation theory of mind-reading. In: Trends in Cognitive Sciences 2(12): 493–501.
Gallese, Vittorio/George Lakoff (2005): The Brain's concepts: the role of the Sensory-motor system in conceptual knowledge. In: Cognitive Neuropsychology 22(5): 455–479.
Garfinkel, Harold (1963): A conception of, and experiments with,"trust" as a condition of stable concerted actions. In: O. J. Harvey (Ed.): Motivation and social interaction. Cognitive determinants. New York: Ronald Press, pp. 187–238.
Garfinkel, Harold (1967): Studies in ethnomethodology. Englewood Cliffs: Prentice-Hall.
Garfinkel, Harold (1986): Ethnomethodological Studies of Work. London: Routledge.
Garfinkel, Harold (1988): Evidence for Locally Produced, Naturally Accountable Phenomena of Order, Logic, Reason, Meaning, Method, etc. In and as of the Essential Quiddity of Immortal Ordinary Society, (I of IV): An Announcement of Studies. In: Sociological Theory 6(1): 103–109.
Garfinkel, Harold (1996): Ethnomethodology's Program. In: Social Psychology Quarterly 59(1): 5–21.
Garfinkel, Harold (2002): Anne Rawls (Ed.): Ethnomethodology's program. Working out Durkheim's Aphorism. Lanham: Rowman & Littlefield.
Garfinkel, Harold (2007): Lebenswelt origins of the sciences: Working out Durkheim's aphorism. In: Human Studies 30(1): 9–56.
Garfinkel, Harold (2008): Editors introduction. In: Anne Warfield Rawls (Ed.): Toward a Sociological Theory of Information. Boulder: Paradigm Publishers.
Garfinkel, Harold/Kenneth Liberman (2007): Introduction: The Lebenswelt origins of the sciences. In: Human Studies 30(1): 3–7.
Garfinkel, Harold/Eric Livingston (2003): Phenomenal field properties of order in formatted queues and their neglected standing in the current situation of inquiry. In: Visual Studies 18(1): 21–28.
Garfinkel, Harold/Michael Lynch/Eric Livingston (1981): The work of a discovering science construed with materials from the optically discovered pulsar. In: Philosophy of the social sciences 11(2): 131–158.
Garfinkel, Harold/Harvey Sacks (1970): On formal structures of practical actions. In: John C. McKinney/Edward A. Tiryakian (Eds.): Theoretical Sociology. Perspectives and developments. New York: Meredith, pp. 337–366.
Garfinkel, Harold/Larry Wieder (1992): Two incommensurable, asymmetrically alternate technologies of social analysis. In: Graham Watson/Robert M. Seiler (Eds.): Text in context: Contributions to ethnomethodology. London: Sage, pp. 175–206.
Gauthier, Isabel/Marlene Behrmann/Michael J. Tarr (2011): Can Face Recognition Really be Dissociated from Object Recognition? In: Journal of Cognitive Neuroscience 11(4): 349–370.
Gauthier, Isabel/Pawel Skudlarski/John C. Gore/Adam W. Anderson (2000): Expertise for cars and birds recruits brain areas involved in face recognition. In: Nature Neuroscience 3(2): 191–197.
Gauthier, Isabel/Pepper Williams/Michael J. Tarr/James Tanaka (1998): Training "greeble" experts: a framework for studying expert object recognition processes. In: Vision Research 38(15–16): 2401–2428.
Gebauer, Gunter (1999): Bewegte Gemeinden. Über religiöse Gemeinschaften im Sport. In: Merkur (605–606): 936–952.
Gebauer, Gunter (2000): Habitus, intentionality, and social rules: A controversy between Searle and Bourdieu. In: SubStance 29(3): 68–83.

References 595

Gebauer, Gunter (2001): Taktilität und Raumerfahrung bei Wittgenstein. In: ARCH+. Zeitschrift für Architektur und Städtebau (157): 91–96.
Gebauer, Gunter (2008): Das Sprachspielkonzept und der Sport. In: Franz Bockrath/Bernhard Boschert/Elk Franke (Eds.): Körperliche Erkenntnis. Formen reflexiver Erfahrung. Bielefeld: transcript Verlag, pp. 41–52.
Gebauer, Gunter (2009): Wittgensteins anthropologisches Denken. München: C.H. Beck.
Gebauer, Gunter/Thomas Alkemeyer/Uwe Flick (Eds.) (2004): Treue zum Stil: Die aufgeführte Gesellschaft. Bielefeld: transcript Verlag.
Gehlen, Arnold (1987): The crystallization of social forms. In: Volker Meja/Dieter Misgeld/Nico Stehr (Eds.): Modern German sociology. New York: Columbia University Press.
Gehlen, Arnold (1988): Man, his nature and place in the world. New York: Columbia University Press.
Geisler, Tobias (2003): Jugendliche Sportszenen zwischen Kult und Kommerz. Eine Fallstudie zu Freeskiing. Magisterarbeit im Fach Soziologie. Universität Konstanz.
Geisler, Tobias (2004): Szene-Sport, Medien und Marketing. Jugendliche Erlebniswelten zwischen Kult und Kommerz. Saarbrücken: VDM.
Gelder, Ken/Sarah Thornton (1997): The Subcultures Reader. London: Routledge.
Gibbs, Raymond W. (2006): Embodiment and cognitive science. Cambridge University Press.
Gibson, James J. (1986): The ecological approach to visual perception. Boston, Mass.: Houghton Mifflin.
Gibson, Will (2006): Material culture and embodied action: sociological notes on the examination of musical instruments in jazz improvisation. In: The Sociological Review 54(1): 171–187.
Giddens, Anthony (1984): The constitution of society: Outline of the theory of structuration. Berkeley: University of California Press.
Giddens, Anthony (1987): Erving Goffman as a systematic social theorist. In: Social theory and modern sociology. Stanford: Stanford University Press, pp. 109–139.
Gladwell, Malcolm (2005): Blink: the power of thinking without thinking. London: Little, Brown and Co.
Glasersfeld, Ernst von (1996): Radical constructivism: a way of knowing and learning. London: Routledge Falmer.
Glock, Hans-Johann (2010a): Aspektwahrnehmung. In: Wittgenstein-Lexikon. Darmstadt: Wissenschaftliche Buchgesellschaft, pp. 42–47.
Glock, Hans-Johann (2010b): Intentionalität. In: Wittgenstein-Lexikon. Darmstadt: Wissenschaftliche Buchgesellschaft, pp. 177–182.
Gobo, Giampietro (2008): Doing ethnography. London: Sage.
Goffman, Erving (1955): On face-work: an analysis of ritual elements in social interaction. In: Psychiatry: Journal for the Study of Interpersonal Processes 18(3): 213–231.
Goffman, Erving (1959): The Presentation of Self in Everyday Life. New York: Doubleday.
Goffman, Erving (1963): Behavior in public places. Glencoe: Free Press.
Goffman, Erving (1967): Interaction Ritual. Essays on Face-to-Face Behavior. New York: Doubleday.
Goffman, Erving (1971a): Relations in Public: Microstudies of the Public Order. New York: Basic.
Goffman, Erving (1971b): Normal appearances. In: Relations in Public: Microstudies of the Public Order. New York: Basic, pp. 282–388.
Goffman, Erving (1974): Frame Analysis. An essay on the Organisation of Experience. Cambridge: Harvard University Press.
Goffman, Erving (1983): The Interaction Order: American Sociological Association, 1982 Presidential Address. In: American Sociological Review 48(1): 1–17.
Goldman, Alvin (2010): Social Epistemology Edward N. Zalta (Ed.): In: The Stanford Encyclopedia of Philosophy (Summer 2010 Edition).

Goodale, Melvyn A./David Milner (1992): Separate visual pathways for perception and action. In: Trends in Neurosciences 15(1): 20–25.
Goodale, Melvyn A./David Milner/L. S. Jakobson/D. P. Carey (1991): A neurological dissociation between perceiving objects and grasping them. In: Nature 349(6305): 154–156.
Goodman, Nelson (2001): Ways of worldmaking. Indianapolis: Hackett Publishing.
Goodwin, Charles (1994): Professional Vision. In: American Anthropologist 96(3): 606–633.
Goodwin, Charles (1995): Seeing in Depth. In: Social Studies of Science 25(2): 237–274.
Goodwin, Charles (2000a): Action and embodiment within situated human interaction. In: Journal of Pragmatics 32: 1489–1522.
Goodwin, Charles (2000b): Practices of seeing, visual analysis: An ethnomethodological approach. In: Theo van Leeuwen/Carey Jewitt (Eds.): Handbook of visual analysis. London: Sage, pp. 157–182.
Goodwin, Charles (2003): Pointing as Situated Practice. In: Sotaro Kita (Ed.): Pointing: Where language, culture and cognition meet. Mahwah, NJ: Lawrence Erlbaum, pp. 217–241.
Goodwin, Charles (2007): Participation, stance and affect in the organization of activities. In: Discourse Society 18(1): 53–73.
Goodwin, Charles/Marjorie H. Goodwin (1996): Seeing as a Situated Activity: Formulating Planes. In: David Middleton/Yrjö Engeström (Eds.): Cognition and Communication at Work. Cambridge: Cambridge University Press, pp. 61–95.
Goodwin, Charles/Marjorie H. Goodwin (2001): Emotion within Situated Activity. In: Alessandro Duranti (Ed.): Linguistic anthropology. Malden: Wiley-Blackwell, pp. 293–256.
Gourlay, Stephen (2006): Towards conceptual clarity for 'tacit knowledge': a review of empirical studies. In: Knowledge Management Research & Practice 4(1): 60–69.
Graybiel, Ann M. (1995): Building action repertoires: memory and learning functions of the basal ganglia. In: Current Opinion in Neurobiology 5(6): 733–741.
Graybiel, Ann M. (1998): The Basal Ganglia and Chunking of Action Repertoires. In: Neurobiology of Learning and Memory 70(1–2): 119–136.
Greeno, James G. (1994): Gibson's affordances. In: Psychological Review 101(2): 336–342.
Greiffenhagen, Christian/Wes Sharrock (2009): Mathematical equations as Durkheimian social facts? In: Geoff Cooper/Andrew King/Ruth Rettie (Eds.): Sociological objects: reconfigurations of social theory. London: Ashgate, pp. 119–135.
Grey, Donald M./D. H. Male (Eds.) (1981): Handbook of Snow: Principles, Processes, Management and Use. Oxford: Pergamon Press.
Gugutzer, Robert (Ed.) (2006): Body Turn. Bielefeld: transcript Verlag.
Gurwitsch, Aron (1964): The field of consciousness. Pittsburgh: Duquesne University Press.
Gurwitsch, Aron (1970): Towards a Theory of Intentionality. In: Philosophy and Phenomenological Research 30(3): 354–367.
Gurwitsch, Aron (1979): Studies in Phenomenology and Psychology. Evanston: Northwestern University Press.
Hacker, Peter M. S./Joachim Schulte (2009): Editorial preface to the fourth edition and modified translation. In: Ludwig Wittgenstein: Philosophical investigations – Philosophische Untersuchungen. Chichester: John Wiley, pp. viii–xxiii.
Haggard, Patrick (2005): Conscious intention and motor cognition. In: Trends in Cognitive Sciences 9(6): 290–295.
Hahn, Alois (2009): Körper und Gedächtnis. Wiesbaden: VS Verlag.
Hals, Endre (2007): Flex curves and SFI 2008. http://www.friflyt.no/files/SFI_2008.pdf (accessed November 24, 2008).
Hals, Endre (2011): Introducing the Ski Flex Index (SFI). http://www.endrehals.no/ (accessed June 22, 2011).
Hammersley, Martyn/Paul Atkinson (1983): Ethnography. Principles in practice. London: Tavistock.
Hammersley, Martyn/Paul Atkinson (2007): Ethnography: principles in practice. 3rd ed. London: Taylor & Francis.

References

Haraway, Donna J (1991): Simians, Cyborgs, and Women: The Reinvention of Nature. London: Routledge.
Hargadon, A./R. I. Sutton (1997): Technology Brokering and Innovation in a Product Development Firm. In: Administrative Science Quarterly 42(4): 716–749.
Harrington, Brooke (2003): The Social Psychology of Access in Ethnographic Research. In: Journal of Contemporary Ethnography 32(5): 592–625.
Hausendorf, Heiko (1992): Das Gespräch als selbstreferentielles System. Ein Beitrag zum empirischen Konstruktivismus der ethnomethodologischen Konversationsanalyse. In: Zeitschrift für Soziologie 21(2): 83–95.
Häusl, Stefan (2008): Skill Drill Big Mountain Lines. Die Kunst der Freeride Pros. In: skiing (38): 22–26.
ten Have, Paul (2002): The Notion of Member is the Heart of the Matter: On the Role of Membership Knowledge in Ethnomethodological Inquiry. In: Forum Qualitative Sozialforschung / Forum: Qualitative Social Research 3(3): Art. 21.
ten Have, Paul (2004): Understanding qualitative research and ethnomethodology. London: Sage.
ten Have, Paul (2007): Ethnomethodology. In: Clive Seale et al. (Eds.): Qualitative Research Practice. Concise Paperback Edition. London: Sage, pp. 151–179.
Heath, Christian (2004): Analysing face-to-face interaction. Video, the visual and material. In: David Silverman (Ed.): Qualitative research: theory, method and practice. London: Sage, pp. 266–282.
Heath, Christian/Jon Hindmarsh (2002): Analysing Interaction: Video, Ethnography and Situated Conduct. In: Thomas May (Ed.): Qualitative Research: An international guide to issues in practice. London: Sage, pp. 99–121.
Heath, Christian/Dirk vom Lehn (2004): Configuring Reception. In: Theory, Culture & Society 21(6): 43–65.
Heath, Christian/Paul Luff (1992): Collaboration and control: Crisis management and multimedia technology in London Underground line control rooms. In: CSCW Journal 1(1–2): 69–94.
Heath, Christian/Paul Luff (2000): Technology in action. Cambridge: Cambridge University Press.
Heath, Christian/Paul Luff/Dirk vom Lehn/Jun Yamashita/et al. (2009): Enhancing remote participation in live auctions: an 'intelligent' gavel. In: Proceedings of the 27th international conference on Human factors in computing systems. Boston, MA, USA: ACM, pp. 1427–1436.
Hebdige, Dick (1979): Subculture: The Meaning of Style. London: Taylor & Francis.
Heidegger, Martin (1962): Being and time. Malden: Wiley-Blackwell.
Heidegger, Martin (1971): On the origin of the work of art. In: Poetry, language, thought. London: Harper & Row, pp. 17–87.
Heidegger, Martin (1977): The Age of the World Picture. In: William Lovitt (Ed.): The Question Concerning Technology and Other Essays. London: Harper, pp. 115–154.
Heidegger, Martin (1982): Basic Problems of Phenomenology. Bloomington: Indiana University Press.
Heider, Fritz (1926): Ding und Medium. In: Symposium. Philosophische Zeitschrift für Forschung und Aussprache 1: 109–157.
Heiskala, Risto (2011): The Meaning of Meaning in Sociology. The Achievements and Shortcomings of Alfred Schutz's Phenomenological Sociology. In: Journal for the Theory of Social Behaviour 41(3): 231–146.
Heritage, John (1984): Garfinkel and Ethnomethodology. Cambridge: Polity Press.
Heßler, Martina/Dieter Mersch/Ulrich Richtmeyer (Eds.) (2009): Logik und Aisthesis. Wittgenstein über Negationen, Variablen und Hypothesen im Bild. In: Logik des Bildlichen: Zur Kritik der ikonischen Vernunft. Bielefeld: transcript Verlag, pp. 139–162.
Hester, Stephen/David Francis (Eds.) (2000): Local educational order: enthnomethodological studies of knowledge in action. Amsterdam: John Benjamins.
Hilgers, M. (2009): Habitus, Freedom, and Reflexivity. In: Theory & Psychology 19(6): 728–755.

Hillebrandt, Frank (2009): Praxistheorie. In: Georg Kneer/Markus Schroer (Eds.): Handbuch Soziologische Theorien. Wiesbaden: VS Verlag, pp. 369–394.
Hindmarsh, Jon/Christian Heath/Paul Luff (2000): Workplace Studies: Recovering Work Practice and Informing System Design. Cambridge: Cambridge University Press.
Hindmarsh, Jon/Christian Heath/Paul Luff (2010): Video in Qualitative Research. London: Sage.
Hirschauer, Stefan (1991): The Manufacture of Bodies in Surgery. In: Social Studies of Science 21(2): 279–319.
Hirschauer, Stefan/Jörg Bergmann (2002): Willkommen im Club! Eine Anregung zu mehr Kontingenzfreudigkeit in der qualitativen Sozialforschung – Kommentar zu A. Nassehi und I. Saake in ZfS 1/2002. In: Zeitschrift für Soziologie 31(4): 332–336.
Hitzler, Ronald/Thomas Bucher/Arne Niederbacher (2005): Leben in Szenen : Formen jugendlicher Vergemeinschaftung heute. Wiesbaden: VS Verlag.
Hitzler, Ronald/Thomas S. Eberle (2007): Phänomenologische Lebensweltanalyse. In: Uwe Flick/Ernst von Kardorff/Ines Steinke (Eds.): Qualitative Forschung. Ein Handbuch. Reinbek bei Hamburg: Rowohlt, pp. 109–118.
Hitzler, Ronald/Anne Honer/Michaela Pfadenhauer (Eds.) (2008): Posttraditionale Gemeinschaften. Wiesbaden: VS Verlag.
Hitzler, Ronald/Michaela Pfadenhauer (2004): Die Macher und ihre Freunde. Schließungsprozeduren in der Techno-Party-Szene. In: Ronald Hitzler/Stefan Hornbostel/Cornelia Mohr (Eds.): Elitenmacht. Wiesbaden: VS Verlag, pp. 315–328.
Hochschild, Arlie Russell (1979): Emotion Work, Feeling Rules, and Social Structure. In: The American Journal of Sociology 85(3): 551–575.
Hochschild, Arlie Russell (1983): The managed heart: commercialization of human feeling. Berkeley: University of California Press.
Hoffman, Steve G./Gary Alan Fine (2005): The Scholar's Body: Mixing It Up with Loïc Wacquant. In: Qualitative Sociology 28(2): 151–157.
Honer, Anne (1995): Bodybuilding als Sinnprovinz der Lebenswelt. Prinzipielle und praktische Bemerkungen. In: Joachim Winkler/Kurt Weis (Eds.): In: Winkler, J./Weis, K.(Hg.): Soziologie des Sports. Theorieansätze, Forschungsergebnisse und Forschungsperspektiven. Opladen: Westdeutscher Verlag, pp. 181–186.
Honer, Anne (2007): Lebensweltanalyse in der Ethnographie. In: Uwe Flick/Ernst von Kardorff/Ines Steinke (Eds.): Qualitative Forschung. Ein Handbuch. Reinbek bei Hamburg: Rowohlt, pp. 194–213.
Honer, Anne/Christoph Maeder (Eds.) (1994): Expertenwissen: die institutionalisierte Kompetenz zur Konstruktion von Wirklichkeit. Opladen: Westdeutscher Verlag.
Hörning, Karl H. (2004): Soziale Praxis zwischen Beharrung und Neuschöpfung. Ein Erkenntnis- und Theorieproblem. In: Julia Reuter/Karl H. Hörning (Eds.): Doing Culture – Neue Positionen zum Verhältnis von Kultur und sozialer Praxis. Bielefeld: transcript Verlag, pp. 19–39.
Hörning, Karl H./Julia Reuter (Eds.) (2004): Doing Culture – Neue Positionen zum Verhältnis von Kultur und sozialer Praxis. Bielefeld: transcript Verlag.
Hoyt, Christopher (2007): Wittgenstein and religious dogma. In: International Journal for Philosophy of Religion 61: 39–49.
Huber, Tine (2009): Tine Huber – Freeskier. About me. http://www.tinehuber.com/about%20me/about%20me.html (accessed December 13, 2010).
Hui, Allison (2012): Things in motion, things in practices: How mobile practice networks facilitate the travel and use of leisure objects. In: Journal of Consumer Culture, 12(2), 195–215.
Hui, Allison (2017): Variation and the intersection of practices. In: Allison Hui/Theodore Schatzki/Elizabeth Shove (Eds.): The nexus of practices: Connections, constellations, practitioners. Milton Park: Taylor & Francis, pp. 52–67.
Humphreys, Duncan (2003): Selling out snowboarding: The alternative response to commercial co-optation. In: Robert E. Rinehart/Synthia Sydnor (Eds.): To the extreme: Alternative sports, inside and out. Albany: SUNY Press, pp. 407–428.

Hunt, Jennifer C. (1995): Divers'accounts of normal risk. In: Symbolic Interaction 18(4): 439–462.
Huq, Rupa (2006): Beyond subculture. London: Routledge.
Husserl, Edmund (1973): Ulrich Claesges (Ed.): Ding und Raum: Vorlesungen 1907. Den Haag: Martinus Nijhoff.
Husserl, Edmund (1991a): Ideas Pertaining to a Pure Phenomenology and a Phenomenological Philosophy I: General Introduction to Pure Phenomenology. Dordrecht: Kluwer.
Husserl, Edmund (1991b): On the phenomenology of the consciousness of internal time. Dordrecht: Kluwer.
Husserl, Edmund (1997): Thing and Space. Lectures of 1907. Dodrecht: Kluwer.
Hussey, Elizabeth (2005): The Man Who Changed the Face of Alpine Skiing. In: Skiing Heritage Journal 17(4): 7–12.
Hutchby, Ian (2001): Technologies, Texts and Affordances. In: Sociology 35(2): 441–456.
Hutchby, Ian (2003): Affordances and the Analysis of Technologically Mediated Interaction: A Response to Brian Rappert. In: Sociology 37(3): 581–589.
Hutchins, Edwin (1995): Cognition in the Wild. Boston: MIT Press.
Hutchins, Edwin (1996): Response to reviewers. In: Mind, Culture, and Activity 3(1): 64–68.
Hutchins, Edwin/Klausen (1998): Distributed cognition in an airline cockpit. In: Yrjö Engeström/ David Middleton (Eds.): Cognition and communication at work. Cambridge: Cambridge University Press, pp. 15–34.
Hutto, Daniel D. (2006): Knowing What? Radical Versus Conservative Enactivism. In: Phenomenology and the Cognitive Sciences 4: 389–405.
Huybers-Withers, Sherry M./Lori A. Livingston (2010): Mountain biking is for men: consumption practices and identity portrayed by a niche magazine. In: Sport in Society: Cultures, Commerce, Media, Politics 13(7): 1204.
Ingold, Tim (1993): The Temporality of the Landscape. In: World Archaeology 25(2): 152–174.
Ingold, Tim (2000): The perception of the environment: essays on livelihood, dwelling and skill. London: Routledge.
Ingold, Tim (2007): Lines: a brief history. London: Routledge.
Ingold, Tim (2009): Against space: Place, movement, knowledge. In: Peter Wynn Kirby (Ed.): Boundless worlds: an anthropological approach to movement. Oxford: Berghahn Books, pp. 29–44.
Ingold, Tim (2010): The textility of making. In: Cambridge Journal of Economics 34(1): 91–102.
Ingold, Tim (2011): Being Alive: Essays on Movement, Knowledge and Description. London: Routledge Chapman & Hall.
Ingram, Jack/Elizabeth Shove/Matthew Watson (2007): Products and Practices: Selected Concepts from Science and Technology Studies and from Social Theories of Consumption and Practice. In: Design Issues 23(2): 3–16.
Jacob, Pierre (2008): What Do Mirror Neurons Contribute to Human Social Cognition? In: Mind & Language 23(2): 190–223.
Jacob, Pierre/Marc Jeannerod (2003): Ways of seeing: the scope and limits of visual cognition. Oxford: Oxford University Press.
Jacob, Pierre/Marc Jeannerod (2005): The motor theory of social cognition: a critique. In: Trends in Cognitive Sciences 9(1): 21–25.
Jay, Martin (1994): Downcast eyes: the denigration of vision in twentieth-century French thought. Berkeley: University of California Press.
Jayyusi, Lena (1988): Toward a socio-logic of the film text. In: Semiotica 68(3–4): 271–296.
Jensen, Rasmus Thybo (2009): Motor intentionality and the case of Schneider. In: Phenomenology and the Cognitive Sciences 8(3): 371–388.
Johnson, Doyle Paul (1990): Security versus Autonomy Motivation in Anthony Giddens' Concept of Agency. In: Journal for the Theory of Social Behaviour 20(2): 111–130.
Jonas, Michael/Beate Littig/Angela Wroblewski (2017): Methodological Reflections on Practice Oriented Theories. Cham: Springer.

Jonasson, Kalle/Jesper Thiborg (2010): Electronic sport and its impact on future sport. In: Sport in Society 13(2): 287–299.
Jordan, Robert Welsh (2000): Time and Formal Authenticity: Husserl and Heidegger. In: Lester E. Embree/John Barnett Brough (Eds.): The many faces of time. Dodrecht: Kluwer, pp. 38–65.
Kalthoff, Herbert/Stefan Hirschauer/Gesa Lindemann (2008): Theoretische Empirie. Zur Relevanz qualitativer Forschung. Frankfurt a. M.: Suhrkamp.
Kassat, Georg (2000): ...doch die Piste dreht die Ski: Die eine Ski-Technik und die Ein-Ski-Methodik. Rödinghausen: Fitness-Contur.
Kassat, Georg (2009): Not the skier – but the slope turns the skis. In: Erich Mueller/Stefan Lindinger/Thomas Stöggl (Eds.): Science and Skiing IV. Aachen: Meyer & Meyer, pp. 292–303.
Kastl, Jörg M. (2001): Grenzen der Intelligenz: Die soziologische Theorie und das Rätsel der Intentionalität. München: Wilhelm Fink.
Kastl, Jörg M. (2004): Habitus als non-deklaratives Gedächtnis-zur Relevanz der neuropsychologischen Amnesieforschung für die Soziologie. In: Sozialer Sinn 2: 195–226.
Kastl, Jörg M. (2007): Habitus. In: Rainer Schützeichel (Ed.): Handbuch Wissenssoziologie und Wissensforschung. Konstanz: UVK, pp. 375–387.
Kaufmann, Jean-Claude (1996): Frauenkörper – Männerblicke. Konstanz: UVK.
Kay, Joanne/Suzanne Laberge (2002): Mapping the field of "AR": adventure racing and Bourdieu's concept of field. In: Sociology of Sport Journal 19(1): 25–46.
Kay, Joanne/Suzanne Laberge (2003): Oh Say Can You Ski? Imperialistic Construction of Freedom in Warren Miller's Freeriders. In: Robert E. Rinehart/Synthia Sydnor (Eds.): To the extreme: Alternative sports, inside and out. Albany: SUNY Press, pp. 381–400.
Keller, Reiner/Michael Meuser (2011a): Wissen des Körpers – Wissen vom Körper. In: Reiner Keller/Michael Meuser (Eds.): Körperwissen. Wiesbaden: VS Verlag für Sozialwissenschaften, pp. 9–27.
Keller, Reiner/Michael Meuser (Eds.) (2011b): Wissen des Körpers – Wissen vom Körper. Körper- und wissenssoziologische Erkundungen. Wiesbaden: VS Verlag.
Kelly, Sean Dorrance (2000): Grasping at straws: Motor intentionality and the cognitive science of skilled behaviour. In: Mark A. Wrathall/Jeff Malpas (Eds.): Heidegger, coping, and cognitive science. Essays in Honor of Hubert L. Dreyfus, Volume 2. Boston: MIT Press, pp. 161–177.
Kendon, Adam (1990): Conducting Interaction: Patterns of Behavior in Focused Encounters. Cambridge: Cambridge University Press.
Kerig, William A. (2008a): The Edge of Never: A Skier's Story of Life, Death, and Dreams in the World's Most Dangerous Mountains. Milford: Stone Creek Publications.
Kerig, William A. (2008b): The Edge of Never. http://www.theedgeofnever.com/ (accessed October 17, 2011).
Kerig, William A. (2009): The edge of Never. A true story of skiing's Big-Mountain tribe. EON Productions.
Kissmann, Ulrike Tikvah (2009): Video Interaction Analysis: Methods and Methodology. Peter Lang.
Knoblauch, Hubert (1994): Erving Goffmans Reich der Interaktion. In: Hubert Knoblauch (Ed.): Erving Goffman: Interaktion und Geschlecht. Frankfurt a. M.: Campus, pp. 7–49.
Knoblauch, Hubert (2001): Fokussierte Ethnographie. In: Sozialer Sinn 1(2001): 123–141.
Knoblauch, Hubert (2002): Fokussierte Ethnographie als Teil einer soziologischen Ethnographie. Zur Klärung einiger Missverständnisse. In: Sozialer Sinn 3(1): 129–136.
Knoblauch, Hubert (2003): Habitus und Habitualisierung. Zur Komplementarität von Bourdieu mit demSozialkonstruktivismus. In: Boike Rehbein/Gernot Saalmann/Hermann Schwengel (Eds.): Pierre Bourdieus Theorie des Sozialen: Probleme und Perspektiven. Konstanz: UVK, pp. 187–201.
Knoblauch, Hubert (2005a): Wissenssoziologie. Konstanz: UVK.

Knoblauch, Hubert (2005b): Focused Ethnography. In: FQS Forum Qualitative Sozialforschung / Forum: Qualitative Social Research 6(3).
Knoblauch, Hubert (2008): The Performance of Knowledge: Pointing and Knowledge in Powerpoint Presentations. In: Cultural Sociology 2(1): 75–97.
Knoblauch, Hubert (2010): Von der Kompetenz zur Performanz. Wissenssoziologische Aspekte der Kompetenz. In: Thomas Kurtz/Michaela Pfadenhauer (Eds.): Soziologie der Kompetenz. Wiesbaden: VS Verlag, pp. 237–256.
Knoblauch, Hubert/Bernt Schnettler/Jürgen Raab/Hans-Georg Soeffner (Eds.) (2006): Video Analysis-Methodology and Methods: Qualitative Audiovisual Data Analysis in Sociology. Frankfurt a. M.: Peter Lang.
Knorr Cetina, Karin (1981): The manufacture of knowledge. An essay on the constructivist and contextual nature of science. Oxford: Pergamon Press.
Knorr Cetina, Karin (1988): The micro-social order: towards a reconception. In: Nigel G. Fielding (Ed.): Actions and structure: research methods and social theory. London: Sage, pp. 21–53.
Knorr Cetina, Karin (1995): Laboratory studies: The cultural approach to the study of science. In: Sheila Jasanoff et al. (Eds.): Handbook of science and technology studies. London: Sage, pp. 140–166.
Knorr Cetina, Karin (1997): Sociality with Objects: Social Relations in Postsocial Knowledge Societies. In: Theory, Culture & Society 14(4): 1.
Knorr Cetina, Karin (1999): Epistemic Cultures: How the Sciences Make Knowledge. Cambridge: Harvard University Press.
Knorr Cetina, Karin (2003): From Pipes to Scopes: The Flow Architecture of Financial Markets. In: Distinktion 7: 7–23.
Knorr Cetina, Karin (2004): How are global markets global? The architecture of a flow world. In: Karin Knorr Cetina/Alex Preda (Eds.): The sociology of financial markets. Oxford: Oxford University Press, pp. 38–61.
Knorr Cetina, Karin (2005): Complex Global Microstructures: The New Terrorist Societies. In: Theory Culture Society 22(5): 213–234.
Knorr Cetina, Karin (2009): The Synthetic Situation: Interactionism for a Global World. In: Symbolic Interaction 32(1): 61–87.
Knorr Cetina, Karin/Alex Preda (2007): The Temporalization of Financial Markets: From Network to Flow. In: Theory, Culture & Society 24(7–8): 116–138.
Kockelmans, Jospeh J. (1979): Deskriptive oder interpretierende Phänomenologie in Schütz' Konzeption der Sozialwissenschaft. In: Walter Michael Sprondel/Richard Grathoff (Eds.): Alfred Schütz und die Idee des Alltags in den Sozialwissenschaften. Stuttgart: Enke, pp. 26–42.
Koffka, Kurt (1999): Principles of Gestalt Psychology. London: Routledge.
Köhler, Wolfgang (1969): The Task of Gestalt Psychology. Princeton: Princeton University Press.
Kojima, Hiroshi (2002): From dialectic to reversibility: A critical change of subject-object relation in Merleau-Ponty's thought. In: Ted Toadvine/Lester E. Embree (Eds.): Merleau-Ponty's reading of Husserl. Dordrecht: Kluwer, pp. 95–114.
Kourtzi, Zoe/Nancy Kanwisher (2000): Activation in Human MT/MST by Static Images with Implied Motion. In: Journal of Cognitive Neuroscience 12(1): 48–55.
Kracauer, Siegfried (1947): From Caligari to Hitler: a psychological history of the German film. Princeton: Princeton University Press.
Kremer, Kirsten (2003): May 27, 1998. In: Synthia Sydnor/Robert E. Rinehart (Eds.): To the Extreme. Alternative Sports, Inside and Out. Albany: SUNY Press, pp. 375–379.
Krieger, Richard Alan (2002): Civilization's quotations: Life's ideal. New York: Agora Publishing.
Kuhn, Thomas S. (1962): The structure of scientific revolutions. Chicago: University of Chicago Press.

Kusz, Kyle (2003): BMX, extreme sports, and the white male backlash. In: Robert E. Rinehart/Synthia Sydnor (Eds.): To the Extreme. Alternative Sports, Inside and Out. Albany: SUNY Press, pp. 153–175.

Ladner, Gerhart B. (1967): Homo Viator: Mediaeval Ideas on Alienation and Order. In: Speculum 42(2): 233–259.

de Laet, Marianne/Annemarie Mol (2000): The Zimbabwe Bush Pump. Mechanics of a Fluid Technology. In: Social Studies of Science 30(2): 225–263.

Landwehr, Jan R/Ann L McGill/Andreas Herrmann (2011): It's Got the Look: The Effect of Friendly and Aggressive "Facial" Expressions on Product Liking and Sales. In: Journal of Marketing 75: 132–146.

Lash, Scott (1994): Reflexivity and its doubles: structure, aesthetics, community. In: Ulrich Beck/Anthony Giddens/Scott Lash (Eds.): Reflexive modernization: politics, tradition and aesthetics in the modern social order. Stanford: Stanford University Press, pp. 110–173.

Latour, Bruno (1991): Technology is Society Made Durable. In: John Law (Ed.): A sociology of monsters: essays on power, technology and domination. London: Routledge, pp. 103–131.

Latour, Bruno (1996a): On Interobjectivity. In: Mind, Culture, and Activity 3(4): 228–245.

Latour, Bruno (1996b): Cogito ergo sumus! Or psychology swept inside out by the fresh air of the upper deck... A review of: Ed Hutchins' Cognition in the Wild. In: Mind, Culture, and Activity 3(1): 54–63.

Latour, Bruno (1996c): Aramis, or the love of technology. Cambridge: Harvard University Press.

Latour, Bruno (2000): 'The Berlin key or how to do things without words'. In: Paul Graves-Brown (Ed.): Matter, Materiality and Modern Culture. London: Routledge, pp. 10–21.

Latour, Bruno/Steve Woolgar (1986): Laboratory life: The construction of scientific facts. Princton: Princeton University Press.

Laurier, Eric (2011): Driving: Pre-cognition and driving. In: Tim Cresswell/Peter Merriman (Eds.): Geographies of Mobilities: Practices, Spaces, Subjects. Farnham: Ashgate, pp. 69–82.

Lave, Jean (1988): Cognition in practice. Mind, mathematics, and culture in everyday life. Cambridge: Cambridge University Press.

Lave, Jean/Etienne Wenger (1991): Situated learning: legitimate peripheral participation. Cambridge: Cambridge University Press.

Law, John (1994): Organizing modernity. London: Blackwell.

Law, John (2003): Making a mess with method. Lancaster. Working Paper, Centre for Science Studies, Lancaster University.

Law, John (2004): After method: mess in social science research. London: Routledge.

Law, John (2009): Seeing Like a Survey. In: Cultural Sociology 3(2): 239–256.

Law, John/Annemarie Mol (Eds.) (2002): Complexities: social studies of knowledge practices. Durham: Duke University Press.

Leder, Drew (1990): The absent body. Chicago: University of Chicago Press.

Lee, Daniel B/Achim Brosziewski (2007): Participant Observation and Systems Theory: Theorizing the Ground. In: Soziale Welt (58): 255–269.

Lee, Jooyoung (2009): Battlin' on the Corner: Techniques for Sustaining Play. In: Social Problems 56(3): 578–598.

Lefebvre, Henri (2007): The production of space. Malden: Blackwell.

vom Lehn, Dirk/Christian Heath (2007): Perspektiven der Kunst – Kunst der Perspektiven. In: Heiko Hausendorf (Ed.): Vor dem Kunstwerk. München: Wilhelm Fink, pp. 147–170.

Lert, Wolfgang/Morton Lund (1999): Bill Klein in Donner Pass. A ski teacher from beginning to end. In: Skiing Heritage Journal 11(2): 14–23.

Lévi-Strauss, Claude (1966): The savage mind. Chicago: University of Chicago Press.

Levinson, Stephen C. (2005): Living with Manny's dangerous ideas. In: Discourse Studies 7(4–5)71: 431–453.

Liberty Skis (2010): Skis 2010. http://libertyskis.com/2010/skis.php (accessed February 17, 2010).

Lind, David A./Scott P. Sanders (2010): The Physics of Skiing: Skiing at the Triple Point. New York: Springer.
Livingston, Eric (1986): The ethnomethodological foundations of mathematics. London: Routledge.
Livingston, Eric (2006a): The Context of Proving. In: Social Studies of Science 36(1): 39–68.
Livingston, Eric (2006b): Ethnomethodological studies of mediated interaction and mundane expertise. In: Sociological Review 54(3): 405–425.
Livingston, Eric (2008a): Ethnographies of Reason. Bodmin: MPG Books.
Livingston, Eric (2008b): Context and detail in studies of the witnessable social order: Puzzles, maps, checkers, and geometry. In: Journal of Pragmatics 40(5): 840–862.
Lizardo, Omar (2007): "Mirror Neurons," Collective Objects and the Problem of Transmission: Reconsidering Stephen Turner's Critique of Practice Theory. In: Journal for the Theory of Social Behaviour 37(3): 319–350.
Lizardo, Omar (2008): Understanding the Flow of Symbolic Goods in the Global Cultural Economy. In: International journal of contemporary sociology 45(1): 13–34.
Lizardo, Omar (2009): Is a "Special Psychology" of Practice Possible? In: Theory & Psychology 19(6): 713–727.
Lizardo, Omar (2011): Embodied culture as procedure: Cognitive science and the link between subjective and objective culture. In: Alan Warde/Dale Southerton (Eds.): Habits, Culture and Practice: Paths to Sustainable Consumption. Helsinki: Helsinki Collegium of Advanced Studies.
Lizardo, Omar (2012): The Three Phases of Bourdieu's U.S. Reception: Comment on Lamont. In: Sociological Forum 27(1): 238–244.
Lizardo, Omar/Michael Strand (2010): Skills, toolkits, contexts and institutions: Clarifying the relationship between different approaches to cognition in cultural sociology. In: Poetics 38(2): 205–228.
Loland, Sigmund (1992): The Mechanics and Meaning of Alpine Skiing. Methodological and Epistemological Notes on the Study of Sport Technique. In: Journal of the Philosophy of Sport 19(1): 55–77.
Loland, Sigmund (2007): Outline of a phenomenology of snowboarding. In: Mike J. McNamee (Ed.): Philosophy, risk and adventure sports. London: Routledge, pp. 108–117.
Loland, Sigmund (2009): Alpine skiing technique – practical knowledge and scientific analysis. In: Erich Mueller/Stefan Lindinger/Thomas Stöggl (Eds.): Science and Skiing IV. Aachen: Meyer & Meyer, pp. 43–58.
Löw, Martina (2001): Raumsoziologie. Frankfurt a. M.: Suhrkamp.
Löw, Martina (2008): The Constitution of Space. The Structuration of Spaces Through the Simultaneity of Effect and Perception. In: European Journal of Social Theory 11(1): 25–49.
Luckmann, Benita (1978): The Small Life-Worlds of Modern Man. In: Thomas Luckmann (Ed.): Phenomenology and Sociology. Harmondsworth: Penguin, pp. 275–290.
Luckmann, Thomas (1973): Philosophy, Science, and Everyday Life. In: Maurice A. Natanson (Ed.): Phenomenology and the Social Sciences. Evanston: Northwestern University Press, pp. 143–186.
Luckmann, Thomas (1979): Phänomenologie und Soziologie. In: Walter Michael Sprondel/ Richard Grathoff (Eds.): Alfred Schütz und die Idee des Alltags in den Sozialwissenschaften. Stuttgart: Enke, pp. 196–206.
Luckner, Andreas (2008): Heidegger und das Denken der Technik. Bielefeld: transcript Verlag.
Luhmann, Niklas (1984): Soziale Systeme. Grundriss einer allgemeinen Theorie. Frankfurt a. M.: Suhrkamp.
Luhmann, Niklas (1990): Complexity and meaning. In: Essays on self-reference. New York: Columbia University Press, pp. 80–85.
Luhmann, Niklas (1995a): Social systems. Stanford: Stanford University Press.
Luhmann, Niklas (1995b): Instead of a preface to the english edition: On the concepts "subject" and "action." In: Social systems. Stanford: Stanford University Press, pp. xxxvii–xliv.

Luhmann, Niklas (1996a): Zeit und Gedächtnis. In: Soziale Systeme: Zeitschrift für soziologische Theorie 2: 307–330.
Luhmann, Niklas (1996b): Die neuzeitlichen Wissenschaften und die Phänomenologie. Wien: Picus Verlag.
Luhmann, Niklas (1997): Die Gesellschaft der Gesellschaft. Frankfurt a. M.: Suhrkamp.
Luhmann, Niklas (1999): Die Wirtschaft der Gesellschaft. Frankfurt a. M.: Suhrkamp.
Luhmann, Niklas (2000a): Art as a social system. Stanford: Stanford University Press.
Luhmann, Niklas (2000b): Organisation und Entscheidung. 2nd ed. Opladen: Westdeutscher Verlag.
Luhmann, Niklas (2000c): The Reality of the Mass Media. Stanford: Stanford University Press.
Luhmann, Niklas (2005): The paradox of decision making. In: Advances in organization studies 14: 85–106.
Lund, Morton (1993): The films of Hannes Schneider. In: Skiing Heritage Journal 5(1): 8–11.
Lund, Morton (1995): A bird of passage. The journey from ski instructor at St. Anton to Hollywood director-producer. In: Skiing Heritage Journal 7(1): 33–40.
Lund, Morton (1996a): A short history of Alpine skiing. From Telemark to today. In: Skiing Heritage Journal 8(1): 5–19.
Lund, Morton (1996b): Skiing down those golden years with John Jay. In: Skiing Heritage Journal 8(2): 6–26.
Lund, Morton (2005): They taught America to ski. In: Skiing Heritage Journal 17(3): 19–25.
Lund, Morton/Peter Miller (1998a): Roots of an Olympic sport: freestyle. Part II: Freestyle comes of age. In: Skiing Heritage Journal 10(3): 17–29.
Lund, Morton (1998b): Roots of an Olympic sport: freestyle. Part I. In: Skiing Heritage Journal 10(1): 11–20.
Lund, Morton/Doug Pfeiffer (1993): The curious, capricious career of the carved turn. In: Skiing Heritage Journal 16(2): 14–19.
Lunn, Arnold (1949): The mountains of youth. London: Eyre & Spottiswoode.
Lynch, Michael (1992a): Extending Wittgenstein: The pivotal move from epistemology to the sociology of science. In: Andrew Pickering (Ed.): Science as practice and culture. Chicago: University Of Chicago Press, pp. 215–265.
Lynch, Michael (1992b): From the "will to theory" to the discursive collage: A reply to Bloor's "Left and right Wittgensteinians." In: Andrew Pickering (Ed.): Science as practice and culture. Chicago: University Of Chicago Press, pp. 283–300.
Lynch, Michael (1993): Scientific practice and ordinary action: ethnomethodology and social studies of science. Cambridge: Cambridge University Press.
Lynch, Michael (1997): Theorizing Practice. In: Human Studies 20(3): 335–344.
Lynch, Michael (1999): Silence in Context: Ethnomethodology and Social Theory. In: Human Studies 22(2): 211–233.
Lynch, Michael (2000): Against Reflexivity as an Academic Virtue and Source of Privileged Knowledge. In: Theory Culture Society 17(3): 26–54.
Lynch, Michael (2001): Ethnomethodology and the logic of practice. In: Theodore R. Schatzki/Karin Knorr Cetina/Eicke von Savigny (Eds.): The Practice Turn in Contemporary Theory. London: Routledge, pp. 131–150.
Lynch, Michael (2002): From naturally occurring data to naturally organized ordinary activities: comment on Speer. In: Discourse Studies 4(4): 531–537.
Lynch, Michael (2006): Cognitive activities without cognition? Ethnomethodological investigations of selected 'cognitive' topics. In: Discourse Studies 8(1): 95–104.
Lynch, Michael (2009): Working out what Garfinkel could possibly be doing with "Durkheim's Aphorism." In: Geoff Cooper/Andrew King/Ruth Rettie (Eds.): Sociological objects: reconfigurations of social theory. London: Ashgate, pp. 101–118.
Lynch, Michael/Steve Woolgar (1990): Representation in Scientific Practice. Boston: MIT Press.
Lyon, Margot L. (1997): The Material Body, Social Processes and Emotion: 'Techniques of the Body' Revisited. In: Body & Society 3(1): 83–101.

Maanen, Hans van (2010): How to study art worlds: on the societal functioning of aesthetic values. Amsterdam: Amsterdam University Press.

Macbeth, Douglas (2000): On an actual apparatus for conceptual change. In: Science Education 84(2): 228–264.

Madary, Michael (2011): The dorsal stream and the visual horizon. In: Phenomenology and the Cognitive Sciences 10: 423–438.

Maeder, Christoph/Achim Brosziewski (1997): Ethnographische Semantik. Ein Weg zum Verstehen von Zugehörigkeit. In: Ronald Hitzler/Anne Honer (Eds.): Sozialwissenschaftliche Hermeneutik. Eine Einführung. Opladen: Leske+Budrich, pp. 335–362.

Maffesoli, Michel (1996a): The contemplation of the world: figures of community style. Minneapolis: University of Minnesota Press.

Maffesoli, Michel (1996b): The time of the tribes: the decline of individualism in mass society. London: Sage.

Malle, Bertram F. (2004): How the mind explains behavior: folk explanations, meaning, and social interaction. Boston: MIT Press.

Malle, Bertram F./Joshua Knobe (1997): The Folk Concept of Intentionality. In: Journal of Experimental Social Psychology 33(2): 101–121.

Malle, Bertram F./Louis J. Moses/Dare A. Baldwin (Eds.) (2003): Intentions and intentionality: foundations of social cognition. Boston: MIT Press.

Mandl, Heiko (2009): Österreichs wilder Osten. Ein Freeride-Trip in die Steiermark. In: skiing – the next level (42): 64–68.

Mannheim, Karl (1972): Essays on the sociology of knowledge. London: Routledge & Paul.

Manning, Phillip (2009): Three Models of Ethnographic Research: Wacquant as Risk-Taker. In: Theory & Psychology 19(6): 756–777.

Marcoulatos, Iordanis (2003): John Searle and Pierre Bourdieu : Divergent Perspectives on Intentionality and Social Ontology. In: Human Studies 26(1): 67–96.

Marcus, George E. (1995): Ethnography in/of the World System: The Emergence of Multi-Sited Ethnography. In: Annual Review of Anthropology 24: 95–117.

Marres, Noortje (2004): Reality is... Review of Annemarie Mol, The Body Multiple. In: EASST Review 23(2).

Marslen-Wilson, William D. (1985): Speech shadowing and speech comprehension. In: Speech Communication 4(1–3): 55–73.

Martinez-Conde, Susana/Stephen L. Macknik/David H. Hubel (2004): The role of fixational eye movements in visual perception. In: Nature Reviews Neuroscience 5(3): 229–240.

Masia, Seth (2005): The evolution of modern ski shape. In: Skiing Heritage Journal 17(3): 33–37.

Mattens, Filip (2010): Kinästhesie. In: Hans-Helmuth Gander (Ed.): Husserl-Lexikon. Darmstadt: Wissenschaftliche Buchgesellschaft, pp. 170–172.

Matthews, Ben (2009): Discerning the Relations Between Conversation and Cognition. In: Human Studies 32(4): 487–502.

Mauss, Marcel (1973): Techniques of the Body. In: Economy and Society 2(1): 70–88.

Maynard, Douglas W. (2006): Cognition on the ground. In: Discourse Studies 8(1): 105–115.

McGrenere, Joanna/Wayne Ho (2000): Affordances: Clarifying and Evolving a Concept. In: Proceedings of Graphics Interface 2000. Montreal.

McNeill, David (1992): Hand and mind. What gestures reveal about thought. Chicago: University of Chicago Press.

McNeill, William (1999): The glance of the eye: Heidegger, Aristotle, and the ends of theory. Albany: SUNY Press.

Merleau-Ponty, Maurice (1964): An unpublished text by Maurice Merleau-Ponty: A prospectus of his work. In: James M. Edie (Ed.): The primacy of perception: and other essays on phenomenological psychology, the philosophy of art, history and politics. Easton: Northwestern University Press, pp. 3–11.

Merleau-Ponty, Maurice (1968): Claude Lefort (Ed.): The visible and the invisible. Followed by working notes. Evanston: Northwestern University Press.
Merleau-Ponty, Maurice (1969): Eye and mind. In: Alden L. Fisher (Ed.): Essential Writings. New York: Harcourt, Brace & World, pp. 252–286.
Merleau-Ponty, Maurice (1974): Phänomenologie der Wahrnehmung. 6th ed. Berlin: Walter de Gruyter.
Merleau-Ponty, Maurice (2002): Phenomenology of perception. London: Routledge.
Mersch, Dieter (2006): Wittgensteins Bilddenken. In: Deutsche Zeitschrift für Philosophie 54(6): 925–942.
Messmer, Heinz (2004): Gesellschaft als Kommunikation – Kommunikation als Gesellschaft? Plädoyer für die Berücksichtigung ethnomethodologischer Konversationsanalyse in Niklas Luhmanns Gesellschaftstheorie. In: Soziale Systeme 13(1/2): 480–490.
Meyer, Christian/Ulrich v. Wedelstaedt (2017): Moving Bodies in Interaction–Interacting Bodies in Motion: Intercorporeality, interkinesthesia, and enaction in sports. Amsterdam: John Benjamins.
Mills, C. Wright (1940): Situated Actions and Vocabularies of Motive. In: American Sociological Review 5(6): 904–913.
Milner, David/Melvyn A. Goodale (1995): The visual brain in action. Oxford: Oxford University Press.
Mohanty, J. N. (1996): Kant and Husserl. In: Husserl Studies 13(1): 19–30.
Mol, Annemarie (2002): The body multiple. Durham: Duke University Press.
Mol, Annemarie/John Law (2002): Complexities: an introduction. In: John Law/Annemarie Mol (Eds.): Complexities: social studies of knowledge practices. Durham: Duke University Press, pp. 1–22.
Molder, Hedwig te/Jonathan Potter (2005): Conversation and cognition. Cambridge: Cambridge University Press.
Moll, Sebastian (2009): Skiweltmeister gegen Hitler. In: einestages. http://einestages.spiegel.de/external/ShowAuthorAlbumBackground/a3912/l10/l0/F.html#featuredEntry (accessed April 3, 2009).
Mondada, Lorenza (2011): Reassembling fragmented geographies. In: Monika Büscher/John Urry/Katian Witchger (Eds.): Mobile Methods. New York: Taylor & Francis, pp. 138–163.
Mondada, Lorenza (2012). Video analysis and the temporality of inscriptions within social interaction: the case of architects at work. In: Qualitative Research 12(3): 304–333.
Moseley, Jonny (2002): Convocation speech at the University of California, Berkeley.
Munter, Werner (1997): 3x3 Lawinen. Garmisch-Partenkirchen: Pohl & Schellhammer.
Nassehi, Armin (2009): Der soziologische Diskurs der Moderne. Frankfurt a. M.: Suhrkamp.
Nassehi, Armin/Irmhild Saake (2002a): Kontingenz: Methodisch verhindert oder beobachtet. In: Zeitschrift für Soziologie 31(1): 66–86.
Nassehi, Armin/Irmhild Saake (2002b): Begriffsumstellungen und ihre Folgen-Antwort auf die Replik von Hirschauer/Bergmann. In: Zeitschrift für Soziologie 31(4): 337–343.
Natanson, Maurice (1979): Phenomenology, Anonymity, and Alienation. In: New Literary History 10(3): 533–546.
Nelson, Wade (2010): The historical mediatization of BMX-freestyle cycling. In: Sport in Society: Cultures, Commerce, Media, Politics 13(7): 1152.
Newen, Albert/Andreas Bartels (2007): Animal Minds and the Possession of Concepts. In: Philosophical Psychology 20(3): 283.
Nicolini, Davide (2012). Practice theory, work, and organization: An introduction. Oxford: OUP.
Nietzsche, Friedrich Wilhelm (1967): Beyond good and evil. Prelude to a philosophy of the future. Charleston: Forgotten Books.
Nietzsche, Friedrich Wilhelm (1996): Human, All Too Human. Lincoln: University of Nebraska Press.
Nissen, M. J./P. Bullemer, (1987): Attentional requirements of learning: evidence fromperformance measures. In: Cognitive Psychology 19: 1–32.

Noë, Alva (2004): Action in Perception. Boston: MIT Press.
Nohl, Dixi (2005): When Krucki ruled the world. In: Skiing Heritage Journal 17(1): 7–12.
Nonaka, Ikujiro (1994): A dynamic theory of organizational knowledge. In: Organization Science 5(1): 14–37.
Norman, Donald A. (1988): The psychology of everyday things. New York: Basic.
Noton, David/Lawrence Stark (1971): Scanpaths in saccadic eye movements while viewing and recognizing patterns. In: Vision Research 11(9): 929–942, IN3–IN8.
Obernhaus, Mark (2008): Steep. Sony Pictures Classic.
Pacherie, Elisabeth (1997): Motor-images, self-consciousness, and autism. In: James Russell (Ed.): Autism as an executive disorder. Oxford: Oxford University Press.
Pacherie, Elisabeth (1999): Leibhaftigkeit and representational theories of perception. In: Jean Petitot et al. (Eds.): Naturalizing phenomenology: issues in contemporary phenomenology and cognitive science. Stanford: Stanford University Press, pp. 330–371.
Pacherie, Elisabeth (2003): Is collective intentionality really primitive. In: American Journal of Economics and Sociology 62(1).
Pacherie, Elisabeth (2006): Toward a dynamic theory of intentions. In: Susan Pockett/William P. Banks/Shaun Gallagher (Eds.): Does consciousness cause behavior? Boston: MIT Press, pp. 145–167.
Pacherie, Elisabeth (2008): The phenomenology of action: A conceptual framework. In: Cognition 107(1): 179–217.
Palmer, Catherine (2004): Death, danger and the selling of risk in adventure sports. In: Belinda Wheaton (Ed.): Understanding Lifestyle Sport: Consumption, Identity and Difference. London: Routledge, pp. 55–69.
Palmer, Stephen E. (1999): Vision science: photons to phenomenology. Boston: MIT Press.
Pavan, Andrea/Luigi F. Cuturi/Marcello Maniglia/Clara Casco/et al. (2011): Implied motion from static photographs influences the perceived position of stationary objects. In: Vision Research 51(1): 187–194.
Pellegrino, G./L. Fadiga/L. Fogassi/Vittorio Gallese/G. Rizzolatti (1992): Understanding motor events: a neurophysiological study. In: Experimental brain research 91(1): 176–180.
Petrasch, Christian (2008): Regelgeleitetes Verhalten. Zur soziologischen Relevanz des Spätwerks Wittgensteins. Kassel: Kassel University Press.
Pichard, Peter (2005): Wedeln heads west. In: Skiing Heritage Journal 17(3): 4.
Pletz, Hendrik (2010): Diskursiver Wandel und technische Praxis. In: Achim Landwehr (Ed.): Diskursiver Wandel. Wiesbaden: VS Verlag für Sozialwissenschaften, pp. 311–333.
Plueddeman, Charles (1994): The mechanichs of speed skiing. Skiing's ultimate speed event is the next best thing to freefall. In: Popular Mechanics (2).
Pollner, Melvin (1991): Left of Ethnomethodology: The rise and decline of radical reflexivity. In: (Vol. 56): 370–380.
Pollner, Melvin/Robert M. Emerson (2001): Ethnomethodology and ethnography. In: Paul Atkinson et al. (Eds.): Handbook of ethnography. London: Sage, pp. 118–135.
Polzer, Klaus (2009): Stefan Häusl. Der erfolgreiche Selfmade-Pro im Interview. In: skiing – the next level (43): 40–46.
Potter, Jonathan (2002): Two kinds of natural. In: Discourse Studies 4(4): 539–542.
Preda, Alex (2000): Order with Things? Humans, Artifacts, and the Sociological Problem of Rule-Following. In: Journal for the Theory of Social Behaviour 30(3): 269–298.
Preda, Alex (2006): Socio-Technical Agency in Financial Markets: The Case of the Stock Ticker. In: Social Studies of Science 36(5): 753–782.
Pressing, Jeff (1988): Improvisation: Methods and models. In: John A. Sloboda (Ed.): Generative processes in music: The psychology of performance, improvisation, and composition. New York: Clarendon, pp. 129–178.
Prinz, Sophia (2014): Die Praxis des Sehens. Über das Zusammenspiel von Körpern, Artefakten und visueller Ordnung, Bielefeld: transcript.

Prinz, Sophia (2016): Dispositive und Dinggestalten. Poststrukturalistische und phänomenologische Grundlagen einer Praxistheorie des Sehens. In: Schäfer, Hilmar (Ed.): Praxistheorie. Ein soziologisches Forschungsprogramm, Bielefeld: transcript, pp. 181–198.
Prinz, Sophia (2020): Zwischen Selbst- und Fremdführung. Die Praxis der Freiheit bei Michel Foucault und Maurice Merleau-Ponty. In: Barbara Ulrike Kadi/Gerhard Unterthurner (Eds.): Macht – Knoten – Fleisch. Topographien des Körpers bei Foucault, Lacan und Merleau-Ponty. Berlin: Metzler, pp. 27–48.
Pritchard, Roy M. (1961): Stabilized images on the retina. In: Scientific American 204(6): 72–78.
Protevi, John (1998): The "Sense" of "Sight": Heidegger and Merleau-Ponty on the Meaning of Bodily and Existential Sight. In: Research in Phenomenology 28(1): 211–223.
Putnam, Hilary (1979): Reflections on Goodman's Ways of Worldmaking. In: The Journal of Philosophy 76(11): 603–618.
Pylyshyn, Zenon W. (1999): Is Vision Continuous with Cognition? The Case for Cognitive Impenetrability of Visual Perception. In: Behavioral and Brain Sciences 22(3): 341–365.
Pylyshyn, Zenon W. (2000): Situating vision in the world. In: Trends in Cognitive Sciences 4(5): 197–207.
Pylyshyn, Zenon W. (2001): Visual indexes, preconceptual objects, and situated vision. In: Cognition 80(1–2): 127–158.
Raab, Jürgen (2007): Die 'Objektivität' des Sehens als wissenssoziologisches Problem. In: sozialer sinn 3: 287–304.
Raab, Jürgen (2008): Visuelle Wissenssoziologie. Theoretische Konzeptionen und materiale Analysen. Konstanz: UVK.
Rammert, Werner (1998): Technik und Sozialtheorie. Frankfurt a. M.: Campus.
Rammert, Werner (2007a): Nicht-explizites Wissen in Soziologie und Sozionik: Ein kursorischer Überblick. In: Technik – Handeln – Wissen: zu einer pragmatistischen Technik- und Sozialtheorie. Wiesbaden: VS Verlag, pp. 147–166.
Rammert, Werner (2007b): Technik–Handeln–Wissen. Zu einer pragmatistischen Technik-und Sozialtheorie. Wiesbaden: VS Verlag.
Rang, Bernhard (1990): Husserls Phänomenologie der materiellen Natur. Frankfurt a. M.: Vittorio Klostermann.
Rapic, Smail (1991): Einleitung zu 'Ding und Raum'. In: Karl-Heinz Hahnengress/Smail Rapic (Eds.): Ding und Raum: Vorlesungen 1907. Hamburg: Meiner Verlag, pp. XI–LXXVII.
Rappert, Brian (2001): The Distribution and Resolution of the Ambiguities of Technology, or Why Bobby Can't Spray. In: Social Studies of Science 31(4): 557–591.
Ratcliffe, Matthew (2002): Heidegger's attunement and the neuropsychology of emotion. In: Phenomenology and the Cognitive Sciences 1(3): 287–312.
Rawls, Anne Warfield (1987): The Interaction Order Sui Generis: Goffman's Contribution to Social Theory. In: Sociological Theory: 136–149.
Rawls, Anne Warfield (2002): Editor's Introduction. In: Harold Garfinkel: Ethnomethodology's program. Working out Durkheim's Aphorism. Lanham: Rowman & Littlefield, pp. 1–64.
Rawls, Anne Warfield (2009): Communities of practice vs. traditional communities: The state of sociology in a context of globalization. In: Geoff Cooper/Andrew King/Ruth Rettie (Eds.): Sociological objects: reconfigurations of social theory. London: Ashgate, pp. 81–100.
Rawls, Anne Warfield (2011): Wittgenstein, Durkheim, Garfinkel and Winch: Constitutive Orders of Sensemaking. In: Journal for the Theory of Social Behaviour 41(4): 396–418.
Reay, Diane (2004): 'It's All Becoming a Habitus': Beyond the Habitual Use of Habitus in Educational Research. In: British Journal of Sociology of Education 25(4): 431–444.
Reckwitz, Andreas (1997): Struktur. Zur sozialwissenschaftlichen Analyse von Regel und Regelmäßigkeiten. Opladen: Westdeutscher Verlag.
Reckwitz, Andreas (2000a): Die Transformation der Kulturtheorien. Weilerwist: Velbrück Wissenschaft.
Reckwitz, Andreas (2000b): Der Status des ‚Mentalen' in kulturtheoretischen Handlungserklärungen: Zum Problem der Relation von Verhalten und Wissen nach Stephen Turner und Theodore Schatzki. (German). In: Zeitschrift für Soziologie 29(3): 167–185.

Reckwitz, Andreas (2002a): Toward a Theory of Social Practices: A Development in Culturalist Theorizing. In: European Journal of Social Theory 5(2): 243–265.
Reckwitz, Andreas (2002b): The Status of the Material in Theories of Culture: From Social Structure to Artefacts. In: Journal for the Theory of Social Behaviour 32(2): 195–217.
Reckwitz, Andreas (2003): Grundelemente einer Theorie sozialer Praktiken – Eine sozialtheoretische Perspektive. In: Zeitschrift für Soziologie 32(4): 282–301.
Reckwitz, Andreas (2004a): Die Reproduktion und die Subversion sozialer Praktiken. Zugleich ein Kommentar zu Pierre Bourdieu und Judith Butler. In: Karl H. Hörning/Julia Reuter (Eds.): Doing Culture. Neue Positionen zum Verhältnis von Kultur und sozialer Praxis. Bielefeld: transcript Verlag, pp. 40–54.
Reckwitz, Andreas (2004b): Die Entwicklung des Vokabulars der Handlungstheorien: Von den zweck- und normorientierten Modellen zu den Kultur-und Praxistheorien. In: Manfred Gabriel (Ed.): Paradigmen der akteurszentrierten Soziologie. Wiesbaden: VS Verlag, pp. 303–328.
Reckwitz, Andreas (2006a): Die Transformation der Kulturtheorien. Studienausgabe. Zur Entwicklung eines Theorieprogramms. Mit Nachwort "Aktuelle Tendenzen der Kulturtheorien." 2nd ed. Weilerwist: Velbrück Wissenschaft.
Reckwitz, Andreas (2006b): Das hybride Subjekt. Eine Theorie der Subjektkulturen von der bürgerlichen Moderne zur Postmoderne. Weilerwist: Velbrück Wissenschaft.
Reckwitz, Andreas (2006c): Nachwort: Aktuelle Tendenzen der Kulturtheorien. In: Die Transformation der Kulturtheorien. Zur Entwicklung eines Theorieprogramms. Studienausgabe. Weilerwist: Velbrück Wissenschaft.
Reckwitz, Andreas (2008): Praktiken und Diskurse: Eine sozialtheoretische und methodologische Relation. In: Herbert Kalthoff/Stefan Hirschauer/Gesa Lindemann (Eds.): Theoretische Empirie. Zur Relevanz qualitativer Forschung. Frankfurt a. M.: Suhrkamp, pp. 188–209.
Reckwitz, Andreas (2012): Die Erfindung der Kreativität: Zum Prozess gesellschaftlicher Ästhetisierung. Frankfurt a. M.: Suhrkamp.
Reindl, Peter (2004): Tourengeher auf Schipisten. In: Alpenverein (5): 12–13.
Rentschler, Eric (1990): Mountains and Modernity: Relocating the Bergfilm. In: New German Critique (51): 137–161.
Reuter, Martina (1999): Merleau-Ponty's Notion of Pre-Reflective Intentionality. In: Synthese 118(1): 69–88.
Rheinberger, Hans-Jörg (1997): Toward a history of epistemic things: synthesizing proteins in the test tube. Stanford : Stanford University Press.
Richtmeyer, Ulrich (2009): Vom Bildspiel zum Sprachspiel. Wieviel Kompositphotographie steckt in der Logik der Familienähnlichkeit? In: V. A. Munz/K. Puhl/J. Wang (Eds.): Language and World. Preproceedings of the 32nd International Wittgenstein Symposium, Kirchberg a. Wechsel. pp. 354–358.
Riis, Ole/Linda Woodhead (2010): A Sociology of Religious Emotion. Oxford: Oxford University Press.
Rinehart, Robert E. (2003): Dropping into sight: Commodification and co-optation of in-line skating. In: Robert E. Rinehart/Synthia Sydnor (Eds.): To the extreme: Alternative sports, inside and out. Albany: SUNY Press, pp. 27–51.
Rinehart, Robert E./Synthia Sydnor (Eds.) (2003): To the Extreme. Alternative sports, inside and out. Albany: SUNY Press.
Rizzolatti, Giacomo/Corrado Sinigaglia/Frances Anderson (2008): Mirrors in the brain: how our minds share actions, emotions. Oxford: Oxford University Press.
Robinson, Victorie (2004): Taking risks. Identity, masculinities and rock climbing. In: Belinda Wheaton (Ed.): Understanding Lifestyle Sports. Consumption, identity and difference. London: Routledge, pp. 113–130.
Rodemeyer, Lanei M. (2006): Intersubjective Temporality. It's about time. Dordrecht: Springer.
Rössel, Jörg (1999): Konflikttheorie und Interaktionsrituale. Randall Collins' Mikrofundierung der Konflikttheorie. In: Zeitschrift für Soziologie 28: 23–43.

Roth, Wolff-Michael (2010): Researching Living/Lived Mathematical Work. In: FQS Forum Qualitative Sozialforschung / Forum: Qualitative Social Research 12(1).
Rouse, Joseph (2000): Coping and its Contrasts. In: Mark A. Wrathall/Jeff Malpas (Eds.): Heidegger, coping, and cognitive science. Essays in Honor of Hubert L. Dreyfus, Volume 2. Boston: MIT Press, pp. 7–28.
Saake, Irmhild (2004): Theorien der Empirie. Zur Spiegelbildlichkeit der Bourdieuschen Theorie der Praxis und der Luhmannschen Systemtheorie. In: Gerd Nollmann/Armin Nassehi (Eds.): Bourdieu und Luhmann. Ein Theorienvergleich. Frankfurt a. M.: Suhrkamp, pp. 85–117.
Sacks, Harvey (1994): On doing 'being ordinary'. In: J. Maxwell Atkinson/John Heritage (Eds.): Structures of social action: Studies in conversation analysis. Cambridge: Cambridge University Press, pp. 413–429.
Salmon, Paul et al. (2007): What Really Is Going on? Review, Critique and Extension of Situation Awareness Theory. In: Don Harris (Ed.): Engineering Psychology and Cognitive Ergonomics. Lecture Notes in Computer Science, Heidelberg: Springer, pp. 407–416.
Schäfer, Eckehart Velten (2020): Dogtown und X-Games – die wirkliche Geschichte des Skateboardfahrens. Körper, Räume und Zeichen einer Bewegungspraktik zwischen Pop-und Sportkultur. Bielefeld: transcript.
Schäfer, Hilmar (2010): Eine Mikrophysik der Praxis – Instanzen diskursiver Stabilität und Instabilität im Anschluss an Michel Foucault. In: Achim Landwehr (Ed.): Diskursiver Wandel. Wiesbaden: VS Verlag, pp. 115–132.
Schäfer, Hilmar (2016): Praxistheorie. Ein soziologisches Forschungsprogramm (Ed.), Bielefeld: transcript.
Schalow, Frank (1991): The anomaly of world: From Scheler to Heidegger. In: Man and World 24(1): 75–87.
Schatzki, Theodore R. (1987): Overdue analysis of Bourdieu's theory of practice. In: Inquiry 30(1–2): 113–135.
Schatzki, Theodore R. (1996): Social Practices: A Wittgensteinian Approach to Human Activity and the Social. Cambridge: Cambridge University Press.
Schatzki, Theodore R. (1997): Practices and Actions. A Wittgensteinian Critique of Bourdieu and Giddens. In: Philosophy of the Social Sciences 27(3): 283–308.
Schatzki, Theodore R. (2001): Introduction: Practice Theory. In: Theodore R. Schatzki/Karin Knorr Cetina/Eicke von Savigny (Eds.): The Practice Turn in Contemporary Theory. London: Routledge, pp. 1–16.
Schatzki, Theodore R. (2002): The Site of the Social: A Philosophical Account of the Constitution of Social Life and Change. University Park: Pennsylvania State University Press.
Schatzki, Theodore R. (2005): The Sites of Organizations. In: Organization Studies 26(3): 465–484.
Schatzki, Theodore R. (2006a): The time of activity. In: Continental Philosophy Review 39(2): 155–182.
Schatzki, Theodore R. (2006b): On Organizations as they Happen. In: Organization Studies 27(12): 1863–1873.
Schatzki, Theodore R. (2007): Early Heidegger on Sociality. In: Hubert L. Dreyfus/Mark A. Wrathall (Eds.): Oxford: Blackwell, pp. 233–247.
Schatzki, Theodore R. (2009): Timespace and the organization of social life. In: Elizabeth Shove/Frank Trentmann/Richard Wilk (Eds.): Time, consumption and everyday life: practice, materiality and culture. New York: Berg, pp. 35–48.
Schatzki, Theodore R. (2010a): The Edge of Change: On the Emergence, Persistence, and Dissolution of Practices. Lancaster. Paper presented at the Symposium on Climate Change and Transitions in Practice; Lancaster, 6–7 July 2010.
Schatzki, Theodore R. (2010b): The timespace of human activity: On performance, society, and history as indeterminate teleological events. Lanham: Lexington Books.
Schatzki, Theodore R. (2010c): Materiality and Social Life. In: Nature and Culture 5: 123–149.

Schatzki, Theodore R./Karin Knorr Cetina/Eicke von Savigny (2001): The Practice Turn in Contemporary Theory. London: Routledge.

Schau, Hope Jensen/Albert M. Muniz/Eric J. Arnould (2009): How Brand Communitiy Practices Create Value. In: Journal of Marketing 73(5): 30–51.

Schegloff, Emanuel A. (1972): Notes on a conversational practice: Formulating place. In: Studies in social interaction: 75–119.

Schegloff, Emanuel A. (1988): Goffman and the analysis of conversation. In: Paul Drew/Anthony Wootton (Eds.): Erving Goffman: Exploring the interaction order. Oxford: Polity, pp. 89–135.

Schindler, Larissa (2009): Das sukzessive Beschreiben einer Bewegungsordnung mittels Variation. In: Thomas Alkemeyer et al. (Eds.): Ordnung in Bewegung: Choreographien des sozialen. Körper in Sport, Tanz, Arbeit und Bildung. Bielefeld: transcript Verlag, pp. 51–63.

Schindler, Larissa (2010): Kampfkünste: Die Produktion von Sicherheit durch das Training verletzlicher Körper. In: Unsichere Zeiten: Herausforderungen gesellschaftlicher Transformationen. Verhandlungen des 34. Kongresses der Deutschen Gesellschaft für Soziologie in Jena. Wiesbaden: VS Verlag.

Schindler, Larissa (2011): Teaching by Doing: Zur körperlichen Vermittlung von Wissen. In: Reiner Keller/Michael Meuser (Eds.): Wissen des Körpers – Wissen vom Körper. Körper- und wissenssoziologische Erkundungen. Wiesbaden: VS Verlag, pp. 335–350.

Schivelbusch, Werner (1986): The railway journey: The industrialization of time and space in the 19th century. Berkeley: University of California Press.

Schlicht, Tobias (2008): Ein Stufenmodell der Intentionalität. In: Patrick Spät (Ed.): Zur Zukunft der Philosophie des Geistes. Paderborn: Mentis, pp. 59–91.

Schlicht, Tobias (2010): Enactive social cognition. In: Proceedings of the Meeting of the Cognitive Science Society. Portland, OR.

Schmidt, Robert (2002): Pop – Sport – Kultur. Praxisformen körperlicher Aufführungen. Konstanz: UVK.

Schmidt, Robert (2006): Technik, Risiko und das Zusammenspiel von Habitat und Habitus. In: Gunter Gebauer (Ed.): Kalkuliertes Risiko: Technik, Spiel und Sport an der Grenze. Frankfurt a. M.: Campus, pp. 78–95.

Schmidt, Robert (2008): Stumme Weitergabe. Zur Praxeologie sozialisatorischer Vermittlungsprozesse. In: Zeitschrift für Soziologie der Erziehung und Sozialisation 28(2): 121–136.

Schmidt, Robert (2009): Soziale Praktiken und empirische Habitusforschung. Zu Desideraten der Bourdieuschen Praxeologie. In: Maria A. Wolf/Bernhard Rathmayr/Helga Peskoller (Eds.): Konglomerationen – Produktion von Sicherheiten im Alltag. Theorien und Forschungsskizzen. Bielefeld: transcript Verlag, pp. 33–47.

Schmidt, Robert (2012): Soziologie der Praktiken. Konzeptionelle Studien und empirische Analysen. Berlin: Suhrkamp.

Schmidt, Robert (2015): Neue Analyse- und Wissenspraktiken im Profifußball. In: Sport und Gesellschaft = Sport and society 12: 171–186.

Schmidt, Robert (2016): The methodological challenges of practicising praxeology. In: Machiel Lamers/Gert Spaargaren/ Don Weenink (Eds.): Practice Theory and Research: Exploring the Dynamics of Social Life. Abingdon: Routledge, pp. 43–59.

Schmidt, Robert (2017): Reflexive knowledge in practices. In: Allison Hui/Theodore Schatzki/Elizabeth Shove (Eds.): The nexus of practices: Connections, constellations, practitioners. Milton Park: Taylor & Francis, pp. 153–166.

Schmidt, Robert (2022): Toward a Culture-Analytical and Praxeological Perspective on Decision-Making. In: Human studies 45.4: 653–671.

Schmidt, Robert/Jörg Volbers (2011a): Siting Praxeology. The Methodological Significance of "Public" in Theories of Social Practices. In: Journal for the Theory of Social Behaviour 41(4): 419–440.

Schmidt, Robert/Jörg Volbers (2011b): Öffentlichkeit als methodologisches Prinzip. In: Zeitschrift für Soziologie 40(1): 24–41.

Schmidt, Robert/Max Weigelin/Kristina Brümmer/Stefan Laube/Hilmar Schäfer (2022): Bodies and embodiment in practices of valuation. Challenging the sociology of valuation with the sociology of the body. In: Österreichische Zeitschrift für Soziologie 47: 217–223

Schneider, Wolfgang Ludwig (2000): The Sequential Production of Social Acts in Conversation. In: Human Studies 23(2): 123–144.

Schneider, Wolfgang Ludwig (2004): Grundlagen der soziologischen Theorie 3: Sinnverstehen und Intersubjektivität- Hermeneutik, funktionale Analyse, Konversationsanalyse und Systemtheorie. Wiesbaden: VS Verlag.

Schneider, Wolfgang Ludwig (2008): Systemtheorie und sequenzanalytische Forschungsmethoden. In: Herbert Kalthoff/Stefan Hirschauer/Gesa Lindemann (Eds.): Theoretische Empirie. Zur Relevanz qualitativer Forschung. Frankfurt a. M.: Suhrkamp, pp. 129–163.

Schnettler, Bernt/Hubert Knoblauch (2007): Powerpoint-Präsentationen: Neue Formen der gesellschaftlichen Kommunikation von Wissen. Konstanz: UVK.

Schnettler, Bernt/Frederik S. Pötzsch (2007): Visuelles Wissen. In: Rainer Schützeichel (Ed.): Handbuch Wissenssoziologie und Wissensforschung. Konstanz: UVK, pp. 472–484.

Schnettler, Bernt/Jürgen Raab (2008): Interpretative Visual Analysis. Developments, State of the Art and Pending Problems. In: FQS Forum Qualitative Sozialforschung / Forum: Qualitative Social Research 9(3).

Schön, Donald A. (1983): The reflective practitioner. How professionals think in action. New York: Basic Books.

Schouten, John W./James H. McAlexander (1995): Subcultures of Consumption: An Ethnography of the New Bikers. In: Journal of Consumer Research 22(1): 43.

Schroer, Markus (2005): Soziologie des Körpers. Frankfurt a. M.: Suhrkamp.

Schroer, Markus (2006): Räume, Orte, Grenzen: auf dem Weg zu einer Soziologie des Raums. Frankfurt a. M.: Suhrkamp.

Schulz-Schaeffer, Ingo (2000): Sozialtheorie der Technik. Frankfurt a. M.: Campus Verlag.

Schulz-Schaeffer, Ingo (2004): Regelmässigkeit und Regelhaftigkeit. Die Abschirmung des technischen Kerns als Leistung der Praxis. In: Julia Reuter/Karl H. Hörning (Eds.): Doing Culture – Neue Positionen zum Verhältnis von Kultur und sozialer Praxis. Bielefeld: transcript Verlag, pp. 108–126.

Schulz-Schaeffer, Ingo (2009): Handlungszuschreibung und Situationsdefinition. In: KZfSS Kölner Zeitschrift für Soziologie und Sozialpsychologie 61(2): 159–182.

Schulz-Schaeffer, Ingo (2010): Praxis, handlungstheoretisch betrachtet. In: Zeitschrift für Soziologie 39(4): 319–336.

Schutz, Alfred (1945): On Multiple Realities. In: Philosophy and Phenomenological Research 5(4): 533–576.

Schutz, Alfred (1953): Common-sense and scientific interpretation of human action. In: Philosophy and Phenomenological Research: 1–38.

Schutz, Alfred (1954): Concept and theory formation in the social sciences. In: The Journal of Philosophy 51(9): 257–273.

Schutz, Alfred (1962): Choosing among projects of action. In: Maurice Alexander Natanson (Ed.): Collected Papers Vol. I: The problem of socialreality. The Hague: Martinus Nijhoff, pp. 67–98.

Schutz, Alfred (1967): The phenomenology of the social world. Chicago: Northwestern University Press.

Schutz, Alfred (1972): Choice and the Social Sciences. In: Lester E. Embree (Ed.): Life-World and Consciousness. Essays for Aron Gurwitsch. Evanston: Northwestern University Press, pp. 565–590.

Schutz, Alfred/Thomas Luckmann (1973): The structures of the life-world. Evanston: Northwestern University Press.

Searle, John R. (1980): Minds, Brains, and Programs. In: Behavioral and Brain Sciences 3(03): 417–424.

Searle, John R. (1983): Intentionality. An essay in the philosophy of mind. Cambridge: Cambridge University Press.

Searle, John R. (2000): Limits of Phenomenology. In: Mark A. Wrathall/Jeff Malpas (Eds.): Heidegger, coping, and cognitive science. Essays in Honor of Hubert L. Dreyfus, Volume 2. Boston: MIT Press, pp. 71–92.
Seel, Martin (1992): Arnold Fanck oder die Verfilmbarkeit von Landschaft. In: Film und Kritik 1: 71–82.
Shannon, C. E. (1948): A mathematical theorie of communication. In: The bell system technical Journal 27: 379–423, 623–656.
Sharrock, Wes/Graham Button (1991): The social actor: Social action in real time. In: Graham Button (Ed.): Ethnomethodology and the human sciences. Cambridge: Cambridge University Press, p. 137–175.
Sharrock, Wes/Jeff Coulter (1998a): On J.J. Gibson. In: Theory & Psychology 8(2): 177–181.
Sharrock, Wes/Jeff Coulter (1998b): On What We Can See. In: Theory & Psychology 8(2): 147–164.
Sheller, Mimi/John Urry (2006): The new mobilities paradigm. In: Environment and Planning A 38(2): 207–226.
Shilling, Chris (2003): The body and social theory. 2nd ed. London: Sage.
Shove, Elizabeth (2003a): Converging conventions of comfort, cleanliness and convenience. In: Journal of Consumer Policy 26(4): 395–418.
Shove, Elizabeth (2003b): Comfort, cleanliness and convenience: the social organization of normality. London: Berg.
Shove, Elizabeth (2007): The design of everyday life. London: Berg.
Shove, Elizabeth (2010): Beyond the ABC: climate change policy and theories of social change. In: Environment and Planning A 42(6): 1273–1285.
Shove, Elizabeth/Mika Pantzar (2005a): Fossilisation. In: Ethnologia Europaea – Journal of European Ethnology 35(1–2): 59–63.
Shove, Elizabeth/Mika Pantzar (2005b): Consumers, Producers and Practices: Understanding the invention and reinvention of Nordic walking. In: Journal of Consumer Culture 5(1): 43–64.
Shove, Elizabeth/Mika Pantzar (2007): Recruitment and Reproduction: The Careers and Carriers of Digital Photography and Floorball. In: Human Affairs 17(2): 154–167.
Shove, Elizabeth/Mika Pantzar/Matt Watson (2012): The Dynamics of Social Practice: Everyday Life and How It Changes. London: Sage.
Shove, Elizabeth/Frank Trentmann/Richard Wilk (Eds.) (2009): Time, consumption and everyday life: practice, materiality and culture. New York: Berg.
Shove, Elizabeth/Matt Watson/Nicola Spurling (2015): Conceptualizing connections. Energy demand, infrastructures and social practices. In: European Journal of Social Theory, 18(3), 274–287.
Siewert, Charles (2006): Consciousness and Intentionality. In: Stanford Encyclopedia of Philosophy. http://plato.stanford.edu/entries/consciousness-intentionality/ (accessed September 16, 2010).
Silverman, David (1993): Interpreting qualitative data. London: Sage.
Simmel, Georg (1911): Die Alpen. In: Philosophische Kultur. Gesammelte Essais. Leipzig: Klinkhard Verlag, pp. 147–154.
Simmel, Georg (1913): Philosophie der Landschaft. In: Das Individuum und die Freiheit. Frankfurt a. M.: Fischer, pp. 130–139.
Simmel, Georg (1976): The style of life (1) and (2). In: Peter A. Lawrence (Ed.): Georg Simmel: Sociologist and European. London: Nelson, pp. 173–222.
Singer, Alan (1997): Aesthetic Community: Recognition as an Other Sense of Sensus Communis. In: boundary 2 24(1): 205–236.
Singer, Alan (1998): Beautiful Errors: Aesthetics and the Art of Contextualization. In: boundary 2 25(1): 7–34.
Sinigaglia, Corrado (2009): Mirror in action. In: Journal of Consciousness Studies, 16 6(8): 309–334.

skibuilders.com (2004): How to – Testing. http://www.skibuilders.com/howto/testing/ (accessed November 24, 2008).
skibuilders.com (2006): Accurate, replicable method of measuring ski flex (long). http://www.skibuilders.com/phpBB2/viewtopic.php?t=407&postdays=0&postorder=asc&start=0 (accessed June 22, 2011).
skiCrystalMtn (2010): Skiing Crystal Mountain, Washington 2010 Powder 8's Competition Part 1.
skiinfo (2003): Tiefschnee-Weltmeisterschaft in Blue River (Kanada) vom 12. bis 19. April. http://magazin.skiinfo.de/220-tiefschnee-weltmeisterschaft-in-blue-river-kanada-vom-12-bis-19-april.html (accessed November 23, 2010).
Skoyles, John R. (2000): Gesture, language origins, and right handedness. In: Psychology 11(24).
Smith, David Woodruff (1992): Consciousness in action. In: Synthese 90(1): 119–143.
Smith, David Woodruff (2007): Husserl. London: Taylor & Francis.
Smith, David Woodruff/Ronald McIntyre (1982): Husserl and intentionality: a study of mind, meaning, and language. Dordrecht: Reidel.
Soeffner, Hans-Georg (1995): Stil und Stilisierung. Punk oder die Überhöhung des Alltags. In: Die Ordnung der Rituale. Die Auslegung des Alltags II. Frankfurt a. M.: Suhrkamp, pp. 76–101.
Solum, Lawrence B. (1987): On the Indeterminacy Crisis: Critiquing Critical Dogma. In: The University of Chicago Law Review 54(2): 462–503.
Sørensen, Estrid (2009): The Materiality of Learning. Cambridge: Cambridge University Press.
Spencer-Brown, George (1971): Laws of form. London: Allen & Unwin.
Spender, J. C. (1996): Organizational knowledge, learning and memory: three concepts in search of a theory. In: Management 9(1): 63–78.
Spiegel Online (2010): Neue Ski-Form: Tiefschneefahren für alle. http://www.spiegel.de/reise/aktuell/0,1518,676580,00.html (accessed February 8, 2010).
Spinney, Justin (2007): Cycling the city: Non-place and the sensory construction of meaning in a mobile practice. In: Paul Rosen/Peter Cox/David Horton (Eds.): Cycling and society. London: Ashgate, pp. 25–45.
Srubar, Ilja (2007a): Heidegger und die Grundfragen der Sozialtheorie. In: Phänomenologie und soziologische Theorie: Aufsätze zur pragmatischen Lebensweltheorie. Wiesbaden: VS Verlag, pp. 35–62.
Srubar, Ilja (2007b): Phänomenologie und soziologische Theorie: Aufsätze zur pragmatischen Lebenswelttheorie. Wiesbaden: VS Verlag.
Srubar, Ilja (2008): Die pragmatische Lebenswelttheorie. In: Phänomenologie und Soziologie. Wiesbaden: VS Verlag für Sozialwissenschaften, pp. 41–51.
Stamenov, Maksim/Vittorio Gallese (Eds.) (2002): Mirror neurons and the evolution of brain and language. Amsterdam: John Benjamins.
Stempel, Carl (2005): Adult Participation Sports as Cultural Capital. In: International Review for the Sociology of Sport 40(4): 411–432.
Stengel, Kathrin (2003): Das Subjekt als Grenze. Ein Vergleich der erkenntnistheoretischen Ansätze bei Wittgenstein und Merleau-Ponty. Berlin: Walter de Gruyter.
Stengel, Kathrin (2004): Ethics as Style: Wittgenstein's Aesthetic Ethics and Ethical Aesthetics. In: Poetics Today 25(4): 609–625.
Stern, David (2000): Practices, Practical Holism, and Background Practices. In: Mark A. Wrathall/Jeff Malpas (Eds.): Heidegger, coping, and cognitive science. Essays in Honor of Hubert L. Dreyfus, Volume 2. Boston: MIT Press, pp. 53–70.
Stern, David (2002): Sociology of science, rule following and forms of life. In: Michael Heidelberger/Friedrich Stadler (Eds.): History of Philosophy of Science – New Trends and Perspectives. Amsterdam: Kluwer, pp. 347–367.
Stern, David (2003): The practical turn. In: Stephen P. Turner/Paul Andrew Roth (Eds.): The Blackwell guide to the philosophy of the social sciences. London: Wiley-Blackwell, pp. 185–206.

Stern, Martin (2009): Stil-Kulturen: Performative Konstellationen von Technik, Spiel und Risiko in neuen Sportpraktiken. Bielefeld: transcript Verlag.
Stock, Jessica (2011): Eine Maschine wird Mensch? Von der Notwendigkeit, Technik als integralen Bestandteil sozialer Praktiken zu akzeptieren. In: Technical University Technology Studies Working Papers (2): 1–58.
Stoddart, Mark CJ (2011): Constructing masculinized sportscapes: Skiing, gender and nature in British Columbia, Canada. In: International Review for the Sociology of Sport 46(1): 108–124.
Stranger, Mark (1999): The Aesthetics of Risk: A Study of Surfing. In: International Review for the Sociology of Sport 34(3): 265–276.
Stranger, Mark (2010): Surface and substructure: beneath surfing's commodified surface. In: Sport in Society: Cultures, Commerce, Media, Politics 13(7): 1117–1134.
Streeck, Jürgen (1996): How to Do Things with Things: Objets Trouvés and Symbolization. In: Human Studies 19(4): 365–384.
Suchman, Lucy (1987): Plans and situated actions: the problem of human-machine communication. Cambridge: Cambridge University Press.
Suchman, Lucy (1994): Do categories have politics? In: Computer Supported Cooperative Work (CSCW) 2(3): 177–190.
Suchman, Lucy (2007): Human-machine reconfigurations. Plans and situated actions 2nd edition. Cambridge: Cambridge University Press.
Suchman, Lucy/Jeanette Blomberg/Julian Orr/Randall Trigg (1999): Reconstructing technologies as social practice. In: American Behavioral Scientist 43(3): 392–408.
Suchman, Lucy/Randall Trigg/Jeanette Blomberg (2002): Working artefacts: ethnomethods of the prototype. In: The British Journal of Sociology 53(2): 163–179.
Sudnow, David (1978): Ways of the hand. The organization of improvised conduct. Cambridge: Harvard University Press.
Summa, Michela (2011): Das Leibgedächtnis. Ein Beitrag aus der Phänomenologie Husserls. In: Husserl Studies 27(3): 173–196.
Swidler, Ann (1986): Culture in Action: Symbols and Strategies. In: American Sociological Review 51(2): 273–286.
Sydnor, Synthia (2003): Soaring. In: Synthia Sydnor/Robert E. Rinehart (Eds.): To the Extreme. Alternative Sports, Inside and Out. SUNY Press, pp. 127–141.
Tarr, Michael J./Yi D. Cheng (2003): Learning to see faces and objects. In: Trends in Cognitive Sciences 7(1): 23–30.
Taylor, Charles (1971): Interpretation and the Sciences of Man. In: The Review of Metaphysics 25(1): 3–51.
Taylor, Charles (1995): Lichtung or Lebensform: Parallels between Heidegger and Wittgenstein. In: Philosophical arguments. Cambridge: Harvard University Press, pp. 61–78.
tetongravity.com (2006): Ski comparison graphs. [Archive]. In: Teton Gravity Research Forums. http://www.tetongravity.com/forums/archive/index.php?t-68512.html (accessed June 22, 2011).
Thornton, Sarah (1996): Club Cultures: Music, Media, and Subcultural Capital. Middletown, CT: Wesleyan University Press.
Thorpe, Holly (2008): Foucault, Technologies of Self, and the Media: Discourses of Femininity in Snowboarding Culture. In: Journal of Sport and Social Issues 32(2): 199–229.
Thorpe, Holly (2010): Bourdieu, Gender Reflexivity, and Physical Culture: A Case of Masculinities in the Snowboarding Field. In: Journal of Sport & Social Issues 34(2): 176–214.
Thrift, Nigel (2004a): Driving in the City. In: Theory Culture Society 21(4/5): 41–59.
Thrift, Nigel (2004b): Still Life in Nearly Present Time: The Object of Nature. In: Body & Society 6(3/4): 34–57.
Thrift, Nigel (2007): Non-representational theory: space, politics, affect. London: Routledge.
Toadvine, Ted/Lester E. Embree (Eds.) (2002): Merleau-Ponty's reading of Husserl. Dordrecht: Kluwer.

Treisman, Anne (1985): Preattentive processing in vision. In: Computer Vision, Graphics, and Image Processing 31(2): 156–177.
Tugendhat, Ernst (1970): Der Wahrheitsbegriff bei Husserl und Heidegger. Berlin: Walter de Gruyter.
Turner, Stephen P. (1994): The social theory of practices: tradition, tacit knowledge, and presuppositions. Chicago: University of Chicago Press.
Turner, Stephen P. (1997): Bad Practices: A Reply. In: Human Studies 20: 345–356.
Turner, Stephen P. (2001): Throwing out the Tacit Rule Book: Learning and Practices. In: Theodore R. Schatzki/Karin Knorr Cetina/Eicke von Savigny (Eds.): The Practice Turn in Contemporary Theory. London: Routledge, pp. 120–130.
Turner, Stephen P. (2007): Mirror Neurons and Practices: A Response to Lizardo. In: Journal for the Theory of Social Behaviour 37(3): 351–371.
Turner, Victor W./Richard Schechner (1988): The anthropology of performance. New York: PAJ Publications.
Ullman, Shimon (1984): Visual routines. In: Cognition 18(1–3): 97–159.
Ullman, Shimon (2000): High-level vision: object recognition and visual cognition. Boston: MIT Press.
Urry, John (1990): The tourist gaze: Leisure and travel in contemporary societies. London: Sage.
Urry, John (2000): Sociology beyond societies. Mobilities for the twenty-first century. London: Routledge.
Urry, John (2007): Mobilities. Cambridge: Polity.
Urry, John/Mimi Sheller (Eds.) (2004): Tourism mobilities: places to play – places in play. London: Routledge.
Vaisey, Stephen (2009): Motivation and justification: a dual-process model of culture in action. In: AJS; American Journal of Sociology 114(6): 1675–1715.
Vongehr, Thomas (2010): Handlung Hans-Helmuth Gander (Ed.): In: Husserl-Lexikon: 129–131.
v. Wedelstaedt, Ulrich/Christian Meyer (2017): Intercorporeality and interkinesthetic gestalts in handball. In: Christian Meyer/Ulrich v. Wedelstaedt (Eds.): Moving Bodies in Interaction–Interacting Bodies in Motion: Intercorporeality, interkinesthesia, and enaction in sports. Amsterdam: John Benjamins, pp. 57–91.
Wacquant, Loïc (2004): Body & Soul. New York: Oxford University Press.
Wacquant, Loïc (2005a): Carnal Connections: On Embodiment, Apprenticeship, and Membership. In: Qualitative Sociology 28(4): 445–474.
Wacquant, Loïc (2005b): Habitus. In: M. Zafirovski (Ed.): International encyclopedia of economic sociology. London: Routledge, pp. 315–319.
Wacquant, Loïc (2009): Habitus as topic and tool. Reflections on becoming a prizefighter. In: William Shaffir/Antony Puddephatt/Steven Kleinknecht (Eds.): Ethnographies Revisited. New York: Routledge.
Wade, Nichoals J. (2007): Scanning the seen: Vision and the origins of eye-movement research. In: Roger P. G. Van Van Gompel et al. (Eds.): Eye movements: a window on mind and brain. Amsterdam: Elsevier, pp. 31–63.
Wagemans, Johan (2001): High-level Theory of Vision. In: Neil J. Smelser/Paul B. Baltes (Eds.): International Encyclopedia of the Social & Behavioral Sciences. Oxford: Pergamon, pp. 16228–16232.
Wagner, Helmut R. (1984): The limitations of phenomenology: Alfred Schutz's critical dialogue with Edmund Husserl. In: Husserl Studies 1: 179–199.
Walker, Robin/Melanie Doyle (2003): Multisensory Interactions in Saccade Generation. In: Jukka Hyönä/Ralph Radach/Heiner Deubel (Eds.): The mind's eye: cognitive and applied aspects of eye movement research. Amsterdam: Elsevier, pp. 89–102.
Walsh, J. P./G. R. Ungson (1997): Organizational Memory. In: Prusak, Laurence (Ed.): Knowledge in Organizations. Newton, MA: Butterworth-Heinemann, pp. 177–213.
Walter, Richard (2008): Powder 8 – Europäischen Tiefschneemeisterschaften. http://www.powder8.at/Articles/home.html (accessed November 23, 2010).

Warde, Alan (2005): Consumption and Theories of Practice. In: Journal of Consumer Culture 5(2): 131–153.
Warde, Alan (2010): What sort of a Practice is eating? Working paper presented at the Climate Change and Transitions in Practice Working Group Meeting. Lancaster University, 7th of June 2010.
Warnier, J. P. (2001): A praxeological approach to subjectivation in a material world. In: Journal of Material Culture 6(1): 5–24.
Watson, Matthew/Elizabeth Shove (2006): Materialising consumption: products, projects and the dynamic of practice. Working Paper Series of the ESRC-AHRC Research Programme Cultures of Consumption. Birkbeck College.
Watson, Matthew/Elizabeth Shove (2008): Product, Competence, Project and Practice. DIY and the dynamics of craft consumption. In: Journal of Consumer Culture 8(1): 69.
Wegener, Detlef/Friederike Ehn/Maike K Aurich/F Orlando Galashan/Andreas K Kreiter (2008): Feature-based attention and the suppression of non-relevant object features. In: Vision Research 48(27): 2696–2707.
Weigelin, Max (2022): Entscheidungen und ihre Bewertungen. Zur Mikrosoziologie des Schiedsrichter-Pfiffs. Österreichische Zeitschrift für Soziologie 47: 225–246.
Weigert, Andrew J. (1975): Alfred Schutz on a Theory of Motivation. In: The Pacific Sociological Review 18(1): 83–102.
Wenger, Etienne (1999): Communities of practice. Cambridge: Cambridge University Press.
Wenger, Etienne (2007): Communities of practice. Learning, meaning, and identity. 15th ed. Cambridge: Cambridge University Press.
Wheaton, Belinda (2000a): New Lads? Masculinities and the new sport participant. In: Men and Masculinities 2: 436–458.
Wheaton, Belinda (2000b): Just do it: Consumption, commitment, and identity in the windsurfing subculture. In: Sociology of Sport Journal 17(3): 254–272.
Wheaton, Belinda (2003): Windsurfing. A subculture of commitment. In: Robert E. Rinehart/Synthia Sydnor (Ed.): To the Extreme. Alternative Sports, Inside and Out. Albany: SUNY Press, pp. 75–101.
Wheaton, Belinda (2004a): Understanding Lifestyle Sports: Consumption, Identity and Difference. London: Routledge.
Wheaton, Belinda (2004b): Mapping the lifestyle sport-scape. In: Belinda Wheaton (Ed.): Understanding Lifestyle Sports. Consumption, identity and difference. London: Routledge, pp. 1–27.
Wheaton, Belinda (2007): After Sport Culture: Rethinking Sport and Post-Subcultural Theory. In: Journal of Sport and Social Issues 31(3): 283–307.
Wheaton, Belinda/Becky Beal (2003): 'Keeping It Real': Subcultural Media and the Discourses of Authenticity in Alternative Sport. In: International Review for the Sociology of Sport 38(2): 155–176.
White, Philip/Brian Wilson (1999): Distinctions in the stands. In: International Review for the Sociology of Sport 34(3): 245–264.
Whittington, Richard (1996): Strategy as practice. In: Long Range Planning 29(5): 731–735.
Wilkins, D. (2003): Why pointing with the index finger is not a universal (in sociocultural and semiotic terms). In: Sotaro Kita (Ed.): Pointing: Where language, culture and cognition meet. Mahwah: Lawrence Erlbaum, pp. 171–215.
Williams, Trevor/Peter Donnelly (1985): Subcultural Production, Reproduction and Transformation in Climbing. In: International Review for the Sociology of Sport 20: 3–16.
Willig, Carla (2008): A Phenomenological Investigation of the Experience of Taking Part in 'Extreme Sports'. In: Journal of Health Psychology 13(5): 690–702.
Wilson, Brian (2007): New media, social movements, and global sport studies: A revolutionary moment and the sociology of sport. In: Sociology of Sport Journal 24(4): 457–477.
Windhager, Sonja et al. (2008): Face to Face. The Perception of Automotive Designs. In: Human Nature 19: 331–346.

Wittgenstein, Ludwig (1984a): Vermischte Bemerkungen. Eine Auswahl aus dem Nachlass. In: Heikki Nyman/Georg Henrik von Wright (Eds.): Ludwig Wittgenstein Werkausgabe Band 8. Frankfurt a. M.: Suhrkamp, pp. 445–573.
Wittgenstein, Ludwig (1984b): Peter Winch (Ed.): Culture and value. Chicago: University of Chicago Press.
Wittgenstein, Ludwig (1990): Tractatus logico-philosophicus. London: Routledge.
Wittgenstein, Ludwig (1995a): Joachim Schulte (Ed.): Vortrag über Ethik und andere kleine Schriften. Frankfurt a. M.: Suhrkamp.
Wittgenstein, Ludwig (1995b): Anhang B: Können wir etwas außer den Daten erkennen? In: Joachim Schulte (Ed.): Vortrag über Ethik und andere kleine Schriften. Frankfurt a. M.: Suhrkamp, pp. 127–129.
Wittgenstein, Ludwig (2006): Anthony John Patrick Kenny (Ed.): The Wittgenstein reader. London: Wiley-Blackwell.
Wittgenstein, Ludwig (2009): Peter M. S. Hacker/Joachim Schulte (Eds.): Philosophical investigations – Philosophische Untersuchungen. 4th ed. Chichester: John Wiley.
Woermann, Niklas (2010): Subcultures of Prosumption. Differenzierung durch Prosumtion in der Freeski-Szene. In: Birgit Blättel-Mink/Kai-Uwe Hellmann (Eds.): Prosumer Revisited. Zur Aktualität einer Debatte. Wiesbaden: VS Verlag, pp. 169–187.
Woermann, Niklas (2011). „The phenomenon exhibits its staff as a population." Die reflexive Akteurskonzeption der Ethnomethodologie. In: Nico Lüdtke/Hironori Matsuzaki (Eds.): Akteur – Individuum – Subjekt. Fragen zu 'Personalität' und 'Sozialität'. Wiesbaden: VS Verlag, pp. 117–148.
Woermann, Niklas (2012a): On the Slope Is on the Screen. Prosumption, Social Media Practices, and Scopic Systems in the Freeskiing Subculture. In: American Behavioral Scientist 56(4): 618–640.
Woermann, Niklas (2012b): Wittgenstein, Switch Misty 7er und die Beredsamkeit von Praktiken. Zur Zugehörigkeit von Technik zu Techniken der Zugehörigkeit. In: Paul Eisewicht/Tilo Grenz (Eds.): Techniken der Zugehörigkeit. Karlsruhe: KIT Scientific Publishing, pp. 29–56.
Woermann, Niklas (2013): Die unmögliche De-Visualisierung von Wissen. Über einige Sehpraktiken einer extremen Gemeinschaft. In: Rene Tuma/Petra Lucht/Lisa-Marian Schmidt (Eds.): Visuelles Wissen und Bilder des Sozialen. Aktuelle Entwicklungen in der visuellen Soziologie. Wiesbaden: VS Verlag, pp. 87–103.
Woermann, Niklas (2017): "It's really strange when nobody is watching." Enactive intercorporeality and the Spielraum of practices in freeskiing. In: Christian Meyer/Ulrich v. Wedelstaedt (Eds.): Moving Bodies in Interaction–Interacting Bodies in Motion: Intercorporeality, interkinesthesia, and enaction in sports. Amsterdam: John Benjamins, pp. 215–242.
Woermann, Niklas (2018): Focusing Ethnography: Theory and Recommendations for Effectively Combining Video and Ethnographic Research, In: Journal of Marketing Management, 34(5–6): 459–83.
Wolff, Stephan (2007): Wege ins Feld und ihre Varianten. In: Uwe Flick/Ernst von Kardorff/Ines Steinke (Eds.): Qualitative Forschung. Ein Handbuch. Reinbek bei Hamburg: Rowohlt, pp. 334–349.
Wrathall, Mark A./Jeff Malpas (Eds.) (2000): Heidegger, coping, and cognitive science. Essays in Honor of Hubert L. Dreyfus, Volume 2. Boston: MIT Press.
Wylie, John (2006): Depths and folds: on landscape and the gazing subject. In: Environment and Planning D: Society and Space 24(4): 519–535.
Zaboura, Nadia/Jo Reichertz (2006): Akteur Gehirn – oder das vermeintliche Ende des handelnden Subjekts. Eine Kontroverse. Wiesbaden: VS Verlag.
Zahavi, Dan (1994): Husserl's phenomenology of the body. In: Études phénoménologiques 19: 68–84.
Zahavi, Dan (2002): Merleau-Ponty on Husserl: A reappraisal. In: Ted Toadvine/Lester E. Embree (Eds.): Merleau-Ponty's reading of Husserl. Dordrecht: Kluwer, pp. 3–29.

Zehetmayer, Hans (2005): Zur Interdependenz von Skitechniken und Ski-Ideologien. Ein Beitrag zur Skigeschichte. In: Alfred Grüneklee/Herbert Heckers (Eds.): Skifahren und Snowboarden heute. Düsseldorf: Skimedia, pp. 9–50.

Index

A

Action, 2, 5, 7, 9, 11, 14, 17, 22, 23, 25, 40, 56, 57, 71, 75–77, 79, 84, 86, 93, 96, 99, 103, 107–109, 123, 125, 130, 133, 140, 141, 146, 148, 150–152, 155, 160, 162, 163, 169, 171, 176, 178, 188, 192, 209, 213, 214, 234–236, 238, 239, 241, 243, 252, 257, 265, 266, 268, 273–275, 279, 284, 286, 291, 293, 294, 296, 297, 299, 302, 303, 309–312, 315, 317, 318, 321, 323, 324, 326, 328, 329, 333, 334, 336, 338, 340–342, 345–351, 353, 355, 357–360, 363, 365, 369, 370, 372, 374–382, 386, 394, 397, 400, 402, 407, 409, 412, 414, 416, 418, 420, 423, 424, 433, 434, 442, 446, 450, 459, 534, 536, 537, 539, 544, 545, 558, 560, 562–565, 574

Action understandings (vs. basal understandings), 378–382, 407, 412, 558

Activity, 20, 24, 56, 75, 77, 86, 92, 137, 138, 140, 141, 145, 149, 153, 156, 163, 186, 188, 192, 235, 240, 243, 265, 272, 273, 284, 291, 296–300, 311, 312, 324–328, 334, 336, 349, 350, 353, 355, 361, 372, 385, 405, 407, 413–418, 427, 441, 443, 467, 484, 537, 538, 555, 558, 563

Affordances, 56–59, 61, 64, 133, 140, 143, 162, 268, 312, 313, 321, 351, 385, 409, 417, 443, 456, 460, 517, 532

Amalgam of practice, 21, 24, 123, 125, 126, 128, 134, 152, 160, 161, 166, 169, 175, 184, 190, 191, 193, 217, 308, 322, 330, 332, 449, 475, 480, 504, 542, 567

ANT, 26, 52, 58, 61, 142, 160, 162, 172, 177, 179, 185, 192, 239

Art, 31, 216, 430, 435, 437, 439–443, 485

Authenticity, 214, 217, 230, 232, 235, 249, 411, 430, 495, 502, 507, 515, 527, 528, 533

B

Basal elements, 27, 97, 189

Basal understandings (vs. action understandings), 378, 380, 407, 412

C

Circulation of elements, 74, 179, 190, 197, 449, 456, 457, 459, 466, 474, 489, 491, 505, 515, 518

Cognition, 50, 60, 89, 91, 92, 96, 146, 151, 153, 154, 161, 267, 292, 333, 368, 370, 398, 414, 418, 476, 539

Coherence, 6, 7, 9, 63, 72, 76, 88, 93, 94, 103, 132, 134, 177, 178, 182, 184, 194, 198, 200, 232, 254, 294, 326, 347, 377, 395, 397, 400, 412, 447, 452, 457, 460, 469, 481, 491, 537, 542

Complementary practices, 5, 23, 26, 59, 64, 77, 91, 97, 147, 197, 252, 298, 331, 452, 475, 478, 484, 485, 527, 547

Consciousness, 11, 14, 33, 49, 58, 79, 89, 91, 93, 94, 99–101, 103, 105, 107–112, 114, 124, 126, 131, 133–136, 138, 140–142, 148, 153, 154, 160, 162, 164, 169, 187, 189, 235, 236, 244, 245, 249, 292, 315, 317, 318, 323, 336–338, 341, 343, 347, 349, 351, 355, 357, 359, 369, 376, 377, 391, 406, 414, 416–418, 428, 437–439, 441, 490, 535, 539, 554
Conversation analysis, 35, 75, 79, 489, 569
Crucial point (Knotenpunkt), 11, 41, 56, 81, 129, 145, 166, 291, 314, 317, 319–324, 331, 342, 388, 407, 409, 427, 447, 480

D
Deliberation of practices, 99, 186, 375, 401, 471, 475, 479, 480, 483, 487, 489, 495, 498, 503, 576
Dispersed practices (vs. integrative), 6, 24, 26, 79, 97, 226, 265, 299, 303, 314, 375, 378, 385, 489, 537
Dissemination of practices, 17, 62, 186, 190, 200, 203, 219, 222, 226, 228, 231, 246, 392, 437, 448, 451, 454, 459, 466, 468, 474, 483, 484, 487, 489, 491, 493, 495, 496, 498, 506, 511, 512, 515, 517, 525, 527, 532, 546

E
Embodiement, 3, 8, 10, 15, 40, 46, 48, 51, 55, 59, 74, 87, 103, 106, 109, 127, 137, 138, 144–148, 151, 161, 162, 164, 165, 169, 177, 185, 192, 196, 200, 204, 209, 213, 233, 235, 236, 238–241, 244, 247, 249, 254, 268, 270, 283, 287, 307, 317, 320, 323, 329, 330, 345, 348, 368, 369, 372, 375, 376, 383, 387, 392, 400, 401, 403, 411, 430, 438, 447, 455, 458, 461, 462, 464, 467, 469, 470, 472–477, 479, 481, 484, 486, 488, 490, 493, 495, 497, 499–501, 503, 505, 506, 510, 513, 520–522, 525, 535, 541
Emotion, 21, 120, 144, 151, 176, 184, 213, 247, 261, 262, 268, 270, 271, 283, 292, 295, 383, 421, 500
Entification, 365, 401, 425
Epistemic seeing (vs. pragmatic seeing), 149, 151, 152, 383

Epistemology, 6, 13, 15–17, 63, 72, 149, 162, 180, 183, 186, 357, 359, 550
Ethnography, 4, 73, 76, 123, 127, 172, 179, 215, 247, 248, 326, 507, 561, 573, 576
   ethnomethodologically informed, 551, 569, 572
Ethnomethodology, 5, 7, 26, 50, 74, 75, 78–80, 135, 177, 243, 265, 267, 334, 365, 437, 535, 550, 551, 558, 561, 570
   studies of work, 573
Evolution, 17, 30, 62, 167, 199, 204, 219, 222, 226, 231, 233, 392, 396, 435, 437, 438, 446–449, 451, 452, 457, 461, 463, 465, 466, 471, 474, 483, 484, 489, 493, 496, 502, 504, 516, 517, 525, 527, 532, 546
Eyeball movement, 83, 85, 87, 88, 90, 93, 102, 104–108, 110–112, 114, 115, 123, 127, 139, 149, 272, 327, 336, 338, 342, 408, 416

F
Family resemblance, 13
Fields, 3, 6–8, 12, 13, 24–26, 36, 50, 73, 76, 78, 82, 84, 85, 87, 88, 90–95, 97, 98, 102–104, 106–109, 111, 112, 114, 123, 131–133, 135, 139–142, 147, 148, 153, 161, 175–177, 189, 222, 229, 233, 235, 241, 246, 247, 252, 266, 277, 281, 284, 296, 297, 309, 311, 318, 320, 321, 332, 337, 338, 342, 344, 351, 372, 373, 385, 397, 406, 408, 409, 413, 418, 424, 427, 434, 464, 478, 479, 496, 502–508, 517, 518, 527, 528, 534, 537, 544, 546, 548, 553, 560–564, 570, 573, 574, 576, 577, 580–582
Figuring out, 16, 38, 67, 80–82, 92, 98, 112, 145, 190, 193, 195, 198, 307, 312, 319, 338, 388, 394, 401, 407, 421, 465, 576
Flow, 5, 32, 74, 92, 119, 141, 166, 181, 189, 194, 232, 267, 272, 288, 300, 306, 307, 310–314, 316, 319, 321, 322, 325–327, 329–332, 334, 335, 337, 338, 341, 353, 354, 360, 365, 392, 395–398, 420–422, 425–430, 443, 447, 451, 459, 489, 502, 504, 518, 521, 523, 533, 545, 567
Foreground/background, 85, 98, 114, 123, 125, 126, 129, 133, 147, 161, 170,

Index 623

184, 186–188, 193, 195, 285, 291, 337, 424, 452, 542, 544, 560
Freeride, 22, 24, 28, 29, 55, 76, 87, 158, 170, 191, 192, 215, 306, 325, 327, 391, 398, 421, 423, 425, 427, 436, 445, 453, 455–457, 459, 472, 482, 520–522, 524, 527, 562, 570, 571, 580
Freestyle, 4, 11, 142, 157, 165, 215, 223, 258, 261, 262, 264, 268, 270–274, 281, 287, 299, 328, 350, 363, 370, 382, 385, 388, 390, 392, 402–405, 407, 409, 420, 430, 458, 482, 484, 487, 488, 498, 504, 508, 509, 511–513, 515, 517, 523–526, 562, 580
  Oldschool freestyle, 6, 165, 363, 383, 390, 405, 430, 459, 513, 517, 524, 525

G
Gestalt, 13, 17, 87–96, 98, 99, 101, 103–105, 107–109, 111, 113–115, 125, 129, 132, 146, 149, 173, 174, 184, 186, 188, 190, 195, 200, 294, 333, 337, 365, 401, 404, 407, 442, 461, 475, 542
Gestures, 27, 34, 36, 41, 45, 48, 51, 53, 75, 76, 210, 212, 219, 230–233, 235–237, 281, 283, 333, 352, 360, 364, 365, 374, 375, 378, 380–382, 528, 569

H
Hybrid, 192, 306, 515, 574

I
Identity, 11, 16, 24, 79, 81, 103, 111, 162, 178, 187, 208, 212, 214, 216, 217, 219, 229, 233, 237, 243, 254, 271, 293, 305, 336, 346, 369, 381, 391, 413, 449, 532, 534, 538, 542, 543, 547, 568
Improvisation, 212, 306, 351, 506
Indexicality, 39, 178, 194, 237, 457
Innovation, 164, 165, 168, 198–200, 203, 233, 438, 448, 453, 455, 460, 465, 466, 468, 472, 477, 503, 505, 506, 508, 509, 526, 527, 548, 551
Instruction, 20, 27, 36, 41, 46, 52, 59, 60, 73, 78, 88, 96, 131, 172, 175, 177, 197, 199, 200, 202, 242, 317, 330, 348, 390, 423, 425, 465, 466, 472,

473, 483, 486–489, 491, 496–502, 510–514, 525, 527, 529, 570, 571
Integrative practices (vs. dispersed), 24, 63, 385
Intentionality, 7, 100, 136, 147, 162, 264, 288, 323, 337, 339, 342, 350, 375, 376, 415–418, 424, 539
Intersubjectivity, 94, 140, 141, 302, 368, 447, 559, 567, 573

K
Knowledge, 2, 8, 11, 14–16, 20, 32, 46, 48, 51, 57, 72, 88, 91, 93–95, 103, 112, 130, 147, 151, 160, 162, 168, 169, 176, 178, 181, 183, 187, 196, 216, 235, 236, 239, 243, 245, 246, 252, 273, 284, 295, 324, 334, 336, 339–341, 345–352, 355, 356, 358, 359, 368, 372, 374, 375, 379, 381, 383, 387, 437, 447, 449, 465, 481, 491, 495, 503, 507, 529, 535, 536, 541, 559–561, 566, 569, 573, 582
  embodied knowledge, 10, 15, 162, 185, 236, 239, 241, 268, 369, 372, 462

L
Landscape, 25, 30, 56, 90, 98, 131, 135, 144, 148, 221, 298, 299, 302, 317, 484
Language game, 97, 138, 229, 232, 241, 247–250, 253, 431, 476, 479, 535
Learning, 3, 17, 72, 78, 125, 126, 129, 130, 171, 203, 238, 243, 245, 246, 265, 306, 308, 317, 329, 331, 335, 341, 346, 348, 350, 368, 373, 374, 379, 382, 407, 429, 447, 453, 463, 466, 469, 470, 472, 474, 487, 488, 490, 497, 501, 503, 507, 513, 515, 520, 525, 532, 533, 548, 559, 562, 570, 571, 574, 582
Lifestyle, 2, 6, 8, 22, 23, 77, 213, 214, 217, 219, 220, 222, 226, 228–231, 234, 236–238, 250, 254, 271, 295, 390, 391, 431–434, 452, 461, 462, 508, 520, 522, 523, 531–533

M
Mainstream, 31, 65, 198, 200, 212, 217, 230, 274, 479, 485, 495, 502, 505–507, 510, 513, 518–521, 524, 526
Media, 7, 17, 22, 24, 31, 59, 65, 75, 167, 186, 188, 198, 200, 212, 214, 219, 221, 224, 226, 228, 230, 231, 255,

295, 386, 390, 392, 396, 399, 401, 402, 407, 420, 425, 429, 436, 438, 441, 442, 447, 455, 459, 466, 471, 475, 481–484, 486, 487, 489, 491, 494–496, 503–505, 507, 508, 510, 513–515, 517–520, 522–527, 532, 533, 543, 545–547, 561, 568, 571, 576, 582
   mass media, 217, 267, 440, 469, 484, 504, 505, 517, 518, 521, 522, 525, 526
   media formats, 483, 519, 524, 527, 546, 571
Memory, 25, 130, 161, 185, 216, 235, 244, 356, 386, 418, 429, 534, 577
Mirror system, 9, 72, 245, 368, 370, 372–375, 377–379, 381, 414, 535, 540

N

Neural pluralism, 243, 244, 414, 534, 538, 548
Normality, 3, 35, 55, 65, 74, 83, 87, 94, 113, 115, 119, 125, 129, 132, 141, 190, 194, 195, 200, 215, 272, 278, 279, 295, 308, 330, 337, 366, 380, 396, 397, 423, 424, 451, 460, 472, 476, 481, 503, 529, 564–568, 571, 578, 579

O

Observation, 4, 8, 16, 17, 21, 24, 33, 35, 51, 53, 57–60, 62, 75, 78, 79, 91, 97, 109, 110, 124, 130, 136, 145, 148, 151, 152, 161, 164, 168–175, 178, 184, 186, 188, 189, 191–193, 195, 196, 200, 208, 219, 222, 227, 230, 231, 233, 234, 236, 238, 244, 246, 251, 252, 254, 255, 260, 262, 264, 270, 273, 274, 288, 295, 298, 303, 309, 317, 318, 323, 325, 326, 328, 330–332, 335, 346, 352, 354, 364, 365, 370, 372, 373, 377, 379–382, 384, 386, 387, 391–393, 397, 399, 401–403, 418, 420–422, 424, 425, 427, 429, 436–443, 447, 450, 458, 459, 463, 465, 466, 473, 474, 479, 498, 499, 509, 514, 517, 520, 521, 523, 536, 542, 543, 545, 546, 552, 553, 561–563, 565, 571, 572, 575, 580, 582
Ontology, 2, 10, 13–15, 24, 33, 35, 58, 94, 115, 126, 128, 134, 138, 153, 161, 163, 178, 180–182, 189, 194, 235, 247, 252, 254, 265, 284, 295, 309, 343, 346, 357–359, 412, 419, 456, 457, 465, 490, 535, 537, 539–541, 549, 558, 565, 567
Optical illusion, 96, 150
Organizations, 7, 93, 111, 123, 125, 140, 147, 153, 162, 185, 199, 219, 234, 248, 252, 291, 301, 322, 330, 332, 390, 396, 412, 414, 429, 447, 449, 451, 453, 463, 466, 471, 493, 495–498, 500–502, 505, 508, 512, 513, 515, 517, 518, 527, 529, 539, 556, 559, 581
Orientation, 7, 24, 36, 41, 48, 55, 60, 64, 66, 71, 73, 76, 77, 79, 86, 88, 92, 102, 107, 124, 135, 143, 146–148, 153, 209, 225, 226, 228, 243, 259, 272, 277, 279, 286, 289, 292, 293, 297, 298, 300, 303, 308, 309, 314, 316, 317, 319–323, 325, 330, 332, 346, 351, 352, 355, 361, 368, 380, 385, 391, 392, 396, 418, 426, 428, 433, 434, 436, 441, 443, 450, 452, 457, 458, 464–466, 469–471, 474, 475, 479, 486, 487, 489, 491, 496, 505, 509, 515, 516, 518, 522–524, 533, 534, 541, 545, 556, 557, 559, 560, 576

P

Phenomenal field, 13, 96, 126, 131, 133, 135, 139–142, 147, 148, 152, 160, 176, 184, 186, 192, 225, 273, 309–311, 320, 354, 394, 401, 402, 409, 413, 424, 426, 427, 452, 461, 490, 537, 543, 544, 560, 567, 576
Phenomenology, 10, 13, 15–17, 56, 81, 84, 85, 89, 97–102, 107, 111, 113, 114, 124, 128, 135–138, 140, 149, 152, 164, 187–190, 194, 233, 284, 311, 325, 327, 334, 343, 349, 357, 359, 377
Pivotal moment, 390, 523
Place, 4, 6, 13, 14, 20, 21, 31, 48, 50, 51, 65, 75, 85, 100, 102, 109, 112, 113, 117, 118, 120, 132, 133, 142, 160, 165, 178, 181, 186, 192, 198, 213, 214, 218, 222, 233, 237, 247, 254, 261, 265, 268, 269, 271, 273, 274, 277–279, 288, 291, 292, 294, 295, 297, 300, 302, 303, 311, 315, 320, 323, 324, 330, 345, 347, 352, 355, 356, 359, 363, 365, 369, 374,

Index

384, 389–391, 394, 396, 398, 399, 402, 404, 406, 407, 411, 420, 421, 429, 432, 436, 441, 445, 446, 449, 454, 456, 458, 466, 467, 471, 472, 474–476, 480, 483, 493, 495, 497, 504, 506, 509, 520, 522, 526, 529, 532, 537, 542, 545, 553, 557, 559, 561, 574
Practical intelligibility, 123, 140, 141, 155, 188, 273, 295, 313, 322, 324, 327, 328, 330, 347, 351, 355, 360, 402, 409–414, 471, 473, 485, 534, 536, 538, 544, 558, 559, 563
Practical understanding, 123, 133, 169, 175, 177, 272, 295, 332, 346, 347, 351, 377, 410–414, 425, 448, 461, 469, 470, 473, 484, 511, 512, 517, 525, 534, 536, 538, 544, 556, 558, 574
Pragmatic seeing (vs. epistemic seeing), 152, 312, 318, 332, 383, 384, 386, 401, 443, 533
Pragmatism, 104, 162, 169, 235, 239, 240, 245, 273, 358, 428, 450, 535, 541, 566
Praxeological validity, 176, 197, 199, 200, 423, 479, 481, 498
Praxeology, 10, 137, 235, 240, 247, 251, 252, 334, 369, 372, 535, 541, 551, 554
Professional vision, 53, 55, 74, 79

R

Regularity, 6, 9, 16, 182, 183, 237, 241, 243, 265, 281, 290, 293, 294, 337, 345, 352, 372, 377, 387, 392, 400, 414, 448, 480, 482, 513, 514, 516, 518–520, 524, 535, 539, 541–543, 565, 568
Riding, 16, 22, 24, 25, 29, 39, 41, 42, 46, 48, 52, 55, 58, 63, 70, 76, 77, 119–124, 128–130, 136, 143, 145, 146, 153, 158, 160, 165, 190, 192, 193, 195, 197, 198, 203, 211, 219, 243, 305–307, 309, 310, 312, 317, 319, 322–324, 327, 329, 330, 332, 335, 341, 350, 354, 361, 385, 392, 393, 405, 420–422, 424–427, 436, 447, 460, 462, 472, 479, 482, 488, 493, 500, 502, 507, 509, 518, 520, 522–524, 528, 566, 567
Ritual, 9, 265, 266, 288–290, 292–294, 296, 300, 382, 521
  interaction ritual, 74, 264, 266, 288, 289, 332

Routines, 3, 12, 51, 55, 64, 74, 75, 83–86, 91–96, 98, 100, 108, 111, 112, 114, 119, 121, 123, 124, 126, 128, 130, 134, 138, 145–147, 149, 150, 152, 162, 165, 166, 183, 192, 195, 197, 201, 235, 240, 241, 263, 265, 303, 316–318, 320, 322, 323, 332, 341, 344, 345, 347, 349, 352, 354, 365, 366, 368, 379, 383, 386, 396, 401, 406, 408, 412, 414, 415, 436, 441, 443, 449, 459, 462–464, 469, 472, 474, 480, 484, 491, 497, 500, 504, 505, 533, 536, 539, 541, 543, 544, 548, 570, 576
Rule-following, 9, 61, 130, 232, 238, 241, 247, 249, 251, 424, 425, 431, 434, 442, 535, 545
Rules, 9, 16, 27, 61, 127, 130, 138, 177, 200, 232, 233, 238–241, 243, 246, 247, 249–251, 289, 293, 296, 301, 327, 333, 336, 351, 378, 380, 383, 390, 394–398, 400, 405, 411, 423–425, 431, 433–435, 440, 442, 448, 450, 453, 458, 461, 470, 471, 473–475, 477, 479–482, 489, 491, 493, 501–504, 506, 507, 516, 523, 524, 534, 535, 543, 545, 558, 567, 568, 571

S

Sequentiality, 53, 64, 85, 93, 109, 293, 325, 337, 401
Similarity, 9, 128, 266, 294, 315, 337, 355, 377, 386, 387, 414, 419, 448, 539, 559, 565, 571
Site, 5, 10, 16, 20, 21, 68, 75, 76, 89, 91, 92, 95, 99, 100, 132, 134, 142, 154, 178, 198, 221, 247, 265, 267, 268, 273, 277, 279, 281, 288, 293, 295, 300, 312, 314, 315, 324, 340, 355, 357–359, 410, 412, 434, 524, 537, 555, 557, 558, 573
Situatedness, 3, 6, 7, 10, 12, 16, 20, 22, 27, 28, 33, 35–39, 42, 46, 48, 49, 51, 55, 56, 60, 62, 63, 69, 73–79, 82, 86, 87, 94, 96, 100, 106, 109, 111, 126, 127, 130, 131, 133, 135, 139, 141, 142, 146, 147, 151, 152, 155, 160, 162, 164, 177, 178, 181, 184, 196, 197, 202, 208, 216, 222, 223, 225, 230, 233, 235, 249, 254, 255, 261, 265, 266, 269, 272, 273, 277, 279, 288–290, 292, 294–297, 302, 303,

309, 313, 314, 318, 321, 322, 325, 330, 332, 334, 338–340, 346, 349, 350, 352, 353, 355, 356, 359, 365, 368, 371, 374, 377, 379, 381, 384, 386, 387, 392, 394, 396, 400–403, 406, 407, 409, 411, 414, 415, 417, 421, 423–425, 428, 429, 435, 437, 438, 441, 443, 447, 448, 450, 453, 457, 461, 471, 474–476, 479–481, 485, 487, 489, 491, 495, 510, 524, 533, 536, 537, 539, 541–543, 545, 548, 553, 555, 557, 559–566, 568–570, 573, 574, 576, 577, 581

Situation theory, psychological, 35

Spectacle, 113, 114, 274, 278, 300, 301, 392, 397, 516

Stabilization of practices, 219, 437, 451, 453, 461, 475, 484, 517, 524

Style, 5, 6, 9, 12, 17, 22, 24, 25, 31, 56, 76, 144, 146, 159, 165, 169, 186, 192, 194, 195, 203, 206, 208–211, 213–215, 217, 219–221, 223, 226, 228–230, 232–234, 236, 237, 246, 248, 252–254, 257, 261, 270, 271, 277, 281, 283, 286, 289, 295, 297, 300, 302, 303, 326, 328, 329, 332, 360, 363–365, 368, 371, 375, 381–384, 386–388, 390, 391, 393, 395, 398, 400, 402–404, 408, 411, 420, 421, 425, 429–438, 444–447, 451–454, 457, 458, 460, 461, 463–466, 470–472, 474, 475, 477, 478, 480–484, 486–489, 493, 495, 497, 498, 501–507, 509, 511, 512, 514, 516, 518, 520–522, 524–527, 529, 531–533, 545, 546, 559, 562, 567, 568, 570, 572, 575

Subculture, 2, 4, 6, 8, 11, 12, 24, 31, 47, 59, 62, 68, 73, 101, 167, 208, 213, 216, 219, 221, 226, 231, 233, 236, 246, 273, 303, 305, 328, 383, 392, 461, 464, 489, 494–496, 519, 531, 572, 574, 580

Subjectivity, 7, 11, 20, 23, 33, 49, 51, 58, 61, 62, 74, 79, 81, 101, 102, 104, 107, 110, 112, 122, 124, 125, 133, 136, 137, 140, 141, 169, 208, 217, 230, 233, 235, 236, 245, 253, 260, 266, 269, 273, 283, 292, 310, 320, 326, 336, 340, 341, 343, 345–349, 355, 357, 359, 365, 369, 372, 373, 376, 381, 413, 414, 416, 419, 434, 435, 437, 447, 451, 465, 467, 487, 496, 507, 512, 522, 529, 532, 537, 539, 552, 557, 560, 563, 565, 569, 573

Symbiotic system, 464, 496, 503–506, 508, 517, 518, 527, 546

T

Techniques, bodily, 17, 23, 34, 40, 46, 51, 55, 59, 125, 144, 165, 196, 200, 204, 209, 233–236, 238–241, 243, 249, 270, 307, 317, 329, 330, 348, 354, 360, 375, 447, 451, 455, 458, 459, 466, 467, 469–473, 475–477, 479, 481, 484, 486, 488, 490, 493, 495, 497, 499–503, 505–507, 509, 510, 512, 516, 520–522, 525, 535, 541, 582

Technology, 21, 26, 62, 75, 164, 165, 167, 179, 196, 198, 200, 203, 230, 239, 240, 267, 270, 353, 415, 430, 455, 462, 467, 471, 475–477, 484, 486, 488, 493, 496, 502, 505, 506, 510, 517, 521, 523, 525, 526, 528, 532, 562, 574, 581

Temporality, 2, 17, 23, 78, 79, 92, 93, 111, 132, 134, 139, 153, 177, 178, 298, 303, 306–308, 311, 312, 314, 315, 322, 324–328, 334, 338–340, 342, 343, 350, 355, 360, 364, 397, 398, 413, 426, 441, 508, 545, 557

V

Vision science, 9, 17, 60, 90–93, 96, 114, 123, 124, 146, 149–151, 154, 243, 244, 308, 317, 322, 331, 333, 367, 368, 370, 372, 374, 376, 378–381, 383, 386, 400, 406, 414, 418, 429, 436, 442, 534, 535, 538, 541, 547, 548

Visual cognition, 60, 90–92, 96, 114, 123, 149, 331, 333, 406, 414, 539, 548